Great American Folklore

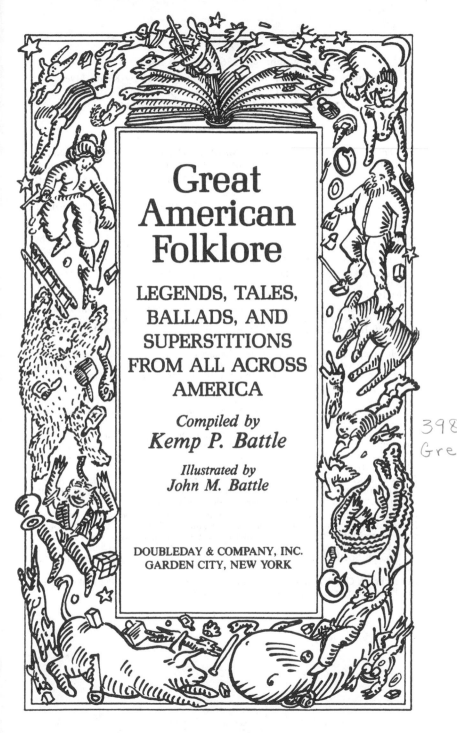

Great American Folklore

LEGENDS, TALES, BALLADS, AND SUPERSTITIONS FROM ALL ACROSS AMERICA

Compiled by
Kemp P. Battle

Illustrated by
John M. Battle

DOUBLEDAY & COMPANY, INC.
GARDEN CITY, NEW YORK

GRATEFUL ACKNOWLEDGMENT IS MADE TO THE FOLLOWING FOR PERMIS-
SION TO REPRINT THEIR COPYRIGHTED MATERIAL. EVERY REASONABLE
EFFORT HAS BEEN MADE TO TRACE THE OWNERSHIP OF ALL COPYRIGHTED
STORIES INCLUDED IN THIS VOLUME. ANY ERRORS THAT MAY HAVE OC-
CURRED ARE INADVERTENT AND WILL BE CORRECTED IN SUBSEQUENT
EDITIONS, PROVIDED NOTIFICATION IS SENT TO THE PUBLISHER.

Abernathy, Francis—"Running the Fox," from *The Sunny Slopes of Long Ago,* by
Francis Abernathy. Copyright © 1966 by the Texas Folklore Society, SFA Station,
Nacogdoches, Texas 75962. Reprinted by permission of the publisher.

Anderson, Mary T.—"Well-Dressed Turkeys," from *Mountain People,* by Mary T.
Anderson. Copyright © 1960 by Tennessee Folklore Society. Reprinted by permission
of the Tennessee Folklore Society.

Asbury, Herbert—"The Blacksmith Duel," from *The French Quarter: An Informal
History of the New Orleans Underworld,* by Herbert Asbury. Copyright 1936 by Alfred
A. Knopf, Inc., and renewed 1964 by Edith Evans Asbury. Reprinted by permission
of the publisher.

Aswell, James R.—"De Ways of de Wimmens," "Fiddler's Dram," and "Pretty
Baby," from *God Bless the Devil!: Bench Tales,* edited by James R. Aswell and others
of the Tennessee Writers' Project. Copyright 1940 by the University of North Carolina
Press. Reprinted by permission of the publisher.

Beath, Paul—"Febold Feboldson, the Most Inventingest Man," from *Febold Feboldson,* by Paul Beath. Copyright 1948 by Paul R. Beath. Reprinted by permission of
Phoebe Beath Catlin.

Bechdolt, Fredrick—"Butch Cassidy Robs the Payroll Train" and "Snake Thomson, a
Good Fiddler," from *Tales of the Old Timers,* by Fredrick Bechdolt. Copyright 1924
by The Century Company. A Hawthorne Book. Reprinted by permission of E. P.
Dutton, a division of New American Library.

Bethke, Robert—"Mart Moody's Bird Dog," from *Adirondack Voices,* by Robert
Bethke. Copyright © 1981 by the Board of Trustees of the University of Illinois.
Reprinted by permission of the University of Illinois Press.

Boatright, Mody—"The New Telephone Wire," from *The Golden Log,* by Mody
Boatright. Copyright © 1962 by the Texas Folklore Society, SFA Station, Nacogdoches, Texas 75962. Reprinted by permission of the publisher. "East Texas Episode,"
"The Boardinghouse," and "An Oilman Helps Out," by Mody Boatright. Copyright
© 1963 by Southern Methodist University Press. Reprinted by permission of the
publisher.

Burns, Frank C.—"Granny Frone" and "Old Ferro." Copyright 1952 Duke University Press. Reprinted by permission of the publisher.

Stevens, James—"Why the Great Lakes Have No Whales," from *The Saginaw Paul Bunyan*, by James Stevens. Copyright 1932 by Alfred A. Knopf, Inc. Reprinted by permission of the publisher.

Thompson, Harold W.—"Bill Greenfield, a Great Liar" and "John Darling, an Even Bigger Liar," from *Body, Boots and Britches*, by Harold W. Thompson (J. B. Lippincott Company). Copyright 1939 by Harold W. Thompson. Renewed 1967 by Dr. Marion Thompson. Reprinted by permission of Harper & Row Publishers, Inc.

Thorp, Jack—"Lost in Heaven" (originally titled "A Lonesome Cowboy"), "Calamity's Bet," "On the Dodge," and "Outlaw Women," from *Pardner of the Wind*, by Jack Thorp, 1945, The Caxton Printers, Ltd., Caldwell, Idaho. Reprinted by permission of the publisher.

Vestal, Stanley—"Old Gabe to the Rescue," from *Jim Bridger*, by Stanley Vestal. Copyright 1946 by Walter Stanley Campbell. Reprinted by permission of William Morrow & Company.

Wright, Richardson—"The Hag of Plymouth," from *Grandfather Was Queer: Wags and Eccentrics in Early America*, by Richardson Wright (J. B. Lippincott Co.). Copyright 1939 by Richardson Wright. Reprinted by permission of Harper & Row Publishers, Inc.

To Carolyn Battle, partner in all things,
and Cicero Griffin, my friend.

CONTENTS

Chapter 13   Paul Bunyan and His World

ACKNOWLEDGMENTS

I am grateful above all to those whose creativity fills this volume. I am also indebted to the Library of Congress, the staff of the American Folklife Center, the Widener Library at Harvard University, the New York Public Library, the Braswell Library in Rocky Mount, North Carolina, the United States Library at the University of London, and the British Museum. To the many librarians at these institutions I offer my sincere appreciation. As well, thanks is due the many dedicated folklorists for the fine work they have done exploring a fascinating and often complex subject. Chief among them one must mention Richard Dorson, John and Alan Lomax, Benjamin Botkin, Mody Boatright, Frank Dobie, A. P. Hudson, Vance Randolph, Carl Carmer, Roark Bradford, George Korson, Zora Neale Hurston, the Federal Writers Project of the W.P.A., the Caxton Printers, the editors of the *Journal of American Folklore, Tennessee Folklore Quarterly,* the Texas Folklore Society, *Southern Folklore Quarterly,* though the list could go on and on.

I also offer my continuing gratitude to the following people who in one way or another helped to shape my own love of storytelling: James Taylor and Mrs. Cicero Griffin, Miss Edith Parker, Shotgun Charlie, Fred, Regina and Greg Ledet, Joe and Phyllis Darcey, John White, John Finley, Mr. Miller, Ashby and Jean Adams, John and Peggy Moore, A. R. Wood, Mrs. Karl Illava, James Calvert, Alex Hoyt, J. Craig La Driere, Malcom Cowley, Kinney, "Skipper" Chilton, Matthew Murray, Bill Kirkpatrick, V. C. Finch, Peter Cohen, Pamela Burr, Ronnie, Boomer and the Knotts Island crowd, Mort Johnson, Kemp Nye, Dwight Miller, Burriss Young, Jimmy Nalley, John Joseph, "Slappy" (who took me over the Huey P. Long Bridge at one hundred miles an hour), Clifton Crane, "St. Francis" and the crowd on the Boston Common, Mrs. Frank House, Kermit Hummel and the entire staff of the *American Voice,* the boys at Blackie's Store, the President and Treasurer of the Tucker Club, the Locomotive League, all the old voyagers who sang their stories to me in rooming houses from Richmond to Los Angeles, Noni, Mamie, Hunky, old Joe Dobbins, Uncle Kemp, Jimmy "Il Mig" Meier, Mish, Tom, Emily, Alice Beresford, and my brothers—in particular to John M. Battle, who has generously contributed his splendid drawings for this volume and, of course, to my mother and father, who each taught me to listen to the sounds the past can make.

Last but not least, thanks to the good souls in the Doubleday London office—in particular Sarah Birdsey—for their help, as well as Val Ransome at the University of London. To Barbara Greenman, who started it all off; Liz Murphy, who assisted me in countless ways; and Mary Sherwin, my able and patient editor, who waded through a thousand stories, good and bad, and still had time to hear "just one more," I am indebted.

INTRODUCTION

AMERICA IS ALIVE with folklore. She is a country of yarns and legends, ghosts and superstitions, teeming with tradition and song. Her people have more folklore in their heads than a hundred books could hold. Wander from Maine to Oregon and you will see this is true. Go to Bangor, where the fog gets so thick that a woman has to shovel herself out of her house; or Dallas, where the ranches are so big the sun sets somewhere between the back porch and the stables. In Arizona you can see where the legendary Pecos Bill rode a cyclone bareback, using a lightning bolt as his quirt. Along the Mississippi you will find the place where Mike Fink, king of the flatboatmen, raced the steamers with his log-lashed raft and pole. Follow the endlessly winding country roads and you'll pass through towns like Dime Box and Duck Sneeze, Fancy Gap, Hog Eye, Looneyville, Oatmeal, Toadsuck, and Bug Scuffle. If you find yourself in Carrolltown, Alabama, visit the old courthouse known for the mysterious face in the windowpane. They say it is the face of a man who was lynched nearby, and no matter how many times they replace the glass, the face returns. Or perhaps if you're lucky, you might catch sight of one of America's ghosts: Billy the Kid with his deadly smile, or Wild Bill Hickock with his long dark hair blowing in the wind. Some folks in Ohio say they've seen a barefoot boy they swear is Johnny Appleseed, casting his apple seeds like rain on the springtime earth, while others claim the great John Henry, mighty hammers in his hands, still stalks the countryside around the Big Bend Tunnel, where he lost his life.

In any event, when your wandering is done, you will know that America's folklore is endless, that there is no place without its distinctive stories and characters; and you will feel certain that if there is anyone who can outboast a Texan, outfight a Rebel, outwit a Yankee or outwork a cowboy, he hasn't been heard of yet in America.

Folklore has always been too impatient, too spontaneous to stand still for definition. The term is elusive and has caused no lack of mischief among the very scholars who claim to know it best. Folklore is primarily, though not exclusively, an oral tale or tradition passed from one person to another, one generation to the next. Taken as a whole, it represents a people's culture as seen through the changing prism of its stories, beliefs, legends, superstitions, and songs. Taken in its parts, folklore is as varied and unending as the people who create it.

Folklorists have always had a difficult task in following the tenuous oral migration of a legend or tale as it trekked across the years, miles, and cultures. They know better than most that great stories and songs often die with the passing of local raconteurs and folksingers, so they travel the land with their notebooks and tape recorders, collecting the authentic folk voice before it disappears. They find, with astonishing regularity, that tales transform themselves and adapt constantly to new surroundings.

Vast amounts of American folklore, of course, are not American at all in origin. Her scant three centuries are but a blink to the older cultures that have had time to refine their lore into a measurable body of work. American folklore is a rich inheritance of hundreds of different traditions. Every time a Greek or a Scot, an African or an Arab made his home in America, he brought his folklore with him. The devil tales, and so many of the superstitions about snakes and dogs, fishes and weather that flourished here, sprang from seeds blown from across the seas. Br'er Rabbit and Br'er Fox were tricking each other in Africa long before they met up with Uncle Remus. Even the exploits of Davy Crockett have their parallel in the feats of the Celtic and Norse heroes. One needs only to browse through Stith Thompson's monumental *Motif Index of Folk Literature* to realize that what seems a wonderful American yarn was told a thousand years ago in Italy, while the ballad hummed yesterday in Kansas was sung in London when Shakespeare was a boy.

There are further difficulties in identifying America's folklore. America was unique in being semiliterate at the very moment she was shaping some of her most enduring legends. Kit Carson was scouting and path-finding the West, for example, while back East they were turning out stacks of dime-novel biographies acclaiming the new hero, the fearless Mountain Man. It is small wonder that when a friend read to Carson one of these dramatic accounts of the reticent explorer's life, he is said to have remarked, "That feller laid it on a leetle thick, I think." So too, Davy Crockett, one of America's earliest frontier heroes, was largely a creation of the newspapers and popular almanacs of his day. They reported his folksy speeches in Congress and recounted the most fabulous frontier tales under his name. By the time of his death at the Alamo, Crockett's enormous legend, midwived by the growing power of print, was fully grown.

The role of printed material has long been at the center of the debate over what constitutes our authentic folk heritage. The tale your grandfather told you, the same one you spun for your children, certainly passes as folklore, but what of the tales read between the covers of a book, adorned with the special touches of the writer? American folklore is full of great figures whose origins are not derived solely from oral sources. Paul Bunyan, mighty logger of the Big Onion Camp, was invented by an enterprising copywriter for a lumber company who thought Paul might help sell lumber. Pecos Bill, greatest of all the cowboys, came from the pen of Edward O'Reilly in a *Century Magazine* article in 1923, and Tony Beaver, the Bunyanesque lumberjack from Pennsylvania, owes his life to Margaret Montagu's *Up Eel River*. Folklorists may have dismissed all of the above, and many more, as lacking authenticity, but they cannot ignore the popularity of these characters among people all over America.

For if there were no Bunyan, there would still be a race of magnificent loggers for whom Bunyan stands as a symbol. If there was no proof that John Henry ever challenged the steam drill with his twenty-pound hammers, he is, nonetheless, immortal for thousands of laborers, black and white, whose dignity has been threatened by machines. And perhaps, as some historians will say, Billy the Kid was shot stealing a side of beef, but once you've read Walter Noble Burns's account of the Kid's last night, will you still believe he was a thief? When I tell my children the Burns version, surely they will not ask me my source.

The fact remains that American folklore flows from mouth to print and back again. History blurs with folk legends and folklore feeds off history. Outside the strict boundary set by the folklorists is a crowd of zesty figures of dubious folk ancestry determined to enter.

From Mickey Mouse to Casey and his bat, from Paul Bunyan to Superman, the figures are already among us, populating our favorite stories. And they are here to stay.

The American imagination has created a very particular lore, not so much of kings and fairies or wishes from a lamp, but a treasury of knee-slapping humor and outrageous invention. Wherever we look— at the wisdom of the frontier woman, the yarns of the trapper, the ironic wit of the black man—we find vital clues to our national character that suggest why Americans are so impatient and restless, so determined to find bigger and better dreams.

A book on classic American folklore is, at best, only a selection. It is bound to reflect the compiler's own taste and experience, no matter how diligent he or she might be about covering the diverse forms of our folklore. For every tale that follows, every song or superstition, there are a dozen more that others will swear go one better. And they are probably right. Such is the delight and challenge of American folklore that a story's best purpose is to inspire the telling of a second and a third and so on—until the voice cracks, the child sleeps, or the jug runs dry.

The following chapters are broad baskets for a wide harvest. The material chosen follows no strict method, nor is it intended to represent any precise geographical or historical consistency. A contemporary story might be placed alongside a tale popular a century before, provided the two have a common theme. The goal is, above all, to entertain. Yarns of explorers and travelers, hunters and cowboys, preachers and gunslingers, have been gathered together in their appropriate places along with chapters on the boundless activity of folk life: love and marriage, boasting, jesting, and fighting. If an entry was too regional it was discarded in favor of something more national in its appeal, and entries more properly classified as history were avoided, no matter how interesting or relevant they might have seemed.

In the main, my sources are scores of books, almanacs, folklore journals and quarterlies, newspapers, and folk archives. Sometimes I have retold tales from these sources, and often I have spun a number of the tales I myself heard. I served an odd apprenticeship to the study of American folklore during years of travel across America. As I dug ditches, slaughtered hogs, stretched fences, primed tobacco, and did a thousand odd jobs from one coast to the other that earned me a bed or a meal, I had occasion to hear many great stories. One learns quickly to recognize the familiar rhythms of a true storyteller. Some, like Shotgun Charlie, a black tenant farmer with a booming laugh and an endless repertoire of legend and humor, appear in the following pages attached to a few of their favorite tales.

I have concentrated on lore that bears most directly on the general life in the United States, with the result that certain ethnic minorities have been bypassed as too regional in their appeal. The rich folklore of dozens of ethnic groups in cities and towns across America must be left to the admirable scholarship of professional folklorists. The black man, on the other hand, has had an immense influence on American folklore and is well represented throughout the collection, as is the native American Indian who, though not as influential, receives some well deserved attention.

Wherever possible I have left the dialect of a story unchanged. There are some people who claim that there is something demeaning in reproducing dialect, as if there were some mockery intended in the use of the untutored and local tongue. Perhaps this was true in another age, when stories were written with an unfortunate tone of condescension, often with needless misspelling, which suggested an added ignorance on the part of the speaker. Any sensible person need not be reminded today, though, of the beauty and the clarity of folk speech. To edit it is to translate it, and there are few translators worthy of the task.

One last reminder: never forget that folklore is all around us. We have heard its voice in the songs our mothers sang us at bedtime or the tales our fathers told while waiting for the fish to bite. We can hear it in the voices of the old when their memories return to them full of mystery and power. Folklore lurks behind the names we choose for our streets and baseball teams, hound dogs and race-horses. It is in the traditions that bring dried corn husks to every door in November or encourage the child to write his dreams to

Santa Claus. Like a river that is fed from innumerable tiny streams and brooks, folklore takes its strength from many sources, and as it grows it carries all of us, young and old alike, along its wayward journey.

Great
American
Folklore

CHAPTER 1

Where the Road Forks and the River Bends: Travelers' Tales

"Davy Crockett and the Fiddler in the River"

"And miles to go before I sleep."
—Robert Frost

THERE ARE FEW real journeys anymore—speed brings our destination magically close and reduces travel to a quick leaping through the changing landscape of time zones. Not so long ago, one was forced to live more adventurously while going from one place to another. On horseback, stagecoach, wagon, raft, steamboat, or train, there was plenty of time to learn a thing or two about those with whom you traveled, or the country through which you passed. A journey brought strangers into the intimate circle of fellow voyagers: "Where are you going? Where did you come from? Did you hear what happened to the stage that took this route last month?" The dangers and tedium that faced the travelers in frontier America inevitably encouraged good-natured talk and the telling of tales. Indeed, folklore of all kinds spread most swiftly on the young nation's roads and rivers, passed from one traveler to the next like good gossip. While the crowded stage in "The Hoosier and the Salt Pile" cannot help but amuse us, it also reminds us how local pride and prejudice could prosper when folks from widely differing backgrounds were thrown together.

The lone traveler experienced a very different sort of journey. His solitary figure on the horizon was treated by the locals with more suspicion than goodwill. There is a wealth of American lore recounting the friction that often passed between local wag and traveling stranger. They approached one another with caution, and it usually wasn't very long before mutual distrust erupted into verbal combat. To the sharpest wit went the spoils! The city fellow who got his comeuppance from the country lad in "Ain't Lost," or poor Mr. Flufkin, who suffered for his ignorance in his disastrous trip to Boston in "Nehemiah Flufkin's Visit to the City," are but two popular examples in the following pages.

The confrontation between the traveler and the local doesn't have to end in victory for either. One of the best-loved American yarns, "The Arkansas Traveler," produces a memorable draw, as the elegant stranger and his fiddling counterpart found their common ground. The best of all worlds is where a traveler establishes himself to the local's satisfaction. If wits are matched, or dexterity with a rifle, a fiddle, or a jug of moonshine proven, then the lone journeyer could find himself as welcome as a prodigal son.

America has always been a restless place. Her roads have long been crowded with people in search of a new Eden, in flight from an old one, or perhaps just curious about what lay around the next bend in the river. When Davy Crockett ran for Congress one last time, in 1835, his message to the voters of Tennessee was direct: "Elect me or not, as you choose. If you don't, Tennessee can go to hell and I'll go to Texas." To Texas he went, joining an endless migration of traveling Americans which has yet to cease.

Such restlessness is why America has always cherished her roamers. We look with nostalgia on the wanderings of Johnny Appleseed as he crossed the land planting his beloved apple orchards. We remember with admiration the great steamboats that raced each other up and down the Mississippi, or the crowded stagecoaches that plied the treacherous roads West. And who among us does not feel a nameless longing at the sound of a distant train's whistle as it rushes on into the night? A drop of the hobo's blood is in our veins and always will be.

The following stories are from an earlier America, but substitute car for horse, highway for river, and they could have taken place yesterday. There will always be poor roads and late trains, strange little towns and intimidating cities, and there will always be someone, maybe even you, in a new place for the first time with only his wit to guide him.

The Arkansas Traveler

A tall, well-dressed stranger made his way through the backwoods of Arkansas, a place where the roads weren't but dirt paths and the cabins scarce as hens' teeth. Suddenly he came to a small clearing, in the middle of which sat an old cabin. It had sagging walls and a mighty poor roof, and out on the porch, sitting on a whiskey barrel playing the fiddle, was an old, bearded man. The stranger, who has come to be known as the Arkansas Traveler, heard the old fellow playing the same notes over and over again as if he couldn't bear to part with them. The Traveler rode up, and all during their conversation the old man continued right on playing those same notes.

Arkansas Traveler: Hello, stranger.

Fiddler: Hello, yourself.

T: Sir, can you tell me where this road goes to?

F: It ain't never been any whar since I've lived here. Least it's always thar when I git up in the mornin'.

T: Well, I'm supposed to take it to where it forks. How far is it to there?

F: It don't fork at all, but it shore splits up like the devil.

T: Have you any spirits here?

F: Lots of 'em. Sal saw one last night by that ol' holler gum tree, and it nearly skeered her out of her skin.

T: You don't understand what I mean, sir. Have you any liquor?

F: Had some yesterday, I did, but ol' Blue he got in and lapped it right up out of the pot.

T: No, I don't meant pot liquor. I mean whiskey. I'm wet and cold and would like some whiskey. Have you got any?

F: Oh, sure I do. Certain. Why, I drank the last this very day.

T (growing more annoyed): Well, I'm as hungry as I am thirsty. I haven't eaten since this morning. Might you have something to eat?

F: Stranger, thar ain't a damned thing in the house and that's a fact. Not a mouthful of meat, not even the dust of a meal round here.

T: Can you give my horse something?

F: Got nothin' to feed him on.

T: Sir, I'm not likely to get to another house tonight and I would be very grateful if you would let me sleep in yours. I'll tie my horse to that tree and will just have to do without anything to eat or drink.

F: Cain't. See, my house leaks. Thar's only one dry spot in it and me and Sal sleeps on that'n. As for your horse, that thar tree is the ol' lady's persimmon tree. You cain't tie to it, 'cause she don't want it shuk off. She aims to make beer off it.

T (staring hard at the fiddler): Why don't you repair your roof and stop the leaks?

F: It's been rainin' all day long.

T: Why don't you do it when the weather is dry?

F: It don't leak then.

T: How far is it to the next house?

F: Stranger, I don't know. I ain't never been thar.

T: Well, do you know who lives here?

F: I do.

T (waiting to hear): Who, then?

F: I do.

T: If I may be so bold, what might be your name?

F: It might be Tom and it might be Dick, but it lacks a damned sight of it.

T: This place of yours is pretty quiet. Seems the only thing alive is you. How do you do for a living here?

F: Perty well, thank you. How do you do yerself?

T: I mean what do you do for a living, sir?

F: Keep a tavern and sell whiskey.

T (exasperated): I told you that was what I wanted!

F: Stranger, hear tell of this. I bought a bar'l more'n a week ago. Me and Sal we went shares. But after we got the bar'l here, we found we only had a bit 'tweenst us, and Sal she didn't want to use her'n first, nor me mine. I had me a spiggin' in one end and she had her a spiggin' in t'other. So, you see, Sal takes a drink out of my end and pays me the bit fer it. Then I'd take one out'n her'n and give her the bit back. My, we was getting along fust rate, 'til Tom, damned skunk that he be, bored a hole on the bottom to suck at and the next time I went to buy myself a drink from Sal, they weren't none thar.

T (giving up): Well, sir, I'm sorry your whiskey's all gone.

The Arkansas Traveler had finally gotten the message and turned his weary horse away from the porch determined to follow the road until he found a place more hospitable. He heard those crazy fiddle notes going over and over, and couldn't resist a parting shot at the old man on the porch.

T: My friend, why in the hell don't you play the balance to that tune?

F: It's got no balance to it.

T: I mean that you aren't playing the whole tune, just part of it.

F: Stranger, kin you play the fiddle?

T: Yes, a little, sometimes.

F: Well, you don't look like a fiddler to me, but if you think you got a tune in you or if you think you kin pull any more out'n the tune I been playing, you kin just git down and try.

The Traveler climbed off his horse and stepped up onto the man's porch. He took up the fiddle and played those same notes, only he added a whole music book more. He played the whole tune, and then some.

F: Stranger, take a half a dozen chairs and set down here. Sal, stir yourself round like a six-horse team in a mud hole. Go round in the holler whar I killed that buck this mornin', cut off some of the best pieces, and bring 'em up for me and this gentleman directly. Raise up the board under the head of the bed and git that old black jug I hid from Tom (the skunk ain't so smart as he'd have me think), and give us some whiskey. Thar's plenty in thar. Mose, drive ol' Blue out of the bread tray, then climb up in the loft and git that rag that's got the sugar tied in it. Dick, carry the gentleman's hoss 'round the back and under the shed and give him some fodder and corn, as much as he can eat.

Mose: Daddy, thar ain't enough knives for to set the table.

F: Whar's big butch, little butch, ol' case, cob-handle, granny's knife, and the one I handled yesterday? That's enough to set any gentleman's table with. Damn me, stranger, if you cain't stay as long as you please, and I'll see to it that you git all the plenty you need to eat and drink. Will you have coffee for supper?

T: Yes, sir.

F: Play away, stranger. You kin sleep on the dry spot tonight.

T (after playing steadily for two hours): Friend, can you tell me about the road I'm to travel tomorrow?

F: Tomorrow! Stranger, you won't git out'n these diggings fer six weeks and a day. But when it gits so you can start, you see that big sloo over thar? Well, you have to git cross that, then you take the road up the bank, and in about a mile you come to a two-acre-and-a-half corn patch; the corn is mightily in the weeds, but you needn't mind that one bit, just ride on. About a mile and a half, maybe two miles from that, you'll come to the damnedest swamp you ever struck in all your travels; it's boggy enough to mire a saddle blanket. Thar's a fust-rate road near about six feet under thar.

T: How am I to get at it?

F: You can't git at it nary time till the weather stiffens down some. Well, about a mile beyon', you come to a place whar thar's two roads. You can take the right-hand road if'n you want to, and you'll follow that a mile or so 'til you find it runs out. So then you got to come back and try the left hand road. When you git about two miles down that-a-one, you'll know fer certain you're on the wrong path, for thar ain't any road thar. You'll then figure you're mighty lucky if'n you can find your way back to my house, whar you can come and play that tune fer as long as it suits you.

Davy Crockett and
the Fiddler in the River

My companions did not intend seeing me farther on my way than the Washita River, near fifty miles. Conversation was pretty brisk, for we talked about the affairs of the nation and Texas; subjects that are by no means to be exhausted, if one may judge by the long speeches made in Congress, where they talk year in and year out; and it would seem that as much still remains to be said as ever. As we drew nigh to the Washita, the silence was broken alone by our own talk and the clattering of our horses' hoofs, and we imagined ourselves pretty much the only travelers, when we were suddenly somewhat startled by the sound of music. We checked our horses, and listened, and the music continued. "What can all that mean?" says I. "Blast my old shoes if I know, Colonel," says one of the party. We listened again and we now heard, "Hail, Columbia, happy land!" played in first-rate style. "That's fine," says I. "Fine as silk, Colonel, and leetle finer," says the other; "but hark, the tune's changed." We took another spell of listening, and now the musician struck up, in a brisk and lively manner, "Over the water to Charley." "That's mighty mysterious," says one; "Can't cipher it out nohow," says another; "A notch beyond my measure," says a third. "Then, let us go ahead," says I, and off we dashed at a pretty rapid gait, I tell you —by no means slow.

As we approached the river we saw to the right of the road a new clearing on a hill, where several men were at work, and they were running down the hill like wild Indians. There appeared to be no time to be lost, so they ran, and we cut ahead for the crossing. The music continued all this time stronger and stronger, and the very notes appeared to speak distinctly, "Over the water to Charley."

When we reached the crossing we were struck all of a heap, at beholding a man seated in a sulky in the middle of a river, and playing for life on a fiddle. The horse was up to his middle in the water; and it seemed as if the flimsy vehicle was ready to be swept away by the current. Still the fiddler fiddled on composedly, as if his life had been insured, and he was nothing more than a passenger. We thought he was mad and shouted to him. He heard us, and stopped his music. "You have missed the crossing," shouted one of the men from the clearing. "I know I have," returned the fiddler. "If you go ten feet farther you will be drowned." "I know I shall," returned the fiddler. "Turn back," said the man. "I can't," said the other. "Then, how the devil will you get out?" "I'm sure I don't know: come you and help me."

The men from the clearing, who understood the river, took our horses and rode up to the sulky, and after some difficulty, succeeded in bringing the traveler safe to shore, when we recognised the worthy parson who had fiddled for us at the puppet show at Little Rock. They told him that he had had a narrow escape, and he replied that he had found that out an hour ago. He said he had been fiddling to the fishes for a full hour, and had exhausted all the tunes that he could play without notes. We then asked him what could have induced him to think of fiddling at a time of such peril; and he replied that he had remarked, in his progress through life, that there was nothing in universal nature so well calculated to draw people together as the sound of a fiddle; and he knew that he might bawl until he was hoarse for assistance, and no one would stir a peg; but they would no sooner hear the scraping of his catgut than they would quit all other business, and come to the spot in flocks. We laughed heartily at the knowledge the parson showed of human nature. And he was right.

How Uncle Steve Interpreted Spanish

During slavery time in Texas it was the custom among some of the owners of land and slaves to go every year on one or two horse-trading expeditions into old Mexico. If the owner could not speak Spanish, he usually carried along some Mexican living in the vicinity as an interpreter.

Master Phil Potts had his plans all made to leave for the border on a horse-trading expedition the following Monday morning. On Sunday he received word that the Mexican he had engaged to go along as interpreter was sick and could not go. Without an interpreter the trip would be useless. An interpreter had to be found.

Now, Steve, a sharp slave, had for a long time wanted to make a trip into Mexico. On more than one occasion he had tried to maneuver his master into taking him along as a hand, but had never succeeded. Here, he thought, was his opportunity. So he hunted up Master Phil and told him he could interpret Spanish. Master Phil was rather surprised to learn of Steve's linguistic accomplishments, but, as there was no choice, agreed to take him.

Everybody in the expedition was in high spirits except Steve, who was wondering what he was going to say when the test came. They traveled all day and did not see a soul until close to sundown. Then, as they approached a water hole, they saw some Mexicans camped there. One of the Mexicans had a very fine-looking bay horse that at once caught the eye of Master Phil.

"Steve," he said, "ask that Mexican how much he will take for that horse."

"Boss," said Steve, "dat Mescan don't wanna sell dat hoss. Mescans don't trade on Mondays, no-how."

"That's all right," answered his master. "Go on and ask him what he wants for the horse."

"Aw right, Boss," agreed Steve, "but Ah jes' knows he ain' gonna sell 'im terday."

"Oh, hombre," called out Steve, "fo' how muchee you sellee de hossy?"

The Mexican, disgusted at Steve's attempt to speak Spanish, replied, "Usted no bueno," which means "You are no good."

"What did he say, Steve?" asked his master.

"He sez," answered Steve, "that he did not want to sell 'im till Wednesday."

"Ah, go on," said the master. "Tell him we will give him a good price, that we really want the horse."

"Aw right, Boss," answered Steve, "Ah'll tell 'im, but Ah done tol' yuh dat Mescans don' trade on Mondays."

"Oh, hombre," said Steve, "no sellee de hossy sho' nuffee?"

"No sabe," answered the Mexican, meaning "I do not understand."

"Well," asked the boss, "what did he say this time, Steve?"

"He sez he don' wanna sell 'im till Sat'day now, Boss. Ah done tol' yuh dese Mescans don't trade on Monday."

"Now," replied the master, "we have just got to have that horse. He is a wonderful animal. Go on and tell him that we will pay him a big price for the horse."

"Aw right, Boss. But yuh sho' is wastin' yo' time, though, 'cause Ah knows dat Mescan ain't gwine trade on Monday."

"Oh, hombre," said Steve, "no sellee de hossy fo' biggee de mon?"

The Mexican, who had some wood piled up beside the road, now thought that Steve, who was pointing in its direction, was asking him the price of it, and replied, "Cinco pesos" (five dollars).

"What did he say this time, Steve?" asked his master.

"Boss, he sho' done gone an' talk foolish dis time. He sez sometimes dat hoss is trottin' an' he thinks he's pacin'.' "

"All right," said his master, "let's go on to Mexico."

How Johnny Appleseed Brought Apple Blossoms to the West

Of all the tales that Pennsylvanians tell, I think they like best the story of a strange fellow who rode into Pittsburgh on the lazy-board of a Conestoga wagon back in 1794. He said his name was Jonathan Chapman, and he built himself a log cabin on Grant's Hill.

It's a long time for a story to carry by word of mouth, but there are some people who say he told it around Pittsburgh that he had been born in Boston in the year of the Battle of Bunker Hill and that the first thing his baby eyes ever saw was a branch of apple blossoms outside the window of his home. If that is true, the sight must have influenced the whole rest of his life, for as soon as he had his house built in Pittsburgh he planted a big apple orchard. There, on the hill now known as Pittsburgh's Hump, the bees in Jonathan Chapman's hives made honey from the apple blossoms and Jonathan gave it away to his neighbors because, he said, the bees didn't charge him anything for it.

In the twelve years he lived in Pittsburgh an idea kept growing in Jonathan Chapman's brain until it got a powerful hold on him. He would take a load of apple seeds westward to the pioneers on the frontier so that they might have flowering, fruitful orchards like his own. Some folks say he would never have really got started with that load, that the idea would have stayed an idea, if Jonathan's girl hadn't jilted him. I met an old lady once who said of him, "He wasn't quite right in the head, you know; my grandmother called him 'love-cracked.' "

Whatever the truth about that may be, in 1806 Jonathan loaded two canoes with apple seeds and started down the Ohio River. When he got to the Muskingum he followed that to White Woman Creek, and he finally ended up along Licking Creek where his load of seeds ran out. Behind him farmers were rejoicing in their seedlings—soon to be waving orchards—and they talked about the strange man who had brought them. They called him Johnny Appleseed.

Johnny went back to the Pennsylvania cider mills to get more seeds. They're still talking about him around Shadeland and Blooming Valley and Coolspring—the queer, blue-eyed man with long hair hanging to his shoulders, barefooted, wearing ragged clothes. When he had disposed of a second load and come back to Pennsylvania for seeds again, his appearance had changed still more. On his head as a cap he wore a tin kettle in which, when he needed it, he cooked his food. His only garment now, winter or summer, was a coffee sack with holes cut in it for his arms and legs.

Strange stories came out of the western wilderness.

Hostile Indians treated Johnny Appleseed kindly and helped him on his way.

A trapper had come upon Johnny Appleseed playing with three bear cubs while their mother looked on placidly.

Johnny Appleseed was entertaining frontier families by showing them how he could stick pins and needles through his flesh without hurting himself.

Johnny Appleseed knew direction by instinct and never carried a compass in the trackless woods.

Johnny Appleseed did not feel the cold of winter and could walk barefoot in below-zero weather without freezing his toes.

Johnny Appleseed had saved the people living in the fort at Mansfield, Ohio, from massacre by Indians, by running sixty miles through the dense woods in five hours to obtain aid.

Hundreds of Ohio acres were abloom with pink blossoms now, and Pennsylvania seeds had reached the banks of the Wabash. Everywhere Johnny Appleseed was welcomed by the grateful farmers. When he sat down at table with them, he would not eat until he was sure that there was plenty of food for the children. After he had eaten he would stretch himself out on the floor, take out the Bible he carried inside the coffee sack, and read aloud what he called "news fresh from heaven"—the Sermon on the Mount. His voice, one good housewife said, was "loud as the roar of wind and waves, then soft and soothing as the balmy airs that quivered the morning-glory leaves about his gray beard."

One day he trudged along for twenty miles to reach the home of a friend near Fort Wayne, Indiana. He sat down on the doorstep to eat his evening meal of bread and milk. He read aloud from the Bible for a while. Then he went to sleep, stretched out on the floor, and he did not wake up.

When the news reached Washington, old Sam Houston, Texas Sam Houston, made a speech about Johnny Appleseed in the American Congress. He said: "This old man was one of the most useful citizens of the world in his humble way. Farewell, dear old eccentric heart. Your labor has been a labor of love, and generations yet unborn will rise up and call you blessed."

This is just what the farmers who own apple orchards along Johnny Appleseed's path over a territory of a hundred thousand square miles have been doing ever since. And all the folks in western Pennsylvania bless Johnny Appleseed, too, for they know that when spring comes to the land known now as the Middle West hundreds of thousands of Ohio and Indiana acres will be pink and white with Pennsylvania apple blossoms.

Nail Soup

A beggar man once was passing through a town and he stopped at the richest man's house in town to beg for something to eat. The man wasn't at home and his wife was stingy and selfish and didn't have no love for anybody but herself. When the beggar knocked on the door she come out and he said, "Could I please have a piece of bread and maybe a bowl of soup?"

"Not a thing in this house to eat," she said.

"Well, never mind," he said, "but I guess you have a nail in the house you would give me."

She said, "What do you want with a nail?"

Said, "Why, I can make some purty good soup off of a nail."

The old woman was in a quandary about that and he went on and told her he could make good soup with a nail and a pan of water. So she wanted to know how it could be done, figured it would be a cheap way to have something on the table. She went in and hunted a nail and brought it and a pan of water out to him. He took it and put the nail in the water and went to stirring it. The old woman bent right over him watching every move he made. Then he said, "If only I had just a pinch of salt to go in now," and she went and brought that out and went to watching him again.

After while he said, "Looks like it needs just a few cabbage leaves, that would set it off just right." She went in the garden and got a few leaves. He stirred them in. Purty soon he had her to bring a few little 'taters and then just a carrot or two. She brought them to him and he kept on stirring the pot over the fire.

At last he said, "It's getting about done." Said, "Why not throw in a few green peas and then some butter to season it all just right." She went and got them and kept watching the pot. Then he called for some bowls and spoons to eat it with. She brought them and he dipped out two big bowls of the soup, said, "Now just taste that." She began to eat it and he asked her if that wasn't purty good soup.

She ate her whole bowl and said, "Yes, that's a good soup, very good." She studied a minute and then said, "But what about the nail, what did it do for it?"

He said, "Oh, the nail?" Said, "Why it seems to be purty hard yet. You'll have to keep on cooking it. Goodbye, and thanks for the soup."

He took out the back door and left her there cooking the nail.

Ohio Roads

A weary way-farer, who journeyed through Ohio a few years ago, illustrated his remarks upon the badness of the roads, by relating the following curious fact. He was floundering through the mire, as many an honest gentleman flounders through life, getting along with difficulty, but still getting along; sometimes wading to the saddle-girth in water, sometimes clambering over logs, and occasionally plunged in a quagmire.

While carefully picking his way by a spot more miry than the rest, he espied a man's hat, a very creditable beaver, lying with the crown upwards in the mud, and as he approached, was not a little startled to see it move. This happened in a dismal swamp, where the cypress waved its melancholy branches over the dark soil, and the frogs croaked as mournfully as they did of old, under the reign of King Stork, and as incessantly as if an influenza had invaded their borders; and our traveler's flesh began to creep at beholding a hat move without the agency of a head. "When the brains are out the head will die," thought he, "and when the head is out, the hat, by the same rule, should receive its *quietus.*"

Not being very superstitious, and determined to penetrate the mystery, the solitary rider checked his nag, and extending his long whip, fairly upset the hat—when, lo! beneath it appeared a man's head, a living, laughing head, by which our inquisitive traveler heard himself saluted with "Hullo, stranger! who told you to knock my hat off?"

The person thus addressed was so utterly astonished as not to be able for a moment to understand that the apparition was no other than a fellow-creature up to the neck in the mire; but he no sooner came to this conclusion than he promptly apologized for the indecorum of which he had been guilty, and tendered his services to the gentleman in the mud puddle.

"I will alight," said he, "and endeavour to draw you forth."

"Oh, never mind," said the other, "I'm in rather a bad fix it is true, but I have an excellent horse under me, who has carried me through many a worse place than this—we shall get along."

A Pallet on the Floor

One time a fellow was traveling through the country, and it was a-raining, and he was looking for a place to sleep. Just before sundown he come to a little old log house. There was a man and a woman there, with three young ones. They only had one bed, but the man he allowed there's always room for a traveler. "You can have the bed," says he. "Me and my woman will sleep on a pallet with the kids."

After supper they set around and swapped whoppers awhile, and when the children got sleepy, the woman put them in the bed. Pretty soon two of the kids was sound asleep, and the man he picked them up careful and moved them to the pallet on the floor. So then the folks talked some more, and the other boy he went to sleep, and they laid him on the pallet, too. "The bed's all your'n, stranger," says the man. "You just turn in whenever you get ready. There's plenty of room on the pallet for me and the old woman." So the fellow went to bed. He was tired from riding all day, and he slept fine.

When the traveler woke up next morning it was still pretty dark, and seemed like the bed had got awful hard. But he just laid there till dawn. And then he seen that he wasn't in the bed at all. He was laying on the pallet with the kids. The man and the woman was in the bed, both of them a-snoring like they was sawing gourds. The fellow got up quiet and went outdoors awhile. He set out by the barn till he heard somebody splitting wood. When he come back to the house everybody was up and the woman was cooking breakfast. "You sure do get up early, stranger," says the man. "If you'd slept a little longer, me and the old woman would have put you back in bed. We always do strangers thataway, and mighty few of 'em ever know the difference."

The Six Thousand Year Principle

There once was an old man named Isaac Vanbibber, a wealthy old coot and as eccentric as a three-legged bullfrog. Some folks say he was an adopted son of Daniel Boone himself and grew up with Boone's oldest boy, Nathan, in St. Charles County, Missouri. Old man Vanbibber ran a tavern most all his life and was pretty well known for his unique philosophy. He used to take every opportunity that came around to declare his everlasting faith in what he called his "six thousand year principle"; that is, every six thousand years the same events in the history of the world and of everybody who ever lived would recur. He used to say that Caesar and Napoleon, Washington, even old man Vanbibber himself would all be coming 'round the mountain for another performance when their time was due. (Six thousand years from this very moment, reader, you'll be reading this book—this very tale—at least according to Vanbibber.) He was an active, persistent defender of this strange notion and spent many long evenings at his tavern boldly laying out his philosophy to disbelieving listeners. Vanbibber took a lot of jabbing and ridicule from everybody on the matter, but he stuck to his ideas.

One day, three Kentuckians rode up to Isaac's tavern and stayed the night. As usual, Vanbibber launched into his six thousand year principle, and the travelers, like everybody else, argued with him for a while, then took to making fun of him. The next morning, the three men decided to play a joke on Vanbibber and put his philosophy to a practical test. They said to the old man that according to his principle they would be back in this very tavern in six thousand years. Vanbibber agreed. The men then offered to give him a joint note, signed by all three, for payment of their bill at 10 percent interest per year payable when they returned in six thousand years.

For a minute the old man was quiet; then he addressed the three travelers. "Boys, ye are right smart fellers from Kaintuck, and I would at once take ye up and accept yer note and let ye go on yer way sure as shootin' in the sartinty that six thousand years from this day ye'd be here owin' me a buckboard full of gold. But I've been thinkin' on ye boys since ye got here and if I remember right ye were here six thousand years ago and left without payin' yer bills. I ain't gonna be taken agin, fellers, so shell out." And shell out they did.

Ain't Lost

A fine city man had a brand-new buggy and a prizewinning pair of trotters that he wished to try out. He drove along the country roads, speeding a little here and walking a little there, studying the good points and admiring the beauty of his new rig. He was so delighted with the prospect that he failed to notice the road. Later on, he realized that he was lost, but he hoped by driving on to find his way, or at least to meet someone who could tell him how to get back to the city.

But it was a long, lonesome road. For a long time he followed the windings, hoping every hilltop would bring him within sight of some dwelling. When it was almost dark he saw in front of him a cotton patch and a good-sized country boy chopping away in the rows. He reined his tired team near the fence and called out, "Hello, boy."

"Hello yourself," the boy replied, still wielding his hoe.

"Where does this road go to?"

"Hain't never seed it go nowhars. Hit allus stays right whar hit is," said the boy, still digging away.

"How far is it to the next town?"

"Don't know; never measured it," replied the boy.

Thoroughly disgusted, the man said with some heat, "You don't know anything. You are certainly the biggest fool I ever saw."

The boy looked a long time in the man's eyes; then he said with contempt, "I knows I don't know nothing. I knows I'se a fool. But I ain't lost."

Lodging in Kansas

I tell you what, stranger, I have gone in for a great majority of different sorts o' lodging an' sleeping, in the course o' my travels. I have slept alongside o' a log, and peeled off the bark for a coverlid; I've slept on a big rock with the snow for a blanket; I've roosted up a tree with a wildcat for a pillow; but the style of lodging in Kansas Territory beats all that clean out o' creation. You see, you can't lie upon a board or plank, because there ain't any there; you can't lie on the ground, because it is covered with water; you can't lie on the old rocks, because they're covered with rattlesnakes: so the only way left to get yourself into the snoreifferous state is to hook your two arms on to the lower limbs of a tree, with the ground and water for a foot-bard, an' there, like a man upon the gallows, you can swing yourself into a gentle slumber, keep off the snakes an' redskins, and no one can say that you ain't getting your lodging in an upright manner. This is a downright fact; if it ain't, take my narves for telegraph-wires!

Michigan Bedbugs

The hero of this story stopped at a hotel in Kalamazoo. When he retired for the night, the fun began. "Well, just as the shivers began to ease off, I kinder felt suthin' tryin' to pull off my shirt and diggin' their feet into the small of my back to get a good hold. I wiggled and twisted, doubled and puckered—all to no use—and it kept goin' like all sin. By-an'-by I got up and struck a light to look around a spell—found about a peck of bedbugs scattered around, and more droppin' off my shirt and runnin' down my legs every minit. Swept a place on the floor, shook out a quilt, lay down, and kivered up for a nap. No use—mounted right on to me like a parcel of rats on a meal tub—dug a hole in the kiver, and crawled through and gave me fits for trying to hide. Got up agin, went downstairs, and got the slush bucket from the wagon, brought it up, and made a circle of tar on the floor—lay down on the floor on the inside, and felt comfortable that time, anyhow. Left the light burnin' and watched 'em. See them get together and have a camp meetin' about it, and they went off in a squad with an old grey-headed one at the top, right up on the wall, on the ceiling, till they got on the right spot, then dropped right plump into my face. Fact, by thunder. Well, I swept them up agin and made a circle on the ceiling, too. Thought I had 'em foul that time, but danged if they didn't pull straws out of the bed and build a bridge over it—and some of them walked across on stilts."

A Yankee Finishes His Meal

There was once this stagecoach route in Texas that ran through a little town called Camden, where a notorious tavern was situated. A stage full of folks was nearing Camden one evening when one man aboard remarked to another, "We aren't but five miles from town."

"Pesky glad to hear it," said a Yankee-lookin' feller. "I'm as hungry as a hound."

"Sorry for you, then," answered the other man. "I'm as hungry as you, but we won't get three mouthfuls down before the stage is ready to leave. It's an old trick at the tavern."

"Trick or no trick," said the Yankee, "I'll have a hearty dinner."

"You might at that," said the man, "but you'll lose your seat on the stage for sure."

The Yankee smiled and looked at everyone. "I'll bet you supper for this whole group that I get my dinner and I don't lose my seat."

"I hate to steal your money, but I'll take that bet, because I know this tavern too well. You can throw cigars and wine into the deal too, for we'll be in Columbus later on this evening in time for a real supper."

Sure enough, when the stage got to Camden, the dinner that was supposed to be for the passengers wasn't ready yet. When it was, a man stood at the door and taxed folks four bits apiece as they went in to eat. But before the passengers could get four bits apiece worth of food down their throats, the tavern-keeper came in shouting that the stage was ready, mail was behind time, and the driver wouldn't wait a minute not even for his own grandmother. The travelers raced outside as fast as they could, no one wanting to miss his seat on the stage and get stuck in Camden, except for the Yankee, who stayed where he was and continued to eat. Plate after plate, he made those vittles walk down his throat most amazingly fast.

"You'll lose your seat, friend," said the tavern-keeper.

"Don't care much. I want the dinner I paid for, and then some," replied the Yankee, eating his way through a turkey that no one else had had time to touch. "And to finish up," he said to the tavern-keeper, "I guess I'll take a bowl of bread and milk."

The keeper went out of the room and presently came back and put the bowl down before his customer.

"Thank you kindly," the Yankee said. "I reckon I'll need a spoon, though, to eat this stuff with; cain't be eatin' bread and milk with my fingers."

"Spoon, sir!" said the keeper, his eyes popping out of his head. "There were a dozen spoons on the table just a while ago, and they were real silver spoons at that!"

"Well, there may have been," said the Yankee, "but you cain't blame them folks on that stage, now, can you? They weren't goin' to pay four bits an' come away with nothin' to show for it."

"Thunder and lightning!" roared the keeper. "If I don't bring the whole lot of those thieves to justice, then there's not a snake to be found in Virginny!" and he rushed to his horse out back.

About a half an hour later, after the Yankee had finished every scrap of food on the table, the same stage returned, rattling and clattering. The Yankee got up, went outside, and climbed aboard the stage among the passengers.

"Hold on! Hold on, stranger!" yelled the keeper, who had brought the stage back with the sheriff. Quite a crowd had gathered. "I want you to point out the robbers that took those spoons. Now I got the law and some friends and they'll help me straighten these thieves out for good."

"Well, mister," drawled the Yankee, "I guess if you look in your coffeepot, I calc'late you'll find them spoons. Seems I made a mistake. Goodbye, and thanks for the best meal I ever got for four bits. And don't be tellin' this to the next stage, neither."

Away went the stage, the driver cussin' because his stage was late, the passengers roarin' with laughter, and behind them a tavern-keeper who was madder than a blind hornet.

A Frequent Mover

There is a man in one of the Western states who has moved so often that whenever a covered wagon comes near his house, his chickens all march up and fall on their backs and cross their legs, ready to be tied and carried to the next stopping place.

The Hoosier and the Salt Pile

It is very refreshin' in these days of progress, after rattlin' over the country for days and nights, at the rate of twenty miles an hour in a railroad car—with your mouth full of dust and smoke, and with such an everlastin' clatter in your ears that you can't hear yourself think —to git into a good, old-fashioned stagecoach. There's something sociable and cosy in stagecoach travelin', so different from the bustle and confusion of a railroad, whar people are whirled along "slam bang to eternal smash," like they were so many bales and boxes of dry-goods and groceries, without so much as a chance of seein' whar they're gwine, or of takin' any interest in their feller sufferers. I love to hear the pop of the whip and the interestin' conversation between the driver and his horses; and I like the constant variation in the motion of the stage, the rattle of the wheels over the stones, the stillness of the drag through the heavy sand, the lunging and pitching into the ruts and gullies, the slow pull up the steep hills, the rush down agin, and the splashin' of the horses' feet and the wheels in the water and mud. And then one has time to see the country he's passin' through, to count the rails in the panels of the fences, and the women and children in the doors of the houses, to notice the appearance of the crops and the condition of the stock on the farms, and now and then to say a word to the people on the roadside. All these things is pleasant, after a long voyage on the railroad. But what's still more agreeable about stage-coach travelin', is that we have a opportunity of makin' the acquaintance of our feller passengers, of conversin' with 'em and studdyin' their traits of character, which from the strikin' contrast they often present, never fail to amuse if they don't interest our mind.

Some years ago I had a tolerably fair specimen of a stagecoach ride from Warrenton to Milledgeville. The road wasn't the best in the world, and didn't run through the most interestin' part of Georgia, but we had a good team, a good stage, and a first-rate driver, what could sing like a camp-meetin' and whistle like a locomotive, and the company was jest about as good a one as could be jumped up for such an occasion. There was nine of us besides the driver, and I don't believe there ever was a crowd of the same number that presented a greater variety of characters. There was an old gentleman in black, with big round spectacles, and a gold headed cane; a dandy gambler, with a big diamond breast-pin and more gold chains hangin' round him than would hang him; an old hardshell preacher, as they call 'em in Georgia, with the biggest mouth and the ugliest teeth I ever seen; a circus clown, whose breath smelled strong enough of whiskey to upset the stage; a cross old maid, as ugly as a tar-bucket; a beautiful young school-gal, with rosy cheeks and mischievous bright eyes; a cattle-drover from Indiany, who was gwine to New Orleans to git a army contract for beef, and myself.

For a while after we started from Warrenton nobody didn't have much to say. The young lady put her green veil over her face and leaned her head back in the corner; the old maid, after a row with the driver about her band-boxes, sat up straight in her seat and looked as sharp as a steel-trap; the old gentleman with the spectacles drummed his fingers on his cane and looked out of the coach-winder; the circus man tried to look interestin'; the gambler went to sleep; the preacher looked solemn; and the hoosier stuck his head out of the winder on his side to look at the cattle what we passed every now and then.

"This aint no great stock country," ses he to the old gentleman with the specs.

"No, sir," ses the old gentleman. "There's very little grazing here. The range in these parts is pretty much worn out."

Then there was nothing said for some time. By-an'-by the hoosier opened agin.

"It's the d—st place for 'simmon-trees and turkey-buzzards I ever did see."

The old gentleman didn't say nothin', and the preacher fetched a long groan. The young lady smiled through her veil, and the old maid snapped her eyes and looked sideways at the speaker.

"Don't make much beef down here, I reckon," ses the hoosier.

"No," ses the old gentleman.

"Well, I don't see how in the h——l they manage to live in a country whar there aint no ranges, and they don't make no beef. A man aint considered worth a cuss in Indiany what hasn't got his brand on a hundred head or so of cattle."

"Yours is a great beef country, I believe," ses the old gentleman.

"Well, sir, it aint nothing else. A man that's got sense enough to foller his own cow-bell with us, aint in no danger of starvin. I'm gwine down to Orleans to see if I can't git a contract out of Uncle Sam, to feed the boys what's been lickin' them infernal Mexicans so bad. I spose you've seed them cussed lies what's been in the newspapers about the Indiany boys at Bona Vista?"

"I've read some accounts of the battle," ses the old gentleman, "that didn't give a very flattering account of the conduct of some of our troops."

With that, the Indiany man went into a full explanation of the affair, and gittin' warmed up as he went along, begun to cuss and swear like he'd been through a dozen campaigns himself.

The old preacher listened to him with evident signs of displeasure, twistin' and groanin' every time he uttered a big oath, until he couldn't stand it no longer.

"My friend," ses he, "you must excuse me, but your conversation would be a great deal more interestin' to me, and I'm sure it would please the company much better, if you wouldn't swear so terribly. It's very wicked to swear so, and I hope you'll have respect for our religious feelins, if you hain't got no respect for your Maker."

If the hoosier had been struck with a clap of thunder and lightning he couldn't have been more completely took aback. He shut his mouth right in the middle of what he was sayin', and looked at the preacher, while his face got as red as fire.

"Swearin'," continued the old hardshell, "is a terrible bad practise, and there aint no use in it no how. The Bible says, 'Swear not at all,' and I spose you know the commandments about taking the Lord's name in vain."

The hoosier didn't open his mouth.

"I know," ses the old preacher, "a great many people swear without thinkin', and that some people don't believe in the Bible."

And then he went on to preach a regular sermon agin, and to quote the Scripture like he knowed the whole Bible by heart. In the course of his arguments he undertook to prove the Scriptures to be true, and told us all about the miracles and prophecies and their fulfillment. The old gentleman with the cane took a part in the conversation, and the hoosier listened without ever once openin' his head.

"I've jest heard of a gentleman," said the preacher, "what has been to the Holy Land, and went all over the Bible country. It's astonishin' what wonderful things he seed thar. He was at Soddom and Gomorrow, and seed the place whar Lot's wife fell!"

"Ah?" ses the old gentleman with the specs.

"Yes," ses the preacher. "He went to the very spot, and what's the most remarkablest thing of all, he seed the pillar of salt what she was turned into."

"Is it possible?" ses the old gentleman.

The hoosier's countenance all at once brightened up, and he opened his mouth wide.

"Yes, sir; he seed the salt standin thar to this day."

The hoosier's curiosity was raised to a point beyond endurance. "What!" ses he, "real genewine good salt?"

"Yes, sir, a pillar of salt jest as it was when that wicked woman was punished for her disobedience."

All but the gambler, who was snoozin' in the corner of the coach, looked at the preacher—the hoosier with an expression of countenance that plainly told that his mind was powerfully convicted of an important fact.

"Standin' right out in the open air?" he axed.

"Yes, sir,—right out in the open field where she fell."

"Well," ses the hoosier, "all I've got to say is, *if she'd dropp'd in Indiany, the cattle would lick'd her up long ago!*"

William T. Thompson

A White Elephant

Into an early mining town in Idaho one morning, there came a pack train of eleven mules, ten of them loaded with whisky and one with flour. A group of miners left a saloon and sauntered out to inspect the freight; and upon seeing what the cargo was on most of the mules, they were pleased. At last, however, one came to the cargo on the eleventh mule and fell back, appalled. He turned to his companions. "What in the name of hell," he asked, "are we going to do with all that flour?"

Hands Up!

Jack Shea tells one time about being held up. It was in Colorado, and he's travelin' on a coach. There's five passengers, and one of them is a middle-aged woman. There's been a lot of stick-up men on this road, and this old lady is worried. She's got fifty dollars, and she's tryin' to get to her daughter somewhere up North. This fifty is all she's got, and if she loses it she's on the rocks.

"There's an old man in the bunch that's got all the earmarks of a cowman," says Shea. "He tells her to stick her roll under the cushions, and slips her a couple of dollars, sayin' that it will pacify these road robbers.

"We ain't gone five mile when the coach stops sudden and a gent outside says, 'Step out, folks, an' keep your hands up while you're doin' it.' We all know what we're up against and ain't slow gettin' out. There's one gent at the leaders, got the driver and the outside passenger covered; another that's waitin' for us. They're both wearin' blinds and heeled till they look nasty. This stick-up seems to know the old cowman and speaks to him. The old man steps out of line and whispers something to him. None of us get any of his talk, but when the hold-up gets through trimmin' us he reaches into the coach, flips the cushion, and grabs the old lady's roll. Then we all return to our seats and the hold-up gives the driver his orders and the coach pulls out.

"We're all trimmed; the old lady's cryin', and the rest of us ain't sayin' much, but we're doin' lots of thinkin'. From what we get, it looks like the old cowman stands in with the hold-ups. He's tellin' the lady not to take it so hard. When one of the passengers wants to know what the low talk is between him and the stick-up, the cowman don't turn a hair but tells us all he double-crossed the lady; then he tells this hold-up that twenty dollars is his bank roll, but if he'll pass him up he knows where there's fifty. The hold-up agrees, and he tips off the old lady's cash to protect himself. He tells it like he ain't ashamed, and finishes, sayin', 'If you don't take care of yourself, nobody else will.'

"This talk makes the whole bunch wolfy. The passenger that's doin' the talkin' is for stoppin' the coach, and if there's a rope there'll be a hangin'. 'We don't need no rope; what's the matter with a lead rein? If he's as light in pounds as he is in principle, we'll slip a boulder in his pants to give him weight. This skunk is dirtier than any hold-up on the road, and the sooner we pull this party, the better it suits me.'

"We're gettin' worked up on all this talk when the cowman, that ain't turned a hair, says, 'If you gentlemen will let me play my hand out you'd find out who wins, but if you're bound to, go through with this hangin'.'

"By this time, the old lady's beggin' for the cowman. She don't want to see him strung up, but thinks jail is strong enough. But these passengers are frothin' at the mouth, and it sure looks like the cowman's end is near. The driver has heard the story and stopped.

" 'Well,' says the old man, 'if you're bound to hang me—' and he don't scare worth a dam—'I'll slip my boots. I've been a gambler all my life,' says he, draggin' off his right boot, 'but none of you shorthorns ever was; you never played nothin' but solitaire. This lady stakes me to fifty,' says he, 'and I always split my winnin's in the middle with them that stakes me.' And takin' a thousand dollars he's got tucked in his sock, he counts off five one-hundred-dollar bills, and hands them to the lady. 'That's yours,' says he.

"Nobody says nothin'. The old lady's shakin' hands, and, between sobs, thankin' this old cross-roader. Somebody tells the driver to drive on, and we're just pullin' into town when the man that's strong for hangin' pulls a pint from his hip and says, 'To show you there's no hard feelin's, we'll all take a drink—barrin' the lady.' When the bottle comes back to its owner, it's near dry, but before he empties it, he says, 'Here's to the gambler that pays his stakes!' Then he empties her and throws her out the window, and we all shake hands."

An Experienced River Pilot

The steamboat got caught in a bad fog at a time when the tide was low. In order to get through the fog without mishap, the captain thought it best to bring in a local pilot to steer the boat to safety. As the boat left the docks, the captain said to his new pilot, "Are you sure you know where all the rocks are, sir?" "Yep," replied the pilot. And with that came a grinding crash as the steamboat abruptly listed to the left. The pilot shook his head. "There's one of 'em now, damn it."

Mississippi Sounding Calls

OFTEN THE ONLY way to safely navigate a river was to "heave the lead," i.e., drop a rope overboard with a lead pipe attached to the end, the rope marked along its length to indicate the water's depth. The soundings were called out in a rhythmic chant to the pilot and could be heard, often in fog or darkness, up and down the river. These melodious leadsmen were said to have inspired the young Samuel Clemens in his search for a writing name. Listen to them now as they call out shallower and shallower water to the pilot:

No bottom,
Mark Four,
Quarter less four,
Quarter less five,
Half twain,
Quarter twain,

Quarter less four,
Half twain,
Quarter twain,
Mark twain,
Quarter less twain,
Nine and a half feet,
Nine feet,
Eight and a half feet.

Steamboats Are Dangerous

In a backwoods settlement, in Arkansas, lived two brothers whom we shall distinguish as Jim and Ned. Jim had seen a good deal of the world, had been present at one or two militia trainings and a cock-fight, and had actually seen a live steamboat. He was looked upon, consequently, in his immediate neighbourhood as considerable of a traveler. Ned was principally remarkable for his intense admiration for, and implicit obedience of, his learned brother's opinions and advice. Now, Ned had usually stayed at home "attending to things," while Jim performed the part of the prodigious son abroad. But one time when Jim was about starting, he determined to avail himself of his brother's experience and knowledge of the world, to see a little life himself.

Bright and early one fine fall morning, clad in the bright-green blanket-coat, and broad-brimmed hat, which form the principal features in the costume of the *élégants* of their section, and mounted on two raw-boned steeds, they started for the Mississippi, and reached a small town on its banks on the afternoon of the following day. Just as they arrived, the *Gen. Jackson* had hauled up to the miniature levee, and lay puffing, and paddling, and jerking cotton bales over her bow, and looking for all the world like an infernal big frame house with the kitchen wall knocked out. Now was the time for Jim to display his knowledge. So dismounting from his horse and giving Ned the reins to hold, and having cautioned him to wait until he had assured himself of the absence of all danger, he sauntered leisurely down towards the boat. It was a pleasant sight to see the air of knowingness and determination not to be taken in with which he nodded to every one he met, at the same time winking with his right eye, and jerking the raised forefinger of his right hand, as much as to say, "It's all very well, stranger, but they can't take *me* in; I know all about steamboats, I *should* think!" So he went on nodding and winking, until finally, not without great inward trepidation, he placed his foot on the boiler deck. Hardly had he done so, when splash went the wheels, the escape pipes sounded their tremendous *phlooow,* and he was enveloped in a cloud of steam. Jim could not stand this, but plunging into the stream, soon stood red and dripping by his bewildered brother. "Ned," says he, "she's blowed, and I'm the only one left alive to tell the tale! Let's go home."

"No, Jim," says Ned, "she hasn't blowed!"

"Well, if she hasn't blowed, she will blow—let's go home!" and springing on his frightened nag he disappeared, followed by his brother, from the eyes of the amused and astonished spectators.

Some weeks after their return, and after their settlement had somewhat got over the wonderful story Jim had regaled them with, a new hero entered upon the scene—one Mr. Thompson, who had been chopping in a woodyard on the Mississippi for six months, and whose adventures created a good deal of excitement among his wondering fellow-citizens. Every one crowded down to hear his stories, and among the rest came our two brothers. Ned sat with open ears and eyes, wondering at all he heard, but Jim listened with a cynical smile on his face, like a man who was not to be humbugged—and occasionally chimed in with a "Very true, Mr. Thompson—you needn't tell us that—we've seen all that before"—and then he would wink and shake his finger at Ned. At length Mr. T. incidentally mentioned the bursting of a steamboat at his yard. This arrested Jim's attention. "Stop, Mr. Thompson," said he, winking at Ned, "had she a d—d tall thing like a bee-martin pole stuck up forard?"

"Yes," rejoined Mr. Thompson.

Jim again winked at Ned. "And had she two great black things, like jackasses' ears in her middle?"

"Yes," replied Mr. Thompson.

Again Jim winked his expressive wink and nodded at his brother. "And had she two blasted big things splashing and grappling in the water alongside?"

Mr. Thompson assented—and Jim repeated his wink. "And was there a small boat pulling along behind, and trying to come up all she knew how?"

"Yes," said Mr. T.

"Ned," said Jim, solemnly, and concentrating all his powers in one determined wink—"*I knowed it was her, didn't I tell you she'd blow?*"

"It's All Right, Captain"

As the fleet steamer *R*. was coming up the Mississippi, several way passengers came on board at Vicksburg, and among others, a giant-looking, middle-aged Kentuckian, who very soon became the subject of curiosity, wonder, and general remark. After traveling a short distance, the party, except our hero, made their way to the captain's office, and paid their fare to the place of destination. The next day, the clerk made bold to call on the delinquent passenger, who had taken no berth, but had passed the greater part of the time in sleeping in his chair, and with his usual urbanity of manner, asked the Kentuckian to give him his place of destination, as it would help him in making up his book, intending his question also as a gentle hint for him to pay his fare.

The giant rose from his lethargy, and replied:

"I'm going up the river a-piece. It's all right, Mr. Clerk."

The clerk not being much the wiser from this answer, again politely asked.

"At what point do you intend to land, sir?"

"Don't land at *no point,* Mr. Clerk. It's all *right,* though."

Here the clerk left our old hero and went to consult the captain, who at once lost his wonted good humor, as the clerk related the result of his interview with the delinquent customer. The captain proceeded forthwith to bring the matter to a focus, and accosted the Kentuckian, saying:

"How far are you going to bear us company up the river, Uncle?"

"Oh! I'm going a-piece up with ye—but it's all *right,* Captain!"

"But, sir," said the captain, "you have neither paid your fare nor given the clerk your place of destination, and you are old enough to know the custom of steamboat men, that when a man refuses to pay his fare, or to give a good reason for not paying, we put him ashore immediately."

"We-l-l, Captain, 'spose 'tis your custom, but it's *all right!"*

Here the captain lost his patience, and resolved to put him ashore forthwith, and accordingly ordered the pilot to land, and told him to make ready to go ashore, to which he very graciously replied:

"It's *all right,* Captain."

The boat landed; and the plank put out, the giant was told to walk, to which he readily assented, saying:

"It's all right."

After getting on terra firma, the captain gave him a short blessing for giving him the trouble to land, and threatened him a top-dressing if he ever saw him again, &c. To which the man responded again, with an air of triumph, pointing to a fine-looking cottage just above him on the bank:

"It's all right, Captain, that's my house. It's *all right!*"

Nehemiah Flufkins's Visit to the City

Nehemiah Flufkins was one of those unfortunate specimens of the genus homo, that seem by some accident to have barely escaped shooting out of the ground in the form of a cabbage, and to have been born with all the outward semblance of humanity. Despite his awful greenness, Flufkins was an observant chap, anxious to look about the world, and, to use his own words, be "some pumpkins." He came to Boston one day to see the elephant, and innocently suffered all manner of tricks to be played upon him, such as paying twenty-five cents to go inside the Common, a charge made by a cunning boy, who discovered that Flufkins had "just come down." Another of the "b'hoys," who had received his cue from the lad who charged the entrance fee to the public Common, stopped Nehemiah as he came out and passed down Tremont Street, and politely tapping him on the arm, he said:

"Fifty cents fine, sir," at the same time holding out his hand for the money.

"Fifty cents! Creation, what fur?"

"The mayor's house, sir."

"Wot of that?" asked Flufkins, looking at the house designated by the other.

"You have passed it just now, *without taking off your hat!*"

"How yer talk. S'posin' I did?"

"Why, that's fifty cents fine in Boston."

"No!"

"Certainly; and unless you pay it, I shall be obliged to take you to the Police Office."

"W-h-e-w! Well, here's a half. Let's see which house it is," said Nehemiah, taking off his hat.

"That's it, sir, the next one to where we stand."

"Wall, I won't git caught agin, anyhow," said the innocent Flufkins, as he walked back and forth before the house of a green grocer, and fixed the spot in his mind!

Scarcely had Nehemiah Flufkins turned another corner, before he was stopped by a third person, who had got the hint from the other two operators.

"What's the matter *now!*" asked Nehemiah, "I haven't passed *another* mayor's house, have I?"

"No, but you forgot your landing fee."

"Landin' fee—what's that?"

"Why, head money."

"Head money! Do yer have to pay for keepin' yer head on?" asked Nehemiah, innocently.

"No—you don't understand, my friend. I perceive that you must be a stranger to the city."

"Wall, I guess I am."

"You see the law is, that any person arriving in town for the first time, shall pay seventy-five cents head money."

"Do tell."

"Yes. What route did you come by?"

"Fitchburg Railroad."

"That's it!" exclaimed his persecutor, as though he had made a discovery.

"What's it?" asked Nehemiah.

"Why, you are the fellow the police are after."

"After me, what fur?"

"For slipping away without paying your head money."

"Wall, look a' here, nabor, it's pretty expensive business, 'pears to me; but there's three quarters, will that fix it?"

"Yes, that is all right—you are free now to look about the town," said the other, walking away with a suppressed chuckle.

"Thank ye," said Flufkins; "only to think of the perleece after me! Well, that *was* an escape."

If there was one thing above another for which Nehemiah had a weakness, it was smoking. At home, his pipe was in his mouth half the time, and seeing some cigars in a window, he felt the desire come over him, and so he walked in, purchased a "long nine," lit it, and walked out into the street, smoking as he went along, looking into the shop windows in Washington Street. The fact was, Nehemiah was now really breaking a city ordinance, and laying himself liable to a fine. It was not long before a policeman, with his badge of office on his hat, accosted him.

"Sir, you must put out that cigar and walk with me," said the officer, with an air of decision that staggered Nehemiah.

"What fur?" stammered Flufkins.

"Smoking in the street."

"Is there a fine fur that too?"

"Yes, sir."

"How much?"

"Five dollars."

"Creation! Five dollars. I haven't got but six left."

"Can't help it, you must go with me."

"Look a' here—hold on!" said Nehemiah; "I don't want to go no whar."

"But you must," said the officer, at the same time looking about him slyly, and seeing no one very near, he added: "If you choose to pay *me*, why it will save your being locked up."

"*Locked up?* Creation! Here, there's five dollars," said Nehemiah, handing the officer the money, who pocketed the change, and walked away—leaving Mr. Flufkins standing alone seemingly afraid to move backwards or forwards, for fear he should incur another fine.

And this was the case; Flufkins was afraid to move lest he should break some other unknown law of the city. He thought the matter over, as well as he could in his confused state of mind, and remembering that he had just one dollar left, enough to carry him home in the cars, he looked all about him for a moment, to see that no one was by to stop him, and then "scratched gravel" like a new one, back towards the depot. As he approached the grocer's house, that had been pointed out to him as the mayor's, he pulled off his hat and only ran the faster, until he was out of sight of it.

At the head of Hanover Street, he was partially stopped by some one who wished to ask the way to some other part of the city, being, like himself a stranger—but Nehemiah had eyes and ears for only one thing, and misunderstanding the question, halloed out:

"Can't help it if 'tis a fine to run; I haven't got no money." And he dashed on like mad towards the railroad station.

Nehemiah didn't let on much about his visit to Boston, but merely said he didn't stay long, it was so pesky expensive.

On a Slow Train Through Arkansaw

It was down in the state of Arkansaw I rode on the slowest train I ever saw. It stopped at every house. When it came to a double house it stopped twice. They made so many stops I said, "Conductor, what have we stopped for now?" He said, "There are some cattle on the track." We ran a little ways further and stopped again. I said, "What is the matter now?" He said, "We have caught up with those cattle again."

We made pretty good time for about two miles. One old cow got her tail caught in the cow-catcher and she ran off down the track with the train. The cattle bothered us so much they had to take the cow-catcher off the engine and put it on the hind end of the train to keep the cattle from jumping up into the sleeper. A lady said, "Conductor, can't this train make any better time than this?" He said, "If you ain't satisfied with this train, you can get off and walk." She said she would, only her folks didn't expect her till the train got there.

A lady handed the conductor two tickets, one whole ticket and a half ticket. He said, "Who is the half ticket for?" She said, "My boy." The conductor said, "He's not a boy; he's a man. Under twelve, half fare, over twelve, full fare." She said, "He was under twelve when we started."

The news agent came through. He was an old man with long gray whiskers. I said, "Old man, I thought they always had boys on the train to sell the pop corn, chewing gum and candy." He said he was a boy when he started. They stopped so often one of the passengers tried to commit suicide. He ran ahead for half a mile, laid down on the track, but he starved to death before the train got there.

We had a narrow escape of being killed. Just as we got on the middle of a high bridge the engineer discovered it was on fire, but we went right across. Just as the last car got over, the bridge fell. I said, "Conductor, how did we ever get across without going down?" He said, "Some train robbers held us up."

There was a lady on the train with a baby. When the conductor asked her for her ticket, she said she didn't have any, the baby had swallowed it. The conductor punched the baby.

There were three kinds of passengers who rode on that train. First class, Second class and Third class. I said, "Conductor, what is the difference between the First class and Third class passengers, they are all riding in the same car?" He said, "Just wait a while and I will show you." We ran a little ways and stopped again. The conductor came in and said, "First class passengers, keep your seats; Second class passengers, get off and walk; Third class passengers, get off and push."

For a crooked road, she was the limit. In order to get the engine around the curves they had a hinge in the boiler. The fireman had a wooden leg and was crossed-eyed, half of the time he was shoveling coal in the headlight instead of the fire-box. It was so crooked we met ourself coming back. The curves were so short they called them corners. The engineer had to shave every day to keep the rocks from knocking off his whiskers.

The conductor was the tallest man I ever saw. I said, "Conductor, what makes you so tall?" He said it was because he had had his leg pulled so often. He said he was born in the top of a ten story building. He came high, but they had to have him.

An old lady said to the porter, "I gave you a dollar, where is my change?" He said, "This car goes through; there is no change."

There was a Dutchman on the train, he was trying to ride on a meal ticket. The conductor told him he would have to pay his fare. He said, "How much does it cost to ride to the next station?" The conductor said, "Thirty cents." The Dutchman said, "I will give you twenty-five." The conductor told him it would cost him thirty. The Dutchman said, "Before I will give more than twenty-five I will walk." The conductor stopped the train and put him off. The Dutch-man ran ahead of the engine and started to walk. The engineer began to blow the whistle. The Dutchman said, "You can vissel all you vant, I von't come back."

The Ballad of Casey Jones

Come all you rounders if you want to hear
The story told of a brave engineer;
Casey Jones was the rounder's name,
A high right-wheeler of mighty fame.

Caller called Casey about half-past four;
He kissed his wife at the station door,
Climbed into the cab with his orders in his hand,
Says, "This is my trip to the Holy Land."

Through South Memphis yards on the fly,
He heard the fireman say, "You got a white eye."
All the switchmen knew by the engine's moan
That the man at the throttle was Casey Jones.

It had been raining some five or six weeks;
The railroad track was like the bed of a creek.
They rated him down to a thirty-mile gait—
Threw the southbound mail some eight hours late.

Fireman says, "Casey, you're running too fast.
You ran the block board the last station we passed."
Casey says, "Yes, I believe we'll make it through,
For she steams better than ever I knew."

Casey says, "Fireman, don't you fret.
Keep knocking at the fire door; don't give up yet.
I'm going to run her till she leaves the rail
Or make it on time with the southern mail."

Around the curve and down the dump,
Two locomotives were bound to bump.
Fireman hollered, "Casey, it's just ahead!
We might jump and make it, but we'll all be dead!"

'Twas round this curve he spied a passenger train.
Rousing his engine, he caused the bell to ring.

Fireman jumped off, but Casey stayed on.
He's a good engineer, but he's dead and gone.

Poor Casey Jones was all right,
For he stuck to his duty both day and night.
They loved to hear the whistle and ring of No. 3
As he came into Memphis on the old I. C.

Headaches and heartaches and all kinds of pain
Are not apart from a railroad train.
Tales that are earnest, noble and grand
Belong to the life of a railroad man.

Lingo of the Rails

A timid little man sat at a railroad lunch counter and ordered ham and eggs. He looked bewildered when the waiter turned his face toward the kitchen and called casually, "A Mogul with two headlights."

A few seconds later the customer said, "Beg your pardon, sir, but I would like to have the eggs turned over."

"Blanket the headlights!" yelled the waiter.

Just then an engineer took a seat at the counter and called for "Wheatcakes and coffee."

"Running orders," shouted the waiter and turned to a third customer, who had just come in.

"A steak well done," said the last arrival.

"A hotbox and have it smoking," was the information given to the cook.

"Scrambled eggs," piped up an old lady with trepidation, and the waiter relayed her order as, "A wreck on the main line."

Then a boomer brakeman noisily set down his lamp and mounted one of the stools. "Let's see your switch list," he commanded. "Give me a coupla battleships, a pan of Murphies on the main line, and a string of flats on the siding."

It was the waiter's turn to look mystified.

"Cut the cow car off the Java train," continued the boomer, "and switch me a coupla life preservers for a Consolidation. It's a long drag to the next feed tank, and you had better fill the auxiliary to its full capacity."

"Say," cried the biscuit shooter, "I've only been on here a week, and you left me behind at the last stop."

"Excuse me," returned the brakeman. "I thought you were an old head. Give me a coupla pork chops, fried potatoes, and a side order of wheatcakes. Also a cup of black coffee and doughnuts. Fill the lunch basket, too, for it'll be some time before I get to the next restaurant. Put the coffee in the bottom and fill the upper deck with sandwiches and pie."

"I get you, Steve," beamed the waiter.

Traveling Superstitions

When you leave on a trip, toss an old shoe behind you for good fortune.

If you have a rooster, never leave on a trip before he crows.

Do not start a journey on Friday. Try never to leave on the thirteenth of the month.

Postpone a journey and you will never make it.

Never look back at your house when you leave it.

If you sneeze seven times you will take a long journey; so too if you trim your fingernails on Saturday.

Itching feet means you will go to a strange country. If your right foot itches, you're bound to have a good journey; if your left foot itches, your trip will end in sorrow.

If you see geese overhead as you depart on a trip, that is a good sign. If you see hogs in the road, turn back. Rabbits crossing your path is bad luck; if they run alongside the path you're on, that's very good luck.

If you see a whirlwind—even a small one—as you leave on a trip, go back home.

You'll have a long, happy journey if a bird's droppings fall on your head.

If you find a pin on the road, pick it up; it's good luck. If you see a spoon, let it be! Some folks are known to throw out a spoon when their luck is going badly, hoping that a passerby will pick it up and take the bad luck with him.

When you pass through a crossroads, slap your right leg for good luck.

Hold your breath while traveling past a cemetery.

To make a guest leave, turn a broom upside down behind the door.

Always tend to your traveling companions, be they horse, dog, woman, or friend, before you tend to yourself while traveling.

The Traveler's Homecoming

"Well haloo, Ben, how's everythin' been gettin' on since I been gone?"

"Right fine, boss. Right fine. 'Cept fer yer ol' bird dog, everythin's been right quiet."

"My bird dog?"

"Yessir, boss. Poor ol' dog jist plain died."

"Damn! She weren't but a puppy."

"Yessir, a perty puppy too. She just ate too much hossflesh, I guess."

"Hossflesh?"

"Yes, boss."

"Where in the hell did she get any hossflesh?"

"Well, there was sure plenty of it around afta the barn burned down. De hosses was just layin' about."

"The barn?"

"Yessir. De barn burned right down an' took all de stock up with it."

"All my stock? That barn was almost new an' I ain't even finished with the bank man about it."

"Yessir. Perty barn, perty barn."

"Well, damn it, how did the barn catch fire, Ben?"

"From de big house, boss. Jimmy says he saw it catch fire from de big house."

"De big house?"

"Yessir. De big house done burned to de groun' since you been gone. Boss, ain't nuthin' else happened though. It's been right quiet."

"Good God, how did the big house catch fire?"

"Don't know 'zactly, boss. I heard tell that one of them candles caught the house up."

"What candles?"

"The ones the preacher put 'round yer wife's momma's coffin. Dat's how it happened, so I heard."

"My wife's momma is dead?"

"Yessir. I was gettin' to dat."

"How did she die?"

"Shock, boss. Folks say it was de shock."

"Of the house burning down?"

"No, boss. De house went up afta she passed away. Dey say it was de shock when she heard yo' wife took up wid dat salesman fella and lit outa town."

CHAPTER 2

The Hills Beyond:
Pioneer Tales

"A Savage Santa Claus"

For we cannot tarry here,
We must march, my darlings, we must bear the brunt of
danger,
We the youthful sinewy races, all the rest on us depend,
Pioneers! O Pioneers!

          —Walt Whitman

HE WAS AMONG the first heroes of American folklore, dressed in his buckskin leggings and carrying his long rifle. We know him by many names—Daniel Boone, Davy Crockett, Jim Bridger, Kit Carson, old Bill Williams—but he is really one hero. He is the American explorer, the restless and solitary searcher who set out into the unknown wilderness of the New World and blazed a thousand paths for others to follow.

From the colonial days, America had been a nation of pioneers; a land of men and women who had gone West to seize and tame their own unruly dreams. Their faith was nourished and sustained by the adventures of explorers who crossed the wide rivers and daunting ranges so the rest could come after and claim it for themselves. The Alleghenies, the Mississippi, the Great Plains, the Rockies—each was an awesome barrier surmounted by lone searchers in moccasins. And soon enough, the explorers were made into giants by an adoring American public who needed to believe in the virtues of self-reliance, ingenuity, and courage. Dime novels and newspapers of the nineteenth century sang their exploits and made them the saints of the new frontier.

It is important to remember how folklore tends to focus on a chosen few. We shall never know the names of many a brave trapper and scout, or many a courageous pioneer, but their exploits live on, immortalized in the biographies of better-known heroes. Thus, the exploits of Peg-Leg Smith or Captain Billy Sublette were eventually attributed to Jim Bridger, while the adventures of James McBride and John Findlay were absorbed in the legend of Daniel Boone. So too, few may know of funny old Muldrow and his wife, or brave Mrs. Merrill, but their stories were told around the fire countless times, though Muldrow might have been called Smith, or Merrill named Jones. No matter. Let the historians argue over who actually did what. Good folklore is not as interested in getting the names right as in getting the stories told.

As different as the explorers might have been from one another—loud like Crockett and Bridger, shy and quiet like Carson or Boone, even surly like old Bill Williams—they were all men who could shoot straight and had mastered their fear of the unknown. They all understood that to survive in the wilderness you had to keep a certain wildness alive in yourself. Explorer lore is filled with violence. The best frontier tales are not about the discovery of the Great Overland Pass but about Indian fights and brushes with death. The explorer scalped so many Indians and slaughtered so many animals, we may sometimes doubt his humanity, yet the fact remains that were he any less fierce the wilderness would have devoured him and left no trace of his passing.

In spite of all the violence, the explorer possessed a deep intimacy with the landscape. The forest and valleys, the plains and the mountain passes all became part of the explorer's identity and past. Look at "Daniel Boone's Tale of the Three Notches" and you'll see how a tree not only solves a riddle but reminds Boone of his lost Kentucky. Even today's roadmaps of the West read like a directory of Mountain Men, their names forever linked to the places and routes they discovered so long ago.

This intimacy extended to the explorer's relations with the Indian as well. The explorer had to prove, through cunning and courage, that he could live on the land in the manner of the Indian. Once he did, he was admired and respected. Not infrequently the white explorer was adopted as a son or brother by a powerful chief, though the bond was strained when conflicts arose. It was still commonplace, though, that a man like Jim Bridger, who could speak in the sign of so many tribes, would sit surrounded by a hundred warriors and entertain them with his stories, only to find himself a week later in a deadly fight with those very same braves. Yet the explorer and the red men were denizens of the same unforgiving landscape, and for all their antagonisms, they understood one another far better than they did the maelstrom of settlers who were to sweep them both aside.

As America reached the Pacific, her first explorers passed away:

Boone grew old and lonely in Tennessee; Bridger and Carson died peacefully in their sleep; Bill Williams perished up in the Rockies (his end is chronicled in this chapter in "Death of a Mountain Man"). Yet, whatever their fate, these pioneers live on today as distinctly American heroes, dogged explorers whose eyes were always fixed on the hills beyond.

Captain John Smith and Pocahontas

One of America's earliest legends was the story of Captain John Smith's rescue by a little Indian girl. Despite the fact that nearly every schoolchild knows the story, evidence suggests the event never took place. Such is the marvel of legend, though, that a story can capture enough of the essence of truth to make irrelevent whether it actually happened or not. As Captain Smith recounted, his remarkable rescue happened soon after he was captured by the Indians near the settlement of Jamestown, which he had founded.

He was brought before the great Indian chief Powhatan, who sat in front of a roaring fire, covered in a robe made from raccoon skins, with bushy tails hung like so many tassels along its edge. On either side of Powhatan sat two beautiful young women, their lovely faces painted in bright colors, their hair full of feathers. All about him were his grim warriors, staring at Captain Smith as if he were a monster from the center of the earth. Their heads and shoulders were painted a fiery red, and some carried proud plumes of feathers in their hair as well; the effect was an array of color and spectacle the likes of which the young Englishman had never before seen. All the warriors wore bright white beads around their necks that sparkled in the firelight.

As Captain Smith was dragged in, a shout arose from the crowd. The queen of Appamatuck was appointed to bring him water to wash his hands, while another brought him feathers, not a towel, to dry himself. A great feast was held and after singing and eating, the crowd quieted and a council followed. As Captain Smith didn't know what they were saying, he could not know of their plans, but no interpreter was needed when he saw them bring out two great stones, followed by a fearsome brave with a huge club. His head was laid upon the stones as a dozen hands held his body steady and another cheer rose from the assembled audience. Powhatan stood up and prepared to signal to the brave who lifted the club above his head, when suddenly from the crowd darted a little girl, Powhatan's favorite daughter, whom he called Pocahontas. She covered Smith's head with her own and held tight to his body with her hands.

The braves dared not touch the Chief's daughter, and the Chief's own mighty voice could not dissuade her. It was a courageous act and it touched all those who witnessed it. Something in the Englishman's face had warmed the heart of the great Indian's daughter, and her quick and certain loyalty did more than save one white man's life. It shifted dramatically the delicate relations between the first white settlers of Jamestown and their red neighbors.

Young Pocahontas later married an English settler herself and went with him to England, where she was treated as a princess. She died there and was buried in the English town of Gravesend.

Daniel Boone's Tale of the Three Notches

I was once on a hunting expedition on the banks of the Green River, when the lower parts of Kentucky were still in the hands of nature, and none but the sons of the soil [the Indians] were looked upon as its lawful proprietors. We Virginians had for some time been waging a war of intrusion upon them, and I, among the rest, rambled through the woods, in pursuit of their race, as I now would follow the tracks of any ravenous animal. The Indians outwitted me one dark night and I was as unexpectedly as suddenly made a prisoner by them. The trick had been managed with great skill; for no sooner had I extinguished the fire of my camp, and laid me down to rest, in full security, as I thought, than I felt myself seized by an indistinguishable number of hands, and was immediately pinioned, as if about to be led to the scaffold for execution. To have attempted to be refractory, would have proved useless and dangerous to my life; and I suffered myself to be removed from my camp to theirs, a few miles distant, without uttering even a word of complaint. You are aware, I dare say, that to act in this manner, was the best policy, as you understand that by so doing, I proved to the Indians at once, that I was born and bred as fearless of death as any of themselves.

When we reached the camp, there was great rejoicing. Two squaws, and a few papooses, appeared particularly delighted at the sight of me, and I was assured, by very unequivocal gestures and words, that, on the morrow, the mortal enemy of the red-skins would cease to live. I never opened my lips, but was busy contriving some scheme which might enable me to give the rascals the slip before dawn. The women immediately fell to searching about my hunting-shirt for whatever they might think valuable, and fortunately for me, soon found my flask, filled with Monongahela (that is, reader, strong whiskey). A terrific grin was exhibited on their murderous countenances, while my heart throbbed with joy at the anticipation of their intoxication. The crew immediately began to beat their bellies and sing, as they passed the bottle from mouth to mouth. How often did I wish the flask ten times its size! I observed that the squaws drank more freely than the warriors, and again my spirits were about to be depressed, when the report of a gun was heard at a distance. The Indians all jumped on their feet. The singing and drinking were both brought to a stand; and I saw with inexpressible joy, the men walk off to some distance, and talk to the squaws. I knew that they were consulting about me, and I foresaw, that in a few moments the warriors would go to discover the cause of the gun having been fired so near their camp. I expected the squaws would be left to guard me. Well, sir, it was just so. They returned; the men took up their guns and walked away. The squaws sat down again, and in less than five minutes they had my bottle up to their dirty mouths, gurgling down their throats the remains of the whiskey.

With what pleasure did I see them becoming more and more drunk, until the liquor took such hold of them that it was quite impossible for these women to be of any service. They tumbled down, rolled about, and began to snore; when I, having no other chance of freeing myself from the cords that fastened me, rolled over and over toward the fire, and after a short time burned them asunder. I rose on my feet; stretched my stiffened sinews; snatched up my rifle, and, for once in my life, spared the Indians. I now recollect how desirous I once or twice felt to lay open the skulls of the wretches with my tomahawk; but when I again thought upon killing beings unprepared and unable to defend themselves, it looked like murder without need, and I gave up the idea.

But, sir, I felt determined to mark the spot, and walking to a thrifty ash sapling, I cut out of it three large chips, and ran off. I soon reached the river; soon crossed it, and threw myself deep into the canebrakes, imitating the tracks of an Indian with my feet, so that no chance might be left for those from whom I had escaped to overtake me.

It is now nearly twenty years since this happened and more than five since I left the whites' settlements, which I might probably never have visited again, had I not been called on as a witness in a lawsuit that was pending in Kentucky and which, I really believe, would never have been settled, had I not come forward, and established the beginning of a certain boundary line. This is the story, sir.

Mr. ——— moved from old Virginia into Kentucky, and having a large tract granted to him in the new state, laid claim to a certain parcel of land adjoining Green River, and as chance would have it, he took for one of his corners the very ash tree on which I had made my mark, and finished his survey of some thousands of acres, beginning, as it is expressed in the deed, "at an ash marked by three distinct notches of the tomahawk of a white man."

The tree had grown much, and the bark had covered the marks; but, some how or other, Mr. ——— heard from some one all that I have already said to you, and thinking that I might remember the spot alluded to in the deed, but which was no longer discoverable, wrote for me to come and try at least to find the place on the tree. His letter mentioned that all my expenses should be paid; and not caring much about once more going back to Kentucky, I started and met Mr. ———. After some conversation, the affair with the Indians came to my recollection. I considered for a while, and began to think that after all, I could find the very spot, as well as the tree, if it was yet standing.

Mr. ——— and I mounted our horses, and off we went to the Green River bottoms. After some difficulties, for you must be aware, sir, that great changes had taken place in these woods, I found at last the spot where I had crossed the river, and waiting for the moon to rise, made for the course in which I thought the ash tree grew. On approaching the place, I felt as if the Indians were there still, and as if I was still a prisoner among them. Mr. ——— and I camped near what I conceived the spot, and waited till the return of day.

At the rising of the sun I was on foot, and after a good deal of musing, thought that an ash tree then in sight must be the very one on which I had made my mark. I felt as if there could be no doubt of it, and mentioned my thought to Mr. ———. "Well, Colonel Boone," said he, "if you think so, I hope it may prove true, but we must have some witnesses; do you stay hereabout, and I will go and bring some of the settlers whom I know." I agreed. Mr. ——— trotted off, and I, to pass the time, rambled about to see if a deer was still living in the land. But ah! sir, what a wonderful difference thirty years make in the country! Why, at the time when I was caught by the Indians, you would not have walked out in any direction for more than a mile without shooting a buck or a bear. There were ten thousand buffaloes on the hills in Kentucky; the land looked as if it would never become poor; and to hunt in those days was a pleasure indeed. But when I was left to myself on the banks of the Green River, I dare say for the last time in my life, a few signs only of deer were to be seen, and as to a deer itself, I saw none.

Mr. ——— returned, accompanied by three gentlemen. They looked upon me as if I had been Washington himself, and walked to the ash tree which I now called my own, as if in quest of a long lost treasure. I took an axe from one of them and cut a few chips off the bark. Still no signs were to be seen. So I cut again, until I thought it time to be cautious, and I scraped and worked away with my butcher knife, until I *did* come to where my tomahawk had left an impression in the wood. We now went regularly to work, and scraped at the tree with care, until three hacks, as plain as any three notches ever were, could be seen. Mr. ——— and the other gentlemen were astonished, and, I must allow, I was as much surprised as pleased, myself. I made affidavit of this remarkable occurrence in the presence of these gentlemen. Mr. ——— gained his cause. I left Green River, for ever, and came to where we now are; and, sir, I wish you a good night.

Bewildered Boone

After coming back from many months in the forests of Kentucky, Daniel Boone was talking one time with some settlers. "Daniel, did you ever get lost?" they asked the great explorer. "Lost?" said Boone. "No, I can't say I was ever lost, but I was bewildered once for three days."

"That's John's Gun!"

At the disastrous battle of the Blue Licks there were a few reported slain who had been captured, and, after running the gauntlet, had been allowed to live. Among them was a certain husband, who, with eleven other captives, had been painted black as a signal of death. The whole twelve were stripped and placed on a log, the husband being at one extremity. The cruel savages now slaughtered eleven, one by one, but when they came to this one, though they drew their knives and tomahawks over him ready to strike, they paused and had an animated powwow, ending in sparing his life—why he never could find out.

For over a year his wife awaited his return, hopeful against all arguments to the contrary. She almost gave up at last, but, wooed by another, she postponed the day from time to time, declaring she could not shake off the belief that her husband would yet come back. Her friends reasoned on her folly; she reluctantly yielded, and the nuptial day was fixed. But, just before it dawned, the crack of a familiar rifle was heard near her lonely cabin. At the welcome sound she leaped out, ejaculating as she sprang, "That's John's gun! That's John's gun!" It was John's gun, sure enough, and in an instant she was again in her beloved husband's arms. Nine years later, however, that same husband did really fall at St. Clair's defeat, and the same persevering lover renewed his suit and at last won the widow.

A Mighty Strange Turkey

This is a story they tell about Jesse Hughes, who was one of early Virginia's greatest hunters. During a particularly violent Indian war, Hughes was in the fort at Clarksburg, where most of the people had gathered until things quieted down. He passed a young boy who was busy cleaning his gun.

"Planning to shoot somebody, Jim?" asked the famed hunter.

The boy looked up, determined. "There's a turkey on the hillside out there and I'm going to bring him home for dinner."

Hughes listened a bit, then said, "I don't hear a turkey."

"Listen," said the boy. "There. Can't you hear that? He's a big gobbler for sure."

Hughes again listened and this time caught the familiar sound of the turkey feeding. "Jim," he said, "how about I go and get that turkey? It does sound like a big one."

"Oh no, sir," said the boy, "thanks all the same. I heard it and I aim to kill it." He picked up his gun.

Hughes put his hand on the boy's shoulder. "Hold on now, Jim," he said, "it's your turkey. I know that. But you know I'm more familiar with shooting than you are, and I know your folks could use that meat."

The boy hesitated.

"I'm not saying that you'd miss, lad, but with things being as they are, a miss might make more fuss than a hit."

The boy reluctantly agreed and watched as the hunter left the fort on the opposite side from the gobbling turkey. He was gone about ten minutes before the boy heard a shot. Everybody ran to the wall and looked over at the hillside, where they saw Jesse Hughes coming back toward them empty-handed. The boy waited with a crowd at the gate.

"What's up, Jesse?" asked people as he came through.

"Why, Jim saw a big turkey and we drew straws to see who'd bag it and I won. Only, I missed the turkey altogether," Jesse answered.

"Mr. Hughes, I'd have gotten that turkey, I know it," Jim said proudly. Everyone laughed at the boy's audacity.

Later, Hughes called the boy over to the stable, where they could be alone. "Jim, do you know what kind of a turkey that was?" Hughes asked.

"No sir," came the reply, "but I know it was a big one and would have fed my family for a week, if only I had had a crack at it."

Hughes smiled. "Well, it was an unusual kind, my young friend. Ever seen one with feathers like this?" The hunter slapped down a bloody scalp fresh from an Indian's head. The boy said nothing; he just stared at those "feathers" and slowly rubbed his own hair.

"Yessir," said Jesse Hughes, "it's best to know just what you're hunting before you go to hunt it."

A Pioneer Woman Fights Back

The year 1791 saw a most remarkable instance of a woman's heroism. A settler named Merrill lived in a lonely cabin in Nelson County, Virginia, his family consisting of his wife, one daughter just budding into womanhood, and other, smaller children. As usual where much of the food for the family must be obtained by the chase, there were many dogs about the place. One night these kept up an unusual noise. Thinking that perhaps they were barking at some belated traveler who had come to ask for shelter or to inquire his road, the hospitable pioneer started out to investigate. As he opened the door, thus throwing his figure into clear relief against the fire blazing at the other side of the room, there was a sharp report, a shot struck him, and he fell backward upon the floor. There could be but one explanation; and even while the yells of the dusky foes were yet sounding, the wife and daughter had drawn him farther into the room, and closed and barred the door.

The instant that the shot was fired, the savages had rushed forward, hoping that the door would not be closed in time to prevent their entrance; but the promptness of the two women had defeated this intention. Nothing daunted, however, by the interposition of the planks between them and their prey, they began to belabor the barrier with their tomahawks. A breach was soon made, and the foremost endeavored to squeeze through this into the room.

But the courageous woman within was ready for him. Her husband lay suffering, perhaps dying; her little children were screaming with fright; the eldest daughter knelt at her father's side, white and trembling, but endeavoring, with the rude surgery of the frontier, to stanch the flow of blood and bind up the wound. The exulting yells without showed how secure of success were the assailants. Seizing an ax, she dealt the intruder a swinging blow upon the head. He died without a groan, and the intrepid woman dragged his body into the room. His companion, supposing that he had entered of his own will, prepared to follow, but met with the same fate. Again and again was this repeated, and four Indians lay on the floor of the cabin.

But the suspicions of those without were now aroused; they did not see why their companions within the cabin should be so silent, why the door had not been opened to admit them. Retreating to some little distance, they tried to get a fair view of the interior. There lay the wounded father, the daughter bending over him; there stood the heroic wife, ax in hand, awaiting the approach of another enemy. The bodies of their fated comrades they could not see, they having been dragged to one side. It was evident that some new plan of attack must be adopted.

There were three Indians yet remaining, of the party of seven. It was agreed that two of these should climb to the roof of the cabin and descend the chimney; while the other, waiting until this had been accomplished, and the attention of the inmates diverted, should enter through the breach in the door. Silently as they might steal up to the house, they could not reach the roof without noise, and Mrs. Merrill speedily detected their purpose. The thrifty woman had provided huge feather beds for her family, and one of these she directed her little son to drag to the fireplace. The united efforts of the boy and his sister placed the huge mass in the very center of the glowing embers. The cotton cover caught fire and kindled the feathers. As the two savages descended the wide-mouthed chimney, a suffocating smoke arose from the burning feathers. Half insensible by reason of it, they were unable to climb to the roof or even to remain where they were, and fell, helpless to the hearth. The wounded man roused himself and dispatched them before they recovered from their insensibility; while the wife still kept guard at the door.

Having allowed what he considered a sufficient time for his comrades to effect their entrance, the one remaining savage crept up to the door, and tomahawk in hand, sprang forward. Once again that ax descended, but with less fatal effect than before; he was wounded, not killed. Howling with pain and dismay, he took himself off to the woods, and never paused until he reached the village of his tribe. A white prisoner, who afterward escaped, overheard his account of it.

"What news?" asked a warrior.

"Bad news," answered the fugitive; "damn bad news. Long-knife squaw fight worse than the warriors of her people."

There is, we believe, no further record of the Merrills in border history; from which we infer that the escaped Indian's story made his kindred afraid to attack the cabin again.

How Muldrow Found His Neighbor

There was once a man named Muldrow, an early pioneer of Kentucky, who took his wife and went to live in the wilderness. They settled on a rocky hill covered with scrub trees and brambles, though why they chose to live there, when down below them were the green and lovely valleys of Kentucky, nobody knows. Muldrow and his wife liked that desolate hill and that was that. They lived there for nearly a year and never once saw another human being.

One day, Muldrow was out hunting when he heard a dog's bark somewhere behind him. He had left his own dogs penned many miles back, so he wasted no time stepping behind a big tree and priming his gun. A few moments later the dog came along, nose to the ground, obviously worked up over Muldrow's scent. Stopping a few feet from Muldrow, the dog growled a warning, its teeth yellow, sharp, and long. Muldrow saw the bushes behind the dog rustle and then part for the dog's owner, a tall, strong-looking man armed with a rifle, a tomahawk, and a hunting knife. While his dress was deerskin like a white man's, his complexion was the dark shade of an Indian.

Muldrow thought of the poor pioneer whose clothes the savage now wore, and though it wasn't really his business, Muldrow was determined to avenge the victim with one shot. He raised his gun but the redskin heard the click of the hammer and leapt behind another tree before Muldrow could shoot. The two adversaries then began to stalk one another from tree to tree, bush to bush, each trying to draw the first fire of the other.

After a few moments, Muldrow, who was impatient with all these stratagems, shouted angrily, "Why don't you shoot, you red heathen?" Back came a voice, equal in anger and challenge, "I'm just waiting for you, you ambushing coward!" Old Muldrow, madder than a wet hen, fumed, "I ain't no coward!" Then there was silence, followed by a good-natured voice saying, "Pilgrim, if you ain't no coward, I sure ain't no heathen. What do you say if we both come to the same side of the Lord?" Sure enough, Muldrow realized his mistake: This fellow was no Indian, just a pioneer like himself. The two men came out and shook hands while the stranger's dog jumped happily at their feet.

It seemed the other fellow had been out shooting game for over a week. He'd come to this country a month before and had left his wife in a new cabin some twenty miles back. He made Muldrow promise to bring his wife for a visit soon, and after hunting a while together the ruddy-faced hunter left. Muldrow went home and told his wife the story. When he finished she just sighed. "Well, it's starting to get crowded again." "You're right," said the old pioneer, "We need elbow room. Best be pushing on before folks get right in under our feet."

Soon after, they left. Nobody else ever did live on that desolate hill, and it is still called Muldrow's Hill, to this very day.

A Savage Santa Claus

"Talkin' about Christmas," said Bedrock, as we smoked in his cabin after supper, an' the wind howled as it sometimes can on a blizzardy December night, "puts me in mind of one I spent in the '60s. Me an' a feller named Jake Mason, but better knowed as Beaver, is trappin' an' prospectin' on the head of the Porcupine. We've struck some placer, but she's too cold to work her. The snow's drove all the game out of the country, an' barrin' a few beans and some flour, we're plum out of grub, so we decide we'd better pull our freight before we're snowed in.

"The winter's been pretty open till then, but the day we start there's a storm breaks loose that skins everything I ever seed. It looks like the snow-maker's been holdin' back, an' turned the whole winter supply loose at once. Cold? Well, it would make a polar bear hunt cover.

"About noon it lets up enough so we can see our pack-hosses. We're joggin' along at a good gait, when old Baldy, our lead pack-hoss, stops an' swings 'round in the trail, bringin' the other three to a stand. His whinner causes me to raise my head, an' lookin' under my hat brim, I'm plenty surprised to see an old log shack not ten feet to the side of the trail.

" 'I guess we'd better take that cayuse's advice,' says Beaver, pointin' to Baldy, who's got his ears straightened, lookin' at us as much as to say: 'What, am I packin' fer Pilgrims; or don't you know enough to get in out of the weather? It looks like you'd loosen these packs.' So, takin' Baldy's hunch, we unsaddle.

"This cabin's mighty ancient. It's been two rooms, but the ridge-pole on the rear one's rotted an' let the roof down. The door's wide open an' hangs on a wooden hinge. The animal smell I get on the inside tells me there ain't no humans lived there for many's the winter. The floor's strewn with pine cones an' a few scattered bones, showin' it's been the home of mountain-rats an' squirrels. Takin' it all 'n all, it ain't no palace, but, in this storm, it looks mighty snug, an' when we get a blaze started in the fireplace an' the beans goin' it's comfortable.

"The door to the back's open, an' by the light of the fire I can see the roof hangin' down V-shaped, leavin' quite a little space agin the wall. Once, I had a notion of walkin' in an' prospectin' the place, but there's somethin' ghostly about it an' I change my mind.

"When we're rollin' in that night, Beaver asks me what day of the month it is.

" 'If I'm right on my dates,' says I, 'this is the evenin' the kids hang up their socks.'

" 'The hell it is,' says he. 'Well, here's one camp Santy'll probably overlook. We ain't got no socks nor no place to hang 'em, an' I don't think the old boy'd savvy our foot-rags.' That's the last I remember till I'm waked up along in the night by somethin' monkeyin' with the kettle.

"If it wasn't fer a snufflin' noise I could hear, I'd a-tuk it fer a trade-rat, but with this noise it's no guess with me, an' I call the turn all right, 'cause when I take a peek, there, humped between me an' the fire, is the most robust silvertip* I ever saw. In size, he resembles a load of hay. The fire's down low, but there's enough light to give me his outline. He's humped over, busy with the beans, snifflin' an' whinin' pleasant, like he enjoys 'em. I nudges Beaver easy, an' whispers: 'Santy Claus is here.'

"He don't need but one look. 'Yes,' says he, reachin' for his Henry, 'but he ain't brought nothin' but trouble, an' more'n a sock full of that. You couldn't crowd it into a wagon-box.'

"This whisperin' disturbs Mr. Bear, an' he straightens up till he near touches the ridge-pole. He looks eight feet tall. Am I scared? Well, I'd tell a man. By the feelin' runnin' up and down my back, if I

---

* A kind of grizzly bear.

had bristles I'd resemble a wild hog. The cold sweat's drippin' off my nose, an' I ain't got nothin' on me but sluice-ice.

"The bark of Beaver's Henry brings me out of this scare. The bear goes over, upsettin' a kettle of water, puttin' the fire out. If it wasn't for a stream of fire runnin' from Beaver's weapon, we'd be in plumb darkness. The bear's up agin, bellerin' an' bawlin', and comin' at us mighty warlike, and by the time I get my Sharp's workin', I'm near choked with smoke. It's the noisiest muss I was ever mixed up in. Between the smoke, the barkin' of the guns an' the bellerin' of the bear, it's like hell on a holiday.

"I'm gropin' for another ca'tridge when I hear the lock on Beaver's gun click, an' I know his magazine's dry. Lowerin' my hot gun, I listen. Everythin's quiet now. In the sudden stillness I can hear the drippin' of blood. It's the bear's life runnin' out.

" 'I guess it's all over,' says Beaver, kind of shaky. 'It was a short fight, but a fast one, an' hell was poppin' while she lasted.'

"When we get the fire lit, we take a look at the battle ground. There lays Mr. Bear in a ring of blood, with a hide so full of holes he wouldn't hold hay. I don't think there's a bullet went 'round him.

"This excitement wakens us so we don't sleep no more that night. We breakfast on bear meat. He's an old bear an' it's pretty stout, but a feller livin' on beans and bannocks straight for a couple of weeks don't kick much on flavor, an' we're at a stage where meat's meat.

"When it comes day, me an' Beaver goes lookin' over the bear's bedroom. You know, daylight drives away ha'nts, an' this room don't look near so ghostly as it did last night. After winnin' this fight, we're both mighty brave. The roof caved in with four or five feet of snow on, makes the rear room still dark, so, lightin' a pitch-pine glow, we start explorin'.

"The first thing we bump into is the bear's bunk. There's a rusty pick layin' up against the wall, an' a gold-pan on the floor, showin' us that the human that lived there was a miner. On the other side of the shack we ran onto a pole bunk, with a weather-wrinkled buffalo robe an' some rotten blankets. The way the roof slants, we can't see into the bed, but by usin' an ax an' choppin' the legs off, we lower it to view. When Beaver raises the light, there's the frame-work of a man. He's layin' on his left side, like he's sleepin', an' looks like he cashed in easy. Across the bunk, under his head, is an old-fashioned cap-'n-ball rifle. On the bedpost hangs a powder horn an' pouch, with a belt an' skinnin' knife. These things tell us that this man's a pretty old-timer.

"Findin' the pick an' gold-pan causes us to look more careful for what he'd been diggin'. We explore the bunk from top to bottom, but nary a find. All day long we prospects. That evenin', when we're fillin' up on bear meat, beans and bannocks, Beaver says he's goin' to go through the bear's bunk; so, after we smoke, relightin' our torches, we start our search again.

"Sizin' up the bear's nest, we see he'd laid there quite a while. It looks like Mr. Silvertip, when the weather gets cold, starts huntin' a winter location for his long snooze. Runnin' onto this cabin, vacant, and lookin' like it's for rent, he jumps the claim an' would have been snoozin' there yet, but our fire warmin' up the place fools him. He thinks it's spring an' steps out to look at the weather. On the way, he strikes this breakfast of beans, an' they hold him till we object.

"We're lookin' over this nest when somethin' catches my eye on the edge of the waller. It's a hole, roofed over with willers.

" 'Well, I'll be damned. There's his cache,' says Beaver, whose eyes has follered mine. It don't take a minute to kick these willers loose, an' there lays a buckskin sack with five hundred dollars in dust in it.

" 'Old Santy Claus, out there,' says Beaver, pointin' to the bear through the door, 'didn't load our socks, but he brought plenty of meat an' showed us the cache, for we'd never a-found it if he hadn't raised the lid.'

"The day after Christmas, we buried the bones, wrapped in one of our blankets, where we'd found the cache. It was the best we could do.

" 'I guess the dust's ours,' says Beaver. 'There's no papers to show who's his kin-folks.' So we splits the pile an' leaves him sleepin' in the tomb he built for himself."

The Trapper's Hello

BACK IN THE 1820s and 1830s the West had its own name for the explorer: he was the mountain man, the rugged trapper who came down out of the Rockies loaded with furs and tall tales of a country few white men had ever seen. Like the Indian, the mountain man knew every tree stump, dried creek-bed, and badger hole from Arkansas to the Pacific. He could read the weather in the flight of an eagle or tell from a broken twig that a dozen Sioux had passed ahead of him several hours before. Long months alone taught him to rely on himself, and though he was suspicious of people he didn't know, he was never scared of them. When he saw strangers, he rode steadily toward them with his gun in the hollow of his arm—a fearless, though wary, approach. If, however, he recognized them as fellow trappers he would rein in his horse, lay his rifle across the saddle, and wait for them. Perhaps, as they met, the conversation might go something like this:

"Where from, stranger?"

"The divide, an' to the bayou fer meat; an' you are from there, I see. Any buffalo come in yet?"

"A heap, and seal-fat at that. What's the sign out on the Plains?"

"War-party of 'Rapahos passed Squirrel at sundown yesterday, and nearly raised my animals. Sign too, of more on left fork of Boiling Spring. No buffalo between the Snake and Broken Arrow Canyon. Do you feel like camping?"

"*Well,* we do. But whar's yer campanyeros?"

"I'm alone."

"Alone! Wagh! How d'ya get your animals along?"

"I go ahead, an' they follow the hoss."

"Well, that beats all! That's a smart-lookin' hoss now; and runs some, I'm thinkin'."

"Well, it does."

"Whar's them mules from? They look like Californy."

"Mexican country—away down South."

"Hell! Whar's yerself from?"

"There away too."

"What's beaver worth in Taos?"

"Dollar."

"In St. Louiy?"

"Same."

"Hell! Any call fer buckskin?"

"A heap! The soldiers in Sante Fe are half froze fer leather; and moccasins fetch two dollars, easy."

"Wagh! How's trade in Arkansa, an' what's doin' at the fort?"

"Cheyennes at Big Timber and Bert's people are tradin' right smart. Jim Waters got hisself a hundred pack right off, and I hear tell there's a lot more to be had whar that come from."

"Whar's old Bill Williams?"

"Ain't nobody seen him. Gone under, they say. The Crows took his hair, I think."

"Well. How's powder goin'?"

"Two dollars a pint."

" 'Bacca?"

"A plew* a plug."

"Got any about you?"

"Have *so.*"

"Give us a chaw and let's camp."

The Trappers' Camp

Brown's hole, at certain seasons of the year, becomes a place of considerable note, and presents many of the features of a western settlement on a holiday. It was interesting to us to note the avariciousness of the traders, and the careless indifference of the trappers, in disposing of their commodities. Dropping in daily—sometimes singly and sometimes in parties from two to ten, loaded with pelts and furs, in value from one to several thousand dollars—the latter would barter them for powder, lead, tobacco, alcohol, coffee, and

* A trapper's name for prime beaver skin, one of which would buy a plug of tobacco.

whatever else they fancied, receiving each article at the most exorbitant price, without uttering a word of complaint. I have seen powder sold to the mountaineers at the enormous sum of from three to four dollars a pint; alcohol at double this price, the same measure; coffee ditto; tobacco two and three dollars per plug, and every thing else in proportion. Money here was out of the question, as much as if it had never been in existence—furs, pelts, and robes, being substituted therefor. Here I witnessed gambling on every scale, from the highest to the lowest—from thousands to units—while every doubtful or mooted point was sure to result in a bet before decided. It was nothing uncommon to see a trapper "come in" with three or four mules, and furs to the amount of several thousand dollars, and within a week from his arrival, be without the value of a baubee he could call his own—furs, mules, rifle, every thing, sacrificed to his insatiable love of gambling. The mountaineer over his cups is often quarrelsome, and an angry dispute is almost certain to be settled in an honourable way (?)—that is, rifles at thirty yards—when one or the other (sometimes both) rarely fails to pay the forfeit of his life. I had not been many days in Brown's Hole ere I witnessed a tragedy of this kind, which, even now, as I recall it, makes my blood run cold with horror.

The actors in this bloody scene were two trappers of the better class, of intelligent and respectable appearance, neither of whom had seen over thirty years, and who as a general thing were of very sober and quiet habits. They were from the same part of the country—had been boys together—had started together upon their adventurous and perilous occupation, and were, moreover, sworn *friends.*

Some three days after our arrival, they had made their appearance, well packed with pelts and furs, which they immediately proceeded to dispose of to the traders. As their trip had been an unusually profitable one, they of course felt much elated, and taking a drink together, sat down to a friendly game of cards, to while away their leisure hours. More strict in their habits than most of their associates, they rarely gambled, and then only for diversion. On the occasion alluded to, they at once began playing for liquor, and having at length drunk more than their wont, proceeded to stake different articles. As the game progressed, they became more and more excited, until at last their stakes ran very high. One was peculiarly fortunate, and of course the luck of the other was exactly the reverse, which so mortified and vexed him, that he finally staked all his hard earnings and lost. On this his companion took another drink, grew more and more merry at his own success, which he attributed to his superior skill in handling the cards, and finally bantered the other to put up his mules. No sooner said than done, and the result was the same as before. He was now, to use the phrase of some of the bystanders, who had crowded around the two to watch the game, "han'somely cleaned out." He had staked all, and lost all, and was of course rendered not a little desperate by the circumstance.

"Why don't you bet your body fixins?" cried one.

Like a drowning man at a straw, he caught at the idea, and the next moment he and his companion were deciding the ownership of his costume by the game of euchre. As might have been supposed, the result was against him, and he was at last completely beggared.

Seizing the half-emptied can of liquor by his side, he drained it at a draught, and in a tone of frenzy cried:

"Somebody lend me somethin! By ——! I must have my fixins back."

"Luck's agin ye now," answered one. "Better wait till another time."

"No! now—now!—by——! now!" he fairly screamed. "I'll show Jim yet that I'm his master at cards any day he —— pleases. Who'll lend me somthin, I say?"

None seemed inclined, however, to assist one so signally unfortunate; and having waited a sufficient time, and finding his appeal likely to prove fruitless, the disappointed man rose, and in a great passion swore he would leave "such outlandish diggins, and the heathenish set that inhabit them."

"Whar'll ye go?" asked his companion, in unusual glee.

"Whar no such —— scamps as you can find me."

"But afore you leave, I s'pose you'll pay your debts!" retorted the other.

"What debts?"

"Didn't I jest win your body fixins?"

"Well, do you claim them, too? I thought as how you'd got enough without them."

"Claim all my property wherever I can find it," returned the other, more in jest than earnest. "Of course ef you're goin' to leave, so as I won't see you agin, I can't afford to trust."

"You're a villain!" cried the loser, turning fiercely upon his friend: "A mean, dirty, villainous thief, and a liar!"

"Come, come, Sam—them's hard words," replied the one called Jim, in a mood of some displeasure.

"Well, they're true, you know it, and you darn't resent 'em."

"By ——!" cried the other, his eyes flashing fire, and his whole frame trembling with a newly roused passion, "I dare and will resent it, at any time and place you please."

"The time's now then, and the place hereabouts."

"And what the way?"

"Rifles—thirty paces."

"Enough, by ——!" and both proceeded to get their rifles and arrange themselves upon the ground—a spot some forty yards from the encampment—whither they were followed by a large crowd, all eager to be eager witnesses of a not-uncommon, though what often proved a bloody scene, as was the case in the present instance.

Selecting a level spot, the parties in question placed themselves back to back, and having examined their rifles, each marched forward fifteen paces, and wheeled face to his antagonist. Sam then called out,

"All ready?"

"Ready," was the reply.

"Somebody give the word, then," returned the first speaker, and at the same instant both the rifles were brought to the faces of the antagonists.

For a moment a breathless silence succeeded, which was broken by the distinct, but ominous word,

"Fire!"

Scarcely was it uttered, when crack went both rifles at once; and bounding up from the earth, with a yell of pain, Sam fell back a corpse, pierced through the brain by the bullet of his friend. Jim was unharmed, though the ball of the other had passed through his hat and grazed the top of his head. Dropping his rifle, with a look of horror that haunts me still, he darted forward, and was the first to reach the side of his dead friend. Bending down, he raised the body in his arms, and wiping the blood from his face with its hands, called out, in the most endearing and piteous tones,

"Sam! Sam!—look up!—speak to me!—it's Jim—your friend. I did not go to do it. I was mad, or drunk. Sam! Sam! speak to me!—for Heaven's sake speak, if only once, and say you forgive me! Sam, why don't you speak? Oh! I shall go distracted! My brain seems on fire! You know, dear Sam, I would not murder you—"

"He'll never speak agin," said one of the by-standers. "His game is up."

The Day Jim Bridger Ran Off

THE GREATEST AND MOST colorful of the mountain men was "Old Gabe," better known as Jim Bridger. His rise to legend was meteoric. He was born in Virginia in 1804 and taken west to the wilds of Kansas City as a little boy. At fourteen he was an orphan, at eighteen a seasoned trapper, and at twenty-six the discoverer of the Great Salt Lake, the Overland Pass, and the mysterious country of boiling water we now know as Yellowstone National Park. He could speak in the tongues of a dozen Indian tribes and follow a trail in a blizzard. He knew every inch of the West, including some places no one ever could find, though Bridger told whopping tales about them (like Echo Canyon, where he could shout, "Get Up, Jim," at night and wake to the call eight hours later!). Around every western campfire somebody had a Bridger whopper to tell. Yet before Jim Bridger became king of the mountain men he had lessons to learn, and one of them, that you don't give up on a partner, was learned the hard way.

Weak from short rations, stiff from wounds still unhealed, on foot because there were scarcely enough horses to pack the supplies, Major Andrew Henry's tired little band of thirteen trappers trudged out of Fort Kiowa some time around September 1st and began the long, heartbreaking trek through nearly four hundred miles of hostile wilderness to Fort Henry. And they stumbled into that never-never land where history and legend merge and become one. For it was on this journey that one of the great, immortal folk tales of the American West was born. Five days' march up the Grand River from its junction with the Missouri, an old gray-bearded giant of a man named Hugh Glass, out ahead hunting for fresh meat, suddenly motioned to a companion named George Harris to wait, and then began a slow, silent stalk through a stream-side thicket. He had heard splashing sounds. He was hoping to surprise a fat buffalo cow.

Instead, he surprised an old sow grizzly with two yearling cubs.

There was no time for aiming. Glass could only shove the muzzle of his flintlock against the mountain of fur that was smashing down on him, pull the trigger, and try to roll out of the way. But the shaggy thousand-pound beast pounced like a cat, sank her long claws into him, and pinned him tightly. The great jaws attempted to close down on his head. He kicked, twisted, and even got out his knife and began swinging it. But it was almost useless against the enraged bear. Glass knew his hunting companion was his only hope.

Harris heard the terrible snarling of the female grizzly, skirted the thicket and ran up the riverbank. One of the yearlings saw him and charged. He backed out into chest-deep water, shot the cub instead of the mother bear, and then shouted for help with all the strength in his lungs.

When Jim Bridger and the other trappers rushed up to the scene, they found the old man still fighting desperately for his life. They killed the remaining yearling, but it seemed impossible to fire at the determined sow bear without hitting Hugh Glass. They could only aim their rifles, and wait.

Finally the old graybeard lay limp on the ground. The huge grizzly dug her claws into him once more to make sure he was lifeless, then turned to face the other men. Instantly, a half-dozen rifle balls smashed into her chest. With a bawling roar of pain, she whirled about and pounced on Glass again. While the trappers were frantically trying to reload, the grizzly began gnawing at the old hunter's head.

The agonizing pain brought Hugh Glass back to life. Screaming, he doubled his legs against the chest of the bear, kicked out with the crazed strength of desperation, and then managed to push to his feet and even start climbing a tree. But the grizzly rushed him, reared up on her hind legs, slammed him to the ground with a tremendous blow to the head, and then began savagely ripping and tearing at him once more. By this time the other trappers had finished reloading and were firing at the big bear again. Suddenly she slumped down and fell directly on top of the old man. There was no sign of life in either of them.

But when the trappers rolled the heavy carcass aside and examined what was left of the graybeard more closely, they found he was still breathing. One side of his face seemed to have been scraped away, and a great flap of scalp hung down over his ear. His ribs had been crushed and his entire body was torn and bleeding, but somehow life still remained in the tough old giant.

As the men attempted to lift him, his eyes opened and he began screaming with pain. It was decided that moving him would almost certainly kill him, and camp for the night was made on the spot. Major Henry ordered his wounds washed with cold water, and then sewn up with the sinew that served as mending thread for buckskins. A crude splint of a thick willow limb and bindings of rawhide was improvised for the broken leg. Still, not one man in the group thought Glass had a chance of lasting through the night. In the morning, Henry announced, they would bury the old man and be on their way.

But when dawn came Hugh Glass was holding stubbornly onto life. His face was as gray as his beard, and his half-open eyes were rolled back like those of the dead. But he was still breathing slightly. His heartbeat was very rapid, and his entire body burned with fever.

Major Henry called his men together for a council. Disposing of a corpse was a routine fur-trade matter. But alive, the old man presented a problem. Like swarms of wasps whose nest has been shattered, bands of Arikaras were determinedly scouring the entire region. The little detachment of whites was still a great distance from Fort Henry, and a much greater distance yet from the streams they hoped to trap. Glass couldn't be moved, and his outfit couldn't wait for him.

"I won't risk all your scalps for one man," the major decided. "We'll have to leave him. I want two volunteers who'll stay here, bury him when he dies, and then move fast to catch up."

The dozen trappers kept their eyes to themselves. With the Arikaras on the warpath, everyone knew how little chance whoever stayed behind would have of catching up.

"Come on," the major demanded. "Who'll stay with the old man?"

There was another heavy piece of silence. Then, with a shrug that was intended to appear casual and matter of fact, Jim Bridger stepped forward and stood alone before the circle of men.

"Hell, I'll stay," he announced. Like his shrug, his mild profanity rang false in his ears.

Major Henry stared at him for what seemed a long time, a stare that blended mild amusement with concern. "How old are you, Bridger?"

Jim hesitated, wondering whether to lie. "Nineteen," he admitted.

The major watched him a while longer, then looked slowly at the others. One by one, he saw eleven pairs of eyes drop silently before him. Abruptly, he exploded "I said two volunteers! You want me to leave a boy here alone?"

At last an older man, John S. Fitzgerald, spoke up. "Major can I say somethin'?" He hadn't stepped forward to volunteer. Everyone turned to watch him. "Like you say, Major, a man's riskin' his scalp t'stay behind. But he's riskin' more'n that. You'n' the general signed us on, promisin' half the beaver we took. Waitin' here, a man's takin' a chance on missin' out on the whole fall hunt, on gettin' nothin' for half a year's work. Just bein' a few days late, it'll still cost him. S'posin' you make it wuth-while? S'posin' you put up . . . say $40 apiece for them that's stayin'? Fair enough?"

Major Henry thought about it. "You'll stay, then?"

Fitzgerald nodded.

"All right," the major agreed. "We'll let it go at that."

Camp was broken very quickly. In less than a half-hour the ten-man brigade was fording the river and moving to the northwest once more. Andrew Henry took a last look at old Hugh.

"I don't see any chance of him recovering enough to be moved," he told Fitzgerald and Bridger. "Fact is, I don't know what's keeping him alive now. Bury him when it's over. Then get out of here—fast!" He turned and hurried after the others.

John Fitzgerald watched the detachment disappear beyond the growth near the stream. Then his eyes searched the cover on all sides, his rifle held ready in his lap. "Sure hope he don't take too long t'die," he said softly.

Jim winced. "Don't talk that way. S'posin' he can hear us."

The older man looked at him, then snorted and shook his head. He walked over and knelt beside Glass. "Get it done with, old man," he muttered aloud. "Ain't nobody goin' t'bury you if the Rickarees find us."

Jim Bridger turned away in silence, but secretly he envied the man who could so coldly reckon their chances. Imitating Jed Smith by stepping out in front of his hesitant companions had seemed a dramatic and satisfying thing to do at the time. But now the chilling realization of just what he had taken on himself moved over him like clouds across the early autumn sun. Hour after hour they waited, but old Glass still clung determinedly to life.

"You know, boy," John Fitzgerald muttered, "the longer we put off makin' a try at catchin' up, the more Rickaree country we got t'cross."

"What else we goin' t'do?" Jim asked. "We cain't just leave him."

The older man seemed about to say more, then merely turned away and went on keeping watch. The sun went down, and the two of them took turns standing guard through the long, uneasy night that followed. But when daylight came, the big gray-haired man still lay there with his eyes partly opened and his chest still rising and falling slightly with his breathing.

"He's goin' t'die anyway!" John Fitzgerald said angrily. "Why the hell's he got t'take us with him?"

Another day and night went by. Then another. Hugh Glass remained exactly the same, locked in a trance, more dead than alive but not dead enough to bury. When the fourth day came with no change in the old man's condition, John Fitzgerald looked him over closely, then shook his head.

"We're givin' him just one more day," he told Bridger flatly. "If he don't go ahead and get it done with, we'll have t'leave him anyway."

This time the boy didn't argue.

A little before sunset on the fifth day, Fitzgerald examined Glass for the last time. The old man's skin was cooler now, and it was impossible to be sure of a pulse. But there was still a slight suggestion of breathing. John Fitzgerald shook his head and began readying his pack.

"We—We just goin' t'leave him like he is?" Jim Bridger asked.

"Rickarees been huntin' out this country ever since that fracas over on the river," the older man told him. "We used up all our luck lastin' this long."

Jim still hung back, undecided.

"You want t'get swung from your heels, boy?" Fitzgerald snorted. "Swung over a fire? Or maybe tied to a tree'n' skinned alive? They'll have fun with you."

"Least we could put him out of his misery."

"You want t'do the shootin'?"

Jim Bridger stood silent.

"Well, I wouldn't let you if you did. Sound of a shot'd bring the Rickarees swarmin' around here like wolves. Our only chance is t'get out quick and quiet."

"You ain't goin' t'take his rifle?" young Bridger blurted out in surprise.

"We ain't leavin' him nothin'!" Fitzgerald told him angrily. "What d'you think we'd tell the major? Left him alive? We got some extra money comin'. We earned it and we're sure as hell gettin' it. You don't leave a good rifle with a buried man, boy. You don't even leave a knife."

As Jim watched in shocked horror, Fitzgerald tied all of Glass's equipment to his pack, then started on down toward the ford. "Comin' or stayin'?" he called back.

Jim Bridger hesitated only a moment longer, then walked slowly after him.

Traveling hard at night and keeping out of sight in the daytime, the two made their way safely through the remaining stretches of Arikara country and finally reached Fort Henry. They had been very lucky, they discovered. The main party had been attacked, with two men killed and two more wounded.

"If I'd a knowed the old man was goin' t'take five days t'die, I'd of asked for twice the money," John Fitzgerald told Andrew Henry.

"He was a tough one, all right," Henry agreed.

"We sealed him up proper with stones," Fitzgerald went on glibly. "Wolves'll never dig him up."

Jim Bridger stood silent, wondering if he dared tell the major what had really happened, and finally decided to say nothing. The hurried work of abandoning the post was completed, and the garrison moved up the Yellowstone River, straining at the paddles as they fought the current in overloaded dugout canoes. Near the mouth of the Powder River, Andrew Henry managed to buy forty-seven new horses from a tribe of Crow Indians, outfitted a small trapping brigade, and set it on a fall hunt southwest toward the mountains. Then he led his main party on up the Yellowstone to build a new Fort Henry near the mouth of the Big Horn.

Jim discovered that the veteran trappers were treating him with a new degree of respect. But there was a gnawing feeling deep within him that kept reminding him how little he deserved it.

No one ever knew how many more days Hugh Glass lay in that trance of concussion and shock. But gradually, like one waking from a long, nightmare-plagued sleep, he became aware of the world around him. Clearly and vividly, he could remember two voices:

Sure hope he don't take too long t'die!

S'posin' he can hear us.

He tried to reconstruct exactly what had happened. He thought of the battle with the grizzly, of the massacre and sham skirmish with the Arikaras that had come earlier. These things were as dim as childhood memories. But the two voices were sharp and insistent. When his forehead had throbbed with fever, every word had burned permanently into his numbed mind:

Get it done with, old man!

We just goin' t'leave him like he is?

Hugh Glass knew he had been abandoned. He knew who had abandoned him. For the first time since he had kicked free of the bear's deadly grip and attempted to climb the tree, he decided to fight for his own life a little. He was an old man, and staying alive might not have been worth the effort and torture involved except for one thing: he wanted to confront the men who had left him; he wanted to see their faces for just a few seconds before he shot them. *Any reason he's got t'take us with him?* With a lunge that dimmed his consciousness like a candle in wind, he pushed up to a sitting position. Depths of pain he had never before known existed shuddered throughout his entire body. His left leg grated horribly when he tried to stand, and he fell back and then began crawling down to the stream. Moving about had reopened his wounds, but he went on, painting the riverbank bright with his blood, because now he had a reason for living. *We ain't leavin' him nothin'!* He drank deeply, then rolled back and rested. There was a twisting sensation inside him that he could feel above everything else. He was starving.

It was a good sign. Dying men were never hungry. Once again he clenched his teeth against the pain and began dragging himself toward a wild plum thicket. He caught the trunks of saplings in his powerful arms, bent and broke them down with his weight. He chewed and swallowed the sour fruit until his stomach revolted. Then he lay still and tried to think.

He was a full two hundred miles from the nearest source of help, the French Fur Company post of Fort Kiowa. And he had nothing, nothing to help him face the impossible odds but his bare hands and his hatred. "If you'd just left my rifle and knife!" he pictured himself telling John Fitzgerald and Jim Bridger before he killed them.

His anger had become stronger than his pain. As he began crawling downstream through the shore growth, the miles of wilderness that lay between him and Fort Kiowa seemed unimportant. "Might as well go under movin' as layin' still," he told himself, over and over. When darkness fell that night, he was still within sight of the thicket where he had started. In dreams that were as clear and as real as life, he hunted men.

On the second day Glass spent several hours searching for a piece of deadwood that could be used as a crutch, but he found nothing that would support his weight. Finally he gave up and crawled to the edge of the wooded area that bordered the river. There on the open plain buffalo were grazing. He tried to remember the taste of fresh meat. When he reminded himself that he could be feasting right now if his rifle hadn't been taken from him, hatred drove him nearly insane. He had been able to find nothing for food but wild cherries, roots, and buffalo berries.

On the morning of the third day, striking directly out across the open grasslands, he dragged himself into a fringe of bushes beside a small creek and heard voices up ahead. He crawled cautiously on, parting the brush with one hand, pulling his body through with the other. All at once, he found himself at the edge of a small clearing. Not twenty feet away, he saw the back of an Indian's head.

He had blundered into the camp of an Arikara raiding party.

He tried to crawl back, but the rustling sounds he made seemed hopelessly loud. All through the hours of daylight he lay perfectly still in the cover. Only when darkness came to hide him, and an evening wind stirred up the bushes to drown out the noise of his movement, did he work his way back to crawl in a wide circle around the camp.

After that, he lost track of the days. On and on he dragged his tortured, half-useless body, inching his painful way over great distances of the prairie. Sometimes his arms gave out before he had crawled a mile; sometimes he went for days at a time without water; but always he moved ahead until he found it again. When there was no wild fruit to be picked, he chewed grass or even the soft upper branches of prairie bushes.

He reached the Moreau River at a spot where it widened and ran swiftly through rock-strewn shallows. After resting his torn and broken body for a night on the bank, he eased himself into the stream. Caught immediately by the force of the current, his arms were wrenched free of their grip on the rocky bottom. Striking frantically out toward the center, he was smashed against boulders where the rapids began. He wrapped his arms around one wet stone after another, and his body trailed like a banner in the racing stream as he worked his way across, clutching at the rocks. His grip failed again, and the river hurled him mercilessly over gravel bars and into another stretch of white water, where boulders hammered at him and deep pools tried to drown him. Just as Glass was certain he couldn't keep his head above the surface any longer, he was tossed into a quiet eddy beside the shore. He swam the last few strokes with leaden arms, dragged his body to the security of a dense thicket, and collapsed.

Early the next morning he searched the growth beside the river until he finally found a forked deadwood limb strong enough to be used as a crutch. For the first time in weeks he stood upright. When he hobbled out across the open plain once more, he covered more ground during the first day than he had in a week of crawling.

He was still living on berries and roots when he reached the Cheyenne River. But with two-thirds of the distance behind him, he no longer had the slightest doubt that he was going to make it. Climbing a ridge, he heard the sharp, ringing cries of wolves running buffalo on the open plain ahead. He hobbled up to the crest just in time to see one of the great humpbacked beasts pulled down by the gray killers. He waited until the wolves had eaten their fill and trotted heavily away. Then he stumbled over to fall upon the carcass and gorge himself with raw flesh.

When the men at Fort Kiowa opened the gates for a graybearded dirt-encrusted giant in tattered buckskins who looked more like a bear than a man, no one believed the fantastic story he told. Glass shrugged off their doubts. He wasn't interested in being believed. All he wanted, he told trader Joseph Brazeau, was the loan of a rifle. And he would be on his way for a showdown at the Yellowstone, where there were a couple of men who needed killing.

Brazeau was outfitting a six-man party to trade at the Mandan villages. Old Toussaint Charbonneau, a Frenchman who had guided Lewis and Clark, the estranged husband of the already legendary Shoshone Indian woman Sacajawea, was going along as interpreter, and he had serious doubts about their chances of getting safely upriver through Arikara country. But Hugh Glass jumped at the opportunity to join them. The Mandan villages were right on his way, his way to Fort Henry, where he expected to find Fitzgerald and Bridger.

Sometime around November 20th, after six weeks of upstream paddling, the trading party neared its destination. Charbonneau argued that it would be safest to proceed overland, that the Arikaras might very likely be camping near the Mandans. The others refused to listen to him, and the old Frenchman took to the shore alone. But Glass thought about what Charbonneau had said, and a short time later, some ten miles below the Mandan villages, he too decided to go on by land.

Limping directly toward the new Columbia Fur Company post of Tilton's Fort that had been established among the Indians, he pushed out through the streamgrowth. Suddenly he met several squaws and recognized them as Arikaras, not Mandans. They ran at the sight of him, and Glass staggered on toward the little trading house as fast as he could hobble. He had gone only a short distance when a number of Arikara braves burst out of the woods, gaining on him rapidly.

They were less than two hundred yards away, and Glass was about to turn and make a stand, to get at least one of them with the single charge in his rifle, when a pair of mounted Mandan Indians galloped out from the little post to help him. One of them swung the crippled old man up behind him, and they raced back to the safety of the fort. Here Glass learned that the Arikaras had ambushed the dugout a short time after he had left it and that he and Charbonneau were the only survivors. Fate seemed very much in accord with his grim determination to stay alive.

Charbonneau stayed on with William Tilton, patiently waiting for a chance to get downriver in safety. But Hugh Glass left that same night, slipping across the Missouri in a borrowed canoe and hiking on upstream along the left bank, alone and afoot. For two more weeks he stumbled through country where wolf runways were the only roads. Prairie winter, North Dakota winter, roared down from the north, fogging the air solidly with white. The layers of snow on the ground deepened and drifted. Even the wolves faced long months of near starvation. But Hugh Glass kept on going.

Early in December he reached the mouth of the Yellowstone, fastened two logs together with strips of bark, then struggled on across the icy river and stumbled into Fort Henry with his borrowed rifle ready. But he found only a few friendly Sioux Indians living there. He learned from them that his brigade had gone upriver toward the mountains.

Hugh Glass spent just one night at the dying fort, then recrossed the Yellowstone, and went on. For twenty-four more days he fought his way through the winter wilderness, across what is now southeast Montana, going without food for days on end, and sleeping in thickets with only a fire to warm him. Finally, in the middle of a late-December night when a screaming blizzard was at its height, he staggered into the new little post near the Big Horn.

Old friends stared at him as if he were a ghost. Then they recovered enough to swarm around him, to clench his hand and slap him on the back. But he shoved them all roughly aside.

"Where's Fitzgerald?" he demanded. "Where's Bridger?"

The group went dead quiet. Finally Major Andrew Henry stepped out and faced the huge gray-bearded trapper.

"Where's them two wuthless whelps?" Glass shouted.

"There'll be no killing here!" the major told him.

"Where are they?" the old man roared. But suddenly his shoulders began to shake, and the rifle dropped from his hands. He pitched forward, and his big body crumpled to lie limp and huddled on the earthen floor.

White-faced with guilt and shame, young Jim Bridger stood beside Major Henry and watched Hugh Glass wake up in a bed of buffalo robes on a pile of evergreen branches.

"He told me the whole story, Glass," the major said softly.

The old man stared at Bridger. "Why'd you do it?" he finally asked.

Jim lowered his head and said nothing.

"He's just a boy," Andrew Henry offered, but his words seared Jim Bridger more than any threat or shouted abuse could have done.

"Yeah." The old trapper kept staring at him. "Yeah, I reckon he's done somethin' he ain't got years enough yet t'answer for."

Still Jim stood silent.

"I recollect some things now," Glass went on. "I heard more'n you knowed. Old John Fitzgerald talked you into runnin' out, didn't he, boy?"

"I ain't makin' no excuses," Jim finally muttered, almost angrily.

Hugh Glass watched him a moment longer, then turned to the major. "Yeah, I sort o' forget he were just a kid."

"There's something else you forgot too."

"How's that?"

"Out of the whole bunch, back there on the Grand, he was the only one to speak up and say he'd stay behind with you. You study on that a while."

"Maybe." The old man was quiet for some time. "But I still want John Fitzgerald, Major," he finally decided. "He ain't no kid. He knew what he were doin'. Don't get in my way with Fitzgerald!"

Major Andrew Henry shrugged. "I've got no say on that. Fitzgerald's no longer working for me. I sent an express to Ashley back around the first of October. John Fitzgerald and another fellow quit and went along. Either the Rickarees got them or else you passed them somewhere on the river." His face relaxed, now that the threat of trouble had passed. "I've lost another four men on this fall hunt. I can't have the few I've got left shooting each other."

There was little else the major and the old trapper could say. There was nothing Jim Bridger could say. Through the days that followed, the nineteen-year-old boy who had run off, leaving a man to die, and who had then known the sick horror of seeing him return, kept entirely to himself, unapproachable as a wild animal crawling off to lick its wounds. If he had been older and wiser, he might have rationalized what had happened—comparing himself with the men who had been afraid to stay behind, considering the futility of sacrificing two lives for one that seemed already lost. As it was, he knew only that he had done a cowardly thing. And there between the ice-locked river and the snow-smothered mountain slopes, with too little to do and too much time to think, Jim Bridger studied on himself for a long while.

Old Gabe to the Rescue

Trapping was not a business which could be carried on profitably by large parties of men. Though the main camp might contain many campkeepers, squaws, children, packers, and horse guards, the men who harvested the fur had to operate in small groups or alone. When Jim Bridger's brigade moved over from the headwaters of Snake

River to Yellowstone country, Joseph L. Meek went on far ahead alone.

On the fifth day out from camp, a large war party of Crows caught up with him. They were on the prairie and Meek was forced to skip to the creek bottom, quirting his mule for all he was worth with the swarming Indians hard on his trail, yelling and firing a random shot now and then as they closed in on him. Unfortunately the beaver had drained the water out of the creek and made dams, and Meek's mule mired down in the swamp.

By the time the Indians were within about two rods' distance, he was ready for them and brought old *Sally*, as he called his rifle, up to his face, ready to fire his last shot. As he puts it: "I knew it war death this time unless Providence interfered to save me: and I didn't think Providence would do it."

The Crow chief was in the lead, but when he found himself looking down the muzzle of Meek's gun, slowed up and yelled to him, "Lay down your gun and you will live."

Meek's state of mind was easily understood: "Well, I liked to live —being then in the prime of life; and though it hurt me powerful I resolved to part with *Sally*. I laid her down. As I did so, the chief picked her up, and one of the braves sprang at me with a spear, and would have run me through, but the chief knocked him down with the butt of my gun."

So far, so good. They led Meek out to the high prairie south of the stream. There they all halted and turned him over to the three squaws while the warriors sat down in a circle to smoke and decide on his fate. Meek, however, never lost his nerve. While they debated, he coolly counted them. There were 187 warriors, 9 boys, and the 3 squaws guarding him.

They puffed and palavered for what seemed three long hours. Then the head chief, named The Bold, summoned Meek into the ring. He said, "I have known the whites for a long time, and I know them to be great liars, deserving death; but if *you* will tell the truth, you shall live."

Meek thought to himself: *They will fetch the truth out of me, IF thar is any in me.*

The chief went on, "Tell me where are the whites you belong to; and what's your captain's name."

Meek looked the chief in the eye and said proudly, "Bridger is my captain's name; or, in the Crow tongue, Casapy, the Blanket Chief."

That gave the Crow chief something to think about. He thought for quite a while. Then he demanded, "How many men has he?"

Now Meek knew that Bridger's camp contained some 240 men— enough to lick the hindsides off the Crow war party. But he also knew that, if he told the truth as to their numbers, the Crows would high-tail it out of there and take him with them—or kill him. His chances of seeing Bridger again would be almighty slim.

On the other hand, if he lied to the Indians and so encouraged them to go looking for Bridger's camp, it was certain the Crows would want to kill him when they found he had lied to them. But Meek was one of the bravest of the Mountain Men. He answered: "Forty."

The Crows relaxed. The chief laughed. "We will make them poor," said he, "and you shall live, but they shall die."

Meek thought "Hardly," but kept a poker face and said nothing.

When the chief asked him where he expected to rejoin Bridger's camp, Meek gave him an honest answer and told him how many days before Bridger would reach the appointed place. Meek *wanted* the Crows to find that camp.

So then the Indians began to hustle around, packing up for the march to meet Bridger. Two of them mounted Meek's mule, and the women loaded him down with packs of moccasins stuffed with dried meat. A war party always carried its pemmican packed in new moccasins to save weight, for as fast as the ration was consumed new moccasins were needed to replace those worn out on the march.

Scouts preceded the party. Seventy warriors formed the advance guard. Meek marched with the women and boys in the middle, and the rest of the warriors followed. To amuse themselves, the squaws prodded their captive with sticks to keep him moving, saying over and over again with much laughter, "White man very poor now." Meek was glad there were only three women along to keep poking him.

They traveled till late that night, then camped. The Indians slept in a circle with Meek in the center. He did not sleep very well. All next day they marched in the same manner, Meek keeping his temper with difficulty and saying nothing. That evening they put him to cooking for the party, and again on the third and fourth days.

On that last day, Meek was feeling pretty bad. Bridger was bound to show up soon, and if anything went wrong, he knew the Crows would rub him out.

On that last day the Indian scouts left their horses on the slope of the ridge ahead and crept up to peer over. Right away one of them came running back, mounted his horse, and rode rapidly in a large circle—to indicate a big party of enemies over the ridge. All the warriors sat down, but immediately after, the scouts signaled that the white men were going to camp.

Meek could only trust to luck. He understood the signals of the scouts perfectly; now the time had come. They all rode to the top of the hill overlooking the Yellowstone River and the vast plains beyond. About three miles away Meek recognized Bridger's big camp with hundreds of horses grazing about it. His heart beat double-quick about that time, and every once in a while he put his hand to his head to feel if his scalp war still thar. Then Meek saw Bridger's horse guard make the signal which indicated that he had discovered the Injuns. It was the showdown.

Says Meek: "I thought the camp a splendid sight that evening. It made a powerful show to me, who did not expect ever to see it after that day, and it war a fine sight anyway from the hill whar I stood. About 250 men, and women and children in great numbers, and about a thousand horses and mules. Then the beautiful Plain, and the sinking sun; and the herds of buffalo that could not be numbered; and the cedar hills, covered with elk—I never saw so fine a sight as all that looked to me then!" When he turned his eyes on that savage Crow band and saw the chief standing amazed with his hand over his open mouth, saw the warriors' tomahawks and spears glittering in the sunlight, his heart shrunk up to about half its right size. The chief turned on him with a terrible scowl: "I promised that you should live if you told the truth; but you have told me a great lie."

All the warriors gathered round with their weapons in hand. But Meek knew better than to show any weakness. He kept his eyes fixed on Bridger's horse guard, who was riding up the hill to drive in the horses. This movement distracted the chief and his warriors, and when the horse guard had come to within about 200 yards of the Crows, the chief ordered Meek to yell to him to come to them.

Meek stepped forward and yelled as loud as he could: "Keep off, or you'll be killed. Tell Old Gabe to try to talk with these Injuns and help me get away."

By that time the horse guard was between the Crows and Bridger's horses. He headed them back to camp on the dead run.

When Jim Bridger got the word that his old compañero Joe Meek was a captive and in danger of death, he wasted no time. After a few questions, he called his leaders together, gave instructions, caught up his rifle, and mounted his big white horse. Then Jim rode out alone until he was within about 300 yards of the war party. There he reined up. Scanning the line of Injuns on the ridge, his eyes caught a familiar figure.

"What tribe are they, Meek?" he shouted.

Meek's yell came, "Crows."

Then Bridger knew how to go ahead. He shouted, "Tell the big chief to send one of his little chiefs to smoke with me."

Jim saw Meek turn to The Bold to translate the message. After a little thought, the Crow chief beckoned Little Gun to go forward and smoke with the Blanket Chief.

Meanwhile Jim, scanning the line of Injuns on the ridge, could see all the warriors openly preparing for a fight, shaking out their war bonnets, which had been carried in taper rawhide cases, stripping the covers from their round shields, painting their faces, straightening their best arrows, loading their guns.

Then Jim saw Little Gun coming, and dismounted. Jim knew the Crow rules of warfare; he began to strip off his clothing. He threw down his hat, pulled off his long-tailed hunting coat, shed his shirt, and kicked off his buckskin leggings until he stood naked in moccasins and breechclout. Little Gun also halted and undressed, laying his weapons ready on top of his buckskins. Then both men, holding their open palms high, walked forward to meet—both naked, so that neither could be carrying a concealed weapon.

As Little Gun came on, Jim saw that he was a big ugly fellow with long hair hanging to his heels and a stiff pompadour smeared with red paint standing high over his painted forehead. Little Gun was strutting. He felt sure that Jim had no heart to attack him, for then Meek would be gone beaver.

When the two men met, they lowered their arms to hug and kiss each other, according to custom. But as they embraced, Bridger took care to stand so that Little Gun's back was turned toward a gully which cut through the ridge a little to one side.

"Sho-dá-gee," said Jim, in hearty welcome—how hearty Little Gun hardly guessed. That Crow was greasy and sweaty and smeared with paint. But Jim kept on hugging him and kissing his ugly face— all the time looking anxiously over the Injun's shoulder, keeping his eyes glued to that gully. It seemed to Jim that he would have to hug that lousy Injun all day before he caught sight of his five armed trappers, who suddenly showed themselves at the end of the gully within easy rifle-shot. Little Gun was cut off and held prisoner. *Wagh!* Bridger did not need to hug him any longer. He turned the Injun loose and quickly stepped back.

The tricked Crows on the ridge howled their anger and dismay, and began to mount their horses and line up for a charge on the five trappers to recover their naked chief. Little Gun heard the yelling, looked round, and saw how he was trapped. Angrily he turned towards Bridger. Jim thought he might try to grab him and use his body as a shield against the bullets until his warriors could ride the trappers down. But before Little Gun or his friends could do anything, one hundred Mountain Men popped out of the gully and came trotting towards Bridger, forming a line to repel the charge. The milling Indians on the ridge hung poised.

The iron was hot. Bridger struck, yelling to Meek, "Tell the chief to send you to me and I will let Little Gun go."

Jim saw Meek turn to the scowling chief. He knew The Bold would give in. Sullenly the Crow said, "I cannot afford to give a chief for one white dog's scalp." Bridger saw Meek making tracks away from the cussed Injuns.

When Meek had safely passed Little Gun's clothes and weapons, Jim gave the Crow the signal to be on his way. Meek and Little Gun kept their eyes skinned, and gave each other a wide berth. And when Meek came up, thar was some *real* huggin', sartin sure. . . .

That evening the Crow chief with forty of his warriors came peacefully into Bridger's camp to make a truce for three moons. The chief explained very plausibly that the Crows had formerly been at war with white men. "But now," he said affably, "we want to be friends with your camp, so that we can all fight together against the wicked Blackfeet, who are everybody's enemies." To make the truce firm, the Crows brought in Meek's mule, his gun *Sally*, and all his plunder. Old Gabe and his Mountain Men sat in a ring with the Crows and gravely smoked that pipe of temporary peace.

But before the Crows left Jim's camp, their chief walked up to Meek, gazed fixedly into his eyes, and said, "Today I give you a new name—*Shiam Shaspusia*, for *you* can out-lie the Crows."

Joe Meek's Mule

Speakin' of Joe Meek puts me in mind of the old story of Joe Meek's mule. That mule was the hardest-headed creature God ever made and it seemed like Joe was always swearin' and cussin' it top to tail.

Once, on the Oregon trail, Joe's party was ambushed by Indians, and though he tried and tried he couldn't get that mule to lift a leg. Seein' that he wasn't goin' anywhere, Joe shouted to his fleein' friends, "Hold still, boys, we can take 'em. There ain't but a dozen of 'em."

About that time, Joe Meek's mule took an arrow in the rump and set off with Joe at a mighty gallop. With that, Joe yelled out to his friends as he passed them, "Git goin', boys, git goin'. There must be a thousand of 'em."

Watch What You Say

The big-game hunter William Stewart had hired a few men as his personal camp tenders, and among them was a young half-breed named Marshall, a lazy thieving pork eater Bridger had kicked out of his brigade for insubordination. Ignoring Jim's warnings, Captain Stewart felt sorry for the man and signed him on. At the first opportunity, Marshall lit out with one of the captain's finest rifles and two of his best horses. While Jim Bridger chuckled over the incident, his guest Stewart cursed the thief with Highland expletives to match anything in a mountain man's vocabulary.

"I'd give five hundred dollars for his scalp!" he raged.

Stewart still had a great deal to learn about mountain men. A trapper named Markhead listened quietly, then mounted up and rode out of camp. At sundown he was back leading two horses and carrying the expensive rifle, with a bloody topknot hanging from its barrel. The Scottish nobleman stared in horror as the scalp was nonchalantly thrust toward him, and he knocked it away angrily.

"I didn't mean—mean for you to—" he stuttered helplessly.

"Cap'n," Markhead asked him evenly, "you wouldn't be tryin' t'get out o' givin' me what's owin' now, would you?"

William Stewart paid up. Jim Bridger and his men were still laughing about it when they rode up to rendezvous on a Green River creek they called Ham's Fork—a new thread to weave into their legends, a new story to tell around the campfires as they waited for the supplies and liquor to come from the East.

A Long Way for Advice

WHEN JIM BRIDGER grew old he left behind his beloved West and a lifetime of scouting to move to St. Louis. One can imagine what he must have thought as he headed east, passing the enthusiastic and hopeful settlers who teemed the trails he had opened to Oregon and California. He used to sit by the fire and tell tales to an old fiddling miller named Stubbins Watts. "Stubbins," said Jim once, "I told 'em about the boilin' water of Yellowstone and they said I was the damnedest liar that ever lived. That's what ya git fer tellin' the truth!" Yet even in the age of trains and surveyors, the old pathfinder's eyes were still invaluable, as the following tale will prove.

At one time early in the 1860s while the engineers of the proposed Union Pacific Railway were temporarily in Denver, then an insignificant hamlet, they became somewhat confused as to the most practicable point in the range over which to run their line. After debating the question, they determined, upon a suggestion from some of the old settlers, to send for Jim Bridger, who was then in St. Louis. A pass, via the overland stage, was enclosed in a letter to him, and he was urged to start for Denver at once, though nothing of the business for which his presence was required was told him in the text.

In about two weeks the old man arrived, and the next morning, after he had rested, Bridger asked why he had been sent for from such a distance. The engineers explained their dilemma. The old mountaineer waited patiently until they had finished and then demanded a large piece of paper. He was handed a sheet of manila paper used for drawing the details of bridge plans. The veteran pathfinder spread it on the ground, took a dead coal from the ashes of the fire, drew a rough outline map, and pointing to a certain peak just visible on the horizon, said, "There's where you fellers kin cross with yer road, an' nowheres else without more diggin' an cuttin' than you think of." Then, with a look of disgust on his withered countenance, he added, "I coulda told you fellers all that in St. Louis, an' saved you the expense of bringin' me out here."

The Death of a Mountain Man

You may have heard of old Bill Williams, though he wasn't as well known as Jim Bridger or Daniel Boone. He was a mountain man, broad-shouldered and strong, with blue eyes and fiery red hair. He lived most of his life among the Osage Indians, because he disliked the company of white men, and fathered two half-breed daughters who carried his bright hair like a birthright. Some say he knew Greek and Latin, though no one knows for sure. He was a tireless walker and a tough fighter who talked to himself when he wasn't talking to his beloved mustang pony, and this fostered the notion among some trappers that Bill Williams was crazy as a coot. Crazy or not, his life was full of adventure, and his long career established him as one of the greatest of the mountain men. No one knows for sure how he died, but this is one story they tell that sounds like the truth.

Old Bill disappeared in the fall, and was last seen on his pony with a trail of mules shuffling behind. His traps, with "William S. Williams M.T. [Master Trapper]" carved on them, hung on the mules like ponderous decorations. After some months when no one had seen a trace of him at any of the posts, rumors started that he had died and that his bones rested somewhere off in the mountains. Stories began circulating of his end—old Bill losing his hair to the Sioux, or the Blackfeet, one of his wives shooting him, Bill falling off a cliff with all his mules loaded with prime pelts—you know how people talk.

In late winter a group of trappers made their way with their horses high up into the Rockies, higher than any of them had ever been before. Pushing ahead in the freezing weather, one of the trappers discovered that a thicket of dwarf pine and cedar trees gave way to a protected clearing. Filled with relief, they thought it was a perfect place to camp, safe from attack by Indians. It would be difficult to find even if you knew where to look for it.

To their astonishment, when the trappers made their way through the trees, there in the middle of the clearing stood a horse. They rode up to find an old grizzled mustang shivering with cold and fatigue. Its ears were cropped, its tail was ragged, and its bones poked through stiffened skin. The cold had nearly finished its deadly work.

One of the trappers came forward and said to no-one in particular, "I know that horse. It belongs to Bill Williams." The others knew he was right, for this pitiful mustang was the proud Nez-Percé pony that had carried Bill out of a thousand scrapes in the past.

"If you are right and that is his horse," said another, "then Bill ain't gonna be far off." They searched only a moment before they found the remains of a fire, charred pine logs sticking through the snow. Beyond it, half covered with snow, was the reclining figure of the old mountaineer. Here was Bill Williams—his snow-crested head bent far over his chest; his hunting coat of fringed elk, made by one of his red-haired daughters, was stiff and discolored. Strewn about him were his packs and traps. His rifle rusted away at his side.

Awestruck, the trappers approached the body and found it hard as stone—there was no way of knowing how long he had been frozen there. A jagged rent in the coat and the dark stains around it showed he had been wounded before his death. But had the wound killed him or had he frozen to death in the majestic cold? What caused the solitary end of Bill Williams? None of them knew, and as Bill himself might have said, "It surely weren't nobody's business."

A friendly bullet cut short the last remaining hours of the trapper's faithful pony. Then, after burying Bill as well as they were able, the trappers agreed to move on, for they had no wish to make a bed on a fellow trapper's grave. There they left Bill Williams, in a spot so wild and remote that only the wind and the stars would know the secret of his last remains.

CHAPTER 3

The
Fightin'
Spirit

"The Hatfield-McCoy Feud: How It Started"

"He's so tough you got to chain him down to die."
—a country saying

AMERICANS LOVE a good fight. Frontier America was marked by an
enthusiasm for the brawl that came, not from love of muscle or
meanness, but from an unwavering sense of entitlement. "I've got the
prettiest sister, fastest horse, and ugliest dog in the district," shouted
Mike Fink, the legendary boatman of the Mississippi, "and I can
outrun, outjump, throw down, drag out, and whip any man from
here to anywhere!" Such is the sound of America's exuberant voice
in the early-nineteenth century, when she brimmed with self-confi-
dence, sure of her absolute inheritance of a new continent. It is no
surprise that a reader of the newspapers and almanacs of the period
finds endless examples of the boasting we see in "Too Long Between
Fights" and the Mike Fink tales.

We all know about the promised land in America. We have heard
the immigrant's song of our gold-studded streets, perhaps even sung
it ourselves. But ever since the first pilgrim at Plymouth, newcomers
to our shores have had to have a taste for adversity in order to make
it here. The faint of heart did not survive; it was only the determined
and the feisty who found a home. America did not sweep west in a
cinematic tide of unqualified hope but, rather, in an endless series of
fresh struggles, fought round by exhausting round.

Out of this singular process, in which the promised land had to be
redeemed again and again, a national appreciation for the fighter
emerged. Survival demanded tenacity and character, and a fight was
the quickest, surest way to test both. It might be a bout with a bear
or a mountain lion, a showdown with an Apache or a crosstown
rival, but when the moment of challenge came, you couldn't back
away. If you deserved your ground, you held it, but, win or lose, the
outcome of the fight stood always as final judge and jury. Of course,
life didn't work that way, but the illusion that it did was vital to the
storytellers, whose fighting tales sustained a people struggling with
life's adversities.

The fighting lore reinforced a moral at the heart of the young
democracy; it was not greater strength or passion that brought tri-

umph, but a surer sense of right and wrong. When Bobby Durham challenges Bill Stallion in A. B. Longstreet's classic "The Fight," it is Durham's outraged sense of honor that gives him the crucial margin of incentive. John Henry's immortal defiance of the steam drill is inspired by his faith in the worth of man over machine. And Strap Buckner, the Texas hero who loved to knock men down, learned the limits of strength and pride when he fought the devil in an oak grove. Sometimes, of course, the fight has no moral at all. It's just a joyous, free-swinging affair, but there is usually a straightforward quality to American fighting lore that awards victory to the just.

The Civil War is an important turning point. The generation that could laugh and cheer the raucous fisticuffs of Fink and Buckner gave way to a generation steeped in the grisly reality of Shiloh and Gettysburg. After the Civil War, the fighting lore centered on killers, outlaws, and gunplay. The land was filled with bitter refugees from the South, men like Jesse James and the Younger brothers, who vowed never to forgive the society that had defeated them in the war. You could no longer tell the good guy as easily from the bad, and justice wasn't necessarily served when the fight was finished. When Crockett thrashed a man, he left him dazed and admiring, a sure vote in the next election. When Jesse James or Billy the Kid bested a man, he left him dead, another notch for a pitiless gunfighter.

This chapter deals with the kind of fight that, even at its most deadly, was more a matter of honor than vengeance, spontaneity than malice. Behind the tales of Mormon Zack, Silver Jack, Mose Humphreys, and Snake Thomson, there is a good-humored agreement that no one will take things too seriously and that when the fight is done the winner and loser will brush themselves off and go in for a drink.

Too Long Between Fights

I was ridin' along the Mississippi on my horse when I came across a feller floatin' downstream, sittin' in the stern of his boat fast asleep. He looked to be a sizable feller and, as I hadn't had a fight in ten days and was gettin' thinner all the time, I thought I'd stir him up. So says I, "Halloo, stranger. If you don't wake up, your boat is liable to run off and leave you." He woke, slanted his eyes at me, and told me to mind my own business.

Well, it wasn't long before I had that feller so riled he ran his boat up on shore and stood before me flappin' his arms and crowin', "Mister, I can whip my weight in wildcats an' ride straight through a crab-apple orchard on a flash of lightnin'. My fingernails is related to a sawmill on my mother's side, and my daddy could lick a steamboat!"

Now, that boy was right where I wanted him, and not to be outdone I answered, "Pardner, watch out. In one word, I'm a screamer. I'm half horse, half alligator, and a touch of an earthquake tossed in. My daddy could whip any man in Kentucky and I can whip my daddy, and my momma wore a hoop snake for a handkerchief. I can out-talk a room full of politicians and give 'em a two-hour headstart. I can outstare a panther, walk like an ox, swim like an eel, run like a fox, yell like an Indian, fight like the devil, dive deeper, stay under longer, and come out drier than any man on either side of the Mississippi. Son, I can swallow a man whole without choking if you butter his head and pin his ears back."

Well, that did it. We had a whopper of a fight by the river until I heard my wife callin', so we both quit and went our separate ways.

Yankee Doodle

THERE IS NO certain origin for this most American of songs. We know it came out of the first days of the Revolutionary War, supposedly written by a British Army doctor who was ridiculing the tattered American colonists.

The Americans, in typical style, turned the mockery to their own advantage and sang this song throughout the war, most loudly at the surrender of Lord Cornwallis at Yorktown. We have sung it ever since, with many variations, and it has always had a fighting pluck.

Father and I went down to camp
Along with Captain Goodwin,
And there we saw the men and boys
As thick as hasty pudding.

Yankee Doodle, keep it up,
Yankee Doodle dandy!
Mind the music and the steps,
And with the girls be handy!

There was Captain Washington
Upon a slapping stallion,
Giving orders to his men,
I guess there was a million.

And there they had a swamping gun
As big as a log of maple,
On a deuced little cart,
A load for father's cattle.

And every time they fired it off,
It took a horn of powder;
It made a noise like father's gun,
Only a nation louder.

And there I saw a little keg,
Its heads were made of leather—
They knocked upon it with little sticks
To call the folks together.

The troopers, too, would gallop up
And fire right in our faces,
It scared me almost half to death
To see them run such races.

But I can't tell you half I saw,
They kept up such a smother,
So I took off my hat, made a bow,
And scampered home to mother.

Yankee Doodle, keep it up,
Yankee Doodle dandy!
Mind the music and the steps,
And with the girls be handy!

VARIATIONS

Yankee Doodle went to town
A-riding on a pony,
He stuck a feather in his hat
And called it macaroni!

Yankee Doodle went to town,
He bought a bag of peaches,
He rode so fast a-coming back,
He smashed them all to pieces!

Yankee Doodle, find a girl,
Yankee Doodle dandy,
Take her to the fair today
And buy a box of candy!

How Mike Fink Beat Davy Crockett in a Shooting Match

I expect, stranger, you think old Davy Crockett was never beat at the long rifle; but he was, tho'. I expect there's no man so strong, but what he will find someone stronger. If you haven't heerd tell of one Mike Fink, I'll tell you something about him, for he was a helliferocious fellow, and made an almighty fine shot. Mike was a boatman on the Mississip, but he had a little cabin on the head of the Cumberland, and a horrid handsome wife, that loved him the wickedest that ever you did see. Mike only worked enough to find his wife in rags, and himself in powder, and lead, and whiskey, and the rest of the time he spent in knocking over bears and turkeys, and bouncing deer, and sometimes drawing a lead on an injun.

So one night I fell in with him in the woods, where him and his wife shook down a blanket for me in his wigwam. In the morning says Mike to me, "I've got the handsomest wife, and the fastest horse, and the sharpest shooting iron in all Kentuck, and if any man dare doubt it, I'll be in his hair quicker than hell could scorch a feather."

This put my dander up, and says I, "I've nothing to say agin' your wife, Mike, for it can't be denied she's a shocking handsome woman, and Mrs. Crockett's in Tennessee, and I've got no horses. Mike, I don't exactly like to tell you you lie about what you say about your rifle, but I'm damned if you speak the truth, and I'll prove it. Do you see that cat sitting on the top rail of your potato patch, about a hundred and fifty yards off? If she ever hears agin, I'll be shot if it shan't be without ears."

So I blazed away, and I'll bet you a horse, the ball cut off both the old tom cat's ears close to his head, and shaved the hair off clean across the skull, as slick as if I'd done it with a razor, and the critter never stirred, nor knew he'd lost his ears till he tried to scratch 'em. "Talk about your rifle after that, Mike!" says I.

"Do you see that sow away off furder than the end of the world," says Mike, "with a litter of pigs round her," and he lets fly. The old sow give a grunt, but never stirred in her tracks, and Mike falls to loading and firing for dear life, till he hadn't left one of them pigs enough tail to make a tooth-pick on. "Now," says he, "Colonel Crockett, I'll be pretticularly obleedged to you if you'll put them pig's tails on again," says he.

"That's onpossible, Mike," says I, "but you've left one of 'em about an inch to steer by, and if it had a-been my work, I wouldn't have done it so wasteful. I'll mend your host," and so I lets fly, and cuts off the apology he'd left the poor cretur for decency. I wish I may drink the whole of Old Mississip, without a drop of the rale stuff in it, if you wouldn't have thought the tail had been drove in with a hammer.

That made Mike kinder sorter wrothy, and he sends a ball after his wife as she was going to the spring after a gourd full of water, and nocked half her comb out of her head, without stirring a hair, and calls out to her to stop for me to take a blizzard at what was left on it. That critter stood still as a scarecrow in a cornfield, for she'd got used to Mike's tricks by long practice.

"No, no, Mike," says I, "Davy Crockett's hand would be sure to shake, if his iron war pointed within a hundred mile of a woman, and

I give up beat, Mike, and as we've had our eye-openers a-ready, we'll now take a flem-cutter, by way of an anti-fogmatic [let's have a drink], and then we'll disperse."

Mike Fink and the Deacon's Bull

As we have seen, Mike Fink was contemporary with the celebrated Davy Crockett, and his equal in all things pertaining to human prowess. It was even said that the animals in his neighborhood knew the crack of his rifle, and would take to their secret hiding places on the first intimation that Mike was about. Yet strange, though true, he was but little known beyond his immediate "settlement."

When we knew him, he was an old man—the blasts of seventy winters had silvered o'er his head and taken the elasticity from his limbs; yet in the whole of his life was Mike never worsted, except upon one occasion. To use his own language, he never "gin in, used up, to anything that travelled on two legs or four, but once."

"That *once*, we want," said Bill Slasher, as some dozen of us sat in the bar-room of the only tavern in the "settlement."

"Gin it to us now, Mike—you've promised long enough, and you're old now, and needn't care," continued Bill.

"Right, right! Bill," said Mike, "but we'll open with a *licker* all round fust, it'll kind o' save my feelin's, I reckon—"

"Thar, that's good. Better than t'other barrel, if anything!"

"Well, boys," commenced Mike, "you may talk of your scrimmages, tight places and sich like, and subtract 'em altogether in one all-mighty big 'un, and they hain't no more to be compared to the one I war in, than a dead kitten to an old she b'ar! I've fout all kinds o' varmints, from an Ingin down to a rattlesnake, and never was willin' to quit fust, but this once—and 'twas with a bull!

"You see, boys, it was an awful hot day in August, and I war nigh runnin' off into pure *ile,* when I war thinkin' that a *dip* in the creek mout save me. Well, thar was a mighty nice place in ole deacon Smith's medder for that partic'lar bizziness. So I went down amondst the bushes to unharness. I jist hauled the old red shirt over my head, and war thinkin' how scrumptious a feller of my size would feel a wallerin' round in that ar water, and was jest 'bout goin' in, when I seed the old Deacon's Bull a makin' a B-line to whar I stood.

"I know'd the old cuss, for he'd skar'd more people than all the parsons o' the 'settlement,' and cum mighty near kill'n a few. Thinks I, Mike you're in rather a tight place—get your fixins' on, for he'll be a drivin' them big horns o' his in yer bowels afore that time! Well, you'll hev to try the old varmint naked, I reck'n.

"The Bull war on one side o' the creek and I on t'other, and the way he made the 'sile' fly for a while, as if he war a diggin my grave, war distressin!

"Come on ye bellerin', old heathin, said I, and don't be a standin thar; for, as the old Deacon says o' the devil, 'yer not comely to look on.'

"This kind o' reach'd his understandin', and made him more vishious; for he hoofed a little like, and made a drive. And as I don't like to stand in anybody's way, I gin him plenty searoom! So he kind o' passed by me and come out on t'other side; and, as the Captain o' the Mud-Swamp Rangers would say, ' 'bout face for 'nother charge.'

"Though I war ready for 'im this time, he come mighty nigh runnin' foul o' me! So I made up my mind the next time he went out he wouldn't be alone. So when he passed, I grappled his tail, and he pulled me out on the 'sile,' and as soon as we war both a' top of the bank old brindle stopp'd and war about comin' round agin when I begin pull'n t'other way.

"Well, I reck'n this kind o' riled him, for he fust stood stock still and look'd at me for a spell, and then commenc'd pawin and bellerin, and the way he made his hind gearin play in the air, war beautiful!

"But it warn't no use, he couldn't tech me, so he kind o' stopped to get wind for suthin devilish, as I jedged by the way he stared! By this time I had made up my mind to stick to his tail as long as it stuck to his backbone! I didn't like to holler for help, nuther, case it war agin my principle, and then the deacon had preached at his house, and it wan't far off nuther.

"I knowed if he hern the noise, the hull congregation would come down; and as I warn't a married man, and had a kind o' hankerin arter a gal that war thar, I didn't feel as if I would like to be seed in that ar predicament.

"So, says I, you old sarpent, do yer cussedest! And so he did; for he drug me over every briar and stump in the field, until I war sweatin and bleedin like a fat bear with a pack o' hounds at his heels. And my name ain't Mike Fink, if the old critter's tail and I didn't blow out sometimes at a dead level with the varmint's back!

"So you may kalkelate we made good time. By-an'-by he slackened a little, and then I had 'im for a spell, for I jist drapped behind a stump and thar snubbed the critter! Now, says I, you'll pull up this 'ere white oak—break yer *tail!* or jest hold on a bit till I blow!

"Well, while I war settin thar, an idea struck me that I had better be a gettin out o' this in some way. But *how,* adzackly, was the *pint!* If I let go and run he'd be a foul o' me sure!

"So lookin at the matter in all its bearins, I cum to the conclusion that I'd better let somebody *know* whar I was! So I gin a *yell* louder than a locomotive whistle, and it wan't long afore I seed the Deacon's two dogs a comin down like as if they war seein which could get thar fust.

"I know'd who they war arter—they'd jine the Bull agin me, I war sartain, for they war orful venemous and had a spite agin me.

"So, says I, old brindle, as ridin is as cheap as walkin, on this rout, if you've no objections, I'll jist take a deck passage on that ar back o' yourn! So I wasn't long gettin astride of him, and then if you'd bin thar, you'd 'ave sworn thar warn't nothin human in that ar *mix!* the sile flew so orfully as the critter and I rolled round the field—one dog on one side and one on t'other, tryin to clinch my feet!

"I pray'd and cuss'd, and cuss'd and pray'd, until I couldn't tell which I did last—and neither warn't of any use, they war so orfully mixed up.

"Well, I reckon I rid about an hour this way, when old brindle thought it war time to stop to take in a supply of wind and cool off a little! So when we got around to a tree that stood thar, he nat'rally halted!

"Now, says I, old boy, you'll lose *one* passenger sartain! So I jist clum upon a branch kalkelatin to roost thar till I *starved,* afore I'd be rid round in that ar way any longer.

"I war a makin tracks for the top of the tree, when I heard suthin a makin an orful buzzin overhead. I kinder looked up and if that war'nt—well ther's no use a swearin now, but it war the biggest *hornet's nest* ever built!

"You'll 'gin in' now, I reckon, Mike, case thar's no help for you! But an idea struck me then that I'd stand heap better chance a ridin' the old Bull than where I war. Says I, 'old feller, if you'll hold on, I'll ride to the next *station!* any how, let that be whar it will!'

"So I jist drapped aboard him agin, and looked aloft to see what I'd gained in changin quarters; and, gentleman, I'm a liar if thar war'nt nigh a half a bushel of the stingin varmints ready to pitch into me when the word 'go' was gin!

"Well, I reckon they got it, for 'all hands' started for our *company!* Some of 'em hit the dogs—about a *quart* stuck me, and the rest charged on old brindle.

"This time, the dogs led off fust, 'dead' bent for the old deacon's, and as soon as old brindle and I could get under way, we *followed!* And as I war only a deck passinger, and had nothin' to do with steerin the craft, I swore if I had we shouldn't have run that channel, any how!

"But, as I said afore, the dogs took the lead—brindle and I next, and the hornets dre'kly arter. The dogs yellin—brindle bellerin, and the hornets buzzin and stingin! I didn't say nothin, for it warn't no use.

"Well, we'd got about two hundred yards from the house, and the deacon hern us and cum out. I seed him hold up his hand and turn *white!* I reckoned he was prayin, then, for he didn't expect to be called for so soon, and it wan't long, nither, afore the hull congregation, men, women and children, cum out, and then all hands went to yellin!

"None of 'em had the fust notion that brindle and I belonged to this world. I jist turned my head and passed the *hull* congregation! I seed the *run* would be up soon, for brindle couldn't turn an inch from a fence that stood dead ahead!

"Well, we reached that fence, and I went *ashore,* over the old critter's head, landing on t'other side, and lay thar stunned. It warn't long afore some of 'em as war not so scared, come round to see what

I war! For all hands kalkelated that the Bull and I belonged *together!* But when brindle walked off by himself, they seed how it war, and one of 'em said, 'Mike Fink has got the *wust of the scrimmage once in his life!'*

"Gentlemen, from that day I drapped the *courtin* bizziness, and never spoke to a gal since! And when my hunt is up on this yearth, thar won't be any more FINKS! and it's all owin to Deacon Smith's Brindle Bull!"

Tough Fighters

A gentleman tells of a fight he witnessed in the backwoods of Kentucky. He says a gang of men had assembled at a drinking house, and a quarrel and fight ensued. So desperate was the conflict that every man in the party had his eyes gouged out, and when none could see where to strike, they would get down on the floor, feel around till they had found an eye, then, placing it in a socket, would take a squint through it and "go at it again."

Bingo

A few years ago I attended the superior court for the county of ————. The court adjourned late in the night, and the judge and bar being very weary, retired to their beds immediately thereafter. We were all in the same room, and immediately adjoining to us was the bar-room, and the chinks or vacant spaces in the partition enabled us to see and hear all that was going on. Shortly after we had retired, about forty men "pretty well corned, and up to everything," entered the liquor room. No sooner had they arrived than they commenced boasting. "I'm the step-father of the earth!" said one. "I'm the yellow blossom of the forest!" exclaimed another, and requested his fellow-citizens then and there being "to nip the bud if they dare." "I'm kin to a rattlesnake on the mother's side!" shouted the earth's ancestor. This seemed to be a *"socdoliger"* (which, translated into Latin, means a *ne plus ultra); for* the "yellow blossom" stopped to consider what answer he could possibly make to this high claim of ancestry. A happy thought struck him. "Will you drink or fight?" roared he in a voice of thunder.

A silence ensued, or at least a subdued murmur, " 'twixt which and silence there was nothing." Perhaps a more embarrassing question could not have been propounded. The rattlesnake's son was exceedingly thirsty—the sands of Africa were not more so; and liquor was the idol of his heart. He loved it dearly, but he loved fighting also; and here was a glorious chance to "lick" an adversary he had longed to get at. *Curia vult advisare.* He was deliberating between these equally pleasant alternatives, when it occurred to him that it was possible to accomplish both.

"Both!" responded he, "both. I'll drink first—I'll fight afterwards."

A loud shout of approbation rose from the crowd. The liquor was called for—a pint of buck-eye whiskey—and impartially divided into two tumblers. The adversaries each took one, and grasping each other with their left hands, and touching the glasses together in token of amity, drained their respective glasses to the last drop, and then smashed them over the heads of each other, and at it they went. A clamour ensued, so terrific that the English language has no word that would be sufficiently expressive of it. All sorts of encouragement were offered by the friends of each combatant, and an amateur, who had no particular predilection for either, jumped upon the counter, and commenced singing a poetic description of all the naval battles of America from the time of Columbus to the present day (which somebody has had the barbarity to put into miserable verse), keeping time with his heels on the counter. Just as he got to the one hundred and ninety-ninth verse, and was in the midst of what he called "The Wasp and Hornet engagement," his melody was stopped by a shrill cry from the "yellow blossom of the forest," who began to fall into the sere and yellow leaf, and gave manifest symptoms of being whipped.

"He bites!" screamed he.

"I get my livelihood by biting," said the other, relaxing his hold for a moment, and then taking a fresh start.

"'Nuff! 'nuff! take him off!"

Up rose the rattlesnake amidst loud cheering. His first impulse was to crow like a cock; then he changed his genus very suddenly, and declared that he was a "sea-horse of the mountain," and that he had sprung from the Potomac of the earth; then he was a bear with a sore head; a lion with a mangy tail; a flying whale; in short, he announced himself to be every possible and every impossible bird, beast, and fish, that the land or the sea has ever produced.

His wit having exhausted itself, some fresh excitement or novelty was requisite. "Let's have *'Bingo!'* " suggested a by-stander. "Huzza for Bingo," echoed the crowd. Well, thought I, I don't know who and what Bingo is, but I do know, that when things reach their worst condition, any change must be for the better; and as any change from this terrible riot must be for the better, I say too, "Huzza for Bingo!" Alas!—as the sequel proved, I deceived myself greatly.

A gallon of whiskey with spice in it, and a gallon of Malaga wine, were placed on a large round table, around which about forty men seated themselves, having first elected a president *vivâ voce.* The president elect commenced the game by singing at the top of his voice:—

> "A farmer's dog sat on the barn-door,
> And Bingo was his name, O!"

And they all shouted in chorus—

> "And Bingo was his name, O!"

"B," said the president, "i" said the next, "n" the third, "g" the fourth, "o" the fifth; and then the chorus, taking up the letter "o," again shouted—

> "And Bingo was his name, O!"

If either missed a letter, or said "n" for example when he should have said "i," his penalty was to take a drink, and the company, as a privilege, drank with him; and with such slight interruptions as the time for drinking would occupy, this continued for about six hours.

At last the patience of the judge (who was quite a young man, and who is not more than a squirrel's jump from me while I write) became exhausted, and he called for the landlord. Our host, who was a tailor by trade, and who was also one of the Bingo fraternity, made his appearance with a candle in his hand, and a very affectionate and drunken leer upon his countenance.

"Go, sir," said the judge, "into the next room, and tell those drunken lunatics that if they don't stop their beastly noise, I'll commit every one of them to jail in the morning, for contempt of court."

"Oh, judge!" answered our host, holding up his unoccupied hand in token of his amazement; "Oh, judge, you'll give me the *double-breasted horrors!* Why, judge, work is *scarce,* and people's pertikler; and if I was to preliminary your orders to that crowd of gentlemen, why, judge, I'd pick up a thrashing in a little less than no time;" and off he staggered. Bingo was forthwith resumed, until gradually the chorus became more confused and indistinct. Chaos had come again. The actions of the virtuous gentlemen there assembled ceased to be above board, and were carried on under the table. Some were snoring, others hiccuping. Bingo had ceased to be, except when some sleeper, feeling some painful sensation from his attitude, etc., would exclaim "Oh!" which would wake up his immediate neighbour, who, the ruling passion strong in death, would exclaim—"And Bingo was ——," and then relapse into such silence as a drunken man generally falls into.

Years have passed away since that awful night. Joys have blessed me; afflictions pained me; but all the vicissitudes of life have failed to drive out of my memory that terrible game and tune of Bingo. It haunts me like a dun in the day, like a ghost in the night. If I hear any one say "Oh!" the sequel immediately occurs to me—"And Bingo was his name, O!" I am not much of an anatomist, but I am satisfied that when a post-mortem examination is had upon me, the whole matter of Bingo will be found incorporated with my pia-mater, or dura-mater, or some other portion of my brain. I can't tell the process or the manner by which, and in which, it has become a part and parcel thereof; but this much I know, that if my operator is a skilful surgeon, he will find there developed, in characters that *he* can read, the distinct statement that there was a farmer, who had a dog, whose peculiar habit and custom it was to sit upon the barn door, and that he answered to the classical and melodious name of "Bingo."

Snake Thomson, a Good Fiddler

There was a fiddler in one of these establishments by the name of Snake Thomson, who had drifted down into the country from Dodge City in the early days to build himself a cabin by the Rifle Pits on the North Paladuro. There he had established what was then known as a whisky ranch; and, as freight rates were high, he had brewed his own stock after a recipe furnished by some amateur chemist. What ingredients he used were never known, but they must have been potent, for when he tried out the concoction on his first customer, a passing buffalo hunter, the man took one drink and died. Whereat the other buffalo hunters drove the proprietor out of the country because, they maintained, he had put snake heads in his liquor to give it strength. Hence the name Snake Thomson, although there were some who called him Dobe Jake, having seen him in Old Fort Clarendon making adobe bricks for a living subsequent to the episode of the venomous whisky.

He fiddled well, and his music had much to do with keeping the dance hall crowded; but the bullets from the revolvers of the male partners often buzzed so closely by his ears as to mar his execution somewhat. The waltzes began to limp; the quadrilles were disturbed by inharmonious passages. So he built himself a platform at shoulder height and beside it drew a line in charcoal on the whitewashed wall, which he surmounted by a printed legend to the effect that he whose lead flew above the mark must be prepared to meet reprisals. And, to bear out his statement, he kept his Winchester beside his chair where all could see it. Thereafter he fiddled undisturbed.

The Texas Rangers

The Texas Rangers were a tough breed. The meanest killers always found a place to hide when the Rangers were around. One time, a riot broke out in a town near Austin. The streets were littered with broken glass and bodies by the time the mayor wired the governor for a company of Texas Rangers to come and put the riot down. The governor wired back that help was on the way and said they would be on the afternoon train. When the train finally pulled into the station, the mayor was anxiously waiting with his staff to welcome the town's saviours. Needless to say, he was horrified to see only one ranger climb down off the train and stroll up the track. "Only one ranger?" cried the mayor. Looking slightly bewildered, the ranger calmly replied, "There ain't but one riot, is there?"

The Fight

In the younger days of the Republic there lived in the county of ——— two men, who were admitted on all hands to be the very *best men* in the county; which, in the Georgia vocabulary, means they could flog any other two men in the county. Each, through many a hard-fought battle, had acquired the mastery of his own battalion; but they lived on opposite sides of the Courthouse, and in different battalions: consequently, they were but seldom thrown together. When they met, however, they were always very friendly; indeed, at their first interview, they seemed to conceive a wonderful attachment to each other, which rather increased than diminished as they became better acquainted; so that, but for the circumstance which I am about to mention, the question, which had been a thousand times asked, "Which is the best man, Billy Stallions (Stallings) or Bob Durham?" would probably never have been answered.

Billy ruled the upper battalion, and Bob the lower. The former measured six feet and an inch in his stockings, and, without a single pound of cumbrous flesh about him, weighed a hundred and eighty. The latter was an inch shorter than his rival, and ten pounds lighter; but he was much the most active of the two. In running and jumping he had but few equals in the county; and in wrestling, not one. In other respects they were nearly equal. Both were admirable specimens of human nature in its finest form. Billy's victories had generally been achieved by the tremendous power of his blows, one of which had often proved decisive of his battles; Bob's, by his adroitness in bringing his adversary to the ground. This advantage he had never failed to gain at the onset, and, when gained he never failed to improve it to the defeat of his adversary. These points of difference have involved the reader in a doubt as to the probable issue of a contest between them. It was not so, however, with the two battalions. Neither had the least difficulty in determining the point by the most natural and irresistible deductions *à priori;* and though, by the same course of reasoning, they arrived at directly opposite conclusions, neither felt its confidence in the least shaken by this circumstance. The upper battalion swore "that Billy only wanted one lick at him to knock his heart, liver, and lights out of him, and if he got two at him, he'd knock him into a cocked hat." The lower battalion retorted, "that he wouldn't have time to double his fist before Bob would put his head where his feet ought to be; and that, by the time he hit the ground, the meat would fly off his face so quick, that people would think it was shook off by the fall." These disputes often led to the *argumentum ad hominem,* but with such equality of success on both sides as to leave the main question just where they found it. They usually ended, however, in the common way, with a bet; and many a quart of old Jamaica (whiskey had not then supplanted rum) were staked upon the issue. Still, greatly to the annoyance of the curious, Billy and Bob continued to be good friends.

Now there happened to reside in the county just alluded to a little fellow by the name of Ransy Sniffle: a sprout of Richmond, who, in his earlier days, had fed copiously upon red clay and blackberries.

This diet had given to Ransy a complexion that a corpse would have disdained to own, and an abdominal rotundity that was quite unprepossessing. Long spells of the fever and ague, too, in Ransy's youth, had conspired with clay and blackberries to throw him quite out of the order of nature. His shoulders were fleshless and elevated; his head large and flat; his neck slim and translucent; and his arms, hands, fingers, and feet were lengthened out of all proportion to the rest of his frame. His joints were large and his limbs small; and as for flesh, he could not, with propriety, be said to have any. Those parts which nature usually supplies with the most of this article—the calves of the legs, for example—presented in him the appearance of so many well-drawn blisters. His height was just five feet nothing; and his average weight in blackberry season, ninety-five. I have been thus particular in describing him, for the purpose of showing what a great matter a little fire sometimes kindleth. There was nothing on this earth which delighted Ransy so much as a fight. He never seemed fairly alive except when he was witnessing, fomenting, or talking about a fight. Then, indeed, his deep-sunken gray eye assumed something of a living fire, and his tongue acquired a volubility that bordered upon eloquence. Ransy had been kept for more than a year in the most torturing suspense as to the comparative manhood of Billy Stallings and Bob Durham. He had resorted to all his usual expedients to bring them in collision, and had entirely failed. He had faithfully reported to Bob all that had been said by the people in the upper battalion "agin him," and "he was sure Billy Stallings started it. He heard Billy say himself to Jim Brown, that he could whip him, *or any other man in his battalion;"* and this he told to Bob; adding, "Dod darn his soul, if he was a little bigger, if he'd let any man *put upon* his battalion in such a way." Bob replied, "If he (Stallings) thought so, he'd better come and try it." This Ransy carried to Billy, and delivered it with a spirit becoming his own dignity and the character of his battalion, and with a colouring well calculated to give it effect. These, and many other schemes which Ransy laid for the gratification of his curiosity, entirely failed of their object. Billy and Bob continued friends, and Ransy had begun to lapse into the most tantalizing and hopeless despair, when a circumstance occurred which led to a settlement of the long-disputed question.

It is said that a hundred gamecocks will live in perfect harmony together if you do not put a hen with them; and so it would have been with Billy and Bob had there been no women in the world. But there were women in the world, and from them each of our heroes had taken to himself a wife. The good ladies were no strangers to the prowess of their husbands, and, strange as it may seem, they presumed a little upon it.

The two battalions had met at the Courthouse upon a regimental parade. The two champions were there, and their wives had accompanied them. Neither knew the other's lady, nor were the ladies known to each other. The exercises of the day were just over, when Mrs. Stallings and Mrs. Durham stepped simultaneously into the store of Zephaniah Atwater, from "down east."

"Have you any Turkey-red?" said Mrs. S.

"Have you any curtain calico?" said Mrs. D. at the same moment.

"Yes, ladies," said Mr. Atwater, "I have both."

"Then help me first," said Mrs. D., "for I'm in a hurry."

"I'm in as great a hurry as she is," said Mrs. S., "and I'll thank you to help me first."

"And, pray, who are you, madam?" continued the other.

"Your better, madam," was the reply.

At this moment Billy Stallings stepped in. "Come," said he, "Nancy, let's be going; it's getting late."

"I'd a been gone half an hour ago," she replied, "if it hadn't a' been for that impudent huzzy."

"Who do you call an impudent huzzy, you nasty, good-for-nothing, snaggle-tooth gaub of fat, you?" returned Mrs. D.

"Look here, woman," said Billy, "have you got a husband here? If you have, I'll *lick* him till he learns to teach you better manners, you *sassy* heifer you." At this moment something was seen to rush out of the store as if ten thousand hornets were stinging it; crying, "Take care—let me go—don't hold me—where's Bob Durham?" It was Ransy Sniffle, who had been listening in breathless delight to all that had passed.

"Yonder's Bob, setting on the Courthouse steps," cried one. "What's the matter?"

"Don't talk to me!" said Ransy, "Bob Durham, you'd better go long yonder, and take care of your wife. They're playing h—l with her there, in Zeph Atwater's store. Dod etarnally darn my soul, if any man was to talk to my wife as Bill Stallions is talking to yours, if I wouldn't drive blue blazes through him in less than no time."

Bob sprang to the store in a minute, followed by a hundred friends; for the bully of a county never wants friends.

"Bill Stallions," said Bob, as he entered, "what have you been saying to my wife?"

"Is that your wife?" inquired Billy, obviously much surprised and a little disconcerted.

"Yes, she is, and no man shall abuse her, I don't care who he is."

"Well," rejoined Billy, "it an't worth while to go over it; I've said enough for a fight: and, if you'll step out, we'll settle it!"

"Billy," said Bob, "are you for a fair fight?"

"I am," said Billy. "I've heard much of your manhood, and I believe I'm a better man than you are. If you will go into a ring with me, we can soon settle the dispute."

"Choose your friends," said Bob; "make your ring, and I'll be in with mine as soon as you will."

They both stepped out, and began to strip very deliberately, each battalion gathering round its champion, except Ransy, who kept himself busy in a most honest endeavour to hear and see all that transpired in both groups at the same time. He ran from one to the other in quick succession; peeped here and listened there; talked to this one, then to that one, and then to himself; squatted under one's legs and another's arms and, in the short interval between stripping and stepping into the ring, managed to get himself trod on by half of both battalions. But Ransy was not the only one interested upon this occasion; the most intense interest prevailed everywhere. Many were the conjectures, doubts, oaths, and imprecations uttered while the parties were preparing for the combat. All the knowing ones were consulted as to the issue, and they all agreed, to a man, in one of two opinions: either that Bob would flog Billy, or Billy would flog Bob. We must be permitted, however, to dwell for a moment upon the opinion of Squire Thomas Loggins; a man who, it was said, had never failed to predict the issue of a fight in all his life. Indeed, so unerring had he always proved in this regard, that it would have been counted the most obstinate infidelity to doubt for a moment after he had delivered himself. Squire Loggins was a man who said but little, but that little was always delivered with the most imposing solemnity of look and cadence. He always wore the aspect of profound thought, and you could not look at him without coming to the conclusion that he was elaborating truth from its most intricate combinations.

"Uncle Tommy," said Sam Reynolds, "you can tell us all about it if you will; how will the fight go?"

The question immediately drew an anxious group around the squire. He raised his teeth slowly from the head of his walking cane, on which they had been resting; pressed his lips closely and thoughtfully together; threw down his eyebrows, dropped his chin, raised his eyes to an angle of twenty-three degrees, paused about half a minute, and replied, "Sammy, watch Robert Durham close in the beginning of the fight; take care of William Stallions in the middle of it; and see who has the wind at the end." As he uttered the last member of the sentence, he looked slyly at Bob's friends, and winked very significantly; where upon they rushed, with one accord, to tell Bob what Uncle Tommy had said. As they retired, the squire turned to Billy's friends, and said, with a smile, "Them boys think I mean that Bob will whip."

Here the other party kindled into joy, and hastened to inform Billy how Bob's friends had deceived themselves as to Uncle Tommy's opinion. In the mean time the principals and seconds were busily employed in preparing themselves for the combat. The plan of attack and defence, the manner of improving the various turns of the conflict, "the best mode of saving wind," &c., &c., were all discussed and settled. At length Billy announced himself ready, and his crowd were seen moving to the centre of the Courthouse Square; he and his five seconds in the rear. At the same time, Bob's party moved to the same point, and in the same order. The ring was now formed, and for a moment the silence of death reigned through both battalions. It was soon interrupted, however, by the cry of "Clear the way!" from Billy's seconds; when the ring opened in the centre of the upper battalion (for the order of march had arranged the centre of the two battalions on opposite sides of the circle), and Billy stepped into the ring from the east, followed by his friends. He was stripped to the trousers, and exhibited an arm, breast, and shoulders of the most tremendous portent. His step was firm, daring, and martial; and as he bore his fine form a little in advance of his friends, an involuntary burst of triumph broke from his side of the ring; and, at the same moment, an uncontrollable thrill of awe ran along the whole curve of the lower battalion.

"Look at him!" was heard from his friends; "just look at him."

"Ben, how much you ask to stand before that man two seconds?"

"Pshaw, don't talk about it! Just thinkin' about it's broke three o' my ribs a'ready!"

"What's Bob Durham going to do when Billy lets that arm loose upon him?"

"God bless your soul, he'll think thunder and lightning a mint julep to it."

"Oh, look here, men, go take Bill Stallions out o' that ring, and bring in Phil Johnson's stud horse, so that Durham may have some chance! I don't want to see the man killed right away."

These and many other like expressions, interspersed thickly with oaths of the most modern coinage, were coming from all points of the upper battalion, while Bob was adjusting the girth of his pantaloons, which walking had discovered not to be exactly right. It was just fixed to his mind, his foes becoming a little noisy, and his friends a little uneasy at his delay, when Billy called out, with a smile of some meaning, "Where's the bully of the lower battalion? I'm getting tired of waiting."

"Here he is," said Bob, lighting, as it seemed, from the clouds into the ring, for he had actually bounded clear of the head of Ransy Sniffle into the circle. His descent was quite as imposing as Billy's entry, and excited the same feelings, but in opposite bosoms.

Voices of exultation now rose on his side.

"Where did he come from?"

"Why," said one of his seconds (all having just entered), "we were girting him up, about a hundred yards out yonder, when he heard Billy ask for the bully; and he fetched a leap over the Courthouse, and went out of sight; but I told them to come on, they'd find him here."

Here the lower battalion burst into a peal of laughter, mingled with a look of admiration, which seemed to denote their entire belief of what they had heard.

"Boys, widen the ring, so as to give him room to jump."

"Oh, my little flying wild-cat, hold him if you can! and, when you get him fast, hold lightning next."

"Ned, what do you think he's made of?"

"Steel springs and chicken-hawk, God bless you!"

"Gentlemen," said one of Bob's seconds, "I understand it is to be a fair fight; catch as catch can, rough and tumble: no man touch till one or the other halloos."

"That's the rule," was the reply from the other side.

"Are you ready?"

"We are ready."

"Then blaze away, my game cocks!"

At the word, Bob dashed at his antagonist at full speed; and Bill squared himself to receive him with one of his most fatal blows. Making his calculation from Bob's velocity, of the time when he would come within striking distance, he let drive with tremendous force. But Bob's onset was obviously planned to avoid this blow; for, contrary to all expectations, he stopped short just out of arm's reach, and, before Billy could recover his balance, Bob had him "all under-hold." The next second, sure enough, "found Billy's head where his feet ought to be." How it was done no one could tell; but, as if by supernatural power, both Billy's feet were thrown full half his own height in the air, and he came down with a force that seemed to shake the earth. As he struck the ground, commingled shouts, screams, and yells burst from the lower battalion, loud enough to be heard for miles. "Hurra, my little hornet!" "Save him!" "Feed him!" "Give him the Durham physic till his stomach turns!" Billy was no sooner down than Bob was on him, and lending him awful blows about the face and breast. Billy made two efforts to rise by main strength, but failed. "Lord bless you, man, don't try to get up! *Lay* still and take it! you *bleege* to have it!"

Billy now turned his face suddenly to the ground, and rose upon his hands and knees. Bob jerked up both his hands and threw him on his face. He again recovered his late position, of which Bob endeavoured to deprive him as before; but, missing one arm, he failed, and Billy rose. But he had scarcely resumed his feet before they flew up as before, and he came again to the ground. "No fight, gentlemen!" cried Bob's friends; "the man can't stand up! Bouncing feet are bad things to fight in." His fall, however, was this time comparatively light; for, having thrown his right arm round Bob's neck, he carried his head down with him. This grasp, which was obstinately maintained, prevented Bob from getting on him, and they lay head to head, seeming, for a time, to do nothing. Presently they rose, as if by mutual consent; and, as they rose, a shout burst from both battalions. "Oh, my lark!" cried the east, "has he foxed you? Do you begin to feel him! He's only beginning to fight; he ain't got warm yet."

"Look yonder!" cried the west; "didn't I tell you so! He hit the ground so hard it jarred his nose off. Now ain't he a pretty man as he stands? He shall have my sister Sal just for his pretty looks. I want to get in the breed of them sort o' men, to drive ugly out of my kinfolks."

I looked, and saw that Bob had entirely lost his left ear, and a large piece from his left cheek. His right eye was a little discoloured, and the blood flowed profusely from his wounds.

Bill presented a hideous spectacle. About a third of his nose, at the lower extremity, was bit off, and his face so swelled and bruised that it was difficult to discover in it anything of the human visage, much more the fine features which he carried into the ring.

They were up only long enough for me to make the foregoing discoveries, when down they went again, precisely as before. They no sooner touched the ground than Bill relinquished his hold upon Bob's neck. In this he seemed to all to have forfeited the only advantage which put him upon an equality with his adversary. But the movement was soon explained. Bill wanted this arm for other purposes than defence; and he had made arrangements whereby he knew that he could make it answer these purposes; for, when they rose again, he had the middle finger of Bob's left hand in his mouth. He was now secure from Bob's annoying trips; and he began to lend his adversary tremendous blows, every one of which was hailed by a shout from his friends. "Bullets!" "*Hoss*-kicking!" "Thunder!" "That'll do for his face; now feel his short ribs, Billy!"

I now considered the contest settled. I deemed it impossible for any human being to withstand for five seconds the loss of blood which issued from Bob's ear, cheek, nose, and finger, accompanied with such blows as he was receiving. Still he maintained the conflict, and gave blow for blow with considerable effect. But the blows of each became slower and weaker after the first three or four; and it became obvious that Bill wanted the room which Bob's finger occupied for breathing. He would therefore, probably, in a short time, have let it go, had not Bob anticipated his politeness by jerking away his hand, and making him a present of the finger. He now seized Bill again, and brought him to his knees, but he recovered. He again brought him to his knees, and he again recovered. A third effort, however, brought him down, and Bob on top of him. These efforts seemed to exhaust the little remaining strength of both; and they lay, Bill undermost and Bob across his breast, motionless, and panting for breath. After a short pause, Bob gathered his hand full of dirt and sand, and was in the act of grinding it in his adversary's eyes, when Bill cried "ENOUGH!" Language cannot describe the scene that followed; the shouts, oaths, frantic gestures, taunts, replies, and little fights, and therefore I shall not attempt it. The champions were borne off by their seconds and washed; when many a bleeding wound and ugly bruise was discovered on each which no eye had seen before.

Many had gathered round Bob, and were in various ways congratulating and applauding him, when a voice from the centre of the circle cried out, "Boys, hush and listen to me!" It proceeded from Squire Loggins, who had made his way to Bob's side, and had gathered his face up into one of its most flattering and intelligible expressions. All were obedient to the squire's command. "Gentlemen," continued he, with a most knowing smile, "is—Sammy—Reynold—in—this—company—of—gentlemen?"

"Yes," said Sam, "here I am."

"Sammy," said the squire, winking to the company and drawing the head of his cane to his mouth with an arch smile as he closed, "I—wish—you—to—tell—cousin—Bobby—and—these—gentlemen here present—what—your—Uncle—Tommy—said—before—the—fight—began?"

"Oh! get away, Uncle Tom," said Sam, smiling (the squire winked), "you don't know nothing about *fighting.*" (The squire winked again.) "All you know about it is how it'll begin, how it'll go on, how it'll end; that's all. Cousin Bob, when you going to fight again, just go to the old man, and let him tell you all about it. If he can't, don't ask nobody else nothing about it, I tell you."

The squire's foresight was complimented in many ways by the bystanders; and he retired, advising "the boys to be at peace, as fighting was a bad business."

Durham and Stallings kept their beds for several weeks, and did not meet again for two months. When they met, Billy stepped up to Bob and offered his hand, saying, "Bobby, you've *licked* me a fair fight; but you wouldn't have done it if I hadn't been in the wrong. I oughtn't to have treated your wife as I did; and I felt so through the whole fight; and it sort o' cowed me."

"Well, Billy," said Bob, "let's be friends. Once in the fight, when you had my finger in your mouth, and was pealing me in the face and breast, I was going to halloo; but I thought of Petsy, and knew the house would be too hot for me if I got whipped when fighting for her, after always whipping when I fought for myself."

"Now that's what I always love to see," said a bystander. "It's true I brought about the fight, but I wouldn't have done it if it hadn't o' been on account of *Miss* (Mrs.) Durham. But dod etarnally darn my soul, if I ever could stand by and see any woman put upon, much less *Miss* Durham. If Bobby hadn't been there, I'd o' took it up myself, be darned if I wouldn't, even if I'd o' got whipped for it. But we're all friends now." The reader need hardly be told that this was Ransy Sniffle.

Thanks to the Christian religion, to schools, colleges, and benevolent associations, such scenes of barbarism and cruelty as that which I have been just describing are now of rare occurrence, though they may still be occasionally met with in some of the new counties. Wherever they prevail, they are a disgrace to that community. The peace-officers who countenance them deserve a place in the Penitentiary.

Augustus Baldwin Longstreet

The Talking Match

A talking match lately came off at New Orleans for five dollars a side. It continued, according to the *Advertiser*, for thirteen hours, the rivals being a Frenchman and a Kentuckian. The bystanders and judges were talked to sleep, and when they woke in the morning, they found the Frenchman dead and the Kentuckian whispering in his ear.

The Blacksmith Duel

One of the famous duelists of early New Orleans was Bernard Marigny, a member of one of Louisiana's oldest and most influential families, who was a master swordsman and a crack shot with a pistol. He was elected to the state Legislature in 1817 as a member of the House of Representatives and took an active and a leading part in the many disputes that arose between the Creoles and the Americans. At the same time Catahoula Parish was represented by James Humble, a blacksmith and a former resident of Georgia, who was noted for his great stature—he stood almost seven feet in his stockings. The Georgian replied to one of Marigny's most impassioned speeches, and made various allusions so pointed and personal that the Creole considered himself grievously insulted, and challenged the blacksmith to a duel. Humble sought the advice of a friend.

"I will not fight him," he said. "I know nothing of this dueling business."

"You must," his friend protested. "No gentleman can refuse a challenge."

"I'm not a gentleman," Humble retorted. "I'm only a blacksmith."

Humble was assured that he would be ruined both politically and socially if he declined to meet the Creole. His friend pointed out that as the challenged person the blacksmith had the choice of weapons and could so choose as to put himself on equal terms with his adversary. Humble considered the matter for a day or two and then sent this reply to Marigny:

"I accept your challenge, and in the exercise of my privilege I stipulate that the duel shall take place in Lake Pontchartrain in six feet of water, sledge-hammers to be used as weapons."

Since Marigny was less than five feet and eight inches tall and so slight that he could scarcely lift a sledge-hammer, this was giving Humble an equal chance with a vengeance. The Creole's friends urged him to stand on a box and run the risk of having his skull cracked by the huge blacksmith's hammer, but Marigny declared that it was impossible for him to fight a man with such a sense of humor. Instead he apologized to Humble, and the two became firm friends.

The Last Duel in Ohio

Our ears, since war began, have become so accustomed to the recitals of deeds of blood, that I fancy the senses of my readers will not be shocked by my account of the last duel fought in Ohio—which came off in 1834. Excepting some half dozen instances, where the citizens of Ohio, living on the border of the State, have gone over the river into Kentucky, and taken a crack or two at each other, the case I am about to speak of, was positively the last, where Buckeyes have gone out to redress their grievances by single combat.

It is true, as the Vermonter said, "if you give a Buckeye the lie, or the likes o' that, he will, in a manner, knock you right deown, and fall to hurtin' on you; and not dew as they dew in Varmont, where, if a man calls you a liar you set right deown and argy it out of him." Yet Buckeyes do not now-a-days shoot one another, although they will fight the enemies of their country, until their hides cannot hold shucks for the bullet holes. But about the duel.

In the early part of the year named, a party of some twenty "good fellows" assembled, by the invitation of Mr. W. (a great favourite of theirs) at the Pearl Street House, Cincinnati. W. was about to "pull up stakes" and locate in a neighbouring city; and the expected separation from his old cronies, induced him to invite them, on the night of his departure, to join him in a few bottles of wine. Such things were more common in those days than since the advent of Madam Temperance into this, then wicked world.

The invitations went out, and, strange to say, not a single "regret" was sent in; but all came. Toasts were drank—songs were sung—speeches got off, and the "Old Pearl" fairly rung again with the revellings in its halls. In spite of all, the night *would* roll on. Three o'clock came, and the thundering of heavy wheels over the pavement told of the approach of the stage that was to take away "the favourite."

The stage-agent opened the door of the dining-hall, and called for "the passenger." Here *was* a scene! All had evidently been joyful overmuch, and a proportionate relaxation had succeeded. Some, incapable of rising or speaking, leaned back in their arm-chairs, and their eyes lolled out upon their wine-gorged cheeks, looking like so many boiled onions stuck upon sun-flowers; while others, who carried lesser sized "turkies," were toddling about the room in groups of two and upwards, muttering delightful sentiments, and swearing that their friendship to each other should last as long as it should please God to let them live.

"Where is Mr. W——?" called out the agent.

"N-n-not here, Mr. C-c-campbell," answered some one;—"he's d-dead!—b-b-been dead t-two hours!"

"Dead! Great God! what do you mean?"

"Ay, dead!—stepped out!—d-d-dead as Tecumseh!"

Mr. C., now beginning to comprehend that life was not quite extinct, added—

"W—— is to go in the stage—and it is now waiting for him at the door."

"Stage? All the world's a stage! Ha, ha!—good. Yip! Yip! Ypsylanti! C-c-campbell, my dear fellow, tell the g-g-gentleman that steers your old w-w-wagon, to haul in that plank—cr-cr-crack on the steam —and let her *r-r-rip,* for W—— *can't go!"*

"But he must go. Where is he?"

"Well, if he *m-m-must* go, and you *will* see him, *there* he is! (pointing under the table), down there among the cast off cr-crockery. D-d-d—n it, see how he hugs the best brands. S-s-sensible to the last!"

Mr. C. looked under the table, and there lay W. snoring, and holding in his embrace a pair of champaigne bottles as closely as a young mother would clasp her twinned babes. So pulling him out by the heels, C. righted him up, and partly dragging, partly lifting him, rolled "the favourite" into the coach. Crack went the whip—the horses plunged forward, and whirled W—— away from his companions, without even a parting tear. In the mean time they had all lain down in the supper-room to rest, singing—

"We won't go home till morning—till broad daylight appears."

W., with some difficulty, at last got fixed in the coach, and fell into a doze. Had he been wakeful, he would probably have discovered that the landlord had, in a joke, placed in the side pockets of his overcoat a bottle of good old Bourbon whiskey, and one of "Cognac."

W.'s seat was on the middle bench of the coach, and directly in front, sat a six-and-a-half foot Tennesseean. W. got into a habit of pitching forward, and would sometimes bring up plump against the abdomen of his vis-a-vis. Several times the Tennesseean passed it over, and actually assisted W. in righting himself up into his seat. Presently a sudden jolt of the vehicle threw "the favourite" upon the breast of the Tennesseean, with a tremendous concussion. The six-and-a-half footer became wrathy, and exclaimed—

"Stranger, if you tumble on me again, in that way, I'll send you over to t'other end of this mill-hopper, pretty d—n quick!"

"N-n-not on to the f-f-femenines on the back seat, I t-t-trust, old Stub-and-twist."

Old "Stub-and-twist," as W. called him, made no reply; but after a while down came W. again upon him, when he pushed him roughly back, and said—

"By G—d, sir, I tell you—meaning no disrespect to the ladies— that if you don't keep your seat, I'll split you plum in two!"

"Sp-sp-split me in two, eh? Let me inform you that I am a g-g- gentleman and never carry the d-d-deadlies. But if I f-f-find you are a g-g-gentleman, I'll attend to your case in the morning, about the b-b- break o' day!"

"Very well, sir; I'll be thar!"

Here "the favourite," by request, changed his seat to one that proved more stationary, and soon fell asleep.

Morning came, and the sudden stopping of the coach at a water- ing-place aroused W. from his sleep. He awoke spitting little wads of cotton, his mouth being as dry and dusty as Broadway in fly-time, and, jumping out, "broke" for the well. Before he reached it, he looked back and saw one leg of the Tennesseean coming out of the coach. Suddenly the recollection of the challenge he had given flashed upon his mind, and the leg then appeared to him to be about fourteen feet long.

"Now I *am* in a fix," said he to himself.

"Well, stranger," said the Tennesseean, advancing, "how do you feel by this time?"

"Tolerably well," replied W.; "but I should like some apology for your insult to me last night."

"No apology from me, sir; not a word. You proposed to fight me this morning, and I am *here!*"

"Very well, sir, but I have no weapons."

"Here—take this," said the Tennesseean—showing him a bowie knife—"*these* are enough for me"—holding out his clenched fist. "You go to that fence—I will remain here, and when you say 'ready,' we will advance at pleasure, and each take his chance for the result."

"Agreed," said W. And he went to his post. While taking off his overcoat he discovered the bottles in his pockets, and suspecting what might be in them, called out to his antagonist to renew negotia- tions in these words:

"I find, sir, I have a pair of loaded pistols in my pockets, and now propose that you take your choice: this will place us more on an equal footing," advancing at the same time with the muzzles for- ward.

The Tennesseean nodded assent, and advanced also, evidently admiring the Buckeye's sense of chivalry. It was yet so early in the gray of the morning, that they drew very near each other before the Tennesseean discovered the shape of the pistols. When he did so a playful smile lit up his countenance; but he spoke not a word until he had deliberately drawn their corks and applied each bottle to his smeller; when he quietly remarked:

"If this is the sort of a man you are, I think I'll take a little of the 'Old Bourbon.' "

The two then exchanged a "shot in the neck," and were that day the life of the coach. And thus terminated the last meeting on the "field of honour" that ever came off in the "Bonnie Buckeye State."

The Good Old Rebel

O I'm a good old rebel,
   Now that's just what I am;
For the "fair land of freedom,"
   I do not care a dam';
I'm glad I fit against it,
   I only wish we'd won,
And I don't want no pardon
   For anything I done.

I hate the Constitution
   This great republic, too;
I hate the freedman's buro,
   In uniforms of blue.
I hate the nasty eagle,
   With all his brags and fuss;
The lyin' thievin' Yankees,
   I hate 'em wuss and wuss.

I hate the Yankee nation
   And everything they do;
I hate the Declaration
   Of Independence, too.

I hate the glorious Union
    'Tis dripping with our blood;
I hate the striped banner,
    I fit it all I could.

I followed Ole Marse Robert
    For four years near about,
Got wounded in three places
    And starved on Point Lookout.
I cotch the roomatism
    A-campin' in the snow,
But if I killed a chance of Yankees,
    I'd like to kill some mo'.

Three hundred thousand Yankees
    Is stiff in Southern dust;
We got three hundred thousand
    Before they conquered us;
They died of Southern feaver,
    And Southern steel and shot,
I wish it wuz three million
    Instead of what we got.

I can't take up my musket
    And fight 'em now no mo';
But I ain't a-goin' to love 'em,
    Now that is certain sho'.
And I don't want no pardon
    For what I wuz and am;
I won't be reconstructed,
    And I don't give a dam'.

The Yank Reunion

One time the G.A.R. [Grand Army of the Republic] boys had a big reunion in our town, and there was old soldiers come from all over the country. Most of them was getting along in years, and there was lots of white whiskers a-blowing around. But every man had a little copper badge in his buttonhole, and lots of 'em wore blue coats with brass buttons. And every once in a while you would see a black hat with crossed sabers on the front, like they used to wear in the Yankee cavalry.

There was a few old soldiers had money to spend, but lots of them was busted. The folks that run the saloons and sporting houses would be glad to kick their ass right out in the street, but they was afraid to do it. Them old soldiers claimed if it wasn't for the Federal Army the whole country would have been ruined, so the people would be living in caves to this day, without nothing to eat, only wild onions. It was as much as a man's life is worth to lay a finger on a veteran. He would just holler "Hog up! Hog up!" and more old soldiers would come a-running, to bust everything in the place. They wrecked the Red Onion Saloon, and smashed them big mirrors that cost seven hundred dollars. When some old fool lost his wallet at Blanche Tucker's whorehouse they swarmed in like hornets, and set the beds afire, and run the girls right out in their shirttail. They'd have burnt the house plumb down, if the firemen hadn't got there just in the nick of time.

Things looked so bad that lots of the businessmen just boarded up their store windows. The best people in town was mostly Southerners, and they just stayed in their houses. They locked the doors, and kept the children home from school. The only good thing about the reunion was that it only lasted three days. By that time the old soldiers was mostly sick and wore out, so pretty near all of 'em had went home.

On the fourth morning there was just one left, and he was a cripple. He'd got one leg shot off in the war, and his left arm was gone. His face was all scarred up, with a black patch over one eye. He set on the sidewalk in front of the First State Bank, and held out his big black hat with the crossed sabers on it. People was putting nickels and dimes in the hat, so the old soldier could get back to Iowa or wherever it was he come from.

Pretty soon old Colonel Fordyce walked out of the bank. He pulled out his wallet, and put a five-dollar bill in the hat. "Thank you, Comrade," says the old soldier. "Seems to me I seen you somewheres. Wasn't you a sergeant in the Ioway First?" Old Fordyce throwed his shoulders back and turned red in the face. "No, sir!" says he. "I rode with Forrest's cavalry."

The crippled man looked at him kind of funny. "Mister," says he, "my own people give me nickels and dimes, or sometimes a quarter. But this is the first help I ever got from a Confederate. Would you mind telling me how-come you throwed in that five-dollar bill?" Colonel Fordyce grinned. "Not at all, sir. The sight of you does my old heart good. You're the only Yank in this town that's trimmed up to suit me." And with that Colonel Fordyce walked down the street.

The old soldier just set there awhile, but he didn't say nothing. And pretty soon he got onto the northbound train, and that is the end of the story.

Mormon Zack Wastes No Time

Mormon Zack Larson was an old Swede and a cook on the cattle trail. One fall after the roundup he decided he was going to winter in Bull Hook, a town they call Havre now, out in Montana. The cowboys ribbed the old cook about how tough Bull Hook was and that, sure as shootin', if he went there, Zack would get beaten up and run out of town. So aboard the cattle train to Bull Hook old Zack got pretty liquored up, readying himself to face a rough town.

When he got off the train at the depot, Zach saw a man standing on the platform. Calmly, he walked over to the fellow and knocked him flat on his back. When the surprised victim got to his feet, he rubbed his jaw and muttered, "Why the hell do you want to start a fight with me?"

Zack wobbled a little, then fairly shouted, "By God, stranger, I got nothin' agin you but I'm goin' to winter in this gawldarned town and I want that understood right from the start."

Silver Jack

I was on the Drive in eighty,
    Working under Silver Jack,
Which the same was now in Jackson
    And ain't soon expected back.
And there was a fellow 'mongst us
    By the name of Robert Waite
Kind of cute and smart and tonguey,
    Guess he was a graduate.

He could talk on any subject,
    From the Bible down to Hoyle,
And his words flowed out so easy,
    Just as smooth and slick as oil.
He was what they call a sceptic,
    And he loved to sit and weave
Hifalutin words together
    Telling what he didn't believe.

One day we all were sittin' round
    Waiting for a flood,
And hearing Bob expound.
    Hell, he said, was all a humbug,
And he made it plain as day
    That the Bible was a fable;
And we 'lowed it looked that way.
    Miracles and such like
Were too rank for him to stand;
    And as for him they called the Savior,
He was just a common man.
    "You're a liar!" some one shouted,
"And you've got to take it back."
    Then everybody started—
'Twas the words of Silver Jack.
    And he cracked his fists together
And he stacked his duds and cried,
    "Twas in that thar religion
That my mother lived and died;

And though I haven't always
  Used the Lord exactly right,
Yet when I hear a chump abuse him
  He must eat his words or fight."

Now, this Bob he weren't no coward,
  And he answered bold and free,
"Stack your duds and cut your capers,
  For there ain't no flies on me."
And they fit for forty minutes,
  And the crowd would whoop and cheer
When Jack spit up a tooth or two,
  Or when Bobby lost an ear.

But at last Jack got him under
  And he slugged him onct or twist,
And straightway Bob admitted
  The divinity of Christ.
But Jack kept reasoning with him
  Till the poor cuss gave a yell,
And 'lowed he'd been mistaken
  In his views concerning hell.

Then the fierce encounter ended
  And they riz up from the ground,
And some one brought a bottle out
  And kindly passed it round.
And we drank to Bob's religion
  In a cheerful sort o'way,
But the spread of infidelity
  Was checked in camp that day.

The Sissy from Hardscrabble County

The men that work in the rock quarries of Hardscrabble County are so tough they crack great big rocks just by spitting on them. The farther you go west in the county the tougher the men get, and the rock quarries are right on the western boundary line. When they set off a blast, those bullies are right out there with ten-year-old white oaks in their hands batting those big boulders around, or else they're playing catch without any gloves.

When they get constipated in the rock quarry camp they never use anything but blasting powder, and they whip their children with barbwire until the kids get to be ten years old and thrash their parents.

Strangers almost never travel into the rock quarry country, because no man, woman, beast, or child that dared to try it ever returned to tell about it, no more than any soul ever fetched back a report from hell.

When the quarrymen leave their camp, everybody but invalids, little children, and cripples take to the hills till danger's past. It's lucky that they usually come in a drove, and you can see their dust for miles away and hear their fearsome blackguarding and whooping for a good hour and a half before they strike the city limits.

Gentlemen, it's no lie nor fairy tale when I tell you that those Hardscrabble County quarrymen are enough to plague a saint. They use them in the farm villages to scare little children and make them behave, but the grownups are even scareder than the young ones.

One day, a lone wolf got right into town before anybody knew he was on the way. He came riding two snapping, snarling panthers, straddling them with a foot on each, and he was lashing them into a lather with a whip made of three six-foot rattlesnakes knotted together.

This fellow was a sight to behold, and everybody knew in a minute that he was a quarryman. He stood a good eight feet without tiptoeing, and not enough fat on him to grease a one-egg skillet. That man was muscled like a draft mule, and he moved around like a bolt of lightning on its holiday.

First thing, he went to the shoe store and bought a pair of brogans. Then he got a nickel's worth of stout roofing nails from the hardware store and asked for the loan of a hammer. He drove those roofing nails right through the soles and heels of the shoes and put the shoes back on his feet. He wore a size fifteen.

"That's the way I like it," he said. "It gives you a good ground grip and all you got to do when your foot itches is to wiggle it around a little."

"I want to get prettied up a little," the quarryman said, and went into the barbershop. The barber took the edge off his shears when he tried to cut his hair.

"Ain't you got no tinsmith in this town?" asked the quarryman. "Get a pair of tin-snips, extra large. And fetch a blowtorch from the plumber's. I ain't had a decent shave for a month of Sundays."

He dropped in the Blue Moon Saloon then and asked for a good, stiff drink, talking as polite as chips. The bartender planked down a bottle of his strong brand of fortyrod. Some of it sloshed over and ate a spot of varnish off the bar the size of a five-dollar bill. The quarryman lost his temper then, and snorted and fumed, fit to kill.

"None of that bellywash for me!" he howled. "I'd as soon have a pinky, sticky ice-cream sody with a cherry on it."

"What sort of a charge do you crave, stranger?" asked the bartender, his false choppers almost shaking out of his mouth.

"Gimmie a prussic acid cocktail with a little sulphuric for a chaser," ordered the quarryman, "and see that you don't go diluting it with no carbolic, neither. What are you, anyway? One of them temperance cranks? You must think I'm a plumb teetotaler!"

The bartender dashed out the back way and hotfooted it to the drug store and got the stuff for the drinks. The quarryman got in a little better humor then, and began passing the time away by spitting on the floor and burning holes right through to the ground underneath.

"Not bad!" he said. "A little weak. Only trouble with this tipple is that it's hell on underwear. Every time you break wind it burns a hole in them."

"I guess you aim to get back to the quarries before nightfall, don't you, stranger?" said the bartender, hoping to God it was so.

"No, no!" answered the quarryman, shaking his head kind of sad. "I don't reckon I'll *ever* go back."

He grabbed a can of tomatoes off the shelf behind the bar and gulped it down without chewing it open.

"Don't it lay heavy on your stomach, stranger?" asked the bartender, terribly put out that the quarryman wasn't leaving that night.

"Not long," answered the quarryman. "I soon digest the can from around the tomatoes. It's easy. A door knob is harder, but I can do it easy as pie when I set my head to it."

"You aim to make your home in our little Magic City?" asked the bartender, still hoping he had heard wrong.

"Hell's fire and damnation no, man!" yelled the quarryman, so riled he bit a foot-long chunk out of the mahogany bar and spat it right in the bartender's face. "I wouldn't live here for love nor money. I wouldn't be caught dead here."

"Well, then," said the bartender, getting a little bolder, "why did you leave the quarries?"

"Aw, I didn't *want* to," answered the quarryman. "I had to."

"You had to? Why? Get in a fight or some kind of trouble there?"

"A fight? Are you plumb stark, staring looney, man? Whoever heard of a man getting into trouble over fighting in the Hardscrabble County rock quarries?"

"Why did you have to leave, then?"

"Well, I might as well own up," said the quarryman, looking like a sheep-killing dog. "They made me. They chased me out because they said I was too much of a sissy to live among the Hardscrabble County quarrymen."

Jack Conroy

John Henry, the Steel-Drivin' Man

". . . You sure sounds happy, John Henry," says Polly Ann. "I hope it's like you say it in the song—that we've found our home. For I's powerful tired of this life of roamin', John Henry, powerful tired."

"I got me a hunch that's more than a hunch," John Henry said. "I knows. We've had plenty of signs of this, too, Polly Ann. Look what year it is—1872. Add one and eight, and you gets nine. Add seven and two, and you gets nine, likewise. My lucky number is nine, Polly Ann. They's nine letters in my natural-born name. I weighed thirty-three pounds, on the dot, when I was born, and three times three is nine. This is bound to be my lucky year, sure as you born. Listen!"

What they heard when they listened was the ring of hammers on steel off in the distance, and the songs of black men working.

"That's finest music I ever heard," John Henry told his Polly Ann. "It 'minds me of the time when I's a little bitty boy and I played with my pappy's hammer. I been huntin' a hammer all this livelong time, and now I knows it."

When they got to the place where the hammers were ringing, it was a mountain. And the men that were hammering and singing were at work building the Big Bend Tunnel for the C. & O. Railroad.

This wasn't much of a railroad, so far as size went. But it was an important one, just the same. For one thing, it's just about the only railroad that will get into this history. For another thing, it stood for something mighty big that was happening in America along about this time: people were building a whole mess of railroads—the Union Pacific, the Santa Fe, the Southern Pacific, the Northern Pacific and the Great Northern, to name just the biggest of them. Finally, it was going to be on this railroad that a hero, namely John Henry, would have it out with a machine.

Captain Tommy was the boss of the men that were working in the Big Bend Tunnel, down there in West Virginia. These men had the job of driving long rods of steel deep into the rock. When the holes were deep enough, and the men had gone far enough away, other men would put nitroglycerin or mica powder or dualin into the holes and blow away the rock, huge hunks at a time.

"You look big and strong," says Captain Tommy when John Henry braced him for a job, "and maybe we can make a steel-drivin' man out of you, sure enough."

John Henry answered him back, in his thunder voice, "Course I's big and strong—bigger and stronger than any black man a-workin' in the Big Bend Tunnel. But you don't need to *make* a steel-drivin' man out of me, cause I already *is* one. Bring me a twelve-pound hammer, and get me a shaker, and stand out of my way, cause I can drive more steel than any nine men at work in this here tunnel."

"Oh! Oh!" says Captain Tommy. "Sounds to me as if this man that came to me and asked me for work might be just bragful and uppity. Here, you, Li'l Bill, come and shake for this big-mouthed black man. And the rest of you stand back and be ready to laugh till you bust, because here's somebody that talks mighty big, and if his say-so is bigger than his do-so, we'll laugh him out of camp."

The shaker held the steel, and John Henry got himself organized to swing the hammer. Chiefly, to get organized, he got a feel of rhythm in his legs, in his stomach, in his chest, in his shoulders, in his arms, and in his head. Also, he started to sing, in time with the rhythm, and he brought down the hammer in time with the tune. He sang:

> *Oh, my hammer,* (WHAM!)
> *Hammer ring,* (WHAM!)
> *While I sing, Lawd,* (WHAM!)
> *Hear me sing!* (WHAM!)

(The whams came in on the rest of the song, the way they did on this verse, but I'll leave them out, because all those whams may be tiresome.)

> *Ain't no hammer,*
> *Rings like mine,*
> *Rings like gold, Lawd,*
> *Ain't it fine?*

> *Rings like silver,*
> *Peal on peal,*
> *Into the rock, Lawd,*
> *Drive the steel.*

> *If'n I dies, Lawd,*
> *I command,*
> *Bury the hammer*
> *In my hand.*

When John Henry first sang about his hammer ringing better than any other, the steel drivers laughed, "Yugh, yugh, yugh," and hit their knees with the palms of their hands. "Ain't never heard such bragful singin' in all our born days!" they said. But when they watched the way John Henry's hot hammer swung in a rainbow arc around his shoulder, and when they saw the way Li'l Bill, the shaker, had to work to loosen and turn the steel after each ringing wham of the hammer, they stopped laughing and their eyes grew round as dinner plates.

Finally, Captain Tommy said, "Stop for a while, John Henry,

while I see the work you've done." Then, when Captain Tommy had looked, he said, "Well, well, John Henry, looks like your do-so is as good as your say-so, and you aren't just bragful and uppity, the way I thought you were. You drove steel as good as you promised—more than any nine men at work in the Big Bend Tunnel."

"Course he did," says Polly Ann, grinning with her pearl-white teeth. "He's not bragful and he's not uppity. He's a natural-born steel-drivin' man, and what he say, he mean. Praise the Lawd, we's done found our home."

"You work for me," Captain Tommy told John Henry, "and I'll give you four dollars a day and the rent of a company house and enough vittles for you and Polly Ann. I like the way you make that hammer ring and the way the steel goes down."

"Thanks politely, Captain Tommy," John Henry answered him back. "I be proud to work for you, but I wants to ask one little favor. When you goes to town, I'd like to have you get me two twenty-pound hammers so I can make 'em ring and drive the steel."

"Anyone else asked for two twenty-pound hammers, I'd laugh right square in his face," Captain Tommy said. "But I've seen what you can do with a swinging hammer, so I'll get you what you want. Now pitch in and let me hear that steel ring, because you're working for me from now on."

So John Henry was working for Captain Tommy, and his loving Polly Ann was keeping house in one of the company houses.

It was hard work in the tunnel, of course. The smoke from the blackstrap lamps and the dust from the hard red shale were so thick that a tall man working in the tunnel couldn't see his own feet without stooping almost double. The thick air was hot, and the men stripped to their waists before working.

But John Henry was the best steel-driving man in the world. He could sink a hole down or he could sink it sideways, in soft rock or hard—it made no difference. When he worked with two twenty-pound hammers, one in each hand, it sounded as if the Big Bend Tunnel was caving in, the ring of the steel was so loud.

And John Henry and his sweet Polly Ann were as happy as singing birds, for their roaming days were over, and they felt they'd found a home.

Everything was going fine until a man came along and tried to peddle his steam drill to Captain Tommy. This man had pictures of the steam drill in a book, and he had a wagging tongue in his head. "This steam drill of mine," he said, "will out-drill any twenty men. It doesn't have to rest or eat, either, so it'll save you lots of money."

"Hm, maybe," Captain Tommy said, *"maybe.* But I've got one steel-driving man here that's the finest in the world, and I'm mighty fond of big John Henry. So I'll tell you what I think we might do. We might have a race between the steam drill and this man of mine. If the steam drill wins, I'll buy it. But if John Henry wins, you give me the steam drill and five hundred dollars."

"I heard about John Henry, all right, and I know he's good," the man said. "But I know a man is nothing but a man. So I'll have that race, the way you say."

"Fine," says Captain Tommy, "except for one thing: I've got to ask John Henry, but I know pretty well what he'll say." So he went to John Henry and asked him if he'd race that drill for a favor and a hundred dollars to boot.

John Henry said, "Course I'll race it, and course I'll beat it. For I's a natural-born steel-drivin' man that can beat any nine men or any of the traps that ever drove steel. I don't want any old machine to take my place at the happiest work I's ever found. So before I let that steam drill beat me, I'll die with my hammer in my hand."

The day of the race, country folks and all the steel-driving gangs in the whole section came to see whether John Henry meant what he said. The race was to be outside the mouth of the tunnel—out there by the blacksmith shops where the steels were sharpened and the hammers were fixed—a place where everybody could see. The steam drill, with a boiler about twenty feet long to make the steam, was on the right-hand corner, and the spot where John Henry was to drive was on the left. The crowd was sprinkled all around the edges of the quarry.

At the time the race was to start, the blacksmiths had sharpened piles of drills, the steam drill had its steam up, and the carriers were ready with pads on their shoulders to carry the sharpened steels from the shop and the dull ones back to be sharpened. When there was one minute to go, the steam drill whistled, and John Henry lifted one of his twenty-pound hammers. Then Captain Tommy dropped his hat, and the race started.

Says John Henry to Li'l Bill, the shaker, "Boy, you'd better pray. Cause if I miss this piece of steel, tomorrow be your buryin' day, sure as you born."

Then the steam drill was chugging and John Henry was swinging and singing—singing "Oh, My Hammer," "Water Boy, Where Is You Hidin'," "If I Die a Railroad Man" and other hammer songs he could keep time to. The steel rang like silver, the carriers trotted to and from the blacksmith shops, and the crowd watched with all its might and main.

It wasn't long after the start that John Henry took the lead. The steam drill salesman wasn't worried, though—or if he was his talk didn't show it. "That man's a mighty man," he said. "But when he hits the hard rock, he'll weaken." Then, when John Henry hit the hard rock and kept driving fast as ever, the salesman said, "He can't keep it up."

John Henry did keep it up, though, swinging those two hammers and driving down the steel, stopping only once an hour, maybe, to take a drink of water from the dipper Polly Ann had carried in her slender little hands. Six hours—seven hours—eight hours of that nine-hour race, he made his hammer ring like gold. And though Li'l Bill got plumb played out and a new shaker had to take his place, all through the eighth hour John Henry was going strong as ever, with the rhythm in every muscle and joint helping him wham the steel.

It wasn't until the ninth hour that John Henry showed any signs of getting tired. Then, when Captain Tommy came up to ask him how things were going, he answered him back, "This rock is so hard and this steel is so tough, I feel my muscles givin' way. But," he went on to say, "before I let that machine beat me, I'll die with my hammer in my hand."

After that, the crowd that was watching could see signs that John Henry was a weary man—very, very tired and weary.

And John Henry wasn't singing any more. All you could hear was the ring of the hammer on the steel and the chug-chug of the steam drill.

When Captain Tommy, at the end of the ninth hour, looked at his watch and yelled, "The race is over," and when the drills stopped going down, everything was as still as a graveyard. Captain Tommy was looking at the holes. Then, when Captain Tommy said, "John Henry won—three holes ahead of the steam drill," everybody cheered—everybody, that is, excepting the salesman and the steam-drill crew—and John Henry.

When the crowd looked at John Henry, they saw the great man was lying on the ground, and his loving Polly Ann was holding his head. John Henry was moaning, and he sort of mumbled, "Before I let that steam drill beat me, I'll die with my hammer in my hand." (Sure enough, he had *two* hammers in his big black hands.)

Then he said, "Give me a cool drink of water 'fore I die."

Polly Ann was crying when she gave him the water.

Then John Henry kissed his hammer and he kissed his loving Polly Ann. She had to stoop down so he could kiss her. Then he lay very still, and Polly Ann cried harder than ever—sounded mighty loud in that quiet quarry.

Just at that minute, there was the sound of hoofs, and a coal-black preacher came riding up on a gray mule. "You got troubles, sister?" he said to Polly Ann. "Can I help you?"

"Only way you can help," she answered him back, "is to read the buryin' service for my lovin' John Henry. 'Cause his home ain't here no more."

So the coal-black preacher read the burying service. They buried John Henry on a hillside—with a hammer in each hand, a rod of steel across his breast, and a pick and shovel at his head and feet. And a great black cloud came out of the southwest to cover the copper sun.

The Hatfield-McCoy Feud:
How It Started

The Hatfield-McCoy Feud, Being a True and Historical Account of the Extraordinary Origin in 1873 of the Famous Feud That Was to Cost Many Lives and Last for Many Decades and Become the Very Symbol of Bad Blood in American History:

"Floyd Hatfield, that thar ain't yo' hog!"
"Why ain't it, Randolph McCoy?"
"Cause hit's mine!"
" 'Tisn't."
" 'Tis."
"We'll see about that!"
"We shore will."

Mose Humphreys,
the Fighting Fireman

Oddly enough, he was by trade a printer; a compositor in the office of Beach's *Sun*—which doesn't seem logical. It is difficult to fancy those huge fingers picking tiny slivers of type out of a case and ranging them in neat rows. He should have been a blacksmith or a stevedore or a truckman. But he was what he was, the undefeated pride of No. 40, and one of the most vicious sluggers, eye-gougers, and hobnail-stampers in all New York's rowdy history. When not serving valiantly at a fire (and there were no braver men on a ladder or under a tottering wall than most of these brawlers) he was usually seeking honorable distinction against rival firemen or the gangsters of the Five Points. Rooster Kelly, of 30, claims that "I kin remember the night him and Orange County, our foreman, had it nip and tuck, and Orange County kinder got the bulge on him after a four-hours' tussle"; but no one else seems to recall this shading of the battle.

But Old Mose, like all other conquerors, finally met his Waterloo; met it at the hands of Henry Chanfrau in a great battle royal which was a landmark in fire department history and was talked of for sixty years thereafter. On one summer Sunday in 1838 a small fire occurred on South Street. Returning from it, the Lady Washington and Peterson companies trotted side by side up Pearl Street. All other crews were jealous of the Petersons, and there was particularly bad blood between them and No. 40. The ropes were fully manned, as always on Sundays; in fact, overmanned, for chroniclers assert that counting outside sympathizers who were pulling or pushing from behind, there were probably five hundred men in direct attendance on each machine; and in addition to this a crowd of partisans and the merely curious followed, hoping and expecting to see a fight. It had been rumored that 40 was spoiling to attack 15 and explode her boasted invincibility; and the presence at the Lady Washington ropes of several husky fighters from 30, 34, and 44 seemed to lend color to the belief that a conspiracy against 15 was on foot. Among the "ringers" were Orange County of 30 and the giant Jeroloman of 44, who now for the first time appeared in 40's ranks.

The two machines wheeled into Chatham Street, and 15 turned eastward on its regular course towards Chrystie Street. The Lady Washingtons would ordinarily have turned off at Mulberry Street, but instead, they kept alongside the others into Chatham Square, which plainly revealed their hankering for trouble. The chaffing between the rivals became more venomous at every step. Foreman Colladay of No. 15 and Assistant Foreman Carlin, who was in charge of 40, passed up and down the line, ostensibly demanding peace, but in reality egging on their cohorts. "Now, boys, no fighting!" shouted Colladay, and then in a lower tone, "But if they will have it, give it to 'em good!" "Be quiet, men!" bellowed Carlin, and then *sotto voce,* "until they begin, then lam hell out of 'em!"

At the head of No. 15's rope was Country McClusky; opposite him on 40 was the formidable Jim Jeroloman. At the rear of 15's line Henry Chanfrau found himself opposite the mighty Mose Humphreys—a post calculated to pale the cheek of the hardest warrior. Henry Chanfrau was known as a sturdy fighter, but no one in the department would have believed that he could hold his own with Mose. It was his stout heart that carried him through.

Traversing Chatham Square it was evident that the conflict was imminent, and both sides began to "peel" for it, some even taking off their shirts. Jim Jeroloman removed his earrings and put them in his pocket. As they passed into the narrow bottle neck at the beginning of the Bowery, the pressure of the crowds on either side forced the two lines into collision. Instantly Jeroloman dropped his rope and swung at McClusky, and the battle was on.

Like a flash through a train of powder, the fray was joined all along the ropes, a distance of nearly a block, and near a thousand men were fighting. The din was frightful—curses, yells, the whack of huge fists against hard skulls and massive torsos, the roar of the onlooking mob, greedy for action and gore. The fighters were so crowded that a defeated brave scarcely had room to fall, and more than one man knocked cold was held upright by the jam around him. If he fell, he was in danger of being trampled to death by the boots of friend and foe.

For more than half an hour the battle raged. The Petersons fought like men inspired. At the end of thirty minutes a hitherto unknown champion named Freeland was getting the better of Orange County. And then suddenly Country McClusky bowed his head and butted Jeroloman in the stomach, doubling him up and sending him to earth like a closed jackknife—following this up, as might be expected, by jumping upon him and stamping him. It was the beginning of the end, and No. 40 began to give ground; for, to the amazement of every one, Mose Humphreys had not been able to down Hen Chanfrau. While the conflict roared, Frank Chanfrau, then a boy of fourteen, watched it from the top of an awning post in front of Alvord's hat store, shrieking again and again in lulls of the battle, "Give it to him, Hen! Julia is looking at you!"

Julia, Henry Chanfrau's sweetheart, lived near by and was a spectator of the fray. Whether Frank's shrill cry reached Henry's ears or whether he saw Julia's pale face at the window and drew inspiration therefrom we do not know; but at last he landed a blow on the point of Mose's jaw which sent that burly champion reeling. Quickly he followed up his advantage—and then, to the horror of No. 40, the mighty Mose was down!—prone under the milling feet of the contending armies!

That was enough; the Lady Washingtons gave way, and some fled in disorder. Two of them dragged the fallen Mose to his feet and supported him away, tottering between them. And then the frenzied Petersons proceeded to wreak their vengeance on their fallen opponents' engine. It was dragged to a pump and deluged with water for hours, until its beautiful white and gold paint and its portraits of Martha Washington were almost completely washed off. Then it was taken in triumph to No. 15's engine house, and Carlin was later permitted to haul it away at the tail of a cart.

No. 40 never recovered from the disgrace of that defeat. Mose Humphreys vanished from his old haunts soon after the fight, and was next heard of as the proprietor of a pool and billiard hall in Honolulu and reputed chum of the Hawaiian king. He married a native woman and reared a family said to have numbered thirty children.

Strap Buckner, the Fightingest Man

Let me tell you the story of Strap Buckner, the fightingest fellow that ever lived, just as I heard it. The old yarn-spinner who told me Strap's sad tale lived but a mile from Buckner Creek all his life and once even sat on Bill Smotherall's knee. Bill, as you will soon find out, was Strap's last and best friend.

The yarn-spinner began his tale. "Nobody knows where Strap was born or what he did in the early part of his life. He was just a young man when he first came to Austin, Texas, a big boy (maybe that's how he got the name Strap, since he was a strapping fellow), with hair bright red like a prairie fire. Strap was well-mannered, and in the eyes of the ladies of Austin, a handsome lad, but he had a habit that unnerved people: he loved to knock men down. He would walk into a crowd of the meanest or biggest men and knock them all down, one after the other. He wasn't bad-tempered, mind you, because he used to help them each to their feet and dust them off. Then he would knock them down again. It sounds odd to you, I'll bet, as it does to me, but Strap Buckner couldn't resist a fight. Folks said he had a genius for it, and I believe he did. Some are born to dance, some are born to preach; Strap was born to fight.

"He whipped everybody in Austin in the days when it was the toughest town in Texas. One time, Strap fought a big black bull called Noche that had appeared on the streets of Austin. Strap said he'd fight the bull with his fists, and everyone came from all over to see the two go at it. That bull was the width of a locomotive and some of Strap's friends pleaded with him to let the bull alone, but Strap wouldn't hear of such a thing. He knocked the animal out with one mighty blow to the forehead, and no one ever saw that black bull again. But that's another story.

"Strap loved to hunt. He carried only an iron pestle, which he could throw with such accuracy that he could wipe a hummingbird's nose from a hundred yards. Sometimes he put the pestle down and fought the mountain lions and the wolf packs with his bare hands. He was so strong and fierce that after a while all the wild animals pushed west in search of a place where they could win a fight now and then.

"The mayor of Austin went to see Strap, because he had chased all the game away, but before they could talk about the problem, Strap knocked him down. Then the mayor came back with the whole town council, but before they could talk to him Strap knocked them all down as quick as a wink. Somebody had to tell Strap he was becoming a nuisance, but no one wanted the job, so the mighty men of Austin did a smart thing: they sent a little girl, a pretty child named Emily, over to Strap's cabin. Most of Austin waited and watched that cabin for over an hour. From time to time people thought they could hear laughter or crying from Strap's place, but no one was too sure. Finally little Emily came out, holding Strap's hand. He had his things in a bundle over his shoulder, and not looking at anyone as he passed by, Strap walked away from Austin forever. Folks were a bit saddened by the sight, but after a while people forgot about him.

That is, all except Little Emily, who grew up to be quite a proud Texas lady. She never told anyone what went on in that cabin, but they say even as an old woman she refused to let any man or woman speak ill of Strap Buckner.

"After leaving Austin, Strap went West, knocking over tall trees and mountainsides along the way for exercise. At last he came to a little store where two white men, Bill Smotherall and Bobby Turkett, were trading with the local Indians. Strap liked them both right away and knocked each of them down with such grace and ease that neither took offense. 'Any man who can knock me off my feet so fast is a friend of mine,' said Bill. So Strap settled nearby along the bend of a stream, and that's how it came to be called Buckner's Creek."

Now, I don't know about you, but when that old yarn-spinner stopped his story there, I was mighty unsatisfied. I knew how Buckner's Creek got its name, but I hadn't learned what became of Strap Buckner. The old man had had enough talking for the moment, and I had to wait until after dinner before he picked up Strap's tale once more.

"Well, Strap liked the creek well enough," the yarn-spinner continued, "but he made trouble for his two friends by knocking down every Indian in the territory, including the great chief Tuleacahoma, who had never been knocked down in his life. The Indians called Strap the Red Sun of the Blue Thunder, and after a while they didn't come around to Bobby and Bill's store when Strap was nearby. Even Bill got tired of getting whipped, and the store would stay locked for days at a time.

"By now Strap was getting frustrated. He had left Austin in sadness, and now he could see that people wanted him to leave his new home. So Strap started drinking, which was unusual for him, since he hadn't ever tasted whiskey before. Strap began to feel that his genius was a curse, because he could find no challenger worthy of his fists, and his friends were few. The whiskey and the hurt, mixed together, made a powerful brew. The more he drank the more he hurt, and the more he hurt the more he drank. Soon Strap was walking outside his cabin flapping his arms madly and crowing in a voice so loud that the Great Salt Lake got whitecaps and the snow melted in the Rockies.

"Bill Smotherall, who was coming to bring Strap food, since he hadn't seen him in weeks, stood on the hill near Strap's cabin and saw his friend's madness. Strap's hair flew out in all directions, and he paced like a cougar with a thorn in his paw as he cried out, 'Hear me now! I am Strap Buckner, the greatest fighter of all time! I am the fightin'est fool, the champion of all the world and I've got no match in heaven or in hell. I defy all living things to find one among you who can challenge me! Ah, but there is nobody! I've already whipped them all. Even the Devil himself would duck me. Yes, the Devil himself, the scrawny little imp, would never dare to challenge my genius!'

"Now, most folks brag from time to time and some men feel they got to brag before a fight just to keep their courage up, but challenging the Devil, and meaning it, is looking for some real trouble. Actually Strap challenged Heaven, too, but the Lord doesn't have anything to prove. The Devil, on the other hand, won't ever miss a chance. So the words had not burst from Strap's lips when far off there was a low rumbling, a great murmur that grew louder and louder. The sky got dark and filled with lightning, and Strap's shouting was lost in the fearsome howl of the wind. A momentous gust blew him back into his cabin, and then, through the cabin door, came a little black figure with bright red eyes. He was shaped like a man though he wasn't but three feet high. He had horns in his head and cloven hoofs, a hooked nose like an eagle's, and his skin was wrinkled. He danced about the room before the baffled Strap Buckner and thumbed his nose. Strap had had too much to drink to know then what you and I already know, and he tried to think who the creature might be. When the strange figure unfurled a long tail with a point on the end which he gently laid on Strap's knee, Strap still had no idea.

" 'Keep your tail to yourself,' said Strap.

" 'Skin for skin,' said the visitor. Then he flung his tail into the wood mantel like a spear.

" 'Who are you?' asked Strap.

" 'Skin for skin,' repeated the little man.

" 'Skin for skin? Is that your name or can't you say anything else?' demanded Strap, getting angry.

"The little man's smile faded and his eyes shone like two torches on a moonless night. His voice hissed and crackled. 'Men call me by many names, my friend Strap Buckner. But you have called me a scrawny little imp, and were that not insult enough, you have had the audacity to challenge me to a fight. I would have ignored you had I not realized you were fool enough to believe in your own strength. So I accept your challenge, Strap Buckner. Skin for skin.'

"Strap sat back astonished. 'Well, Mr. Devil, it's you. Now, hold on and take a chair. You wouldn't want to fight a drunk man, would you? I'll be good to my word and knock you flat, but can't we do it tomorrow, when I can see straight? It's only as it should be.'

"The Devil's eyes narrowed. He had spent eternity tricking and being tricked, and he looked hard into Strap's eyes for a sign of treachery. The Devil is a smart fellow, and all he saw in those eyes was the certainty of a strong man who fully intended to do what he said he would do. The Devil smiled.

" 'Give me your hand, Strap Buckner. Skin for skin. Tomorrow morning at nine under the oaks by the creek. If you lose, you come with me. Same old deal,' hissed the Devil.

" 'Suits me,' said Strap.

" 'And if you win,' queried the Devil, 'what riches do you seek?'

"Strap shrugged. 'I don't care for riches. Just give me a good fight, that's all I want. It's been a long time.'

"The Devil laughed aloud and said, 'Sleep well, Strap Buckner. Tomorrow you are mine.' Then the little man turned for the door. Strap reached good-naturedly to open it for him, but in a whoosh of air the Devil was through the keyhole and gone, leaving the cabin with a smell of burnt ash and sulphur.

"Now, what would you do if you had to fight for your soul the next day with the Devil himself? I suppose it shows how great Strap was that he could put the jug away and go off to sleep like a baby all night long. Bill Smotherall crept down from the hill where he had been and peeked through Strap's window. He said later that Strap looked so peaceful that he didn't have the heart to wake him.

"The next morning, Strap awoke fresh and cheerful. He sang to himself as he washed in the creek. Some say that a terrific rainstorm gave him a scrubbing, while lightning brushed his hair, but that's nonsense. The truth was that the day was as pretty as a wedding dress. Strap ate a hearty breakfast and set off for the oak grove near the creek, his iron pestle in his hand.

"After arriving at the grove, he didn't have long to wait. Unlike the Devil's entrance the night before, his appearance on this bright morning was quiet, almost ghostly. The Devil stepped from behind a tree and faced the brave fighter.

" 'Strap Buckner, the hour has arrived,' he said.

" 'Yes, indeed,' said Strap happily, 'let's get on with it.'

"As if that were a signal, the Devil's body began to grow. He soon was bigger than Strap, bigger than the trees, bigger even than the hillside itself. Up he swept until he was almost a hundred feet tall, his awesome tail flung up into the sky until it struck and stuck into a passing cloud.

"Strap stared up at his adversary. 'I've no objection to this change in size,' he shouted, 'if that's what you want. But it does strike me as a bit cowardly.'

"The Devil glowered at him and replied, 'I'll return to a fair size if you'll put away that pestle.' Strap agreed and the Devil shrank back to the size of a normal giant, all except his tail, which remained stuck in the cloud above.

"Strap and the Devil began to circle one another like boxers, each waiting for the other to strike a blow. Then the Devil began to grimace and dropped his arms to his sides. It seems the cloud was moving off and painfully dragging the Devil with it, so he couldn't concentrate on the fight. Strap, seeing the problem, never considered taking advantage of the situation.

" 'Get your damned tail out of that cloud; I'll wait,' he said.

"The Devil rolled up the length of his tail, pulled it from the cloud, and dropped back to earth with renewed purpose. The two of them did not wait any further but lit into one another like two wildcats. How can one describe this awesome contest? It was as if the earth were shaking apart from within. The ground trembled and the air was filled with thunder. First Strap seemed to have struck the winning blow, then the Devil. But each would get up again and return to the fight. It was a wondrous struggle and it went on all day long.

"Meanwhile Bill Smotherall, Bobby Turkett, and the Indians were all huddled in a cave miles away, waiting for this magnificent earthquake to pass away. They held tight to one another and watched the mountains and valleys shudder. As darkness came, the earthquake had not abated, and by midnight it seemed worse than ever. Then all at once there was the most terrific noise, as if the world had cracked open. Then there was silence. Stillness. They waited and watched from the mouth of the cave, and then one of the Indians cried out and pointed into the sky.

"Across the night sky went the glowing form of a red monkey. He sat astride a black bull, and under his arm was the limp body of a man. He rose high into the night, and then bull, monkey, and man dropped straight down. There was a distant thunder and then silence.

"In the morning they all rushed to Strap's cabin. The door was ajar, the cabin empty. Down the creek where an oak grove had been, there was only a barren hill. A broken cloven hoof lay steaming by a rock and bits of red hair lay strewn about the ground. The iron pestle was by the creek. Bill Smotherall bore it gravely back to his store, and the procession from Strap's cabin was somber and sad.

"There are many stories that Strap was seen again. They say he came at night on the back of a black bull, that he appeared in strange places at odd times with a weird look in his eye and that he never answered to his name. Bill Smotherall says he saw him only once more, during a rainstorm, when the creek flooded (it took Strap's cabin with it) and Strap waved sadly to him; but Bill was an old man by then and you know how old men see things. To this day, though, when a Buckner's Creek baby cries, whether from surliness or colic, only say to it, 'Strap Buckner,' and you'll hear no more from that baby for hours. One thing is certain, there's not been a fighting man since like Strap Buckner. And if you don't believe all this, which is your right, you can have a look at this."

With that, the old yarn-spinner took me to an oak box he had in the corner of his house. I looked inside, and there, as real as could be, was an iron pestle. It seemed to shine. I tried to lift it but it was too heavy for me.

"Yes, sir," said my host, "whenever the thunders roar and the tempest howls, and wherever a proud man thinks he is the greatest in the world, well, Strap Buckner's sure to be close at hand."

The Death of Crockett

WHEN DAVY CROCKETT joined Jim Bowie and dozens of other men to fight the Mexicans at the Alamo, he was assured a prominent place among America's great folk heroes. Whatever the myths about his life, the reality of his brave death was undeniable. He had risen from the backwoods much as Andrew Jackson had, and lent his western exuberance to the wit and politics of the fledgling democracy. Whether he spoke in Congress or through the yarns the newspapers loved to recount, he embodied the spirit of his age. The following "epitaph" serves as a final note to that great age when honor and glory were to be had through the "fightin' spirit."

Thar's a great rejoicin' among the bears of Kaintuck, and the alligators of the Mississippi rolls up thar shining ribs to the sun, and has grown so fat and lazy that they will hardly move out of the way for a steamboat. The rattlesnakes come up out of thar holes and frolic within ten foot of the clearings, and the foxes goes to sleep in the goose-pens. It is because the rifle of Crockett is silent forever, and the print of his moccasins is found no more in our woods. His old fox-skin cap hangs up in the cabin, and every hunter, whether he are a Puke, a Wolverine, or a Sucker, never looks at it without turnin' away his head and droppin' a salt tear.

Luke Wing entered the cabin the other day and took down old Killdevil to look at it. The muzzle was half stopped up with rust, and a great green spider run out of it and made his escape in the cracks of the wall. The varmints of the forest will fear it no more. His last act to defend it, war when the poor gallant Kurnill drew a lead on a pesky Mexican and brought him down. Crockett went to put "Big Butcher" into another, and the feller on the ground turned half over, and stuck a knife into him. Another come up behind and run his bayonet into Crockett's back, for the cretur would as soon have faced a hundred live mammoths as to have faced Crockett at any time.

Down fell the Kurnill like a lion struck by thunder and lightning. He never spoke again. It war a great loss to the country, and the world, and to ole Kaintuck in particklar. Thar were never known such a member of Congress as Crockett, and never will be agin. The painters and bears will miss him, for he never missed them.

He died like a member o' Congress ought to die. While he war about to do his country some sarvice, and raise her name as high as her mountains, he war cut down in the prime o' life, and at a time when he war most wanted. His screams and yells are heard no more, and the whole country are clouded with a darkness for the gallant Kurnill. He war an ornament to the forest, and war never known to refuse his whiskey to a stranger. When he war alive, it war most beautiful to hear his scream coming through the forest; it would turn and twist itself into some of the most splendifferous knots, and then untie itself and keep on till it got clar into nowhere.

But he are a dead man now, and if you want to see old Kaintuck's tears, go thar, and speak o' her gallant Kurnill, and thars not a human but what will turn away and go behind some tree and dry up thar tears. He are dead now, and may he rest forever and a day arter.

CHAPTER 4

Hunting
and
Fishing Yarns

"The Tale of the Dog with the Upside, Downside Legs"

CHAPTER 4

Hunting
and
Fishing Yarns

"The Tale of the Dog with the Thame Downside Leg"

They riseth in the early morning,
They goeth forth full of hope,
Mighty are their prospects.
When the day is spent they returneth
Smelling of strong drink—
And the truth is not in them.
—a sign pinned to a wall
in a Minnesota hunting lodge

HUNTING AND FISHING are enduring rituals. We may no longer share the frontier hunter's preoccupation with fresh game and animal pelts; the woods that were once thick with deer and rabbit, and the streams that were crowded with bass may be fewer and less abundant, but some things never change. To stand waist-deep in the cold bright water while you cast your fly toward a lazing trout; to wait in a cramped, dark blind for the dawn and the first ducks to come; to sit after dinner by the fire and listen to the stories of the hunters—these are timeless moments that are as magical for you or me as they surely were for our ancestors.

As for the stories that the hunters and fisherfolk tell, they don't change much either. In lodges and hunting camps all across America you are bound to hear a hunter tell of his most spectacular shot—like the fellow in Pennsylvania who saw a branch with a dozen partridges roosting on it. With his last bullet he split the branch down the middle just long enough to open and then close on the whole row of partridge feet. Then the fellow sawed off the branch and carried his trophy home.

You are likely to hear tales by hunters who love their dogs with a sure devotion. One man had a dog so smart that it knew what to hunt by looking at what its master carried out of the house on hunting days. If he carried a rifle, the crafty dog went sniffing for deer; if he carried a shotgun, it was sure to point for quail; if he carried a lantern, it went treeing coons. One morning, the hunter carried his wife's ironing board outdoors. The poor dog got so confused it let out a mournful howl and died.

There are also plenty of tales for those who love to fish. Every stream has a shrewd and arrogant creature, like Old Joe the catfish, who has bested every local fisherman for decades. And is there one trout fisherman alive who has not seen a trout as big as a shark, and very nearly caught him?

Shotgun Charlie once told me that he didn't know who told bigger whoppers, the fisherman or the hunter, but that there was a difference between them. The fisherman, he said, always lied about what got away: the perch he wrestled with for an hour soon became a hundred-pound perch he fought all day long and lost. The hunter, on the other hand, lied about what he got: his two rabbits became four by the next hunt and ten by the hunt after. Why did number matter to the hunter and not the fisherman? " 'Cause," said Shotgun Charlie, "de fisherman cain't be blamed for havin' his weeny ol' line broke by de mightiest catfish in de land, but de hunter ain't got no one to blame if he come home empty-handed but his own po' shootin' self."

In any event, the comradery of the hunt where stories could be spun is as much a part of the experience as the hunt itself. The following yarns may or may not be true, but they are part of that ongoing ritual—a distinguished, often hilarious lore that is renewed every time someone baits a line or loads a shell.

But we are wasting time with all this talk. In the words of Shotgun Charlie on a moonlit night in the woods of North Carolina with the hunt about to begin: "Let's git on, de dogs is scentin'."

How Jack Wood Got Thin

It was during my autumnal trip of 1849, to the backwoods of Pennsylvania, that I became acquainted with the hero of this sketch. He was about thirty-five years old, six feet two in height, and stout in proportion—a noble specimen of a man, quite an Ajax in size and courage. His hair was long and black, and fell in a curly mass down his shoulders. He could walk as far, run as fast, and shoot or fight as well, as "the next one."

He always prided himself on his hunting dress, and always looked neat in his person; his usual dress was a thick blanket hunting frock, of a dark brown colour, bound round the neck, skirt, and sleeves, with strips of beaver skin; his stout homespun breeches was met at the knees by heavy buckskin leggings, his feet encased in strong Indian moccasins, and on his head he wore a sort of skull-cap of grey fox-skin, with the tail sewed on the left side, and hanging down on his shoulder. His breast was crossed by two fancy beaded belts of buckskin, one supporting an ox-horn so white and transparent that the dark powder could be seen through it, the other holding a fancy leather scabbard, into which was thrust a heavy hunting-knife. His waist was encircled by a stout leather belt, in which he carried his bullets and caps, and through which was thrust his small but sharp tomahawk. His rifle was of the best make, and he prided himself in keeping it in good order.

Having run from home when but eighteen years of age, he worked his way out to the western country, where he adopted the hunter's life, and joined a roving band of half-Indians and half-whites, with whom he strolled till the breaking out of the Mexican war. He then joined a company of rangers, and fought under old Zack till the close of the war, and while there, displayed that courage and daring that has always marked his life.

The war over, he came to Philadelphia, and finding father and mother dead, and both sisters married, he went out west again, and commenced the roving life he so much liked.

Jack's only partner of his joys and sorrows was his hound, for he hated all of the womankind.

Last fall I visited Jack's neighbourhood, and stopped at the same tavern as when I sojourned thither in '49, and after seeing my horse well taken care of, I entered the barroom and lighted my cigar, thinking to have a smoke. Seated by the old-fashioned wood stove, I puffed away quite leisurely, when in stalked the tallest, thinnest, and queerest specimen of a man I had ever seen. He was in full hunting rig, and dropping the butt of his rifle heavily on the floor, he leaned on the muzzle, and looked me full in the face. After he seemed fully satisfied, he walked towards me, and when within three feet of me, stopped and took another look; then seizing me by the hand, he shouted out—

"Harry Huntsman, as I'm a sinner! Old boy, how d'ye do?"

"Stranger," replied I, "you certainly have a little the advantage of me."

"Stranger!" roared he, "d——e if I don't like that! Call me a stranger! Old Jack Wood a stranger to you! Ha, ha, ha! You're the stranger!"

"Why, Jack, that aint you?" I foolishly asked.

"Yes, Harry, what's left of me—just about three-quarters of the original."

"Three-quarters!" replied I; "why, Jack, say one quarter, and you will be nearer the mark. But how came this great change?—been sick, or in love?"

"Love! No, sir-ee! As for sickness, I don't know what you mean; but the cause of my being so thin is"—

"What?" I eagerly asked.

"Panthers."

"Panthers," laughed I, "why, Jack, they didn't eat the best part of you away, did they?"

"No, worse than that, they scared it off. It makes my flesh crawl to think of it."

At this, my curiosity was riz, as the Yankee says, and I was anxious for particulars.

"Come, Jack, out with it, don't let me die in ignorance."

"Well, Harry, here goes; but first and foremost, you know I never was a coward; and never will be. All I want is fair play, but to cut a man's throat when he's asleep, can be done by any coward; just such

a way them panthers served me. Three days after you left, last fall—
that was the fifth of December, I believe"—

I nodded assent.

"Well, three days after you left, I found my fire-wood rather low,
and came to the conclusion that I'd better cut a *few* before the heavy
snows came—for I don't much fancy wood chopping in two feet of
snow. So that morning, early, I shouldered my axe and put off for the
swamp, about a mile to the right of my shanty—but you know where
it is. I left everything at home—rifle, gun, and knife—as I never like
the idea of doing anything by half and half; when I want to hunt I
hunt, and when I go to chop wood, I go for that purpose only. Well, I
reached the swamp and fell to work, and chopped for about four
hours, when I thought a little rest and a pull at the flask would be
just the thing. So down I sat on a log, and took one or two, or
perhaps three, good pulls, but not more. Then lighting my pipe, I
commenced to blow a cloud. Hardly had I gave three whiffs, when I
heard a rustling motion among the low brush directly to my right;
this was followed up by a low growl, and before I could get my axe
out, up walked two great big panthers. Here, thinks I, for a run; so
off I put, and the two devils right after me. Fright seemed to lend
wings to my feet, for I scarcely touched the ground I ran over, and I
knew I went over an amazing quantity in a remarkably short space of
time. After a hard run I came to the conclusion to climb a tree, and
rather foolishly selected a small one, when there were just as many
large ones.

"On they bounded to the foot of the tree, and there they treed me,
and such an infernal caterwauling, growling, and half-a-dozen other
noises as they kept up, made my hair rise right up. They then jumped
up at me, shaking the tree at every bound. I hallooed, whooped,
screamed, and swore, but it was no use—there they were. Finally I
suppose they got tired and hungry, so one went away while the other
stopped to keep watch, and thus they relieved each other every now
and then; and, Harry, I'll be shot if they didn't keep me up there four
days.

At last Bill Smith, happening to be running turkeys, came that
way. I shouted as loud as I could, and he heard me, came over and
shot one of the varmints, and the other "ran off." He then helped me

down, and when I touched the ground, I was just as thin as you see me now, and my hair nearly white. I had sweated and fretted myself all to nothing. I'm just as strong and hearty as ever, but get no fatter." Here he leaned over to me, and shouted out—"But, Harry, I'm down on all panthers since that day, and I don't intend to stop hunting them till every one of them is extinct."

The Tale of the Dog
with the Upside, Downside Legs

Up in the Catskill Mountains there was rainbow gladness. The sun shone warmer than warm, the mountaintops were greener than green, the pools and the streams gleamed brighter than bright, and the little birds sang for the joy of living. But gladdest of all was Johnny Darling, walking with a spring-sapling kind of walk like a king in his realm.

Under his arm was Nevermiss, his trusty gun, and by his side ran Dee, the finest hunting dog in all the land, given him by old man Reinheimer.

"It's the season for hunting fine, fat deer to salt away the meat for the lean winter days—and to soften deerskins for moccasins, too," spoke Johnny to his dog.

"Hi there, Dee, you are nosing the ground busier'n a flea on a hot day. Come, show me that you deserve the name o' the finest hunting dog in the land. Find me a fine, fat deer."

Doggone if that dog didn't do the very thing then and there. His nose went suddenly into the ground, he let out a low, powerful growl, and then flew off like sizzling lightning on a summer's day. He was tearing in and out the trees and went so fast you couldn't see that dog at all, only white and black streaks. For Dee was black on one side and white on the other. There he was, now a white streak! now a black streak! now a white streak! now a black streak!

He did this for only a short time, when there leaped out in the distance a deer fit for a hunter's dream. But it was too far for shooting.

"Hi, Dee! run 'r down," shouted Johnny, trying to keep up with the dog.

The deer flew on and Dee after it, faster'n galloping fire. The best Johnny could do was trail behind.

"Faster, Dee," cried Johnny, "and you'll have deer meat to bust."

Dee heard his master's voice and put all his legs in that run. He ran so fast he was just a weaving line through the trees. He never saw brush nor briar nor anything. That's why he never saw a fine, slender white birch standing like a ship's mast. Phizzzz!!! he went bang into it! And Dee was sliced in two as if it had been done by a master butcher.

It happened in a split second—so quick that dog never felt anything at all.

Johnny was up and at him and looked at the finest dog in all the land lying in two halves, one on each side of the birch, while the deer was still running ahead, burning the trail behind him.

Now, you know Johnny Caesar Cicero Darling was the fastest-thinking man ever lived in the Catskills. He looked at the dog he loved, cut in two, and yonder outside o' shooting range was a prize deer.

Quicker'n a shot he picked up the two halves of his dog and put 'em together. Then, without let or leave, he tied 'em together with hide thongs he always carried, figuring on Mother Nature to do the rest.

The trick worked, and Dee hopped off quick as a jack rabbit after that deer, and Johnny after him.

The dog ran even faster than before. He ran so fast now he couldn't catch himself, only this time there was something queer the way he ran. Johnny couldn't tell just what it was. Every once in a while the dog seemed to be kind o' flopping through the air instead of running. But he was getting nearer and nearer to that deer. It's a fact, but the deer was tiring while the dog was still fresh as the morning, running and flopping and flopping and running. Soon the animal slowed down and stopped in a clearing that had just one balsam tree. Johnny came up within gunshot, raised Nevermiss, and the prize deer of the season was his.

The dog rushed to the clearing and so did Johnny, but when he got near he stopped as if a boulder had struck him straight between the eyes. He just kept on looking at Dee, for he was a sight to kill.

There was that dog standing on his two white legs, while the two black legs and half of his face were pointing upward in the air.

Do you know what Johnny had done? Why, he was in such a mighty hurry he had put the two parts of Dee together half up and half down.

"By gor!" cried Johnny, "so that's how you ran that deer down! When you got tired o' running with the downside legs you rolled around and ran ahead with the rested upside legs. Land o' Goshen! Now I'll surely have the finest and fastest dog in the land, for he can run double fast as any living creature. Hey juberju!"

From that day on Dee could run easy a hundred and fifty miles a day as the crows fly, and he was known as the fastest hunting dog in the East.

Mart Moody's Bird Dog

Mart Moody from Tupper Lake used to tell this tale. "I went out one day and here was a big flock of ducks out on Tupper Lake. And I had this good dog. And I shot. And I sent the dog out there. She was heavy with pups, and I didn't know whether I should send her out there. It was a cold day in the fall. Well, she took right off and away she went. And it got dark and she never showed up. And I got to worrying about her. I worried about that dog. She was a good dog, a real good retriever. She'd get anything I'd shot at. So the next morning I woke up and I thought I'd go see if I could find her. And I got down by the shore of the lake and I looked out. And I see something coming. And this dog, she come into shore. She had three ducks in her mouth. And behind her she had seven pups. And each one of the pups had a duck in his mouth."

Pretty Baby

Let a bunch be setting around telling hunting tales and he could always tell one better. Like the time Alec Barrs told about his dog jumping a big rabbit up on the ridge, the biggest rabbit he'd ever seen —but it got away.

" 'Tain't nothing to the size of what Pretty Baby can do," Windy Peevyhouse said as usual. "Why, no more than last week that dog jumped a rabbit over close to Littleton Lake, and Pretty Baby must of knowed I was a far piece away for he just treed that cottontail up a tree and stood there a-baying and a-wagging his tail to let me know what he'd done."

Him telling outlandish things like that for the truth was what got him the name Windy. He was always blowing off at the mouth and making his self the laughingstock of Littleton's Cross Roads and further away than that. But people sniggering at him didn't stop him none. Seemed to make him worse.

Old Man Abb Littleton would speak up sometime like the time he said to Windy about trapping, "There's them as says yore ketch-dog trees them varmints in a trap you've set, Windy." And Old Man Littleton laughed fit to kill.

Abb could say most anything he wanted to just anybody. He owned most of the land holdings thereabouts and the store too. So nearly everbody generally owed him for something and had to be beholden to him.

But Abb nor nothing couldn't stop Windy from breezing off about his dog, Pretty Baby. Claimed he was the best retriever that ever brung in a piece of game. Of course Windy always done too much talking for his own good too. Like when he told about Pretty Baby retrieving the duck on Littleton's Lake. Now Abb Littleton was fonder of that lake and the ducks and the fishes he'd stocked it with than all his other holdings. He didn't like no meddling in his lake nor anywheres about.

"You shoot a duck over my lake again," he told Windy, "and I'll law you to the last frazzling law court in the land. I'll do it if you fish a fish out of there, either," Abb says good and loud. "That goes for the rest of you-ens, too. And the first time I ketch that ketch-dog around my lake I aim to—well, that ketch-dog will ketch his self some cold death, that's all."

Now Windy didn't know nothing more about fishing than a frog knows about bed sheets, and if he'd thought of fishing in the lake before then, didn't nobody know about it. But right soon after Abb Littleton dared him to fish in the lake, Windy was seen to be a-digging red worms. Folks knowed he was going fishing and they thought they knowed where.

"Ain't you ketching any, Windy?" Old Man Sam Burley asked him once.

"Won't bite them red worms, Sam," says Windy. "Old Man Littleton shore as anything feeds them fish of his something."

"Can't you ketch none a-tall?" said Old Sam.

Windy says, "Oh, just some little minners about fitten for a cat. I am shore fish hongry too! Ain't you, Sam?"

"You bet I am," says Sam.

"What's the best way you know to fish, Sam?" Windy asks.

"Dynamite."

"Dynamite!" says Windy. "And have Old Abb Littleton shooting our britches off? You shore are up the wrong tree this time, Sam. He'd hear the rumpus of the dynamite and how would we git any fish and him coming to his lake like a shot?"

Sam thought and then he says, "I allow we might do it on a day the same time of a thunder storm. Of a nighttime would be better to do dynamiting. I figger it wouldn't come as near being heard by so many. Wish that lake was four miles away instead of just one."

That's how Windy and Sam skummed up that scheme. But they had to wait. Seemed like there was more fair weather for a spell than anybody ever remembered of for a long time.

So Windy kept on bragging about what a fine retrieving dog old Pretty Baby was. He showed everbody around Old Abb Littleton's store, just with sticks and things, how Pretty Baby never got too wore out to bring back whatever it was he throwed away. His tales got bigger about the game meat he killed and Pretty Baby dragged in to him. The game got bigger with every kill too. So folks just got so they didn't take no pains to listen special to what Windy said. They knowed he snuck off most days in the late after-dinner part of the day with his gun and dog and always brought in game meat. But nobody never heard a shot, nor he didn't ever buy no gun cartridges from Abb Littleton's store, which was right queer, it being the nearest for ten miles away.

Well, a cloudy day finally come along. Windy and Sam was out around eyeing the sky and whittling around like they didn't have a care in the world, which they didn't much.

"How many fish you figger we'll git, Windy?" says Sam.

Windy says, "I reckon on a big wagon load. Ought to seine that many."

"Them people over at the county seat," says Sam, "ought to pay a good price too. Them having so much money and all. Don't you think so?"

"Yeah," says Windy. "Well, we'll go over, come the first good start of rain, and even if it don't thunder none, maybe Old Abb Littleton will think it's thunder. That's all we aim to fool."

So about dark, here they went, Sam and Windy, hotfooting it over to the lake, only they never went in that direction. They went over towards the Barfieldses' place like they was just rambling around, and Pretty Baby tagging along under Windy's heels as usual. They circled around till they come to the lake. About that time the fireworks started in the clouds.

Windy says, "Just like as if we'd planned it to the minute, Sam."

"Yeah," says Sam, "the Lord's on our side even if Old Abb Littleton ain't. I bet he'll just swell up and bust when he finds out about his fish being killed and sold."

"After all this planning I sort of hate to do it to him in a way, Sam," says Windy.

Sam give a big hoot. "Not me, not to Abb Littleton! He owns more than the law ought to allow anyway. Besides, he dared us. Can't nobody git away with that, can they, Windy?"

"No," says Windy, "nobody can't. He brought it stump down on his self."

Well they got out that dynamite stick and fixed it all up with a fuse like they wanted it and flung it over in the lake.

Then their eyes popped out of their heads.

Pretty Baby, that lop-eared long-legged retrieving fool of a dog, dove off into the lake and started swimming straight as a good old dog can swim right towards the place where the dynamite had struck on the water.

"My Lord!" yells Windy. "If that don't beat a pig a-pecking! Run for yore life. That fool ketch-dog aims to bring back that dynamite!"

"It will blow us both clear to the pearly gates too!" says Sam.

Well, them men got away from that lake a heap faster than they ever left any place before, and Sam shied of Windy like he had a case of lepersy.

"That dog ain't going to be looking for me," thinks Sam, "because I ain't never taught him to bring me no sticks. I shore don't want this one he's a-bringing!"

Pore old Windy like to of run his self to death in that minute or two. Pretty Baby was a-doing his best to catch up with Windy.

Then a sad thing happened. That dynamite done what it was supposed to do. But not in the lake. And the last Windy saw of his retrieving dog was his hind legs waving farewell.

Well, the next morning Old Abb's store opened up uncommonly soon. And, naturally, Windy wanted to be there and about to see if anybody had learned anything of what happened.

So he went creeping in the store sort of hacked-like. And, as common, the whole frazzling bunch of the usual lie-swappers was gathered up.

"Where's yore dog, Windy?" Old Man Littleton says, puffing on his corncob pipe like as if he was awful wise about something.

"Pore old faithful Pretty Baby," says Windy. "He was retrieving in a cub of a painter last night and the mama painter come along and got mad and et him up. There ain't even a piece left of him to bury. Pore old faithful dog!" moaned Windy, and everbody knowing they wasn't no painters left around in these parts.

"That's shore bad about yore dog, Windy," says Abb. "I know you must be some put out and sad about him."

Old Abb piddled around behind the counter and then come out to where Windy set.

"Because I know you feel so bad," he says, "I aim to give you this mess of catfish I fished out of the lake last night. It will make you feel some better. And I want you to know I think a heap of any dog that can put up such a fight with a she-painter and make her roar like that one did last night."

Still a-piddling around not looking at nobody as he talked, Old Abb was.

"It would of made a body think they was dynamite about somewheres," he says. "But, of course, they wasn't because ain't been none sold—except one stick of Sam Burley more than eight weeks ago. That was to blow up a stump, wasn't it, Sam?"

Well all the time Windy was squirming around and finally he couldn't stand it no longer.

"Abb," he says, "seeing as you given me these fishes, I can't bear to lie to you. That's just the way it was. I mean Pretty Baby was blowed up with dynamite just like you done reasoned out someways. I was a-lying all the time, but I never wanted you fellers to know that I same as kilt my own ketch-dog—me a-teaching him all them retrieving tricks. Why, Pretty Baby thought it was just another stick to play a game with, that dynamite. Pore old Pretty Baby."

Windy heaved a sigh and says, "And this morning it was shore lonesome a-gitting up with Pretty Baby not here around a-licking me in the face to unwaken me. But before I got my pants on, I heard a lumbering falling racket in the top of the old horseapple tree next on to the cowshed and when I looked out the door, there was old Pretty Baby out there with the prettiest little old pink-faced angel you ever seen or heard tell of in his jaws. He'd retrieved it in just like always when he ketches meat for me."

"A angel!" the whole bunch of them lie-swappers bellered out.

"Where is it now?" Old Abb says, all the time gitting up off the nail keg he was setting on like as if he aimed to go see for his self.

"Well sir," says Windy, "that angel and Pretty Baby just played around the back lot and around like as if Pretty Baby was a-showing that little bitty thing all the chickens. And the old cow just mooed like she thought it was the doggonedest thing she ever seen and I reckon it was. Then, I swan if that angel didn't git Pretty Baby up on its back and the last I seen they was flying off the prettiest you ever seen. I reckon he must of taken a fancy to that ketch-dog of mine and was a-toting him back to wherever Pretty Baby had got him."

"A angel!" snorted Old Abb. "Aw git out, Windy!"

"A angel it was for fair!" says Windy. "All them that disbelieve can come up to the house and see the feathers that come out of them pretty little wings when it come through the limbs with my ketch-dog. Of course, some might say they was goose feathers. But they ain't. They's a angel's feathers for shore."

So after that folks just decided nothing wouldn't hack Windy for long.

Julia Willhoit

A Hand-Caught Rabbit

There was this fella down here one time and he had a wonderful rabbit dog. Well, this dog died and he decided that he had to do something to remember him by, so he had him skinned and made himself a pair of gloves out of that dog's hide. One time, he was out in the forest working, and he pulled his gloves off and laid them on this stump and set down to eat his lunch. All of a sudden this rabbit run out of the underbrush and those two gloves jumped off of that stump and grabbed the rabbit and choked him to death.

Running the Fox

There never were two old men who liked to fox hunt as much as Dad Wilson and Bert Tunstall from up at Woodville. They were both older than the courthouse and so deaf they couldn't hear it thunder.

Every day you could find them on the square talking at the tops of their voices to each other and the other old-timers, and any time there was a big fox hunt on, Dad and Old Bert would be there talking dogs and trying to hear who was running. They judged most of the bench shows in Tyler County and kept a pretty good bunch of blue-tick hounds to run whenever they could get somebody to go along and help them around.

Dad's grandson Charlie took them out east of Hillister one cold spring night, and they cast the dogs about nine o'clock. The pack struck a trail right off, so they drove to the top of a sand hill near the railroad right-of-way and fired up some pine knots and settled down to enjoy the race. Their conversation was always sort of short during the running and generally was about which dog was leading or which one was just babbling or running the trail the wrong way. And this was a cold, still night and you could hear the pack nearly all the time, especially when they topped a hill, even though they were taking the fox away.

"There's old Jug leading the race again," said Dad.

"Too coarse-mouthed for Jug," replied Bert. "Sounds like Sadie to me."

"Sadie ain't that fast."

"Jug never led anything but his tail."

And this went on till the pack had run out of hearing, and they were getting ready to get in the pickup to find a better stand. About that time, though, the T. & N.O. freight out of Shreveport topped a rise and blew for a crossing about a mile off.

"I-God," Dad said, "don't tell me that ain't Jug."

"You better gitcha a hearing aid," Old Bert told him back.

And that T. & N.O. kept coming up one hill and going down another, blowing at ever logging road on the line.

Bert said, "Damn, they shore are coming, ain't they?"

And the old man said, "They *shore* are."

By that time the freight had hit the hilltop and was blowing the long whistle for the Hillister crossing, and the ground was trembling and the trees were shaking, and the two old men just stared into the fire. It had passed in a couple of minutes, and you could barely hear the sound of the engine as the tracks took the train through Big Turkey Creek bottom.

Old Man Tunstall shook his head and spit into the fire. "Well, sir, I don't know whether that was Jug or Sadie leading, but, by God, *that* was a race!"

And Dad said, "I-God, it *shore* was!"

A Shooter with a Heart

"I kin hit," said Old Tex at Sam Tait's place, "a sagehen at a distance of a hundr'd yards, but I gotter be loaded."

Someone "loaded" Old Tex with what his personal muzzle needed (a shot of good whiskey), and then went out looking for a target. Long before one offered itself, the effect of Tex's private charge had worn off, and he demanded more internal explosives.

"I kin hit," he proclaimed, patting his lusty fowling piece, "any sagehen with Old Bess here at a hundr'd 'n' twenty-five yards."

Again the proper charge was rammed home to Old Tex's vitals, and his audience waited for a bird. Before one appeared, Tex was really ready to assert how Old Bess could shoot.

"I kin hit," he promised, "any object that runs 'r flies at a distance of a hundred 'n' fifty yeards—not an inch less."

This time a gay-crested roadrunner was spied down the slope at just about the distance Old Tex craved. The arrival was busily turning over stones and cakes of mud for crickets and millipedes.

One more charge for Tex, a mighty clicking of Old Bess's hammers, and the long weapon was up to its owner's eye and shoulder. For a moment he held it there, and all stood waiting. Then he lowered the fowling piece. "Shucks," he said, "I kin do it. But I haven't got the heart to strain the gun."

Accommodating Deer

"Round heah," said Shotgun Charlie, "folks don't do no deer huntin'. We jist go into de woods an' light a fire an' de deer come right outta de trees an' turn deir backsides to de flame. When de meat git right, you kin cut yo'self a piece o' steak right off 'em. Cicero tol' me he had some deer come back in de mawnin' to give cold cuts, but I 'spect he's lyin'."

Why I Never Shoot Bears

Fred Jennes, veteran woods guide of Greenville, Maine, tells this tall tale and swears by all the Bibles in Piscataquis County that it is gospel truth:

"Do you know why I don't kill bears?" he asked. "No! Well, it's this way. Three years ago this June I was on a fishing trip up to Grand Lake. I had been out on the water pretty nearly all of one day and, getting tired, paddled back to camp. I hauled the canoe up on the sandy beach and started for the shack.

"When I got within about 100 feet of the place I saw the front door was open. I peeked in. There stood a big black bear just pulling the cork out of my molasses jug with his teeth. Out came the sticky syrup all over the floor. Bruin lapped up some of it and then rubbed his right paw into the rest—smeared it all over.

"So I crept around behind the camp, stuck my head in the window and yelled. He shot through the door like a bullet and headed for the lake. I never saw such an odd gait on a bear before—sort of mixture of running and galloping. And all on three legs. He was holding up the paw daubed with molasses.

"From where I stood it looked as if the critter had sat down on the shore and was holding his sweetened paw up to the air. It was June and the air was full of flies, mosquitoes and black midges. I could see that they were swarming around that molasses foot. Soon it was covered with flies feasting on that stuff.

"Suddenly he waded out in the water and stood up. He was in to his shoulders. He placed the sweetened paw down close to the surface and the next thing I saw a fine trout jump clear of the water at those flies.

"Every time a fish leaped clear of the water, Bruin would give it a cuff that sent it ashore and far up the beach.

"Finally as he saw the pile of trout on the sand he seemed to think he had enough. He waded ashore lapping off the insects and I expected he would sit down and gobble every fish. I recalled that all I had caught that day was two small fish.

"Well, sir, he had a fine feed, and when he had eaten half a dozen fine big trout, he paused, looked over at the bushes where I was and actually laid the remaining fish in a row. Then he ambled off up the shore and oddly enough kept looking back over his shoulder.

"I walked down to the beach and true enough there were half a dozen wonderful trout. At the edge of the woods the bear stopped and was standing up. As loud as I could, I yelled, 'Thanks, old man!' Do you know he actually waved a paw at me and dove into the thicket. I honestly think he left me those fish to pay for my spilled molasses. No, *sir,* I never shoot bears."

Fred Jennes

Bee Hunting in the Ozarks

" 'Bout all a feller needs t' go bee huntin'," he said, "is a can of water an' sugar mixed purty thick t' use fer bait. I soak a corncob in th' sweet'nin' over night an' then lay hit on a stump or th' top of a rail fence where I have seen bees a workin'. Purty soon a yaller bee'll come buzzin' along an' load up on th' sugar. Hit takes on all it can carry an' then makes two or three circles above th' bait 'fore hit goes bee-line fer th' tree. A feller's got t' have a good eye t' keep up with th' critter while it's makin' them circles. When I git th' direction it goes, I don't lose no time gittin' through the woods. If'n I know th' country, I have a purty good idey where the tree is fer bees have a way o' flyin' that lets a feller know 'bout how fur they're goin'. Sometimes I set a second bait 'bout fifty steps away frum th' first one an' let a bee take off frum thar. Hardly ever have t' set more'n two baits t' git th' right direction. But even then it ain't easy t' find th' tree. I keep my eyes peeled fer a big holler oak. When I git close enough I can hear th' buzzin', an' if th' wind is jist right, I can smell th' honey, too.

"When I sight th' tree I walk 'round till I see th' hole they're usin', then I cut a big X deep through th' bark with my barlow. A tree that's marked can't be teched by nary other bee hunter. 'Tis sort of a unwritten law of th' woods, this marked-tree business. Ever'body knows what it means. Nobody but a low-down skunk would cut a marked-tree in these here hills. Even if it is on th' other man's land don't make no difference.

"I usually chop or saw th' tree purty soon after I find hit, some-times on th' same day if it ain't too late. Lots o' mornin's I'm out a hour by sun waitin' with my bait an' that gives me time t' do all th' work in one day. Most of my bee huntin' is done on Sunday since pap died an' I had t' take over th' runnin' of th' shop.

"One time when I wus a kid of a boy, pap found a bee tree right at th' head o' this here holler. We wus needin' some sweet'nin' purty bad, so he took his rifle gun an' went up on th' ridge an' killed a buck deer. He brought it home an' skinned it an' hung th' meat in th' smokehouse. He got a feller who lived down on th' crick t' go with him t' cut th' tree. Hit wus shore a rich one and they sewed-up close t' eighty pounds o' honey in the deerskin. Jist as they wus ready t' start home a couple o' wild turkeys flew over an' lit about a quarter up th' holler. Pap an' th' feller with him had their guns along so they decided t' foller th' turkeys. They wus a big holler stump 'bout seven feet high standin' close by an' pap drapped th' skin o' honey into it. They wus gone a couple o' hours and brought back a big gobbler. When they got t' whar they had cut th' bee tree, they heerd a awful noise inside that stump they had left th' honey in. Sich scratchin' an' takin' on ye never heerd. They slipped up t' th' stump an' pap swung hisself up an' looked in. What d'ye think, a half-grown bar wus in that thar stump after th' sweet'nin'! Hit had clumb up th' outside an' drapped in, but after loadin' up on th' honey, hit couldn't climb out. Thar hit wus all stuck-up frum ears t' tail an' takin' on turrible. But pap soon put it out o' misery. He clumb a tree an' shot th' critter between th' eyes. Th' honey wus mostly ruint but we had plenty o' meat at our house fer quite a spell."

A Fine Bloomin' Shot!

Many years ago I worked in a drift on Big Mountain. When the weather was nice I used to crawl through the air hole and eat my dinner on the surface. I always carried a shotgun with me, seein' as the woods around the mine were full of game. One nice summer day I was a-sittin' under a tree eatin' cherry pie made for me by the little lady back in the shanty. I dropped the cherry pits on the grass there right in front of me.

Well, sir, as I was a-sittin' there, didn't a buck deer suddenly come out of the woods and stop within fifty feet of me! My gun had nothing but birdshot into it so I picked me a handful of the cherry pits and filled my gun with them. I took careful aim of the buck, and ye know, I shot him square in the head. That did not kill him. He stood as if stunned. Then suddenly, he shook his antlers, turned around, and bounded back into the woods. Behold ye! the next summer to the very day the same deer returned and stood before me. How did I know it was the same deer? Out of his head a cherry tree spread in full bloom.

The Buck or the Bullet

Cicero leaned back and wiped his forehead with his hand. We'd been under the sun all day long setting posts along the road, and our shirts hung on the last post like flags on a windless day. After a while we got to talking about hunting, because Cicero's grandson had shot a deer the weekend before and more quail than he could carry.

"Yessir," Cicero said, "it's right nice huntin' on this farm. Always has been. Can't be walkin' too far before you're gonna step on somethin' worth shootin' fer dinner. Course I grew up on the side of Roundabout Mountain, an' that was the toughest place to hunt there ever was. See, a man jist couldn't get hisself a shot off, 'cause everytime you got close, the deer or turkey would turn the corner on you and be gone. My pappy once took off after a big buck and followed him through the woods right to the base of Roundabout. Sure enough, that buck seemed always to turn the corner right when Pappy was gonna take his shot. Eventually Pappy got tired of losin' him on the curve and come up with a smart idea. He bent his gun around till it suited him an' then he shot it and laid down to wait. Sure enough, three times he saw that buck go by and three times he saw the bullet come after it, each time gainin' just a bit. What a sight it must'a been to see 'em runnin' by, wonderin' which of 'em would tire first, the buck or the bullet."

Cicero leaned back and shut his eyes. "I b'lieve the buck tired after the fifth time by," he said.

"Then what happened?" I asked.

"Well," said Cicero, getting to his feet, "folks got to exaggeratin', you know how folks get sometimes. They said the bullet caught the buck right between the eyes when it turned to see how close it was. But that ain't the truth. Fact was, Pappy missed. That buck ran off, wore out but mighty relieved."

Major Brown's Coon Story

"I was down on the crick this morning," said Bill Gates, "and I seed any amount of coon tracks. I think they're agoin' to be powerful plenty this season."

"Oh, yes," replied Tom Coker, "I never hearn tell of the likes before. The whole woods is lined with 'em. If skins is only a good price this season, I'll be worth somethin' in the spring, sure's you live, for I've jest got one of the best coon dogs in all Illinois."

"You say you never hearn tell o' the like o' the coons?" put in Major Brown, an old veteran who had been chewing his tobacco in silence for the last half hour. "Why, you don't know ennything 'bout 'em! If you'd a come here forty years ago, like I did, you'd a thought coon! I jest tell you, boys, you couldn't go amiss for 'em. We hardly ever thought of pesterin' 'em much, for their skins weren't worth a darn with us—that is, we couldn't get enough for 'em to pay for the skinnin'.

"I recollect one day I went out a bee huntin'. Wal, arter I'd lumbered about a good while, I got kinder tired, and so I leaned up agin a big tree to rest. I hadn't much more'n leaned up afore somethin' give me one of the allfiredest nips about the seat o' my britches I ever got in my life. I jumped about a rod, and lit a runnin', and kept on a runnin' for over a hundred yards; when, Think, sez I, it's no use runnin', and I'm snake-bit, but runnin' won't do enny good. So I jest stopt, and proceeded to examine the wound. I soon seed it was no snake bite, for thar's a blood-blister pinched on me about six inches long.

"Think, sez I, that rether gits me! What in the very deuce would it a bin? Arter thinkin' about it a while, I concluded to go back, and look for the critter, jest for the curiosity o' the thing. I went to the tree and poked the weeds and stuff all about; but darned the thing could I see. Purty soon I sees the tree has a little split a runnin' along up it, and so I gits to lookin' at that. Dreckly I sees the split open about half a inch, and then shet up agin; then I sees it open and shet, and open and shet, and open and shet, right along as regular as a clock a tickin'.

"Think, sez I, what in all creation can this mean? I know'd I'd got pinched in the split tree, but what in thunder was makin' it do it? At first, I felt orfully scared, and thought it must be somethin' dreadful; and then agin I thought it moutn't. Next I thought about hants and ghosts, and about a runnin' home and sayin' nothin' about it; and then I thought it couldn't be enny on 'em, for I'd never hearn tell o' them a pesterin' a feller right in open daylight. At last the true blood of my ancestors riz up in my veins, and told me it 'ud be cowardly to go home and not find out what it was; so I lumbered for my ax, and swore I'd find out all about it, or blow up. When I got back, I let into the tree like blazes, and purty soon it cum down and smashed into flinders—and what do you think? Why, it was rammed and jammed smack full of coons from top to bottom. Yes, sir, they's rammed in so close that every time they breathed they made the split open."

A Coon-Hunt in a Fency Country

'Tis really astonishin what a monstrous sight of mischief there is in a pint of rum. If one of 'em was to be submitted to an analization, as the doctors call it, it would be found to contain all manner of devilment that ever entered the head of man, from cussin and stealin up to murder and whippin his own mother, and nonsense enough to turn all the men in the world out of their senses. If a man's got any badness in him, it'll bring it out jest as sassafras tea does the measles, and if he's a good for nothin sort of a feller, without no bad traits in pertikeler, it'll bring out all his greenness. It affects different people in different ways—it makes some men monstrous brave and full of fight, and some it makes cowards—some it makes rich and happy, and some poor and miserable; and it has a different effect on different people's eyes—some it makes see double, and some it makes so blind that they can't tell themselves from a side of bacon. One of the worst cases of rum-foolery that I've heard for a long time, took place in Pineville last fall.

Bill Sweeney and Tom Culpepper is the two greatest old coveys in our settlement for coon-huntin. The fact is, they don't do much of anything else, and when *they* can't ketch nothin you may depend coons is scarce. Well, one night they had everything ready for a regular hunt, but owin to some extra good fortune, Tom had got a pocket-pistol, as he called it, of reglar old Jimmakey, to keep off the rumatics. After taking a good startin horn, they went out on their hunt, with their lite-wood torch a blazin, and the dogs a barkin and yelpin like forty thousand. Evry now and then stoppin to wait for the dogs, they would drink one another's health, till they begun to feel very comfortable, and chatted away bout one thing and another, without mindin much which way they was gwine. By-an'-by they cum to a fence. Well, over they got, 'thout much difficulty.

"Who's fence is this?" ses Bill.

" 'Taint no matter," ses Tom, "let's take suthin to drink."

After takin a drink they went on, wonderin what on earth had cum of the dogs. Next thing they cum to a terrible muddy branch.* After pullin through the briers and gettin on t'other side, they tuck another drink, and after gwine a little ways they cum to another branch, and a little further they cum to another fence—a monstrous high one this time.

"Whar upon earth is we got to, Culpepper?" ses Bill, "I never seed sich a heap of branches and fences in these parts."

"Why," ses Tom, "it's all old Sturlin's doins—you know he's always buildin fences and making infernal improvements, as he calls 'em. But never mind—we's through them now."

"Guess we is," ses Bill; "here's the all-firedest tall fence yet."

Shure enuff, thar they was right agin another fence. By this time, they begun to be considerable tired and limber in the gints, and it was sich a terrible high fence—Tom drapped the last piece of the torch, and thar they was in the dark.

"Now you is done it," ses Bill.

Tom know'd he had, but he thought it was no use to grieve over

* A brook.

spilled milk, so ses he, "Never mind, old hoss—cum ahead, and I'll take you out," and the next minit kerslash he went into the water.

Bill hung on to the fence with both hands like he thought it was slewin round to throw him off.

"Hellow, Tom," ses he, "whar in the world is you got to?"

"Here I is," ses Tom, spoutin the water out of his mouth, and coughin' like he'd swallowed something. "Look out, thar's another branch here."

"Name a' sense, whar is we?" ses Bill. "If this isn't a fency country, dad fetch my buttons."

"Yes, and a branchy one, too!" ses Tom; "and the highest, and deepest, and thickest that I ever seed in my born days."

"Which way is you?" ses Bill.

"Here, rite over the branch."

The next minite in Bill went, up to his middle in the branch.

"Cum ahead," ses Tom, "let's go home."

"Cum thunder! in such a place as this, whar a man hain't more'n got his cote tail unhitched from a fence, fore he's over his head and ears in the water."

After gettin out and feelin about in the dark a little, they got together agin. After takin another drink, they sot out for home, denouncin the fences and the branches, and helpin one another up now and then; but they hadn't got more'n twenty yards fore they brung up all standin in the middle of another branch. After gettin thro' the branch and gwine about ten steps, they was brung to a halt by another fence.

"Dad blame my pictur," ses Bill, "if I don't think we is bewitched. Who upon earth would build fences all over creation this way?"

It was but a ower's job to get over this one, but after they got on the top they found the ground on t'other side 'thout much trouble. This time the bottle was broke, and they come monstrous near having a fight about the catastrophy. But it was a very good thing, it was, for after crossin two or three more branches, and climbin as many more fences, it got to be daylight, and they found out that *they had been climbin the same fence all night,* not more'n a hundred yards from whar they first cum to it.

Bill Sweeney ses he can't account for it no other way but that the licker sort o' turned their heads, and he says he does really believe if it hadn't gin out they'd be climbin that same fence and wadin that same branch till yet. Bill promised his wife to jine the Temperance Society if she won't never say no more bout that Coon-Hunt.

William T. Thompson

Davy Crockett Meets His Match

Well, Billy told me of a time when Davy Crockett was walkin' home in the late afternoon, right afore sunset. He hadn'a done much in the way of shootin', and knowin' Crockett's temper like folks around here did, Billy said he was mighty put out. "If you wanta make a hunter madder'n a bridled bull, jist keep him from bringin' meat home after a full day of walkin'," they say.

Billy told how Davy was passin' under a mighty tall tree near the Great Gap when he looked up and spied a fat furry coon starin' down at him. He was just about to raise his gun when he saw the coon lift his paw and say, "Excuse me, is your name Davy Crockett?"

"It is," Crockett said as he lowered his gun Old Betsy.

Well, Billy says that coon put on the saddest face you ever saw and he said to Davy, "Then, you needn't take any more trouble. I'm comin' down."

The coon climbed on down that tree just as slow and mournful as could be. He just plain considered himself shot. Davy got to thinkin' that such a courteous coon deserved better than bein' skinned, so when the coon waddled up to him he bent down and patted the little feller on the head.

"You're a right thoughtful feller," Crockett said. "I won't hurt you none."

The coon didn't seem surprised at all; instead he just started backin' himself off into the woods saying, "That's mighty kind, Mr. Crockett."

"Hey, now," said Davy, "what's yer hurry?"

"Well, Mr. Crockett, it's not that I doubt you. No, sir. It's just that you might change your mind."

And with that, the coon was gone. Billy said that Davy *did* change his mind, but by the time he did, that smart coon was long gone. Even Davy laughed. It was the first, and last, coon who ever out-talked Davy Crockett.

An Underwater Robbery

"Did you ever hear of the scrape that I and uncle Zekiel had duckin' on the Connecticut?" asked Jonathan Timbertoes, while amusing his old Dutch hostess, who had agreed to entertain him under the roof of her log cottage for and in consideration of a bran' new tin milk pan. "No, I never did; do tell it," said Aunt Pumkins.

"Well—you must know that I and uncle Zeke took it into our heads on Saturday's afternoon to go a gunning after ducks, in father's skiff; so we got and sculled down the river; a proper sight of ducks flew backwards and forwards I tell ye—and by-an'-by a few of 'em lit down by the marsh, and went to feeding. I catched up my powder horn to prime [load], and it slipped right out of my hand and sunk to the bottom of the river. The water was amazingly clear, and I could see it on the bottom.

"Now, I couldn't swim a jot, so sez I to uncle Zeke, you're a pretty clever fellow, just let me take your powder horn to prime. And don't you think, the stingy critter wouldn't. Well, says I, you're a pretty good diver, an' if you'll dive and get it, I'll give you primin'.

"I thought he'd leave his powder horn; but he didn't, but stuck it in his pocket, and down he went—and there he staid"—here the old lady opened her eyes with wonder and surprise, and a pause of some minutes ensued, when Jonathan added, "I looked down, and what do you think the critter was doin?" "Lord!" exclaimed the old lady,

"I'm sure I don't know." "There he was," said our hero, "setting right on the bottom of the river, pouring the powder out of my horn into hizen."

When We Isn't We

It was a very rainy, cold day on the Hornsby plantation, and consequently there was no outside work the slaves could do. Some of them remained at home telling tales, while others went hunting. Among those who went hunting were Clem and Jim. Clem had a gun and Jim had none. Jim went along just for company. They had not gone very far when Clem shot and killed a rabbit.

"We killed uh rabbit, didn't we?" said Jim.

"Yeah," said Clem, "we killed uh rabbit."

A little farther on, Clem looked up in a tree, sighted a squirrel, and shot him down.

"We killed uh squirrel, didn't we?" said Jim.

"Yeah, we killed uh squirrel," said Clem.

On the way back home a fox crossed in front of them. Clem took aim with his gun and shot the fox.

"We killed uh fox, didn't we?" said Jim.

"Yeah," answered Clem, "we killed uh fox."

Just as they neared the edge of the woods leading to the big house, they saw a wild turkey perched on a rail fence. Clem raised his gun and fired, but the turkey flew away and the bullet that missed it killed a mule. The master, hearing the shot and seeing the mule fall, came up to the two slaves and angrily demanded, "Who killed my mule?"

"We did," answered Clem.

"We nuffin'," said Jim. "Yuh killed dat mule yo'se'f. Ah ain' got no gun."

Hunting Superstitions

Hunt geese when the wind is blowing cold and hard.

Horsehair on your wrist makes for straight shooting.

A wet bird won't fly at night.

The better the day, the worse the ducks. If the day breaks beautifully, have a wedding, not a duck hunt.

Shoot your gun once in the yard before you leave, for good luck.

Never look up at the birds; they can see your face, and they'll flare.

When shooting with others, never claim your shot took the bird. It's bad luck for you and bad manners.

It's bad luck to kill a cricket on a hunting trip.

Don't take your dog out when the wind is strong, or he'll run in circles.

When your dog points, walk right up his tail, legs on either side of his ribs. If you don't, you'll miss your shot.

Never shoot a rabbit that won't run or a duck that won't fly.

Lots of rabbits, few quail; lots of quail, few rabbits.

Kiss your shotgun shells before you load them and you won't miss your shot.

Never count your game; you're a fool if you do. Always divide game evenly among hunters.

Shotgun Charlie Goes Fishing

Charlie always told me that nothing "eases a body like fishin'." One day some summers back, I went to see a cousin who lived about two miles past Charlie's favorite fishing hole. As I passed the pond, I could see Charlie laying up under the shade of a big tree, his line in the water. I stopped and we talked for a while. Every now and then he pulled in his line and tossed it back, and I noticed he had no bait on the hook. I kept still about it, because Shotgun Charlie has his own ways, and finally, after a few minutes, I left.

Some hours later I was going home and once again passed the pond. Charlie was still there, cap low on his head and his line still in the water.

"Catch anything?" I asked.

"Nope."

"Aren't they biting?"

"Might be, might not. Cain't tell."

"Shotgun," I said, unable to resist, "there isn't any bait on your hook."

"Dat's right," he said, tipping his cap ever forward to block the late afternoon sun from his eyes. "An' dat's how it'll stay. If I put worms on dis hook, dem ol' fishes'll worry me to death."

A Hard-Drinking Snake

Shotgun Charlie and I went fishing once in a place he knew along the Tar River. "We might ketch 'em; we might not. No tellin'," he had said to me. It was the Fourth of July, hot and still, and we got onto the river and close to a spread of tree-shaded lily pads. "Now, right dere," said Charlie in his soft voice, as if he were putting me to sleep, "I b'lieve we'll take ourselves a whole string of 'em if we can feed 'em dinner nice and easy."

With that, Charlie dropped a cast in a soft plop along the edge of the pads and handed me the rod. I hadn't done much fishing, so he had probably saved us a tangled line in the nearby trees. Dinner was worms, squirming and fresh from the riverbank, but it didn't seem to inspire the hidden fish. After some quiet hours, Charlie said, "Well, it don't look like dey's crazy for worms."

Just then I saw a black water snake moving through the water with a frog in his mouth, and it dawned on Charlie and me about the same time that frogs might be tastier to our lazy fish than worms. As the snake went by the boat, Charlie hooked it with the net, grabbed it behind the head, and started to pull the frog loose. That snake just wouldn't let go and bit into the frog harder, as if to say "Oh, no you don't." Charlie pried and pried, to no avail. "I guess this fella is mighty hungry," he said. "Seems a shame to make him turn over what he done earned hisself, but he can get 'em a whole sight easier'n we can."

Charlie leaned down and took up a flask of locally brewed moonshine that I had insisted we might need and he asked me to open it. Now, Charlie wasn't a drinking man and it seemed a strange time to be offering me a swallow, but when I handed him the open flask he did the strangest thing. He tipped a few drops of that most precious fluid (the best in the county, Clifton had said to me in the back of his store when we tested it) down the throat of that snake. The snake shook and wriggled and let loose of the frog right there. Charlie tossed the snake into the river, where it floated belly up like it was dead; then, with a convulsion, it rolled over and disappeared. He smiled at me and said quietly, "Don't you be tellin' no tales, now. Clifton'd run me outta the state if he knowed I was usin' his 'medicine' on snakes instead of me."

Well, we carved up the frog and they suited the fish just right. We each reeled in some nice fat perch and were baiting the hooks again when I heard a soft slapping on the side of the boat. I thought it was the water, but the river was still and calm, so I looked down by the oar and what did I see? There, tapping the boat, was that damned snake with another frog in his mouth.

The Fish Rider

One day, a trout fisher fastened his hand line (a large, strong line whose hook is thrown off thirty or forty yards in the river) to his leg, finding the multiplicity of his tackle inconvenient to manage. A large catfish, weighing forty-eight pounds, seized the bait, and before our fisherman was well aware of the fact, he was posting down the river faster than a towboat astern of a steamer. Luckily, the catfish, as much alarmed as its follower, did not keep the deep channel, but attempted to pass a sandbar, which nearly crossed the stream. Here our almost breathless acquaintance caught hold of something which brought the fish to a sudden halt, and the fisherman was enabled to avenge himself for his temporary discomfiture.

The other case occurred only a few miles above the city. The sturgeon in the heat of a summer is very sluggish and will lie panting like a hog in the coolest parts of the stream, regardless of the approach of danger. Our friend found one of these animals seven and a half feet long in a shallow part of the river, and being much of a man, thought he could master him by jumping astride of him and, at the same instant, clapping his hands into his gills. He jumped and was successful in placing the fingers of both hands in the fish's gills. Instantly the animal darted down the river like a racehorse, sometimes under water, sometimes out. The rider could neither stop him nor get his hands out of his gills, which clasped them like a vise. Fortunately, the frighted animal bolted into one of our friend's own fish traps, and there the spectators who had pursued on the bank finally found him swearing, in the most positive manner, it was the last sturgeon he would ever ride.

The Saucer-Back Halibut

Whiskery as a "porkypine," tanned to the color of an old leather boot, Jereboam Thacher of Provincetown, longshore fisherman, looked old enough to have fished in the Flood. One leg, missing from the knee joint, was pieced out with the loom of an oar.

"How did I lose my leg?" asked he. "It's a tale that would turn your hair gray. I don't often tell about it, for folks won't believe me. Haint nobody left these days that kin remember what the fishin' was like when I was a young feller. But I'm tellin you life was different when a man could walk alongshore with a pitchfork and load up an oxcart with squiteague, and when the cod schooled right in to the rocks and laid there for days. In them times the lobsters used to crawl in on the marshes and bed down for the winter as soon as the weather cooled up, and men dug em out by the bushel along in Januwary—Febuwary.

"Twas a halibut took my leg off, although the critter didn't mean no harm. Used to be a lot of em around inshore in them days, big fellers, shaped like a sole or a flounder, broad, with both eyes on one side of their heads; spotted light and dark brown on the back and dead white underneath. Only place they git 'em now is well offshore, but in them days they used to run right in to the beach. And they run from twenty-five pound weight up to, waal, no man ever knew how big the biggest one was. They get 'em now that run to three-four hundred pound. There was bigger ones than that when I was young.

"A halibut is a bottom fish, but there's times when they come up. They'll skitter acrost-water, jump out clean, and then there's times when they'll lay almost awash, with their sides and fins curled up like a saucer. Jest lay there. What for? The Lord only knows.

"Waal, this day, I had run offshore into the bay, haulin' lobster pots, doin' a little hand-linin' and managin' to git a hundred er two pounds of lobsters and 'bout as many fish. I was runnin' right along under sail in my smack-boat, makin' good time before a light southerly that was blowin', and glad of it, too, because the fog was makin'. I must have been three mile from land when all to oncet I fetched up solid. Pretty nigh capsized. Figgered 'twas a piece of driftin' wreck, and I went forrad to shove clear and look for damage, but it wasn't a wreck at all. It looked like bottom, but no bottom that I ever seen before. Besides, there was forty foot of water there.

"I got clear, put her on the other tack and stood off, wonderin' about it. I run on for mebbe twenty minutes, then tacked inshore and bingo! I was aground agen! 'Bout six times I hit before I fin'lly tuk in that there was somethin' between me and home. What it was I couldn't tell, but it was there. And then, jest as I was pushin' off the last time, I noticed a flurry some fathoms ahead of me, and I see somethin' big break water, a oval brown thing that opened and shet.

It was a head, but, Godfreys, what a head! I could see two eyes, twice the length of a whaleboat oar apart. Lookin' around they was.

"By-an'-by I realized what the eyes belonged to. A halibut! Layin' awash. And I had been sailin' acrost his saucer-back for nigh on an hour!

"Things didn't look too good to me, but I wasn't real worried. How to git clear, that was the question. Fin'lly I figgered that I'd run on to his fin agen, climb out, stand on it, and hang onto my boat, which might be lightened enough to ride over. I trimmed aft my sheet and headed for where I knew his side laid. I miscalkerlated some, and hit it before expected, hit it hardish, too. Then I passed the slack of my halliards round me, and jumped over the bow. Something hit my knee, and I never felt sech pain before. I crawled over the gunnel, more dead than alive, saw that my leg was bleedin' bad, and wound a line tight around it. Then I took an oar, and dizzy with pain, I tried to shove the boat over. As she moved ahead, and went clear, I saw what had done the damage:

"I had struck that fish solid and started up a couple of scales. There they laid, four foot acrost, standin' half on edge, sharp as a meat-axe, hard as flint. I had stumbled onto the edge of one, and later, when some of the bunch picked me up, they found that my leg was so nigh cut off that they had to finish the job."

Old Joe, the Legendary Catfish

The old-time fishermen who live near the falls of the Brazos, tell many yarns about "Old Joe," a legendary catfish whose home is in the Sumpter Hole, a deep and dangerous whirlpool just below the falls. He is the oldest, biggest, and the most dreadful catfish that ever lived in the river.

No man has ever seen him, but in the deep silence of the night many folk have heard his splash, and in the mornings they have seen the undisputed evidences of his dirty work.

The locals' favorite fishing tackle is the throw line, a long, strong line with a weight and two or three hooks fastened to one end, and the other tied to the top of a small willow pole stuck upright into the ground, with a small bell fastened on the top so that it will ring when a fish is caught. The fisherman baits his hooks and throws them far out into the river. Then he waits patiently for the fish to bite. Sometimes the bell rings loudly and the fisherman runs to find line, pole, bell, and all gone. Whereupon he mumbles to himself, "Old Joe done gone and got my line."

Often when a party is out late at night on the river, something strikes the boat with great force. After the frightened fishermen right it, with much effort, they shout, "Old Joe is after us! Old Joe is after us!"

In a dangerous place like this where many inexperienced people come to fish, there are many accidents. So whenever anyone is drowned, the fishermen all remind each other solemnly, "Old Joe done got ernother man."

Many amateur fishermen have made elaborate plans to catch "Old Joe," but he is too old and too wise to be caught napping, and too strong to be trifled with. It is always the same old story. A broken line or a broken hook, but never an "Old Joe" on the string. And he will continue to haunt the river and to destroy the hooks and lines. He will always be bumping boats, splashing the water, and scaring the fishermen. And, surest of all, he will every year "get ernother man."

Crooked Stream

We went fishing last summer to a brook, within a dozen miles of here, that was so crooked that our companion, after trying several times to jump across and landing on the same side every jump, at last gave it up in despair and concluded to go round!

Grant's Tame Trout

The sage of Beaver Camp sat sunning himself on the bench beside the cook camp, the bench so widely known as the scene of countless weary hours of that perpetual toiler. He seemed to be smoking an old black pipe, whereas he was only dropping matches into its empty bowl at intervals of three minutes, agreeable to the terms of his contract with the American Match trust.

As he so sat and pondered, the writer, at the time a recent arrival, approached and said: "Mr. Grant, I wish you would give me the true history of your wonderful success in taming a trout. I have heard of it in all parts of the world, but I have always longed to hear the story direct from headquarters."

"Well, it really ain't so much of a story," replied the famous chronicler. "It was this way. Nine year ago the eleventh day of last June, I was fishin' out there in the pads, and right under the third yaller leaf to the right of the channel—yes, that one with the rip in it —I ketched a trout 'bout six inches long. I never see a more intelligent-lookin' little feller—high forehead, smooth face, round, dimpled chin, and a most uncommon bright, sparkling, knowin' eye.

"I always allowed that with patience and cunning a real young trout (when they gets to a heft of 10 or 15 pounds there ain't no teachin' them nothin') could be tamed jest like a dog or cat.

"There was a little water in the boat and he swims around in it all right till I goes ashore and then I gets a tub we had, made of the half of a pork barrel, fills it with water and bores a little small hole through the side close down to the bottom and stops the hole with a peg.

"I sets this tub away back in a dark corner of the camp and every night after the little fellow gets asleep I slip in, in my stockin' feet, and pulls out the peg softly and lets out jest a little mite of the water. I does this night after night so mighty sly that the little chap never suspected nothin' and he was a-livin' hale and hearty for three weeks on the bottom of that tub as dry as a cook stove, and then I knowed he was fit for trainin'.

"So I took him out o' doors and let him wiggle awhile on the path and soon got to feedin' him out of my hand. Pretty soon after that, when I walked somewhat slow (I'm naturally quite a slow walker, some folks think) he could follow me right good all round the clearin', but sometimes his fins did get ketched up in the brush jest a mite and I had to go back and swamp out a little trail for him; bein' a trout, of course he could easy follow a spotted line.

"Well, as time went on, he got to follerin' me most everywhere and hardly ever lost sight of me, and me and him was great friends, sure enough.

"Near about sundown one evening, I went out to the spring back of the camp, same one as you cross goin' to Little Island, to get some butter out of a pail, and, of course, he comes trottin' along behind. There was no wind that night, I remember, and I could hear his poor little fins a-raspin' on the chips where we'd been gettin' out splits in the cedar swamp. Well, sir, he follered me close up and came out onto the logs across the brook and jest as I was a-stoopin' down over the pail I heard a kee-plunk! behind me and Gorry! if he hadn't slipped through a chink between them logs and was drownded before my very eyes before I could reach him, so he was." Here a tear started from the good old man's eye on a very dusty trip down his time-stained cheek.

"Of course I was terribly cut up at first—I couldn't do a stroke of work for three weeks—but I got to thinkin' that as it was comin' on cold (it was in late November then) and snow would soon be here and he, poor little cuss, wasn't rugged enough for snow-shoein' and he couldn't foller me afoot all winter no how, and as he couldn't live without me, mebby it was jest as well after all he was took off that way. Do you know, mister, some folks around here don't believe a word of this, but if you'll come down to the spring with me, right now, I'll show you the very identical chink he dropped through that night, so I will. I've never allowed anyone to move it. No, sir! nor I never will."

Fishing Superstitions

Fish bite better in the dark of the moon. If mosquitoes are biting, fish will bite too.

Wind in the east, fish bite least.

Wind in the west, fish bite best.

Wind in the south, they'll take bait in the mouth.

Wind in the north, go back home.

If you want worms for bait, slap the ground with your hand. The worms think it's raining and will come to the surface.

When worms are on the ground, don't fish. The fish can get them as easily as you can and they won't be hungry.

If you see a fish break water before your first cast, you won't catch anything.

It's bad luck to change fishing rods or poles.

Don't carry your rod into the house before your trip, or you'll catch nothing. Never step over your rod.

Whenever you cast, it's good luck to say the name of your first love.

Talking scares fish away.

Turn your pockets inside out while fishing, and you can't miss.

Never throw your first catch back. Other people say to always throw your first catch back for good luck.

Never take your dog with you when fishing, or the fish won't bite.

Don't ever fish on Sunday.

The greatest fishing days are always the seventeenth and eighteenth of every month.

Letting your shadow fall upon the water while you're fishing will scare the fish away.

Absolutely never count your fish. It brings bad luck.

Anything a Man Can Do, a Woman Does Better

Beekman De Peyster was probably the most passionate and triumphant fisherman in the Petrine Club. He angled with the same dash and confidence that he threw into his operations in the stock market. He was sure to be the first man to get his flies on the water at the opening of the season. And when we came together for our fall meeting, to compare notes of our wanderings on various streams and make up the fish stories for the year, Beekman was almost always "high hook." We expected, as a matter of course, to hear that he had taken the most and the largest fish.

It was so with everything that he undertook. He was a masterful man. If there was an unusually large trout in a river, Beekman knew about it before any one else, and got there first, and came home with the fish. It did not make him unduly proud, because there was nothing uncommon about it. It was his habit to succeed, and all the rest of us were hardened to it.

When he married Cornelia Cochrane, we were consoled for our partial loss by the apparent fitness and brilliancy of the match. If Beekman was a masterful man, Cornelia was certainly what you might call a mistressful woman. She had been the head of her house since she was eighteen years old. She carried her good looks like the family plate; and when she came into the breakfast room and said good morning, it was with an air as if she presented every one with a check for a thousand dollars. Her tastes were accepted as judgments, and her preferences had the force of laws. Wherever she wanted to go in the summertime, there the finger of household destiny pointed. At Newport, at Bar Harbor, at Lenox, at Southampton, she made a record. When she was joined in holy wedlock to Beekman De Peyster, her father and mother heaved a sigh of satisfaction and settled down for a quiet vacation in Cherry Valley.

It was in the second summer after the wedding that Beekman admitted to a few of his ancient Petrine cronies, in moments of confidence (unjustifiable, but natural), that his wife had one fault.

"It is not exactly a fault," he said, "not a positive fault, you know. It is just a kind of a defect, due to her education, of course. In everything else she's magnificent. But she doesn't care for fishing. She says it's stupid—can't see why anyone should like the woods—calls camping out the lunatic's diversion. It's rather awkward for a man with my habits to have his wife take such a view. But it can be changed. I intend to convert her. I shall make an angler of her yet."

And so he did.

The new education was begun in the Adirondacks, and the first lesson was given at Paul Smith's. It was a complete failure.

Beekman persuaded her to come out with him for a day on Meacham River and promised to convince her of the charm of angling. She wore a new gown, fawn color and violet, with a picture hat, very taking. But the Meacham River trout was shy that day; not even Beekman could induce him to rise to the fly. What the trout lacked in confidence the mosquitoes more than made up. Mrs. De Peyster came home much sunburned, and expressed a highly unfavorable opinion of fishing as an amusement and of Meacham River as a resort.

"The nice people don't come to the Adirondacks to fish," said she; "they come to talk about the fishing twenty years ago. Besides, what do you want to catch that trout for? If you do, the other men will say you bought it, and the hotel will have to put in another for the rest of the season."

The following year, Beekman tried Moosehead Lake. Here he found an atmosphere more favorable to his plan of education. There were a good many people who really fished, and short expeditions in the woods were quite fashionable. Cornelia had a camping costume of the most approved style made by Dewlap on Fifth Avenue—pearl-gray with linings of rose-silk—and consented to go with her husband on a trip up Moose River. They pitched their tent the first evening at the mouth of Misery Stream, and a storm came on. The rain sifted through the canvas in a fine spray, and Mrs. De Peyster sat up all night in a waterproof cloak, holding an umbrella. The next day they were back at the hotel in time for lunch.

"It was horrid," she told her most intimate friend, "perfectly horrid. The idea of sleeping in a shower bath, and eating your breakfast from a tin plate, just for sake of catching a few silly fish! Why not send your guides out to get them for you?"

But, in spite of this profession of obstinate heresy, Beekman observed with secret joy that there were signs, before the end of the season, that Cornelia was drifting a little, a very little but still perceptibly, in the direction of a change of heart. She began to take an interest, as the big trout came along in September, in the reports of the catches made by the different anglers. She would saunter out with the other people to the corner of the porch to see the fish weighed and spread out on the grass. Several times she went with Beekman in the canoe to Hardscrabble Point and showed distinct evidences of pleasure when he caught large trout. The last day of the season, when he returned from a successful expedition to Roach River and Lily Bay, she inquired with some particularity about the results of his sport; and in the evening, as the company sat before the great open fire in the hall of the hotel, she was heard to use this information with considerable skill in putting down Mrs. Minot Peabody of Boston, who was recounting the details of her husband's catch at Spencer Pond. Cornelia was not a person to be contented with the back seat, even in fish stories.

When Beekman observed these indications he was much encouraged, and resolved to push his educational experiment briskly forward to his customary goal of success.

"Some things can be done, as well as other," he said in his masterful way as three of us were walking home together after the autumnal dinner of the Petrine Club, which he always attended as a graduate member. "A real fisherman never gives up. I told you I'd make an angler out of my wife; and so I will. It has been rather difficult. She is 'dour' in rising. But she's beginning to take notice of the fly now. Give me another season, and I'll have her landed."

Good old Beekman! Little did he think— But I must not interrupt the story with moral reflections.

The preparations that he made for his final effort at conversion were thorough and prudent. He had a private interview with Dewlap in regard to the construction of a practical fishing costume for a lady, which resulted in something more reasonable and workmanlike than had ever been turned out by that famous artist. He ordered from Hook & Catchett a lady's angling outfit of the most enticing description: a split-bamboo rod, light as a girl's wish and strong as a matron's will; an oxidized silver reel with a monogram on one side and a sapphire set in the handle for good luck; a book of flies, of all sizes and colors, with the correct names inscribed in gilt letters on each page. He surrounded his favorite sport with an aureole of elegance and beauty. And then he took Cornelia in September to the Upper Dam at Rangely.

She went reluctant. She arrived disgusted. She stayed incredulous. She returned— Wait a bit and you shall hear how she returned.

The Upper Dam at Rangely is the place, of all others in the world, where the lunacy of angling may be seen in its incurable stage. There is a cozy little inn, called a camp, at the foot of a big lake. In front of the inn is a huge dam of gray stone, over which the river plunges into a great oval pool, where the trout assemble in the early fall to perpetuate their race. From the tenth of September to the thirtieth, there is not an hour of the day or night when there are no boats floating on that pool and no anglers trailing the fly across its waters. Before the late fishermen are ready to come in at midnight, the early fishermen may be seen creeping down to the shore with lanterns in order to begin before cockcrow. The number of fish taken is not large—perhaps five or six for the whole company on an average day—but the size is sometimes enormous—nothing under three pounds is counted —and they pervade thought and conversation at the Upper Dam to the exclusion of every other subject. There is no driving, no dancing, no golf, no tennis. There is nothing to do but fish or die.

At first, Cornelia thought she would choose the latter alternative. But a remark of that skillful and morose old angler McTurk, which she overheard on the verandah after supper, changed her mind.

"Women have no sporting instinct," said he. "They only fish because they see men doing it. They are imitative animals."

That same night, she told Beekman, in the subdued tone which the architectural construction of the house imposes upon all confidential communications in the bedrooms, but with resolution in every accent, that she proposed to go fishing with him on the morrow.

"But not on that pool, right in front of the house, you understand. There must be some other place, out on the lake, where we can fish for three or four days, until I get the trick of this wobbly rod. Then I'll show that old bear McTurk what kind of an animal woman is."

Beekman was simply delighted. Five days of diligent practice at the mouth of Mill Brook brought his pupil to the point where he pronounced her safe.

"Of course," he said patronizingly, "you haven't learned all about it yet. That will take years. But you can get your fly out thirty feet, and you can keep the tip of your rod up. If you do that, the trout will hook himself, in rapid water, eight times out of ten. For playing him, if you follow my directions, you'll be all right. We will try the pool tonight and hope for a medium-sized fish."

Cornelia said nothing, but smiled and nodded. She had her own thoughts.

At about nine o'clock Saturday night, they anchored their boat on the edge of the shoal where the big eddy swings around, put out the lantern, and began to fish. Beekman sat in the bow of the boat, with his rod over the left side; Cornelia in the stern, with her rod over the right side. The night was cloudy and very black. Each of them had put on the largest possible fly, one a "Bee-Pond" and the other a "Dragon"; but even these were invisible. They measured out the right length of line and let the flies drift back until they hung over the shoal, in the curly water where the two currents meet.

There were three other boats to the left of them. McTurk was their only neighbor in the darkness on the right. Once, they heard him swearing softly to himself and knew that he had hooked and lost a fish.

Away down at the tail of the pool, dimly visible through the gloom, the furtive fisherman, Parsons, had anchored his boat. No noise ever came from that craft. If he wished to change his position, he did not pull up the anchor and let it down again with a bump. He simply lengthened or shortened his anchor rope. There was no click of the reel when he played a fish. He drew in and paid out the line through the rings by hand, without a sound. What he thought when a fish got away, no one knew, for he never said it. He concealed his angling as if it had been a conspiracy. Twice that night, they heard a faint splash in the water near his boat, and twice they saw him put his arm over the side in the darkness and bring it back again very quietly.

"That's the second fish for Parsons," whispered Beekman; "what a secretive old Fortunatus he is! He knows more about fishing than any man on the pool, and talks less."

Cornelia did not answer. Her thoughts were all on the tip of her own rod. About eleven o'clock, a fine, drizzling rain set in. The fishing was very slack. All the other boats gave it up in despair; but Cornelia said she wanted to stay out a little longer, they might as well finish up the week.

At precisely fifty minutes past eleven, Beekman reeled up his line and remarked with firmness that the holy Sabbath day was almost at hand and they ought to go in.

"Not till I've landed this trout," said Cornelia.

"What? A trout! Have you got one?"

"Certainly; I've had him on for at least fifteen minutes. I'm playing him Mr. Parsons' way. You might as well light the lantern and get the net ready; he's coming in towards the boat now."

Beekman broke three matches before he made the lantern burn; and when he held it up over the gunwale, there was the trout sure enough, gleaming ghostly pale in the dark water, close to the boat, and quite tired out. He slipped the net over the fish and drew it in—a monster.

"I'll carry that trout, if you please," said Cornelia as they stepped out of the boat; and she walked into the camp, on the last stroke of midnight, with the fish in her hand, and quietly asked for the steel-yard.

Eight pounds and fourteen ounces—that was the weight. Everybody was amazed. It was the "best fish" of the year. Cornelia showed no sign of exultation until just as John was carrying the trout to the icehouse. Then she flashed out:

"Quite a fair imitation, Mr. McTurk—isn't it?"

Now, McTurk's best record for the last fifteen years was seven pounds and twelve ounces.

So far as McTurk is concerned, this is the end of the story. But not for the De Peysters. I wish it were. Beekman went to sleep that night with a contented spirit. He felt that his experiment in education had been a success. He had made his wife an angler.

He had indeed, and to an extent which he little suspected. That Upper Dam trout was to her like the first taste of blood to the tiger. It seemed to change, at once, not so much her character as the direction of her vital energy. She yielded to the lunacy of angling, not by slow degrees (as first a transient delusion, then a fixed idea, then a chronic infirmity, finally a mild insanity), but by a sudden plunge into the most violent mania. So far from being ready to die at Upper Dam, her desire now was to live there—and to live solely for the sake of fishing—as long as the season was open.

There were two hundred and forty hours left to midnight on the thirtieth of September. At least two hundred of these she spent on the pool; and when Beekman was too exhausted to manage the boat and the net and the lantern for her, she engaged a trustworthy guide to take Beekman's place while he slept. At the end of the last day her score was twenty-three, with an average of five pounds and a quarter. His score was nine, with an average of four pounds. He had succeeded far beyond his wildest hopes.

The next year, his success became even more astonishing. They went to the Titan Club in Canada. The ugliest and most inaccessible sheet of water in that territory is Lake Pharaoh. But it is famous for the extraordinary fishing at a certain spot near the outlet, where there is just room enough for one canoe. They camped on Lake Pharaoh for six weeks, by Mrs. De Peyster's command; and her canoe was always the first to reach the fishing ground in the morning, and the last to leave it in the evening.

Someone asked him, when he returned to the city, whether he had good luck.

"Quite fair," he tossed off in a careless way; "we took over three hundred pounds."

"To your own rod?" asked the inquirer, in admiration.

"No-o-o," said Beekman, "there were two of us."

There were two of them, also, the following year, when they joined the Natasheebo Salmon Club and fished that celebrated river in Labrador. The custom of drawing lots every night for the water that each member was to angle over the next day, seemed to be especially designed to fit the situation. Mrs. De Peyster could fish her own pool and her husband's too. The result of that year's fishing was something phenomenal. She had a score that made a paragraph in the newspapers and called out editorial comment. One editor was so inadequate to the situation as to entitle the article in which he described her triumph "The Equivalence of Woman." It was well meant, but she was not at all pleased with it.

She was now not merely an angler, but a "record" angler of the most virulent type. Wherever they went, she wanted, and she got, the pick of the water. She seemed to be equally at home on all kinds of streams, large and small. She would pursue the little mountain brook trout in the early spring, and the Labrador salmon in July, and the huge speckled trout of the northern lakes in September, with the same avidity and resolution. All that she cared for was to get the best and the most of the fishing at each place where she angled. This she always did.

And Beekman—well, for him there were no more long separations from the partner of his life while he went off to fish some favorite stream. There were no more homecomings after a good day's sport to find her clad in cool and dainty raiment on the verandah, ready to welcome him with friendly badinage. There was not even any casting of the fly around Hardscrabble Point while she sat in the canoe reading a novel, looking up with mild and pleasant interest when he caught a larger fish than usual, as an older and wiser person looks at a child playing some innocent game. Those days of a divided interest between man and wife were gone. She was now fully converted, and more. Beekman and Cornelia were one; and she was the one.

The last time I saw the De Peysters, he was following her along the Beaverkill, carrying a landing net and a basket, but no rod. She paused for a moment to exchange greetings and then strode on down the stream. He lingered for a few minutes longer to light a pipe.

"Well, old man," I said, "you certainly have succeeded in making an angler of Mrs. De Peyster."

"Yes, indeed," he answered, "haven't I?" Then he continued, after a few thoughtful puffs of smoke, "Do you know, I'm not quite so sure as I used to be that fishing is the best of all sports. I sometimes think of giving it up and going in for croquet."

CHAPTER 5

Love
and
Marriage

"Crockett Pops the Question"

> *Kiss me quick and go, my honey,*
> *Kiss me quick and go.*
> —old folksong

EVERY DAY, IN EVERY CITY, town, and village, the sweet flush of love stirs, and in that cycle of courtship, love, and marriage familiar to us all, one can find the oldest and best-loved forms of folklore. The ballads of love won and lost, the spectacular feats accomplished by those in search of a mate's approval, the sad, bitter lament from love's ruin, fill the folklore of every nation.

America has been an enthusiastic contributor to the folklore of love and marriage for a variety of reasons. Frontier life itself put an enormous pressure on the family—it was a social and economic necessity to marry and have children. Sons were needed to work the field, daughters to keep house, and there was little time to waste. The single life was simply unacceptable for all except hermits, nuns, and riverboat gamblers, so at a certain point, whatever your sex, you put your pride behind you and took any mate you could find. Advertisements often appeared in the eastern press recruiting women for the men out West in the mining camps: "Women Needed! All Shapes and Sizes! Guaranteed Husband! Come Quickly!" The country had to be settled and it couldn't be done alone.

That is not to say that America in those days was without romance. Nothing melted a heart like frontier ballads, even if they were sweet and sad like "Joe Bowers" or "I Once Loved a Young Man." The ballad tradition in America is derived principally from the Scottish and English ballads, but they were enormously popular and claimed by the new nation instantly as "American" tunes. Some, like "Clementine" and "Frankie and Johnnie," have that unmistakable trace of American energy, worthy rivals to the other, older songs. And one should not forget the square dance, that frontier institution, which made many a country match. When new love bloomed during the fiddling, those who had once been similarly in love looked on with nostalgia and perhaps some envy. But once a marriage proposal was made and accepted, the romance was done and it was on to the business of married life.

Women in America had a difficult time. Their life on the frontier was much tougher than a man's. He could excuse himself for the adventure of the hunt or Indian wars, but his wife's world was compressed by the needs of her children and the duties of her home. Read the recently found journals written by frontier women and you see the unending tasks and backbreaking toil that was their daily lot. Consequently, the folklore that women found most useful were the wisdoms from their own experience: superstitions of courtship, marriage, health, and pregnancy, the catalog of proverbs and sayings that could be used for the instruction of children. Midwives, for example, were undisputed authorities. If they warned that sweeping under the bed of a new mother would kill the infant, dust gathered under that bed for a year. If a child grew up mean, it was inevitably an old midwife who remembered that the child's mother had kicked a stray dog when she was six months pregnant.

The inevitable conflict between men and women living together also provided wonderful folktales. The old cliché that the woman is the real boss finds fresh expression in "The Queen of the Bull-Whackers" and "De Ways of de Wimmens." There are plenty of infidelities to recount, as well as stories of henpecked husbands and beleaguered wives. "A Patient Wife" is, in fact, a classic of the bleak American humor that marriage so frequently encourages.

In any event, there is a good deal in the following section that highlights the laughter and pathos to be found on the shifting ground where men and women meet. When love comes to a heart, it will cause a song to be sung or a tale to be told, happy or sad, and that is the only certainty in love and marriage.

High Horse's Courting:
A Sioux Love Story

You know, in the old days, it was not so very easy to get a girl when you wanted to be married. Sometimes it was hard work for a young man and he had to stand a great deal. Say I am a young man and I have seen a young girl who looks so beautiful to me that I feel all sick when I think about her. I can not just go and tell her about it and then get married if she is willing. I have to be a very sneaky fellow to talk to her at all, and after I have managed to talk to her, that is only the beginning.

Probably for a long time I have been feeling sick about a certain girl because I love her so much, but she will not even look at me, and her parents keep a good watch over her. But I keep feeling worse and worse all the time; so maybe I sneak up to her tepee in the dark and wait until she comes out. Maybe I just wait there all night and don't get any sleep at all and she does not come out. Then I feel sicker than ever about her.

Maybe I hide in the brush by a spring where she sometimes goes to get water, and when she comes by, if nobody is looking, then I jump out and hold her and just make her listen to me. If she likes me too, I can tell that from the way she acts, for she is very bashful and maybe will not say a word or even look at me the first time. So I let her go, and then maybe I sneak around until I can see her father alone, and I tell him how many horses I can give him for his beautiful girl, and by now I am feeling so sick that maybe I would give him all the horses in the world if I had them.

Well, this young man I am telling about was called High Horse, and there was a girl in the village who looked so beautiful to him that he was just sick all over from thinking about her so much and he was getting sicker all the time. The girl was very shy, and her parents thought a great deal of her because they were not young any more and this was the only child they had. So they watched her all day long, and they fixed it so that she would be safe at night too when they were asleep. They thought so much of her that they had made a rawhide bed for her to sleep in, and after they knew that High Horse was sneaking around after her, they took rawhide thongs and tied the girl in bed at night so that nobody could steal her when they were asleep, for they were not sure but that their girl might really want to be stolen.

Well, after High Horse had been sneaking around a good while and hiding and waiting for the girl and getting sicker all the time, he finally caught her alone and made her talk to him. Then he found out that she liked him maybe a little. Of course this did not make him feel well. It made him sicker than ever, but now he felt as brave as a bison bull, and so he went right to her father and said he loved the girl so much that he would give two good horses for her—one of them young and the other one not so very old.

But the old man just waved his hand, meaning for High Horse to go away and quit talking foolishness like that.

High Horse was feeling sicker than ever about it; but there was another young fellow who said he would loan High Horse two ponies and when he got some more horses, why, he could just give them back for the ones he had borrowed.

Then High Horse went back to the old man and said he would give four horses for the girl—two of them young and the other two not hardly old at all. But the old man just waved his hand and would not say anything.

So High Horse sneaked around until he could talk to the girl again, and he asked her to run away with him. He told her he thought he would just fall over and die if she did not. But she said she would not do that; she wanted to be bought like a fine woman. You see she thought a great deal of herself too.

That made High Horse feel so very sick that he could not eat a bite, and he went around with his head hanging down as though he might just fall down and die any time.

Red Deer was another young fellow, and he and High Horse were great comrades, always doing things together. Red Deer saw how High Horse was acting, and he said: "Cousin, what is the matter? Are you sick in the belly? You look as though you were going to die."

Then High Horse told Red Deer how it was, and said he thought he could not stay alive much longer if he could not marry the girl pretty quick.

Red Deer thought awhile about it, and then he said: "Cousin, I have a plan, and if you are man enough to do as I tell you, then everything will be all right. She will not run away with you; her old man will not take four horses; and four horses are all you can get. You must steal her and run away with her. Then afterwhile you can come back and the old man cannot do anything because she will be your woman. Probably she wants you to steal her anyway."

So they planned what High Horse had to do, and he said he loved the girl so much that he was man enough to do anything Red Deer or anybody else could think up.

So this is what they did.

That night late they sneaked up to the girl's tepee and waited until it sounded inside as though the old man and the old woman and the girl were sound asleep. Then High Horse crawled under the tepee with a knife. He had to cut the rawhide thongs first, and then Red Deer, who was pulling up the stakes around that side of the tepee, was going to help drag the girl outside and gag her. After that, High Horse could put her across his pony in front of him and hurry out of there and be happy all the rest of his life.

When High Horse had crawled inside, he felt so nervous that he could hear his heart drumming, and it seemed so loud he felt sure it would wake the old folks. But it did not, and afterwhile he began cutting the thongs. Every time he cut one it made a pop and nearly scared him to death. But he was getting along all right and all the thongs were cut down as far as the girl's thighs, when he became so nervous that his knife slipped and stuck the girl. She gave a big, loud yell. Then the old folks jumped up and yelled too. By this time High Horse was outside, and he and Red Deer were running away like antelope. The old man and some other people chased the young men but they got away in the dark and nobody knew who it was.

Well, if you ever wanted a beautiful girl you will know how sick High Horse was now. It was very bad the way he felt, and it looked as though he would starve even if he did not drop over dead sometime.

Red Deer kept thinking about this, and after a few days he went to

High Horse and said: "Cousin, take courage! I have another plan, and I am sure, if you are man enough, we can steal her this time." And High Horse said: "I am man enough to do anything anybody can think up, if I can only get that girl."

So this is what they did.

They went away from the village alone, and Red Deer made High Horse strip naked. Then he painted High Horse solid white all over, and after that he painted black stripes all over the white and put black rings around High Horse's eyes. High Horse looked terrible. He looked so terrible that when Red Deer was through painting and took a good look at what he had done, he said it scared even him a little.

"Now," Red Deer said, "if you get caught again, everybody will be so scared they will think you are a bad spirit and will be afraid to chase you."

So when the night was getting old and everybody was sound asleep, they sneaked back to the girl's tepee. High Horse crawled in with his knife, as before, and Red Deer waited outside, ready to drag the girl out and gag her when High Horse had all the thongs cut.

High Horse crept up by the girl's bed and began cutting at the thongs. But he kept thinking, "If they see me they will shoot me because I look so terrible." The girl was restless and kept squirming around in bed, and when a thong was cut, it popped. So High Horse worked very slowly and carefully.

But he must have made some noise, for suddenly the old woman awoke and said to her old man: "Old Man, wake up! There is somebody in this tepee!" But the old man was sleepy and didn't want to be bothered. He said: "Of course there is somebody in this tepee. Go to sleep and don't bother me." Then he snored some more.

But High Horse was so scared by now that he lay very still and as flat to the ground as he could. Now, you see, he had not been sleeping very well for a long time because he was so sick about the girl. And while he was lying there waiting for the old woman to snore, he just forgot everything, even how beautiful the girl was. Red Deer, who was lying outside ready to do his part, wondered and wondered what had happened in there, but he did not dare call out to High Horse.

Afterwhile the day began to break and Red Deer had to leave with the two ponies he had staked there for his comrade and girl, or somebody would see him.

So he left.

Now when it was getting light in the tepee, the girl awoke and the first thing she saw was a terrible animal, all white with black stripes on it, lying asleep beside her bed. So she screamed, and then the old woman screamed and the old man yelled. High Horse jumped up, scared almost to death, and he nearly knocked the tepee down getting out of there.

People were coming running from all over the village with guns and bows and axes, and everybody was yelling.

By now High Horse was running so fast that he hardly touched the ground at all, and he looked so terrible that the people fled from him and let him run. Some braves wanted to shoot at him, but the others said he might be some sacred being and it would bring bad trouble to kill him.

High Horse made for the river that was near, and in among the brush he found a hollow tree and dived into it. Afterwhile some braves came there and he could hear them saying it was some bad spirit that had come out of the water and gone back in again.

That morning the people were ordered to break camp and move away from there. So they did, while High Horse was hiding in his hollow tree.

Now Red Deer had been watching all this from his own tepee and trying to look as though he were as much surprised and scared as all the others. So when the camp moved, he sneaked back to where he had seen his comrade disappear. When he was down there in the brush, he called, and High Horse answered, because he knew his friend's voice. They washed off the paint from High Horse and sat down on the river bank to talk about their troubles.

High Horse said he never would go back to the village as long as he lived and he did not care what happened to him now. He said he was going to go on the war-path all by himself. Red Deer said: "No, cousin, you are not going on the war-path alone, because I am going with you."

So Red Deer got everything ready, and at night they started out on the war-path all alone. After several days they came to a Crow camp just about sundown, and when it was dark they sneaked up to where the Crow horses were grazing, killed the horse guard, who was not thinking about enemies because he thought all the Lakotas were far away, and drove off about a hundred horses.

They got a big start because all the Crow horses stampeded and it was probably morning before the Crow warriors could catch any horses to ride. Red Deer and High Horse fled with their herd three days and nights before they reached the village of their people. Then they drove the whole herd right into the village and up in front of the girl's tepee. The old man was there, and High Horse called out to him and asked if he thought maybe that would be enough horses for his girl. The old man did not wave him away that time. It was not the horses that he wanted. What he wanted was a son who was a real man and good for something.

So High Horse got his girl after all, and I think he deserved her.

Buffalo Gals

THE ZEST AND FLAIR of American courtship is celebrated in this delightful song. Though it was written over 140 years ago, it has lost little of its charm. Some used to sing it as "Charleston Gals," others as "New York Gals," and still others as "Louisiana Gals," but wherever the gals came from, you can bet they always danced by the light of the moon:

> As I was walking down the street,
> Down the street,
> Down the street,
> A pretty gal I chanced to meet
> Under the silvery moon.
>
> > Buffalo gals won't you come out tonight,
> > Come out tonight, come out tonight,
> > Buffalo gals won't you come out tonight
> > And dance by the light of the moon.
>
> I asked her if she'd stop and talk,
> Stop and talk,

Stop and talk,
Her feet covered up the whole sidewalk,
She was fair to view.
    Chorus.
I asked her if she'd be my wife,
Be my wife,
Be my wife,
Then I'd be happy all my life,
If she'd marry me.
    Chorus.

Jemima, What Have You Done to Me?

Delicious Miss Jemima: What have you done to me! Ever since the "corn shucking" when I had you for a pardner for two "hoe-downs" and a "double-shuffle," I hain't had one good night's rest. Just as soon as I lay down and git the heading all fixed to my notion, and the kivering nicely tucked in, I begins right straight to think of you, an' it 'pears to me I ken see you just as plain with them black eyes of yourn, and them plump round cheeks, and soft pulpy lips, as if you was right clost to me sure enough. This makes me restive an' uneasy, an' I kicks an' tumbles about till I gits into a cold sweat, an' then when at last I do go off into a cat nap, I'm sure to wake up immediately with the kivering rolled up in a hard knot round my neck, an' my nose stopped as tight as a bottle, an' all the next day I am going about the house sneezing like a dog that has had his head hilt over tar and feathers for the distemper. I have gone off my feed entirely, and look as lean as a shad after spawning time. Even middling and white head cabbage (of which in gineral I am uncommon fond) aint nigh so satisfactory as they used to be afore I knowed you. Oh Jemima, Jemima, what have you done to me? Only this mornin' Mammy made a whole lot of buck wheat cakes for breakfast, an' as I'm powerful fond of 'em, I smeared a pile about as big as a hatters block with fresh butter and honey, but arter I had got 'em all fixed to my notion, I thought of them ar' soft pulpy lips of yourn, an' I couldn't have tuck a bite if it had been to save me. I tell you what, Jemima, when I leaves hot buck wheat cakes an' honey without a considerable scuffle, you may depend ther's something or nother the matter with me sure. The other day my Mammy says to me, says she,

"Jake, I wish you would go to the cowpen an' rope a gentle cow, an' bring her to the door, as I want some warm milk right from the cow to give the baby that's teething."

Well, off I goes, thinking of nothing but you all the time, an' after a while I got back and out comes Mammy to milk the cow, but she stopt all of a sudden an' says she,

"Jake, what on airth do you mean by bringing up that great beast here?" Sure enough when I turned round there stood the old work ox looking as innocent as if he had been used to give a gallon at a milking every day of his life. Only this very morning Mammy asked me to go in the truck patch an' weed it out a little, so off I went, thinking of you all the time, and commenced slashing away among the beets and carrots and flower beds, when all at once I heern Mammy a screechin' out like a sand hill crane; an' sure enuf when I come to myself rightly, I found I had cut up all the old womans yarbs, allecimane and tansey, and every sprig of sage which she had been countin' on strong for making sassenger at next hog-killing time.

"I do declare to goodness," says Mammy, "if the boy hain't got the mazes, worse than when he had the fever an' ager, an' used to sit all day long on the sunny side of the house a flipping flies with a splinter."

But I know it aint the mazes, for it all come to you, Jemima, an', oh, Jemima, do tell what you have done to me!

I suspicioned strong at one time that you had gin me "love powders," an' so a few days ago, I went straight to Dr. Jimisons the Pothecary that lives at the corner, with the big blue bellied bottles in the winder, an' I told him right up I wanted something to carry off the love powders *somebody* had give me. Well, he give me two bolusses [pills] about as big as malagy grapes an' a good deal like 'em, an' told me to take 'em just as I was going to bed and he be bound they'd give me easement. That very nite I tuck 'em both accordin' to directions, an' if you had give me love powders I'm sartin they must have carried 'em off, for every thing else was, an' they made me so orful sick, that I'm free to confess I never thought of you onct till next morning arter my stomick had settled agin.

The only thing that 'pears to do me any good at all now a-days, is to loll about the shady fence corners round your daddy's farm, an' watch you an' your sister Sal a rompin' in the yard, an' when I see you skippin' up an' down like a young fawn an' them ar' beautiful curls of yourn streamin' out behind, it does 'pear to me, if I was sure nobody was lookin at me, that I could knuckle right down an' kiss the very tracks you make in the sand; an' arter you goes back inter the house, it seems to me I haint got no strength to move, an' I ginerally sits for a long time listening to the partridges an' turtle doves a cooin' an' singin' in the thickets (dod rot it, it used to be heap more fun to pop at 'em with my old double barrel) an' the wind a moanin' among the long leaf pines just like bugle horns an' fiddles playing 'way up in the sky.

Oh, Jemima, do tell what you have done to me! Last night I dreamed to see myself a sittin' with you in a nice hewed double log cabin, with a big gallery in front, all kivered with woodbine an' clapboards, an' a nice yard with a well in it, an' a long sweep for the children to ride on, an' a big ash hopper in the corner, an' a tall pole with gourds hanging all 'round it for the martin to lay in, an' you may depend I felt good; but when I woke up an' found 'twant nothing but a dream, I bumped my head agin the wall till the floor was literally kivered with the daubin', I jarred out the cracks. Ever since I seed you last Sunday walking arm an' arm with Bob Sikes (the fust time I catch him I'll beat him till his hide won't hold shucks) it 'pears to me I don't care 'bout nothing—I don't care if the bay filly does lose her foal an' gits beat the next quarter race she runs into the bargain—I don't care what becomes of the sow an' pigs; an' if the meat all spoils at hog killin' time, 'twont make a red cent's difference to me—I don't care if the measles does get among the children an' hooping cough to boot—an' for two dimes I'd jest as soon cut stick an' split for Californy as any other way.

Yourn till death,

JAKE SHORT.

Old Smoky

On top of Old Smoky, all covered with snow
I lost my true lover by courting too slow.

While courting is pleasure and parting is grief,
A false-hearted lover is worse than a thief.

A thief they will rob you and take what you have
But a false-hearted lover will take you to the grave.

The grave will decay you, will turn you to dust
Only one boy out of a hundred a poor girl can trust.

They'll tell you they love you to give your heart ease
As soon as your back's turned they'll court who they please.

'Tis raining, 'tis hailing, this dark stormy night
Your horses can't travel for the moon gives no light.

Go put up your horses and give them some hay
Come sit down beside me as long as you can stay.

My horses aren't hungry, they won't eat your hay
My wagon is loaded, I'll feed on my way.

As sure as the dew drops fall on the green corn
Last night he was with me, tonight he is gone.

I'll go back to Old Smoky, to the mountain so high
Where the wild birds and turtledoves can hear my sad cry.

Way down on Old Smoky all covered in snow
I lost my blue-eyed boy by courting too slow.

Joe Bowers

My name it is Joe Bowers, I've got a brother Ike;
I came here from Missouri, yes, all the way from Pike;
I'll tell you why I left there and how I came to roam,
To leave my poor old mammy, so far away from home.

I used to love a gal there, her name was Sallie Black,
I asked her for to marry me, she said it was a whack;
She says to me, "Joe Bowers, before you hitch for life,
You ought to have a little home to keep your little wife."

Says I, "My dearest Sallie, O Sallie, for your sake,
I'll go to California and try to raise a stake."
Says she to me: "Joe Bowers, you are the chap to win.
Give me a kiss to seal the bargain"—and I throwed a dozen in.

I'll never forget my feelings when I bid adieu to all.
Sal, she cotched me round the neck and I began to bawl.
When I begun they all commenced, you never heard the like,
How they all took on and cried the day I left old Pike.

When I got to this here country, I hadn't nary a red,
I had such wolfish feelings I wished myself most dead.
But the thoughts of my dear Sallie soon made these feelings git;
And whispered hopes to Bowers— Lord, I wish I had 'em yit.

At last I went to mining, put in my biggest licks,
Came down upon boulders just like a thousand bricks.
I worked both late and early in rain and sun and snow,
But I was working for my Sallie; it was all the same to Joe.

I made a very lucky strike, as the gold itself did tell,
For I was working for my Sallie, the girl I loved so well.
I saved it for my Sallie that I might pour it at her feet;
That she might hug and kiss me and call me something sweet.

But one day I got a letter from my dear, kind brother Ike;
It came from old Missouri, yes, all the way from Pike;
It told me the gol-darndest news that ever you did hear,
My heart it is a-bustin', so please excuse this tear.

I'll tell you what it was, boys—you'll bust your sides, I know;
For when I read that letter you ought to seen poor Joe.

My knees gave way beneath me, and I pulled out half my hair;
And if you ever tell this now, you bet you'll hear me swear.

It said my Sallie was fickle, her love for me had fled,
That she had married a butcher, whose hair was awful red;
It told me more than that, it's enough to make me swear—
It said that Sallie had a baby and the baby had red hair.

Now I've told you all that I can tell about this sad affair,
'Bout Sallie marrying a butcher and the baby had red hair
But whether it was a boy or girl the letter never said;
It only said its cussed hair was inclined to be red.

Frankie and Johnny

Frankie and Johnny were lovers, O Lordy, how they could love.
Swore to be true to each other, true as the stars above;
He was her man, but he done her wrong.

Frankie she was a good woman, just like everyone knows.
She spent a hundred dollars for a suit of Johnny's clothes.
He was her man, but he done her wrong.

Frankie and Johnny went walking, Johnny in a brand-new suit.
"Oh, good Lord," says Frankie, "but don't my Johnny look cute?"
He was her man, but he done her wrong.

Frankie went down to Memphis, she went on the evening train.
She paid one hundred dollars for Johnny's watch and chain.
He was her man, but he done her wrong.

Frankie lived in the crib house, crib house had only two doors;
Gave all her money to Johnny, he spent it on those call-house
    whores.
He was her man, but he done her wrong.

Johnny's mother told him, and she was mighty wise,
"Don't spend Frankie's money on that parlor Alice Pry.
You're Frankie's man, and you're doing her wrong."

Frankie and Johnny were lovers, they had a quarrel one day,
Johnny he up and told Frankie, "Bye-bye, babe, I'm going away.
I was your man, but I'm just gone."

Frankie went down to the corner to buy a glass of beer.
Says to the fat bartender, "Has my lovingest man been here?
He was my man, but he's doing me wrong."

"Ain't going to tell you no story, ain't going to tell you no lie,
I seen your man 'bout an hour ago with a girl named Alice Pry.
If he's your man, he's doing you wrong."

Frankie went down to the pawnshop, she didn't go there for fun;
She hocked all of her jewelry, bought a pearl-handled forty-four
    gun
For to get her man who was doing her wrong.

Frankie she went down Broadway, with her gun in her hand,
Sayin', "Stand back, all you livin' women, I'm a-looking for my
    gambolin' man.
For he's my man, won't treat me right."

Frankie went down to the hotel, looked in the window so high,
There she saw her loving Johnny a-loving up Alice Pry.
Damn his soul, he was mining in coal.

Frankie went down to the hotel, she rang that hotel bell.
"Stand back, all of you chippies, or I'll blow you all to hell.
I want my man, who's doing me wrong."

Frankie threw back her kimono, she took out her forty-four,
Root-a-toot-toot three times she shot right through that hotel
    door.
She was after her man who was doing her wrong.

Johnny grabbed off his Stetson, "Oh, good Lord, Frankie, don't
    shoot!"
But Frankie pulled the trigger and the gun went root-a-toot-toot.
He was her man, but she shot him down.

Johnny he mounted the staircase, crying, "Oh, Frankie, don't you
    shoot!"
Three times she pulled that forty-four a-root-a-toot-toot-toot-toot.
She shot her man who threw her down.

First time she shot him he staggered, second time she shot him he
    fell.
Third time she shot him, O Lordy, there was a new man's face in
    hell.
She killed her man who had done her wrong.

"Roll me over easy, roll me over slow,
Roll me over on my left side for the bullet hurt me so.
I was her man, but I done her wrong."

"Oh my baby, kiss me, once before I go.
Turn me over on my right side, the bullet hurt me so.
I was your man, but I done you wrong."

Johnny he was a gambler, he gambled for the gain,
The very last words that Johnny said were, "High-low Jack and
the game."
He was her man, but he done her wrong.

Frankie heard a rumbling away down in the ground.
Maybe it was Johnny where she had shot him down.
He was her man and she done him wrong.

Oh, bring on your rubber-tired hearses, bring on your rubber-tired
hacks,
They're taking Johnny to the cemetery and they ain't a-bringing
him back.
He was her man, but he done her wrong.

Eleven macks a-riding to the graveyard, all in a rubber-tired hack,
Eleven macks a-riding to the graveyard, only ten a-coming back.
He was her man, but he done her wrong.

Frankie went to the coffin, she looked down on Johnny's face,
She said, "Oh, Lord, have mercy on me. I wish I could take his
place.
He was my man and I done him wrong."

Frankie went to Mrs. Halcomb, she fell down on her knees,
She said to Mrs. Halcomb, "Forgive me if you please.
I've killed my man for doing me wrong."

"Forgive you, Frankie darling, forgive you I never can.
Forgive you, Frankie darling, for killing your only man.
He was your man, though he done you wrong."

The judge said to the jury, "It's as plain as plain can be.
This woman shot her man, it's murder in the second degree.
He was her man, though he done her wrong."

Now it was not murder in the second degree, it was not murder in
the third.
The woman simply dropped her man, like a hunter drops his bird.
He was her man and he done her wrong.

"Oh, bring a thousand policemen, bring them around today,
Oh, lock me in that dungeon and throw the key away.
I killed my man 'cause he done me wrong."

"Oh, put me in that dungeon. Oh, put me in that cell,
Put me where the northeast wind blows from the southwest corner
of hell.
I shot my man 'cause he done me wrong."

Frankie walked up the scaffold, as calm as a girl can be,
And turning her eyes to heaven she said, "Good Lord, I'm coming
  to thee.
He was my man, and I done him wrong."

A New England Courtship

Jonathan Dunbatter saw Prudence Feastall at the meeting. Jonathan sidled up to Prudence after the meeting, and she kind of sidled off. He went closer and axed her if she would accept the crook o' his elbow. She resolved she would, and plumped her arm right 'round his. Jonathan said the text "seek and ye shall find" was purty good readin'. Prudence hinted that "ask and ye shall receive" was better. Jonathan thought so too, but this axing was a puzzler. A feller was apt to git into a snarl when he axed, and snarlin' warn't no fun. Prudence guessed strawberries and cream was slick. Jonathan thought they warn't so slick as Pru's lips. "Now, don't," said Pru, and she guv Jonathan's arm an involuntary hug. He was a leetel started, but thought his farm wanted some female help to look after the house. Pru knew how to make rale good bread. "Now, don't," said Pru. "If I should," said Jonathan. "Now, don't," said Pru. "Maybe you wouldn't—" and Jonathan shuck all over, and Prudence replied, "If you be coming that game, you'd better tell feyther." "That's jist what I want," said Jonathan, and in three weeks Jonathan and Prudence were "my old man" and "my old woman."

A Frontier Love Story

Having come to the years of maturity, and being a stout lad of his age, young Harding began to look around for a wife. Having heard of one Betsey Buzzard, a good stout gal, not very high, but making up what she wanted in longness by being pretty thick through and as round as an apple, he cut out for the house where she lived. Ben considered himself a whole team, and went about trapping this gal just as he would tree a bear.

He felt pretty queer when he had got near the house where she lived, and had a good mind to turn back and not go in, as he was afeard she would have nothing to say to him, but he knowed that "faint heart never won fair lady," and so he stood still awhile to wait till his courage got up; but he found the longer he stood, the more his courage went away, and he began to fear if he stood much longer, he should not dare to go at all. So he thought he would take only one long step towards the house, as there couldn't be anything decisive in that. Then he took another step, and so on until he had only one step to take to the house, and now he found that that last step was just as much as if he hadn't taken any steps before, for he was puzzled just as much how to go ahead as he was before he stopped at all. The way his heart bobbed up and down was a caution. He dassent so much as look over his shoulder, and much less look ahead; he was stuck in the mud like a Mississippi sawyer, and thought he would rather face a whole regiment of wildcats than look Betsey in the face, but 'twa'nt because he didn't love her, only 'twas a dubious thing to make the first attempt, and not know nothing about how he would be received.

Just then the door opened, and Betsey herself come out all rigged up in her best bib and tucker, and Ben was dumb-foundered right away, and his heart came up into his throat, specially as Betsey was cross-eyed, and he thought she was looking right at him, whereas she was looking towards the hovel where the horses was kept. There she stood right on the door stone, and Ben felt it would be impossible for him to speak to her, but, pretty soon, another fellow come out of the barn, leading along a horse towards Betsey. Then Ben forgot his bashfulness all at once, and his dander riz right up. "I say, stranger," said he, "do you make purtentions to this gal?"

The fellow let go the horse and looked right at Ben, as if he would eat him up alive! Ben knew what would come next very well, and sure enough the other fellow made a dive at one of his eyes, but Ben jumped up his whole length and lit right on the other feller's head. Both of them tumbled together against an old gate, leading into a watermillion patch, and the way the vines was snarled about their legs and the watermillions got squashed was a caution. Sometimes he was uppermost and sometimes the tother; until at last, Betsey, who had taken a notion to Ben, jumped astraddle of the other feller's back when he was down, and began pounding him with a stone over the head, until he called for quarter. When he seed that, he give over right away, for it went so to his heart that his gal should turn agin him that he couldn't fight. He got on his feet and shook himself, and he turned all colors when he seed Ben go right up to Betsey and give her a smack on the cheek. Says Ben to himself, "Mister, I think you are most catawampiously chawed up." The feller said not a word but turned his tail and went straight off, and was never heered on arterwards.

So, the gal then told Ben that she was just a going to set out with that feller for camp meeting, and that if he liked, he might take his place on the horse. So Ben got right up on the horse, and took Betsey up behind him, and they drove off to camp meeting, at the distance of about ten miles. On the road they courted with all their might, till Ben got her to agree to have him, though she little thought, all that time, that he would one day be a member of Congress.

When they reached the camp, they found the preachers all very earnestly engaged, some a praying and some a preaching and some a singing sams. There was one feller in perticular that hollered so you could hear him as far as a catamount, and he stamped worse than a fulling mill. There was guards placed all round to prevent the gals running after the fellers. There was a great many tents where the ministers penned up the gals to convert them; and some on 'em was hollerin like they were going mad.

At last one minister come along and asked Ben and Betsey to be converted—so he got up on the trunk of a tree to preach them a sarment, when just in the middle of it, he slumped in, for it was a holler tree, and he sunk clean down out of sight, but he was so arnest that he kept on preaching in the tree, till a great bear that was inside with him woke up and begun to move, when he hollered out that the devil was gouging him most ridiculous. Then Betsey laughed right out, for she knowed it was a bear; and she climbed up the tree, so as to lower down a rope to him and help him out.

Finally, somehow or somehow else, they got the minister out of the holler tree, and he said he had been swallered up in a whale like Jonah. But presently the bear come breaching from the tree like a steamboat. Then such a scratching and hollerin as there was you never see. They thought the devil had broke loose upon them sure enough. They upset the tents in their hurry to cut out, and there was one minister that was so fat he couldn't run very fast, and the bear gained upon him every step he took. When Betsey walked right up to him and stuck him with a knife.

Howsomever there was no more praying or preaching that day, and as Ben and Betsey had a great deal of courting to go through with they cut out for home. Ben had some serious talk with the gal, on the way home, but she told him he would be seriouser still, when they were married, and so he was, which happened on the very next week.

Crockett Pops the Question

"Every human in our clearing always thought it war thar duty to take a vartuous gal, and replenish the airth, especially in our parts o' the world, whar folks war pesky scarce, and the painters and bears war ennermost all the population, speckled with crocodiles and rattlesnakes. Thar war a gal that lived a smart piece from my cabin that I had seed flog two bears, for eatin' up her under petticoat; an' every blow she hit 'em, war a Cupid's arrow goin' into my gizzard. So I put on my best raccoon-skin cap and sallied out to see her.

"When I got within three miles of her house I began to scream, till you could see my voice a-goin' through the air like flashes of lightning on a thunderbolt—it sounded most beautiful to her, for it went through the woods like a harrycane, and I warn't far behind it. When she heered it pretty nigh, she come out, and climbed up the biggest tree thar; and when she reached the top, she took off her barr skin petticoat, the one she died red with tiger's blood the day her mother kicked the bucket; and then she tied it fast to a big limb, and waved it most splendiferous. I soon came up to her, and she made one jump down to meet me. I cotch'd her in my arms, and gin her such a hug that her tung stuck out half a foot, and then we kissed about half an hour, and arter that I popped the question. She 'greed to have me if I'd promise to have no babies; but she let me off from that agreement pesky quick arter we war tied together."

How Daniel Boone Found His Wife

Daniel Boone was out hunting one night with a friend. They were on a "fire hunt," a backwoods way of hunting in which one goes ahead with a torch while another follows, watching the woods for the reflection of the torch on the eyes of nearby deer, elk, or coons. They were down in a heavily timbered bottom, near a small stream that ran along the land belonging to Mr. Morgan Bryan, a local pioneer. It was there that Daniel thought he "shined" the eyes of a deer. He crept off into the woods and circled the animal and, sure enough, he saw the two eyes again, bright in the dark and very near.

Daniel raised his rifle and sighted the deer, but something made him hesitate. Later he would say that never in all his life did his trigger finger tremble save that one fateful night, and tremble it did. Hesitating cost him a clear shot of his quarry, for without warning it broke off through the brush and ran like the wind.

Daniel lit off after the deer, determined not to hesitate the next time, and oh what a chase it was! Taking logs and bushes at a leap, Daniel could hear the deer always just ahead of him and he couldn't seem to gain on his prey. Through the forest they went, branches cracking, leaves scattering, until Daniel came out into an open clearing by Mr. Bryan's cabin. The deer was gone and he found himself surrounded by a pack of growling, barking dogs. Old man Bryan came to the door and hailed the exhausted hunter, who was so out of breath Bryan laughed and made Daniel come inside and rest.

"What makes a young man like you so winded?" said Bryan.

Before Daniel could tell him of the great chase, a little boy rushed in shouting, "Pa! Pa! Sister was down at the creek to check my fishin' lines and was chased by a panther or somethin'. She's too skeered to tell me anythin', but she looks like she done run for her life!"

Daniel turned to see standing there in the doorway a young girl, and her eyes were the same bright eyes he had "shined" a moment before. They belonged to young Rebecca Bryan, and I don't suppose it will come as any surprise to you that not long after this remarkable meeting that little deer became Rebecca Boone, Daniel's beloved and capable wife.

Black-Eyed Susie

All I want in this creation's
A pretty little wife and a big plantation.
  Hey, pretty little black-eyed Susie,
  Hey, pretty little black-eyed Susie.

I love my wife, I love my baby,
I love my biscuits sopped in gravy.

All I want to make me happy,
Two little boys to call me pappy.

All I want in this creation's
A pretty little wife and a big plantation.
  Hey, pretty little black-eyed Susie,
  Hey, pretty little black-eyed Susie.

Superstitions: Love and Marriage

If you count nine stars every night for nine nights and put a mirror under your pillow the last night, you will dream of your true love.

Name the four corners of a room that you have never slept in before and the first corner you see when you wake will be your mate.

Never walk between sweethearts, or they'll quarrel.

When a girl places a man's hat on her head, she wants to be kissed.

A white spot on your fingernail tells you you have a romantic admirer. Some people have more than one.

When you see a redbird, your love is coming to you.

When you see a redbird, start saying your ABC's. The letter you are saying when the bird flies is the first letter of your lover's name. You will marry that person unless the bird lands on a fence.

If your eye quivers, your love is thinking about you. If your ear burns, your love is talking about you.

If you have two lovers, place an apple seed—one for each lover—over each eyelid and blink. The one that stays on longest will be your true love.

On the first morning of May, a girl should rise without speaking a word, go outside, and turn around three times under a cedar tree. Then she should listen. If she hears singing, she will be happily married.

If the wind blows on your wedding day, you'll have many quarrels. Rain is very good luck.

If it snows on your wedding day, you will be very happy and very rich.

Always marry when the hand of the clock is rising. Your marriage will rise with it.

If a man is younger than his wife, he'll have good luck raising sheep.

If you want to know if your spouse will be faithful, sleep with a piece of your wedding cake under your pillow and the answer will come in your dreams.

Weddings, Frontier Style

For a long time after the first settlement of a country, the inhabitants in general married young. There was no distinction of rank, and very little of fortune. On these accounts the first impression of love resulted in marriage, and a family establishment cost but a little labor and nothing else. A wedding engaged the attention of a whole neighborhood, and the frolic was anticipated by old and young with eager expectation. This is not to be wondered at when it is told that a wedding was almost the only gathering which was not accompanied with the labor of reaping, log-rolling, building a cabin, or planning some scout or campaign.

In the morning of the wedding day, the groom and his attendants assembled at the house of his father, for the purpose of reaching the mansion of his bride by noon, which was the usual time for celebrating the nuptials, which for certain must take place before dinner. The gentlemen dressed in shoepacks, moccasins, leather breeches, leggins, and linsey hunting shirts, all home made; the ladies, in linsey petticoats, and linsey or linen short gowns, coarse shoes and stockings, handkerchiefs, and buckskin gloves, if any. If there were any buckles, rings, buttons or ruffles, they were relics of old times—family pieces from parents or grandparents.

The horses were caparisoned with old saddles, old bridles or halters, and pack-saddles, with a bag or blanket thrown over them; a rope or string as often constituted the girth as a piece of leather. The march in double file was often interrupted by the narrowness and obstructions of our horse-paths, as they were called, for we had no roads; and these difficulties were often increased, sometimes by the good, and sometimes by the ill will of neighbors, by felling trees and tying grape-vines across the way. Sometimes an ambuscade was formed by the way-side, and an unexpected discharge of several guns took place, so as to cover the wedding company with smoke.

Another ceremony commonly took place before the party reached the home of the bride. It was after the practice of making whiskey began, which was at an early period. When the party were about a mile from the place of their destination, two young men would single out to run for the bottle; the worse the path—the more logs, brush and deep hollows the better, as these obstacles afforded an opportunity for the greater display of intrepidity and horsemanship. The English fox chase, in point of danger to riders and horses, is nothing to this race for the bottle.

The start was announced by an Indian yell; logs, brush, muddy hollows, hill and glen were speedily passed by the rival steeds. The bottle was always filled for the occasion, so that there was no use for judges, for the first who reached the door was presented with the prize. On returning in triumph he announced his victory over his rivals by a shrill whoop. At the head of the troop he gave the bottle, first to the groom and his attendants, and then to each pair in succession to the rear of the line, and then putting the bottle in the convenient and capacious bosom of his hunting shirt, he took his station in line.

The ceremony of the marriage preceded the dinner, which was a substantial backwoods feast of beef, pork, fowls, and sometimes venison and bear meat roasted and boiled, with plenty of potatoes, cabbage, and other vegetables. During the dinner the greatest hilarity always prevailed, although the table might be a large slab of timber hewed out with a broad axe, supported by four sticks set in auger holes; and the furniture, some old pewter dishes and plates, eked out with wooden bowls and trenchers. A few pewter spoons, much battered about the edges, were seen at some tables; the rest were made of horn. If knives were scarce, the deficiency was made up by the scalping knives which every man carried in sheaths suspended to the belt of the hunting shirt.

After dinner the dancing commenced, and generally lasted till the next morning. The figures of the dances were three and four-handed reels and jigs. The commencement was always a square four, which was followed by what was called "jigging it off": that is, two of the four would single out for a jig, and be followed by the remaining couple. The jigs were often accompanied with what was called "cutting out"; that is, when either of the parties became tired of the dance, on intimation, the place was supplied by some one of the company, without any interruption to the dance. In this way it was often continued till the musician was heartily tired of his situation. Towards the latter part of the night, if any of the company, through weariness, attempted to conceal themselves for the purpose of sleeping, they were hunted up, paraded on the floor, and the fiddler ordered to play "Hang out till tomorrow morning."

About nine or ten o'clock a deputation of the young ladies stole off the bride and put her to bed. In doing this it frequently happened that they had to ascend a ladder instead of stairs, leading from the dining and ball room to a loft, the floor of which was made of clapboards lying loose. This ascent, one might think, would put the bride and her attendants to the blush; but as the foot of the ladder was commonly behind the door, purposely opened for the occasion, and its rounds at the inner ends were well hung with hunting shirts, dresses, and other articles of clothing—the candles being on the opposite side of the house, the exit of the bride was noticed but by few. This done, a deputation of young men, in like manner, stole off the groom and placed him snugly by the side of his bride, while the dance still continued; and if seats happened to be scarce, every young man was obliged to offer his lap as a seat for one of his girls. Late at night refreshment in the shape of "black Betty"—the bottle—was sent up the ladder, with sometimes substantial accompaniments of bread, beef, pork and cabbage. The young couple were compelled to eat and drink of whatever was offered them. The feasting and dancing often lasted several days, at the end of which the whole company were so exhausted with loss of sleep, that many days' rest was requisite to fit them to return to their ordinary labors.

Square-Dance Calls

EVEN IF YOU HAVE never swung a partner to a stamping fiddler's call, it is not hard to imagine a square dance, that exuberant American social occasion in calico and straw. The caller was the most important part of the dance, for it was he who got folks on their feet and made them mix. Many a romance has started from the clever calls of the fiddler who kept a sharp eye out for matchmaking. Here are some of his lively directions. You supply the music and the dancing and see whom you end up with!

Salute your partner! Let her go!
Balance all and do-si-do!
Swing your gal, and all run away!
Right and left, and gents sashay!
Gents to right and swing or cheat!
On to the next gal and repeat!
Balance to the next and don't be shy!
Swing your partner and swing her high!
Bunch the gals and circle around!
Whack your feet until they sound!
Form a basket! Break away!
Swing and kiss and all git gay!
All gents to the left and balance all!
Lift your hoofs and let 'em fall!
Swing your opp'sites! Swing again!
Kiss the sage-hens if you can!
Back to your partners, do-si-do!
Gents salute your little sweets!
Hitch up and promenade to your seats!

The Bride and Groom of Pisgah

Yes, that's the Bride and Groom—the Bride and Groom of Pisgah. Every time the north side of the mountain is covered with snow you can see 'em, jes as plain as life. That's her, standing up, with her veil over her shoulders and that's him, kneeling down by her side. Looks like he's a-holding her hand.

I heerd the tale from my granny, and my granny knowed Peggy Higgins, and Peggy Higgins witnessed the marryin' and helped 'em get away from the revenooers what was after 'em.

Jim Stratton was the young feller and Mary Robinson was his gal, and Mary's pappy, ole man Robinson, I reckon was the cause of the hull trouble. Jes because ole man Robinson thought no feller was good enough for Mary is why he went and done what he did.

Jim and his mammy lived over beyond Big Bald, and Mary and her folks lived across the ridge on t'other side of Frying Pan Gap. That was long before the gov'ment took over the land and before that rich Vanderbilt feller had it, even. There wasn't no roads over the mountain then, jes a few cartways 'round the slopes for the saw-mills, and if you wanted to go over the mountain you had to walk it on the trails.

I reckon Jim and Mary was cut out for each other from the time they was born, but when they was little 'bout the only time they seen each other was once or twicet a year when there was services at the meetinghouse in the cove.

Jim was 'bout seventeen and Mary must a-been 'bout fifteen, my granny said, when Jim began to go over the ridge to Mary's house. First off he pretended not to notice Mary atall. He'd make out that he come on a chore for his mammy, to borrow some meal, or to ask 'bout woodchopping, or something like that. Then he got so's he'd ask Mary did she think it would rain tomorrer, or would she like a little rabbit for a pet. If she say she'd like to have the rabbit, that gives Jim a chance to go back to her house.

Pretty soon ole man Robinson figgers out what's going on, and he tells Jim he reckon there ain't no use for him to be hanging 'round his house none. That put the devilment in young Jim, and he'd keep watch to see when ole man Robinson was working at his still, or had set out for Waynesville, and then Jim'd go over the ridge behind Robinson's cabin, and he'd whistle like a bobwhite, and Mary'd slip out, and the two of 'em would walk around, talking.

Mary told Jim it wa'n't no use; her pappy was dead set agin him, and he'd better not try and see her no more. But Jim wa'n't no Stratton for nothing. He was a strapling feller on the lean side, but big boned. He had sharp, black eyes and a good-stout set to his jaw. His pappy'd been kilt by a sheriff when Jim was a little feller, and Jim hated the law, and he hated anybody what got in his way. He was a sure shot with a rifle. Folks reckoned Jim meant what he said when he said it, and they mostly let him alone.

Nobody blamed him none for courting Mary Robinson. My

granny said she was the pertest little thing anyone ever seen. She wa'n't very big and she wa'n't little, neither, jes about medium, and she had dark brown hair with long curls, and her eyes was brown, and they had long black lashes what made her skin look whiter'n what it really was. She was a good girl, and smart, and she'd make a good wife for any fine feller.

Jim was jes bound to have her, that's all, and so he'd slip over the ridge when her ole man was off, and Mary kept telling him he'll have to stay away or her pappy might kill him when he's not looking.

Some folks thought ole man Robinson was sot agin Jim because Jim was running a liquor still in the ivy thicket behind Bull Ridge, but that didn't make no sense, because ole man Robinson was running a still hisself, and 'most ever'body on the fur side of Pisgah was doing the same. Folks had always run liquor stills in the mountains, 'cause it's 'bout the only way a feller could use up his corn and get any money for it. Of course the revenooers was always trying to break up the stills. But it seem like they never catch nobody unless he stand right in their way. The revenooers got fifty dollars for every still they took, and they didn't get nothing for catching a blockader, so it was jes sort of understood that a blockader knows when they're coming and he better stay away from the still until they cut it up.

Ole man Robinson didn't have no trouble keeping the other fellers away from Mary. If one of 'em come 'round, he'd run 'em off, but that didn't work with Jim, and it looked like they's bound to be trouble between 'em. They's both hotheaded and wa'n't scairt of the devil even.

That's why, when Jim heard that the revenooers was a-coming to break up his still, he was sartin ole man Robinson had turned the law on him. He went over the ridge behind Robinson's cabin, and whistled his bobwhite call, and after while Mary come back to the edge of the timber. He told Mary the law was going to break up his still and he knowed her pappy had set 'em on him.

"Iffen them revenooers axe up my still, I'm a-fixing to settle with your pappy," Jim said.

Mary begged and pleaded, and told Jim she knowed in her heart that her pappy'd had nothing to do with it. She begged Jim to marry her, and they could leave out, and go sommers else to live.

"Jim, honey," she said, "it jes don't pay to fight the law and be mad at your neighbors all the time. A person's got to have peace and has got to live right. Please, honey, let's go away before there's trouble."

But Jim wouldn't have it that way. He'd show the law and he'd show her pappy who Jim Stratton was, and he had some settling to do with the revenooers and some other people too.

The law come up to his still on a afternoon, jes before dark. It was about the middle of December and was turning off cold. They made a lot of noise, beating up the mountain, and their dogs barked, so's anybody could hear 'em. Jim was a-hiding behind a big oak tree, and he had his rifle, and he was a-waiting. The revenooers walked right up to the still—seem like they knowed exactly where it was at. They turned in on it with axes. They chopped up the barrels and let all the mash run out in the branch. They smashed up the copper worm, and they chopped into the boiler. Jes as they was fixing to carry the boiler and worm off, so's they could collect their fifty dollars, Jim cut down on one of the revenooers, and sent a rifle ball through the middle of his forehead. Before he could reload, the others had run off ever which ways, leaving the dead man and the bashed-up still behind.

Now Jim knowed he was in for it, and he must work fast. Seems like he hadn't thought ahead none, 'bout what he would do after he had killed the law.

He kept thinking, "I've got to get ole man Robinson and I've got to get Mary." What worried him most was how he could get Mary to go with him iffen he killed her pappy. But he knowed he had to settle with her ole man.

He took off the left-hand trail, and when he got to where Peggy Higgins lived, he called Peggy out, standing a ways off, behind the meat house. Peggy come to the door and called out, "Who's there?" and Jim answered, "Is anybody in there?" Peggy says she's alone, and Jim steps out and shows himself. He goes in the house with Peggy and tells her what has happened.

Peggy is a ole widder-woman what has lived all to herself as long as anybody can 'member. The neighbors is good to her, helping her out through the winter, and looking after her one way and 'nother.

She is a special friend of Jim's mammy, and right off she makes up her mind to help Jim out of his trouble.

"The law will be back here in no time," she told Jim, "and you better take off, jes like you are, without going home even."

Jim won't hear to it; he say he's a-going to settle with ole man Robinson and he's a-going to take Mary off with him. Peggy did all she could to argue with him, and beg him, but Jim said for Peggy to go and fetch Preacher Ball from down in the cove, and he'll come back in two hours and bring Mary with him.

Peggy knew it's no use arguing any more, so she put on her ole cloak, and tied a shawl over her head, and she took off for the cove and Jim took the upper trail to Frying Pan.

The wind has turned and is blowing in from the northwest, and before Jim got to the ridge it has set in snowing purty good. He was wearing his cotton jeans, and a stout shirt, and a ragged jacket, and a ole felt hat. He was carrying his rifle and didn't have no mittens, and his boots wa'n't much. He didn't mind the snow none, and when it begin getting colder he jes blowed on his hands some and kept warm climbing the trail over the ridge.

On the way he kept thinking how he's going to call ole man Robinson out, and whether he ought to give him a chance. He jes can't make up his mind whether to tell the ole man to come out with his gun. They's a couple of inches of snow on the ground when he gets to the place behind the cabin, and he whistles his bobwhite call. Mary must a-been waiting for him, 'cause she come a-running. She didn't have no coat on, jes a jacket, and she hurried up to Jim and said, "Jim, you must go away, and you must hurry and not lose no time. The law's done been here, and pappy went with 'em, and they're going for more men, and they're meaning to take you, Jim, dead or alive. There's bad trouble, Jim, and you mustn't lose no time."

"Mary, honey," Jim said, quiet and slow like, "in a way I'm sorry your pappy's not here, and in a way I'm glad. You go and get your things and we'll go to Peggy Higgins' house, and Preacher Ball'll be there, and we'll be wedded, you and me, and we'll go sommers and set up and we'll never come back here no more. And I hope your pappy and me don't never cross trails."

Well, Mary ran back in the house and come out in jes a minute with a few little things in her hands, and Jim helped her on with her cloak, and she tied a shawl over her head after they'd done set out on the trail. Her mammy was calling after her to come back, but Mary didn't even answer her mammy. Her little brother follered them up the trail a-ways, to see where they's headed for, and then he turned back.

The snow is over Mary's shoetops when they get to Peggy Higgins' house, but Peggy hasn't got back yet with the preacher.

"What if the preacher wa'n't to home?" Mary asks.

"He's got to be home, but iffen he ain't we'll be wedded sommers else," Jim says.

But in 'bout an hour the preacher and Peggy come up the trail from down in the road where the preacher'd left his horse and wagon.

The preacher didn't fuss none at Jim; he jes asked did he have a ring. This set ole Peggy running 'round the cabin, and she pulled a chest from 'nunder her bed, and she got out a ole white dress and a long white veil.

"This here's what I was wedded in," she said, "and I'm aiming that Mary shall have it and be wedded in it, same as I was."

And she took a gold ring offen her finger and handed it to Jim, and says, "That'll be your wedding ring, too."

The preacher don't no more than start till they hear a dog barking down the lower trail. Peggy told the preacher to hurry, and he hurried, and pronounced 'em man and wife, and jes then they could hear men shouting. Jim, he run to the back door and looked out, and he run to the front door and looked out. Then he said, "Mary, they're coming up the lower trail, grob your things and let's take out."

Mary grobbed her cloak, and let out a kind of a little sob, and she and Jim run out of the front door, and they got inside the timber before the law come up to the house from behind.

Ole Peggy made out she don't know nothing 'bout Jim and Mary, and the preacher don't tell no lie, but he don't tell no truth neither 'cause he ain't got nothing to say atall, and the law—they was six or eight of 'em with dogs—fuss 'round the place, and look under the bed, and tromp 'round the outside.

It was plumb dark now, and the revenooers called for lanterns so's they can search outside. The snow has been falling harder and the lanterns don't show up no sight of Jim and Mary's tracks, but 'casionally the dogs get a scent, and they let out to barking and beat off into timber, but seems like they lose the scent and come back to the house.

The law messed 'round the place all night, sometimes going off with the dogs, and coming back again. Two of the men set out for the Robinson place, and two of 'em went back to the cove with the preacher. When daylight come, some of 'em took out on the upper trail what forks out, one fork going to Bull Ridge and t'other going to the Rat and on around the north side of Big Pisgah.

Peggy prayed to herself all night, and every time the law set out she was scairt most to death, and every time they come back she was cheered some and hoped Jim and Mary would get away.

By morning the snow was almost hip deep. The revenooers what took the upper trail worked up to the forks, and there they saw marks what looked like Jim and Mary had sat down in the snow. The tracks led off t'ord Pisgah, but the revenooers knowed they couldn't get through 'cept they shoveled their way up the trail. So they come back to Peggy's, and they drank some hot coffee, and took off t'ord the road. One of the men was the sheriff.

Before he left he took Peggy off to herself in the kitchen and he said to her: "Peggy, I know what happened, and I know what you done, and I ain't saying nothing. But I'm afeerd Jim and Mary is laying up there sommers around Pisgah. They didn't have a chance. When the snow lifts, we'll have a search."

The snow was on a good spell, and when it thawed down, men from all over the mountains and coves hunted up the trails, and where there was cliffs they climbed down and looked below. They hunted off and on all spring, but they didn't find nothing.

Ole man Robinson wa'n't hisself any more. He allus kept trying to get more people to hunt the mountains, and he even got a lawyer to put notices in the city papers, asking did anybody know where his Mary was at. He wa'n't no good at work, and he jes let his still stand and never ran it no more. He moped around like that a few years and then he died off.

Some say those gov'ment forest fellers found some bones up on the north side of Pisgah a few years ago, but I reckon there wa'n't no truth to it. Nobody knows what become of Jim and Mary, but ever'body knows when the snow is on the north side of the mountain you can see the Bride and Groom there, jes as plain as life.

The Mermaid

Before they had any steam, ships were sailing by sails, you know, across the Atlantic. The Atlantic was fifteen miles deep, and there were mermaids in those days. And if you called anybody's name on the ship, they would ask for it, say, "Give it to me." And if you didn't give it to them they would capsize the ship. So the captain had to change the men's names to different objects—hatchet, ax, hammer, furniture. Whenever he wanted a man to do something, he had to call him, "Hammer, go on deck and look out." The mermaid would holler, "Give me hammer." So they throwed the hammer overboard to her, and the vessel would proceed on. The captain might say, "Ax, you go on down in the kindling room, start a fire in the boiler; it's going dead." Then the mermaid says, "Give me ax." So they have to throw her an iron ax. Next day he says, "Suite of furniture, go down in the stateroom and make up those beds." And the mermaid yells, "Give me a suite of furniture." So they had to throw a whole suite of furniture overboard.

One day he made a mistake and forgot and said, "Sam, go in the kitchen and cook supper." The mermaid right away calls, "Give me Sam." They didn't have anything on the ship that was named Sam; so they had to throw Sam overboard. Soon as Sam hit the water she grabbed him. Her hair was so long she could wrap him up—he didn't even get wet. And she's swimming so fast he could catch breath under the water. When she gets home she goes in, unwraps Sam out of her hair, says: "Oooh, you sure do look nice. Do you like fish?" Sam says, "No, I won't even cook a fish." "Well, we'll get married." So they were married.

After a while Sam begin to step out with other mermaids. His girl friend became jealous of him and his wife, and they had a fight over Sam. The wife whipped her, and told her, "You can't see Sam never again." She says, "I'll get even with you." So one day Sam's girl friends asked him, didn't he want to go back to his native home. He says yes. So she grabs him, wraps him in her hair, and swum the same fastness as his wife did when she was carrying him, so he could catch breath. When she come to land she put him onto the ground, on the bank. "Now if he can't do me no good he sure won't do her none." That was Sam's experience in the mermaid's home in the bottom of the sea.

Then he told the others how nice her home was, all fixed up with the furniture and other things. There weren't any men down there— guess that's why they ain't any mermaids any more. Sam said they had purple lips, just like women are painted today. You see pictures of mermaids with lips like that. In old days people didn't wear lipstick, and I think they got the idea from seeing those pictures.

Sam told the people the mermaid's house was built like the alligator's. He digs in the bank at water level; then goes up—nature teaches him how high to go—then digs down to water level again, and there he makes his home, in rooms ten to twenty feet long. The mermaid builds in the wall of the sea like the alligator. Sam stayed down there six years. If he hadn't got to co'ting he'd a been there yet, I guess.

The Queen of the Bull-Whackers

She was a huge, raw-boned, muscular woman, homely enough to excite pity; as untidy as a Sioux squaw and as fond of chewing tobacco as any woman is of drinking her tea—every inch a queen if these be our standards. Such was Mother Jurgenson, and she was the only woman who ever drove a bull team hauling freight for pay; perhaps this is the reason why she was called Queen.

Nearly all of the freight shipped into the Black Hills before the advent of the railroad was hauled by bull teams. Certainly no more forlorn and pitiable looking animals were ever seen on the face of the earth. The animals grazed their own subsistence when they should have been resting, and could thus transport goods for much less cost than horses and mules that had to be fed. When the grass was short the poor animals were almost starved, and it required all the encouragement of those cruel black-snake whips to keep them moving and pulling their share of the heavily laden wagons. The drivers were of the lowest order of humanity, dirty, rough and cruel.

Now, as I said, Mother Jurgenson drove a bull team, and Mother Jurgenson's husband also drove a bull team. He was no handsomer than she, and only more cleanly because, not having her inches, there was less space to be grimy. He had moods when it was his most agreeable pastime to beat the partner of his daily toils. She must originally have belonged to that class of peasantry in Europe who, travellers tell us, are trained to believe in the supremacy of man, and that it is a husband's privilege as well as duty to chastise his wife. At times the other bull-whackers had noticed a dangerous gleam in Mother Jurgenson's eyes when, at the close of a hard day's work, her husband had whipped her.

On the arrival of the teams in Deadwood, Jurgenson would slip off to the saloon and leave his wife to unload the freight from his wagon as well as her own. Occasionally when very heavy lifting was required, Jurgenson, between drinks, would give his wife valuable advice or hurry her with the work.

One evening, after a very wearisome day's work, Mother Jurgenson was slower than usual about the final unloading. Jurgenson concluded that a little conjugal discipline might quicken her movements, but as it happened, he struck her just one too many times; like a tigress she sprang upon him and rained blow upon blow and fairly wiped the earth with him, while the crowd cheered her on. Jurgenson's astonishment was soon followed by pleas for mercy, but mercy was not for him. Finally, from sheer exhaustion, she ceased, and gathering what remained of her liege lord, and holding him at arm's length, said: "Old man, henceforth I'm boss; you play me for meeks again and I'll break every bone in your cowardly body."

After this there was a great change in the financial condition of the Jurgenson family. Mother Jurgenson collected all the freight bills; she allowed her husband a limited allowance to spend in the saloons, while she unloaded the freight, bought needed supplies and did the banking. When all the business was transacted, and she was ready to start on the overland trip, she would go to the saloon where Jurgenson had been enjoying himself as best he could on his now limited means, and say, "Come, old man, git a move on you"; and he would go at once to his place and drive his bull team right behind hers. She saved money and bought a good ranch, and is now among the prosperous farmers of Dakota.

Birthing, the Frontier Way

Little Lucy Gray was hoeing a long, hard row when we got there. With each contraction, she'd scream and faint. Old Mrs. Blevins was having a fight on her hands just to keep her on the bed. But the good mid-woman had everything ready, boiling water, charred linen, a sharp knife, and heated balm of Gilead bud salve. Without noticing the ailing patient, old Doc plopped down in front of the fire and began chewing the fat with the family folks. It was his usual way. A few jokes and he had the family's mind off the seriousness of the matter at hand to the point they were laughing and joking too.

Little Lucy Gray came too and reared up to look at old Doc. Another contraction seized her and she fell back squalling at the top of her lungs.

"Her water done broke, Doc," the mid-woman cautioned.

Old Doc started in on another joke, paying little heed to the situation.

Little Lucy Gray became frantic and began wailing in a quivering voice, "Do something, Doc, fer God's sake, do something!" and fell back in a dead faint.

Old Doc got up quietly and pulled down the covers. Placing his hands on her abdomen firmly, he manipulated the fetus for several minutes, then smiled at the mid-woman.

"Hit be rearing to come into this here world, got a powerful kick. There, hits shifted 'round like hit ought'a be," he said raising up.

"Set her legs fer the snatching, Mrs. Blevins!"

Turning to an anxious young Pete, he sent him off to the kitchen to fetch some red pepper. Pete gave old Doc a quizzical stare, wondering, but hurried without question and brought a snuff can of powdered red pepper. Looking around, old Doc spotted a yellowed copy of the Belas Hess mail order catalogue, and tore the front page off. Folding the paper into a crease, he slowly sprinkled some red pepper on it. Little Lucy Gray revived and reared up to watch as old Doc sprinkled a little more pepper on the paper, then dusted a little off on the floor as though there must be some exact amount. Little Lucy Gray's eyes fixed on the paper, following it with an almost hypnotic stare as old Doc moved it from side to side until it was close to her face. Old Doc turned to the family and winked, then suddenly blew the pepper squarely into her face. She fell back gasping and wheezing as she clutched her hands to her face. Then, gasping for breath, she sneezed violently.

And sure as shootin, the youngun popped right out into old Doc's waiting hands.

Kemp Nye

Superstitions: Pregnancy and Infants

If a woman swallows a pumpkin seed, she will become pregnant.

To hasten the birth of a child, tickle the mother's nose with a feather.

Never make a bonnet for a baby before it is born, or its birthing will be difficult.

Pants hung over the end of the bed at night will make for an easy delivery.

If a child is born on a stormy night, it will have a stormy disposition.

A mother's head should always be to the north during birth.

A baby born in the afternoon will be rich.

A baby born at the time of a new moon will be very strong and mighty.

The seventh son is always a healer. The tenth son is always a preacher.

A child born on Christmas Day can understand animals, see spirits, and will be generally very lucky.

If a woman holds a newly born baby in her arms on her first visit to see the baby, she will become a mother.

On your first visit to see a baby, kiss the bottom of its feet and you will give it good luck.

It is very lucky for a man to let a newborn male wet on him.

Rub an apple on a baby's tongue and it will have a lovely singing voice.

Never let moonlight fall on a newborn baby.

Always make sure a baby sees a sunrise before a sunset.

Never kiss a baby on the mouth. It's very bad luck.

If a baby's fists are clutched tight, the child will be greedy and selfish. If they are open, the child will be generous and kind.

A baby will acquire the disposition of the first person who carries him outdoors.

A Close Call

There was a woman who lived back of Swift Creek, and her husband was a government man who went all around the county trying to get people to do this or pay that. I don't know what he did, but I knew, as everyone else around here did, that his wife wasn't the kind to wait for him to come home to get warm. No sir.

One night, this other fellow came around to pay the lady in question some sweet talk as her husband was gone for one of his trips. He hadn't been there but a minute or two when they heard boots on the front porch. As this lady's husband was big and short-tempered, the fellow hopped, quick as can be, into a large empty pickle barrel standing in the corner of the room. As it turned out, it wasn't the lady's husband arriving but another caller looking for some sweetness himself.

So the second fellow sits down with this lady, and a moment later they heard steps on the porch. As the door swung open, there stood her husband with a bag and shotgun in his hand. Just then, from the back of the room, the second fellow came forward, rolling the pickle barrel ahead of him. "Thank you kindly, ma'am, for bein' so kind as to lend me an' my wife this pickle barrel," he said, grinning. Then he rolled the barrel out the door as the woman's husband, with a suspicious stare, watched him go by.

The man rolled the barrel down the road and around the corner and then sat down to rest his nerves a bit. "Hoo boy. I'd best be thankin' this barrel for gettin' me out of a close scrape," he mumbled to himself. And with that the other fellow poked his groggy head out of the barrel. "Hell, boss," he said. "I'd best be thankin' *you* for carryin' this damned barrel out!"

I Once Loved a Young Man

I once loved a young man as dear as my life,
He often did promise to make me his wife.
He fulfilled his promise, he made me his wife,
But see what I've come to by being his wife.
Oh, here's my dear children all crying for bread,
My husband's off drinking, and I wish I was dead.

I'm going to Georgia, Georgia to roam,
I'm going to Georgia to make it my home.

I'll build me a log cabin on the mountain so high,
Where the wild beasts and snowbirds will hear my sad cry.

They'll know I'm a poor girl, a long ways from home,
The road's rough to travel, and nowheres to go.

Come all my young ladies, take warning from me,
That you'll never get struck on a green growing tree.

The leaves they will wither, the roots they will die,
The young man will fool you, for one has fooled I.

They'll hug you, they'll kiss you, and tell you more lies
Than the cross-ties on the railroad and the stars in the sky.

A Patient Wife

There once was a rancher's wife whose husband was just about the worst sort of fellow in the world to live with. He swore and gambled and stayed out all night and never had a nice thing to say to his wife. She was patient with him though, loyal as could be, and never did walk out on him though nobody would have blamed her if she had. At last his high living caught up with him and a local rancher found him in a ditch some miles out of town. The doc said he'd had a heart attack and had gone to his just reward.

On the day of his funeral his wife dressed in black and followed behind the hearse that was to take her man to the cemetery. They drove down the dusty road pretty fast and caught a rut and the hearse door swung open and out came the casket with a crash. Everybody was startled but not as much as when they heard from inside the casket the swearing and cussing of the good lady's husband. It appeared that the jolt got his ticker going again. Well, for another ten years that mean old man lived and made life even worse for that patient woman. Seems that his almost dying didn't do him any good at all. Then, while out one night, the old rancher keeled over and fell into a ditch, where a neighbor found him. Again the local doctor said the man's heart had given out. This time, as they got the casket into the hearse for the funeral, the rancher's wife took the driver to one side and said softly, "Now, Sam, let's take this road nice and easy."

A Wise Husband

Abraham Lincoln used to tell a story about a man he knew once named Featherston. Featherston was one of those men who made you feel sorry for him whenever he came to town with his wife. She was the worst nag in the world and was always telling him everything he did was wrong, wrong, wrong. One day, Featherston's wife was seen taking a switch to her husband near their home. A few days later, Featherston met a friend in the street, who said to him, "I've always stood up for you whenever folks say you should stand up to your wife, but I'll do it no longer. Any man who will take being switched in public by his woman deserves to be horsewhipped by her, or worse." Featherston looked at his friend with a smile and a wink and replied, "Now, old friend, calm down. It didn't hurt me any, and you've no idea the power of good it did Sarah Ann."

"Old Whiskers"

One Saturday, a farmer went to town, an' his friends talked him into gettin' his whiskers all shaved off an' gettin' his hair clipped close. That night, he went home late an' his wife was already in bed. He slipped in easy, undressed quietly, an' got into bed softly with his wife. She ran her hand over his smooth face an' said, "Young man, if you're goin' to do anything, you'd better be agittin' at it, 'cause Old Whiskers'll be here pretty soon."

Why Womens Is Sharper dan Mens

Dere was an ole man, you know, he had a daughter, and he tell his daughter he had invited a preacher to his house, and he say, "Daughter, I guine down to de train to meet de Reverend, and bake two ducks and leave 'em dere for him, don't tech 'em." And she said, "No, I ain't gonna tech 'em." And he go to de train to meet de Reverend, and de gal taste de ducks, and dey taste good, and she taste 'em till she taste 'em all up.

And after de ole man come, he never look in de place where he had de ducks, and he went in de other room to sharpen his knife on the oil stove, and de preacher was settin' in de room wid de gal. She knewed her papa was gonna whip her, and she started to snifflin' 'bout it, and de preacher say, "What is de matter, daughter?" And she say, "Dat's all de fault I find wid papa—papa go invite preachers to his house and go and sharpen his knife to cut off both dey ears." And de Reverend say, "What is dat, daughter?" And de gal say, "Yes, papa invite preachers here all de time and cut off both dey ears." And he say, "Daughter, han' me my hat quick." And de gal give him his hat and he run out. And she call her papa and say, "Papa, de preacher got both de ducks and gone." And he run to de door and holler to him and say, "Hey, hey, where you guine? Come back here!" And de preacher answer him and say, "Damned ef you'll git either one of dese."

And he raise a dust de way he flewed down de road. And de ole tales tell you dat womens has always been sharper dan mens.

She Wanted a Divorce

One time, a woman was trying to get a divorce because she claimed her husband ain't no good. But the fellow was a-standing right there in the courtroom, and he says it is an outrageous lie. So the judge says, "Well, how long have you two been married?" and the woman says three years. "How many children have you got?" says the judge, and they showed him the three children.

The judge thought about it awhile. "There ain't no way to divide up three children," says he. "Why don't you live together another year? Then you'll have four kids, and you can take two apiece."

The woman just stood there with her mouth open, but the man spoke up. "That's worse and more of it, judge," says he. "If I top her again, she's liable to have twins."

"Twins!" hollered the woman. "He's just a-bragging, judge. Why, if I'd depended on *him,* we wouldn't even have these three we got!"

The poor husband didn't have no answer to that one, and neither did the judge. So they just give the woman her divorce and called it a day.

Sweet Betsey from Pike

Oh, don't you remember sweet Betsey from Pike,
Who crossed the big mountains with her lover Ike,
With two yoke of cattle, a large yellow dog,
A tall shanghai rooster and one spotted hog.

Singing, goodbye, Pike County, farewell for a while,
We'll come back again when we've panned out our pile,
Singing tooral lal, looral lal, looral lal lay,
Singing tooral lal, looral lal, looral lal lay.

One evening quite early they camped on the Platte,
'Twas near by the road on a green shady flat,
Where Betsey, sore-footed, lay down to repose,
While with wonder Ike gazed on his Pike County rose.

Their wagon broke down with a terrible crash,
And out on the prairie rolled all kinds of trash;
A few little baby clothes done up with great care—
'Twas rather suspicious, though all on the square.

The shanghai ran off and the cattle all died;
That morning the last piece of bacon was fried;
Poor Ike was discouraged, and Betsey got mad,
The dog drooped his tail and looked wondrously sad.

They stopped at Salt Lake to inquire the way,
When Brigham declared that sweet Betsey should stay;
But Betsey got frightened and ran like a deer,
While Brigham stood pawing the ground like a steer.

They soon reached the desert, where Betsey gave out,
And down in the sand she lay rolling about;
While Ike, half distracted, looked on with surprise,
Saying, "Betsey, get up, you'll get sand in your eyes."

Sweet Betsey got up in a great deal of pain,
Declared she'd go back to Pike County again;
But Ike gave a sigh, and they fondly embraced,
And they traveled along with his arm round her waist.

They suddenly stopped on a very high hill,
With wonder looked down upon old Placerville;
Ike sighed when he said, and he cast his eyes down,
"Sweet Betsey, my darling, we've got to Hangtown."

Long Ike and sweet Betsey attended a dance,
Ike wore a pair of his Pike County pants;
Sweet Betsey was covered with ribbons and rings;
Says Ike, "You're an angel, but where are your wings?"

A miner said, "Betsey, will you dance with me?"
"I will that, old hoss, if you don't make too free;
But don't dance me hard, do you want to know why?
Dog on you! I'm chock full of strong alkali!"

This Pike County couple got married, of course,
And Ike became jealous—obtained a divorce;
Sweet Betsey, well satisfied, said with a shout,
"Goodbye, you big lummox, I'm glad you've backed out!"

De Ways of de Wimmens

Most folks say de *six'* day was Sat'd'y, cause on de *seventh* day didn't de Lawd rest an' look his creation over? Now, hit *may* been Sat'd'y dat he done de *work* of makin' man an' woman, but from all de signs, he must *thought up* de first man an' woman on ol' unlucky *Friday.*

Sat'd'y *aw* Friday, de Lawd *made* 'em. Den he made a nice garden an' a fine house wid a cool dogtrot faw dem to set in when de sun git hot. "Adam an' Eve," he say, "here hit is. Git yo' stuff together an' move in."

"Thank you kindly, Lawd," say Eve.

"Wait a minute, Lawd," say Adam. "How we gwine pay de rent? You ain't create no money yet, is you?"

De Lawd say, "Don't worry yo' haid 'bout dat, Adam. Hit's a free gift faw you an' de little woman."

So de man and woman move in an' start to red up de house to make hit comfortable to live in. And den de trouble begun.

"Adam," say de woman, "you git de stove put up while I hangs de curtains."

"Whyn't you put up de stove," say Adam, "an' me hang de curtains? You's strong as me. De Lawd ain't make neither one of us stronger dan de other. Howcome you always shovin' off de heavy stuff on me?"

"Cause dey's man's work and dey's woman's work, Adam," say Eve. "Hit don't look right faw me to do dat heavy stuff."

"Don't look right to who?" say Adam. "Who gwine see hit? You know dey ain't no neighbors yet."

Eve stomp de flo. She say, "Jes' 'cause hit ain't no neighbors yet ain't no reason faw us actin' trashy behind dey backs, is hit?"

"Ain't dat jes like a woman!" say Adam. Den he set down and fold his arms. "I ain't gwine put up no stove!" he say. "An' dat *dat,* woman!"

Next thing he know ol' Eve lollop him in de talk-box wid her fist an' he fall over backward like a calf hit by lightnin'. Den he scramble up an' was all over her like a wildcat. Dey bang an' scuffle round dere till de house look like a cyclone wind been playin' in hit. Neither one could whup, 'cause de Lawd had laid de same equal strenth on dem both.

After while dey's both too wore out to scrap. Eve flop on de baid and start kickin' her feets an' bawlin'. "Why you treat me so mean, Adam?" she holler. "Wouldn't treat a no-count ol' hound like you does po' me!"

Adam spit out a tooth an' try to open de black eye she give him. He say, "If I had a hound dat bang into me like you does, I'd kill him."

But Eve start bawlin' so loud, wid de tears jes' sopping up de bedclose, dat Adam sneak out of de house. Feelin' mighty mean an' low, he set round awhile out behind de smokehouse studyin' whut better he do. Den he go find de Lawd.

De Lawd say, "Well, Adam? Anything 'bout de house won't work? Hit's de first one I ever made an' hit might have some faults."

Adam shake his head. "De house is prime, Lawd. De *house* couldn't be no better dan hit is."

"Whut den, Adam?" say de Lawd.

"To tell de truth," say Adam, "hit's dat Eve woman. Lawd, you made us wid de equal strenth an' dat's de trouble. I can't git de best of her nohow at all."

De Lawd frown den. "Adam!" he say. "Is you tryin' to criticize de Lawd? Course you's of de equal strenth. Dat de fair way to make a man an' woman so dey both pull in de harness even."

Adam tremble an' shake but he so upset an' miserable he jes' has to keep on. He say, "But Lawd, hit reely ain't equal 'tween de two of us."

Lawd say, "Be keerful dere, Adam! You is *de*sputin' de Lawd smack to de face!"

"Lawd," say Adam, "like you says, we *is* equal in de strenth. But dat woman done found 'nother way to fight. She start howlin' an' blubberin' so hit make me feel like I's a lowdown scamp. I can't stand dat sound, Lawd. If hit go on like dat, I knows ol' Eve gwine always git her way an' make me do all de dirty jobs."

"Howcome she learn dat trick?" say de Lawd, lookin' like he thinkin' hard. "Ain't seed no little ol' red man wid hawns an' a pitchfawk hangin' round de place, is you, Adam?"

"Naw, Lawd. Thought I heard Eve talkin' wid somebody down in de apple orchard dis mawnin, but she say hit jes de wind blowin'. Naw, I ain't seed no red man wid hawns. Who would dat be, any-how, Lawd?"

"Never you mind, Adam," say de Lawd. *"Hmmmmmmm!"*

"Well," say Adam, "dis woman trouble got me down. I sho' be much oblige if you makes me stronger dan Eve. Den I can tell her to do a thing an' slap her till she do. She do whut she told if she know she gwine git whupped."

"So be hit!" say de Lawd. "Look at yoself, Adam!"

Well, Adam look at his arms. Where befo' dey was smooth an' round, now de muscle bump up like prize yams. Look like hit was two big cawn pones under de skin of his chest an' dat chest hit was like a barrel. His belly hit was like a washboard an' his laigs was so awful big an' downright lumpy dey scared him.

"Thank you kindly, good Lawd!" say Adam. "Watch de woman mind me now!" So dat Adam high-tail hit home an' bust in de back do'.

Eve settin' down rockin' in de rocker. Eve lookin' mean. Didn't say a mumblin' word when Adam come struttin' in. Jes' look at him, jes' retch down in de woodbox faw a big stick of kindlin'.

"Drap dat stick, woman!" say Adam.

"Say who?" say de woman. "Who dat talkin' big round here?"

Wid dat, she jump on him an' try to hammer his haid down wid de stick.

Adam jes' laugh an' grab de stick an' heave hit out de window. Den he give her a lazy little slap dat sail her clean 'cross de room. *"Dat* who sayin' hit, sugar!" he say.

"My feets must slip aw somethin'," say Eve. "An' you de one gwine pay faw hit out of yo' hide, Adam!"

So de woman come up clawin' an' kickin' an' Adam pick her up an' whop her down.

"Feets slip agin, didn't dey?" say Adam.

"Hit must be I couldn't see good where you is in dis dark room," say Eve. She riz up an' feather into him agin.

So Adam he pick her up an' thow her on de baid. Fo' she know whut, he start laying hit on wid de flat of his hand 'cross de big end of ol' Eve. Smack her wid one hand, hold her down wid t'other.

Fo' long Eve bust out bawlin'. She say, "Please quit dat whackin' me, Adam honey! Aw please, honey!"

"Is I de boss 'round here?" say Adam.

"Yas, honey," she say. "You is de haid man boss."

"Aw right," he tell her. "I *is* de boss. De Lawd done give me de mo' power of us two. From now on out an' *den* some, you mind me, woman! Whut I jes' give you ain't nothin' but a little hum. *Next* time I turn de whole song loose on you."

He give Eve a shove an' say, "Fry me some catfish, woman."

"Yas, Adam honey," she say.

But ol' Eve was mad enough to bust. She wait till Adam catchin' little nap. Den she flounce down to de orchard where dey's a big ol' apple tree wid a cave 'tween de roots. She look 'round till she sho' ain't nobody see her, den she stick her haid in de cave an' holler.

Now, hit *may* been de wind blowin' an' hit *may* been a bird, but hit sho' sound like somebody in dat cave talkin' wid Eve. Eve she sound like she *com*plainin' dat she got a crooked deal an' den hit sound like she sayin', "Yas—Yas—Yas. You means on which wall? De east wall? Oh! Aw right."

Anyhow, Eve come back to de house all smilin' to herself like she know somethin'. She powerful sweet to Adam de rest of de day.

So next mawnin' Eve go an' find de Lawd.

Lawd say, "You agin, Eve? Whut can I do faw you?"

Eve smile an' drap a pretty curtsy. "Could you do me a little ol' favor, Lawd?" say Eve.

"Name hit, Eve," say de Lawd.

"See dem two little ol' rusty keys hangin' on dat nail on de east wall?" Eve say. "If you ain't usin' 'em, I wish I had dem little ol' keys."

"I *de*clare!" say de Lawd. "I done fawgot dey's hangin' dere. But,

Eve, dey don't fit nothin'. Found 'em in some junk an' think maybe I find de locks dey fit some day. Dey been hangin' on dat nail ten million years an' I ain't found de locks yet. If you want 'em, take 'em. Ain't doin' me no good."

So Eve take de two keys an' thank de Lawd an' trot on home. Dere was two do's dere widout no keys an' Eve find dat de two rusty ones fit.

"Aaah!" she say. "Here's de locks de Lawd couldn't find. *Now,* Mister Adam, we *see* who de boss!" Den she lock de two do's an' hide de keys.

'fo' long Adam come in out of de garden. "Gimme some food, woman!" he say.

"Can't, Adam," say Eve. "De kitchen do's locked."

"I fix dat!" say Adam. So he try to bust de kitchen do' down. But de Lawd built dat do' an' Adam can't even scratch hit.

Eve say, "Well, Adam honey, if you go out in de woods an' cut some wood faw de fire, I maybe can git de kitchen do' open. Maybe I can put one dem cunjur tricks on hit. Now, run long, honey, an' git de wood."

"Wood choppin' is yo' work," say Adam, "since I got de most strenth. But I do hit dis once an' see can you open de do'."

So he git de wood an' when he come back, Eve has de do' open. An' from den on out Eve kept de key to de kitchen an' made Adam haul in de wood.

Well, after supper Adam say, "Come on, honey, let's you an' me hit de froghair."

"Can't," say Eve. "De baidroom do' is locked."

*"Dad*blame!" say Adam. "Reckon you can trick dat do' too, Eve?"

"Might can," say Eve. "Honey, you jes' git a piece of tin an' patch dat little hole in de roof an' while you's doin' hit, maybe I can git de baidroom do' open."

So Adam patched de roof an' Eve she unlock de baidroom do'. From den on she kept *dat* key an' used hit to suit herself.

So dat de reason, de very reason, why de mens *thinks* dey is de boss and de wimmens *knows* dey is boss, 'cause dey got dem two little ol' keys to use in dat slippery sly wimmen's way. Yas, fawever mo' an' den some!

An' if you don't know *dat* already, you ain't no married man.

James R. Aswell

Harvey and Myra

One time, there was some people that didn't have but one boy in the family. Harvey was a good worker, and a big stout fellow besides. When he got to be seventeen years old it come in the boy's head to get married. His pappy was kind of worried, because Harvey done most of the farm work, but if he was to leave they'd have to pay a hired man. So pappy thought it would be better for Harvey to play around with some white-trash gals up the creek, and not think about getting married for a while yet.

But Harvey didn't take no interest in them peckerwood floozies, and he got to sparking a pretty girl named Myra that lived over in Lawrence County. Pretty soon it looked like him and Myra would get married sure, so the old man had to do something. "I hate to tell you this, son," says he. "Don't say nothing to your maw about it, but I was over in Lawrence County myself, fifteen years ago." What pappy meant was that he had knowed Myra's mother in them days. Harvey felt awful bad about this, but it won't do to marry your half sister, so he quit going to see Myra.

It wasn't long till Harvey was going steady with another pretty girl that lived at Gum Springs, and her name was Virginia. But, soon as the boy begun to talk about getting married, pappy says he had been over to Gum Springs fourteen years ago, so it won't do for Harvey to marry Virginia, neither. The boy done considerable grumbling this time, but he didn't want to hitch up with no half sister, so he and Virginia quit going together.

One day, the folks heard how Harvey was running after a girl named Kitty that was only thirteen years old, and she lives up near

Neosho. And in about three weeks he begun to talk about getting married. So pappy dragged out the old story again and says he was over there around Neosho thirteen years ago. "It would be sinful for a boy to lay up with his half sister," pappy says, "and maybe against the law besides." Harvey didn't say much, but he done a lot of thinking.

Finally he went and asked his maw about it. "Marry whoever you want, son," she says. "Don't pay no attention to pappy. I don't believe he ever got all them women in trouble. But even if he did, it don't make no difference. The fact is, pappy ain't your father no-how." Harvey was kind of set back when he heard that. But pretty soon he seen the funny side of it, and him and maw both busted out laughing.

When the folks got up next morning, Harvey was gone, and his saddle mare was gone too. They found out later that he had went back to Lawrence County and fixed things up with Myra. So then him and her got married without no more foolishness, and they lived happy ever after.

CHAPTER 6

Preachers
and
Their Congregations

"Bundle of Troubles"

When I see a man preach I like to see him act
as if he were fighting bees.

—Abraham Lincoln

IN AMERICA, RELIGION has a thousand voices. The Lord's word descends from every kind of pulpit, and the answering prayer rises from every sort of pew. Whether at a riverside baptism or in a stone cathedral, during a feast of holy rollers or at a gathering of Quakers, you'll always find, presiding over the event, the preacher.

In America the preacher has always been primarily a storyteller. With a Bible in his hand, he had at his fingertips the world's richest treasury of legend and proverb. If a preacher was known for his sermons, if he knew how to *preach,* it meant he knew how to tell a good story, a talent that could fill his church.

The best preachers were aware of their congregations' insatiable appetite for entertainment. There was once a young deacon in the early days of Texas named Z. N. Morrell. He was the first man of the cloth in the new town, and he soon found his services being interrupted by locals who gathered outside the church to talk and swap stories. Morrell's modest congregation was continually distracted, so the enterprising preacher determined to settle the matter. He challenged the loafers to a tale-telling contest: if Morrell lost, he promised to pack up and leave town, but if he won, he expected the local crowd to join his congregation. When the contest ended, Morrell had won by unanimous and enthusiastic consent, and for years afterward his services were the biggest event in the county.

A preacher and his congregation were often mirrors of one another. In colonial New England, the preacher was held as a stern and sober judge of human conduct, God's unyielding emissary. In an age of witch trials, when all kinds of superstition were treated with high seriousness, he was held in awe. Where else but New England could a reverend like "Handkerchief" Moody, who wore a handkerchief over his face in public and delivered his sermons with his back to the congregation, be treated with the utmost respect and admiration?

It was farther south, in the country where fundamentalism flourished alongside sects of every description, that the preacher was a more lively figure. When he wasn't settling a local feud among Ozark families, he was doing his best to tame and influence a wild and raucous congregation. The stories about him were full of zest and humor, like "The Deacon's Testimony" and "The Fighting Parson," or maybe they illuminated his occasional use of near-Solomonic wisdom, as in "The Stolen Wedges."

The greatest sin for the American preacher, or, for that matter, his congregation, was to be impractical. If a preacher offered platitude instead of advice, cant in place of wisdom, he was mercilessly caricatured for his narrow-minded piety. Stories abound that make fun of folks who sought to find in their religion answers to problems they could best solve themselves. It is a simple fact that religion will always be susceptible to the comic imagination as readily as it will be for the serious philosopher, as the following stories attest.

If Only the Angels Knew

"I gits mighty sick of all dis preachin' to womens 'bout live in de ways of de Lord an' don't have nothin' to do wid no mens. Dese preachers keep on hollerin', an' dey is de biggest rascals of 'em all. You kin hear dey mout' a mile—like God can't hear if dey whisper. But I kin mighty nigh see de ole devil poke up his fire an' lick his tongue out at dey goin's on. Listen to 'em an' dey make you think dey been right up in heaven walkin' 'round arm in arm wid God Almighty wid angels followin' 'em 'round wid milk an' honey.

"If de angels know wha' I know, dey would know dey ain't none of 'em would think heaven fitten widout a jug of liquor where dey could git a drink every time dey turn 'round, but if I is any judge, most of dem big-mout', big-bellied ole bastards is gonna bust hell wide open.

"Dey holler, 'God, Jesus' an' 'Lord,' an' talk 'bout heaven an' you better pray or you'll burn in hell, an' Sunday after dey done preach, den dey will eat up all de grub you kin put on your table, set down an' go to pickin' dey teet' an' lookin' at your baby gal.

"Don't tell me 'bout no preachers."

What Did He Say?

This story is true because I knew the man it happened to and he told me himself. The man, Reverend Braswell, preached a sermon about some local man, a notorious liar, who lived up past Swift Creek. A farmer had told the reverend how this man had gotten sick and had thrown up four black crows; and the reverend, in turn, used the strange occurrence as the main point of his sermon. After the service, the farmer came up to the reverend and told him, "That fellow I told you about threw up only three crows, not four."

"Who was the man who threw up these crows?" the reverend asked the old farmer, wanting to get his story right.

"I didn't know the man personally, but Royce King was there when it happened and he knew the man real well," came the reply.

So Reverend Braswell went and found Royce King and asked him about the three crows, and Royce said that it wasn't three crows, only two—but they were two big ones. "I didn't actually see them myself," Royce said, "but I heard the story from Ada Powell's brother, who was helping the man at the time."

So the reverend drove over to Ada's brother's house and asked him about the two crows, and he nodded his head, saying, "Ah yes, the one big black crow." The reverend was pretty upset by this time, what with the crows dropping off in number one by one. But he patiently listened while Ada Powell's brother told him that he hadn't been there but G. K. Peoples had delivered a load of peanut hay up by Swift Creek that day and had seen the crow himself.

More upset than ever, the reverend went to G. K.'s farm and asked G. K.'s wife about the crow that the man had thrown up. She looked puzzled. "Black crow? There weren't no black crow as I know of. G. K. tol' me that it was just that Billy Hackett had gotten mighty sick an' heaved up somethin' that looked like a black crow."

The Fighting Parson

Ed Sinkler was the bully of the neighborhood. He was tall and muscular, with deep-set black eyes and dark curly hair which, because of infrequent combings, was bushy and unruly. He was known throughout the community as a good and willing fighter. Nobody had ever seen him fight, nor had anybody ever known anybody who had seen him in action, but the idea persisted that he could, and would, whip any man who happened to incur his displeasure.

Ed was a garrulous fellow, given to boasting, and he advertised the fact that he could hold a kicking mule with his bare hands, that he had once twisted the barrel off a rifle-gun, and that he could draw nails out of a board with his teeth. Despite lack of proof of these claims, belief in them grew. Ed Sinkler's prodigious strength became a byword in the community. A man was "as strong as Ed Sinkler" or could "lift as much as Ed Sinkler."

Old Squire Greenup and the new preacher sat on the squire's porch talking. The preacher was a shrewd-looking fellow in his middle thirties who wore his long-tailed black coat with self-conscious dignity. Ed Sinkler ambled up the road and stopped before the gate.

"Howdy, Squar," he said.

"Evenin', Ed. Won't you come up an' take a chur [chair]." Ed came up and the squire introduced him to the new preacher.

"Reckon I ain't got time t' set, Squar," said Ed, assuming a business-like tone. "I jist come down t' see Brother Smithers hyar. I hearn as how he had driv up t' see you'ens."

"Anything private?" asked the squire. "If'n 'tis, I'll go in th' house an' let you fellers talk by yerselves."

"Jist keep yer chur," Ed assured him. "Tain't nothin' private atall. Th' chances are that it'll be knowed from hyar t' yander 'fore nightfall anyhow." He cleared his throat and turned to the preacher. "It's come t' my ears, Brother Smithers, that you've been a-makin' some slurrin' remarks 'bout me, an' I've come down t' ask you 'bout it."

Slowly the preacher rose to his feet. His face indicated no emotion. He was fully five inches taller than Ed, and when he straightened up his head rustled the strings of beans and dried apples that the squire's wife had festooned from rafter to rafter. "I ain't sayin' nothin' one way er 'nuther," the preacher replied quietly. "Until I know what I've been quoted as sayin', I ain't admittin' nothin' nor denyin' nothin'."

Ed struck an antagonistic pose. "I hearn that you said that if I'd come into th' meetin' house while meetin' was goin' on 'stead o' settin' outside with my arm 'round some gal, I'd be a more useful citizen t' th' community. Did you say that?"

"Do you do that, Brother Sinkler?" The preacher's eyes twinkled.

"That ain't th' point," Ed insisted. "I ast you, did you say it?"

"You answer my question fust."

"All right, I'll answer you. 'Tain't none o' yer business. Preachin's yer business, not mindin' my courtin' transactions. Take off yer coat an' come out hyar in th' road. We'll settle this thing right now. Yer guilty, an' I don't want t' mess up Miss Greenup's flower beds a-thrashin' you hyar in th' yard."

"Ed, Ed." Squire Greenup pleaded for peace. "You ain't goin' t' do nuthin' rash, are ye? Ca'm yerselves, fellers, ca'm yerselves." Neither of the men appeared to hear him, and the little squire, his dignity insulted, drew himself up pompously. "Gentlemen," he said in his best magisterial voice, "if ye fight I'll have t' deal with you accordin' t' th' law."

By this time the preacher had removed his coat, loosened his collar, and rolled up his sleeves. His arms were sinewy, and his shirt, clinging damply to his body, disclosed ridges of fine, pliant muscles upon his shoulders and back.

"May I pray?" he asked quietly of his adversary.

"Pray if ye want to. In fact, I'd advise it."

The preacher knelt at the edge of the porch. "O Lord," he prayed in a loud voice, "thou knowest that when I kilt Bill Thompson an' Clate Jennings that I done it in self-defense. Thou knowest, too, Lord, that when I splattered th' brains of Kemp Staples all over his co'n patch that it was forced upon me. An' now, O Lord, when I am jist on th' verge o' puttin' this hyar poor wretch in his grave, I'm askin' ye t' have mercy on his soul. Amen."

The preacher arose, took a long-bladed knife from his pocket and began whetting it on the sole of his shoe. Dismally, plaintively, his voice rose in song.

> *Hark from the tomb the doleful sound,*
> *Mine ears attend th' cry.*

Now, Ed Sinkler was nothing if not resourceful. Living in comparative comfort for thirty years without having engaged in any gainful occupation had sharpened his wits to a remarkable degree. He burst out laughing loudly. The preacher, surprised, stopped whetting his knife. Ed laughed because he had a reputation at stake. To run would be ruinous to that reputation. To fight would be equally ruinous. He had to stand his ground, and craftily he chose his course of action. Striding up to the porch he held out his hand. "Yer all right, parson," he said. "I was jist a-testin' out yer metal. When I hearn that you'd ariv 'mongst us I says t' myself, 'I'm goin' down t' see what kind o' goods that feller's made of fer no feller that ain't got no backbone has got any business in these hyar parts.' "

By this time the preacher had recovered from his surprise. Wrath overcame him. "I want ye t' know I made that thar remark you mentioned. What are ye goin' t' do 'bout it?"

"Nuthin' atall, Brother Smithers. Surposin' you did say it. I reckon th' only way you could feel that way 'bout it is because you ain't never done no sparkin' settin' outside a meetin' house. If you had ever tried it once, you' never say nary word agin it. It's th' most satisfactory courtin'. . . ."

Abruptly the preacher donned his coat. Casually he pulled his chair up beside the one on which the squire had collapsed. "As I was a-sayin', Brother Greenup," he said, as if no interruption had occurred, "thar's baptizin' by sprinklin' an' by pourin', an' thar's baptizin' by dippin', but thar's only one of 'em that's right."

Predestination for the Indian

In the early days of the Republic of Texas when the Indians were especially bad, an old Primitive Baptist preacher was preparing for a long trip across the Indian country. He was especially careful in cleaning and loading the long rifle that was to accompany him. A friend, seeing his preparation and knowing his belief in predestination, said to him, "Uncle Billie, why are you so careful about your gun? If you meet the Indians and you are predestined to die at that time, why, you will die anyway; so why worry about the gun? 'What is to be will be anyway,' you know."

"Yes, I know all about that," said Uncle Billie, "but it might be the Indian's time too."

The Deacon's Testimony

Deacon Jones an' his gal live in a section of de country where dere been a heap of bears. An' one night he been guine to an experience meetin', an' dere been two roads, an' his gal say:

"Papa, le's we don't go through de woods road, kaze I seen a bear dere today."

An' de deacon say:

"I ain' care nothin' 'bout no bear. I'm a Christian an' loves God an' God loves me, an' I puts my trust in Him. I loves God. God is good. I'm guine through dem woods."

An' de gal say:

"Papa, le's we don't make no mistakes. Le's we go 'round."

An' de deacon say:

"I'm guine through dem woods. I trust God. I puts my faith in God. God is good an' will pertec' me."

An' de gal say:

"I ain' trustin' all dat. I'm guine 'round."

An' de deacon say:

"Well, I'm guine through de woods. God is my pertecter."

An' he went through de woods, an' de gal went 'round.

An' when de deacon git half way through de woods, a bear jumped on him an' he had a terrible time fightin' wid dat bear. De bear tored mighty nigh all his clothes off, an' bit him up an' mighty nigh ruint him. But when he git loose, he made his way to de experience meetin'. An' when he git dere, de congregation been tellin' 'bout dey experience wid God an' Jesus an' de devil an' wid angels—an' a passel of lies.

An' den dey spied Deacon Jones in de back of de congregation, an' dey call on him for his experience an' he say he ain' got nothin' to say. An' all dem brother an' all dem sister keep on hollerin' for him. An' after a while de deacon git up an' say:

"My brothers an' sisters, all I kin say is: God is good. God is good.

I loves God. I sho' loves Him, an' I puts my faith in Him. God is good an' He'll help you in a lot of little things, but, my brothers an' sisters, good as God is, He ain' worth a damn in a bear fight."

The Stolen Wedges

One time, there was a preacher named Lorenzo Dow, and he held big camp meetings all over the country. An old-timer kept complaining about how somebody has stole his iron wedges, that they used to split rails with. Preacher Dow says never mind, just give me a wedge like the ones you lost, and I will find out who is the thief.

So that night, right in the middle of the meeting, old Dow had 'em all shouting and praying. All of a sudden he pulled out a big old iron wedge, and waved it over the pulpit like he was going to throw it. "May God carry this straight to the head of the man that stole Brother Ralston's wedges!" he yelled.

Mostly the people just looked kind of surprised, but a fellow in the second row ducked. "That's the guilty man!" says Preacher Dow. So then everybody begun to sing and pray louder than ever. The thief confessed right there, and got religion, and gave the wedges back, and begged everybody to forgive him. Some of them old-time preachers was awful handy when it come to things like that.

Soapy Smith
Preaches to the Damned

One winter night when the snow was falling heavily and the cold was intense, and Smith's saloon was selling hot drinks as fast as a row of bar-tenders could supply them, a shabby and thinly clad man entered the room; his embarrassment made it evident that this was his first visit to a saloon and gambling-hall. He seemed to be looking for an office where he could present his inquiry; not seeing any such place he started toward the bar, then hesitated in a bewildered way, but finally with much diffidence made his way up to the counter. One of the men in white aprons laid a glass in front of him and asked what he would have; he managed to stammer that he had a letter from Mr. Jefferson Smith which he wished to present in person. Smith was seated in the "look-out" chair, watching a game of faro where the bets were heavy; the visitor was directed to this chair and presented the letter, and then stepped back to wait results.

The loafers and hangers-on soon recognized that the new arrival was probably an itinerant circuit rider, and thinking to while away the time by having a little sport with him they were profuse in their offers of tobacco and invitations to drink, and were generally guying him with annoying remarks while Smith was reading the letter. It was from his wife, and was a plea for him to befriend the minister and to assist him with the funds necessary to start a church. He finished reading the letter, and then looking at the men who were tormenting the messenger, started toward them, shaking his fists violently, and said, "Don't you dare to insult my friend; the next d—d cuss that makes fun of the parson I'll fill so full of lead that there will be nothing left of him but solder." There was a hurried standing back, a very polite lifting of hats as Smith led the man by the arm and walked him to the front of the hall where the whole assemblage could be faced. A look-out chair platform was ordered to be brought, and standing on it Soapy began his address: "Gentlemen, you'll please be quiet." The admonition was hardly needed, for the proverbial pin could certainly have been heard. "Every dealer will turn his box down. The bar will serve no more drinks. Me and Jesus are going to run this place for the space of about half an hour, and we'll have no nonsense nor funny business, nor no interruptions to the speaker."

With this introduction, the self-constituted preacher continued: "My brother who stands here by my side has brought me a letter from the truest of the true; from one whose thoughts are as far above mine as the stars of heaven are above the deepest caverns of the earth; whose life has been a bright and shining light amidst the dark shadows of my wanderings; whose name no man could speak lightly of in my presence and live. I will not in the red lights of this hall and to my companions in the rapids mention her name. But she has asked me to assist this minister to start a church here and to befriend him in every way possible, and by G—d I will do it, and the Lord is going to have his innings right here in this whiskey shop."

It was interesting to watch the look of blank astonishment, wonder, disgust and alert curiosity which swept around the room. These men were certainly only too used to hearing the sacred name hurled about, but this was different. However, there was no time to speculate, for Soapy's words came thick and fast.

"I am not very fresh on the trail, and the Book from which to read the text is not handy, but the foundation facts you shall have just the same. When a Man tries to help you even if you don't understand His ways, and when His greatest of all love has been tested by His dying for sinners—and I guess every cuss of you here will come under that heading—I say when such a Friend sends His representative to see you He is entitled to receive your attention and support. A mud hen can't become an eagle nor a burro a lion by any transformation at death, nor can any of us old pioneers of the down grade stack the cards so as to beat the Lord at His own game, and I for one am not going to try climbing the heights of glory when I know that I am ticketed for the through express that doesn't make any stops this side of hell. Some of us may be too late for our brother's ministrations, but there are others here who have only just begun to go down hill, who don't take more than a dozen drinks a day, who haven't killed many men, who hain't recently held up a coach or a train, who haven't stole much and don't bet high at faro, and I just propose to turn them over to this soul-herder. The parson will give his receipt to the Lord for you; then if you don't like the shackles and want to return to the Bad Lands all you have got to do is to ring in a substitute, so as to keep our church number solid. Now, how can a parson corral them unless he has a shop and the right kind of a layout to help on his work. That's the part I'm going to save for lastly, so I'll leave the financial side for a moment and get down to city patriotism.

"I believe a camp thrives best where all kinds of business get a fair show. What would our whiskey shops do if there were no mines?

What would the mines do if there were no engineers, blacksmiths, steam-fitters, timber men and teamsters? What would become of our merchants if we did not get hungry, and if we wore blankets, and the women cared no more for style than a Ute squaw?"

This was a new role for the saloon-keeper, and he was perspiring from the force of his own eloquence, but he was not through yet and did not propose to stop until he had made a clean job.

"Now, I cannot exactly state what present necessity our friend will fill. We have got along thus far tolerably well without religion, but it ain't very inspiring at funerals when the undertaker is the whole works. For my part I don't see what right we've got to call in the minister when we come into this world and when we go out, if we give him the cold shoulder the rest of the time. Perhaps it was lucky that when our friend Bob Ford was killed there was no parson in camp—that is, lucky for the parson, for it ain't fair to speak agin the dead, and I must allow the parson would have been up against a brace game in slinging happy conclusions at his wind-up.

"Some of you miserable whelps over in yonder corner, who are so full you can't keep awake, will find it to your advantage to listen to my sermon or you'll have a longer sleep than you have bargained for, and the services of the parson will be needed sooner than he expected. I mean you, Whistling Dick Jones, and you, too, Barbarian Brown, and a few more of you.

"Then there's another job that the parson can do slicker than any justice of the peace. Perhaps you men have forgotten that you have families 'way back East, but those of you who are eligible and believe in women and children and school-houses can figure with pleasure on a sober dealer at the wedding 'round-up,' and when it comes to the final show down and the kissing of the bride there will be no aroma of whiskey floating round like a sea fog in a dead calm.

"When Sunday comes you'll know it, and there will be other music than the dance-hall bill of fare. I long to hear the war-whoop of salvation resound through these eternal hills and to listen to the paeans of the saints as they shout hallelujah, and with amens roaring like artillery. A regular dose of religion given you once a week will do you as much good as a bath in getting the blue smoke and brimstone out of your systems. So I say, let the effulgent rays of Methodism illumine your dark souls like a lighthouse on a rock-bound coast. We shall get used to the preacher and he will get used to us, and we shan't know how to get along without each other. I tell you what, Creede is behind the times; we've got to have all the things there are on earth, and Creede must have a church, and we are going to build it. Now, boys, the jig is up to you. These everlasting hills that pierce the heavens, and will be here when you and I are dead and gone, must not look down in shame on a miser gang that denied the Lord's shepherd a living. My brother is a worthy man, but he can't play his game without his shop and his tools, and we've got to grubstake him and raise the wad that will raise the temple. Now every man in this room has got to chip in nothing less than a dollar. If you haven't got a dollar, you have no business to be in a gambling-house. If there are any professional loafers and dead beats here, who think that my church is going to be a free-lunch stand, and they don't put in a dollar, 'now is the time to withdraw'—that's a regular parson phrase.

"I'll start the game with a fifty dollars, and while the band plays 'Honey, yo's made a hit with me,' I'll pass round the hat. Any of you who's got credit but with no cash handy, I'll stake, but no nickels and no small change goes." Above the sound of fumbling in pockets could be heard the drop of Soapy's fifty dollars in gold. Not a man in the house save the parson, to whom the opportunity of contributing was not extended, failed to donate according to the limit laid down, though two or three persons borrowed their dollars from Smith. The contribution amounted to three hundred and fifty dollars. Soapy's disappointment was evident. "Parson," he said, "I'm sorry, but I'm afraid that we are a little shy on cash. Three hundred and fifty dollars isn't enough to start in business with; you can't do a good job on a cent less than seven hundred dollars. You don't want a coal-bin for a church, and you ain't going to have it. Why, the Lord and the Devil would both be ashamed of it. Now, if you were a dead game sport, I should ask you to stake the three hundred and fifty dollars on the high card." The poor parson looked a shade paler, as if scared for fear he might be forced to do the Devil's work to earn his money. But Soapy came to his rescue by saying that possibly he might not know a deuce from a king and that he would put a dollar on the high card for the church, and if it won he might get his seven hundred dollars. Whether the dollar on the high card won or lost, the minister could not have told to save his life, but he did know that Soapy Smith handed him seven hundred dollars, and that there was a rousing cheer from the spectators and that he managed to add a loud amen. He also grasped Smith's hand vigorously and tried to thank him, but words failed and tears took their place as they walked to the door where he received a final wish of good luck from Smith.

In three minutes the unusual interruption was a thing of the past and as if it had not been; the games were in full blast and glasses were rattling.

Little Mercies

Two fellows came one Sunday morning to the local Baptist church and idled around the front door during the service. The preacher was a smart man, and when he rose to preach the sermon he looked out over the congregation for a moment. Then he said in a booming voice, "Brethren, may de Lord have mercy on all de scoffers." The church was quiet. "May de Lord have mercy on all de laughers." Another pause. And then in an even louder voice, "May de Lord have mercy on de two peanut-eaters at the back."

A Parson's Supper

A Methodist parson was once traveling in our parts, and he put up at a log house in the woods, where there was a woman of his way of thinking. So them two fell to religionizing for two or three hours, when, at last, he fetched a sigh and said how he wished he was on the seaboard, where he could have a fresh mess of eels for his supper. So she says right away, "You can have eels ready in less time then skinning a badger, if you want," and out she run to get him some for supper. While she was out the minister heard strange noises that he didn't know what to make on. He thought somebody was playing dice, for he heard a tremendous rattling as if a dozen men were shaking dice boxes at once. At last he got up and went out to see what it meant, intending to preach them a sermon against gambling, when what should he see but his landlady with a big knotted club in her hand batterfanging a dozen rattlesnakes that were squirming and twisting around her in all manner of shapes and fashions. One big fellow fetched a leap at her when she dodged him, and wrung off another one's neck that was about to spring on her. The minister thought she was in great danger, and got hold of a stick to help her. "Don't worry yourself, holy sir," said she, "you go into the house and write out your sermon, and leave me to get your supper."

"Supper!" cried he, "I don't understand you!"

"Didn't you order eels?" said she, "and ain't I preparing a nest of the varmints, as fast as I can?"

The minister flung down his club, and run right off, and never stopped till he got home again. He told all the brethren it was no use to go into Kentucky to preach, the very women served up rattlesnakes for supper.

Cheesebox Church

Some folks 'cuses me of not bein' a religious man, and say I's not saved, and all that, jes on account I's perticular 'bout the kinda church I goes to. Iffen I could get to a good brick church I'd go ever Sunday and on prayer-meetin' night, too. But, they ain't nobody what's gwine a-get me in one of them rickety wooden tabernickles, and none of them lil old cheesebox churches what the darkies have in this here neighborhood. Jes look at this busted nose, and look at the place where they ain't no hair growin' on my haid! That comes from goin' into a lil old rickety wooden churchhouse, and I don't mean to git ketched that away agin. No, suh! Not me!

That was near ten y'ar ago, when I was a-livin' on Harricane

Crick, a-workin' for Cap'n Pennybacker. They was a bunch of cullud folks what called 'emselfs the Black Saints of Possom Ridge, and they holds meetin's 'round wherever they finds a place, and fin'ly they gits up some cash money and decides to build 'emselfs a churchhouse.

They didn't git much cash money, and they had to make out best they could, and so they bought 'em some loblolly pine boards, and some tar paper, and some nails, and they puts up a lil old buildin' on Harricane Crick.

I reckon they was 'bout a hunner darkies what belongs to these Black Saints, and when they got that buildin' up what they calls a churchhouse, it looks more like a big hen-house to me than a meetin'house. Anyhow they gits 'em a preacher of the name of Rev. Ambrose Ferebee, and they begins holdin' meetin's in that house.

The boards run up and down, and they warn't hardly any joists to hold 'em tergather. They nailed more boards on for a roof, and then to keep the water and wind out, they went over the hull business, roof and sides, with tar paper, what they tacked on with big tin washers to keep the tacks from pullin' through.

The Rev. Ambrose Ferebee, he was a powerful preacher, and you could hear him a-yellin' and a-stompin' up on his platform for miles 'round. Some of the sistern got to workin' on me, and 'suaded me to come to the meetin's. They was jes lil old wooden benches to set on, 'thout no backs to 'em, and they warn't no floor 'cept the dirt.

After the Rev. Ferebee done preached 'bout a month, he 'nounced one Sunday that they's a-gwine be a revival at the church, and that the Rev. Dooteronomy Simmons is a-comin' to conduck it.

As I done say, the Rev. Ferebee was a pow'ful preacher, and he got a good pair of lungs, and he got a good stout pair of laigs to stomp on the platform, but he ain't in it with this here Rev. Dooteronomy Simmons when he get his first meetin' started.

This Rev. Dooteronomy stand still a long time on the platform, jes a-lookin' at the flock settin' on the benches, then he lift up his long skinny arm, and let out a yell like 'bout 'leben panthers a-screamin' all t'oncet. When he let out that yell, ever'body jump plum offen they bench, and by the time they git set down agin, the Rev. Dooteronomy is yellin' out a stream of preachin' faster'n a horse can run.

The Rev. was long and skinny, like I say, but he got a big barrel chest on him, what look like he's done been blowed up like a pouter pigeon. He'd take a great big breaf, and then he'd yell out them words, thick and fast, till all his breaf done gone. Then he'd stop and take another great big breaf, and light out agin. I never heerd such preachin' in my borned days.

First thing I know, folks settin' on they benches begun weavin' back and forth, jes keepin' time to the preachin'. Then they begun to blow out they breafs while the Rev. Dooteronomy was talkin', and when the Rev. takes in a big breaf, all the folkses settin' there, they takes a big breaf too.

The Rev. was preachin' 'bout sheep and goats, and he say that in this life they is two kinds of folks, sheep and goats. Then he takes a big breaf, and when he gits in the big breaf, he run on and wants to know who's gwine a-be the sheep, and who's gwine a-be the goats. When the Rev. runs out of breaf, the congergation say, all together, "Yea—Lawd," and then they all fills up with a big breaf jes like the Rev. done.

I heerd somethin' crackin', and I looks up, and I sees that ever time the folks takes a breaf together, the walls and the roof of the church suck way in. And when they all let's out they breaf, the walls and roof of the church bulge way out, jes like a rubber balloon bein' blowed up.

I knowed somethin' gwine a-happen, and I lets out a yell as loud as I could, but the folks jes look at me like I's a sinner gettin' grace, and then keeps on drawin' in and blowin' out with the Rev. And the walls and roof of the church keep suckin' and bulgin', a lil more each time.

Fin'ly the Rev. Dooteronomy stop daid still. He take a big breaf, and ever'body take a big breaf. He hold his breaf a minnit and ever'body hold they breaf a minnit, too. Then the Rev. yells out: "Who's gwine a-be the goats?"

Ever'body watch for him to let go his breaf, but he hold it a minnit, and then he let go, and ever'body let go, and then the walls of that there church blow plum out and the roof come bangin' down right on ever'body's haids.

They warn't nobody kilt, but they war a pow'ful lot of cracked haids in that congergation when they got 'em all fished out.

No, suh! Ennybody what wants to can go to one of these here tabernickles, or a cheesebox church, but not me. I goes to a good stout brick church or I don't goes to none, atall.

Faith and Expectation

A good old sister in Zion had long been worried about the mountain that stood in front of her cabin and cut off the view of the great valley beyond. Many times, she had wished that she could pick it up and lay it out of her way. At church one day the preacher discussed the power of prayer. Quoting from Scripture, he declared that if one had sufficient faith, one might say unto the mountain, " 'Be thou removed,' and straightway it would fall into the sea."

The good sister heard with great interest, and that night she prayed long and fervently that the mountain might be removed from her door. Then she slept the sleep of the righteous until the early dawn. She waked and hurried to the door to see whether the mountain were gone. But there it stood just as high and as rugged as ever. In disgust she turned away and said, "Just as I expected."

Powers of Concentration

Two friends were once traveling together on horseback, when, the conversation taking a religious turn, one of them observed that he never could pray without occasionally thinking of something else, and that it was a source of great trouble to him, that he had tried to break himself of the habit, but that he believed instead of decreasing it was growing upon him, and that the more effort to devote his mind intently to the one great object was the very cause of the aberration.

"Well, that may be the case with you," observed the other, "but, as for my part, I never suffer, on such occasions, worldly considerations to have any effect on me. I totally lose sight of them, because I consider them sinful, ungrateful, and—"

"No doubt, no doubt," interrupted the first speaker, "but I have found it so difficult, that I shall be pleased to learn how you gained the faculty of this fixed devotion. I make you this proposal, and then we will talk the matter over afterwards: If you will get down on your knees and say the Lord's Prayer, and when you have done declare to me that you thought of nothing else during the whole time, I will give you my horse."

"Most willingly," answered the other; and dismounting, he knelt on the ground, and commenced the prayer aloud. He had not proceeded more than half way, when, starting up, he seized his friend's hand and exclaimed, *"And did you say the saddle, too?"*

Catching the Lord

It happened that, in an early day, a Methodist circuit rider came to a crossroads in the state of Wisconsin where stood a typical country lad—barefooted, pants rolled up, one suspender, and shirt bosom open. The preacher was mounted on about the poorest horse that had ever been seen in these parts. Addressing the boy, he said, "My son, which one of these two roads will take me to Stoughton?"

The boy paid no attention to the question. He had never seen a respectable man mounted on so sorry a steed. The minister repeated the question, and the boy, looking up, queried, "Who are you?"

Back came the answer, "I am a follower of the Lord."

"Well," said the boy, "it won't make any difference which road you take. You'll never catch him with that hoss."

Last Licks

Patrick O'Neill became wealthy as a mine contractor, and being a bachelor believed in spending his money during his lifetime. His unconventional manner of living and his neglect of the Church of his fathers over a long period of years brought him a reputation as a libertine. He was quite an old man when he had a stroke. His faithful housekeeper called a doctor. It took the doctor but a minute to tell Patrick that he was in a very bad condition.

"I believe I am," muttered Pat.

"Yes, you are, Pat," said the doctor, "and it will cost you a pretty penny before we of the medical profession have anything to do with you."

"What will it cost?" asked Pat, blinking his eyes.

"It will cost at least a thousand dollars," replied the doctor.

"Well, dochtor, don't ye think that's very excessive?"

"Not at all, Pat. You see, never before did we have an opportunity to make a dollar out of you, so it will cost you a thousand dollars before we do anything for you now."

"Very well," says Pat. "I'll give ye the thousand dollars on one condition."

"And what is that?"

"That ye won't let me die without the priest."

"Oh, that will be all right. We can arrange that."

The doctor knew very well that there was no hope for Pat, yet he left him with the feeling that there might be a chance. Several days later, however, he told him the truth. "Well, Pat," says he, "you may call in the priest, for you're not going to get well."

The patient nodded his head in resignation and the priest was sent for.

The priest was an old man himself. When he entered the sick room he took one look at the dying man and said, "Well, you old reprobate, you've sent for me at last. Little you thought of me during the past forty years, running around carousing with nary a thought for the Church of your fathers. And now, Pat, don't you know that after the life you've led it will take a great deal of money for masses, prayers, and offices to be read for you, if your soul's to be saved?"

"What will it cost, fa-ather?"

"It will cost at least a thousand dollars."

"Very well, fa-ather, I'll give ye the thousand dollars on one condition."

"And what may that be?"

"Both ye and the dochtor must be here when I'm dying."

"Oh! very well," said the priest. "I suppose that can be arranged."

So the room was cleared and Pat was given the last rites of the Church. Both the priest and the doctor were there. The doctor leaned over the bed to tell Pat that if he had any last request to make, to make it then.

"You have only a few minutes to live," he said.

"You're there yet, fa-ather?" muttered the patient.

"Yes, yes, I'm here," replied the priest.

"Are ye still there, dochtor?" asked Pat.

And the doctor assured him that he was.

"Well, dochtor," said Pat, "ye come around to the other side of the bed."

The priest hereupon leaned over to Pat and in a kindly but firm voice said, "Tut, tut, now, what nonsense is this you're going on with when it's your rosary you should be saying?"

"Well, fa-ather," said Pat as he breathed his last. "As a young man I went to your Church and many's the time I heard ye say from the pulpit that our Savior died between two thieves. I'd like to die the same way."

An Oilman Helps Out

A Texas millionaire went into a church to pray. He knelt and said: "O Lord, I know everything has to operate according to your will. But I understand you listen to prayers, so here I am. First, Lord, I want to tell you about my ranch out in the hill country. It's not a great big spread, just three thousand cows in my foundation herd, good white-faced stuff. It's getting pretty dry up there, and if it don't rain in a couple of weeks, I'll have to start feeding. So if you could send a rain that way, I sure would appreciate it.

"Then, Lord, I bought some land up in Colorado. Supposed to be uranium land, but I don't know how it'll turn out. But if you could let it turn out good, I sure would be grateful.

"Then, Lord, I've got sixteen oil wells drilling. Of course, Lord, everybody knows that a man can't expect to get oil in every wildcat he drills, and I'm not asking for oil in all sixteen. But, Lord, if you could let me have oil in twelve, I'd sure be obliged to you. Amen."

While the oilman was praying, a man in a threadbare suit had entered quietly and taken a seat. He now knelt to pray. He said, "O, Lord, I've done everything I know to do, and I don't know anything else to do but pray. I'm an accountant, and I lost my job when the firm sold out to another company. That was six months ago and my savings are all gone. It's hard for a man forty-seven years old to find a new job, but I've tried. I've worn out my shoes going from one place to another. Then my suit is beginning to look shabby, and I have a wife in the hospital. The doctor says she can go home, but I owe the hospital a hundred and seventy dollars and they won't let her go. And every day they add twelve dollars to the bill. O Lord, please help me in some way to get on my feet again. Amen."

The oilman pulled out his wallet and peeled off five one-hundred-dollar bills and quietly placed them in the accountant's hand. Then he knelt again and said, "Lord, you needn't bother about this little chicken—I've taken care of him."

How They Sing in the City

One time, a farmer who was a deacon in the church was summoned to serve on a federal grand jury in a city. He was gone two weeks. First thing when he got back home, his wife asked him if he had attended church services in the big city. Of course he had. "Did you know any of the songs they sang?" his wife wanted to know.

"No, I didn't," the farmer replied. "They didn't sing songs. All they sung was anthems."

"Anthems! what on earth is anthems?"

"Well, it's like this," the deacon answered. "Now, if I was to say to you, 'Ma, the cows is in the corn,' that would not be any anthem."

"Of course it wouldn't," Ma put in.

"Wait a minute," the deacon went on. "If I'd say in a long, quavering-out, dying up-and-down voice, 'Ma, Ma, Ma, the cows—the cows—the Holstein cow, the muley cow, the Jersey cow, the old brindle cow, and old Spec, too—all them cows—the co-o-o-w-s—is in—is in—the cow-ow-ows is in—is in—the corn, the corn, the co-oo-rr-n, ah men, men, men,' that would be an anthem."

Advice on Sin

"Dad, it's your turn to take a drink."

"Just a small one, Loye."

"Dad, you say you believe in the Bible?"

"Every word of it, Dickie. There ain't nothing but the truth in them Scriptures."

"Isn't it wrong for Christians to drink corn whisky?"

"No sir, no sir, it ain't sinful to drink corn whisky. The only reason why the blessed Jesus and them disciples drunk wine at the Last Supper was 'cause they couldn't get corn whisky."

"They didn't have corn in those days."

"Yes Dickie, yes, they had corn, that's right, they had corn."

"I thought them Indians in this here country was the first people to eat corn."

"Sure Loye, them Indians was the first people to *eat* corn, but they ain't got no sense nohow."

"They had corn in them days, yes sir, they had corn."

"Jesus was a tramp, wasn't he, Dad?"

"I ain't heard of him going in no business."

"He was a carpenter."

"Only when he was a boy, Loye. He just did a few odd jobs about the house."

"Just suppose the Old Man would send him back again in these here times, what do you think the people would do?"

"Wahl Randy, I guess—"

"Guess! Why, they would arrest him for vagrancy."

"How about them miracles, Dickie?"

"Why the people would think it was a trick or he had a paid troupe that played the towns with him."

"Dickie, it ain't right to talk thataway, no sir, and it ain't going to do nothing but bring you a heap of misery. I knows 'cause when I was your age I was right smart ornery. I use to doubt the Lord God and His blessed ways. I use to play the women."

"You use to do some courtin', Dad?"

"Oh yes son, yes sir."

"What kind of women?"

"I use to like to get some sweet innocent young fryer, one of them apple-face gals that's all candied up to fall in love with me, win her confidence, tell her heaven is right here on earth, and then when I gets things my own way, tell her she's got to die to get to heaven."

"Where did you find them innocent apple-face gals?"

"Wahl, it ain't right of me to tell you, Loye, but I use to go to church and sit in the back where all the young folks is and start talking to one of the gals and kinda hint around 'bout taking her home. It ain't right to do, but it ain't hard to do."

"That's right, that's where I gets all my high-powered decent bitches."

"You can get them gals now just like Dad use to?"

"Yeh."

"What church, Randy?"

"Any of them, Dickie, they's all the same."

"Loye, let's go to church and get a brace of apple-face gals."

"Huh?"

"Huh hell, come on, let's go."

"Dickie, you talk like a man on dope. There ain't no church open on Saturday night."

"Let's go to town."

"You boys set down and mind your conduct."

"Let's all take a drink."

"Tell us some more about your gals."

"Yeh, Dad."

"Wahl sir, I'll never forget the time I went to one of them Holy Roller churches. I was a young scamp, like you boys, and went just for the meanness. When I gets there all the congregation was down on the floor rolling and whooping, so I lays down by a good-looking gal and starts in a-rolling. Wahl sir, the lights went out, but that don't stop them from rolling and howling. Then the old Devil gets the best of me and before I could stop myself I rolls over by this gal and sides up to her like a sick cat to a hot brick. Boy! did she yell, she just whooped and howled something awful, but nobody paid her no mind 'cause they thought she was getting more religion. But I ain't worrying 'bout that black sin 'cause I've made it right with the Old Man, yes sir, and He ain't the kind to hold a grudge against nobody, not Him."

"Amen!"

"Praise be the Lord!"

"Will He forgive all us monkeys that's been a-cutting up and ain't been doing right by Him?"

"Yes sir, He forgives all kinda folks. He ain't particular like most folks is. He ain't got no special gang, He's just a big-hearted old boy that'll do right by all us folks."

"You're sure of that?"

"Yes Randy, I knows it."

"Wahl I ain't going to do no worrying, then. I'm just going 'bout my business and every once in a while ask the Old Man to forgive me."

"Randy, you have never sinned, have you?"

"I ain't done nothing but sin, Dickie. It seems kinda natural for me to sin, so I guess I just got to let it go like that. I'm just a born sinner."

"Wahl sir, I thought I was just a born sinner till I got the salvation and started reading them Scriptures, and then I come to find out that folks is born in the world with sin on their head and it is up to them to leave go of them sins and hitch up with the Lord."

"How do you leave go of your sins, Dad?"

"Loye, it ain't so easy to do and it takes many a year to do it. Young ones is naturally full of the Devil, plumb full, and the only thing they can do 'bout it is to sow them wild seeds they got, and keep on sowing them till they ain't got no more. Then they is ready for the salvation."

"I'm mighty proud to hear that."

"The faster you can sow them wild seeds the better off you'll be, 'cause then you can get the salvation all the sooner. If you just mope along only letting out all that devilment and orneriness a little at a time, you is liable to catch yourself dying and ain't been able to come to the Lord."

"My God! pass me that fruit jar of whisky, the whole jar."

"Save me a drink, Dickie, I don't want to die and go to hell."

Daniel M. Garrison

The Settin' Up

Dere was a fellow that went to one of his fren's' settin-up, and dis fren' was laid out dead on de coolin' board, and in some shape he wanted to go an' relieve him, an' he got down to prayer. Had a crowd of people there too. He was prayin' dere wid his eyes shut, and he say, "Lord be wid dis deceased brother, he gone, he is dead; if it be thy will, raise him; if it is not thy will, God, save his soul. God, he leaves all his sisters, his brothers, his companions here behind him. God, be wid him, have mercy on him, save his soul. Father, it is within thy power to raise him, it is within thy power to save him. Lord, go with his bereaved family he leff behin'."

An' as he was down dere prayin', wid his eyes shut, de man on de coolin' board raise up, an' set up, an' de people saw him an' slipped out an' sneaked out, an' he still prayin' an' he raise up an' open his eyes an' sawed no people but de dead man in front of him an' he backed off de dead man an' grabbed up an ax, an' he say:

"If you don't wait till I git out of here I'll finish killin' you."

An' ever since den, mens has been more perticular 'bout what dey ax God to do.

Dividing Up the Souls

One night, two boys went into Mean Man Bascomb's peanut fields to steal some nuts. They got a sack full and then ran off to a nearby cemetery to hide while they divided up the peanuts. While climbing over the cemetery wall, they dropped two peanuts. Unconcerned, the boys found a tall tombstone to hide behind, and then they got to work counting their booty.

Meanwhile, Mean Man's oldest son was prowling around the area looking out for the culprits who had been stealing peanuts from his father's fields. It didn't matter that Mean Man's fields were overflowing with nuts and a bag or two wasn't going to matter. Mean Man's boy wanted to grow up like his Daddy, who was mean as a stuck snake.

Well, Mean Man's son got outside the cemetery wall and heard two voices inside counting, "One fer you. One fer me. One fer you. One fer me." As quick as he could, Bascomb's boy ran back to his father's house.

"Pa, God an' the Devil are in the cemetery an' they're dividin' up the souls of the dead. Come quick," the boy yelled excitedly.

Mean Man Bascomb nearly whacked his son for being superstitious but nevertheless followed him reluctantly to the cemetery wall. Together they heard the voices counting, "One fer you. One fer me." After a while the first voice said, "That about does it. But wait a minute; what about the two out there by the wall?" "It don't matter to me," the other voice replied. "Well, I'll take 'em," answered the first voice. "I'm jes' gonna roast 'em with the rest of my batch."

Well, they say that Mean Man Bascomb beat his son home by fifty yards. And ever since that night he's been a God-fearing man.

Bundle of Troubles

One night, Mose went to bed 'bout bowed down with his troubles. Seem like all of 'em was a-hoppin' on him at oncet. He turned and twisted, but by-an'-by he went to sleep and then he had the dream.

Seem like, in the dream, ever'body had all a-sudden started fussin' 'bout their troubles. Seem like they couldn't talk 'bout nothin' else. Fin'ly, the debbil, he got tard of all this loose talk 'bout troubles, caze most of 'em was blamed on him. Then one Sadday, 'thout nobody 'spectin' him, he 'peared uptown, jes as the streets was most crowded, and he rung a bell to call all they 'tentions to him.

When ever'body gathered 'round, he say like this:

"I bin hearin' a powerful lot 'bout all you folks's troubles. Yo'all thinks you is got more troubles as anybody. And I's a-gittin' mighty tard a-hearin' 'bout nothing else. Yo'all nussin' you troubles so hard you ain't got no time for no real sinnin'.

"I tell you what I's a-gonna do. I's a-gonna take up all of you troubles. Ever'body what has got troubles, jes wrop 'em up in a bun'le and bring 'em down to the depot checkroom right away and I'll take 'em up and rid each and ever'body of you troubles. Now go home and wrop them troubles up and hurry down to the depot with 'em."

Well, it didn't take Mose more'n a minit to git home. He say he warn't runnin' 'zactly, but he was a-passin' a lot of folks what was.

He got the biggest thing he could find to hold all of his troubles, which was a big paper box with "Saunders Tripe" printed on the outside. Mose didn't think it would begin to hold all his troubles, but he started in a-packin' anyway.

First went in his old rheumatiz, and then his cawns.

"Yo'all bin hurtin' me for many the year," he say, "and I's sho glad to part company with you."

Then in went the lan'lord, and the sto'keeper what Mose owe for his fertilize. Then there was his back church dues what he hadn't paid, and that yeller gal over at Marse John Simmons' place. I don't know why he put her in, but he did. Then he throwed in his sore tooth, and his boy what got drunk all the time, and the old plow what never would foller a straight furrow. Then in went his old black skin, all his gray hair, and his wife's naggin', and the hatchet what would fly offen the handle. He throwed in his old mule, Bess, what kicked the daylights outen him ever time she got a chancet, and that sportin' darkey what was a-slippin' 'round seein' his youngest gal.

He throwed in a heap more of tribalashuns, and it seem like the box jes wouldn't hold all of 'em, but there was allus a lil room at the top.

By-an'-by he had 'em all in, and then he took a big breaf and a piece of old plow line and tie them troubles up hard and fast in the box. He made a nice bun'le and throwed it on his wheelbar and started for the depot.

It took him a long time to git there, caze the streets was packed with folks all loaded down with bun'les. There was old Sis Tompkins what didn't anybody know ever had a trouble in her life, and what was allus a-laffin', and a-jokin', and a-goin' on. She was loaded down with sech a big bun'le that she had three of her lil gran'chillun a-helpin' her tote it. There was the preacher with a good-size load. There was even white folks, and Mose was surprise at that, but they seem to have the biggest bun'les of all. There was old Cunnel LeRoy, the biggest man in the town; even he had a bun'le. It warn't a very big bun'le, 'bout the size of a dozen eggs wropped up, but it was a bun'le jes the same.

When Mose got to the depot, the checkroom was piled up to the ceilin' with bun'les, and the debbil had three-four of his imps a-helpin' him with the checkin'. Mose put down his bun'le, and a perlite lil imp put a check on it and handed Mose a stub.

"What fo' you gimme this check?" say Mose. "I don't want the bun'le back—no time, atall."

" 'Tain't you check," say the perlite lil imp. "It's somebody else's check. You see it's like this: Next Chusday all yo'all what's checked a bun'le of troubles comes back here with these checks and you gits somebody else's bun'le of troubles. Ever'one of you has been a-sayin' that you troubles was worser yit, so the Old Man he gonna let each'n of you trade and git somebody else's troubles."

"Well," say Mose. "I sho won't mind that. Mebbe I git some nice easy troubles like dander, or a good-lookin' wife, or too much money." And then he put out for home.

Long 'bout cain't-see time, when Mose was a-settin' on his porch, he got to thinkin' 'bout the propersition, and the more he think 'bout it the lessen he likes it. He 'members somethin' 'bout old Cunnel LeRoy, and some of the other folks, too. Seem like it jes warn't workin' out like he had thunk. By'n by he got down his hat and his walkin' stick and he went down to the depot to see how things was a-comin'. When he got there, first thing he heered was somebody laffin', and he looked 'round the corner of the pile of bun'les and there was the debbil and the imps a-laffin' fit to kill. Seem like they had jes heered the bestest joke anybody ever told.

"Now look here," say Mose to hisself. "When the debbil gits to laffin', somebody bound to git the worst of it. I ain't never heered of the Old Boy a-doin' anybody a favor yit lessen he gits the best of the deal."

So he went up to the debbil, perlite-like, and he say, "Mister Debbil, mebbe I make a mistook today. I left a big bunch of troubles with you, but I ain't so sure now that I wants to part with 'em. They bin with me so long I thinks that I's growed kinda fond of 'em. Wonder could I get 'em back 'thout nobody axin' me no questions?"

The debbil he open his mouf wide and laff. And when he laff it was worser as when he frowns. His eyes didn't have no whites in 'em and was all shiny like they bin polished. His funny skin was a-twitchin', and his tail was a-lashin' back'rds and for'rds.

"Br'r Mose," he say, 'tween laffs, "I's powerful sorry to tell you, but the check for you bun'le is in somebody else's hands now, and I don't see how you can git it back."

"Well, then," say Mose, "I won'er iffen you can show me what kinda lookin' bun'le this here check of mine calls for?"

"To be sho," say the Old Boy, and he looked at the check, and went 'round comparin' it with the checks on the bun'les.

"Here it is," he fin'ly say, and he holds up the lil bun'le of troubles of Cunnel LeRoy. "Looks like a mighty nice lil bun'le of troubles you gonna git Chusday, Br'r Mose. I congratulates you. Jes a lil bun'le of white folks troubles. That ought'n worry an old darkey like you."

When Mose see that bun'le he scairt most to death.

"Please, suh, Mister Debbil," he say, "please, suh, gimme my old bun'le of troubles back. That's it right over there by that lil green imp, in the box marked with the tripe. I bin a-thinkin' it over and my troubles ain't so bad. I kinda miss the ole cawns, and the rhumatiz, and the game tooth. By rights I owes the lan'lord, and the sto'keeper, and it wouldn't be right not to pay 'em. That yeller gal ain't gonna bother me no more, caze she's gittin' crazy 'bout somebody else. I kin take a firmer hand with the chillun, and I don't mind gittin' mule-kicked, or throwed by the plow, and I kinda misses the old woman's naggin' already. To tell the truf, I don't believe they was troubles after all—jes lil worries, and I misses 'em tubble. Won't you please to give 'em back, suh?"

The debbil he laff agin, and he laff and laff. And Mose begin to back off a lil way. Then the debbil look mad, and he say: "Take you bun'le of troubles, Br'r Mose," he say, "but don't you ever let me hear you fussin' 'bout 'em agin, or I'll give you some sho-nuff troubles."

Mose grab up his troubles and toss 'em up on his shoulder like they was no more'n a box of feathers. It didn't take no wheelbar to git 'em away from that depot.

Why didn't Mose take old Cunnel LeRoy's troubles when he had a chancet? I axes him that.

Mose say he see a coffin in that bun'le, and he 'members jes in time that the Cunnel's trouble was a lil old cancer of the stummick.

Toll 'em Heavy

Once, there was a miller who could "toll 'em heavy" or "toll 'em light" as he ground corn for rich farmers, ordinary farmers, and farmers who made barely enough to eat. As he ground the corn, the miller always carried on a conversation with the devil, who stood behind his shoulder, as to whether or not he should play fair with his customers.

One day, a little before noon, there drove up to the mill a very rich farmer with fifty wagon loads of corn. The miller began to grind.

And as he ground, he turned his head over his shoulder and said, "Devil, he's rich. Must I toll him heavy or toll him light?"

And the devil said to the miller, "He probably got rich being hard on the poor. Toll him heavy."

And the miller tolled him heavy.

Early that afternoon came to the mill just an ordinary farmer with ten wagon loads of corn. And the miller put the corn into the mill and began to grind.

And as he ground, he turned to the devil and said, "This fellow is not poor, he is not rich. How must I toll him, heavy or light?"

And the devil said, "Oh, he'll get along all right. Certainly he will not starve. He is contented with his lot. He is healthy. He is happy. Toll him heavy."

So the miller tolled him heavy.

A little before sundown came to the mill another farmer. He had one sack of corn on his back, about a bushel perhaps. He was tired from walking a long way. He was hungry. And the miller put his corn into the mill and began to grind it.

And as he ground, he turned once more to the devil and said,

"Devil, this fellow certainly is poor. He's tired. He's hungry. What must I do with him, toll him heavy or toll him light?"

And the devil answered, "He's poor, damn him, keep him poor! Toll him heavy."

And the miller tolled him heavy.

George C. Taylor

Superstitions About Faith

A woman who dreams she is in church listening to a preacher will marry one. The same is true if she dreams of white linen.

If you dream of a church, it means your enemies are about, or your habits need changing.

If a knife or a dishrag falls to the floor, the preacher is coming.

If you open the Bible after you have made a wish and you find the words "And it came to pass" under your finger, your wish will come true.

It's bad luck to place something on top of the Bible, or to lose one.

If you see a rainbow, say the Lord's Prayer and you'll have good fortune.

A star shooting in the sky means someone has died. If it shoots to the right, that person has gone to heaven; if it shoots to the left, he's gone to hell.

Don't do anything important on August 1. That is the day the devil was kicked out of heaven, and he always messes up people's plans on that day.

If someone burns food while cooking, he is feeding the devil.

A sudden silence in a room of talking people means an angel is passing through.

If a baby smiles while asleep, angels are talking to it.

The Reformation of Uncle Billy

"Lyin' is lyin', be it about fish or money," remarked the deacon dogmatically, "an' is forbid by Scripter, an' he can't be saved an' freed from sin till he does stop lyin'. That's all there is to it. Billy Matison's got to give up fish-lyin', or he won't never git into the kingdom."

"Well, I reckon you're right, deacon," said Ephraim; "but it ought to be some excuse for Billy that he don't harm no one by his lyin'. Seems to me a lie ain't rightly a lie unless it ketches somebody. Ef you lie about a hoss you're tradin', I'll admit that's wrong, 'cause you'd do the other feller dirt; but Billy's lyin' don't fool nobody, an' it don't cost nobody nothin'. An' then you'd ought to be easy on him, seein' how long he's been at it. Why, Billy Matison's been lyin' 'bout fish off an' on for nigh sixty-six year, an' reg'lar, summer an' winter, for the hull time, at that. Now I leave it to you, deacon; it ain't easy to break off short."

They were sitting in front of the grocery. All were gray-haired men nearing the end of their lives, and all were members of the First Church. So was Billy, but his one sin cast a doubt in the minds of his friends regarding his salvation. Billy did not worry in the least. His regular daily occupation was to fish from the bridge across the river, and there he would sit day after day, catching nothing, or at least very little. But in the evening, among his cronies before the grocery, he told marvelous tales of the fish he had almost landed, of the big bass he had caught; and when the fishing season ended, and the rendezvous was the stove in the grocery, all these tales were retold, while it was observed that they had grown strangely during their period of desuetude.

Billy was such a genial, whole-souled liar about his fish that no one had ever had the heart to suggest the improbability of his tales; but a revival had taken place in the village, and under the fervid words of the evangelist the old men had been brought to a full real-

ization of not only their own, but Billy's sins; and the deacon had
resolved that Billy must be saved in spite of himself.

"No," admitted the deacon; "it ain't easy to break off short, but
it's got to be done. Billy's got to be saved. We know his sin, ef he
don't, an' knowin' a sin an' not doin' our best to stop it 'mounts to
the same as ef it was our sin, an' I ain't goin' to everlastin' fire jest
because Billy Matison lies about the fish he don't ketch."

"That sentiment does you proud, deacon," said Hiram, a weak-
eyed old man with a thin white goatee; "you do yourself proud.
That's lovin' your neighbor *as* yourself."

The deacon felt the delicate flattery, and puffed his pipe in silence
a moment, lest he seem puffed up by the compliment.

"Billy Matison has got to be brung up short," he said, at length;
"he's gittin' old, an' no tellin' when he will drop off. He's got to be
cured now an' at once."

Ephraim had been thoughtfully pushing killikinick into his brier
with his thumb. He struck a match on his trousers and puffed the
tobacco into a glow.

The deacon opened his mouth again. "Billy Matison has—" he
said.

"It's a pity," said Ephraim, interrupting him, "we can't let him
break off gradual. When you come to think how long Billy has told
fish lies, it seems like the shock of quittin' right sudden might be too
much for him—might make him sick, or kill him, mebby. Now, if he
could sort o' taper off like—say, ketch one less fish a day for a week,
or drop off half an inch a day from the size—it might let him down
easy an' not try his constitution so bad."

"It *would* be easier on Billy," said Hiram.

The deacon thought deeply for a minute.

"Jest so," he said; "mebby it might strain him to give up *all* his
lyin' at one time, seein' he takes so much pride in it, an' mebby we
ought to be a *leetle* easy on him. Ef Billy Matison was a young feller
it would be best, but we can't risk his dyin' unsaved. No; we got to
git him to give it up right now. Now is the app'inted time."

"It'll be mortal hard on Billy, come winter," said Amos. "I 'low
Billy won't know how to spend the winter ef he can't lie some."

Hiram shook his head sadly.

"I doubt," he said, "ef Billy can live out the winter ef he don't lie. Fish-lyin' is got to be all he does winters."

The deacon had been thinking again, and did not catch this remark.

"There's one p'int we must be careful on," he said: "Billy's almighty touchy, an' we mustn't let on we think he's lyin'. You know how touchy he is, Hiram."

"Thasso," said Hiram. "We can't let on we think he's *lyin'*, he's so dum touchy. Ef we let on he was lyin', an' that we knew he was lyin', he'd go off mad an' never come nigh us."

"An' then we would have a harder job, a big sight, to cure him," said the deacon.

"But I don't see how we can git at him airy other way," said Amos, "for ef we *don't* let on we know he's lyin' we can't tell him not to lie no more."

"They 's jest one way to do it," said the deacon, "an' that's the way it's got to be did. We got to make him take back what he lies. Ef he lies an' says he caught a big one, we got to make him tell the truth, an' we got to do it gentle, an' not let on he's lyin'. We got to—"

Here the conversation paused, for around the livery-stable corner came Billy Matison, his fishing-pole slung over his shoulder, his bait and lunch-basket slung on the pole, and his cane in his hand. As he approached the group of old men, Billy did not appear a very energetic fisherman. His back was bent far forward, and his hand trembled as it held the pole. His cane was a necessity, and not an ornament. His wrinkled face was small, and appeared still smaller under the great home-made straw hat that rested on his long gray hair. He was an inoffensive, pale-eyed old man, and his toothless gums grasped a blackened clay pipe. Water stood in his eyes. Billy was seventy-eight, and "showed his age."

As he neared the group of old men, they arose. They were but little younger than Billy, and leaned on their canes for support. The straightest of them did not assume the perpendicular at once, but opened gradually from his stooping position, as if his joints had long had the rust of rheumatism.

Billy tottered up to them, unsuspicious of their plot for the safety of his soul. When he reached them, he tremblingly swung his pole and basket to the walk, and sank on the plank bench with a sigh of relief.

Then he took his pipe from his mouth, and holding it out in his shaking hand for emphasis, said in his wavering voice:

"Deacon, I ketched the biggest bass I ever see to-day. I'll warrant it goes four pound."

Amos glanced at Hiram with pity in his eyes. Of all Billy's lies this was the greatest. But the deacon seated himself beside the fisherman, and putting one hand on Billy's shoulder, said:

"Billy, you an' me has knowed each other forty years, an' in all them years we been good friends, ain't we?"

Billy turned slowly and gazed at the deacon. His lower jaw dropped weakly, as was its wont when he was surprised. Words failed him.

"Ain't we?" insisted the deacon.

Billy replaced his pipe between his lips, and said simply, "Yes."

"An' you recollect how I helped you when you was courtin' 'Manthy? You'd never 'a' got her but for me, Billy."

Billy's head shook a slow negative.

"An' how I lent you money to build a new house when yourn burned?"

Billy nodded. His eyes sought the faces of the group, but they were stern, and he could fathom nothing there.

"Billy," continued the deacon, "I'm goin' to ask a favor of you. It ain't much. Won't you say that mebby that bass only weighs three pounds an' a half?"

"Well, mebby it does," Billy admitted.

"Well, won't you say three pounds?"

"That bass—" began Billy, but the deacon interrupted him:

"For old friendship's sake, Billy. It's a special favor."

A few more lines gathered in Billy's brow, but he nodded.

"Billy," said the deacon, "you remember the night I brought your boy Jim home when he got lost? Can't you make it two pounds for that?"

Billy gazed doggedly at the plank walk. It was a hard struggle, but he nodded.

"You remember Gettysburg, Billy, an' how I carried you two mile? Can't you make it one pound for Gettysburg?"

Billy got up. He was trembling with something besides age now. It was anger.

"Deacon, you mean I'm lyin'—"

"No, Billy," said the deacon, soothingly; "I don't. Mebbe me an' Hiram's got a bet up. Gettysburg, Billy! Make it a pound for me an' Gettysburg."

Billy leaned on his stick with both hands.

"It's—a—pound," he said.

"An' now, Billy," said the deacon, laying his hand on Billy's arm, while the old men gathered closer about him, "you remember when your Mary Ann went—when she—she left home, an' you—when she visited us until you wanted her back? For that, Billy, won't you make it no fish at all? Won't you say you didn't ketch no fish at all to-day, Billy?"

Billy straightened up, and two large drops rolled from his eyes down the gutters of his cheeks.

"Deacon," he said, "I wouldn't do it for no one but you, but for you an' Mary Ann I didn't ketch no fish to-day."

For only one moment the deacon stood triumphant. Then each of the old men grasped Billy's hand firmly, and trudged away, leaving Billy alone, wrapped up in his thoughts. The deacon and Hiram went away together, and the deacon said, "Hiram, it's begun." That was enough.

And Billy! Half stunned, he stood gazing after them. He knew it all. He knew these old friends of his thought him a liar, and that they were trying to save him. Perhaps he should not have yielded, but the deacon had certainly been his best friend, and—

A known liar! A notorious liar!

He picked up his basket with a sigh and slipped it from the pole. Then he painfully mounted the two steps into the grocery.

"Billings," he said, as he placed the basket on the counter and raised the lid, "I ketched a big bass to-day; want you to weight it."

Billings took the fish from the basket and dropped it into the tin scoop, where it fell with a slap. He pushed the weight along until the beam swayed evenly.

"Four pound, two ounces," he said.

CHAPTER 7

Witches, Ghosts, and Strange Events

"The Tale of the Talking Eggs"

The religion of one generation is apt to become the superstition of the next.
—Sir James Fraser

THE WITCHES AND GHOSTS seem to have all gone. On Halloween, perhaps, we are reminded of them by the candy-laden impostors who drag their brooms or trail their sheets along the sidewalk, but the spells and the hauntings are no more. This is what the modern, sensible citizen says, anyway. We look with a detached disdain upon the witch trials of Salem, where innocent people were drowned or burned by their suspicious neighbors, and Cotton Mather's accounts of ghostly visitation read like colorful and quaint folklore. Superstitions, too, have lost their hold, and the idea that a corpse bled at the touch of a murderer, or that a cow went dry on the spell of a witch, has no power in an age of medical sophistication and pasteurized milk.

Yet America has always possessed a thriving and serious respect for the supernatural. The pioneer life, with cabins often separated by miles of dark wood, had its share of fear and misgivings. The tracks of an idly fleeing wild boar became the footprints of the devil, while the panther's cry sounded astonishingly like the scream of a woman. Strange lights and odd sounds, of which the wilderness was full, were transformed into chilling tales of the unexplained. And people being what they are, a mystery would attach itself permanently to a place. It is remarkable how local haunts and legends were derived from those first frontier frights.

The witch, of course, was a major figure in these matters. She had long ago established herself in many cultures, and she came to America from across the sea like so many others. Misfortune and disaster, so much a part of frontier life, could always be blamed on her mischief. The witch-masters, who could check a witch's spell, or even kill her (with a silver bullet), were in great demand and took their work very seriously. It was the witch-master who had the best chance of trapping a witch outside her skin, in the guise of a black cat (her favorite costume), and killing her before she could return to her original form.

As for ghosts, America was full of them. The dead remained restless and visible as long as some injustice or unresolved secret had to be settled. Every town and hamlet had their favorite (or their dreaded) spirit. The place where a person drowned or the house in which someone died was soon caught in a gathering mist of rumor. All it took was one reliable witness, swearing total sobriety, to say he saw someone known to be already dead and buried, and a ghost was born. Ghosts were rarely malevolent; it's just that most folks never waited around to see this fact proved. The ones who did often got unexpected results, like the woman in "The Miser's Gold."

However modern we might think we have become, the supernatural has a sure hold on our imagination. Wherever we pass an abandoned house or a graveyard at night, we feel the ripple along our spine. Hoodoo, the magic-conjuring brought by the black man to American life, will always count for something, as long as love, revenge, and desire are as elusive and mysterious as the human heart, while even the most cynical of us will hesitate to mock the sworn sincerity of one who has seen a ghost.

The following stories are examples of mystery and the macabre on the American landscape, and they are part of that ongoing process of storytelling that modern yarn-spinners like Stephen King still exploit. After all, we have not changed at all: we still don't understand the things that scare us, and stories of horror or mystery stay with us long after the lights have been turned off.

Granny Frone

I recollect 'specially a story my mammy used to tell me a long time ago. Yes, I guess I could tell it to you; here, just wait till I get this snuff out of my mouth. I never could talk with snuff in my mouth.

Now as I recollect it, old Uncle Ed Dodson and Aunt Cindy they lived away up yonder in the gap around back about 1880, I guess. Well, it seems as how witches had been pestering of them for a good long spell of time. First one of Ed's steers died, then the cows started in going dry and they couldn't make butter off the milk and that was a sure sign of witches working. Well, next one of Ed's dogs, one of his very best dogs, just laid down and died; and when that happened Ed flew plumb off the handle, my mammy said, and started raving around that he be damned—now that's the very words he used—he be damned if he would stand any more of it. Granny or no Granny, he would put an end to it.

You see, the witch was his own Granny, old Granny Frone that lived over across the hill from him. She got mad at Ed about something or other and that was her way of paying him back.

Well, Ed said damned if he cared whose Granny she was, her picture was going on a young black gum tree with a nail in the heart of it 'fore dark and that he was going to sink her up to the head. You know that was the way you doctored against a witch. You drawed a picture on a tree, put a cross where the heart ought to be and a nail in the heart. Then the witch would be taken ailing right away. Then you keep driving the nail on in and she would get worse and worse till by the time you got the nail driv up she would be dead. That is unless she could borrow something from them. You see, that way she could break the power of the doctoring.

But Ed was that mad he swore that the nail was going plumb up to the head and that nary drap nor grain or anything was she to get off his place. So when old Granny Frone took ailing and begun to send the boys first for some salt, then a little 'baccer, next some fire to kindle with, why nary a thing did she get; and Ed kept driving the nail in. Well, pretty soon he had it sunk nearly to the head and old Granny Frone was just about gone when Mammy said that Aunt

Cindy got to feeling sorry for her and begun to beg Ed to pull the nail out. Aunt Cindy told Mammy that it seemed just like plain murder to her and that all day she had had a terrible feeling that something awful was going to happen, especially after the old rooster came and stood in the door and crowed three times. But Ed, his mind was made up, and he was so sot on what he was doing that he couldn't be stopped.

Well, Mammy said that along towards dark Ed looked out the door and saw old Granny Frone coming down the ridge with her hand over her heart and her hair a-flying. "Lord have mercy on us, Ed," said Aunt Cindy, "yonder's Granny Frone coming here. A-coming to die on this place and leave her witch sperrit wandering around here to go into some of us." And with that Ed grabbed up the hammer and took off up the ridge to pull the nail out. But he was too late a-starting. Granny Frone just got inside the gate and was begging for water and hollering, "You've killed me, you've killed me."

About that time Aunt Cindy run to her with a gourd of water begging her to take it and drink from it, but just as she reached out her hand to take it, why instead of taking it she just threw up her hands and fell and muttered, "You killed me, Ed Dodson, you killed me! But I'm getting even with you now. My sperrit, my witch sperrit —I'm leaving it here, Ed Dodson, to plague you as long as you live." And with that she was gone.

Yes, that's what they say; her spirit went into Ed. He always did act quare [queer] after that, but he never did do anybody any harm that we ever heard of, yet he was afraid of the dark.

Old Ferro

Ye know Eph' Tucker, that used to live on the Hashion. Well he wuz allis counted a mighty truthful man and he used to tell me a sight o' tales about witches. He said when he lived down in Ashe there wuz a man named Ferro who shore could bewitch people. Eph said he wuz a talkin' with Ferro one day and Ferro told him there wuz a man lived clost him that had done him some mean tricks and he wuz a goin' to make that man see some trouble that night.

"Ax him in the mornin'," Ferro says, "and he'll tell ye that he's seed a heap o' trouble last night."

Well, Eph met the man next day and shore 'nough he told Eph he hadn't slep' a bit the night afore. Eph axed him what wuz the matter and he went on to tell about seein' a big thing like a bear a walkin' the jist [joist] over his bed all night; the man said he tried to shoot the thing but his gun wouldn't shoot, and he had to set there and watch that ole bear, or whatever it wuz, all night a walking on the jist backards and forrids right over his bed.

Well, after that Eph sayd he knowed ole Ferro shore wuz a witch and he decided he'd like to be a witch too, so's he could aggervate people that he didn't like. One day, he says to Ferro says he, "I want to learn to bewitch people like you can."

Ferro kindly agreed to show him how to be a witch. He says, "You come with me out in the road." They went out'n the wagon road and Ferro tuck a stick and made a ring in the dirt. "Now you git in that ring," says Ferro. Eph he got in the ring. "Now squat down," says Ferro. Eph he squatted down. "Now," says Ferro, "put one hand under yer right foot and t'other hand on top o' yer head." Well Eph put one hand under his foot and t'other on top of o' his head. "Now," says Ferro, "you say after me, 'Devil take me ring and all.' " Eph said he wuz a gittin' a little bit skeered by this time but he said what ole Ferro told him, "Devil take me ring and all," and about that time the ground begin to sink right under him. Eph says he felt hisself a goin' right down an' down. He shore wuz skeered by this time and he give a jump right out o' the ring and run from that place as hard as he could. He didn't turn his head to look back. After that Eph said he never tried to be a witch anymore.

The Hag of Plymouth

Not so solitary was Aunt Rachel, who once lived alone in a tumble-down fish house hanging over the waterfront near Duxbury, Massachusetts. An ancient, decrepit hag, bundled in whatever tatters she could pick up, her external appearance hid a woman with a keen eye for the sea and a canny knowledge of the seasons.

Her favorite diversion was wandering alone in the night—and the darker the night, the better. She would stumble along the rocky foreshore and "watch the flux of the sea" or penetrate far inland, wherever her feet led her—searching, searching. Searching for what? Who knows?

Most of the respectable natives avoided her, since she had a rough side to her tongue and made no bones about using it; but now and then a minister, a schoolmaster, or a physician would consult her before starting on a journey. It was among the fishermen, though, that she found her sworn allies. From her knowledge of the sea, the wind and the sky, she told them what the weather would be. They would ask her advice before launching their boats. Coming back, they left a choice fish before her hut, and let her help herself from the fish flakes where the salted catch was drying.

This hearty trust and friendship of the fishermen afforded the one bright spot in her drab and lonely existence. It was the anchor that gave stability to her living. No man who went down to the sea in ships from Plymouth ever failed her . . . Then one day the *Betsy,* a sugar boat from Boston, put into the harbor. Strange sailors landed. They thought to make sport of her and pretended to ask her advice. She sensed their insincerity and accused them of being "Moon Cursers"—men who set false beacons and wreck ships for plunder—such as had made her childless and a widow. She laid the poor man's curse on their boat and warned them not to sail on her. "May he who rides upon the pale horse be your guide," she concluded her prophecy. They further teased and harassed the old tatterdemalion, saying they'd "put a stopper in her gab," till her violent temper flared up, and she cursed the lot of them "from Hell to high water."

The next morning, in retaliation, one of the brutes set fire to her hut and the others rushed back to the boat shouting imprecations. At sight of the flames the whole town tumbled down to the waterfront—"every inhabitant but the infants and decrepit." They found Aunt Rachel mounted on a rock. She was wrapped in the remains of an old sail cloth. Her matted hair floated out like streamers upon the wind, her long, bony arms were extended in threatening gestures. She foamed at the mouth and "howled in the most distressing accents." Her eyes seemed starting out of their sockets. She leaned forward in an ecstasy of expectation as she watched the crew climb aboard, watched the anchor creep up the side, watched the sails ripple up the masts and belly in the breeze as the boat headed out to sea. When the brig passed Beach Point the old harridan's ravings increased. She lifted up her voice and laid a curse on them.

Surely enough, the boat struck a reef and sank. The cargo was lost and one man—the one who had fired her hut—was drowned. So enthralled was the populace by the sinking of the vessel that no one noticed Aunt Rachel pitch forward. When someone finally approached the bundle of rags on the rock, he discovered that the old woman was dead.

The town buried her on the spot where her hut had stood. For many years after that, the reef was known as Rachel's Curse.

Hoodoo

THE DARK MAGIC of hoodoo (or voodoo, as most of us know it) has its roots in the witch doctors and conjure chiefs of Africa, but it was not long after the arrival of the slaves in America that the powers of hoodoo were eagerly sought by men and women of all creeds and races. In the early nineteenth century, New Orleans became a city devoted to the subtle spell of hoodoo, and names like Doctor John (who could read minds) and Marie Leveau (the greatest and most feared of the hoodoo queens) lent New Orleans an aura of mystery and taboo. Even today, late at night in New Orleans, there are quiet places where the hoodoo queens wait to tell you how to get your lover back or how to drive an enemy crazy. Hoodoo is powerful, and it is conducted in absolute and ritual secrecy. As long as anyone searches for a magic path to love, revenge, or divination, the dice from a dead man's bones will roll and the snake skins will mix with the lizard's tongue to establish a sorcerer's power.

Below are some samples of hoodoo collected by Zora Neale Hurston; though they were collected in the southern United States, they take us back to another time and another continent.

TO STOP A MAN FROM WANDERING

Take a Barred Rock rooster, name him after the man, and tie him with a long rope to the fence and shorten it one foot every day, and feed him there. Start with a five-foot rope and shorten it to a yard. Feed the chicken three days there at one yard, and the man will never wander.

TO MAKE HUSBANDS STAY HOME

Take sugar and cinnamon and mix together. Write name of husband and wife nine times. Roll paper with names and put in a bottle of holy water with sugar and honey. Lay it under the back step.

TO HOLD A MAN

Take a piece out of the seat of his drawers, tie a ring to it (any ring) and put a fig leaf in the ring. Roll all this together, and carry it on you.

TO KEEP A PERSON ON THE JOB

Write name of boss three times and workman's name four times across it. Set a red light, pour honey around the candle, also spice. Then light the candle.

TO MAKE LOVE CHARMS

Take powdered angleworm dust mixed with love powder and ground John the Conqueror root. Place the above articles in a small bag with a string on each end of the bag so as to meet around the waist. This charm will make your lover or sweetheart come to you and stay.

TO BREAK UP A COUPLE

Write the name of one party eight times and the name of the other party once across the name of the other. Take the heart out of a red onion and put in the paper, together with red pepper and salt. Put the heart back into the onion and bury it upside down with the onion showing slightly above the ground.

TO MAKE SICK OR PUNISH AN ENEMY

Take a soiled undergarment of theirs, hang on a bare rafter, and get some hackberry switches and whip the garment. They will be so sore they can't get out of bed.

TO BREAK A FRIENDSHIP

Take three lemons and cut stem end off (squeeze some juice out). Write one name eight times one way on the paper and the other eight times across it. Roll it up and poke in the lemon, one in each lemon. Bury those lemons in the yard where the sun rises and sets on them. Every day at one o'clock pour one-half cup vinegar on the lemons. Those people will fight and part.

TO FIND OUT SECRET ENEMIES
(People Who Try to Trip You)

Take a new white plate. Make twenty-one marks on the inside and fifty on the bottom outside. Put the plate where no light don't shine. If there is an enemy laying wait to trip you, the plate turns dark. Make marks with very small brush and lampblack. (This is for bootleggers or anyone hiding from police.)

If you want to know if a man friend is coming back or wishes to send anything, take a white saucer and treat as the plate, and it will work on the mind and cause them to do what you want.

For a woman, you use a cup.

TO PROVE IF YOUR FRIEND HAS OR IS TRYING TO HARM YOU

Place a silver dime in your mouth, and if the dime turns black the supposed friend is an enemy to you; if the dime remains white, the friend is true and has not tried to hurt you.

TO OVERPOWER YOUR ENEMIES

Take thirteen nails—all different sizes. Place them all in a black bottle filled with well water. Write the names of your enemies thirteen times on separate pieces of paper and place them in the bottle. Bury the bottle upside down in front of the enemies' gate, under the steps or at the front gate.

PRAYER AGAINST ENEMIES

Recite three times: "O great, strong, and highest God! May it please thee to change the hearts of my enemies and opposers that they may do me good instead of evil, as thou didst in the day of Abraham when he called upon thee by this holy name. Amen." (While reciting the above prayer, you can burn Temple or Oriental Incense.)

TO MOVE NEIGHBORS

Write the name of the person you want to move eight times on paper. Put it in a dark bottle and add four tablespoons of vinegar, one tablespoon of whole black pepper, one guinea pepper, one cayenne pepper, and hang the bottle where the sun can rise and set on it. They will move quickly.

Sweep behind an undesirable roomer every time he goes out, or put hatred powder in the hatband and it will give him a wandering mind.

Take their shoe and throw it in the graveyard—an abandoned graveyard. They will wander about and no one will pay any attention to them.

TO KEEP A HOUSE EMPTY

a. Tie nine red peppers on a string and hang them up the chimney.
b. Nine ten-penny nails driven in sill of the door.

TO GET A PERSON OUT OF A HOUSE

For a woman: Take a flat onion. For a man: a sharp onion. Write the name five times on paper. Core the onion out and stuff paper in there and close it back with the cut-out onion, and when the party goes out, roll the onion behind him before anybody else crosses the door-sill. Make a wish at the same time.

TO CAUSE GENERAL MOVING

Take three pecans. Write the name of the person you want moved, around each pecan three times. Warm them over the fire and throw them against the house, and he will move even if he owns it.

TO KEEP A HOUSE VACANT

Take five cents Epsom salts, some well water, and shake it up with a pinch of cayenne pepper. Throw against the walls before you move, and no one will live in the house.

RUNNING FEET

To give anyone the running feet: Take sand out of one of his tracks and mix the sand with red pepper; throw some into a running stream of water, and this will cause the person to run from place to place until finally he runs himself to death.

The Tale of the Talking Eggs

Now, I kin learn a chile to be good an' I've set a pile of 'em on de right road by tellin' a story I know 'bout two little sisters I done growed up wid. One was named L'il Tater, 'cause folks say she

looked like one when she come into de world, an' t'other was called
Blossom, 'cause her mama loved her so an' she was born in de
spring. Now, Tater's mama didn't treat her right and was always
hollerin' at her. Folks say it was 'cause she weren't as perty as Blossom, but dat L'il Tater was de sweetest chile you could ever hope to
meet. Blossom was surely differ'nt in every way, mean and spiteful,
an' she was always throwin' stones at folks or laughin' at dere
misfo'tunes. Dere mama seemed as blind to Blossom's mischief as
she was to Tater's sweetness. Some mamas is like dat.

One day Tater was told to take de bucket an' go to de well fo'
some water, even dough dat bucket was heavy an' hard to hold. So
Tater dragged de bucket to de well, singin' to herse'f an' countin' de
clouds in de sky, when suddenly she heard a voice from de woods
call out, "Baby, kin you give an ol' woman a sip o' dat water? My
mouf's dry an' hot, an' I ain't got no well." Tater, bein' sweet an'
good, said, "Yes'm, come hea an' I'll give you some o' my water."
An' de voice said, "Thank you, baby, I'm hea."

But Tater didn't see nothin'. She just felt a cool breeze blowin' on
her legs. Den she turned an' saw an' ol' woman standin' by de well.
She musta been a hunnert years ol', wid a shawl pulled up over her
head. De woman came up an' sipped from dat bucket fer de longest
time, den she said, "Bless you, chile, you's a good girl. God is gonna
bless you." An' den she left.

Now, Tater went home wid de bucket o' water an' t'ought no more
'bout de ol' woman. Doin' good things was nat'ral to Tater. As
usual, Tater's mama kept on actin' as if Tater couldn't do no right.
She beat Tater 'round de ears an' Blossom done all kinds of meanness to po' Tater when no one was watchin'. So, one day, Tater ran
off into de woods an' commenced to cryin' an' rubbin' her face wid
her tiny hands. She was so unhappy she didn't see no clouds an'
couldn't even sing no songs.

Just den, Tater heard a voice say, "Don't be cryin', chile. You
come over hea to me." Tater knew right off it was dat ol' woman's
voice even befo' she felt de cool wind on her legs. Sure 'nough, dere
was dat ol' woman standin' by a tree. She came an' took Tater's hand
an' said, "You come wid me awhile." De two walked into a brambly
bush dat opened up fer 'em like it knew dey was comin'. Tater never

told nobody where dis was, but dere are some mighty big brambly bushes back of Swift Creek, so maybe it was dere. When dey walked through dem bushes, de first thing Tater saw was two sharp huntin' knives fightin' wid each other. Tater reckoned it was a strange sight, but she didn't say nothin' fer fear of insultin' de ol' woman. As dey passed, de knives stopped fightin' an' dropped to de ground, de blades stickin' in de grass.

A little further on, de ol' woman led Tater past two arms who were fightin' like de knives. Dis was an even stranger sight, but still she kept her tongue in her head. As dey passed, de arms stopped an' shook hands wid each other. Still further on, dey came upon two heads shoutin' at each other. Dis was de strangest sight of all, an' Tater wanted to hush 'em both, but she was too polite. As dey passed, de heads stopped shoutin' and began to smile. Dey both said in a soft voice to Tater, "Bless you, chile." Tater smiled back an' followed de woman to her cabin.

Once inside de ol' woman's cabin, Tater was told to make a fire. As she was puttin' de kindlin' on, Tater looked over to see de ol' woman take her own head off, plop it like a punkin in her lap, an' commence to brushin' her hair. Tater knew she shouldn't stare none, so she made de fire. Den de ol' woman gave her a bone an' tol' her to put it in de pot fo' dinner. Dat bone made Tater sad, 'cause it had no meat on it an' she was so hungry, but also 'cause dis ol' woman didn't have nothin' to eat neither. But once she put de bone in de pot, Tater smelled somethin' rich and good like meat an' dat ol' pot was bubblin' wid a pow'ful good stew. Dis was surely a strange place.

Den de ol' woman stood up an' complained dat her back itched an' she asked Tater to scratch it fo' her. When Tater did dat, she pulled her hand away and it was all bloody 'cause dat ol' woman's back was like broken glass. Tater tried not to cry but she did a little. De ol' woman quickly blew on her hand an' it was smooth an' good as new.

Tater slept dat night as deep an' peaceful as a baby. De next mo'nin', de ol' woman told Tater to go home an' t'ings would be better. She said, "You is a good girl. You go to de chicken house an' go inside. All de eggs dat are cryin' out, 'Take me! Take me!' well, you take 'em. But if you hea some of de eggs cryin', 'Don't take me!

Don't take me!' well, you let 'em be. Den you start on home an' throw dem eggs one after de next over yo' shoulder." So Tater said good-bye to de ol' woman an' thanked her fo' everythin' an' went to de chicken house. She did as she was told, an' den, wid one last wave to de ol' woman, she walked home. On de way, she tossed de eggs, an' Lawd a'mighty, each time one of dem eggs broke, a most wondrous t'ing spilled out. Dere was gold an' silver an' perty clothes. Dere was even a fine bay horse dat scooped Tater up an' carried her all de way back.

When she got home wid all dese treasures, Tater got shouted at by her mama. "Where did you git all dese things? You tell me, chile!" Tater told her mama, an' all de while, her mama was t'inkin'. When Tater finished, her mama called for Blossom. "Go find dat ol' woman as quick as you kin an' get mo' of dem eggs!"

Blossom went into de woods an' she found de ol' woman an' asked if she could come home wid her. De ol' woman led her into de brambly bushes and past de fightin' knives. Blossom saw dem knives an' laughed at dem. She done de same wid de arms, laughin' an' pointin' her finger an' sayin', "Ain't dat de stupidest thing in de world?" An' when dey passed de heads shoutin' at each other, Blossom rolled on de ground an' laughed fit to bust. "Dis is surely a stupid place," she said to de ol' woman, as de heads went on shoutin'.

Once dey was at de cabin, Blossom waited for de ol' woman to take her head off to brush her hair. Blossom grabbed dat head quick as a lick an' said, "Now, I ain't givin' your head back till you give me all de things you done gave my sister." De ol' woman said, "You is a bad girl an' God'll punish you, but I got to have my body back, so I'll tell you what to do." De ol' woman explained 'bout de eggs, an' to be sure de ol' woman wasn't playin' a trick, Blossom set her head out on de porch while de po' woman's body was gropin' all over de cabin. Inside de chicken house all de eggs was cryin' out, "Take me! Don't take me! Take me! Don't take me!" an' Blossom couldn't hea which was sayin' what, so she just collected 'em all an' ran fo' home.

On de way home, Blossom just started to toss dem eggs on de ground, an' instead of gold an' silver dem eggs was full of snakes an' frogs an' tiny whips dat lashed de air an' snapped at her head. An' instead of a fine horse dat carried her home, Blossom got an old wolf dat chased her through de woods an' all de way to her mama's cabin. Dat wolf an' all his wicked friends chased Blossom an' her mama right out o' dat cabin, an' is surely chasin' dem yet.

Tater, who had gone to de well, came home to a clean an' empty house wid de horse grazin' out front. She's been livin' in dat house ever since, ridin' dat horse, an' givin' children from all 'round de pertiest little pieces of gold an' silver. Most folks call her Louise now, an' you know, she's still as sweet as she can be.

The Black Cats Are Talking

The ole man was a woodcutter. One evenin', as he was comin' home from his work, he saw a passel o' black cats out in the road. He looked to see what they was doin', an' there was nine black cats totin' a little dead cat on a stretcher. He thought, "Well, I never heard o' such a thing as this: nine black cats totin' a little dead cat on a stretcher."

Jes' then, one o' them cats called out to the ole man an' says, "Say, mistuh, please tell Aunt Kan that Polly Grundy's daid."

The ole man nevah answered 'em; he jes' walked on a little faster; but he thought, "Um-m-m! If this ain't the beatin'est thing, them cats a-tellin' me to tell Aunt Kan that Polly Grundy's daid." Who is Aunt Kan? I wonder; an' who is Polly Grundy?

Well, he jes' walked on, an' presently one of 'em hollered ag'in an' say, "Say, ole man, please tell Aunt Kan Polly Grundy's daid."

He jes' walked on ag'in, gittin' a little faster all the time; an' presently all of 'em squall out: "Hey there, ole man, please, suh, tell Aunt Kan Polly Grundy's daid."

Then the ole man he broke into a run, an' he nevah stopped till he got to his house. He thought he wouldn' tell his ole woman nothin' about it. But that night he was settin' befo' de fire eatin' his suppah— ole folks lots o' times eats their suppah befo' de fire—an' while his wife was a-settin' it fo' 'im, he say, "Well, Ole Woman, I guess I'll tell you some'n' dat I didn' think I would tell you."

When he say that, the ole yellow cat got up f'om de corner wheres she was a-layin', an' come ovah an' set down right by his chair, a-lookin' up at 'im.

His ole woman say, "Well, what is it, Ole Man? I knowed they was some'n' on yo' mind when you come in at dat door."

He say, "Well, when I was comin' in from de woods dis evenin', walkin' down de road, right there in de road I seen a whole passel o' black cats. When I went ovah an' looked, there was nine black cats a-totin' a little daid cat on a stretcher; an' them cats squall out to me three different times an' tell me to tell Aunt Kan that Polly Grundy's daid."

When he say that, ole yellow cat jumped up an' say, "Is she? B'God, I mus' go to the buryin'! An' out that door she flew, an' she ain' nevah come back yet!"

The Sick Man's Ghost

Father told me this story. This experience, and another one he had, had a great influence on his life.

Father was in the Civil War. He was pretty young when he joined the army. He fell in with tough companions, and soon he became pretty rough. The men were infidels, and they made a convert of Father.

After the war, Father worked for an old gentleman named Jonathan Froman. Everybody called him Uncle Jonathan. Uncle Jonathan was a fairly wealthy man and pretty widely read.

One time, church was going on in the settlement a little way from Uncle Jonathan's. One night, during the meeting a frolic was held in the same settlement. Father decided to go to the dance instead of going to church. On his way to the dance, he had to pass a farm where an old gentleman was bad sick. This old man had a son about Father's age.

On passing the farm of the sick man, coming from the dance, Father saw a fellow walking down through the field. Father thought it was the old man's son, and he slowed down. He thought the son had been to church, and Father thought he would ask what had happened at church and who was there, like a young fellow will. But just before the son got in speaking distance to him, that fellow turned a little to one side and went over a fence, and he didn't climb or jump the fence. It just seemed that he walked down, raised up in air as he was walking, crossed over the fence, and sank down to the ground on the other side.

Some cattle were grazing along there. They became very much excited and came running down to where Father was. Father turned his eyes to the cattle for a moment, and when he looked back, he couldn't see the man any more. The cattle ran on down on the inside of the fence near Father. It seemed that they wanted companionship. They weren't afraid of Father, but they were afraid of the apparition.

Father said that he talked to old Uncle Jonathan Froman about what he'd seen. Uncle Jonathan said that he had seen the sick man's spirit. "He'll die," said Uncle Jonathan, "and you'll see it." Uncle Jonathan's belief in ghosts was that you can see a man's spirit before he dies but never after. On death the spirit leaves this world never to return.

Sure enough, Father said, the fellow died in the course of about a week.

Father talked about it as long as he lived. It kind of had a bearing on his infidelity. It proved to him that man had a spirit apart from the body. It was no hallucination of Father's. Father wasn't even frightened. He just thought that the man's son was walking down to meet him to tell him something. If Father had seen it alone, he might have thought it was a hallucination, but the cattle saw it too.

He didn't see it again, and the cattle didn't either, for they turned their heads and looked.

The Miser's Gold

In the early days of Pope County there were log cabins scattered here and there over the country, the homes usually of pioneer families. People migrating from Kentucky and Tennessee, however, usually had a hard time finding shelter at night, for, as a rule, the early settler had about as many children as his cabin would hold.

Down in the Gooseneck (which is the name usually given to the southern part of Pope County) there was a deserted log cabin that would have been a blessing to travelers if it hadn't been haunted. A man who had had a lot of money had lived there at one time. The robbers had visited his house one night and killed him. Since then a ghost had haunted the place, and none of the people in the neighborhood would come near it after dark.

One evening a family migrating from Kentucky stopped at the old deserted cabin to spend the night. With wolves and panthers still plentiful enough, most people felt safer behind barred doors. The log cabin offered ample protection; in fact, it was one of the best cabins in the neighborhood, even having a cellar underneath. The children gathered wood and the mother started a fire in the fireplace, while the father took a bucket and went up the road to the next house for water, since the water at the deserted cabin wasn't fit for use.

It was about a mile to the next cabin. When he got there, he was told that the cabin he had stopped at was haunted, or "hainted" as folks said, and that no one could stay there. They told him such awful stories that he was afraid to return. It was beginning to grow dark—which made things look more frightful still. After much debate and hesitation, he decided to spend the night with these people and leave his family to its fate.

His wife, being a devout Christian, got out a candle and lighted it and opened her Bible, which she read every night, and began reading while she waited for her husband to return with the water. But he didn't return.

After a while, when it grew dark, she heard someone walking up to the door, but she supposed it was her husband and thought no more of it, until a strange man walked into the room. He walked slowly and deliberately up to her without a word and didn't stop till he was directly in front. Now, the woman was braver than her husband; being a devout Christian, she put her trust in the Lord. She spoke up and said, "What in the name of the Lord do you want?" Old folks say for one to ask a ghost, "What in the name of the Lord do you want?" Then the ghost will tell you and not return again.

The ghost said, "Follow me."

She took up her candle and her Bible and followed the ghost, trusting in the Lord. He led her down a flight of stairs into the cellar and said, pointing toward the northwest corner, "Dig down there and you will find a pot of gold." After saying that he vanished and was never seen again.

The next morning the husband returned and they dug up the pot of gold, and they were well provided for after that.

They claim that the ghost had haunted the house, trying to tell someone about the pot of gold, but no one had been brave enough to listen to it before the woman.

The Ghostbuster

"There sure is plenty of treasure buried in Louisiana, but you gotta be careful of them spirits. They do some funny things. I knew one real well what would come to my house all the time. He would get behind a door and milk a towel, and all the cows in the neighborhood would go dry."

That is the warning of Gaston la Cocq, who has spent years searching for buried wealth. But Gaston knows how to handle these guardian phantoms.

"You have to take a spirit controller with you," he says. "And you have to be a mixed crowd; some white and some colored. You see, when your controller talks to the ghost that thing's gonna say if white or colored men should dig, and it means one or the other has to do all the work. That's the way it goes.

"All buried treasure has got spirits watching over it. Like Lafitte. You know how he used to do? He would take five or six men along to hide his stuff, and he would tell them all but one who he was gonna have kilt. The one he picked was the one what would be the spirit to watch his treasure forever. After they buried all the gold and silver and jools, Lafitte would say very quiet, 'Now, who's gonna guard my stuff?' and the man who didn't know no better would want to shine with his boss and he'd say, 'I will.' Then he would get kilt. Of course, Lafitte didn't shoot him, himself. He was the general and he always stayed in the back. You know how generals don't never get near to where the shooting is at."

Gaston's spirit controller is named Tom Pimpton, and he's a colored man. He has been hunting for treasure for years too and is one of the best controllers in the state. Practically all his knowledge, you see, has come from the *Book of Hoyle,* the *Book of Moses, Little Albert,* and the *Long-Lost Friend.* He purchased these mystic volumes from a Sears Roebuck catalogue, and he considers them priceless, for you can hardly buy them nowadays. Tom devotes himself exclusively to the supernatural angle of the treasure-hunting business.

"I just masters them spirits," he says, "I don't dig; anybody can do that. I just fights the spirits. There ain't none of 'em can mess with me.

"There's land spirits and there's water spirits, and you gotta know how to talk to both kinds. The land spirits is bad and the water spirits is good. They got seven kinds of land spirits; that's part of the trouble. There is bulls, lions, dogs, babies, snakes, persons, and pearls. When you see a cat, that's a bad one and if you ain't careful your hole's gonna lap up water right as you dig.

"You gotta be careful and you gotta be clean. You gotta suffer, too. The man's gotta suffer and the woman's gotta suffer. You sure can't touch no woman, not even your wife, for four days 'fore you start out.

"If something is wrong, you knows it right away. You can't ever fool a spirit. Your treasure is sure to start sinking and slipping, and once it sinks it ain't coming up again for seven years. Last time I was out, you know, a fool man done gone and forgot and left his Buzz tobacco in his pocket? You can't be careless like that and 'spect to find treasure.

"Sometimes when your treasure slips, you can tie it up, but you gotta use white silk thread. Ain't nothing else gonna hold it.

"When you go out, you use your divining rod or a finding machine until you knows where the treasure is at. Then you drives sticks in the ground in a circle and stretches a clothesline around it. Never use no wire! Your ring's gotta be thirteen feets to the east, thirteen feets to the south, thirteen feets to the west and thirteen feets to the north. You leaves a gate in the east side for your men to come through, then you closes it up. Once your mens get inside that ring, nobody can't talk, nobody can't swear, nobody can't spit. And don't let nobody throw dirt outside that ring, 'cause that brings bad spirits.

"Soon as I gets my mens in the ring I 'noints them on the forehead with special Delivery Oil. That oil's expensive; it costs me five dollars an ounce. You see, I won't mess with none of them cheap oils that has been 'dulterated.

"After everybody been 'nointed, I reads the Twenty-Third Psalm, with them all joining hands and repeating the words after me. Then I reads the Ninety-First Psalm to myself. Next I gotta read page 87 and page 53 from the *Book of Moses.* Page 53 has got the Master's Seal on it and you gotta know that by heart.

"Sometimes I takes liquor along when I go out. Some spirits likes liquor. They is call the drunken spirits.

"I done dug up plenty of treasure in my time. I just made up my budget the other day and I needs $40,000. I'll get it easy. Shucks, that ain't no money. Me and a friend of mine dug up $65,000 apiece over in Gretna one day. Had a big snake standing straight up in the air over it; he was tall as me and big enough around to hug. I just walked up and talked to it like it was a baby, and it crawled away. Underneath we found a great big mess of gold.

"The best treasure I ever found was a diamond the size of a brick out of the *banquette.* It was wrapped in kidskin and had Lafitte's name carved in it. It was worth about $1,500,000, and it was setting in a kettle of $5,000,000 worth of gold coins. I spent all that on my wife when she was sick and I just saved enough out of it to marry this here wife I got now.

"It's an easy way to get money, but you sure gotta be careful. When you is digging, funny things happen. Trees begin to fall, and fences come tumbling down, and the whole earth shakes and makes a loud rumbling sound. Spirits don't never like to give up their treasure."

Supernatural Superstitions

When two people of the same name live in a house, ghosts stay away.

Ghosts hate new things. If you have a persistent ghost, hang something new over your door.

Say, "What in God's name do you want?" when you first see a ghost, and you will know no fear.

A baby born near midnight will have the ability to see ghosts.

A ghost will come and knock on your wall when someone in the house is going to die.

Never strike at a ghost; never get mad at it. You will have very bad luck and the ghost will resent you and plague you for it.

Ghosts enjoy people singing and will listen.

Graveyards at night are lucky places if you stay quiet. Talk and you will be haunted for a week.

Christmas Eve is the favored time for ghosts to walk on earth.

When horses and other animals start acting strange, it's because they see a ghost. Horses that snort at night are seeing a ghost.

Always settle an argument before you sleep, or ghosts will come and bother you.

If someone sees a ghost, look over their left shoulder and you'll see the ghost. If you snip the hair off someone who is dreaming and put it under your pillow, you will have the same dreams.

Death Superstitions

Never carry an ax into the house; it means death.

Only carry a hoe through the same door of your house that you brought it in, or someone in the house will die.

If you miss a row while planting, or hear a crowing hen or rooster after dark, or see the wind blow out a candle, these things mean death.

Beware the sight of a white horse, a little white dog, or a lone white goose.

If an owl comes into your room and sits at the foot of your bed, it's as if an angel is sitting at your bedside, and it means that whoever lies in that bed shall die.

If three people look into a mirror at the same time, the youngest of the three will die.

Never let a swing stop on its own. Stop it yourself or someone close to you will die.

If a bird flies into your house, it's an omen of death.

After someone dies, their picture will begin to fade.

Beware the queen of spades, the death card.

If a dog howls while looking at the ground, it's because he senses that death is very near.

The Mystery Star

Mr. Davidson had moved from his farm in Kentucky and settled near the inland village of Columbus. He owned a large farm of the finest land in the entire community. His acres were tended by numerous slaves, who loved their master. He was never harsh to them, and they exerted every effort to please their master whether in tending stock, sowing or planting grain, or reaping the harvest. Mr. Davidson and his family were good neighbors and friends to everyone in the community. Everyone said that he was doing well as year after year evidences of prosperity crept forth on the Davidson farm.

One evening after the evening chores were done and the slaves had sung their songs in front of their cabin doors and gone to bed, the family was startled by a strange, bright star that seemed to hang suspended in the sky. No one had ever seen the star before, and everyone was curious about its strange appearance. The family soon retired and forgot the presence of the strange star.

The family went about their daily work the next day without any reference to the strange heavenly visitor of the night before. But the next evening while Mr. Davidson and his family were seated at a late-evening meal, the queer phenomenon appeared again. The younger members of the family reveled in its brilliancy and hoped it would always appear thus. The star seemed to be nearer than the night before.

Night after night the star appeared, growing brighter and brighter each evening. Its presence was no longer ignored during the day, and many references were made to its appearance and brilliancy during the day's conversation.

Everyone except Mr. Davidson talked much of its presence. At first he appeared to have little interest in the children's references to the star, but later could be noticed paying utmost attention whenever it was referred to. But never a comment from him.

Finally, the star's proximity to the little farmhouse changed interest into fear. The children stayed closely indoors and scarcely ventured a look toward the bright light that shone as brightly as the noonday sun. Moans and prayers could be heard coming from the slave quarters. The older folk were silent. Mr. Davidson went about his day's work silently and gloomily. He was nervous and fidgety. His wife, a modest, timid, little woman, now scarcely spoke a word while he was around.

One evening the star seemed to be closer than ever. It seemed to hang between the old log barn and the straw-covered shed, near the lower end of the barn-lot that served as a cowshed. The moans and prayers from the slave quarters had changed to screams of terror. Something must be done. Mr. Davidson called his wife and children to him, and kissed each one of them. Then, putting on his coat and boots, he bade them remain indoors while he went out to investigate.

In a few moments he returned pale and haggard. His eyes seemed to stare straight ahead without seeing. He made no answer to the numerous questions asked but went directly to bed. The children, glancing timidly out the windows, failed to see the bright light of the star.

Next morning, after the family had eaten their breakfast in silence, Mr. Davidson called all of his slaves around him and presented each with a written statement signed by himself giving them their freedom.

No one has ever seen the strange star again, nor has anyone ever known what Mr. Davidson saw when he went forth that night to meet his great adventure with the Mystery Star.

The Seven-Year Light on Bone Hill

Bone Hill is located just south of Levasy, Missouri. Its graceful sides slope gently toward the Missouri River bottoms, and from its tall summit one can view the valley for miles around. Why this hill, by far the tallest and most outstanding of any in that community, should be called Bone Hill no one knows exactly. Legend has it that during the early times, before the country was settled, the Indians slaughtered hundreds of buffalo on top of the hill and, after taking what meat and skins they wanted, departed, leaving the carcasses to decay and the bones to bleach in the sun. Years later, pioneers in wagon trains, while making their leisurely way across the plains were surprised to see a tall hill that appeared to be snow-capped. Its summit glittered in the rays of the summer sun as though capped with snow or frost. But they knew that this could not be, for the hill was not high enough to be crowned with snow in midsummer. On closer investigation it was found that thousands of buffalo skeletons were bleaching on its top, and it was their whiteness that reflected the rays of sunshine.

Near the foot of Bone Hill is an old-fashioned stone wall. Crumbling in places, this line of stone still serves its original purpose, that of dividing fields. It also serves as a hiding place for vermin and snakes. Its age is not known exactly. It was built sometime before the Civil War, when slavery was permissible. Human labor was cheap and stone was plentiful.

A legend has grown up about this old stone wall at the base of Bone Hill. During the Civil War, people in this community were harassed by marauders who would rush across the river from Kansas and plunder and rob a few homes and then dash back across the river to safety. At the base of the hill lived a peace-loving farmer who had labored hard and saved his earnings. He converted as much of his property as he could into gold. Bushwhackers learned of his wealth or at least imagined he had much gold hidden on his farm. They made frequent raids but were always unsuccessful. The farmer had torn down a small section of the stone wall, dug deep into the ground, and buried his wealth. He then rebuilt the fence. Time soon erased all evidence of the fence having been tampered with. The family was so harassed and tormented by raiders that they finally moved away and left their gold buried under the fence. They were afraid to move it with them for fear of being robbed. They said that they would return for the gold in seven years if the war was over in that time. But not long after, tragedy overtook the family and they were all killed. With their death, the secret of the hiding place of the gold passed out of existence.

Since the death of the entire family, no one has ever discovered the hidden gold. But it is said that every seventh year at a certain time of day a large flame can be seen along the old stone wall. The flame generally appears at nighttime. It burns for a while and then disappears. Many searchers have looked along the old wall for evidence of the flame having burned the vegetation, but thus far no one has ever found anything burned. If anyone approaches the flame it disappears and does not show up again. Residents have timed the flame and it is said that it appears regularly at a certain time every seven years. At no other time is the flame seen. It is presumed that the departed spirit is looking after the safekeeping of the wealth that he never got to enjoy. People of that community often mention The Seven-Year Light on Bone Hill.

The Death-Watch Tick

A miner was buried alive by a pillar of coal which he was robbing. After his body was dug out, it was discovered that his watch was still in the mine. It was not hanging on a timber in the heading, where he usually kept it, but was buried in the gob, where it ticked away unseen.

It soon gave evidence of being the most amazing timepiece. Its chief function seemed to be to forecast the approach of death, and so uncannily accurate was it that miners feared it more than the devil. It flitted all through the mine, going from one working place to another and inflicting itself upon this miner or that, depending upon whom fate had marked for death. No one could learn in advance where or when it would appear. Always it announced its arrival by ticking. The ticking was slightly louder than that of an ordinary watch but marked by the same relentlessness. There was no use trying to smash it with one's pick, or to blow it up with a stick of dynamite. Sooner could one smash or blow up one's shadow. The death watch eluded all measures of force and merely mocked men's curses. It was as inevitable as death itself. There were stretches of weeks or months when it kept silent. Then, with the suddenness of a fall of top rock, there would come the fateful tick-tock . . .

One night, while on his accustomed tour of inspection, the fire boss was astounded to hear the death-watch tick. It sounded so weird and awesome in that empty mine! There were fear and pity in his heart for Jim Kelly, in whose working place the watch was ticking.

When morning came, the fire boss was in his station along the gangway and waved Jim aside when he came up for his brass check.

"In the name of God, Jim, go back home," he said.

"What's the matter?" asked Jim.

"Now, in the name of God, do as I tell ye. You'll be thankful to me later on."

But Jim, with seven hungry little mouths to feed, could not afford to miss a day, and for that reason insisted on knowing why he was being called off.

"Well, if I must tell ye, Jim, I heard the—the death-watch tick in your heading last night as plain as ever I heard anything. Don't go in there or it's kilt you'll be."

"The death-watch tick!"

Jim turned deathly pale. The dinner pail trembled in his hand. He turned back.

Now, there was gratitude in Jim's heart for being spared the fate, as he thought, of so many of his fellow miners, and he knew of no better way to celebrate his defeat of the death-watch tick than by attending church. Looking at his watch he found that he could still make the eight o'clock mass and so hurried home to change his clothes. To reach the church from his home he had to go over a railroad grade crossing. When he got there he found the gates down. Rather than wait and take a chance of missing the mass, he ran across the tracks. But he was not fast enough. The 7:55 flyer mowed him down.

Fiddler's Dram

Talk about your fiddlers—why, in yonder's times we *had* fiddlers around here! None of your modern-age make-shifters that whip all the tunes till a body can't tell "Rabbit in the Pea Patch" from "Bull Amongst the Yearlings." Nor in them days they didn't make the fiddle sound like a jug full of hungry mosquitoes, neither! No siree! They just made the sweetest music this direction from heaven.

And in all yonder time I verily know there never was a finer hand to fiddle than Ples Haslock. He fiddled for all the square dances and play-parties anywheres around. No gathering of whatever kind amounted to much unless Ples was there, with his long, solemn face and them light blue far-shot eyes, patting his foot and ripping away on his fiddle and calling the figgers.

"Gents, hands in your pockets, back to the wall,
Take a chaw tobaccer and balance all!
Ladies, do-se-do with the gents you know,
Swing your corner and-a here we go!"

He wasn't no old billygoat fiddler with crazy ways and a cracked voice. He was right young and by nature handsome. All the girls sighed, but Ples just didn't deal in women. He said, "Give me my fiddle and a place to pat my foot and they's nothing else in creation I crave." His daddy had got an old fiddlebox in a bunch of junk he'd traded from an Irish Gypsy for a nag, is how Ples got started fiddling. He made his own strings out of catamount guts and the bow from the tail hairs of mare colts. Then he teached his self to fiddle till he laid it plumb over any of the old heads.

Since his daddy died, Ples lived at home by his self over near Post Oak, but he was a man that just didn't stay home much. He liked to ramble and visit around. Wheresoever he went, he was twice as welcome as anybody. He had word of all the latest things and happenings and he could keep a family spell-charmed to the midwarp of the night telling tales he made out of his head. He'd made the young'uns elder-shoot flutes and cornstalk fiddles, and, when asked to, he'd get out his own old fiddle and make it talk—I *mean* talk! You'd sweared to hear it that there was a live mockingbird singing in that fiddlebox or a buzzing cowfly or maybe a little peeping chicken. He could take and mock cats fighting or old gossip women gabbing till folks fell on the floor laughing. And he could fiddle the old tunes to where the meanest man in the county would break under and cry all down his face.

Nothing was too good for Ples Haslock when he visited around. He was welcomed by high and low as long as he wanted to stay, and they begged him to stop longer when he fancied to go.

They had fiddling contests then, but it got so there wasn't a heap of contest to them. Everybody come to know that Ples Haslock was going to win hands down. He always walked off with the gallon jimmyjohn of fine oak-chartered drinking whiskey they give for the prize. Why, it come to the point where they had to give another jug for second prize or they'd never had nobody in the contest but Ples. The other fiddlers only tried to outbeat each other. None of them had any show at all against Ples and they purely all knowed it.

So what happened one time but the wall of the jail at Dukedom fell out and the county court didn't have no money in the poke to fix it. When the squires figgered to get up a fiddling contest to raise the money, everybody says, "We'll have to send over to Post Oak and tell Ples Haslock and notify him."

Coot Kersey was the best fiddler near and around Dukedom, and Coot says, "He may can't come this time. I hear he's a sick man. Down with heart dropsy is what I hear."

"Don't you *hope* so, Coot?" they says, and laughed him to a fair deadstand.

The County Court Clerk says, "I've got to drive my rig over to Post Oak on business tomorrow. I'll tell Ples and notify him."

So the County Court Clerk dropped his hitching block in front of Ples Haslock's the next day and called, "Heyo! You to home, Ples?"

Nobody answered him, so he walked through the weeds to the house, a one-room shack that looked like a good strong puff of air would blow it over. The clapboards was dropping off and the shingles curled up every which way like the feathers of an old Dominecker hen.

When the County Court Clerk climbed the shaky steps to the porch, Ples woke up inside and said, "Who's there?"

"Just me," says the County Court Clerk and give out his name.

"Well, come right in!" says Ples. "Ain't seen you since I don't rightly know when. How're you folks living at Dukedom?"

"Pretty fair, Ples. Can't complain."

The room was one big clutteration of old clothes, pots and pans, and junk, and Ples was setting up in a mess of dirty comforts on his bed at the far end.

Everything else might be knocking around just anywheres it lit, but Ples didn't care a whet so long as his fiddle was safe. He never let go of that fiddle—had it now beside him in bed, running his fingers over it like you'd pet a child. It give the County Court Clerk a shock to see how like death Ples looked, green-faced and shrunk, with big brown liver splotches on his face and hands. He had gone down mightily, but his eyes was just as blue-bright as ever. His nose looked natural. It always had been big and bony.

County Court Clerk said, "How're you feeling, Ples?"

"Well," says he, "I could say I was down in the back. I could say I don't know what I'd do if it wasn't for them kind people that neighbor me round. I could say it and I *do* say it. Three times a day some good neighbor woman brings me some nice something to eat and sets a spell talking. The menfolks come over at night and see that I ain't fell out of bed to my harm. Between whiles, I just lay around and play my fiddle."

"I'd heared you was ailing," says the County Court Clerk.

"It's for a fact," says Ples. "Heart dropsy runs in the Haslock line. Here of late I've been having night flotations, too. But seems like I'm coming around some. Aim to be up and on my feet soon."

The County Court Clerk was of two minds whether to tell him about the contest, but now he figgered it wouldn't do no harm. So he come out about the jail wall and the contest and notified Ples that it would be held at the Dukedom school two weeks come a Monday.

Minute he heard that, Ples peartened up mightily. "I'll be there!" he says. "When the roll is called at Dukedom, Ples Haslock will be there certain sure!"

So the County Court Clerk visited awhile and then had to be on his way. "We'll be looking for you, Ples," he says.

"Get your fiddler's dram ready," says Ples, "for I virtuously aim to win it."

Well, the night of the contest most everybody in the county come to Dukedom in their Sunday best and tramped into the schoolhouse and settled in their seats. Everybody was in a looking-forward mood. You know how them gatherings are. A heap of shouting and high joking back and forth. Old gossip-trots running from one group to another with the latest. Young bloods standing around talking loud and the girls giggling and sneaking looks at them. Little mustards running up and down the aisles, snatching things from each other, having rooster-fights at the back of the hall, and raising a general rumpus. Little girls setting with their folks and sticking out their tongues at the boys when nobody was looking. Babies crying, people coughing, and the lye soap smell pretty strong.

The crowd was getting restless. Little boys, and some not so little, began whistling and banging desks for things to get started.

Old Judge Huley Dunlap was the chairman of the committee and he come out on the stage and give out that the contest was fixing to start. Then he put on his glasses and read off the names of the fiddlers, seven in all.

When he got through, everybody commenced yelling, "How about Ples Haslock?"

"Well," says Judge Dunlap, "we'd hoped he could make it, but till yet he ain't showed up. He's been laid up in bed lately and I reckon he couldn't stand the trip over here from Post Oak. Anybody that wants to can get their admission back at the door."

Some folks grumbled, but everybody stayed set and things quieted down.

So the seven fiddlers came out on the stage and took seats and the contest was ready to break out.

Everybody knowed that five of the seven fiddlers might as well not have got in the contest. They was plain everyday set-in-a-rocker-and-scratch-aways. The contest was between Coot Kersey and Old Rob Reddin, number six and seven. With Ples Haslock down and out, Coot and Old Rob was the best fiddlers you could find anywhere around and about in the county. Everybody figgered Old Rob was the likely one, not because his fiddling was fancier than Coot's but because of the crazy way he carried on.

The five sorry fiddlers sawed away and got through without nobody paying attention in special. Coot and Old Rob would do the real fiddling and they come last.

There was a big laugh when Coot's turn come. Everybody always felt like laughing when they saw Coot. The way his head bobbed up and down on his long, red, wrinkled neck with every step he took, the way his chin ran back and his nose beaked out, and the way a long tag of his hair kept wattling down to the bridge of his nose put everybody in mind of an old turkey gobbler. Coot gobbled when he talked, too.

But one thing sure—Coot could make a fiddle sing. He was the dead-serious kind of fiddler. Had to have his fiddle set just right across his knees before he'd commence, but let him get started and he sure fiddled. His piece was "Leather Britches." He went at it like a boy killing snakes, whipping and scraping away and stamping his foot till he'd worked up a pouring sweat. When he'd finished, he was as limp as an old rag. He drawed down a powerful clap-hand from the listeners.

The gathering set up smart when it come Old Rob Reddin's turn and he hobbled to the front of the stage. Folks started grinning before he'd done a thing. Old Rob was as funny to look at as Coot Kersey, but not because he put you in mind of no bird or animal. He was a lard-fat little man, and when he walked his stomach wobbled in front of him. He'd never been heard to open his mouth without some real funny humor-saying rolling out. If ever by accident he was to have a mournful spell and say anything serious, people would've laughed at him just the same. Seeing Old Rob meant laughing like falling in the creek meant getting wet.

So Old Rob he plumped his self down in the fiddler's chair. He laid his fiddle on his lap and winked at his wife that was setting down front. All on a sudden he yelled, "Hold to your seats, folks! I'm driving wild!"

He give the gathering time to stop howling. Then he lit in fiddling "Hell Turned Loose in Georgia." The way he carried on, a body'd thought he was having some sort of fit if they hadn't knowed better. When he drawed a high note, he'd open his mouth wide, run his eyebrows to his hairline, and shoot his neck up. On low ones he'd bend almost to the floor. Every once in so often he'd throw his bow into the air. While it was coming down he'd bawl out things like *"Eating* hogeye!" and "I *love* chittlins!" and "Ladies, where *was* your man last Saturday night!"

Everybody was still shouting and stamping and whistling when Old Rob come down off the platform. No need to hold the jimmyjohn over the different fiddlers' heads to see who'd get the most applauding. A deaf and dumb blind man could easy see Old Rob had that contest.

Like everybody, the judges was so taken up with watching Old

Rob cut capers because he'd won that they didn't see Ples Haslock till he'd already started playing. The first anybody knowed he was anywheres about was when a fiddle begun on the stage.

The crowd looked to see who it was, and there sat Ples in the chair with his fiddle across his knees, his bow weaving over the strings, and his foot patting steady. Yes, there he set with his eyes shut and his head nodding in time with his foot.

It was a dumbfounder, all right. For just a minute the gathering thought maybe they was seeing things. But there he was, Ples Haslock, all drawed and pale from sickness, fiddling in the contest just a snatch before it was too late.

The minute folks seen it *was* Ples, the hall got still as time in a grave.

It was about nine o'clock when Ples started in and he fiddled over an hour. It was straight, honest fiddling—none of your stunts on the strings like Coot Kersey, none of that loud fool-blabber that was Old Rob Reddin's stock-in-trade.

Folks there had heard fiddlers that could make them laugh and fiddlers that could make them cry, but Ples this night didn't do neither one. When you listened to him you nearly forgot who you was. You just set limp in your seat while your mind tried to remember something cloudy and away far off, something you'd never really seen or done.

Ples played "Poor Wayfaring Stranger" and "The Two Sisters" and "The Elfin Knight" and a dozen or more.

When Ples Haslock did stop, it verily did look like the crowd was going to tear the whole place down and scatter the pieces. They heaved to their feet and whooped, whistled, screamed, and bellered and hammered on the desks. Kept it up while Judge Huley Dunlap handed Ples the jimmyjohn of fine red drinking whiskey and said, "I hereby present and award to Ples Haslock this prize which may he enjoy it as much as the good people of Dukedom done his fiddling." Leastways they seen Judge Dunlap's mouth flapping and knowed he was saying something like that.

Well, Ples stood up, holding his fiddle and his bow under his left arm and heisting the jimmyjohn with a crooked finger of his right hand. He flipped that jimmyjohn over his shoulder, jerked the corncob out of the mouth of it with his teeth, and taken a long pull, his fiddler's dram.

Right then come a crash. For the chair, the jimmyjohn and Ples and his fiddle all landed in a heap on the floor.

Man, woman, and child run up onto the stage. But Judge Huley Dunlap made them stand back. "Get a doctor!" he says. "This man is done for, or near it. I can't feel no heartbeat at all."

So they hushed down and stood looking at Ples where he laid there on the stage.

"Think of it!" they says. "Poor Ples coming thirty miles to Dukedom with the last life in him just to win this contest!"

"He sure was a man that liked to fiddle!"

"Would you look at his clothes," says somebody. "All covered with clay, they are. From the looks of it, he must walked all the way and through the swamp at that."

They kept saying, "It's the beat of all ever happened in Dukedom!"

Before long the doctor come hustling in and knelt down and examined over Ples. He said, "How'd he get in here?"

So they told him. Judge Dunlap says, "He just keeled over dead before our eyes, poor man."

"Keeled over, my granny!" says the doctor. "This here man has been dead for forty-eight hours at the very least. And from the clay he's got on his clothes, I'd say buried, too."

James R. Aswell

An Epitaph

Remember, Friends, as you pass by,
As you are now, so once was I,
As I am now, so you must be,
Prepare for death and follow me.

The Girl with the Lavender Dress

Two Hamilton College juniors, motoring to a dance at Tuxedo Park after sunset of a warm Indian-summer Saturday on the road that runs through the valley of the little Ramapo River, saw a girl waiting. She was wearing a party dress the color of the mist rising above the dark water of the stream and her hair was the color of ripe wheat. The boys stopped their car and asked the girl if they could take her in the direction she was going. She eagerly seated herself between them and asked if they were going to the square dance at Sterling Furnace. The thin, tanned face with high cheekbones, the yellow hair, the flashing smile, the quicksilver quality of her gestures, enchanted the boys and it was soon a matter of amused debate whether they would go along with her to Sterling Furnace or she would accompany them to the dance at the Tuxedo. The majority won and the boys were soon presenting their new friend to the young couple who were their hosts at the Park. "Call me Lavender," she said to them. "It's my nickname because I always wear that color."

After an evening in which the girl, quiet and smiling, made a most favorable impression by her dancing, drifting dreamily through the waltzes in a sparkling cloud of lavender sequins, stepping more adeptly than any of the other dancers through the complications of revived square dances—Money Musk—Hull's Victory—Nellie Gray —the boys took her out to their car for the ride home. She said that she was cold and one of them doffed his tweed topcoat and helped her into it. They were both shocked into clichés of courtesy when, after gaily directing the driver through dusty woodland roads, she finally bade him stop before a shack so dilapidated that it would have seemed deserted had it not been for a ragged lace curtain over the small window in the door. After promising to see them again soon, she waved good night, standing beside the road until they had turned around and rolled away. They were almost in Tuxedo before the chill air made the coatless one realize that he had forgotten to reclaim his property and they decided to return for it on their way back to college the next day.

The afternoon was clear and sunny when, after considerable difficulty in finding the shack, the boys knocked on the door with the ragged lace curtain over its window. A decrepit white-haired woman answered the door and peered at them out of piercing blue eyes when they asked for Lavender.

"Old friends of hers?" she asked, and the boys, fearing to get the girl into the bad graces of her family by telling the truth about their adventures of the day before, said, yes, they were old friends.

"Then ye couldn't a-heerd she's dead," said the woman. "Been in the graveyard down the road fer near ten years."

Horrified, the boys protested that this was not the girl they meant —that they were trying to find someone they had seen the previous evening.

"Nobody else o' that name ever lived round here," said the woman. "Twan't her real name anyway. Her paw named her Lily when she was born. Some folks used to call her Lavender on account o' the pretty dress she wore all the time. She was buried in it."

The boys once more turned about and started for the paved highway. A hundred yards down the road, the driver jammed on the brakes.

"There's the graveyard," he said, pointing to a few weathered stones standing in bright sunlight in an open field overgrown with weeds, "and just for the hell of it I'm going over there."

They found the stone—a little one marked "Lily"—and on the curving mound in front of it, neatly folded, the tweed topcoat.

CHAPTER 8

Animal
Tales

"Two-Toe Tom"

CHAPTER 8

Animal Tales

"Two-Toe Tom"

"Didn't the fox never *catch the rabbit,*
Uncle Remus?"
—Joel Chandler Harris

ANIMAL TALES ARE the oldest and most popular of the folkloric tradition. At their simplest, they are a child's magic door, a peek into a world of talking mice and foxes; at their most profound, they reveal a culture's deepest characteristics. The turtle, with his steady determination, and the rabbit, with his carefree speed, are the seeds of allegory. Put them together in the forest and race them, and your reward will be wisdom. Animals hold up well under the burden of allegory, and they carry the weightiest truth with ease.

The most important of the black man's many gifts to American folklore is his animal tales. He carried into bondage with him a formidable oral tradition of creation and trickster tales, in which animals were the principal characters. The creation tales had less relevance on this side of the Atlantic, since they explained the origins of a world the black man no longer inhabited, but he used the trickster tales to great advantage.

The Uncle Remus stories, by Joel Chandler Harris, are a good case in point. They have entertained us for over a hundred years. Yet many of us who listen in rapture as Br'er Rabbit punches the Tar Baby or is heaved into his beloved brier patch, fail to remember that, though written by a white man, these tales were the offspring of an enslaved race. Within so many of these tales was a message the white man frequently missed, but one that often sustained the black spirit: Every time Br'er Rabbit danced off through the briers, a faith was strengthened that the world did not belong solely to the strong, that guile and intelligence counted for more. The clever rabbit's last laugh surely heartened the slave, whose own life was as much at the mercy of his master's whim as Br'er Rabbit's was in Br'er Fox's grip.

Though the American Indian also has a rich and varied tradition of trickster and creation tales, it is perhaps the Indian's creation tales that have become more popular with Americans. How the buffalo came to be, or the Rocky Mountains, or why there are no trees on the plain, all described the origins of our native soil and thus possessed an intrinsic interest. Nonetheless, one can see the difference in trickster folkloric traditions by comparing the Pawnees' Coyote tale with "Sheer Crops," a popular example of Afro-American folklore. Both are splendid examples of animal trickster tales, but, as you will see, how different they are! The Pawnee tale has the cold, stark quality of myth, while "Sheer Crops" is steeped in bitter experience and possesses a biting irony and humor.

Whatever solemn significance we ascribe to these animal tales, however, they are pure entertainment. The colorful dialect has been eased, and though the reading might be a little difficult, what life and richness would be lost if one were to try to wring the regional flavor from it.

Coyote Turns into a Buffalo:
A Pawnee Myth

Coyote, starving, met a Buffalo bull grazing. Coyote watched the Buffalo eat grass and said: "Grandfather, how you eat!" The Buffalo did not notice Coyote. After a while Coyote began to run around in front of the Buffalo bull. The Buffalo bull stopped eating, looked at Coyote, and said: "My grandson, why do you run around and bother me?" Coyote said: "Grandfather, you have grass to eat all over this country, and here I am starving because I can find nothing to eat." The Buffalo said: "My grandson, what you say is true, but I know you and I can not help you. You are tricky. I might do something for you, but you would do something which was wrong and you would be killed." But Coyote said: "No, my grandfather. I do not think that if you take pity on me I shall do anything wrong." The Buffalo then looked up and said: "If you are in earnest and want to be like me, go and hunt a buffalo wallow."

The Coyote went and found a buffalo wallow, then he came back and told the Buffalo bull that he had found a buffalo wallow. They went along together and the Buffalo bull ran towards Coyote, and when the Buffalo bull made a motion to hook, Coyote jumped to one side and the Buffalo went by. Then the Buffalo said: "I see that what I said is true. You are not in earnest. You jump to one side. I can not do anything for you." Three times the Buffalo ran towards Coyote and every time Coyote jumped aside. The Buffalo became angry and was going away, but Coyote begged hard for him to take pity on him once more. Coyote made up his mind that he would rather be killed than starve to death, and so he stood in the buffalo wallow.

The Buffalo ran towards him and tried to hook him, but when his horns touched Coyote he turned into a Buffalo, and there the two Buffalo fought with locked horns, pushing one another about. Then the Buffalo said: "My grandchild, there you are. Now you can eat all of this good grass that you see over this land. Stay with me for several days, and learn our powers. Graze upon high hills so that you can see a long distance, and when you see people coming, always run. In the night follow the ravines, and when you have come to a bunch of grass and weeds, sit down in the center of the weeds. In the morning go again upon the high hills and graze."

Coyote-Buffalo remained with the Buffalo. After a while the Buffalo told Coyote-Buffalo to go on and do as he had told him. He told him that whenever he sat down to always have his nose towards the wind, so that if any people should come he could smell them for a long distance and could run from them. While Coyote-Buffalo was grazing he saw a Coyote sitting near him, and Coyote-Buffalo said: "My grandchild, what do you want?" Coyote said that he was starving and would like to be like the Buffalo, so that he could get plenty of grass to eat. Coyote-Buffalo said: "That is easy. I was a Coyote, but I was turned into a Buffalo. You find a buffalo wallow and I will take pity upon you and make you like a Buffalo. You must be brave, and then you shall be like me."

The Coyote found a buffalo wallow and they went to it. Coyote-Buffalo put the Coyote into the buffalo wallow and told him to stand there. Then Coyote-Buffalo ran toward the Coyote, thinking that he would have the power to turn the Coyote into a Buffalo. He ran, and when he tried to hook the Coyote, the Coyote turned around and tried to bite him. As Coyote-Buffalo struck the Coyote he turned into a Coyote again and there were two Coyotes with their mouths locked together. When he got loose, Coyote who had been a Buffalo began to call the other Coyote names, and said: "You have done me a great wrong. I am now a Coyote again." The other Coyote ran away.

Coyote who had been a Buffalo went back to the Buffalo and said: "Grandfather, I am sorry. When I was running I fell down and I turned into a Coyote again. Take pity upon me and I will be more careful after this." The Buffalo told Coyote to find another buffalo wallow. Coyote found it and stood in the buffalo wallow, and the Buffalo ran, and as his horns struck Coyote, he again turned into a Buffalo. He said: "Now, do not try to turn Coyotes into Buffalo, but stay with me."

After they were together for several days, Coyote-Buffalo said: "I will travel towards the west," and the Buffalo said: "Good! On your way you will meet twenty Buffalo running fast. There will be nineteen Buffalo cows and one bull. When the bull sees you and stops he will say: 'Join us; let us go where the people are, so that we may receive smoke.' Do not listen to him. You must not go with him. You must stay away from him." Coyote said: "Grandfather, I will do as you say."

Coyote-Buffalo went west. For several days he traveled, and one evening he heard Buffalo coming, running fast. He jumped up and stood in the pathway. The Buffalo cows passed, but when the bull came up he said: "My brother, let us go where the people are, so that we may receive smoke." Coyote-Buffalo said: "Good! I will go with you." They began to run. Towards evening they overtook the Buffalo cows and they went on together.

In the evening the Buffalo sat down to rest. Then the Buffalo bull said: "It is not far to go where we are going, and there we shall receive smoke." Coyote-Buffalo said: "Let us, then, start again and get there as soon as we can." The Buffalo arose, and they ran for some time in the night. When they came to ravines they squatted down and Coyote-Buffalo said: "My brother, let us now smoke." The Buffalo bull said: "Why, do you not know what I mean when I say that we are going for smoke?" Coyote-Buffalo did not know, but he said: "Oh, I had forgotten. We are not to get smoke yet." In the morning they started again. Every time they stopped, Coyote-Buffalo would say: "Let us now smoke." The Buffalo would say: "Why, do you not know what I mean when I say that we are going for smoke?" Coyote would say: "I had forgotten. I remember now what it is." Then the Buffalo started on again and at last they came close to the village. They squatted down in the ravine and sat there.

Early in the morning, scouts were sent out from the people and they found the Buffalo sitting in the ravine. The scouts went and told the people that there was a herd of Buffalo close to the village. The old men cried through the village and told the men to surround the Buffalo. The men went out, surrounded the Buffalo, and they killed all the Buffalo. The men said that the Buffalo were holy and that their meat was to be taken to the lodge of the priest. Several men ran after one Buffalo that could run faster than the others. They ran this Buffalo over some hills, and just as one man got near the Buffalo, the Buffalo came to a place where there was a high precipice. The Buffalo fell as the man was about to shoot, and as he fell the Buffalo turned into a Coyote and ran away.

The men were surprised when they saw the Buffalo turn into a Coyote. They went home and told about it. The old people said that this Coyote must have been turned into a Buffalo by some other Buffalo. Coyote ran back to where the Buffalo bull was grazing and said: "My grandfather, I joined those people who went to get smoke from the people. The people ran after me and I stumbled over some bad places. I fell down and turned into a Coyote. Take pity upon me and let me turn into a Buffalo again." Buffalo bull said: "Find me a buffalo wallow." Coyote found a buffalo wallow and they went to it. Coyote stood in the wallow and the Buffalo bull ran towards him and hooked him and threw him up into the air. Before he struck the ground he hooked him again and again, until he killed him. Ever since that time, the Coyotes have been willing to be Coyotes, and the Buffalo have always disliked Coyotes.

The Wonderful Tar-Baby Story

"Didn't the fox *never* catch the rabbit, Uncle Remus?" asked the little boy the next evening.

"He come mighty nigh it, honey, sho's you born—Br'er Fox did. One day after Br'er Rabbit fool 'im wid dat calamus root, Br'er Fox went to work an' got 'im some tar, an' mixed it wid some turpentine, an' fixed up a contraption dat he called a Tar-Baby, an' he took dis 'ere Tar-Baby an' he set 'er in de big road, an' den he lay off in de bushes for to see what de news was gonna be. An' he didn't have to wait long, neider, 'cause by-an'-by here come Br'er Rabbit pacin' down de road—lippity-clippity, clippity-lippity—just as sassy as a jay-bird. Br'er Fox, he lay low. Br'er Rabbit come prancin' along 'til he spied de Tar-Baby; an' den he reared up on his 'hind legs like he was 'stonished. De Tar-Baby, she sat dere, she did, an' Br'er Fox, he lay low.

" 'Mornin'!' says Br'er Rabbit, 'Nice weather dis mornin'.'

"Tar-Baby ain't sayin' nothin' an' Br'er Fox, he lay low.

" 'How you come on, den? Is you deaf?' says Br'er Rabbit. ' 'Cause if you is, I can holler louder.'

"Tar-Baby stayed still, an' Br'er Fox, he lay low.

" 'You're stuck-up, dat's what you is,' says Br'er Rabbit, 'an' I'm gonna cure you, dat's what I'm gonna do,' says he.

"Br'er Fox, he sorta chuckled in his stomach, he did, but Tar-Baby ain't sayin' nothin'.

" 'I'm gonna learn you how to talk to 'spectable folks if it's de last thing I do,' says Br'er Rabbit. 'If you don't take off dat hat an' tell me howdy, I'm gonna bust you wide open,' says he.

"Tar-Baby stayed still, an' Br'er Fox, he lay low.

"Br'er Rabbit kept on askin' 'im, an' de Tar-Baby, she keep on sayin' nothin', till presently Br'er Rabbit drew back with his fist, he did, an' blip he took 'er side of de head. Right dere's where he broke his molasses jug. His fist stuck, an' he couldn't pull loose. De tar held 'im. But Tar-Baby stayed still, an' Br'er Fox, he lay low.

" 'If you don't lemme loose, I'll knock you agin,' says Br'er Rabbit, an' wid dat he fetched a swipe with d'other hand, an' dat stuck. Tar-Baby, she ain't sayin' nothin', an' Br'er Fox, he lay low.

" 'Turn me loose, 'fore I kick de nat'ral stuffin' out of you,' says Br'er Rabbit, but de Tar-Baby, she ain't sayin' nothin'. She just held on, an' then Br'er Rabbit lost de use of his feet in de same way. Br'er Fox, he lay low. Den Br'er Rabbit screamed out dat if de Tar-Baby didn't turn 'im loose he'd butt 'er crank-sided. An' den he butted, an' his head got stuck. Den Br'er Fox, he sauntered fort', lookin' jist as innocent as one of yo' mammy's mockin'-birds.

" 'Howdy, Br'er Rabbit,' says Br'er Fox. 'You look sorta stuck up dis mornin',' says he, an' den he rolled on de ground, an' laughed an' laughed till he couldn't laugh no more. 'I 'spect you'll take dinner with me dis time, Br'er Rabbit. I done laid in some calamus root, an' I ain't gonna take no excuse,' says Br'er Fox."

Here Uncle Remus paused, and drew a two-pound yam out of the ashes.

"Did the fox eat the rabbit?" asked the little boy to whom the story had been told.

"Dat's how far de tale goes," replied the old man. "He might, an' den agin he might not. Some say Judge B'ar come 'long an' loosed 'im—some say he didn't. I hear Miss Sally callin'. You better run along."

How Mr. Rabbit Was Too Sharp for Mr. Fox

"Uncle Remus," said the little boy one evening, when he had found the old man with little or nothing to do, "did the fox kill and eat the rabbit when he caught him with the Tar-Baby?"

"Lawd, honey, ain't I told you 'bout dat?" replied Uncle Remus, chuckling slyly.

"When Br'er Fox found Br'er Rabbit mixed up wid de Tar-Baby, he felt mighty good, an' he rolled on de groun' an' laughed. By-an'-by he up an' say:

" 'Well, I 'spect I got you dis time, Br'er Rabbit,' says he. 'Maybe I ain't, but I 'spect I is. You been runnin' 'round here sassin' after me a mighty long time, but I 'spect you done come to de end of de row. You been cuttin' up yo' capers an' bouncin' 'round in dis neighborhood 'til you come to believe yo'se'f de boss of de whole gang. An' den you is always somewheres dat you got no business being,' says Br'er Fox. 'Who asked you to come an' strike up a 'quaintance wid dis 'ere Tar-Baby? An' who stuck you up dere where you is? Nobody in de roun' world. You jist took an' jammed yo'se'f on dat Tar-Baby widout waitin' for any invite,' says Br'er Fox, 'an' dere you is, an' dere you'll stay 'til I fix up a brush-pile and fire 'er up, 'cause I'm gonna bobbycue you dis day, fer sure,' says Br'er Fox.

"Den Br'er Rabbit talked mighty humble.

" 'I don't care what you do wid me, Br'er Fox,' says he, 'jist so you don't fling me in dat brier-patch. Roast me, Br'er Fox,' says he, 'but don't fling me in dat brier-patch.'

" 'It's so much trouble to kindle a fire,' says Br'er Fox, 'dat I 'spect I'll have to hang you,' says he.

"'Hang me jist as high as you please, Br'er Fox,' says Br'er Rabbit, 'but fer de Lord's sake don't fling me in dat brier-patch,' says he.

"'I ain't got no string,' says Br'er Fox, 'an' now I 'spect I'll have to drown you,' says he.

"'Drown me jist as deep as you please, Br'er Fox,' says Br'er Rabbit, 'but don't fling me in dat brier-patch.'

"'Dere ain't no water nigh,' says Br'er Fox, 'an' now I 'spect I'll have to skin you,' says he.

"'Skin me, Br'er Fox,' says Br'er Rabbit, 'snatch out my eyeballs, tear out my ears by de roots, an' cut off my legs,' says he, 'but please, Br'er Fox, don't fling me in dat brier-patch.'

"Of course Br'er Fox wanted to hurt Br'er Rabbit bad as he could, so he caught 'im by de 'hind legs an' slung 'im right in de middle of de brier-patch. Dere was a considerable flutter where Br'er Rabbit struck de bushes, an' Br'er Fox sorta hung 'round to see what was gonna happen. By-an'-by he heard somebody call 'im, an' way up de hill he saw Br'er Rabbit sittin' cross-legged on a chinkapin log combin' de pitch out of his hair wid a chip. Den Br'er Fox knew dat he'd been fooled mighty bad. Br'er Rabbit was pleased to fling back some of his sass, an' he hollered out:

"'Bred an' born in a brier-patch, Br'er Fox—bred an' born in a brier-patch!' an' wid dat he skipped out jist as lively as a cricket in de embers."

What the Guinea Hen Says

A long time ago, there were many foxes in the county. All the farmers had many chickens upon which the foxes made their depredations. The farmers all obtained dogs to keep the foxes away from their chicken-yards. For a time there were no chicken-raids. The dogs woke their masters in time for them to get their guns and shoot the foxes. But by and by the head dog in the neighborhood was approached by a group of foxes.

"Look here," said the chief fox, "there is no use in our fighting each other this way. After all, we are distant relatives. Wouldn't you like a nice fat hen to eat every night?"

The dog admitted that he would.

"Well then," said the fox, "from now on, you keep quiet until we get a few chickens and then you can bark your head off. In return we'll leave a fat hen, all dressed, in the hollow stump near your farm."

The dog agreed to the proposition, and told his fellow dogs about it. They all decided to join up with the foxes.

From that time on, the farmers lost more chickens than ever. When the foxes had finished their work, the dog would set up a frenzied barking but, by the time the farmer got down with his gun, there was nothing to shoot at. Things went from bad to worse.

But the farmers were not the only ones worried. So were the chickens. They had a conference among themselves and said, "None of us could act as watchdogs. We can't yell loud enough." So they went to the guinea hens and said to them, "Listen, you birds have good strong voices. Will you act as watchdogs to scare off the foxes and wake the farmer?"

At first, the guinea hens said, "No," but the chickens said, "If you don't you'll soon be eaten too, because the foxes will eat all us chickens and will then start to eat you." So the guinea hens agreed.

That night while the dog sat watching, the foxes came sneaking up to the chicken-yard. But before they could get in, the guinea hens started screaming, "Foxes!" "Foxes!" "Foxes!" One of the farmers awoke immediately and, seizing his gun, ran down and shot some of the foxes. He gave the dog a good beating and set him to minding the front yard. He set the guinea hens up as permanent guardians of the barnyard. And so they are today. The first night they yelled, they yelled so hard that they became hoarse. And they are still hoarse today, but if you will listen closely you will hear that they are saying in their hoarse voices, "Foxes! Foxes! Foxes!"

Lissenbee

One time, there was a fellow named Lissenbee, and the trouble was that he couldn't keep nothing to himself. Whenever anybody done anything that wasn't right, Lissenbee would run and blab it all over town. He didn't tell no lies, he just told the truth, and that's what made it so bad. The people would believe whatever Lissenbee said, and there wasn't no way a fellow could laugh it off.

If he saw one of the county officers going to a woman's house when her husband was not home, Lissenbee would tell it right in front of the courthouse, so there would be hell to pay in two families. Or maybe some citizens liked to play a little poker in the livery barn, but there wasn't no way to keep it quiet, on account of Lissenbee. And when our preacher brought some whiskey home, there was Lissenbee a-hollering before we could get the keg out of the buggy. It got so the boys was afraid to swipe a watermelon, even, for fear old blabbermouth Lissenbee would tell everybody who done it.

The last straw was the time Lissenbee found a turtle in the road. It was bigger than the common kind, so he stopped to look at it. The old turtle winked its red eyes, and it said, "Lissenbee, you talk too damn much." Lissenbee jumped four feet high, and then just stood there with his mouth a-hanging open. He looked all 'round, but there wasn't nobody in sight. "It must be my ears has went back on me," said he, "because everybody knows terrapins is dumb." The old turtle winked its red eyes again. "Lissenbee, you talk too damn much," said the turtle. With that, Lissenbee spun 'round like a top, and then he lit out for town.

When Lissenbee got to the tavern and told the people about the turtle that could talk, they just laughed in his face. "You come with me," said he, "and I'll show you!" So the whole crowd went along, but when they got there old turtle didn't say a word. It looked just like any other turtle, only bigger than the common kind. The people were mad because they had walked away out there in the hot sun for nothing, so they kicked Lissenbee into the ditch and went back to town. Pretty soon Lissenbee sat up and the old turtle winked its red eyes. "Didn't I tell you?" said the turtle. "You talk too damn much."

Some people around here say the whole thing was a joke, that it ain't possible for a turtle to talk. They claim some fellow must have hid in the bushes and throwed his voice, so it just sounded like the turtle was a-talkin'. Everybody knows that these here medicine-show doctors can make a wooden dummy talk good enough to fool 'most anybody. There was a boy here in town tried to learn how to talk that way out of a book, but he never done no good at it. The folks never found nobody in these parts that could throw his voice like that.

Well, no matter if it was a joke or not, the story sure fixed old blabbermouth Lissenbee. The folks just laughed at his tales after that, and they would say he better go tell the turtles about it.

Sheer Crops

Br'er Bear an' Br'er Rabbit dey wuz farmers. Br'er Bear he has acres an' acres uf good bottom land, an' Br'er Rabbit has dis small sandy-land farm. Br'er Bear wuz always "raisin' Cain" wid his neighbors, but Br'er Rabbit was most generally raisin' chillun.

After a while, Br'er Rabbit's boys began to git grown, an' Br'er Rabbit decided he's gwine to have to git more land if he makes buckle an' tongue meet.

So he goes ober to Br'er Bear's house, he did, an' he say, sez he, "Morning, Br'er Bear. I craves ter rent yer bottom field nex' ye'r."

Br'er Bear he hem an' he haw, an' den he sez, "I don't 'spect I kin 'commodate yer, Br'er Rabbit, but I might consider it, bein's it is you."

"How does you rent yer land, Br'er Bear?"

"I kin onliest rent by der sheers."

"What is yer sheer, Br'er Bear?"

"Well," said Br'er Bear, "I takes der top of de crop fer my sheer, an' you takes de rest fer yo' sheer."

Br'er Rabbit thinks about it real hard, an' he sez, "All right, Br'er Bear, I took it; we goes ter plowin' ober dere nex' week."

Den Br'er Bear goes back in der house just a-laughin'. He sho is tickled as to how he hez done put one by ole Br'er Rabbit dat time.

Well, 'long in May, Br'er Rabbit done sent his oldest son to tell Br'er Bear to come down to de field to see about dat sheer crop. Br'er Bear he comes a-pacin' down to de field an' Br'er Rabbit wuz a-leanin' on de fence.

Mo'nin', Br'er Bear. See what a fine crop we hez got. You is to have de tops fer yer sheer. Whare is you gwine to put 'em? I wants ter git 'em off so I kin dig my 'taters."

Br'er Bear wuz sho hot. But he done made dat trade wid Br'er Rabbit, an' he had to stick to it. So he went off all huffed up, an' didn't even tell Br'er Rabbit what to do wid de vines. But Br'er Rabbit perceeded to dig his 'taters.

'Long in de fall, Br'er Rabbit he's gwine to see Br'er Bear agin an' try to rent der bottom field. So he goes down to Br'er Bear's house, an' after passin' de time of day an' other pleasant sociabilities, he sez, sez he, "Br'er Bear, how about rentin' der bottom field nex' year? Is yer gwine ter rent it to me agin?"

Br'er Bear say, he did, "You cheat me out of my eyes las' year, Br'er Rabbit. I don't think I kin let yer have it dis ye'r."

Den Br'er Rabbit scratch his head a long time, an' he say, "Oh, now, Br'er Bear, you know I ain't cheated yer. Yer jest cheat yerself. Yer made de trade yerself an' I done took yer at yer word. Yer said yer wanted der tops fer yer sheer, an' I give 'em ter you, didn't I? Now you just think it all ober agin an' see if you can't make a new deal fer yerself."

Den Br'er Bear said, "Well, I rents to you only on dese perditions: dat yer have all de tops fer yer sheer an' I have all de rest fer my sheer."

Br'er Rabbit he twis' an' he turn an' he sez, "All right, Br'er Bear, I'se got ter have more land fer my boys. I'll take it. We go to plowin' in dere right away."

Den Br'er Bear he amble back into de house. He wuz shore he'd made a good trade dat time.

Way 'long in nex' June, Br'er Rabbit done sent his boy down to Br'er Bear's house agin, to tell him to come down ter de field ter see about his rent. When he got dere, Br'er Rabbit say, he did:

"Mo'nin', Br'er Bear. See what a fine crop we hez got? I specks it will make forty bushels to der acre. I'se gwine ter put my oats on der market. What duz yer want me ter do wid yer straw?"

Br'er Bear sho wuz mad, but it wa'n't no use. He done saw whar Br'er Rabbit had 'im. So he lies low an' decided to hisself how he's gwine to git even wid Br'er Rabbit yit. So he smile an' say, "Oh, der crop is all right, Br'er Rabbit. Jes' stack my straw enywheres around dere. Dat's all right."

Den Br'er Bear smile an' he say, "What about nex' year, Br'er Rabbit? Is you cravin' ter rent dis field agin?"

"I ain't doin' nothin' else but wantin' ter rent it, Br'er Bear," said Br'er Rabbit.

"All right, all right, you kin rent her agin. But dis time I'se gwine ter have der tops fer my sheer, an' I'se gwine ter have de bottoms fer my sheer too."

Br'er Rabbit wuz stumped. He didn't know what ter do nex'. But he finally managed to ask, "Br'er Bear, if yer gits der tops an' der bottoms fer yer sheer, what will I git fer my sheer?"

Den old Br'er Bear laff an' say, "Well, you would git de middles."

Br'er Rabbit he worry an' he fret, he plead an' he argue, but it does no good.

Br'er Bear sez, "Take it or leave it," an' jes' stands pat.

Br'er Rabbit took it.

Way 'long nex' summer, ole Br'er Bear 'cided he would go down to der bottom field an' see about dat dere sheer crop he had wid Br'er Rabbit. While he wuz a-passin' through de woods on hiz way, he sez to himself, he did:

"De first year I rents to de ole Rabbit, I makes de tops my sheer, an' ole Rabbit planted 'taters; so I gits nothin' but vines. Den I rents agin, an' der Rabbit is to have de tops, an' I de bottoms, an' ole Rabbit plants oats; so I gits nothin' but straw. But I sho is got dat ole

Rabbit dis time. I gits both de tops an' de bottoms, an' de ole Rabbit gits only de middles. I'se bound ter git 'im dis time."

Jes' den de old Bear come ter de field. He stopped. He look at it. He shet up his fist. He cuss an' he say, "Dat derned little scounderel! He done went an' planted dat fiel' in corn."

Never Hold Your Head Too High

One day, there was a little bantam-cock with a high top-knot who was exceedingly vain though he had so many feathers on his legs that he could hardly walk. Seeing a goose duck her head in passing under a bar at least six feet high, he thus accosted her. "Why, thou miserable, bare-legged caitiff! thou shovel-nosed, web-footed, pigeon-toed scavenger of the highways! thou fool of three elements! not content with ignominiously crawling under a fence, thou must even nod thy empty pate by way of confessing thy inferiority. Behold how we bantams do these things!" So saying, with a deal of puffing and fluttering, with the help of his bill, he managed to gain the top of the fence, where he clapt his wings, and was just on the point of crowing in triumph, when a great hawk that was sailing over his head pounced down upon him, and seizing him by the top-knot, carried him off without ceremony. The goose, cocking her eye and taking a side view of the affair, significantly shook her feathers, and the next time she passed under the bar, bowed her head lower than ever.

How Sandy Got His Meat

Br'er Rabbit an' Br'er Coon wuz fishermuns. Br'er Rabbit fished fer fish an' Br'er Coon fished fer f-r-o-g-s.

After a while, de frogs all got so wild Br'er Coon couldent ketch 'em, an' he hadn't had no meat to his house an' de chilluns wuz hungry an' de ole woman beat 'em over de haid wid de broom.

Br'er Coon felt mighty bad an' he went off down de road wid his head down wundering what he gwine do. Jus' den, ole Br'er Rabbit wuz skippin' down de road an' he seed Br'er Coon wuz worried an' throwed up his ears an' say-ed:

"Mornin', Br'er Coon."

"Mornin', Br'er Rabbit."

"How is yer, Br'er Coon?"

"Porely, Br'er Rabbit, porely. De frogs has all got so wild I cain't ketch 'em an' I ain't got no meat to my house an' de ole woman is mad an' de chilluns hungry. Br'er Rabbit, I'se got to have help. Sumthin' has got to be done."

Old Br'er Rabbit look away crost de river long time; den he scratch hiz ear wid his hind foot, an' say:

"I'll told ye what we do, Br'er Coon. We'll git every one of dem frogs. You go down on de sand bar an' lie down an' play jest like you wuz d-a-i-d. Don't yer move. Be jus' as still, jus' like you wuz d-a-i-d."

Ole Br'er Coon mosied on down to de river. De frogs heard him comin an' de ole big frog said:

"Yer better look aroun'. Yer better look aroun'. Yer better look aroun'."

Another ole frog say-ed:

"Knee deep, knee deep, knee deep."

An' "ker-chug" all de frogs went in de water.

But Ole Br'er Coon lay down on de sand an' stretched out jest like he wuz d-a-i-d. De flies got all over him, but he never moved. De sun shine hot, but he never moved; he lie still jest like he wuz d-a-i-d.

Directly, Ole Br'er Rabbit came runnin' thru de woods an' out on de sand bar an' put his ears up high an' hollered out:

"Hey, de Ole Coon is d-a-i-d."

De ole big frog out in de river said:

"I don't bleve it, I don't bleve it, I don't bleve it."

An' all de little frogs roun' de edge said:

"I don't bleve it, I don't bleve it, I don't bleve it."

But de ole coon play jest like he's d-a-i-d an' all de frogs came up out of de river an' set aroun' where de ole coon lay.

Jest den Br'er Rabbit wink his eye an' said:

"I'll tell yer what I'd do, Br'er Frogs. I'd bury Ole Sandy, bury him so deep he never could scratch out."

Den all de frogs went to dig out de sand, dig out de sand from under de ole coon. When dey had dug a great deep hole wid de ole coon in de middle of it, de frogs all got tired an' de ole frog said:

"Deep er nough—deep er nough—deep er nough."

An' all de little frogs said:

"Deep er nough—deep er nough—deep er nough."

Ole Br'er Rabbit was takin a little nap in der sun, an' he woke up an' said:

"Kin you jump out?"

De ole big frog look up to de top of de hole an' said:

"Yes I kin. Yes I kin. Yes I kin."

An' de little frogs said:

"Yes I kin. Yes I kin. Yes I kin."

Ole Br'er Rabbit told 'em:

"Dig it deeper."

Den all de frogs went to work an' dug a great deep hole way down inside de sand wid Ole Br'er Coon right in de middle jest like he wuz d-a-i-d. De frogs wuz gittin putty tired an' de ole big frog sung out loud:

"Deep er nough. Deep er nough. Deep er nough."

An' all de little frogs sung out too:

"Deep er nough. Deep er nough. Deep er nough."

An' Ole Br'er Rabbit woke up ag'in an' axed 'em:

"Kin yer jump out?"

"I bleve I kin. I bleve I kin. I bleve I kin."

Ole Br'er Rabbit look down in de hole ag'in an' said:

"Dig dat hole deeper."

Den all de frogs went to work throwin' out sand, throwin' out sand, clear till almost sundown and dey had a great deep hole way, way down in de sand, wid de ole coon layin' right in middle. De frogs wuz plum clean tired out an' de ole big frog said:

"Deep er nough. Deep er nough. Deep er nough."

An' all de little frogs said:
"Deep er nough. Deep er nough. Deep er nough."
Ole Br'er Rabbit peeped down in de hole ag'in an' said:
"Kin yer jump out?"
An' de ole frog said:
"No I caint. No I caint. No I caint."
An' all de little frogs said:
"No I caint. No I caint. No I caint."
Den Ole Br'er Rabbit jump up right quick an' hollered out:
"RISE UP, SANDY, AN' GIT YOUR MEAT."
An' Br'er Coon had meat for supper dat nite.

De Knee-High Man

De knee-high man lived by de swamp. He wuz alwez a-wantin' to
be big 'stead of little. He sez to hisself: "I is gwinter ax [ask] de
biggest thing in dis neighborhood how I kin git sizable." So he goes
to see Mr. Horse. He ax him: "Mr. Horse, I come to git you to tell
me how to git big like you is."

Mr. Horse he say: "You eat a whole lot of corn and den you run
round and round and round, till you been about twenty miles and
after a while you big as me."

So de knee-high man, he done all Mr. Horse tole him. An' de corn
make his stomach hurt, and runnin' make his legs hurt and de trying
make his mind hurt. And he gits littler and littler. Den de knee-high
man he set in his house and study how come Mr. Horse ain't help
him none. And he say to hisself: "I is gwinter go see Br'er Bull."

So he go to see Br'er Bull and he say: "Br'er Bull, I come to ax you
to tell me how to git big like you is."

And Br'er Bull he say: "You eat a whole lot o' grass and den you
bellow and bellow and fust thing you know you gits big like I is."

And de knee-high man he done all Br'er Bull tole him. And de
grass make his stomach hurt, and de bellowing make his neck hurt
and de thinking make his mind hurt. And he git littler and littler.

Den de knee-high man he set in his house and he study how come Br'er Bull ain't done him no good. After wile, he hear ole Mr. Hoot Owl way in de swamp preachin' dat de bad peoples is sure gwinter have de bad luck.

Den de knee-high man he say to hisself: "I gwinter ax Mr. Hoot Owl how I kin git to be sizable," and he go to see Mr. Hoot Owl.

And Mr. Hoot Owl say: "What for you want to be big?" and de knee-high man say: "I wants to be big so when I gits a fight, I ken whup."

And Mr. Hoot Owl say: "Anybody ever try to kick a scrap wid you?"

De knee-high man he say naw. And Mr. Hoot Owl say: "Well den, you ain't got no cause to fight, and you ain't got no cause to be mo' sizable than you is."

De knee-high man says: "But I wants to be big so I kin see a fur ways." Mr. Hoot Owl he say: "Can't you climb a tree and see a fur ways when you is clim' to de top?"

De knee-high man he say: "Yes." Den Mr. Hoot Owl say: "You ain't got no cause to be bigger in de body, but you sho' is got cause to be bigger in de BRAIN."

Two-Toe Tom

When Pap Haines bought his forty from the lumber company twenty years ago, folks told him he better not keep any stock on account of old Two-Toe. Two-Toe is a red-eyed 'gator and about fourteen feet long and he can knock a mule into the water with just one flip of his tail. When a farmer sees that track with just two toes on the left forefoot (the rest was cut off by a steel trap long ago), that means he has shore got to pen up his calves and pigs and he can't be too careless with his mules and grown cows either. Got to well-water them for a while instead of letting them wander around just any pond, because you can't never tell which one he is in. But well-watering doesn't look out for calves and pigs enough. Any good-sized 'gator will come right up to the lot or cow-pen at night. And Two-Toe Tom is an eating fool. If the farmer's got a dog, old Two-Toe just says dog-meat is dessert for a 'gator.

But Pap Haines said he'd run his chances on the forty. Said he would keep some light-wood splinters handy for a light and some big hard-tearing pine knots. A pine knot is better than a gun. Ordinary shots shell off an alligator's back like water. But a good hard lick on the back of the head or the neck with a pine knot will tear in and keel him over—then you can kill him on his tender belly. Of course Pap didn't reckon he could do any good with a steel trap. Ever since Two-Toe left the rest of his foot in one he has known more about steel trap layout than the men who set them. But a good dose of dynamite under that red-eye in some pond would make him feel pretty sick.

Pap Haines says he had right bad luck just at first. He has to go back 'way before his son was married to recollect when Two-Toe Tom threw him back for a cow. The 'gator caught her drinking at a pond and he came two nights later and got the calf out of the cow-pen. Then Two-Toe kind of fell out with this neck of the woods. He didn't bother around for ten years or more. Pap's wife died and his son got married and his wife borned four children, about two years apart. The state began building the clay pike, so they began sleeping four man-boarders in one shed room and Pap had to sleep in the room with his son and his wife and all the children because they used the other shed room to eat in. Boarders made good company, living back country, and their rent helped out when times were bad.

Then, after laying-by time, Pap Haines and his son lost another mule. They had been keeping all the stock in the lot by the window at night. In the daytime they turned out the mules but they tried to watch them and not let them get off too far. There was no work to do one morning, and the son decided he would like to go over with the old man and take dinner to the boarders and kind of see how they were coming along with the new road. The old lady and the kids wanted to go too, so they hitched one of the mules to the old buggy and didn't bother about catching up the other mule.

When they got back along towards night they found the mule half eaten down by a pond. A little further along in the mud was that Two-Toe left-forefoot track.

One of the boarders said he was acquainted with a man down close to Brewton that could get any 'gator he set out to. He used a blind and a high-powered rifle, and he had a sharpshooter pin that he got back in the army. The boarder set out in a Model T the next morning and was back with the man by noon. They had stopped at the court-house in Andalusia and found out that that old ten-year-ago hundred-dollar reward for Two-Toe Tom was still in force. Pap Haines said to the man:

"We'll give you twenty-five more and board you even if it takes a week or two."

"It jest takes patience," the man said; "the trouble about a blind, folks generally git too close. A 'gator can smell a man before he gets his head high enough out o' water for the man to see him. I don't like to brag but I most generally git a bad 'gator, give me time enough."

He followed some tracks for a ways and then he said:

"Jedgin' by these tracks he's in one of these three ponds."

Then he climbed high up in a thick-limbed tree with his rifle and his dinner, three hundred yards or more from any one of the ponds. He said the 'gator couldn't see through the limbs that far and he would just naturally come out to the sun in a day or two. It might be a week, the man reckoned, but he would spot that devil's head somewhere, and one look would be enough.

"It jest takes patience," he said.

So the man was patient in the tree for nigh onto a week, every day, until they heard about Two-Toe Tom's track seven or eight miles down the country, where he had killed two calves.

The man went down there, but Two-Toe Tom must have had a good nose, or good eyes, one, for he hasn't yet got clipped off with a rifle.

Pap Haines never had any more trouble with that 'gator till last March. He had begun to reckon somebody had got him, and then one of his mules didn't come up in the morning. Any mule will get contrary sometimes and not come up, so the old man went down in the brush to look for him, not bothering much, not until he saw that track. It came from a pond up yonder in a clump of water oaks and crab grass and followed along a sluggish branch too shallow for fish, much less a 'gator, and went down the hollow.

"Uh-uh," Pap Haines said. "Hell's up now."

Sure enough, over in the bushes where the spring rains had over-flowed the pond he saw the mule lying with his side torn open and a part of the top shoulder and the top ham eaten away. Some of the bushes were bent and torn, showing there had been a struggle. And there in the mud was that track. Two-Toe Tom was still alive and he was on the move again.

Pap Haines and his son didn't wait for breakfast. They got some pine knots and they mortally lit out after those tracks. They didn't have any trouble following them past two ponds and on to another one. And there were no tracks leading out anywhere. It was a good piece to another pond in any direction. No two ways about it, Two-Toe Tom was in that pond all right. The son got to where he could see all 'round the pond and told the old man to hitch the other mule to the buggy and light out to town for some dynamite, some fuses and some caps.

"Make it plenty of dynamite," he said, "and get back quick, and tell my wife to send me some breakfast."

While Pap Haines was gone, his son waited for the old red-eye to come out. He was going to let him get some distance and then cut him off from coming back to the pond and whale into him with pine knots.

But Pap got back with the stuff and nothing had happened. They filled about fifteen syrup buckets with dynamite, packed the sticks tight in dirt and cottonseed and cut off some fuses. They lighted three at a time and threw the buckets in the pond. The water shot way up in the air and roots and trees came up from the bottom. Nothing could have been left alive in that pond. Just the same, every-body, and there were eight of them by now, went stepping around pretty careful.

After they threw the last bucket Pap Haines said:

"We got him now. He'll be a floatin' belly up in this pond by mornin'."

They had all started back toward the house when they heard a big splashing down by the first pool Pap had tracked the 'gator through.

Then somebody began screaming. Everybody ran as fast as he could and the screams kept up, but it was a good ways down there. Pap Haines is over sixty, but he got there first, just in time to see two red eyes sinking under the water. Beside the pond was what was left of his twelve-year-old granddaughter. She had heard the blasting and was coming down to see what it was about.

They spent the rest of the day shooting into the water and they set off some more dynamite, but nothing happened. Two weeks later, a farmer down by Stedman ten miles away lost a couple of shoats and found the two-toed track.

Pap Haines lives alone now. His son and family have moved up north, around Tuskegee. They want him to come there, for he can hardly scrape a living by himself, but he says he has never been above Montgomery and he can't get 'round to it. Besides, he says he plans to kill that red-eyed hell-demon before he dies. He acts a little queer about it and some folks laugh at him.

They tell him Two-Toe Tom has got tunnels all around from one pond to another and lots of secret ways to get in and out of swamps.

"I know that," he says, "but he won't fool me no more."

They tell him Two-Toe Tom has been heard from down Florida way and he won't be back. He says,

"He might be down there, but he'll be back. And I'll be waitin'."

He keeps one old mule and lets him run loose for bait.

The Boll Weevil Song

THERE WAS A TIME not so long ago when the fields of the South were snow-white with the harvests of cotton. The arrival of the boll weevil, an insect that thrived on cotton, put an end to the supremacy of the crop and ruined thousands of farmers and towns that depended upon it as a principal resource. "The Boll Weevil Song" is a famous ode to the hated insect. Throughout the South a rich vein of grim humor about the boll weevil grew, like the time a farmer was asked why he had harvested his cotton so early in the summer. He said he went outside after hearing someone crying and found a big boll weevil beating a little one with an ax handle because the little one could only strip one row of cotton at a time. The farmer figured then and there he ought to get out before the big boll weevil came after him.

Oh, de boll weevil am a little black bug,
    Come from Mexico, dey say,
Come all de way to Texas, jus' a-lookin' for a place to stay.
    Jus' a-lookin' for a home, jus' a-lookin' for a home.

De first time I seen de boll weevil
    He was a-settin' on de square,
De next time I seen de boll weevil, he had all of his family dere,
    Jus' a-lookin' for a home, jus' a-lookin' for a home.

De farmer say to de weevil:
    "What make yo' head so red?"
De weevil say to de farmer, "It's a wondah I ain't dead,
    A-lookin' for a home, jus' a-lookin' for a home."

De farmer take de boll weevil,
    An' he put him in de hot san'.
De weevil say: "Dis is mighty hot, but I'll stan' it like a man,
    Dis'll be my home, it'll be my home."

De farmer take de boll weevil,
    An' he put him in a lump of ice;
De boll weevil say to de farmer: "Dis is mighty cool an' nice,
    It'll be my home, dis'll be my home."

De farmer take de boll weevil,
    An' he put him in de tire.
De boll weevil say to de farmer: "Here I are, here I are,
    Dis'll be my home, dis'll be my home."

De boll weevil say to de farmer:
    "You better leave me alone;
I done eat all yo' cotton, now I'm goin' to start on yo' corn,
    I'll have a home, I'll have a home."

De merchant got half de cotton,
    De boll weevil got de res'.
Didn't leave de farmer's wife but one old cotton dress,
    An' it's full of holes, it's full of holes.

De farmer say to de merchant:
    "We's in an awful fix;
De boll weevil ate all de cotton up an' lef' us only sticks,
    We's got no home, we's got no home."

De farmer say to de merchant:
    "We ain't made but only one bale,

And before we'll give yo' dat one we'll fight an' go to jail,
We'll have a home, we'll have a home."
De cap'n say to de missus:
"What d' you t'ink o' dat?
De boll weevil done make a nes' in my bes' Sunday hat,
Goin' to have a home, goin' to have a home."
And if anybody should ask you
Who it was dat make dis song,
Jus' tell 'em 'twas but a travelin' man wid a pair o' blue duckin's
on.
Ain' got no home, ain' got no home.

Animal Superstitions

If a turtle bites you, he won't let go until he hears thunder.

If you lose your cows, get a daddy longlegs and ask him, "Where are my cows, ol' daddy longlegs?" The first leg he lifts will tell you which way the cows went.

Never kill a toad. If you handle one, you'll get warts.

It's good to see a spider at night. "If you expect to live and thrive, let the spider walk alive."

If you see a spider come toward you in the morning, you'll be in a fight before sundown.

If a cow chases you, by closing your fingers around your thumb and making a fist you'll be safe.

Put a snake in a cider barrel and the cider will turn sweet.

If a rooster crows at the back door, death is on the way; if it crows at the front door, you'll have visitors.

If you hear the sounds of many animals, there'll be rain.

If your cat dies and you get another one, give it the same name. The cat will bring luck to your family.

If you always scratch a dog where it can't scratch itself, your dog will never run away from home.

If you want to stop a dog from howling, turn your shoes upside down.

A horseshoe over the door is good luck.

Whenever you see a white horse, look over your shoulder and you'll see old Mr. Devil.

If a person touches a bird's egg, its mother will never return to the nest.

A white dove flying overhead is a good sign. A woodpecker near your house is an even better sign.

Salt a bird's tail for a lifetime of good fortune.

It's good luck when an animal follows you home.

CHAPTER 9

Country Life
and
Country Laughter

"Little Brown Jug"

CHAPTER 9

Country Life
and
Country Laughter

"Little Brown Jug"

"I ain't sayin' the man's dishonest, mind ya,
but he's got to git someone else to call his hogs in."
—a Tennessean's description
of his neighbor

THERE IS SOMETHING about country living that the city cannot touch. In the city, where life is full of fury and energy, you are a face among faces, while in the country you are someone's child or grandchild. You might be stopped outside the post office by a kindly old man with thick glasses who grips your shoulder and says, "I knew your granddaddy. We fished together on the Tar River when we were boys." In that moment there is a mutual sense of memory; young and old meet together on magic ground, a landscape of laughter and reminiscence.

The following stories serve as a kind of country sampler. The stock characters, such as the simpleton and the country bumpkin, take their place alongside the oft-told favorite rural yarns like "The Razorback Hog" and "Racing the Train." Yet there is something more, too. The folks who live beyond the city lights often see the world more clearly. Our rural cousins consider things, savor them more. They have mastered the art of saying a great deal in a few words (the disgruntled boarder in "The Vinegar Queen's Supper" is a perfect example), and they know, as we learn from "Shotgun Charlie's Sage Advice," that nothing comes easy. Politicians have always had their toughest time in the villages and hamlets where folks listen to what you say, not how you say it. When a recent candidate running for office asked the potential voters to trust him, a man whispered to me, "When a feller says, 'Trust me,' I always make sure my hand's on my wallet."

Some of the brightest spots in the American language appear when locals get to talking with one another. They retain the ability to connect their thoughts directly to the metaphors that make up their life. An attractive girl is "perty as a speckled puppy" and a small child is "jist about fryin' size." None can improve on such observations. "Listen to the People Talk" is just a taste of a few country idioms, uncorrupted and straight.

Trespassers Beware

NOTIS! *tresspassers will B persecuted to the full extent of 2 mungrel dogs which never was over-sochible to strangers & 1 dubble brl shot gun which aint loaded with sofa pillors. Dam if I aint gittin tired of this hell raisin on my place.*

A Melting Story

One winter evening, a country store-keeper in the Green Mountain State was about closing his doors for the night, and while standing in the snow outside, putting up his window-shutters, he saw through the glass a lounging, worthless fellow within grab a pound of fresh butter from the shelf and hastily conceal it in his hat.

The act was no sooner detected than the revenge was hit upon, and a very few moments found the Green Mountain store-keeper at once indulging his appetite for fun to the fullest extent, and paying off the thief with a facetious sort of torture for which he might have gained a premium from the old inquisition.

"I say, Seth!" said the store-keeper, coming in and closing the door after him, slapping his hands over his shoulders, and stamping the snow off his shoes.

Seth had his hand upon the door, his hat upon his head, and the roll of new butter in his hat, anxious to make his exit as soon as possible.

"I say, Seth, sit down; I reckon, now, on such an e-*tar*-nal night as this, a leetle something warm wouldn't hurt a fellow; come and sit down."

Seth felt very uncertain: he had the butter, and was exceedingly anxious to be off, but the temptation of 'something warm' sadly interfered with his resolution to go. This hesitation, however, was soon settled by the right owner of the butter taking Seth by the shoulders, and planting him in a seat close to the stove, where he was in such a manner cornered in by barrels and boxes that while the country grocer sat before him there was no possibility of his getting out, and right in this very place sure enough the store-keeper sat down.

"Seth, we'll have a little warm Santa Cruz," said the Green Mountain grocer, as he opened the stove-door and stuffed in as many sticks as the space would admit. "Without it you'd freeze going home such a night as this."

Seth already felt the butter settling down closer to his hair and jumped up declaring he must go.

"Not till you have something warm, Seth; come, I've got a story to tell you, too; sit down, now;" and Seth was again pushed into his seat by his cunning tormentor.

"Oh! it's too darn'd hot here," said the petty thief, again attempting to rise.

"Set down—don't be in such a plaguey hurry," retorted the grocer, pushing him back in his chair.

"But I've got the cows to fodder, and some wood to split, and I *must* be agoin'," continued the persecuted chap.

"But you mustn't tear yourself away, Seth, in this manner. Set down; let the cows take care of themselves and keep yourself cool, you appear to be fidgety," said the roguish grocer with a wicked leer.

The next thing was the production of two smoking glasses of hot rum toddy, the very sight of which, in Seth's present situation, would have made the hair stand erect upon his head had it not been well oiled and kept down by the butter.

"Seth, I'll give you a toast now, and you can butter it yourself," said the grocer, yet with an air of such consummate simplicity that poor Seth still believed himself unsuspected. "Seth, here's—here's a Christmas goose—(it was about Christmas time)—here's a Christmas goose well roasted and basted, eh? I tell you, Seth, it's the greatest eating in creation. And, Seth, don't you never use hog's fat or common cooking butter to baste with; fresh pound butter, just the same as you see on that shelf yonder, is the only proper thing in natur to baste a goose with—come take your butter—I mean, Seth, take your toddy."

Poor Seth now began to smoke as well as to melt, and his mouth was hermetically sealed up as though he had been born dumb. Streak after streak of the butter came pouring from under his hat, and his handkerchief was already soaked with the overflow. Talking away as if nothing was the matter, the grocer kept stuffing in the wood into the stove, while poor Seth sat bolt upright, with his back against the counter, and his knees almost touching the red hot furnace before him.

"Darnation cold night, this," said the grocer. "Why, Seth, you seem to perspire as if you were warm! Why don't you take your hat off? Here, let me put your hat away!"

"*No!*" exclaimed poor Seth at last, with a spasmodic effort to get his tongue loose, and clapping both hands upon his hat, "No! I must go: let me go out; I aint well; let me go!" A greasy cataract was now pouring down the poor fellow's face and neck, and soaking into his clothes, and trickling down his body into his very boots, so that he was literally in a perfect bath of oil.

"Well, good night, Seth," said the humorous Vermonter, "if you *will* go;" adding, as Seth got out into the road, "neighbor, I reckon the fun I've had out of you is worth a nine pence, so I shan't charge you for that *pound of butter!*"

Racing the Train

There were these two fellers who had never seen a train before, so they figured they'd go out and see one, since there was a track runnin' nearby, ten miles west of Tarboro. When they got to the track, they saw there wasn't anything to see but two long, shiny rails. So they laid down to wait, and pretty soon they heard an awful noise and then they saw comin' the most fearsome, smoke-belchin' thing they'd ever seen. Well, they commenced to runnin' ahead of that train—one fella runnin' along the track and the other speedin' off into the woods. With all the strength he could muster, the fella runnin' along the track yelled out to his buddy, "Bob, if I cain't outrun this damn thing on this here perty road, you ain't never gonna outrun it in them woods."

The New Telephone Wire

Saturday at dinner they loaded on a bale of cotton and this old man carried it to the gin. Then he come back and told his wife, "They're a-puttin' in the outfit that I never heard of in my life."

"Well," she says, "husband, what wuz it?"

"Well," he says, "they call it a telephone wire. I never saw nothin' like it."

"Ooh! I do wish that I could go see it."

"Well," he says, "kindle up, work hard, and if we get out another bale of cotton by next Saturday at dinner, we'll load it on, and I'll carry you up there to see the telephone wire."

Well, she decided that they wasn't gonna quite make it and she hired two children to come and help 'em so they would get out the bale of cotton by Saturday night.

Well, they got there. They got there with the bale of cotton. And she hurried up and walked along under the wire. It was about a mile long then. She'd hold her hand over her eyes and look and watch.

"Well," he says, "now have you saw the telephone wire?"

She says, "Yeah, I saw it. I'm ready to go."

He says, "Old woman, what do ya thinka that?"

"Well, old man, I think it might be all right to send papers and letters on, but when they put a bale a cotton up there, POP she'll go."

When You Don't Know, Guess

There was a young boy from the hill country who didn't know much about anything. When he was old enough, the boy was told by his father that he should get a job helping a cousin down in the town at the cousin's general store. This cousin was an ambitious salesman and he told the boy that he wanted the boy never to turn away any business.

One day, the boy was left to run the store for an hour while his cousin was out on business. Just then, an old man came in with a gold watch. "Think ya kin fix it?" he asked the boy.

"Sartin we kin," the boy replied.

"Now?" asked the old man.

"In a bit, when my cousin gits back," the boy answered, figuring his cousin could fix anything.

Shaking his head, the old man started to leave, saying "Gotta git it fixed now."

Well, the boy went into a panic, because his cousin was always saying that they should never turn away business. "Wait, mister," he blurted out, "I'll fix it fer ya."

Now, the boy had never seen a watch in his life, didn't even know what it was for, but he dutifully pried the watch open from the back to look inside. As he did so, out dropped a bug onto the table. The boy's heart leaped.

"I figgered out what was wrong, mister," the boy said proudly, "Why, the fella that runs this thing is dead!"

The Razorback Hog

The razorback hog is one tough animal, and there is a famous story to prove it. There was this farmer who was clearing some ground for a field he wanted to use. He took down all the trees and then went after the stumps. The best way to get those stumps up, the farmer was told, was to use dynamite, rather than pulling them up with a mule and chain. So the farmer bought some dynamite, took it to the field, and dug a deep hole under the roots of one of the big blackjack oak stumps.

After laying a few sticks under the first stump, the farmer lit the fuses and waited behind a rock. Nothing happened. Obviously the fuses had died, he thought. Just then his wife called him home. So the farmer left the field, figuring that he'd return after dinner to relight the fuses.

Now, this farmer had a big razorback hog, a tough, ugly thing that he let forage around. That hog got to the oak stump, found the dynamite, and did what hogs do when they find things lying around: he ate them. All three sticks. Then the hog made his way back to the barn, where he decided to take a little of the mule's cornfeed for dessert. After breaking into the mule's stall, the hog put his snout into its trough. The mule wasted no time and kicked the hog with a vengeance. It won't surprise you, I suppose, if I tell you that that kick and that dynamite made quite a team.

A neighbor who heard the explosion and saw the smoke ran over. There he found the farmer standing in the ruins of his barn. "Good God Almighty, Tom," he said to the farmer, "it looks right bad."

"Yep," the farmer answered, shaking his head, "my mules is all dead, the barn is gone, every window in my house done blow'd out, and I've got one awful sick hog."

A Family Pet

Acme Sulphide came in from his prospect on Caribou Creek, bringing a big cougar to Larry Frazee's taxidermist shop. "Want him skun out and made into a rug?" asked Larry.

"No sir. Stuff him as is. I wouldn't think of walkun on Petronius."

"Why not? Just a cougar, ain't he?"

"Not by your tin horn. He's an institution, that's what he is. When he was just a kitten I ketched him by the mine shaft. Him and Pluto, they was great friends until Petronius growed up. Then, one evening when I comes back, why Pluto was gone and Petronius wouldn't eat his supper. I was plumb mad, but I figgered Pluto was gettun old and wasn't so much account nohow. Then, by gum, I missed Mary, the goat. When I missed the last of the chickens and Petronius showed up with feathers in his whiskers, I made up my mind to shoot him. But I got to thinkun how that goat could butt, and the hens wasn't layun anyhow. So I let it go. But I shoulda bumped him then.

"Lydie, she's my old woman—or she was. Partner of my joys and sorrows for forty years. One evening when I gets back she was gone. No sign of her anywhere exceptun one shoe. And Petronius didn't want no supper agin. That got me mad, danged if it didn't, and I went for my gun to blast the varmint. Then I got to thinkun. Lydie wasn't much for looks and besides, she was about to leave me. She was all for hittun the trail, so I puts my gun up."

"Then what happened?"

"Well, last night he jumped me on the trail and took a big hunk right out of me. That was too danged much. So mount him up pretty. He represents my whole family."

Pig or Puppy

There was once a man from Nash County, named Wilson, whose best friend lived in the neighboring county. Wilson and his friend both loved dogs and, one Christmas, Wilson gave his gardener a pretty puppy to take to his friend's house as a gift. The gardener was a simplehearted man, and after he got his instructions he put that puppy in a burlap sack, loaded it onto the wagon, and set off.

On the way through town, the gardener stopped at the local bar for a drink and left the wagon unattended. Some mischievous children heard the puppy's whining and, determined to bewilder the gardener, they put a baby pig into the sack in place of the puppy. The poor gardener came out, climbed aboard the wagon, and continued on his way.

When he reached his destination, he took the sack from the wagon and, to his confusion, heard grunting sounds. The man opened up the sack and closed it tight again, turned around and headed for home, saying to himself, "The boss sure didn't want me deliverin' no pig. No sir."

On the way home, he stopped again at the bar, and those same children put the puppy back in the sack. After a quick drink, the gardener came out and off he went, back to his employer's home. Minutes before he arrived there he heard barking from his sack. Looking inside, the gardener shook his head. "Good golly," he said. "In Nash County you is one thing and in Warren County you is another. You best make up your mind and tell me—is you pig or is you puppy?"

Quit While You're Ahead

On the Pleasant plantation, a slave known as Uncle John could tell his master every morning what the master was going to do all that day. The manner in which Uncle John found out about Master Tom Pleasant's plans was by hiding behind the chimney of the fireplace at the big house every evening. The master had a practice of telling his wife soon after supper each night what he planned to do the next day, and Uncle John had found this out.

After the evening eavesdropping, Uncle John was prepared the next morning to tell his master how many slaves were going to pick cotton, how many were going to chop cord wood, how many were going to husk corn, etc. He was often called upon to make such predictions, or rather, as it seemed, to read his master's mind. At length Master Tom Pleasant decided to make a thorough test of the darkey's fortune-telling abilities. The Civil War had commenced, and he considered it dangerous to have a fortune-teller among the slaves.

One Saturday night, shortly after Texas joined the Confederacy, the master told his wife that he was going to whip Uncle John good the next night, and find out whether he was fooling him or not. Uncle John was behind the chimney as usual and heard what the master had to say. The next morning the master called him and said, "John, what am I going to do today?"

"Wal," said John, "Boss, yuh's gonna whip ol' John ternight."

"Yes," said the master, "tonight at nine o'clock you meet me out at the stable and get your whipping."

"Aw right, Massa, aw right," said Uncle John.

The first thing Uncle John did was to go look for Uncle Jeremiah, his best friend. He asked him to get a lantern and an old bugle; to get high up in a tree near the stable shortly before nine o'clock that night, and wave the lantern and blow the trumpet every time he shouted to him to do so.

Uncle Jeremiah did as he was commanded and was in the tree at the hour appointed; Uncle John was at the back steps of the big house, where the master soon appeared.

"Don' whip me, Massa, don' whip me," pleaded Uncle John. "Ef yuh does, Ah's gwine call down Gab'ul f'om de heabens."

"Oh, yes," shouted the master, "I am going to beat you good. You know so much now, stop me from beating you."

"Flash yo' lightnin', Gab'ul, an' blow yo' trumpet!" shouted Uncle John. Uncle Jeremiah, hidden in the tree, started to waving the lantern and blowing the bugle.

"Stop! Stop!" shouted the master, seeing the light and hearing the trumpet. "I'll give you a thousand dollars if you don't have Gabriel come down."

"Naw suh, naw suh," shouted Uncle John. "Flash yo' lightnin', Gab'ul, an' blow yo' trumpet."

"Stop! Stop!" cried the master. "I'll give you your freedom if you don't have Gabriel come down."

"Naw suh, naw suh. Flash yo' lightnin', Gab'ul, an' blow yo' trumpet." Uncle Jeremiah waved the lantern again and blew the trumpet.

"Stop! Stop!" shouted the master. "I will give all of the slaves their freedom if you don't have Gabriel come down."

"Naw suh, naw suh," shouted Uncle John. "Flash yo' lightnin', Gab'ul, an' blow yo' trumpet."

Uncle Jeremiah, who had been very faithful up to this time, but who had just heard the master offer the freedom of all the slaves to Uncle John, now refused to flash the lantern. Instead he shouted from the branches of the tree to Uncle John: "Dat's ernuf. Whut mo' does yuh want?"

Little Brown Jug

Me and my wife and a bob-tailed dog,
Crossed the river on a hickory log,
My wife fell in, the dog got wet,
But I hung to my little brown jug, you bet!

Ha, ha, ha, you and me!
Little brown jug, don't I love thee?
When I am working on my farm,
I take little brown jug under my arm,
Put him under a shady tree,
Little brown jug, don't I love thee?
Chorus.

If I had a cow that gave such milk,
I'd dress her in the finest silk,
I'd feed her on the choicest hay
And milk her sixty times a day.
Chorus.

The rose is red, my nose is too,
The violets blue and so are you,
And yet I guess, before I stop,
I'd better take one last drop.
Chorus.

Moonshiners

Now, the way you begin making whisky, you carry your old barrels to the place, in some holler where they is plenty of water. A still is a thing you can make. You take and get you a sheet of copper the size you want to make your still, large or small, and you take some brass brads and put that thing in the form of a barrel. Then you take plank and make a head for this still. After that you want a hole in this head, so you take a auger and handsaw and saw a round hole in the head for your cap, whatever cap you want. It's a kag about twelve inches, I guess.

But start with your mash first in the copper still. Take and heat your water boiling, then you take meal. Pour your meal in the barrel, and then you pour in your water. You stir this meal up until you cook it good. You keep right on adding meal and water until you cook it right into a mush. Well, when you get it cooked to your notion, you take about a quart of flour to ever' barrel, and put it right down on top of your mash to hold your heat in. 'Ell, we let that set over to the next day, let it get good and cool.

And then we take an old sausage mill to grind our malt corn. We'd sprout what was called malt corn. Take and put corn in a coffee sack in water until it sprouted good, until good long sprouts come on it. Then we'd take this mill and grind this malt corn up, about a kag to a barrel. And we'd go back and put this malt corn in that barrel. And then you take your hands like making dough, and you bust ever' lump in there. Stir just like making gravy, to get it all dissolved just like milk. And then you cover your barrel real good, and in about three days this meal will go to working. You've seen slop, now, be setting in a bucket in hot times, come up in big bubbles and bust. That's the way mash works. It'll work in about three or four days sometimes.

Then it'll clear off, and all that meal will settle back in the bottom. And then we'll go ahead and get a forked stick, and we'll get into them barrels, and we'll stir all that up together. We'll take and build us a fire and heat that until it turns into a simmer, beginning to get ready to boil. Then we take our cap, put a stick with a hole in it down in the cap, and put it in that hole in the still. And then we'll take clay mud and daub all the steam in there. The steam is coming out the hole in your cap. We have a piece of wood, oh, usually about two feet long, sourwood. Take it and bore me a hole in it. Start in at one end and bore as far as I can, and then start at the other end and bore the hole out. We use that fer an arm. We put that in that still cap, and we'll daub it in there. Well, we'll put a worm in it if we're making the old-fashioned way—we'll take our worm then and put in the other end of that arm, and we'll daub her in there good. And of course if we're making it with a crooked worm, we'll have a barrel to put that worm in; and if we're making with a straight worm, we'll have a trough made and a hole bored in each end of it, and the worm would run through it for our water to pour in on.

That goes to boiling in the still, and the steam comes out into that worm and evaporates in the worm, and when it comes out to the end, we catch it and call it singlings. It's an alkiehol, but not high-powered alkiehol. It runs a stream about the size of a number-eight nail.

Well, we'll run these singlings off, about eight or ten gallons, sometimes twelve.

I'll have this still full of singlings and go back and pour 'em in a barrel. I'll go right back and repeat it over and over till I'll get me a barrel of this what I call singlings. Well, now I'll take my old still apart and wash and scrub it. Have to wash ever'thing thoroughly clean—worm, arm, still, cap, and ever'thing. Take you about three hours or three hours and a half to get it cleaned up ready for your second run.

Then I'll put these singlings back in the still. Get 'em on the fire now and get 'em to boiling, just up in the center, like you was a-making sorghum, you know, when they go to foaming up in the pan. I'll cap 'em up like I did in the first place. Well, I'll pull my fire down to a very small fire—you wouldn't want to overheat it. Just heat it enough to get it started to boil good enough, and then just keep a small steady fire under it. Keep about one temperature all the time. About an hour after you capped your still up again, your first shots of alkiehol begin to run. Two hundred proof. You'd catch that in a jar or jug, whatever you wanted to catch 'em in. Set it around. I always mark mine—number one, two, three, four, like that. Catch it in a gallon fruit jar or gallon jug. Sometimes I'd catch it in a gallon jug.

When I'd get this run off down to where it gets so weak it wouldn't bead—you see, it is too strong to bead when it first comes out of a run like we're speaking of; sometimes you can catch ten or twelve gallons too strong to bead—well, then you catch you so much and this is good beading whisky, about ninety to a hundred to a hundred-and-ten proof. Then it runs down until it won't bead a-tall. And we call that backings. Then I'll catch a half a bushel of these backings, and then I'll cut it all off and get ready to make my whisky.

Take my first shots, my middle batch, and my weak batch, and I'll get me two old washtubs. I'll put me so much of one kind in there and so much of another. Take me a stick and keep it stirred up good. I'll keep a-tasting, you know, clear down in the bottom, and shaking it. I'd put some in a bottle and give it three shakes and turn it back upright. Get the bead of the whisky till it would be the size of a squirrel's eye—that's the way I allas judged it. I'd have a hundred-

and-ten proof whisky. And I'd keep on that way till I got my whole batch o' whisky just the way I wanted it. Jar it up and go to selling it then.

Thanks Just the Same

Down in Malad Valley, Big Andy had been drinking; and when time came to go home to his wife, he decided to ride with a man named Jones, because Jones had a load of hay. But, while journeying, most of the load slid off, with Andy atop it, still pulling lustily from his bottle. He must have sat there an hour, drinking and smiling benignly, before another man came along. "Hello," he said, "you want a ride?" "No, thanks," said Andy, waving his bottle, "I'm riding with this guy."

A Little More Cider

One time, there was a fellow had a fine big apple orchard, and soon as the new highway come through he got to selling apples in baskets. He built a little wooden stand down by the road, so pretty near every automobile that come along would stop. Then the fellow got hold of a cider-mill, and after that he sold cider in bottles, with a nice label on it. Finally he fixed up a icebox in the stand, so as to sell cider by the drink. The tourists liked it fine, and the fellow was making pretty good money.

A big bunch of people from St. Louis come along one day, so him and his wife was both down at the stand, and their little boy was a-leaning against the counter. The little boy was about six years old, and he was a cute little fellow. So a big fat tourist woman says, "Sonny, do you like cider?" The boy smiled at her. "Oh yes, ma'am!" says he. The tourist woman laid down another dime and passed the boy a full glass, but the little fellow kind of held back. "Go ahead and drink it," says the tourist woman.

She kept on a-urging him, but the little boy just shook his head. "We got our own cider in the cellar to drink," he says. "This here selling-cider is made out of apples which has got worms in 'em." The tourist woman set her glass right down on the counter, and the other customers didn't drink no more cider, neither. They just looked at each other kind of funny for a minute. Then they all walked out to their big shiny automobiles and drove off down the road.

The fellow and his wife just stood there goggle-eyed till the customers was plumb out of sight. Pretty soon the man cut a switch and tanned the little boy's behind all the way back to the house. He sure laid it on heavy, and you could hear that boy a-hollering clear down to the crossroads.

The old mother-in-law got pretty mad, and she says things has come to a pretty pass when a young-un gets a whipping for telling the truth. The fellow says it ain't so. "I raise my children to be honest," says he. "Why, if Tommy was to tell them tourists that the cider *ain't* made out of wormy apples, I'd give him a licking for lyin'."

The old woman studied awhile. "You whip him if he says the apples is wormy, and then whip him again if he says they ain't! It don't make no sense to me. What are you-uns tryin' to learn that boy, anyhow?"

The fellow just kind of grinned at her. "We're tryin' to learn him to keep his mouth shut," says he.

A Still Tongue Makes a Wise Head

There was once a farmer who was a hard worker, stood well with everybody, and owned his own home in the post oaks on the edge of the Brazos bottom. He was a man of considerable intelligence and raised his three oldest daughters to be schoolteachers. His youngest child was a boy, and by the time he had reached the age of seventeen it dawned upon the father that his son was a fool. The son also began to understand that he was a fool. But the father did not give up hope. He took great pains in trying to train the boy so that he would not act so foolishly.

One day, he said to him: "Son, you talks too much. Dat's how people knows dat you am silly. Ain't yer never heard dat a still tongue makes a wise haid? If you'd keep yer mouf shut, folks wouldn't find out what a fool you is."

The boy took the lesson in good faith and agreed to do his best to keep people from finding out.

Not long after this, the old man and his son took a load of stovewood to town. They drove the wagon up on the square and the old man got down, went into a store, and left the boy sitting on the load of wood.

A merchant across the square saw the wood and hurried over to buy it. Coming up to the wagon, he looked at the boy and called out, "Hello, boy, do you want to sell that wood?"

The boy rolled his eyes but kept his mouth shut.

Again the merchant asked, "How much will you take for that wood?"

Still the boy looked wise and never said a word.

Exasperated and disgusted, the merchant turned on his heel, remarking, "Humph, you must be a fool."

Soon afterwards the old man came out of the store and climbed up on the wagon. The boy looked at him sadly and said, "Pappy, dey's done found it out, an' I ain't opened my mouf."

A Long-Handled Shovel

One time, there was a fool boy up on Cow Creek took a notion to dig him a well in the pasture. He dug down a ways, and then all of a sudden the side of the well caved in. There was some rocks fell down too, and it's God's own luck the poor half-wit didn't get killed and buried right there.

Away along in the night he come a-running up to one of the neighbors' house, a-hollering so loud he woke everybody up. "For God's sake," says he, "give me a long-handled shovel!" The old man says, "This is a hell of a time to raise such a hullabaloo, and if you want to borrow something why don't you come in the daytime?" But the boy just kept on a-hollering. "The well caved in on me! I'm a-dying under all these rocks and dirt! For God's sake give me a long-handled shovel!" The old man was pretty mad by this time. "I ain't going to put up with no more of this foolishness," he says. "Maw, fetch me the shotgun!" And so the boy run a-blubbering down the road.

When he come to the next house the boy hollered everybody up just like he done before. "For God's sake," says he, "give me a long-handled shovel! The well caved in on me! I'm a-dying under all them rocks and dirt! For God's sake give me a long-handled shovel!" The man come to the door and opened it, until he seen who was there. "You ain't a-dying," says he, "you're just drunk." And then the man went back to bed and blowed out the light. The boy hollered around outside for a while. Then he give up and run on down the road.

It was pretty near daylight when he come to the third house, and the fellow that lived there got up and put on his clothes. "For God's sake give me a long-handled shovel!" says the boy. "The well caved in on me! I'm a-dying under all them rocks and dirt! For God's sake give me a long-handled shovel!" The fellow couldn't make no sense out of what the boy says, but he figured something serious was the matter. So he went and got the shovel. The boy grabbed it and run back up the road fast as he could.

The fellow that give him the shovel follered right along behind, to help out. They run pretty near four miles. Then the boy took out across the cow pasture, and jumped down a big hole in the ground. Dirt and rocks begun to fly, so the fellow just stood back out of the way. He figured on doing some shoveling himself, soon as the boy got tired.

Pretty soon the boy come a-climbing out. He wiped the dirt and sweat off his face, and he looked mighty happy about something. "By God, I made it!" says he. "But it was a mighty close call. If you hadn't given me that shovel, I'd be dead as a wagon-tire right this minute!"

The fellow stared at the boy mighty funny, and then he went over and looked down the hole. "Listen, son," says he, "was anybody else down there, when the dirt caved in?" The boy says, "No, I was all by myself. That's what makes well-digging so damned dangerous."

Nobody said anything after that, and you could hear the peter-birds a-singing in the trees. The fellow just set there and thought about it awhile. Pretty soon he picked up his shovel, and started out to walk the four miles back home.

Paw Won't Like This

One time, there was a farm boy coming to town with a big load of hay. Just after they crossed the Cow Creek bridge, the horses got to acting up, and pretty soon they upset the whole business in the road just below the Applegate place. When old man Applegate come out, there was the wagon laying on one side, and a pile of hay big as a mountain. The farm boy was running around wild-eyed, and looked like he was going to bust out crying. "Paw won't like this," says he. "Paw won't like this at all!"

As soon as he seen the horses wasn't hurt, old man Applegate done his best to get the boy calmed down. "Don't you worry, son," says he. "It ain't your fault. Things like that might happen to any-body." So then he says, "You just fetch the team up to my barn, and come and eat dinner with us. After dinner me and the hired man will help you pitch that hay back onto the rack." The boy says he'd like to have dinner, but his paw wouldn't want him to leave the wagon. "Don't you worry about that," says old man Applegate. "I've knowed your paw longer than you have, and I'll tell him all about it." So the boy took his team up to the barn, and fed them. And then he went over to the house and ate a big dinner with the family.

After dinner they all set out on the porch awhile, a-belching and picking their teeth. Everybody tried their best to cheer the boy up, but he acted terrible uneasy. "Paw won't like this," says he, "I better go back to the wagon." The folks just laughed, and says for him not to worry. "The first time I see your paw, I'll tell him you ain't to blame," says old man Applegate. "Maybe I'll tend to it this evening. Is your paw in town today?"

The boy looked at old man Applegate kind of bewildered. "Why no," he says, "paw's under that there hay."

Ask the River

The streams of the Plains are very different in their behavior from ordinary streams. Most streams constantly tend to cut their channels deeper, and are therefore called degrading streams. The streams of the Plains, on the other hand, are building up their channels. The cause is twofold: first, the immense amounts of sand which the streams carry; and second, relatively small amounts of water carried by the streams. In other words, the rainfall along the various rivers is not sufficient to furnish water enough to scour the stream channel, and so the streams are aggrading, or building up their channel.

This in turn means that these streams are constantly changing their courses. They have low, sandy banks, and with every freshet the channel shifts back and forth. This causes destruction of farms, and it is no uncommon thing for a stream that has been bridged to abandon its channel under the bridge and leave the structure high and dry.

People coming to this western country do not always understand the behavior of our rivers and, until they learn better, attempt to treat them as they did the streams in the East. This method of treatment is not always successful.

Some twenty years ago I happened to be down on the South Canadian near Norman and found an Iowa farmer, who had bought a river-bottom farm, building a dike along the riverbank. He had three teams at work with scrapers throwing up a wall of loose sand between his field and the water in the river.

His neighbor, a former cowboy who had lived in Indian Territory all his life and who owned the adjoining farm, came sauntering up to see what was going on. He wore the regulation cattleman's outfit, high-heeled boots and broad-brimmed white hat. He stood for a time watching the teams at work moving dirt.

"Well, neighbor," he said, "what do you reckon you're doing?"

"Building me a dike," said the Iowa farmer.

"Dike? What's it for?" inquired the cowboy.

"Why, to keep out the water, of course."

"Do you reckon it'll do it?" asked the cowboy.

"Don't see why not," replied the farmer, "I built just such a dike back in Iowa and it did the work."

The cowboy said nothing for quite a while. He walked over to the bank, looked up the river and down the river, spit into the water, and turned to the Iowa man. "Did you ask the river?" he said.

The very next rise not only took out the dike but washed away half the farmer's field.

A Mean Grocer

There is a grocer who is said to be so mean that he was seen to catch a flea off his counter, hold him up by his legs, and look into the cracks of his feet to see if he hadn't been stealing sugar.

The Vinegar Queen's Supper

Not far from a Mississippi river town was a boardinghouse that catered to the men who made their living on the river. Included in the weekly rate was an evening meal, usually a foul-tasting stew prepared by a bad-tempered cook that generations of boarders had nicknamed "the Vinegar Queen." Her custom was to bang an old pot with a tin spoon and summon her luckless boarders to the meal. One night, she banged the pot and startled a sleeping hound dog under the table into a loud and mournful howl. As the boarders filed in, one said, glaring at the dog, "What the hell is *he* making such a fuss about? He ain't got to eat it!"

The Boardinghouse

A wildcat well was being put down on a farm in the apple country of Arkansas. The drilling crew was boarding at the house of the farmer. Each morning, there would be fried apples for breakfast. Each noon, there would be stewed apples for dinner. Each night, there would be apple cobbler for supper. This diet was welcomed at first, but as the weeks went by, the men ate with less and less gusto. One day as the apple dish went by, a driller passed it on. The landlady said, "Mr. Green, I'm afraid you don't like apples."

"Oh yes," he said. "I like apples. I'm just not a son of a bitch about them."

East Texas Episode

The standard oil lease is for ten years or until the drilling of a well, and an annual rental is paid the lessor. Usually some bank is designated as the depository agent, and deposit of the rental money in the bank constitutes legal payment. In East Texas during the depression days of the 1930s, some of the banks so designated failed, and the oilmen, in order to retain their leases, found it necessary to tender lease money in person. One day, a representative of an oil company arrived in the Sulphur Bottom country with $120 in currency for a man named Tobe Fails, who owned a rundown farm in the region. He stopped at a filling station and asked how to find the Fails farm.

The attendant pointed to a rusty and topless Model T Ford and said, "That's Tobe turning off the highway now."

The agent overtook Fails on the dirt road, but when he sounded his horn, the old car leaped ahead and began dodging through the trees and around piles of bush where tie cutters had been at work. After a long and circuitous race, the Model T stopped back of a house. The agent stopped in front, got out, and knocked on the door. After a few minutes Tobe opened the door partway and looked out. "What do you want?" he asked.

The oilman held up some bills. "I want to tender you the hundred and twenty dollars rental due you on that oil lease my company bought last year."

"Well, of all the luck!" Tobe said. "You have been chasing me all over hell and half of Texas to pay me a hundred and twenty dollars, and I just throwed two gallons of the best whiskey I ever made in the well."

The Man from Texas

One time, there was a fellow that lived in Arkansas, but he was born and raised in Texas. So most of the time he just sat around bragging about the Lone Star State, and he says Texas is just the same as Paradise. The home folks didn't think much of this kind of talk, because it looked like he was running down Arkansas. Texas is all right, maybe, but anybody that has been there knows it ain't no heaven on earth.

Pretty soon, a man from Yellville begun to tell a story about a Texan that died and he was trying to get into Heaven. Saint Peter talked with him awhile, but the Texan didn't do nothing but jingle his big spurs and brag up Texas. Finally Saint Peter opened the gate, and he says, "Well, you can come in. But I'm afraid you won't like it here." The Arkansawyers all laughed at that story, but the man from Texas says he don't see nothing funny about it.

So then a man from Hot Springs begun to tell a story about another Texan that died, and when he got to the pearly gate they ask, Where did he come from? "I was borned and raised in Texas," says he. The angel opened up the gate. "Come right in, brother," says the angel, "you have been in Hell long enough!" The Arkansawyers all laughed at that story, but the man from Texas says he don't see nothing funny about it.

Next a fellow from Bald Knob told a story about another Texan that died, and when he come to the big gate it was wide open, so he could see what was going on inside. The Texan stood there a-fanning himself with his big hat, and he says, "Gosh, I didn't know Heaven was so much like Texas." The gatekeeper just looked at him kind of sorrowful. "Son," he says, "this ain't Heaven." The Arkansawyers all laughed at that story, but the man from Texas says he don't see nothing funny about it.

Them fellows from Texas can read and write, fiddle and fight, knock up and throw down. They can holler loud, shoot straight, and jump high. But it seems like most of 'em is kind of dumb when it comes to appreciating a funny story.

Keep Going

There is a story that New Yorkers like to tell about their neighbors in New Jersey that goes like this: Not so long ago, a cabin cruiser was shipwrecked off the Carolina coast. The captain was the only survivor and he clung to a piece of a wooden door, drifting for several days until he was finally spotted by a local fishing trawler. The fishermen threw him a line and hauled him alongside. With teeth chattering, the poor, shipwrecked skipper asked, "Where am I?" "New Jersey," came the answer. Gripping his door with resignation, the tired drifter shouted back, "I guess I'll float on a little further."

Oolah! Oolah!

One time, there was a fellow lived just over the line in Oklahoma, and he was running for Congress. There was a lot of Indian farmers out that way, and he got an old chief to round up a lot of them to hear him speak.

"The Government ain't treated you boys right in the past," says he, "but I aim to change all that soon as I get to Washington. After I'm elected, my Indian brothers won't be living in shanties and brush wigwams like they do now. No, siree! Not in my district! I'm going to see that every one of you fellows has got a good house, and fine furniture, and a new cookstove, and a electric ice-box if he wants it."

The Indians acted like they was mighty happy to hear this, and they all clapped their hands and hollered, "Oolah! Oolah!" The old chief looked kind of surprised, but he did not say nothing.

"And furthermore," says the candidate, "my first act as your Congressman will be to get every Indian voter a good farm if he ain't got one already. And I'm going to fix it so every one of you boys can have a nice, late-model car, instead of some old jaloppy. Yes, and we'll build roads fit to drive on, without no mud holes in 'em!"

The Indians was in a fine good humor by this time, laughing and chuckling amongst themselves, and they clapped their hands louder than ever. They was all hollering, "Oolah! Oolah!" till you could hear them half a mile off.

"I'm going to bring better livestock into the district too," says the candidate. "I'll see that good bulls and stallions are available to every Indian stockman, so that our cattle and horses will be second to none in the United States." And with that he set down, and all them Indians was so happy they just laughed and slapped each other on the back. They kept a-hollering, "Oolah! Oolah!" for five minutes anyhow, while the candidate was a-smiling and shaking hands with everybody that come within reach. He says it is the most enthusiastic audience he ever spoke to, and one of the best meetings of his whole campaign. The old chief he just set there poker-faced and never said a word, but anybody that knows Indians could tell he was just as tickled as the rest of them.

On the way back to town the candidate stopped at a big farm where the ranchman wanted to show him some fine cattle. There was one prize bull that they said was worth ten thousand dollars. "A magnificent animal!" says the candidate, and he started to walk right into the pen, but an Indian ranchhand touched his arm. "You better come around this other gate, Mister," he says. "The boys ain't cleaned up that side yet, and if you walk over there you'll get *oolah* on your shoes."

Crockett Gets the Votes

While on the subject of election matters, I will just relate a little anecdote about myself, which will show the people to the east how we manage these things on the frontiers. It was when I first run for Congress. Well, I started off to the Cross Roads, dressed in my hunting shirt, and my rifle on my shoulder. Many of our constituents had assembled there to get a taste of the quality of the candidates at orating. Job Snelling, a gander-shanked Yankee who had been caught somewhere about Plymouth Bay and had been shipped to the West with a cargo of codfish and rum, erected a large shanty and set up shop for the occasion. A large posse of the voters had assembled before I arrived, and my opponent had already made considerable headway with his speechifying and his treating, when they spied me about a rifle shot from the camp, sauntering along as if I was not a party in the business. "There comes Crockett," cried one. "Let us hear the colonel," cried another; and so I mounted the stump that had been cut down for the occasion, and began to bushwhack in the most approved style.

I had not been up long before there was such an uproar in the crowd that I could not hear my own voice, and some of my constituents let me know that they could not listen to me on such a dry subject as the welfare of the nation, until they had something to drink, and that I must treat 'em. Accordingly I jumped down from the rostrum and led the way to the shanty, followed by my constituents shouting, "Huzza for Crockett," and "Crockett for ever!"

When we entered the shanty, Job was busy dealing out his rum in a style that showed he was making a good day's work of it, and I called for a quart of the best, but the crooked critur returned no other answer than by pointing at a board over the bar, on which he had chalked in large letters, *"Pay to-day and trust to-morrow."* Now, that idea brought me all up standing; it was a sort of cornering in which there was no back out, for ready money in the West, in those times, was the shyest thing in all natur, and it was most particularly shy with me on that occasion.

The voters, seeing my predicament, fell off to the other side, and I was left deserted and alone, as Andrew Jackson will be when he no longer has any offices to bestow. I saw, plain as day, that the tide of popular opinion was against me and that, unless I got some rum speedily, I should lose my election as sure as there are snakes in Virginny—and it must be done soon, or even burnt brandy wouldn't save me. So I walked away from the shanty, and not a voice shouted, "Huzza for Crockett." Popularity sometimes depends on a very small matter indeed; in this particular it was worth a quart of New England rum, and no more.

Well, knowing that a crisis was at hand, I struck into the woods with my rifle on my shoulder, my best friend in time of need, and as good fortune would have it, I had not been out more than a quarter of an hour before I treed a fat coon, and in the pulling of a trigger he lay dead at the root of the tree. I soon whipped his hairy jacket off his back, and again bent my way towards the shanty, and walked up to the bar, but not alone, for this time I had half a dozen of my constituents at my heels. I threw down the coonskin upon the counter and called for a quart, and Job, though busy in dealing out rum, forgot to point at his chalked rules and regulations, for he knew that a coon was as good a legal tender for a quart, in the West as a New York shilling, any day in the year.

My constituents now flocked about me and cried, "Huzza for Crockett," "Crockett for ever," and finding that the tide had taken a turn, I told them several yarns, to get them in a good humour, and having soon dispatched the value of the coon, I went out and mounted the stump, without opposition, and a clear majority of the voters followed me to hear what I had to offer for the good of the nation. Before I was half through, one of my constituents moved that they would hear the balance of my speech after they had washed down the first part with some more of Job Snelling's extract of cornstalk and molasses, and the question being put, it was carried unanimously. It wasn't considered necessary to call the yeas and nays, so we adjourned to the shanty, and on the way I began to reckon that the fate of the nation pretty much depended upon my shooting another coon.

While standing at the bar, feeling sort of bashful while Job's rules and regulations stared me in the face, I cast down my eyes and discovered one end of the coonskin sticking between the logs that supported the bar. Job had slung it there in the hurry of business. I gave it a sort of quick jerk, and it followed my hand as natural as if I had been the rightful owner. I slapped it on the counter, and Job, little dreaming that he was barking up the wrong tree, shoved along another bottle, which my constituents quickly disposed of with great good humour, for some of them saw the trick, and then we withdrew to the rostrum to discuss the affairs of the nation.

I don't know how it was, but the voters soon became dry again, and nothing would do but we must adjourn to the shanty; and as luck would have it, the coonskin was still sticking between the logs, as if Job had flung it there on purpose to tempt me. I was not slow in raising it to the counter, the rum followed of course; and I wish I may be shot if I didn't, before the day was over, get ten quarts for the same identical skin, and from a fellow, too, who in those parts was considered as sharp as a steel trap and as bright as a pewter button.

This joke secured me my election, for it soon circulated like smoke among my constituents, and they allowed, with one accord, that the man who could get the whip hand of Job Snelling in fair trade, could outwit Old Nick himself, and was the real grit for them in Congress.

The way I got to the blind side of the Yankee merchant was pretty generally known before the election day, and the result was that my opponent might as well have whistled jigs to a milestone as attempt to beat up for votes in that district. I beat him out and out, quite back into the old year, and there was scarce enough left of him, after the canvass was over, to make a small grease spot. He disappeared without even leaving as much as a mark behind.

After the election was over, I sent Snelling the price of the rum, but took good care to keep the fact from the knowledge of my constituents. Job refused the money, and sent me word that it did him good to be taken in occasionally, as it served to brighten his ideas; but I afterwards learnt that when he found out the trick that had been played upon him, he put all the rum I had ordered in his bill against my opponent, who, being elated with the speeches he had made on the affairs of the nation, could not descend to examine into the particulars of the bill of a vendor of rum in the small way.

Change the Name of Arkansas?

Mr. Speaker: The man who would CHANGE THE NAME OF ARKANSAS is the original iron-jawed, brass-mounted, copper-bellied corpsemaker from the wilds of the Ozarks! Sired by a hurricane, dammed by an earthquake, half-brother to the cholera, nearly related to the small-pox on his mother's side, he is the man they call Sudden Death and General Desolation! Look at him! He takes nineteen alligators and a barrel of whiskey for breakfast, when he is in robust health; and a bushel of rattlesnakes and a dead body when he is ailing. He splits the everlasting rocks with his glance, and quenches the thunder when he speaks!

Change the name of Arkansas! Hell, no! stand back and give him room according to his strength. Blood's his natural drink! and the wail of the dying is music to his ears! Cast your eyes on the gentleman, and lay low and hold your breath, for he's 'bout to turn himself loose! He's the bloodiest son of a wild-cat that lives, who would change the name of Arkansas! Hold him down to earth, for he is a child of sin! Don't attempt to look at him with your naked eye, gentlemen; use smoked glass. The man who would change the name of Arkansas, by gosh, would use the meridians of longitude and the parallels of latitude for a seine, and drag the Atlantic Ocean for whales! He would scratch himself awake with the lightning, and purr himself asleep with the thunder! When he's cold, he would "bile" the Gulf of Mexico and bathe in it! When he's hot, he would fan himself with an equinoctial storm! When he's thirsty, he would reach up and suck a cloud dry like a sponge! When he's hungry, famine follows in his wake! You may put your hand on the sun's face, and make it night on the earth; bite a piece out of the moon, and hurry the seasons; shake yourself and rumble the mountains; but, sir, you will never change the name of Arkansaw!

The man who would change the name of Arkansaw would massacre isolated communities as a pastime. He would destroy nationalities as a serious business! He would use the boundless vastness of the Great American Desert for his private grave-yard! He would attempt to extract sunshine from cucumbers! Hide the stars in a nail-keg, put the sky to soak in a gourd, hang the Arkansas River on a clothesline, unbuckle the belly-band of Time, and turn the sun and moon out to pasture; but you will never change the name of Arkansaw! The world will again pause and wonder at the audacity of the lop-eared, lantern-jawed, half-breed, half-born, whiskey-soaked hyena who has proposed to change the name of Arkansaw! He's just starting to climb the political banister, and wants to knock the hayseed out of his hair, pull the splinters out of his feet, and push on and up to the governorship. *But change the name of Arkansaw, hell, no!*

Fitting Epitaph

Two men were walking through a graveyard when they came across a stone with the following inscription: "Here lies Sam Jones, an honest man and a good lawyer." After a moment's thought, one man turned to the other and remarked, "It sure is unusual for one grave to hold three people in it."

Hog-Thieves Hanging Together

A young district attorney was trying his first case. It was a rather simple one, a clear case of hog theft with no complications. The defendant was an old-timer who lived in the back country and did not seem to be a person of any consequence.

The case was called, and the defendant appeared without a lawyer and announced himself ready for trial. The young attorney explained that the state would furnish a lawyer if the defendant was not able to hire one. The defendant declined and the trial proceeded. The attorney put on his witnesses, developed his evidence, and very courteously turned his witnesses over to the defendant, who, however, did not ask a single question. The attorney closed his case and asked the defendant to put on his witnesses. The defendant had no witnesses.

Then the attorney made his argument before the jury, and the defendant was told that he might make a speech in his own behalf if he wished. The defendant said that he could not make a speech, but if the judge and attorney would permit, he would like to whisper a word or two in the ear of each of the jurymen. This request was granted, and the defendant passed to each member of the jury and whispered something in his ear. Then he sat down. The judge gave the charge and the jury retired. In a few minutes they brought in a verdict of "not guilty."

The attorney was astonished, for the verdict was clearly contrary to both the law and the evidence. The man had been proved guilty. But the jury had cleared him. The more the attorney thought about the case, the less he understood it. Finally he went to the defendant and said, "The jury has declared you not guilty. That makes you absolutely free from the charge. You can never be tried again for that offense. You won your case and I congratulate you. But I cannot understand why. I will give you ten dollars to tell me what you whispered in the ears of those jurymen."

The old man smiled, reached out for the ten, and replied, "I said, 'Now is the time for all us hog-thieves to hang together.' "

How Do You Plead?

There was once a man accused of horse-stealing. It seems that he had all but been caught in the act and the evidence presented by the prosecution amounted to an airtight verdict of guilty. The man's lawyer, though, was a smooth talker, and his summation was a masterpiece of melodrama and emotion. He talked of the man's long history of abandonment by his family and of the cruel and merciless misfortunes that had befallen him since the day he was born. The lawyer spared no detail. At last, he begged the jury to look in the thief's teary eyes to see if they could detect a man who would steal horses from his neighbors. It was no surprise that after this speech—the lawyer's last before he ran for state office—the jury found the man not guilty of any charges and let him go.

After the trial, the acquitted man went drinking in a nearby bar with friends and someone asked him if he had actually stolen the horses. "Well, boys," he said, shaking his head slowly, "I really don't know. I sure thought I did, but after hearin' that speech, I'll be danged if I know fer sure."

Shotgun Charlie's Sage Advice

The way I sees it, yo' generation is jes' too danged impatient. Ya'all got to have everythin' straight away and can't be waitin' for nothin' or nobody. Puts me in mind of the story about the fella who was plowin' his field. All he took with him was some corn cake to eat at noon. He plowed an' plowed an' then stopped to eat some of that cake. It was too hard. Like a stone. So he put it down an' commenced to plowin' some more. A couple of hours later he stopped agin and went to his corn cake. Still too hard. All day that man plowed his field and nearly worked hisself to death and didn't eat nothin'. Finally, when he had finished, he came over, took that corn cake, and ate it right up. Wiping his hands, the fella said to hisself, "I figgered that cake would get good after a while."

Listen to the People Talk

THE PHRASES BELOW are but a handful of examples of what some call "the folk idiom." They are snatches of speech alive with imagination and metaphor. We who live in an age of mass communication so often fail to say what we mean; perhaps we need to remind ourselves of the simple and vivid language all about us in America. The sound of the American folk voice is oftentimes the sound of poetry and wisdom.

Mad as a wet hen

Shy as a colt

He ain't got the brains God give a squirrel

So thin he had to stand twice in the same place to make a good shadow

Skittish as a bridegroom

He ain't got enough sense to pound sand in a rat hole. He jist plain got snow on his roof. [He's foolish]

It scared me pea green

That boy was comin' at me like a bat outta hell

Stiffer'n a lead pipe an' jist as cold

No bigger than a minute, that little gal

We're swingin' on the same gate, pardner

He wears a ten-dollar hat on a five-cent head

Don't know beans from buckshot

He's climbing Fool's Hill in a hurry

All vine an' no 'taters

Sometimes I don't know whether I'm pitchin' or catchin'

The more I see people the more I like dogs

She's got eight acres of hell in her, an' that ain't no lie

A bird cain't fly over that place without takin' some grub with 'im

That land's so poor, a turkey cain't gobble on it

His eyes always be shinin' like new money

He's all tongue and no gut

He could make a meal out'n a keg of ten-penny nails

Swellin' like a bullfrog

Cut your peaches, gals [go about your business]; thunder ain't rain

There ain't room enough to cuss a cat without gettin' a mouthful of
   fur

He ain't much of a shot—couldn't hit the side of a barn with his eyes
   open

Sure as God made little apples and folks to eat 'em

Lots of big cows got little horns

Clean as a hound's tooth

Countin' de stumps ain't gonna clear dat field

Stiff as a mule's tail, ugly as sin, meaner'n a chained dog, chatty as a
   sparrow, perty as a speckled puppy, fat as a Christmas turkey

He's always tellin' tales, always puttin' too much paint on the brush

When you be sweatin' in de short rows, you cain't see de whole field

Fella's so crooked they got to bury him with a corkscrew

Muddy roads make de mileposts lie

Fella's so tall he's gotta climb a ladder to shave hisself

The farther up the street you go, the tougher they are, and that man
   lives in the last house

He's so quick he can jump across the river and back without touching land

Tough as a pine knot

Skinny as a picket fence

Fat and sassy

Come in and set a spell. Don't be rushin' off

I'm just easin' along
I'm fair to middlin'
I'm right sharp today. I feel right stout

Riddles

WE ALL KNOW our share of riddles. We heard them when we were children and sharpened our curiosity on their puzzling clues. The answers were always so plain, uncomplicated, and obvious that we couldn't wait to go off and stump others. There are riddles of all kinds—some that trick or tease, others that are funny or challenge the mind—but the best riddles are the old ones. A few of them follow; if you don't recognize them, maybe your grandparents will.

Round as a saucer, deep as a cup,
Yet the whole Mississippi couldn't fill it up.
          —a strainer

The longer she stands, the lower she grows.
          —a candle

In the water, under the water,
Over the water, and never gets wet or cold.
          —a duck egg

I was four weeks old
When Moses was born,
Not five weeks old yet.
          —the moon

Black we are and much admired,
Men seek for us till they are tired.
We tire the horse, but comfort the man,
Tell me this riddle if you think you can.
          —coal

God never did see,
Abraham Lincoln never done saw,
And we see every day.
          —our equals

House full, room full,
But can't get a spoonful.
                    —smoke

In marble walls as white as milk,
Lined with skin as soft as silk,
With a pool so crystal-clear,
A golden sun doth always appear.
No doors there are to this stronghold,
Yet thieves break in and steal the gold.
                    —an egg

What can a man give to a woman
But can't give to another man?
                    —a husband

If a man was born in England,
Raised in Kansas,
And died in Peking,
What is he?
                    —dead

Round as a biscuit,
Busy as a bee,
Prettiest little thing
You ever did see.
                    —a watch

Green as grass, but is not grass.
Red as blood, but is not blood.
Black as ink, but is not ink.
What is it?
                    —blackberry

You see, the man was riding,
And YET was surely walking.
How is this?
                    —YET is his dog.

Lady has a red pig,
And a dead pig,
A boar pig,
And a poor pig.
How many pigs does the lady have?
                    —one. A dead, red, poor boar pig.

Old man shook it and shook it.
The old lady pulled up her dress and took it.
                    —an apple from the tree

The man who made it didn't use it.
The man who bought it didn't want it.
The man who used it didn't know it.
                    —a coffin

Sisters and brothers have I none,
But that man's father is my father's son.
Who am I?
                    —a man telling of his son

Look me in the eye, I am somebody;
But stand behind me and I am nobody at all.
                    —a mirror

Children's Rhymes

Eeny meeny miny mo.
Catch a tiger by the toe.
If he hollers, let him go.
Eeny meeny miny mo.
O-U-T spells out and
That means You!

One, two, buckle my shoe;
Three, four, knock at the door.
Five, six, pick up sticks;
Seven, eight, lay them straight;
Nine, ten, a big fat hen.

One potato, two potato,
Three potato, four;
Five potato, six potato,
Seven potato, more.

Ring around the rosies,
A pocket full of posies.
Tisha! Tisha!
We all fall down.

Fatty, fatty, two by four,
Hanging 'round the kitchen door,
When that door begins to shake,
Fatty has a bellyache.

Georgy Porgy
Pudding and pie,
Kissed the girls
And made them cry.
When the boys
Came out to play,
Georgy Porgy
Ran away.

Hickory, dickory, dock!
The mouse ran up the clock;
The clock struck one,
And down he run,
Hickory, dickory, dock!

Pease porridge hot,
Pease porridge cold,
Pease porridge in the pot,
Nine days old.

Lady bug, lady bug
Turn around,
Lady bug, lady bug,
Touch the ground.
Lady bug, lady bug,
Fly away home
Your house is on fire,
And your children will burn.

Rich man, poor man,
Beggar man, thief,
Doctor, lawyer,
Indian chief.
Ragman, bagman,
Tinker, tailor,
Junkman, sailor.

Peter Piper's Practical Principles of Plain and Perfect
Pronunciation to Please the Palates of Pretty Prattling Playfellows.
Pray Parents to Purchase this Playful Performance, Partly to Pay
him for his Patience and Pains; Partly to Provide for the Printers
and Publishers; but Principally to Prevent the Pernicious
Prevalence of Perverse Pronunciation.

Peter Piper picked a peck of pickled peppers;
Did Peter Piper pick a peck of pickled peppers?
If Peter Piper picked a peck of pickled peppers,
Where's the peck of pickled peppers Peter Piper picked?

CHAPTER 10

That Wild, Wild West

"Calamity's Bet"

That
Wild, Wild
West

"Calamity's Bar"

"This ain't your fight, Doc."
—Wyatt Earp to Doc Holliday
at the O. K. Corral

THEY CAME out of the dust and the heat of the American West into the cool fame of American legend. You know them: Jesse James, Billy the Kid, Wild Bill Hickock, Sam Bass, Calamity Jane, Wyatt Earp, Pat Garrett, Belle Starr, Butch Cassidy, Annie Oakley, to name but a few. The list could go on and on of men and women forever linked by the lawless and wild lore of the West. Many were gunfighters—quick on the draw, nerveless, deadly, the last image for so many gunfighters who thought themselves faster. Beyond them was a country where banks were robbed and trains held up, where men were hanged for stealing a horse and fined ten dollars for killing another in a saloon brawl.

Back East, the country that lay beyond the Mississippi was a source of fascination. The urbane salons of New York and Philadelphia relished the stories of the Wild, Wild West, where life was tough and death a regular player at every poker table. Famished for tales of the great outdoors, the folks back East showed an endless appetite for Indian fights and the high noon of two men shooting it out in a deserted street. Buffalo Bill, who relentlessly and effectively promoted himself as the very personification of the West, understood that appetite. He toured America and the world with his famous Wild West Show, playing to capacity crowds. In it was every western cliché possible, including a reenactment of Custer's Last Stand. Yet the greatest draw was not the Indians or the cowboys but, rather, a little girl, named Annie Oakley, who could shoot a gun better than anyone on the face of the earth. How the crowds loved a shooter!

But while Oakley shot clay pigeons and silver dollars, it was the gunfighter who gave the West its legendary status and menace. He fought a man or a crowd with the same equanimity, and he never forgot—and rarely forgave—someone who had done him wrong. The best gunfighters had a reputation for kindness to the less fortunate, and they were known for their steady hand and their own private code of conduct. Yet, so often it seemed the main ingredient to a gunfighter's fame was in how he died. His death, much more than his life, decided his place in the lore of the West.

In folklore, a little wickedness must be taken for granted; that is, men had to die in gunfights, banks had to be robbed, and huge posses outwitted, for a real legend to grow. Then, after he had established his ability to kill without getting killed, the gunfighter was ready for his last great performance. Wild Bill Hickock, with his back to the door for the only time in his poker-playing career, was shot dead while holding two pair: aces and eights, ever after called "the dead man's hand." Jesse James dusted a picture with his back turned to the cowardly Charlie Ford, who, having waited for the chance, shot him in the back and ran (they sold the duster at auction two days later for five dollars). Billy the Kid hesitated in the moonlight and was killed by Pat Garrett, who crouched in the shadow. All were little turns of fate that cost the noted killers their lives and catapulted them into legend.

Like traditional heroes in other cultures, these figures died from betrayal. A gunfighter like Clay Allison was a mean and shrewd killer, quick with his six-shooter, but he was never considered a first-rate hero. Was it because he died by falling drunk out of a wagon onto his head? A real hero must die unmastered, wrapped in the mystique of the undefeated.

It is odd to us, perhaps, that these gunfighters earned their immortality as killers. Who was Billy the Kid really? To some, he was a heartless punk who gunned down his mother's lover at twelve and killed with awesome regularity for the next nine years. To others, he was a good man banished to the wrong side of the law for avenging the foul murder of his friend Jim Tunstall. Was Jesse James a cruel bank-robber who killed any brave-hearted citizen who tried to stop him, or was he a virtuous refugee from the Civil War, doomed by the lost honor of his beloved South? These are the kinds of paradoxes from which heroes are made. The historians will argue, but the storytellers will go right on making legends out of the deeds and deaths of the great outlaws.

We shall treasure the memory of the West. It had independence and a raw, lawless energy that appeals to us still. And we will always believe in the heroism of the badmen, not because their wickedness was admirable but because we are sympathetic to their determined and desperate isolation. Billy the Kid may have been a cold-blooded murderer, but not to everyone. In the months following his death, a rude wooden cross appeared over his grave. On it was carved the epitaph *"Duerme Bien, Querido."* Sleep Well, Beloved.

The West

How tough was the West? I'll tell you. In a local paper from a frontier Texas town in the 1840s comes a description of a day's activities: two street fights, one hanging, three men ridden out of town on a rail, a quarter race, some turkey shooting, a gander-pulling, a match dogfight, a rousing sermon by a circuit rider who afterward ran a footrace for applejack all around, and, as if this were not enough, the local judge, after losing his year's salary at poker and horsewhipping a person who claimed he didn't understand the game, went out and helped lynch his grandfather for hog-stealing. And this all happened on a Sunday.

Another View of the West

One of the most famous signs ever seen on the Western frontier was the following, stuck on the side of an abandoned cabin:

> One hundred miles to water
> Twenty miles to wood
> Six inches to hell
> God bless our home
> Gone to live with the wife's folks.

The Shallows of the Ford

Did you ever wait for daylight when the stars along the river
Floated thick and white as snowflakes in the water deep and
    strange,
Till a whisper through the aspens made the current break and
    shiver

As the frosty edge of morning seemed to melt and spread and
    change?
Once, I waited, almost wishing that the dawn would never find
    me;
Saw the sun roll up the ranges like the glory of the Lord;
Was about to wake my pardner who was sleeping close behind me,
When I saw the man we wanted spur his pony to the ford.

Saw the ripples of the shallows and the muddy streaks that fol-
    lowed,
As the pony stumbled toward me in the narrows of the bend;
Saw the face I used to welcome, wild and watchful, lined and
    hollowed;
And God knows I wished to warn him, for I once had called him
    friend.

But an oath had come between us—I was paid by Law and Order;
He was outlaw, rustler, killer—so the border whisper ran;
Left his word in Caliente that he'd cross the Rio border—
Call me coward? But I hailed him—"Riding close to daylight,
    Dan!"

Just a hair and he'd have got me, but my voice, and not the
    warning,
Caught his hand and held him steady; then he nodded, spoke my
    name,
Reined his pony round and fanned it in the bright and silent
    morning,
Back across the sunlit Rio up the trail on which he came.

He had passed his word to cross it—I had passed my word to get
    him—
We broke even and we knew it; 'twas a case of give and take
For old times. I could have killed him from the brush; instead, I
    let him
Ride his trail—I turned—my pardner flung his arm and stretched
    awake;

Saw me standing in the open; pulled his gun and came beside me;
Asked a question with his shoulder as his left hand pointed toward
Muddy streaks that thinned and vanished—not a word, but hard
    he eyed me
As the water cleared and sparkled in the shallows of the ford.

Henry Herbert Knibbs

The Robbers and the Widow

One time, there was a poor woman whose husband got killed in the War Between the States. It was pretty hard sledding for a widow woman in them days, and now a Yankee money-lender was going to take the farm. She was feeling mighty bad about it, when a couple of men come a-riding up and asked her could they get something to eat. The old woman seen they had been in the Confederate Army, so she give 'em a good supper.

Soon as she got the dishes washed, they all set out on the gallery awhile, and the old woman told 'em about the mortgage. The Yankee would be here tomorrow for his four hundred dollars, and she didn't have only fifty dollars saved up. The widow woman was bound to lose her farm, and no help for it. The two men didn't have much to say, and pretty soon they went to bed.

Next morning, she fixed 'em a good breakfast, and then one fellow says, "Ma'am, we are going to lend you three hundred and fifty dollars so you can pay off that mortgage." So they give her the gold, in a leather sack. Then he fixed up a paper for the Yankee to sign, and both of the men got on their horses and rode off. It was pretty near sundown when the money-lender come to see about the mortgage. He acted kind of surprised when the widow woman counted out that gold, but he marked the mortgage *Paid in Full.* He signed the receipt, too, and put the money in his gripsatchel. Then he got in his buggy and drove back towards town.

Away in the night the widow woman heard somebody outside, and it was the same two men that come there before. She got up and made some coffee, and showed them how the mortgage was all paid off. Then she begun to talk how she would try to pay the three hundred and fifty dollars, but the two men just laughed. "You don't owe us nothing," says one, "we done collected off'n that Yankee." The old lady just looked at them two men. Both of them was wearing big pistols now, and she seen they was road agents. One of them laid fifty dollars on the fireboard. "We don't never take nothing from a Confederate soldier, nor his widow, neither," the fellow says.

Then them two men walked out, with their spurs a-jingling. The old woman followed 'em down to the gate, and she wanted to know their names, so she could remember them in her prayers. "That's mighty kind of you, Ma'am," says the one with the whiskers. "I reckon we're a-standing in the need of prayer. My name is Frank James, and this is my brother Jesse."

Jesse James Meets Wild Bill

William Hickock, or, as he was more generally known, "Wild Bill," was in Texas once on some business connected with his government employment. While here, Bill was for a time quite cautious. He recognized the fact that nearly every other man in this state was a "gunfighter," while up in Kansas he could bully almost any man he met. Bill was a "killer," but he was one of those cold-blooded murderers, who gave his enemy no show, but "got the drop" and shot him without mercy. When his enemy was a quick, active, fighting man, not easily taken by surprise, Bill always "took water," as witness his encounter with Bill Thompson at Ellsworth, Kansas. As above stated, Bill had been very quiet and orderly, and kept so until he was ready to leave the town. Having taken a few drinks, he thought he would risk a little bluster and bravado, and seeing a quiet-looking man standing near him, he drew his revolver, fired at a small tree about fifty yards off and put a bullet in the center of it.

"By G—!" he almost howled, "I could just cut a fellow's hair today without touching his head," and he looked significantly at the quiet man. The latter threw both hands to his sides, drew his pistols, straightened out both arms, his revolvers going off simultaneously, and two balls were planted, one above the other, below "Wild Bill's." As he replaced his pistols he quietly said, "Just open up your barbershop as soon as you like." Bill saw that he was no match for the quiet man, who was no other than Jesse James, so he very prudently delayed his tonsorial efforts until some more opportune time, and left the town. [This was a story some folks liked to tell but it never did happen.]

The Fateful Northfield Raid

On that afternoon, the outlaws rode into Northfield in three groups, having met for final consultation in a piece of woods about five miles to the westward. At that meeting, each man was given to know precisely what part he was expected to take in the Northfield job— emergencies, of course, not being lost from the reckoning. The octet divided into three sections. Three men were to enter the bank and get the money—if they could; two were to sit their horses on Division Street, opposite the bank, and keep too-curious people away; three were to occupy posts on Bridge Square as a rear guard, the gang intending to make its getaway by crossing the bridge over Cannon River.

The three who were to rob the bank rode across the bridge about 2 o'clock, crossed the square, dismounted in front of the bank, and threw their reins over hitching-posts. These men were Sam Wells, Bob Younger, and, it is believed, Jesse James. They walked in a leisurely way to the street corner and sat down upon some dry-goods boxes in front of a store. Nonchalantly, in appearance, they began whittling the pine boxes.

In a short time, Cole Younger and Clell Miller rode up Division Street. The three whittlers pocketed their knives, arose, walked slowly to the bank entrance, and went inside. Leaving his horse unhitched, Clell Miller walked to the door of the bank, which the other three had left open. He closed the door and sauntered back and forth on the sidewalk, keeping an eye on the door.

Cole Younger's saddle-girth seemed to be troubling him; anyhow, he got off his horse, in the middle of the street, and pretended to be tightening the girth. He was an excellent actor, but this particular bit of acting failed to go down with the Northfield male element, which already had begun to suspect that the play was a bad one.

One of the spectators who didn't like the prologue was Henry M. Wheeler, a youth of twenty-two who was at home on vacation from Ann Arbor, where he was a senior medical student in the University of Michigan. Henry's father conducted a drugstore on the east side of Division Street. The college student had been sitting under an awning in front of the pharmacy when the horsemen rode up. He arose and walked along until he was opposite the bank and the bandits.

Another spectator who was not impressed with the genuineness of the acting was J. S. Allen, a hardware merchant. When he saw the three strangers enter the bank, he tried to follow. Clell Miller seized him by the scruff of the neck and ordered him to stand back, get away, go inside somewhere else.

"And if you speak a word," said Miller, fingering a large revolver, "I'll kill you!"

Nevertheless, Allen jerked loose, ran around the corner to his store, and shouted so loudly that he was heard all up and down the square:

"Get your guns, boys! Get your guns! Those fellows are robbing the bank!"

Henry Wheeler, who had heard a pistol shot from inside the bank, also was shouting loud alarms. Cole Younger and Miller remounted and ordered young Wheeler to "get inside," firing a shot or two over his head to frighten him. The future physician and surgeon was not of the frightening breed. Nor did he get so excited as to lose his presence of mind.

Whilst Younger and Miller were riding up and down, yelling for everybody to get in, and firing right and left, and the three bandits from the bridge side were dashing into the square and beginning tactics similarly violent, Wheeler dashed into the drugstore to get his gun. He was a huntsman and kept a competent fowling-piece. Suddenly he recollected that he had left the weapon at home, some blocks away. He ran on through the store and into the Dampier Hotel, where he found an old army carbine, a relic of federal use against Southerners of the Sixties, including possibly some of the exguerrillas now invading Northfield.

Three paper cartridges were the only ammunition to be found. Wheeler loaded the carbine with one of these, pocketed the others, ran upstairs, and posted himself at a front window overlooking the scene of the outdoors excitement.

Anselm B. Manning was a business rival of J. S. Allen, being another hardware merchant. But Allen forgot all about business, save that immediately in hand, as he rushed past Manning's store toward his own after he got out of Clell Miller's clutch.

"Get your gun, Manning! They're robbing the bank!"

Manning had a breech-loading rifle in his store window. From his desk he took a box of cartridges. Loading as he ran, he reached the scene of battle in a jiffy. Standing in the open street, he met a shower of bullets. They whistled all about him. Manning was cool and calm.

Allen reached his own store, where he had in stock a number of rifles and shotguns. He began loading them rapidly, passing them out to citizens who could use them. Elias Stacy accepted one and used it well in the subsequent proceedings. Others also made good use of the Allen arsenal stock.

But it was a shotgun in the hands of Stacy, provided and loaded by Allen, that drew first blood from a bandit. Just as Clell Miller was mounting his horse to help Cole Younger drive Henry Wheeler away, Stacy fired at Clell. The gun was loaded with small birdshot. Miller was knocked from his saddle, but he got back at once, his head and shoulders peppered with birdshot.

"Why, this is the very fellow who grabbed me and threatened to shoot me at the bank door," said J. S. Allen, after the battle.

Allen was inspecting the peppered countenance of a corpse; but it was not birdshot that had killed Clell Miller of Clay.

Let the battle scene shift now from the open street and the square to the interior of the First National Bank of Northfield. When the three robbers entered the bank, they found the bookkeeper, Joseph Lee Heywood, at the cashier's desk, substituting for Cashier G. M. Phillips, who was away on an extended trip. A. E. Bunker, teller, and F. J. Wilcox, assistant bookkeeper, were engaged in routine duties.

Only these six—three armed robbers and three unarmed employes— were present. There was, to be sure, a ladylike little pistol on a shelf under the teller's counter; but Bunker, luckily for himself, was not in touch with this weapon at the moment of his surprise by the "hands up" command from one of the three who already had man-sized six- shooters pointing directly at his head.

Before Bunker was able fully to comprehend the situation, the three had climbed over the counter, a makeshift affair not intended for permanent banking use. The man who had uttered the order then coolly notified Bunker and his companions that the purpose of the invasion was to rob the bank.

"And don't any of you fellows holler!" he added. "We've got forty men outside, and it'll be no use to holler. It'll be dangerous if you do."

He flourished his revolver by way of emphasis. The other two indulged in similar flourishing. Each had his eye and his aim on a bank employe.

"Are you the cashier?" the spokesman inquired, turning toward Heywood.

"I am not," replied Heywood.

In the literal sense this was true. Bunker and Wilcox both replied negatively to the same question, put in turn. The robber turned back to Heywood, who sat at the cashier's desk.

"I know you're the cashier," he said angrily. "Now you open that safe, damn quick, or I'll blow your head off!"

The door of the vault, in which the safe was visible, stood open. Sam Wells rushed to the vault and stepped inside. Heywood arose, walked rapidly to the vault and tried to shut Wells inside. Before he could slam the heavy door shut he was seized by both Wells and the leader of the robbing squad.

"Unless you open that safe at once you'll be shot dead!" cried the leader.

"I can't open it—the time lock is on."

"You're lying!"

Repeatedly they demanded that Heywood open the safe. They pulled him back and forth about the big room, cursing him.

"Murder! murder!" Heywood shouted.

The leader struck him on the head with a heavy revolver. Heywood sank to the floor.

"Let's cut his damn throat!" cried Sam Wells, who opened his pocket knife and made a slight cut in the neck of the fallen man. At least a semi-cutthroat was Wells of Jackson County! Then the pair caught Heywood under the armpits and dragged him back to the door of the vault, again insisting that he open the safe.

From time to time the desperate men turned to Wilcox and Bunker, ordering each in turn to unlock the safe. Both replied that they could not unlock it.

Heywood lay upon the floor near the vault, hardly conscious. Wells bent low and fired a shot close by the acting cashier's head— the first shot fired inside the bank. This was done in the hope of inducing Heywood to unlock the safe. The bullet passed through a tin box in the vault, containing valuables left by a special depositor.

Bob Younger was keeping watch on Bunker and Wilcox. He made them get down under the counter, on their knees. Bunker then thought of the pistol on the shelf. He was edging toward the place where it lay, at a moment when Younger had turned his back. Wells, who seemed to see in every direction at once, divined Bunker's intention. Leaping forward, he seized the pistol, which he stuck into one of his pockets.

"Huh! you couldn't do any harm with this little derringer, anyhow," he said.

Bunker arose to his feet. Bob Younger was on guard again.

"There's money here, somewhere, outside the safe," he said. "Where do you keep it? Where's the cash till?"

On the counter was a box containing some fractional currency. The teller pointed to this. Drawing from under his linen duster the inevitable wheat sack, Younger began to stow away the loose change —a pitifully small quantity of loot; and that was all the outlaws got from the bank. In a drawer under the counter, close to the robber's hands, reposed in safety $3000 in paper money.

Bunker, who had been ordered to get back beneath the counter, still stood up. Younger told him to get down and stay down.

"There's more money somewhere here. Where do you keep it? Show me where, or I'll kill you!"

However, he did not kill Bunker. Robert Younger probably never killed any man; there is no record of his having done so. He tried hard that day to kill a man, however—an armed man outside the bank.

Bunker made a dash for liberty. He ran through the bank directors' room to the rear door, which was closed, with inside blinds, which were fastened. He hoped to reach Manning's hardware store, across the alley, and give the alarm, for as yet he was not aware that Manning, Allen, Wheeler, Stacy, and several other citizens already were exchanging hot shots with the five bandits outside.

Sam Wells leaped again to the breach. Bunker was close to the rear door when Wells fired at his head. The bullet went through the door-blind. Bunker burst open the blind and the door, and dashed down the steps outside. Wells pursued him, firing a shot which passed through the teller's right shoulder. The wound was severe but not fatal. Bunker made for a surgeon's office in the adjoining block. He was out of the battle.

Sam Wells got back into the banking room just in time to hear one of the bandits outside the bank shouting that the game was up.

"Come out, boys! come out. They're killing all our men!" was the warning Wells and his two companions heard. The three escaped by way of the teller's window and the front door. Heywood, still dazed from the terrific blow on his head, had managed to get to his feet. He was groping his way toward his desk just as the last of the departing desperadoes was climbing through the teller's window.

This man turned and shot Heywood through the head. The faithful acting cashier dropped to the floor, stone dead. It was a deliberate murder, inexcusable even on the ground of self-defense, for Heywood was unarmed and was virtually helpless from his hurt.

They were not killing all of the raiding party's men, but they were killing just as many as they could. The Northfield defenders had been apt and able. For amateur fighters, they made magnificent records. Their marksmanship turned out to be far better than that of the notorious Missourians who had been regarded as dead shots. As for the Minnesotans, the deadliness of their execution on the edge of the instant was and remains an unsurpassable tribute to the steadiness of their nerves at a time of sudden and violent excitement.

Those Northfielders knew what they were after, and they went straightway and got it. They did not know at the moment that they were beginning to decimate the ranks of the hitherto invincible border bandits, to split in twain the James-Younger confederation of crime; but they did know that they were "getting" some of the most desperate freebooters that ever had raided a bank, and that knowledge no doubt gave them great joy of the battle.

First to fall in the street fight was an innocent aid to the outlaws—one of their splendid saddle-horses. When Merchant A. B. Manning arrived with loaded rifle and stood with bandit bullets zipping past his ears, he saw the horses belonging to the men who had gone in to rob the bank. Above the horses' backs were visible the heads of two highwaymen.

Manning took aim quite deliberately at the head of a selected outlaw, who ducked behind a horse before the merchant was good and ready to pull the trigger. Keeping his rifle leveled and changing his aim slightly, Manning shot the horse nearest him. He had realized, on the instant, that a horseless rider would have upon the invaders a weakening effect as valuable to the local cause as would a riderless horse.

Manning stepped around the corner to reload. The breech-lever jammed. The merchant ran into his store, got a ramrod, ejected the empty shell. Returning to the street corner, he fired at one of the robbers who was near the door of the bank. The bullet struck a post and glanced off, finding for second target Cole Younger and inflicting one of the several wounds which the biggest of the bandits received that day. Cole Younger was such a stalwart that he was hard to miss. Physically, at any rate, Cole was not cut out for a bullet-inviting freebooter; there was too much of him.

The cool-headed Manning reloaded, the ejecting lever working all right again. Glancing around the corner of the building, he saw William Stiles, sole Minnesotan of the outfit, sitting in saddle about eighty yards away. Manning was taking no potshots. He intended that every bullet should count. "Tally!" was the song of his missiles. So deliberate was the man in drawing a bead on Stiles that some fellow-townsmen standing not far away grew impatient, almost indignant.

"Get him! get him! Shoot, man, shoot!" they urged.

Manning took his time. Stiles evidently was posted there on sentry duty; his horse was at a standstill. The merchant's bullet went through the bandit's heart, and the "Bill Chadwell" of several desperate forays cashed in at last, in his old home county. Relieved of his burden, Stiles's horse ran gaily to a livery stable, the subsequent proceedings interesting him no more; the horse was looking for hay. Manning stepped back, reloaded, stepped forward, and watched his chance to get another outlaw.

All this time—and it was but a very few minutes, at that—young Henry Wheeler was busy with the old army carbine he had borrowed. From his second-floor window in the Dampier Hotel, he surveyed the scene, a cool and collected youth. Jim Younger was riding past. Wheeler fired at him and missed. Younger heard the bullet hit a spot beyond him and turned to gaze at that spot. Then he turned about to see whence the missile came. Several citizens were firing at the robbers, and Younger failed to discover the medical student at the window.

Wheeler next observed Clell Miller, bleeding from Elias Stacy's charge of birdshot but still in his saddle and perfectly good for further fighting. The future physician had rammed the second of his paper cartridges down the throat of the old carbine and now aimed coolly at Miller. The bullet that had been intended for some Confederate soldier a dozen or more years earlier and had been preserved as a relic of the Civil War, found now a vital spot in the body of the oldtime Quantrill guerrilla from Clay County, Missouri. Penetrating his right shoulder, it severed the great subclavicle artery. Clell Miller died almost instantly. Tumbling from his saddle, he lay crumpled upon the ground.

Henry Wheeler's third cartridge, and last, had fallen to the floor; the paper covering burst, and the powder was spilled. Eager for more of the same kind of shooting, Wheeler turned to go downstairs in search of more ammunition. He met the hotel clerk coming up with a fresh supply. Wheeler again took position at the window.

Northfield citizenry was up and at it. Shotguns instantly and inadequately loaded were in the hands of James Gregg, Ross Phillips, J. B. Hyde and others. These men did the best they could with what they had to do with. Elias Hobbs, not having even a birdshot weapon such as the other Elias, Citizen Stacy, had used in peppering the now deceased Clell Miller, found somewhere an armful of loose rocks.

"Stone 'em! stone 'em!" shouted Elias Hobbs, and he stoned 'em. Two or three others also stoned 'em. Northfield, in this emergency, got back to primitive methods of warfare. The stones worried the desperadoes but did little or no damage.

Henry Wheeler and Merchant Manning had not had enough of it. The six unslain outlaws were shooting at heads wherever heads were visible, and missing, save in one instance. Nicholas Gustavson, a Swede who understood little English, failed to "get in" when ordered so to do by one of the horsemen; he was shot to death. The raiders were firing also at windows and doors. Glass was crashing in the windows of the Dampier Hotel, and the casements of stores and offices here and there along the square were being shattered.

Henry Wheeler rammed home another paper cartridge and stood awaiting another chance to exercise his trigger finger. Anselm Manning, standing at his corner, saw Bob Younger running toward him. It was Bob's horse that was the victim of Manning's first bullet, and the young outlaw was afoot.

Manning proceeded to take deliberate aim at Younger. At the same moment, Younger leveled his revolver at Manning. Each man moved aside to escape the other's expected bullet. Younger took refuge under the outside stairway of the building in which the bank was located.

Wheeler, at his window, saw Manning and Younger trying to get each other within range and, incidentally, trying to keep out of range. He could see Younger's right arm, with the big weapon gripped in the fingers, but the rest of the bandit's body was invisible. Wheeler fired. The bullet shattered Younger's elbow. Younger shifted his six-shooter to his left hand and kept on trying to get his chance at Manning.

Just then came a lull in the battle. Manning had dashed through a store with the intention of getting on the other side of Younger and driving him from shelter. Wheeler was reloading. The old carbine was renewing its gallant and militant youth, and the young collegian now had full confidence in the retired and re-enlisted weapon.

The surviving robbers had had more than enough of it. Miller's horse, like that of Stiles, had run away when his master was shot from the saddle. Bob Younger's mount being dead, there were but five horses for six men. The youngest of the Youngers, his right arm swinging useless, darted out from under the stairway and up Division Street, where the eldest of the Youngers sat in saddle. Cole helped Bob to climb up behind. It was an enormous burden for the horse, but the fine animal was equal to the demand. With the four other horses, each carrying a survivor of the engagement, he galloped down-street and out of town, southward.

Wheeler was back at his window, Manning again out in the open. But the street showed so many citizens in the wake of the retreating raiders that neither of the marksmen risked another shot.

Church bells had been set ringing. The big bell in the cupola of Carleton College, of which institution the slain Heywood was treasurer, was clanging resonantly. From all points in the little city, people were gathering in Bridge Square. Some were inspecting the corpses of Stiles and Miller. Others had entered the bank and were looking after the body of Heywood, whose devotion to duty had cost him life. Still others, a considerable group, were preparing to mount horses and pursue the six survivors. They felt that at least they should be able to capture or kill Cole and Bob Younger, taking into consideration their horse's handicap.

Though the shattered window-panes and the bullets imbedded in posts and walls proved—if such proof were needed—that the bandits had not been firing blank cartridges, not a single member of the citizens' impromptu shooting force had been hit.

The professional dead-shots had failed miserably; the amateur sharpshooters had carried off all the honors of the day.

Doc Holliday

"I first met Doc Holliday in Fort Griffin, Texas, in 1877," said Wyatt Earp. "I was down in that country from Dodge City after a bunch of cow thieves. There was a woman in town—well, you can call her Doc's inamorata. Her name was Kate Fisher, but in that refined town they called her Big Nose Kate. A name like that might suggest a big, coarse female, but Kate wasn't like that; she was what you might call handsome, in a way. I liked Doc; he was a witty fellow and good company; he asked me a lot of questions about Dodge and thought he and Kate might like to come there. I had to go to Fort Clark for a few days, and when I got back to Fort Griffin, I found the town buzzing with excitement over Doc and Kate.

"Doc had sat in a game of poker one night with a fellow named Ed Bailey. This Bailey was a crooked card man, and he was always monkeying with the deadwood, which is to say, the discards, and Doc admonished him once or twice to quit this and play poker. Finally, a pretty nice pot came along. Doc called and Bailey spread down three kings. Doc didn't say a word but just quietly pulled down the pot and threw his hand away without showing what he held. Of course, Bailey started a big holler.

" 'I saw you palming one of those kings,' said Doc.

" 'Give me that money,' roared Bailey. 'I won it and I'll have it.'

"Doc was stacking the chips in front of him as Bailey reached for them. Doc knocked his hand away. Bailey went for his six-shooter and was coming up with it when Doc drew a long knife from under his coat collar—he had it hanging by a cord down his back—and with a sidewise swipe below the brisket ripped Bailey wide open.

"Doc was arrested. While he was being held in the hotel office under guard of the town marshal and two policemen, Bailey's gambler and cowboy friends gathered in the street. The crowd kept growing and getting uglier. There was talk of getting a rope, and things began to look pretty bad for Doc. Big Nose Kate got word of what was going on and hurried to the hotel. The officers let her in, and she had a little talk with Doc and went away. Now, a big nose generally means a strong, bold character—at least, so I've heard tell—and right now Big Nose Kate lived up to her nose.

"She ordered a couple of horses saddled at a livery and hitched them in an alley. Then she started a blaze in a shed back of the hotel and ran into the street yelling, 'Fire!' When, just as she had figured, the mob deserted the front of the hotel and rushed to the burning building, Kate walked into the hotel office. This time she had on a man's pants, coat, boots, and hat. From a satchel she was carrying, she jerked a pair of six-shooters. Doc grabbed them and ordered the marshal and the two deputies to throw up their hands. While Doc kept the marshals covered, Kate disarmed them, and, stowing their artillery in her bag, she and Doc backed out of the door.

"When the mob got back from the fire, madder than ever and still talking about a lynching, Doc and Kate were galloping hard across the prairies on a four-hundred-mile ride to Dodge City. I found them there on my return, living in style at a hotel, and they laughed as they told me about their adventure and seemed to regard it as a fine joke."

Wyatt Earp Plays a Lone Hand

As McCann and Johnny Behind-the-Deuce rode into Tombstone, the mine whistles on the hill began to boom. News of the murder of the engineer had been telegraphed ahead from Charleston. Miners flocked from the shafts and streamed down the hill toward town.

Wyatt Earp was dealing faro in the Oriental. Doc Holliday lolled in the lookout chair. Virgil Earp lounged against the bar. Business was dull. The place was as quiet as a prayer meeting. McCann and Johnny Behind-the-Deuce burst in upon the peaceful scene.

"Mob coming," McCann broke out breathlessly. "Going to lynch this boy. Hurry up. Do something, for Christ's sake. No time to lose."

Wyatt Earp slid one card off the deck and then another. He took in a bet or two. He paid a few winning wagers. With the skill of old habit, he leveled off the tops of the stacks of chips in the check-rack and carefully evened them along the sides with the backs of his fingers. He overlooked no detail of customary routine. Then he turned up his box. The game, for the present, was over.

"Hold on to your chips, boys," he said to the players. "I'll cash 'em as soon as I've finished with this little business matter."

As a gambler, he pushed back his chair. He rose as an officer of the law. Stepping to the front door, he saw, a block west, at Fifth and Tough Nut streets, an excited crowd gathered about the newly ar-rived horsemen from Charleston. On beyond, the hill was swarming with miners. The situation impressed him as having possibilities. But the Oriental, facing on two streets and with great doors and win-dows, was no place in which to stand off a mob. There was a bowling alley across Allen Street in the next block to the north, narrow and wedged between stores and with doors only at front and rear. A handful of determined men might hold it against a multitude. Wyatt Earp escorted Johnny Behind-the-Deuce to the bowling alley. He posted Virgil Earp at the rear and Doc Holliday behind the locked front door. He was ready now.

He had never met Johnny Behind-the-Deuce before. He had seen him a few times around Tombstone gambling houses and had chuck-led over his strange nickname and the origin of it. He knew nothing of the right or wrong of the killing of the Charleston engineer. But now this little shrimp of a fellow had been placed in his custody; it was his duty as an officer to protect him. This sense of official duty— nothing else—actuated him. If he had to die in performance of his duty, he would die.

An ominous confused murmur rose from the direction of the hill, a deep moaning bellow like that of brutes stirring to fury, the note of menace unmistakable. The mob was starting. Here it came in a rush-ing, crushing mass eastward through Fifth Street. It surrounded the Oriental. A yell went up like a rocket—"He's in the bowling alley." With a roar, the mob turned for the rush to the bowling alley. As it changed front, it came face to face with Wyatt Earp at a distance of twenty paces. He stood alone in the middle of Allen Street, a double-barreled shotgun resting in the crook of his elbow.

"Hold on, boys." Wyatt Earp raised his hand and for a moment kept it poised in air. "Don't make any fool play. There ain't no sense in this."

The mob halted in its forward sweep.

"Where've you got that murdering rat hid?"

"He's right in there." Wyatt Earp jerked his thumb at the bowling alley. "And he's going to stay in there. He's my prisoner now, and you fellers ain't goin' to get him."

"The hell we ain't."

"You boys better disperse." Wyatt Earp said it as calmly as he might have said, "Tut-tut," to naughty urchins in school. "Go on home. Go on back to work. I'm here to take care of this prisoner. And I'm going to take care of him."

The silence was shattered by sudden fierce yells.

"Ki-yi-ki-yi-yip!"

"Wa-wa-wa-wa—wa-hoo!"

The shrieks were broken into wild staccato by tapping the mouth with the hand. There were old Apache fighters in that crowd. The front ranks began to stamp up and down like savages doing a war dance.

"Here we go, boys."

"Smash in the bowling alley."

"String the dirty varmint to a telegraph pole."

Wyatt Earp cocked both barrels of his shotgun.

"Come on, then, you yellow curs. Let's see you get him."

His booming voice was like the roar of a lion at bay as he flung the challenge in the mob's teeth. Again the crowd stood still in wavering indecision.

One foot advanced, his shotgun held tensely across his breast ready for instant action, Wyatt Earp stood, one man against five hundred. Grimly alone. Hopelessly isolated for the moment from all the rest of the world. No help to fall back on, no chance to run, no shelter, no place of refuge. Just a man out there in the middle of the street, all by himself with only his own strength to depend on and only his own courage to save him. Before him a mob thirsting for blood, closing in for the kill, its victim almost within reach. The front line, stretching across the street from wall to wall, bristled with six-shooters and rifles, every face twisted and flaming with passion. One solitary man blocked the road to vengeance.

"That fool's bluffing." The shout was vibrant with impatient resentment. "Call his bluff and watch him quit."

Wyatt Earp brought his shotgun to his shoulder with a snap. At the level of a man's heart, he swung its muzzle very slowly across the crowd from one side of the street to the other and very slowly back again.

"Don't make any mistake," he flung back. "I'll blow the belly off of the first man that makes a move."

The storm was working to the bursting point. This was ridiculous. One man hold back five hundred? Rush him, disarm him, brush him aside.

"What's the matter out there in front?"

"Go on!"

The men behind began to push and shoulder forward. Flickering waves of movement told of gathering momentum for a fresh start. A powerful thrust made the front ranks bend and sway. It was like a ripple presaging the final rush.

"Kill him!"

Wyatt Earp's jaws set. His eyes blazed. His face in that tense moment was so marble-white that his tawny moustache looked black against it. Again he swept the crowd with his leveled gun, and death lurked in the black depths of those twin muzzles.

"Kill me." His voice had a conversational steadiness. "I'm ready. Ought to be easy; there are enough of you. But I'll do a little killing myself. You can get me; but I'll take a few of you to hell with me."

The drama had rushed to crisis. Here was a proposition. They could take it or leave it. He was ready to die. If they were too, all right. Yes, they could kill him. One shot would do the business. They couldn't miss him. But he would take some of them to the grave with him. He might get two or three. Or half a dozen might crumple down under the scattering double charge of buckshot. It was sure death for some of them. Did they want to gamble? Were they willing to take the chance?

Well?

Silence fell. For a space the mob stood motionless, hesitating, undecided, weighing the odds. Then abruptly the tension snapped. Some men in front, looking a little sheepish, drew back into the crowd. Others followed. The front line grew ragged; it was breaking up. Not much sense, after all, in getting killed for a dirty little blackguard like Johnny Behind-the-Deuce. The law might hang him anyhow. This lynching business was pretty wild and crazy if you stopped to think about it. Just as well to let the law take its course. Men at the outer edges began to walk away. Gaps and lanes opened in the thinning ranks. Throngs began to bustle through the side streets like flood waters draining off through sluiceways. Soon all had disappeared except a few small groups that still hung about the corner. The storm had passed; peaceful sunlight once more bathed the empty streets. Wyatt Earp, leaning on his shotgun, stood in silence and watched the mob melt away. Then he stepped with an air of leisureliness over to the sidewalk.

"Go down to the O. K. Corral, Doc," he said to Holliday in the casual voice of one arranging a detail of business routine, "and see if Johnny Montgomery can let us have a spring wagon. I guess I'll send Johnny Behind-the-Deuce over to Tucson."

Johnny Behind-the-Deuce was taken in the spring wagon under strong guard to Tucson. Ten heavily armed men on horseback accompanied him as far as Dennis's ranch but, as no attack developed, turned back to Tombstone. Johnny broke jail at Tucson before his trial, and though Papago Indian trailers were used to track him, he was not recaptured. He disappeared from the Southwest, and whatever became of the murderous little scalawag with the funny pseudonym no one in that country knows to this day.

Shoot-out at the O. K. Corral

Whiskey has made more fight-talk than fights, and more brag has been slept off with its liquor than ever was made good in battle. Frontier benders pretty generally followed the alcoholic rule, but the red-eye that set Ike Clanton's tongue wagging in the Allen Street saloons during the evening of October 25, 1881, was to precipitate the most celebrated encounter between outlaw and peace officer in the history of untamed Arizona. It was also to furnish Ike with dubious immortality through a gun-fight over which the West has wrangled for half a century, and can still argue as heatedly as while the roar of six-shooters echoed in the streets of Tombstone.

Potency under Ike's belt found vent in loose-mouthed boasts that he would kill Wyatt Earp and Doc Holliday before the setting of the next day's sun. When Farmer Daly and Ed Byrnes suggested that the rustler had laid out quite a job, Ike sneered:

"The Earps are not so much. You'll see, tomorrow. We're in town for a showdown."

About midnight Ike went to the Occidental Saloon, where his friends were playing poker. Doc Holliday entered and walked directly to Clanton.

"Ike," Doc said, "I hear you're going to kill me. Get out your gun and commence."

"I haven't any gun," Clanton replied.

"I don't believe you," Doc retorted. "I'll take your word for it this time, but if you intend to open your lying mouth about me again, go heeled."

Morgan Earp, who passed the saloon as Holliday was berating Clanton in picturesque profanity, pulled Doc to the sidewalk. Clanton followed with Tom McLowery, insisting that he was not armed but promising he soon would be and would shoot Doc on sight. Wyatt and Virgil Earp came along and took Doc to his room, where Wyatt ordered the dentist to keep away from Clanton.

"A gun-fight now, with you in it," Wyatt warned Holliday, "would ruin my chance to round up this bunch."

"All right," Doc promised regretfully, "I'll keep away from him."

Half an hour later, Ike found Wyatt at the Eagle lunch-counter.

"You tell Doc Holliday no man can talk about me the way he did and live," Ike began. "I'm wearing a gun now and you can tell Holliday I aim to get him."

"Doc's gone to bed," Wyatt replied. "You're half-drunk. You'll feel better when you've had some sleep."

"I'm stone-cold sober," Ike retorted. "I'm telling you to tell Holliday I'll gun him the first time I see him."

"Don't you tangle with Doc Holliday," Wyatt advised. "He'll kill you before you've started."

"You've been making a lot of talk about me too," Ike said.

"You've done the talking," Wyatt corrected.

"Well, it's got to stop," Ike declared. "You had the best of me tonight, but I'll have my friends tomorrow. You be ready for a showdown."

"Go sleep it off, Ike," Wyatt suggested. "You talk too much for a fighting man."

Virgil Earp came in the door as Ike started out. Ike paused and shouted over his shoulder:

"I said tomorrow. You're to blame for this, Wyatt Earp. What I said for Doc Holliday goes for you and your so-and-so brothers."

Wyatt and Morgan Earp went home about four o'clock. Virgil went to the Occidental to keep an eye on Behan, Clanton, McLowery, and the other cowboys until their game broke up; he reached home after daylight.

The Earps were awakened in the morning of October 26 by word that Ike Clanton was at Fifth and Allen streets, armed with six-guns and a Winchester, bragging that his friends were on the way to Tombstone to help him clean out the Earps. A second message warned that Billy Clanton, Frank McLowery, and Billy Claiborne had just ridden in to join Ike and Tom McLowery and that five outlaws were at Fourth and Allen streets. Ike and Frank had been in several saloons asking if the Earps or Holliday had been around that

morning. In Vogan's they had boasted they would shoot the first
Earp who showed his face in the street.

"Where's Holliday?" Wyatt asked.

"He hasn't been around."

"Let him sleep," Wyatt ordered.

Ike Clanton had not given the Earps much concern, but Billy
Clanton, Claiborne, and the two McLowerys, whatever else they
might be, were game men, crack shots and killers. The McLowerys
were possibly the two fastest men with six-guns in all the outlaw
gang. Frank McLowery was admittedly better on the draw-and-
shoot than Curly Bill or John Ringo, and held by some to surpass
Buckskin Frank Leslie.

Warren Earp was in California with his parents. Jim Earp was
physically unable to take a hand. But, outnumbered as they were,
none of the three brothers, as he buckled on his guns, had any idea
other than that they would go directly to Fourth and Allen streets.

"You and Morg go up Fremont Street," Wyatt instructed Virgil.
"I'll take Allen Street."

He was giving his brothers the better chance of avoiding the outlaws. They knew it, but obeyed, as was their habit.

"If you see Ike Clanton, arrest him," Wyatt said. "But don't shoot
unless Ike does. Take his guns away in front of the whole town, if
you can, and show him up."

At Fourth Street, Virgil and Morgan turned south and reached the
mid-block alley as Ike Clanton eased out of the narrow passage, rifle
in hand, eye on the Allen Street corner.

"Looking for me?" Virgil asked in Ike's ear.

Clanton swung around, lifting the rifle. Virgil seized the Winchester with his left hand, jerked a Colt's with his right, and bent the six-
gun over Ike's head. Virgil and Morgan lugged their prisoner
through the street to Judge Wallace's courtroom, where Morgan
guarded him while Virgil went to find the judge. Several persons who
had seen Ike arrested went into the courtroom, among them R. J.
Coleman, a mining man who figured in later happenings, and Deputy Sheriff Dave Campbell. Ike was raving with fury.

"I'll get you for this, Wyatt Earp!" he yelled as Wyatt came
through the door.

"Clanton," Wyatt answered, "I've had about enough from you and your gang. You've been trying for weeks to get up your nerve to assassinate my brothers and me. The whole town's heard you threaten to kill us. Your fight's against me, not my brothers. You leave them out of this. I'd be justified in shooting you on sight, and if you keep on asking for a fight, I'll give it to you."

"Fight's my racket," Ike blustered. "If I had my guns, I'd fight all you Earps, here and now."

Morgan Earp offered one of Ike's sequestered six-guns, butt foremost, to the owner.

"If you want to fight right bad, Ike," Morgan suggested, "take this. I'll use my fists."

"Quit that, Morg," Wyatt snapped. Deputy Sheriff Campbell pushed Ike into a chair.

"All I want with you," Ike shouted, again identifying Wyatt with a few choice epithets, "is four feet of ground and a gun. You wait until I get out of here."

Wyatt walked from the courtroom. At the door he literally bumped into Tom McLowery, hurrying to Ike's assistance.

"You looking for trouble?" McLowery snarled as he recovered his balance.

"I didn't see you coming," Wyatt answered.

"You're a liar!" McLowery retorted.

Bystanders said Wyatt paled an ominous yellow under his tan.

McLowery's gun was at his hip. Faster than the outlaw could think, Wyatt slapped him full in the face. Tom made no move for his pistol.

"You've got a gun on," Wyatt challenged. "Go after it."

McLowery's right hand dropped downward. Wyatt Earp's Buntline Special flashed and the marshal buffaloed Tom McLowery his full length in the gutter. Wyatt turned his back and walked toward Allen Street.

Judge Wallace fined Ike Clanton twenty-five dollars for breach of the peace. As Ike realized he was to get off thus lightly, more of his bravado returned. The courtroom was filled, and before this audience the outlaw took a fling at Virgil Earp.

"If I'd been a split-second faster with my rifle," he boasted, "the coroner'd be working on you now."

"I'm taking your rifle and six-guns to the Grand Hotel," Virgil replied. "Don't pick them up until you start for home."

"You won't be here to see me leave town," Ike retorted.

Wyatt Earp had posted himself outside of Hafford's. Frank and Tom McLowery, Billy Clanton, and Billy Claiborne passed him, all wearing six-guns, and went into Spangenberg's gun-shop. Virgil Earp came along, carrying Ike Clanton's weapons to the Grand Hotel, and joined Wyatt at a point across Fourth Street from the gunsmith's. They and several Vigilantes who stood with them could see plainly all that went on in the gun-store.

Ike Clanton now hurried into Spangenberg's. He purchased a six-shooter, and the five rustlers loaded their cartridge-belts to capacity. Virgil Earp went on to the hotel. Frank McLowery's horse moved onto the walk in front of the gun-store. Wyatt strode across the road and seized the animal's bit. The two McLowerys and Billy Clanton came running from the store.

"Let go of my horse!" Frank shouted.

"Get him off the walk," Wyatt rejoined.

"Take your hands off my horse!" McLowery insisted.

"When he's where he belongs," Wyatt replied, backed the horse into the road and snubbed him close to the hitching-rail.

The three rustlers had their hands on their gun-butts, spectators later testified.

"That's the last horse of mine you'll ever lay hands on!" Frank McLowery assured Wyatt with a string of oaths.

Wyatt turned on his heel and re-crossed the street.

The cowboys left Spangenberg's in a group, going to the Dexter Corral on the south side of Allen Street, between Third and Fourth streets, owned by Johnny Behan and John Dunbar. Wyatt joined Virgil and Morgan at Hafford's corner, where the brothers stood for possibly half an hour while the rustlers made several trips on foot between the corral and near-by saloons, during which most of Tombstone was apprised of their intention to wipe out the Earps.

Captain Murray and Captain Fronck, with half a dozen Vigilantes, were conferring with Wyatt when R. J. Coleman, heretofore mentioned, reported that he had followed the rustlers to the Dexter Corral and on the way back had met Johnny Behan. Coleman said he had told Behan he should disarm the outlaws, as they were threatening to kill the marshal and his brothers, and that Behan had gone on into the corral. As the Earps and the Vigilantes went into Hafford's to get away from the crowd that gathered, Coleman again went down Allen Street to watch the cowboys.

While Virgil Earp was talking with the Vigilantes, Sheriff Behan entered Hafford's and cut into the conversation.

"Ike Clanton and his crowd are down in my corral making a gun-talk against you fellows," Behan said. "They're laying to kill you. What are you going to do about it?"

"I've been hoping that bunch would leave town without doing anything more than talk," Virgil answered. "I guess they've got to have their lesson. I'm going to throw 'em into the calaboose to cool off. I'll put somebody on to see that they don't walk out, too."

"You try that and they'll kill you," Behan warned Virgil.

"I'll take that chance," Virgil replied. "You're sheriff of Cochise County, Behan, and I'm calling on you to go with me while I arrest them."

Behan laughed. "That's your job, not mine," he said, and left the saloon.

Virgil Earp went into the Wells-Fargo office and returned with a sawed-off shotgun, as Coleman came back to Hafford's with word that the rustlers had transferred headquarters from the Dexter to the O. K. Corral and recruited a sixth to their war-party in the person of Wes Fuller, hanger-on and spy for the Curly Bill crowd. Ike Clanton, Tom McLowery, Billy Claiborne, and Fuller had crossed Allen Street to the O. K. Corral without horses, Billy Clanton had ridden his horse, and Frank McLowery had led his. All were wearing six-guns, Coleman said, while Billy Clanton and Frank McLowery had rifles slung from their saddles. They had gone past the stalls near the Allen Street entrance to the corral and into the rear lot, which opened on Fremont Street. They had posted Wes Fuller on lookout in the alley, and Tom McLowery had gone out into Fremont Street, returning within a few minutes.

The reason for Tom's brief absence was established later by Chris

Billicke and Dr. B. W. Gardiner, who had been standing on the courthouse steps. Tom walked from the corral to Everhardy's butcher-shop, better known as Bauer's. This business had been placed in Everhardy's name after Bauer was indicted as purchaser of cattle which the Curly Bill crowd rustled, but Bauer continued to work at his block. Chris Billicke and Dr. Gardiner saw Tom McLowery talk with Bauer and stuff a roll of bills into his trousers pocket as he left the shop, revealing as he did so the butt of a six-gun at his belt, an item to be noted.

After Tom's return, Coleman started to walk through the corral yard and was stopped by the cowboys, who asked if he knew the Earps. When he replied that he did, Frank McLowery and Ike Clanton gave him two messages, one for the Earps as a whole, the other for Wyatt, in particular.

"Let's have 'em," Wyatt said.

"They told me to tell the Earps that they were waiting in the O. K. Corral, and that if you didn't come down to fight it out, they'd pick you off in the street when you tried to go home."

The strategy which had moved the outlaws from the Dexter to the O. K. Corral now was apparent.

Allen and Fremont streets ran parallel with the numbered streets crossing them at right angles, and with an alley running east and west through each block. The O. K. Corral had its covered stalls on the north side of Allen Street, and an open yard across the alley on the south side of Fremont. On Fremont Street an adobe assay office stood at the west line of the corral yard, while to the east was C. S. Fly's photograph gallery.

On the north side of Fremont Street, facing the yard, was the original Cochise County Courthouse, a rambling two-story adobe with courtroom on the ground floor, and on the upper the offices of county officials. These offices opened onto an outside gallery, the west end of which was about opposite the west line of Fly's studio. Then came the *Epitaph* office, and an adobe store occupied by Mrs. Addie Bourland, a milliner.

To return to the O. K. Corral, the alley which ran between the stalls and yard gave onto Fourth Street, and in this passageway Wes Fuller was stationed to keep an eye on the Allen Street corner.

The Earps, in going to and from their homes at First and Fremont streets, customarily followed Fremont Street past the O. K. Corral yard. The only other direct route available took them by the Allen Street entrance. The Clantons and McLowerys could command with their guns, on a moment's notice, either path; thus outlaw strategy forced the Earps to call the turn or quit the play.

"What's the special message for me?" Wyatt Earp asked Coleman.

"They said to tell you that if you'd leave town they wouldn't harm your brothers," Coleman answered, "but that if you stayed, you'd have to come down and make your fight or they'd bring it to you."

Wyatt looked at Virgil and Morgan. Without a word the three Earps started for the door. Captain Murray stopped them.

"Let us take this off your hands, boys," he offered. "Fronck and I have thirty-five Vigilantes waiting, ready for business. We'll surround the corral, make that bunch surrender, and have them outlawed from Tombstone."

"Much obliged," Wyatt answered for his clan, "but this is our job.

"Come on," he said to Virgil and Morgan.

As the Earps swung out of Hafford's door and started, three abreast, along Fourth Street, Doc Holliday came up on the run.

"Where are you going, Wyatt?" Doc demanded.

"Down the street to make a fight."

"About time," Holliday observed. "I'll go along."

"This is our fight," Wyatt said. "There's no call for you to mix in."

"That's a hell of a thing for you to say to me," Doc retorted. "I heard about this while I was eating breakfast, but I didn't figure you'd go without me."

"I know, Doc," Wyatt said, "but this'll be a tough one."

"Tough ones are the kind I like," the gun-fighting dentist answered.

"All right," Wyatt agreed, and Doc Holliday fell into step with the only person on earth for whom he had either respect or regard.

Holliday was wearing a long overcoat and carrying a cane, as he often did when his physical afflictions bore heavily.

"Here, Doc," Virgil Earp suggested, "let me take your cane and stick this shotgun under your coat where it won't attract so much attention."

Holliday handed over the stick and drew his right arm from the overcoat sleeve, so that the garment hung cape-like over that shoulder. Beneath it he held the short Wells-Fargo weapon. As the four men passed the Fourth Street alley, Wes Fuller ran back into the corral where the Clantons and McLowerys were waiting.

"You ought to have cut him down," Doc Holliday observed.

Beyond this laconic suggestion, not one of the quartet of peace officers spoke as they walked rapidly toward Fremont Street.

Johnny Behan and Frank McLowery had been standing together at the corner of Fourth and Fremont streets as the Earps left Hafford's. The sheriff and the rustler hurried to the corral yard; Behan talked for a moment with the five cowboys, then hastened back toward the corner, some fifty yards away. He had covered less than half the distance when the marshal's posse came into view.

Tombstone's Fremont Street of 1881 was a sixty-foot thoroughfare with the wide roadbed of the hard-packed, rusty desert sand bordered by footpaths at no marked elevation from the road level. The walks, where buildings adjoined, ran beneath the wooden awnings with their lines of hitching-rails. At the O. K. Corral yard, there was necessarily a gap in the awning roofs and rails, which gave unhindered access for the width of the lot. Johnny Behan apparently expected the marshal's force to follow the sidewalk to the corral and hurried along it to meet them.

Along Fourth Street the Earp party had been two abreast, Wyatt and Virgil in the lead, with Virgil on the outside, Morgan behind him, and Doc Holliday back of Wyatt. Each sensed instinctively what could happen if they rounded the corner of Fly's Photograph Gallery abruptly in close order, and at the street intersection they deployed catercorner to walk four abreast, in the middle of the road.

Half a dozen persons who saw the four men on their journey down Fremont Street have described them. The recollections agree strikingly in detail. No more grimly portentous spectacle had been witnessed in Tombstone.

The three stalwart, six-foot Earps—each with the square jaw of his clan set hard beneath his flowing, tawny mustache and his keen blue eyes alert under the wide brim of a high-peaked, black Stetson—bore out their striking resemblance, even in their attire: dark trousers drawn outside the legs of black, high-heeled boots, long-skirted, square-cut, black coats then in frontier fashion, and white, soft-collared shirts with black string-ties to accentuate the purpose in their lean, bronzed faces. Doc Holliday was some two inches shorter than his three companions, but his stature was heightened by cadaverousness, the flapping black overcoat and the black sombrero above his hollow cheeks. Holliday's blond mustache was as long and as sweeping as any, but below it those who saw him have sworn Doc had his lips pursed, whistling softly. As the distance to the O. K. Corral lessened, the four men spread their ranks as they walked. In front of Bauer's butcher-shop, Johnny Behan ran out with upraised hand. The line halted.

"It's all right, boys. It's all right," the sheriff sputtered. "I've disarmed them."

"Did you arrest them?" Virgil Earp asked.

"No," Behan said, "but I will."

"All right," Virgil said. "Come on."

The politician's nerve deserted him.

"Don't go any farther," he cried. "I order you not to. I'm sheriff of this county. I'll arrest them."

"You told me that was my job," Virgil retorted.

The three Earps and Holliday moved on in the road. The sheriff ran along on the walk.

"Don't go down there! Don't go down there!" he cried. "You'll all be killed!"

The four men in the road cleared the line of Fly's studio. Virgil, Wyatt, and Morgan turned sharply left into the corral, Virgil a few feet in the lead, Wyatt and Morgan following in the order named. The wise Doctor Holliday halted with an uninterrupted sweep of Fremont Street. The door of Fly's gallery banged. Johnny Behan had ducked into the building, where a window gave him view of the corral yard and farther along a side-door opened. Across the lot the five rustlers stood, backs to the assay office wall.

The outlaws were vigorous, sinewy fellows—Ike Clanton, burlier than the rest, wearing, as did each McLowery, a thin mustache in Mexican-dandy style—all with a similarity of attire as marked as, but contrasting sharply with, that of the Earps. Huge sand-hued sombreros, gaudy silk neckerchiefs, fancy woolen shirts, tight-fitting doeskin trousers tucked into forty-dollar half boots—a get-up so generally affected by Curly Bill followers that it was recognized as their uniform—set off the lean, sunbaked hardness of these desert renegades. Ike Clanton and Tom McLowery wore short, rough coats, the other three, fancy sleeveless vests in the best cow-country fashion.

Billy Claiborne was farthest of his group from the walk, perhaps thirty feet from the street line. Next, on his left, was Ike Clanton, then Billy Clanton and Frank and Tom McLowery. They had avoided bunching, and Tom McLowery was about ten feet from the street. Posted to blank possible fire from the assay-office corner were two cow-ponies, one Frank McLowery's, the other Billy Clanton's, each carrying a Winchester rifle in a saddle-boot.

One glance at the cowboys revealed that, despite Johnny Behan's declaration, all were armed. Tom McLowery had a six-gun stuck in the waistband of his trousers. Frank McLowery, Billy and Ike Clanton, each had similar weapons slung from their belts. Claiborne had a Colt's at either hip.

The Earps moved in. From the road, Doc Holliday referred to Johnny Behan in one unprintable phrase. Virgil Earp was well into the corral, Wyatt about opposite Billy Clanton and Frank McLowery, Morg facing Tom. Not a gun had been drawn. Wyatt Earp was determined there'd be no gunplay that the outlaws did not begin.

"You men are under arrest. Throw up your hands," Virgil Earp commanded.

Frank McLowery dropped his hand to his six-gun and snarled defiance in short, ugly words. Tom McLowery, Billy Clanton, and Billy Claiborne followed concerted suit.

"Hold on!" Virgil Earp shouted, instinctively throwing up his right hand, which carried Doc Holliday's cane, in a gesture of restraint. "We don't want that."

For any accurate conception of what followed, one thing must be kept in mind: action which requires minutes to describe was begun, carried through, and concluded faster than human thought may pick up the threads. Two witnesses swore that its whole course was run in fifteen seconds, others fixed the time at twenty seconds, Wyatt Earp testified that it was finished thirty seconds after Frank McLowery went for his gun. Also, careful note of that action furnishes, more than any other episode of his life, the key to the eminence of Wyatt Earp.

Frank McLowery and Billy Clanton jerked and fired their six-guns simultaneously. Both turned loose on Wyatt Earp, the shots with which they opened the famous battle of the O. K. Corral echoing from the adobe walls as one.

Fast as the two rustlers were at getting into action from a start with guns half-drawn, Wyatt Earp was deadlier. Frank McLowery's bullet tore through the skirt of Wyatt's coat on the right, Billy Clanton's ripped the marshal's sleeve, but before either could fire again, Wyatt's Buntline Special roared; the slug struck Frank McLowery squarely in the abdomen, just above his belt buckle. McLowery screamed, clapped his left hand to the wound, bent over and staggered forward. Wyatt knew Frank as the most dangerous of the five outlaws and had set out deliberately to dispose of him.

In this fraction of a second, Tom McLowery jumped behind Frank's horse, drawing his gun and shooting under the animal's neck at Morgan Earp. The bullet cut Morgan's coat. Billy Clanton shot a second and a third time at Wyatt, missing with both as Morgan turned loose on him, aiming for Billy's stomach, but hitting the cowboy's gun hand.

Sensing that Tom McLowery was now the most dangerous adversary, Wyatt ignored Billy Clanton's fire as Tom again shot underneath the pony's neck and hit Morg.

Tom McLowery must be forced into the open. Wyatt shot at the pony behind which the cowboy crouched, aiming for the withers. The pony jumped and stampeded for the street, the excitement taking Billy Clanton's horse with him. As his brother's horse started, Tom McLowery grabbed for the rifle in the saddle-boot, but missed it.

At the upper end of the lot, Virgil Earp had been delayed in going for his gun by the position of his hand and his grasp of Doc Holliday's cane. Before Virgil could jerk his Colt's free, Billy Claiborne fired at him twice and missed. Claiborne started across the corral toward the side-door of Fly's gallery, which opened for him, firing point-blank at Virgil as he passed him and missing again. When Ike Clanton saw Johnny Behan open the door for Claiborne, his braggart heart funked. Ike had not drawn his gun; it swung at his hip as in his panic he headed straight for Wyatt Earp.

Tom McLowery's second slug had hit Morgan Earp in the left shoulder, glanced on a bone, ripped across the base of his neck, and torn a gaping hole in the flesh of his right shoulder.

"I've got it!" Morg gasped as he reeled under the shock.

"Get behind me and keep quiet," Wyatt said.

As Morgan was hit, Virgil Earp fired his first shot in the fighting, breaking Billy Clanton's gun-arm as it covered the cowboy's abdomen. Billy worked the "border shift," throwing his gun from right to left hand.

Far from obeying Wyatt's command, Morgan, who saw Billy Clanton's maneuver, shot Billy in the chest as Virgil put a slug into Clanton's body, just underneath the twelfth rib.

Before Wyatt could throw down on Tom McLowery, as the pony plunged away, Ike Clanton had covered the few feet across the corral and seized Wyatt's left arm.

"Don't kill me, Wyatt! Don't kill me!" the pot-valiant Clanton pleaded. "I'm not shooting!"

"This fight's commenced. Get to fighting or get out," Wyatt answered, throwing Ike off. The gallery door was held open and Ike fled after Claiborne.

Tom McLowery was firing his third shot, this at Wyatt as Ike Clanton hung to the marshal's arm, when Doc Holliday turned loose both barrels of his shotgun simultaneously from the road. Tom's shot went wild and McLowery started on a run around the corner of the assay office toward Third Street. Disgusted with a weapon that could miss at such a range, Holliday hurled the sawed-off shotgun after Tom with an oath and jerked his nickel-plated Colt's. Ten feet around the corner, Tom McLowery fell dead with the double charge of buckshot in his belly and a slug from Wyatt Earp's six-gun under his ribs which had hit him as he ran.

Frank McLowery was nearing the road, left hand clutching his abdomen, the right working his gun as he staggered on. Billy

Clanton was still on his feet and following. Frank shot at Wyatt. The slug struck short. So did another he sent at Morg.

Wyatt heard the crash of glass from the side-window of Fly's gallery, where Claiborne and Sheriff Behan stood. Two shots from the window followed.

"Look out, boys!" Wyatt called. "You're getting it in the back!"

Morgan Earp wheeled to face this new danger, stumbled and fell, but Doc Holliday sent two bullets through the window. Shooting from the gallery stopped. At this juncture Ike Clanton darted from a rear door across the alley and into the stalls of the O. K. Corral, flinging his fully loaded six-gun into a corner of the yard as he ran. Doc sent two shots after Ike, but was a split-second late. Doc wheeled to face Frank McLowery, who had reached the street, drawn himself upright and, less than ten feet away, was steeling himself for steady aim at Holliday.

"I've got you, you so-and-so such-and-such," McLowery snarled.

"Think so?" Doc found wit to inquire.

When Morgan fell, he rolled to bring his gun-arm free and brought up at full length on his side facing McLowery and Holliday.

"Look out, Doc!" Morg called, shooting as he lay.

McLowery's, Holliday's, and Morgan Earp's pistols roared together. Doc winced and swore. Frank McLowery threw both hands high in the air, spun on his boot-heels, and dropped on his face. Morg got to his feet. Morgan's bullet had drilled clear through Frank McLowery's head, just behind the ears; Doc's had hit the outlaw in the heart. Either would have killed him instantly, while Wyatt's first shot, which had torn through his abdomen, would have brought death in another few seconds. Frank's last bullet had hit Doc Holliday's hip-holster, glanced, and shaved a strip of skin from his back.

Meanwhile, as Wyatt sent a bullet into Tom McLowery when he ran, Virgil Earp and Billy Clanton were shooting it out. Billy was making for the street, firing as he went, when he hit Virgil in the leg. Virgil kept his feet and returned the fire as Wyatt shifted his attention to Billy Clanton. Wyatt's shot hit Billy in the hips, and as the cowboy fell, Virgil's bullet tore through his hat and creased his scalp. With his last ounce of gameness, the rustler raised to a sitting posture and tried to steady his wavering gun on his knee. While Wyatt and Virgil hesitated over shooting at a man who plainly was done, Billy Clanton slumped in the dust. The firing ceased. Billy Claiborne ran from the rear of Fly's on through toward Allen Street. Holliday's trigger clicked futilely.

"What in hell did you let Ike Clanton get away like that for, Wyatt?" Doc complained.

"He wouldn't jerk his gun," Wyatt answered.

The fight was over.

Frank McLowery was dead in the middle of Fremont Street. Tom McLowery's body was around the Third Street corner. Billy Clanton was still breathing but died within a few minutes.

Virgil's leg-wound and Morgan's, in the shoulder, were ugly, but not serious. Doc Holliday's scratch was superficial. Four of the cowboys had fired seventeen shots; Ike Clanton, whose brag and bluster brought on the battle, none. They had scored just three hits, not one of which put an adversary out of action.

The three Earps and Holliday had fired seventeen shots, four of which Doc Holliday had thrown at random into the gallery window and after Ike Clanton. The remaining thirteen had been hits. Any one of Frank McLowery's wounds would have been fatal. Billy Clanton had been hit six times, three fatally. Either of Tom McLowery's wounds would have killed him, and Wyatt's shot which stampeded the cow-ponies was a bull's-eye; it served Wyatt's exact purpose, stinging the animal to violent action, but not crippling him beyond ability to get out of the way.

As the smoke of battle lifted, Wyatt turned to look up Fremont Street. A yelling mob was headed toward him. The Citizens' Safety Committee had started for the corral in a column of twos, but excitement overcame discipline.

"I distinctly remember," writes John P. Clum, "that the first set of twos was made up of Colonel William Herring, an attorney, and Milton Clapp, cashier of a local bank. Colonel Herring was tall and portly, with an imposing dignity, while Milton Clapp was short and lean and wore large spectacles. The striking contrast in stature and bearing between these two leaders of the 'column' registered an indelible picture which still intrudes as a flash of comedy in an exceedingly grave moment."

Virgil and Morgan Earp were taken to their homes by the Vigilantes and a guard of twenty posted around the Earp property to prevent retaliation by friends of the dead outlaws. Other Vigilante squads patrolled the Tombstone streets.

Ike Clanton was found hiding in a Mexican dancehall, south of Allen Street, and Billy Claiborne near-by. They were taken to the calaboose and guarded to prevent either escape or lynching. Ike, at least, had small desire for freedom; he begged to be locked up and protected.

After his brothers had been cared for, Wyatt Earp walked up Fremont Street with Fred Dodge. Across from the sheriff's office, above the O. K. Corral, Johnny Behan stopped them.

"Wyatt," the sheriff said, "I'm arresting you."

"For what?" Wyatt asked in astonishment.

"Murder," Behan answered.

Wyatt's eye turned cold and his voice hard.

"Behan," he said, "you threw us. You told us you had disarmed those rustlers. You lied to throw us off and get us murdered. *You* arrest *me?* Not today, nor tomorrow either. I'll be where any respectable person can arrest me any time he wants to, but don't you or any of your cheap errand-boys try it."

The sheriff walked away.

That afternoon, a coroner's jury refused to hold the Earps and Holliday for death of the cowboys. Johnny Behan, principal witness at the inquiry, was deeply chagrined. At this time Behan thought himself the sole eye-witness to the fight in the corral, other than the participants. He so boasted to C. S. Fly. Fly had seen something of the battle and had noted other witnesses of whom Behan was unaware. Fly was a Vigilante, and close-mouthed. He reported Behan's belief to the Safety Committee, which sagely decided to give the talkative little sheriff all the rope he'd take.

One item which the coroner did uncover was that the three dead outlaws had, among them, more than six thousand dollars in currency, and that Ike Clanton and Billy Claiborne also had carried large sums of cash into the battle. This substantiated subsequent testimony that the rustlers had planned to kill the Earps and Holliday and ride for Old Mexico to stay until public resentment subsided.

The Cochise County grand jury was sitting at Tombstone at the time of the battle in the O. K. Corral, and the Vigilantes asked that body to investigate the killings immediately. Behan, still believing there were no non-participating witnesses to contradict him, testified before the grand jury, as did Ike Clanton. Numerous Tombstone citizens were called, but the Earps did not appear. The grand jury announced that it could find no reason to indict four duly appointed peace officers for performance of necessary duty.

Stuart N. Lake

Butch Cassidy Robs the Payroll Train

One night he came to Castle Gate. It was the evening before payday, and the coal camp in the Wasatch Mountains was waiting on the morrow. Gambling tables were ready in the saloons, and numbers of the cold-faced fraternity who made their livings by following the paymaster from place to place were here from Denver and Salt Lake. Near the lower end of the street a quiet poker game was going on in one of the drinking establishments.

It was the only activity of its sort in Castle Gate that evening, and it was proceeding listlessly enough when Cassidy entered the place. His worn overalls, soiled sombrero, and high-heeled boots proclaimed him to be a cowboy, and the languid tin-horns who were pitting their skill against one another for the sake of passing away the time were more than ready to let him sit in. As the evening grew older his big face became tighter set, his puckered blue eyes grew harder, and when two hours or so had gone by he shoved back his wide-brimmed hat.

"Well, boys," he said, "you've cleaned me."

With that he sauntered over to the bar and beckoned to the proprietor.

"There's two or three of us camping just outside the town," he explained, "and we're going out with some cattle down Price way in the morning. The boys sent me in to buy three bottles of Old Crow. I kind of hate to go back to them without the whisky."

"Sure," the saloon-keeper told him, for when he is the owner of the game a man can afford to be magnanimous to one who has dropped one hundred and fifty dollars. "That's all right, fellow. The liquor's on me."

He reached to the back bar and wrapped up three bottles.

"Here, take 'em along."

But Cassidy shook his head.

"That ain't the idee," said he. "I'm willing to pay for it. All that I'm asking for is credit."

"Well, if that's the way you feel about it, hand me the money next time you're riding by," the proprietor bade him.

So Cassidy departed with the bottles under his arm, and nobody thought any more about the matter.

It was sometime near noon the next morning when the west-bound passenger-train pulled in, and the miners were lining the sidewalk to watch the big monthly event, the arrival of the paymaster. Those were the days before the first great coal strike in Utah and Colorado, and most of the men were of the old Pennsylvania-Irish breed, as tough a crowd as you could find in any Western camp. Many of them carried weapons and were willing enough to use them on occasion.

Castle Gate lies in the depths of a steep-walled cañon. The main street is within a stone's-throw of the railroad track, and almost opposite the depot there was at that time a two-story stone building which contained the company's offices.

The paymaster alighted from the Pullman with a leather sack of money in either hand, and beside him came his armed guard with two big-caliber revolvers hanging from his belt. They left the depot platform and crossed the street toward the stone building. And the miners were so intent upon the spectacle of those two sacks containing their monthly wages that they did not notice the pair of roughly dressed riders who had come up the thoroughfare from the camp's lower end. So Butch Cassidy and Bob Leigh had swung from their saddles and were facing the paymaster with drawn revolvers before that official, his armed guard, or any one else took any thought of them.

"Han's up," Cassidy bade them.

They say the guard was a good man with his six-shooters, but he had no opportunity to demonstrate his skill that morning. He and the paymaster stood with uplifted arms while Bob Leigh stepped forward, took the money-bags, backed away to his pony, tied the sacks across the horn, and swung into the saddle. Cassidy remained facing the victims, holding his revolver on the two of them, while he walked slowly backward, reaching with his left hand for his pony's reins.

Just then a miner up the street started shooting.

A clerk in the coal company's offices on the second floor of the stone building heard the report, glanced through the window, and, seeing what was going on, seized an old Sharp's single-shot rifle that was hanging on the wall. He ran to the landing of the stair-flight that led up along the outside, took hasty aim, and pulled the trigger. The slug raised a little dust in front of the pony's forefeet, and the bronco shied away with a snort of fright just as Cassidy's fingers were about to close on the reins.

The outlaw held his eyes on the pair before him; his six-shooter remained leveled upon them; he edged toward the horse—without turning his head.

"Whoa, boy," he said soothingly. "Easy now."

The pony backed off still farther. The clerk reloaded, and the old Sharp's boomed again.

"Hurry, Butch," Bob Leigh cried and added an oath for emphasis.

Three or four miners began shooting up the street. Slugs were snarling by, and some of them were coming pretty close. Cassidy's eyes had become two blue pinpoints; they never left the faces of the men before him as he answered evenly over his shoulder:

"Oh, hell. Those fellows don't know how to shoot."

He took another step toward the bronco.

"Easy! Easy!"

He always had a way with horses. His left hand found the reins. Now he stood beside the animal. The armed guard was showing symptoms of uneasiness.

"Just keep 'em up where they be," Cassidy bade him, and swung into the saddle.

Everyone who had a gun took a shot at the pair as they ran their horses down the street, but the outlaw had their marksmanship pretty well appraised. All the bullets went wild.

Now telegraph instruments began clicking frantic summons. The sheriff got out a posse down at Price. They followed the trail of the robbers across the country to Castle Valley. Men in Huntington told them how the fugitives had ridden through the village in broad daylight. The track took the pursuers off into the south; it led them over the desert reaches of the San Rafael swell, down into the bluffs that drop toward the Colorado. But Cassidy and Bob Leigh had got a change of horses somewhere along the route, and they made one hundred miles without a stop across the arid wilderness. The weary posse returned to the railroad on jaded ponies.

In the meantime the saloon-keeper who had given Butch Cassidy the three bottles of whisky had been raising lamentations. No voice in all the camp was so loud against the outlaws; he delved into the depths of an exhaustive vocabulary to find terms fit for their perfidy. For they had taken with them the best horse in his corral.

Just about the time the first members of the posse returned, he changed his tune. The horse had come back, and tied to its crupper there was a packet containing ten dollars of the stolen money and a hastily scrawled note which said:

This is pay for the three bottles of Old Crow.

Stackalee

It was in the year of eighteen hundred and sixty-one
In St. Louis on Market Street where Stackalee was born.
Everybody's talkin about Stackalee.
It was on one cold and frosty night
When Stackalee and Billy Lyons had one awful fight,
Stackalee got his gun. Boy, he got it fast!

He shot poor Billy through and through;
Bullet broke a lookin glass.
Lord, O Lord, O Lord!
Stackalee shot Billy once; his body fell to the floor.
He cried out, Oh, please, Stack, please don't shoot me no more.

The White Elephant Barrel House was wrecked that night;
Gutters full of beer and whiskey; it was an awful sight.
Jewelry and rings of the purest solid gold
Scattered over the dance and gamblin hall.
The can-can dancers they rushed for the door
When Billy cried, Oh, please, Stack, don't shoot me no more.
Have mercy, Billy groaned, Oh, please spare my life;

Stack says, God bless your children, damn your wife!
You stold my magic Stetson; I'm gonna steal your life.
But, says Billy, I always treated you like a man.
'Tain't nothin to that old Stetson but the greasy band.
He shot poor Billy once, he shot him twice,
And the third time Billy pleaded, please go tell my wife.
Yes, Stackalee, the gambler, everybody knowed his name;
Made his livin hollerin high, low, jack and the game.

Meantime the sergeant strapped on his big forty-five,
Says now we'll bring in this bad man, dead or alive.
And brass-buttoned policemen tall dressed in blue
Came down the sidewalk marchin two by two.
Sent for the wagon and it hurried and come
Loaded with pistols and a big gatlin gun.
At midnight on that stormy night there came an awful wail
Billy Lyons and a graveyard ghost outside the city jail.
Jailer, jailer, says Stack, I can't sleep,
For around my bedside poor Billy Lyons still creeps.
He comes in shape of a lion with a blue steel in his hand,
For he knows I'll stand and fight if he comes in shape of man.
Stackalee went to sleep that night by the city clock bell,
Dreaming the devil had come all the way up from hell.
Red devil was sayin, you better hunt your hole;
I've hurried here from hell just to get your soul.

Stackalee told him yes, maybe you're right,
But I'll give even you one hell of a fight.
When they got into the scuffle, I heard the devil shout,
Come and get this bad man before he puts my fire out.
The next time I seed the devil he was scramblin up the wall,
Yellin, come and get this bad man fore he mops up with us all.

II

Then here come Stack's woman runnin, says, daddy, I love you
    true;
See what beer, whiskey, and smokin hop has brought you to.
But before I'll let you lay in there, I'll put my life in pawn.
She hurried and got Stackalee out on a five thousand dollar bond.
Stackalee said, ain't but one thing that grieves my mind,
When they take me away, babe, I leave you behind.
But the woman he really loved was a voodoo queen
From Creole French market, way down in New Orleans.
He laid down at home that night, took a good night's rest,
Arrived in court at nine o'clock to hear the coroner's inquest.
Crowds jammed the sidewalk, far as you could see,
Tryin to get a good look at tough Stackalee.
Over the cold, dead body Stackalee he did bend,
Then he turned and faced those twelve jury men.
The judge says, Stackalee, I would spare your life,
But I know you're a bad man; I can see it in your red eyes.
The jury heard the witnesses, and they didn't say no more;
They crowded into the jury room, and the messenger closed the
    door.
The jury came to agreement, the clerk he wrote it down,
And everybody was whisperin, he's penitentiary bound.
When the jury walked out, Stackalee didn't budge,
They wrapped the verdic and passed it to the judge.
Judge looked over his glasses, says, Mr. Bad Man Stackalee,
The jury finds you guilty of murder in the first degree.
Now the trial's come to an end, how the folks gave cheers;
Bad Stackalee was sent down to Jefferson pen for seventy-five
    years.
Now late at night you can hear him in his cell,
Arguin with the devil to keep from goin to hell.
And the other convicts whisper, whatcha know about that?
Gonna burn in hell forever over an old Stetson hat!
Everybody's talkin bout Stackalee.
That bad man, Stackalee!

                          Collected by Onah L. Spencer

Sam Bass

Sam Bass was born in Indiana, it was his native home
And at the age of seventeen, young Sam began to roam.
He first went down to Texas, a cow-boy bold to be
A kinder hearted fellow, you'd scarcely ever see.

Sam used to deal in race stock, had one called the Denton mare
He watched her in scrub races, took her to the County Fair.
She always won the money, wherever she might be.
He always drank good liquor, and spent his money free.

Sam left the Collins ranch in the merry month of May
With a herd of Texas cattle the Black Hills to see
Sold out in Custer City and all got on a spree
A harder lot of cow-boys you'd scarcely ever see.

On the way back to Texas, they robbed the U. P. train
All split up in couples and started out again.
Joe Collins and his partner were overtaken soon
With all their hard earned money they had to meet their doom.

Sam made it back to Texas all right side up with care
Rode into the town of Denton his gold with friends to share.
Sam's life was short in Texas 'count of robberies he'd do
He'd rob the passengers' coaches, the mail and express, too.

Sam had four bold companions, four bold and daring lads
Underwood and Joe Jackson, Bill Collins and Old Dad
They were four of the hardest cow-boys that Texas ever knew
They whipped the Texas Rangers and ran the boys in blue.

Jonis borrowed of Sam's money and didn't want to pay
The only way he saw to win was to give poor Sam away
He turned traitor to his comrades they were caught one early
    morn
Oh what a scorching Jonis will get when Gabriel blows his horn.

Sam met his fate in Round Rock July the twenty-first
They pierced poor Sam with rifle balls and emptied out his purse.
So Sam is a corpse in Round Rock, Jonis is under the clay
And Joe Jackson in the bushes trying to get away.

Hang Me, O Hang Me

Hang me, O hang me, and I'll be dead and gone,
Hang me, O hang me, and I'll be dead and gone,
I wouldn't mind the hangin', it's bein' gone so long,
It's layin' in the grave so long.

Judge Parker, the Hanging Judge

Judge Parker was the first of the frontier judges to make a difference. Before he came out to Fort Smith, Arkansas, just after the Civil War, there wasn't a judge for a thousand miles who lasted more than a few months. The problem was that every man the judges found guilty had friends who usually took the law into their own hands, and many a judge was known to disappear overnight. But old Judge Parker wouldn't stand for any nonsense and he faced down all those who didn't see the lasting value of law and order. Parker sent eighty-eight men to the gallows and he became known as "the hanging judge."

One story that's told about Judge Parker isn't about a hanging, but it involves a very slick man from back East who was a first-rate thief. This man stole cattle, horses, and a lot else, but he never got caught. Never even got his hands dirty. Many men went to jail or were hanged in this fellow's stead, but never this man. He was always too smart to make a mistake—until one night he got arrested for disturbing the peace and was hauled into Judge Parker's court.

Parker knew all about the man, but he also knew that disturbing the peace was a misdemeanor, so the judge gave the man a tongue-lashing and fined him fifty dollars. The slick man smiled and pulled out a roll of bills. "Sure, Judge," he said. Parker fined him another hundred dollars for his insolent and insulting behavior. Again the man smiled and kept pulling bills from his wad. With that, Judge Parker quickly added, "And twenty years in prison, and let's see you peel that out of your pocket."

Roy Bean as Coroner

This incident actually occurred in 1882, when the Galveston, Harrisburg and San Antonio, more generally known as the Southern Pacific Railroad, was building west from San Antonio to El Paso. The building of that road in the exceedingly rough, canyon-cut country west of Del Rio called for great engineering skill. When the Pecos River was reached, it was spanned by a great cantilever bridge, 320 feet above the riverbed. There were draws and canyons to cross, cuts and fills to make, and the construction of the road proved to be very expensive. A Philadelphia bridge company had the contract to put in all steel bridges, while another company erected the falseworks.

One day while the bridge carpenters were erecting the falsework for an iron span across a deep, rocky canyon, the structure fell. Seven men were killed outright, and three were injured fatally.

It was thirty miles over to Langtry, where Roy Bean was justice of the peace and saloon-keeper. As the nearest coroner, he was summoned to hold an inquest. Mounted on a mule, he hastened to the scene of the accident. When he arrived, he found the seven dead men laid out side by side on the bottom of the canyon, and alongside the corpses lay the three injured men, so near to death that they were scarcely breathing.

Bean immediately selected a jury from the crew of workmen, and, calling them together, viewed the ten silent figures lying in the blistering sun of the hot afternoon. Then he proceeded to examine the bridge timbers, remarking on the size and length of the heavy beams.

Approaching the corpses once more, he examined each one, and remarked, "No doubt but that this man came to his death by them big timbers falling on him." When he came to the dying men, he made the same remark.

At this, one of the jurymen called Bean's attention to the fact that the last three men in the row were not dead.

Bean silenced him. "Say, you gander-eyed galoot," he said, "who's running this hyar inquest? Don't you see them three fellers is bound to die? Do you think I am damn fool enough to ride thirty miles on a sore-backed mule again to hold another inquest? Officially and legally them fellers is dead, and so I pronounce them dead, every mother's son of 'em, and you will accordingly render your verdict that they came to their deaths by them big bridge timbers a-falling on 'em."

The last of the injured men did not die for three days.

J. Marvin Hunter

Law-Abiding Folks

In a tough town out West, a mob was fixing to lynch a man and spirits were running high. Just as they were about to throw a rope on the tree, the local judge appeared. He raised his voice but they didn't hear him, so he took out a six-shooter and fired a few rounds.

"Gentlemen," he said, "don't you be lynching this boy. Our town is a fair place and we're trying to make a name for it as a respectable community."

"He stole hosses, Judge. That ain't respectable," someone yelled.

"I know. All I'm saying is that we ought to give the man a fair trial and then lynch him."

Judge Three-Legged Willie

Have you ever heard of Judge Three-Legged Willie? His real name was Williamson, but nobody knew him by that name. If you saw him come down the street with his peg leg and his cane, you'd know why everyone just took to calling him Three-Legged Willie. Now, Judge Parker may have hung folks when it suited him and Judge Roy Bean may have fined them, but Judge Three-Legged Willie was the toughest of them all. He stumped into Shelby County in Texas in the 1830s, and I can tell you that was when wildcats still lived on the streets.

He came into the county and opened his court by tipping a flour barrel on its end and calling for the culprits. One local stepped forward and said the county didn't have no need of a judge and a court. The old judge demanded, "By what legal authority do you over-rule this court?" The fellow grinned and drove a bowie knife into the top of the flour barrel, saying, "This, sir, is the law of Shelby County." And before that knife could commence to quivering, the judge pulled out a long-barreled pistol and laid it on the barrel top. "If that's the law of Shelby County," he said, "then here's the constitution."

The Death of Billy the Kid

Poe joined Garrett and McKinney at nine o'clock that night at the appointed meeting place at the north end of the double row of cottonwoods and recounted his day's experiences. The suspicion he encountered in Fort Sumner and Rudolph's agitation convinced him, he said, that the Kid was somewhere in the Fort Sumner vicinage. Garrett was not so sanguine.

"But as long as we are here," Garrett said, "we might as well try watching Charlie Bowdre's old home in Fort Sumner. Manuela Bowdre, Charlie Bowdre's widow, still lives there with her mother, and if the Kid's in these parts, he's probably hiding there."

They set off from Fort Sumner through the four-mile avenue of cottonwoods. A quarter of a mile from town, they hid their horses in a grove of trees on the Pecos and took a position in the old peach orchard at the north edge of the village. Just across the road from their place of concealment stood the old military hospital in which Manuela Bowdre had her home. A full moon was in the sky, making the landscape as bright as day, but the peach trees were in full leaf, and in the deep shadows they were safe from chance discovery. For two hours they remained there silently watching the Bowdre door like three cats at a mouse hole. But no sign of the Kid rewarded their patience. It was hard on midnight when they decided to abandon their vigil.

"I had no faith in this trip in the first place," growled Garrett. "I'm willing to bet the Kid ain't in Fort Sumner and never has been here since his escape. We'll go back to our horses now and start for Roswell. Best to put a little distance between us and Fort Sumner before daybreak."

"Let's go see Pete Maxwell before we give it up," insisted Poe doggedly. "If the Kid's in Fort Sumner or has been here, he'll know beyond a doubt. Maybe he'll tell us."

"Maybe," replied Garrett dubiously, "and maybe he won't. If the Kid happened to hear Maxwell had betrayed him, Pete would be due to start on a long journey. But just to satisfy you, Poe, we'll see him."

They crossed the road, white with moonlight, slipped into the sleeping town, stole noiselessly through the streets in the shadows of the houses, and came out into the broad open space that had once been the parade ground of the army post. Before them stood the Maxwell home.

Once used as officers' quarters, it was a large two-story building containing twenty rooms, its lower walls of adobe bricks sustaining a frame superstructure with a row of dormer windows along its gable roof opening from the upper rooms. A wide sheltered veranda ran across its front and along the north and south sides. It faced east on the old parade ground, from which it was separated by a low picket fence that extended fifty feet to the south to a row of adobe houses along the side yard. A cannon, relic of old soldier days, stood outside the fence near the northeast corner. At the southeast corner beside the front gate grew a tall cottonwood tree.

"Pete Maxwell's sleeping room is right there in the southeast corner of the house," said Garrett when they reached the gate. "You fellows wait here outside and I'll go in and have a talk with him."

Garrett stepped across the porch and entered the door of Maxwell's room which, on this warm summer night, had been left open. Poe sat down on the edge of the porch at the gateway. McKinney squatted down on his heels, cowboy fashion, just outside the picket fence and rolled himself a cigarette. The moon was riding westward from the zenith and the two men, sitting in silence, merged into the dark, heavy shadows falling eastward from the building.

Maxwell's room was in deep darkness. Garrett paused just inside the door for a moment until his eyes grew accustomed to the obscurity. Then, groping his way to a chair at the head of the bed, he sat down and gently roused Maxwell.

The room was twenty feet square. There were three windows, two in the front and one in the south wall near the door, but the roof of the porch prevented even a faint reflection of moonlight from entering. Maxwell's bed stood against the south wall, its foot near the door, its head against the front wall. There was a bureau in the northwest corner, a fireplace in the west wall, and a washstand between the fireplace and the door. The floor was carpeted.

Maxwell was surprised when he awoke from a deep sleep and saw Garrett sitting at his bedside. He rubbed his eyes.

"Oh, hello, Pat," he mumbled. *"Qué hace Usted aquí?"*

"About the Kid, Pete," said Garrett in Spanish. "I've had word——"

A voice sounded outside—a voice that Garrett knew. He cut short his words. He sat in tense, sudden silence, listening. . . .

When Garrett and his deputies stole into Fort Sumner from the peach orchard, Billy the Kid was in the house of Saval Gutierrez, Pat Garrett's brother-in-law, which stood at the south edge of the Maxwell side yard not more than fifty feet from the Maxwell home. He had come in only a few minutes before from a sheep ranch several miles south on the Pecos. He was tired. He took off his coat, boots, and hat and threw himself on a bed. He smiled to himself as he thought how neatly he had thrown Garrett off the scent. While the posses were sweeping New Mexico, he had been safe in Fort Sumner among friends. But it was time for him to get out of the country. These bloodhounds on his trail would nose him out sooner or later. He would start for Mexico to-morrow night. And while the Kid dreamed his dream, death was waiting in ambush for him fifty feet away.

"Celsa," he called.

Celsa Gutierrez, Saval's wife, who had been waiting up for the Kid to come in from the sheep camp, stepped into the room from the kitchen.

"I'm hungry, Celsa," said the Kid. "Can't you get me a bite to eat?"

Celsa rummaged through her pantry.

"There is nothing here but some cold tortillas and coffee, Chiquito," she said, "but Pete Maxwell killed a beef to-day. It is hanging in the north porch of the Maxwell house. I'll go cut you off a steak and cook you a good supper."

She went back into the kitchen and got her butcher knife. She was reaching for her *rebozo* hanging on a nail on the wall to throw over her head against the night damp.

"I'll go for the meat," said the Kid, getting up from the bed.

"No, *muchacho,*" protested Celsa. "You must stay here. There is no telling what might happen to you. Danger is always near you. You must not venture out to-night."

On this night of nights, Fate, it might seem, was setting the stage. There was no need for the Kid to come in from the sheep camp. But he had come. There was now no need for him to go for the meat. But he went.

"There is no danger, Celsa," he said. "Give me the butcher knife."

So the Kid started out for the meat just as he was, bareheaded, coatless, with only socks on his feet, the butcher knife in his right hand and, naturally enough, as he was left-handed, his forty-one calibre double-action revolver in its scabbard at his left side. He stepped from the door of Saval Gutierrez's home not more than a minute after Garrett had entered Pete Maxwell's room.

The familiar scene outdoors was more than usually serene in the pale moonlight. The deep hush of midnight lay upon the slumbering town. The great, dark, silent mass of the Maxwell home loomed fifty feet ahead of him. There was no movement, no sound to indicate danger, nothing to warn him to be on guard. He was hungry. The carcass of beef hung in the north porch. He would cut off a good steak for himself. There was no better cook in Fort Sumner than Celsa. He would have a regular feast. . . . He did not see the two deputies sitting in the heavy shadows of the porch. With quick, easy stride, still thinking of his supper, he walked straight toward them, his soul off watch.

Poe saw him coming. McKinney, squatting behind the palings rolling a cigarette, neither saw nor heard him. The Kid's figure stood out clearly in the moonlight as he moved noiselessly on bootless feet over the matted grass. Not a flash of suspicion disturbed Poe's mind that this was the desperado he was hunting, whom he knew he had to kill on sight, who otherwise would kill him instantly and without mercy. Strangely enough at this tense, critical moment of the long chase, the deputy's wits seem to have been wool-gathering. He looked at the approaching figure with only casual interest, wondered in a mildly curious way who this half-dressed youth might be wandering about at midnight, and contented himself with the half-formed, passing thought that probably it was one of Pete Maxwell's sheep herders.

Coming on rapidly, the Kid stepped up on the porch and almost stumbled over Poe before he saw him. If his soul had been off watch before, that instant it sprang to hair-trigger alertness. There was a lightning-quick movement of his left hand and Poe was staring in astonishment into the muzzle of the Kid's revolver.

"*Quién es?*"

The Kid's voice was vibrant with a suddenly awakened sense of danger. Who were these two armed strangers at Pete Maxwell's house at midnight? He began to back away across the porch.

Poe was nonplussed, his mind somehow still out of focus. He thought with a certain touch of pity that, without intention, he had frightened this poor sheep herder. It seemed to him vaguely that he owed the simple rustic some sort of apology. He got to his feet and took a step toward the Kid.

"Don't be scared," he said reassuringly. "I'm not going to hurt you."

The Kid kept backing away.

"*Quién es?*" he snapped out again.

Poe said nothing more. He did not know what to say. He had never seen a sheep herder act like this. The fellow must be crazy. It did not occur to him to draw his six-shooter. He stood there feeling rather foolish, the Kid's gun all the while pointed at his breast. McKinney had stepped up on the porch and was standing now a pace behind Poe. He, too, fancied the Kid a sheep herder and was equally at a loss to understand the situation.

The Kid backed into the doorway of Maxwell's room. There he paused for an instant, half-hidden by the thick adobe wall, his gun still at aim.

"*Quién es?*" he called a third time.

Then he turned and stepped into the black darkness of the chamber; into security, as he fancied; into a death trap, in reality. In the darkness, Death crouched, waiting, ready.

Coming in out of the bright moonlight, the Kid could hardly see his hand before him. But he did not need to see. He knew the room of old, the arrangement of the furniture—every detail. He groped to the foot of the bed, stepped around to the side, leaned slightly over Maxwell.

"*Quiénes son esos hombres afuera,* Pete?" he asked. (Who are those fellows outside?)

Garrett, sitting silent in the darkness at the head of the bed, could have stretched out a hand and touched the Kid. He knew at once this was the Kid. He had recognized his voice when the Kid had flashed his first Spanish question at Poe outside on the porch. He had recognized the familiar figure silhouetted against a patch of moonlight as the Kid came in the door. If no doubt was in his mind of the Kid's identity, neither was there doubt as to what he himself must do and do quickly if he was to live to see the light of another day. His mind was instantly made up.

As the Kid entered, Garrett, still sitting in his chair, reached for his six-shooter. But so quickly did the little drama in the darkness rush to its climax, he was still in the act of drawing his weapon from its scabbard when the Kid, two feet away, was bending over Maxwell with the query that was never answered. The Kid felt, rather than saw, the noiseless movement of Garrett's arm. He caught a sudden, vague glimpse of Garrett's form bulking dimly in the darkness. He sprang back to the middle of the room and threw his revolver to a level.

"*Quién es?*" he demanded sharply.

Dropping over sideways from the chair toward the floor in a tricky, dodging movement, Garrett answered the question with a shot. A flare of lurid flame lighted up the darkness for an instant, the room shook with a sudden crashing explosion, and Billy the Kid fell dead with a bullet through his heart.

Garrett fired a second shot as quickly as his finger could pull the trigger and, bolting for the door, was out of the room in three strides. Pete Maxwell, in wild panic, scrambled over the foot of his bed and, hard on Garrett's heels, dashed outside, a fat, ludicrous figure clad only in his nightshirt. He blundered on the porch into Poe, who shoved his six-shooter into his stomach and would have killed him, had not Garrett, with a hurried explanation, knocked the weapon aside.

"It was the Kid who came in there on to me," Garrett told Poe, "and I think I got him."

"Pat," replied Poe, still under the sheep-herder hallucination, "I believe you have killed the wrong man."

"I'm sure it was the Kid," responded Garrett, "for I knew his voice and could not have been mistaken."

They heard several gurgling gasps inside. Then there was silence. But no one dared enter that room of death. A spectre of fear stood in the darkness like the menacing ghost of the dead . . .

The Death of Wild Bill

. . . Wild Bill was now living in peace with everyone in Deadwood, as he had travelled far from his former conflicts with the bad men of Hays and Abilene. O. W. Coursey, the historian of the Black Hills, now a resident of Mitchell, South Dakota, has made a searching investigation of those wild times. He learned that Bill had a premonition when he entered Deadwood Gulch that his end was near. When the party reached the top of the upland divide (Break Neck Hill) and looked over into Deadwood Gulch for the first time, he said to Colorado Charlie Utter, "I have a hunch that I am in my last camp and will never leave this gulch alive."

"Quit dreaming," retorted Utter.

"No, I am not dreaming," replied Wild Bill. "Something tells me that my time is up, but where it is coming from I do not know, as I cannot think of one living enemy who would wish to kill me."

On the evening before he was killed he was standing up leaning against the jamb of the door to the building in which he was to be assassinated the next day, looking downcast.

"Bill, why are you looking so dumpy tonight?" Tom Dosier asked him.

"Tom, I have a presentiment that my time is up and that I am soon going to be killed," Bill replied.

"Oh, pooh, pooh!" said Tom. "Don't get to seeing things; you're all right."

A letter written by Wild Bill to his wife on that same evening lends reality to this legend:

AGNES DARLING:

If such should be we never meet again, while firing my last shot, I will gently breathe the name of my wife—Agnes—and with wishes even for my enemies I will make the plunge and try to swim to the other shore.

J. B. HICKOK.

On the following afternoon, Wednesday, August 2, 1876, he was engaged in a game of poker in a saloon owned by Carl Mann and Jerry Lewis.

There is some diversity of opinion as to the name of this place. O. W. Coursey says it was No. 6; Harry Young, the barkeeper, in his "Hard Knocks," says it was No. 66; while Brown and Willard, in "Black Hill Trails," give it as No. 10.

Those sitting at the table beside Wild Bill were Carl Mann, Charles Rich, and Captain Massey, the latter a former Missouri River pilot. As the game progressed the quartet were joking and laughing.

For the first time known, Wild Bill was sitting with his back to a door. While he was facing the front door, a rear door was standing open. Charlie Rich had taken Bill's seat next to the wall, just to plague him, and kept it, though several times Bill asked Charlie to exchange places. Rich said afterward that he was the cause of Bill's murder.

Jack McCall, the assassin, entered the saloon in a careless manner, not giving the least hint of his cowardly purpose. He walked up to the bar, at which Harry Young was officiating, and then sauntered around to a point a few yards behind Wild Bill. He then swiftly drew a .45-calibre Colt and fired. The bullet passed through Bill's head, issued beneath his right cheek bone and before it had spent its course, pierced Captain Massey's left arm. The time was 4:10 P. M.

In his letter to the writer Mr. Peirce gives several details that have not heretofore been revealed. Doc Peirce was the impromptu undertaker who took charge of the remains and looked after the details of the burial:

"Now, in regard to the position of Bill's body," writes Mr. Peirce, "when they unlocked the door for me to get his body, he was lying on his side, with his knees drawn up just as he slid off his stool. We had no chairs in those days—and his fingers were still crimped from holding his poker hand. Charlie Rich, who sat beside him, said he never saw a muscle move. Bill's hand read 'aces and eights'—two pair, and since that day aces and eights have been known as 'the dead man's hand' in the Western country. It seemed like fate, Bill's taking off. Of the murderer's big Colt's-.45 six-gun, every chamber loaded, the cartridge that killed Bill was the only one that would fire. What would have been McCall's chances if he had snapped one of the other cartridges when he sneaked up and held his gun to Bill's head? He would now be known as No. 37 on the file list of Mr. Hickok."

It has been stated that Bill occupied a cabin which stood in a little copse near the spot where the Burlington depot now stands in the city of Deadwood; but Doc Peirce states that Bill was living in a tent, a wagon cover stretched over a pole. Colorado Charlie Utter was his tent mate. It was to this tent that the body was taken by Doc Peirce to prepare it for burial.

In a former statement he said: "When Bill was shot through the head he bled out quickly and when he was laid out he looked like a wax figure. I have seen many dead men on the field of battle and in civil life, but Wild Bill was the prettiest corpse I have ever seen. His long moustache was attractive, even in death, and his long tapering fingers looked like marble."

On the Dodge

Bill Muggridge and I were heading north from El Paso with a four-horse team and a wagon loaded with valuable supplies, and approached the Hueco Tanks about dusk, meaning to camp there for the night. The Tanks are a formation of big lava boulders, with natural reservoirs of fresh water, located near the Texas-New Mexico line. Bill, who was my partner in a ranch proposition, was an English remittance man of the kind you've read about. The night before, in El Paso, we had gone to see a minstrel show. A black-face comedian pulled one joke that was a corker; I nearly fell off the seat laughing at it. But poor old Bill sat as solemn as soap, never cracking a smile, because the point failed to percolate his skull. He had slept on it all night, ridden all day, and now, just as we were making for our camping place, he suddenly saw the point and burst out laughing.

"By God! old chap," he exclaimed, "wasn't that a bully wheeze."

Bill might be slow on the uptake with an American minstrel joke, but not otherwise. Suddenly I felt a sharp dig of his elbow. He said nothing, and kept right on laughing, but I followed the direction of his eyes, and in the shadows of the lava boulders saw a man, half-crouched, dragging a rifle.

We carried a Winchester in a holster tied to the wagon bow on my side, but you had to get off the wagon to get it out. I braced myself, sprang to the ground, whirled, and jerked out the gun, all in practically one motion. "Whoops!" I said, throwing down on the skulking figure, "what do you want?"

The man moved out of the shadows in a hurry, waving peaceably. "No harm," he said, "nothing, nothing. I was goin' to cook supper. Jest thought," nervously, "I'd see who was a-comin'."

"Where's your horse?" I asked. I didn't see one staked out, and had noticed no tracks. The stranger admitted that he had come there afoot. This was odd enough in the West, where to travel afoot from the front gallery to the horse corral was quite a *pasear*, but having satisfied ourselves that the stranger was alone and had no designs on us or our property, we asked him to take a load off his feet and share our chuck.

That was the evening of John Collier's first day on the dodge. Bill and I asked him no pertinent personal questions. Too much curiosity about other folks was considered bad form and not too healthy on the range. But we knew perfectly well that our guest had been up to some devilment, even though the nature of it might be no concern of ours. Mentioning the name he was going by, the feller said he was on the lookout for a job, and as Bill and I were drilling a stock-water well and needed help, we hired him. Some time later when I was in El Paso again, the sheriff gave me a letter-perfect description of John Collier, our hired hand.

"I don't know what name he's usin'," the sheriff said, "but I wouldn't much wonder if he headed your way."

"What's he wanted for?" I asked.

"Killin' Diamond Dick—" a Canadian gambler of unpleasant reputation. "The cuss probably needed killin'," the sheriff added. "Still, we need the man that done it. Don't reckon you seen him?"

"Sheriff," I said, "do you know I got just the worst kind of memory for faces!"

He knew what I meant; and I knew that he knew.

Going on the dodge was one of the peculiar institutions of the old West. It corresponded with what is known in certain circles today as "taking it on the lam." There were other rangeland phrases for it, such as hiding out, riding the lone trails, hunting the high places, laying out with the dry cattle—this last referring to cattle that range a long way and come infrequently to water. The country was big, and the spirit was one of live and let live. A man who got into trouble in one place might easily light out and make good somewhere else, if he changed his name and more or less walked in the paths of righteousness henceforth. It was an unwritten rule not to bother a man on the dodge or be too inquisitive about him; but he better behave himself in his new surroundings and not be caught riding horses with the wrong brands or selling the wrong man's beef!

The majority of men on the dodge in the West were not what would be called bad men, judging by those I knew. A good many were like Collier—victims of circumstances, or of quick temper, carelessness, daredeviltry, and thoughtlessness. I never knew exactly what happened between Collier and the gambler he killed. Probably it was hasty words over a game of cards and purely an accident that the gambler collected the bullet in a vital spot instead of Collier. The latter was a great windy, nothing special as a gunman, and he couldn't on any account tell the truth. Bill Muggridge and I put him to work on the well we were drilling, and one day while we were hoisting a slush bucket, he got his right thumb caught in the sprocket chain, smashing it so badly that it had to be amputated. Collier bawled like a baby at the pain. Many years later I dropped into a saloon in Santa Fe and heard him telling a bunch of open-mouthed townies how that thumb had been shot off in a gun battle. Happening to look up and see me listening with considerable interest to the details of his story, of which he was the outstanding hero, he seemed to forget all the last part of it.

The way Collier made his getaway after killing the gambler was rather interesting. He had no horse, and set out afoot from the little town of Isleta, near El Paso, hoping to put as much distance behind him as possible. Now, if he had walked at the side of the road, or straight across the desert, where the going would have been easiest, a man on horseback could have tracked him at a lope, and he soon would have been caught. But Collier was smart enough to walk in the deep sand of the wheel tracks; the loose sand that he displaced dropped right back in, and his tracks were gone as soon as they were made, like other footsteps in the sands of time. He walked through thirty-five miles of that loose sand, in the daytime heat of Texas and southern New Mexico, to get to the Hueco Tanks where we found him.

In fifty-odd years as a cowboy and cattleman, and occasionally as a special officer, I knew a lot of men on the dodge. I hired them, worked cattle with them, camped and ate, drank, sang, and swapped stories with them, and at times trailed and caught them for horse stealing or worse. Some were plenty hard, but as I say, only a small percentage were downright villainous. By accident, or in a passion, a man committed offenses that you or I, in the same fix, might have committed. In a country so lonely, the law was often a long ways off. I have ranched in a spot fifty-five miles from the nearest town, and eighty-five miles from the county seat. I know if I'd got in a tight spot out there, I would have protected myself. Wait for the sheriff? No, sir!

Outlaw Women

A number of women who went on the dodge came from highly respected families. Many were Southerners who, during the turmoil of the Civil War period, became estranged to former ways of living, through their families' sudden loss of fortune. Like most Southern girls of that day, they were excellent horsewomen, and took quite naturally to the adventurous life of the range and the hills. Some of these women outlaws I knew. From old records and letters written by the characters themselves to relatives, lovers, and friends, I traced the lives of more than twenty of them. The evidence is overwhelming that they were more sinned against than sinning, victims of circumstance that they refused to bow down to without a struggle, and they were often unable to gain their ends within the law.

Altar Doane, for example, as a girl of fifteen, left Independence, Missouri, with her father, mother, and brother Jed in a covered wagon drawn by four mules. The family was lured West by reports of rich gold strikes. Altar's father was a strict-living, high-tempered, vindictive man, who, when aroused, was dangerous. Her mother was a meek little woman in failing health, who found the hardships of the journey too much for her, and died before they reached their destination. Altar strongly resembled her father in looks and disposition, and after her mother's death, and even before it, camp duties and responsibilities fell on her young shoulders. Nine months after leaving Missouri, the Doanes pulled into a little gold camp then known as the Essaus Diggings, where they found a few placer miners at work. They made camp and panned the sands here for a while without any special luck, then moved somewhat farther upstream, where at a likely-looking place they built some sluice boxes, and every night added a little gold to the slowly-accumulating hoard in the buckskin bag that was their bank. One morning they struck a pocket under some boulders from which they gathered nuggets worth around five hundred dollars. Somehow the news of this strike, small though it was, became known—probably it leaked out through the boy, Jed, when he went to the store for supplies. The next day, when suppertime came, and her father and brother did not return, Altar went in search of them. She found them sprawled out in the sand, shot through the head, both dead, and the claim jumped.

Altar made her preparations methodically. First she disposed of her mules and outfit, receiving in exchange some cash, a saddle, and a fine thoroughbred horse, very fast, which made her probably the best mounted horsewoman in the state. Then she took her leave, publicly. How far she rode is not known. But apparently she circled around, and came back. The day after she left, the two claim jumpers were found dead, each shot through the head, and lying almost exactly where she had found her father and brother. Altar Doane had become a killer, and though a miner's court might have acquitted her, she chose to go on the dodge.

One other little incident in her career shows her cool nerve. She turned up one day in Montana mounted on her thoroughbred, near where the town of Kalispell now stands. She was sitting on her horse watching a race between two locally-owned horses, neither of which seemed very fast to her. She made a remark to that effect to her neighbor, a hard-looking customer whose name was Marsh, and who, as it turned out, owned a half interest in the horse that won the race. Marsh asked if she would like to run her horse against the winner for some real money. After some talk, she agreed, confident that she could win by five jumps and a hoggin' string. The terms of the race were as follows: distance, four hundred and forty yards; price, a dollar a yard put up by each entrant; time, the next afternoon at four o'clock; weight, each horse to carry one hundred and thirty-five pounds. A stakeholder was agreed on, and the money was put up. Not until that night did Altar learn that the stakeholder owned the other half interest in the horse which her horse was to run against, and that the race was almost certain to be rigged against her somehow.

At the hour agreed on, the two horses with their riders appeared, Marsh's son riding the second horse, and Altar riding for herself. Everybody except the starter went to the far end of the straightaway track to see the finish. The two horses scored a long while, Altar's opponent making several bad breaks. The starter called Altar to bring her horse back to the score each time; and then once, when she was headed the wrong way, he dropped his flag, sending the other horse away to a flying start. Altar whirled and followed, but the other horse by then had a lead of ten lengths. The girl closed the gap, lapping the other horse at the finish, but lost. Naturally, she was mad.

It was dark when she rode back to her hotel. Once more she made her plans methodically. She tied her horse to a post back of the building, then went in and ate her supper. Marsh and another man came in and ate while she was there. Later, Altar went out to the office and sat down. When Marsh went up to his room, she followed, knocked at his door, went in, stuck a gun in his face, and told him to fork over the roll that he and the crooked starter had robbed her of. Marsh took a look at the gun, which she held perfectly steady, and decided it was sweeter to go on living than to enter into any immediate argument. He counted out eight hundred and eighty dollars (her bet and his), and handed the roll over.

"Now, Mister," said Altar, tucking the money in her pocket, "you can have your choice. I'm willin' to kill you here and now. But if you'd rather, you can take a ten-minutes' walk with me, not once makin' a break or openin' your mouth, and if you act nice, I'll spare you your hide." Marsh naturally chose the second alternative. "Remember," she promised, "if you make one false move or say a word to anybody, I'll drop you."

He marched to the lobby with her, as peaceful as a lamb. Altar paid her bill, and Marsh stayed right with her like her little boy, until she reached her horse. Then she mounted and dashed off in the darkness, and left him. She crossed the line into Canada, and the last trace we have of her was in the Rustercruse country, where she is said to have married a member of the Canadian Mounted Police.

Belle Starr, another famous woman outlaw, dealt in stolen horses and had a gang working for her. She was not my idea of complete depravity. "Battle Axe" also dealt in stolen horses. She got her odd nickname from the fact that she was never known to be without a plug of Battle Axe chewing tobacco. She was born and raised west of the line of Arkansas, in "the Strip" (or as some called it, No Man's Land) where even the lilies of the field were born rough and grew spines as they aged. She had a strain of Indian blood in her veins, but was not a full-blooded Indian. Sometimes she worked with a gang, but mostly she carried on alone. Once she stole a bunch of good horses at Bloomburg, Arkansas, and in twenty-four hours turned up with them near Sulphur Bluff, Texas, a distance of almost a hundred miles, and she had no help. The owner of the horses and a deputy sheriff trailed her on this occasion, and the second day, at sunrise, rode up to the post corral where the horses were penned. Battle Axe was camped on the opposite side of the corral, about two hundred feet away. She wore a man's hat, chaps, and brush jacket, and undoubtedly her pursuers thought she was a man. They opened fire with their pistols, but Battle Axe dropped to the ground unhurt, and with her saddle gun killed them both. She then drove the horses north and east to Hart's Bluff, where she sold them.

She partnered for a while with the Broken Bow gang, which headquartered near Broken Bow, Indian Territory, the gang consisting of Jack Spain, Tom Cree, and a few others. This gang was surprised in camp while on a raid near the head of Clover Creek, and Battle Axe's left shoulder stopped a bullet fired by one of the officers. However, she managed to get away, and hid out in the brush. It was her practice never to sleep close to camp, so her saddle and outfit were overlooked by the officers, and she got away from the scene on an old pack horse that was too poor to interest the officers. Late in the afternoon, weak and sick from her wound, she had no alternative when she reached a lonely cabin but to ride right up and hail it. Strangely enough (strange, because women in those parts were scarce, and a "Montgomery Ward wife" was the only chance some cowhands had at matrimony), a woman came to the door. When she saw that her visitor was a woman and wounded, she made her get down and come in. Battle Axe made up a story, saying she had been riding along and heard some shooting, and a stray bullet struck her. There was no doctor within a hundred miles, but Mrs. James, the ranch wife, bathed and bandaged the wound and put her to bed, and Battle Axe lay there for a month before she was able to ride again.

Now, the James woman had a little girl named Ethel May, who was a cripple. The child's leg had been broken by a horse's falling with her, and some quack who tried to set it did such a poor job that the little girl could hardly walk. Battle Axe and Ethel May James became great friends. When Battle Axe was getting ready to pull out, she asked Mrs. James how much she owed her for all the trouble and care. Mrs. James wouldn't take a cent. Battle Axe thanked her and climbed aboard her old pack horse, which had fattened up considerably in the meantime. Not long after she had gone, Mrs. James, making up the bed, found an envelope under the pillow addressed to Ethel May, and inside it this badly scrawled message:

"To pay for having your off hind leg fixed up right."

The enclosure was three hundred dollars in bills.

A turning point in Battle Axe's career occurred at Hot Springs, Arkansas, when she was about twenty-seven years old. She was dressed in woman's clothes, and was not at all bad looking—in fact, quite a lady, medium tall, five feet, six and a half, with an olive skin, black eyes, and a figure that indicated plenty of outdoor activity and good health. She was never in any sense a carouser or wastrel. Although she had never had an opportunity for much education, she could read, she wrote a fairly good hand, and she knew how to save her money. In Hot Springs, on this Saturday afternoon, she went to the races. Two horses in the grand sweepstakes caught her eye. Their names were Spurs and Wings. Both were owned by the same man and were very valuable, having won large purses in Tennessee and Kentucky. After the race, which Spurs won, Wings coming in third, Battle Axe followed the two to their stalls; and having seen that they were at the end of the row, she went back to her hotel for supper. Presently, by messenger, she dispatched a gallon jug of good corn whiskey to the boy who had charge of Spurs, and with it an unsigned note saying the snake poison came with the good wishes of one who had won on the horse that day. When she judged that the liquor would have been used for its intended purpose and produced its proper effect, Battle Axe quietly slipped into Spur's stall and led him out without waking the snoring stable boy, then did the same with Wings. Mounting Spurs bareback, she rode off with both horses. Ten miles out of town she changed to her business clothes, and from then on laid up by day and rode only at night, thus escaping with these prize horses to the camp near Broken Bow. Later she traded both of them to a man from Dallas, Texas, for two hundred head of steeldust breeding mares. These were the foundation stock of the H E L brand, which Battle Axe ran for many years.

Her end was not spectacular. One day she picked up a Fort Smith, Arkansas, paper, and by pure accident came across a message in the "Personal" column intended for her. It said that her sister, with whom she had been out of touch for years, was very sick in Fort Smith, and wanted to see her. She climbed aboard a saddle horse, and with another following, made the hundred-mile ride to Fort Smith in less than sixteen hours. There she stayed, nursing the sick woman until she died. Battle Axe's sister left a five-year-old daughter, for whom Battle Axe felt a fondness and proposed to take home. The girl's father agreed to let her go. Since Battle Axe had now stolen enough to be well fixed, and had a good ranch, hundreds of good horses, and considerable cash in the bank as the wages of her crimes, she determined to turn over a new leaf, be respectable, and do the best she could for her niece. She had a talk with her ranch hands and friends, and spread the word that she wanted the girl to have the right kind of bringing up and a good safe home, so that she might grow up to be a lady and respect her aunt. So the old nickname, Battle Axe, was barred from that time forward. And while old-timers were welcome to a meal and a bed any time when they came by, the old life was out too. For many years Battle Axe continued to ride broncs and break them fearlessly on her H E L Ranch. One night she passed out peacefully in her sleep. She hadn't hesitated to take what she wanted, and she had shot to kill to keep what she got, and the lawyers have names for a lot of things she did. But who's going to stand up and say that she was all bad and completely rotted away with sin?

The old lady was buried at the forks of Little River under her right name, Helen Law.

Calamity's Bet

There were all sorts of crazy horse races run in the West, one of the craziest being one that was proposed and won by Calamity Jane herself. She was sitting in front of a saloon beside her horse, Jim, when a stranger rode up and invited her to trade horses. He was willing, he said, to prove that his horse could outrun hers under any conditions, for money, marbles, or whiskey. She said the idea of a race sort of appealed to her and inquired if she might name the distance and conditions. The stranger said he was willing, and each of them put one hundred dollars in the hands of a stake holder, winner to take all. Calamity Jane then had a notary write down the terms of the race, and it was signed and witnessed by two passing gamblers. The terms she dictated were as follows: "We'll start twenty feet back of the platform where the horses are now standing, jump the horses up on the platform, ride into the saloon, take a drink, ride out through the back door, enter the next saloon by the back door, have a drink there, and out the front, enter the next saloon, and so on all the way down the street until all eleven saloons and dance halls on that side of the street are visited in turn. First horse at the bar of the last saloon gets the money." Her horse had been trained to do this stunt and had done it for years, and when he got to a bar, he could even take a bottle in his teeth, up-end it, and drink just like a man—and with about the same physical consequences. Calamity Jane won the race by three saloons and four drinks.

Annie Oakley Makes Her Name

On a bright November day when the last yellow leaves were fluttering from the trees on Grand Street, Lyda Stein led her sister up the steep streets of Fairmount. From the ridge Annie saw Cincinnati spreading across the basin and the hills of Kentucky rising beyond the river.

"Not much like North Star, is it?" Lyda kept pointing over the city as though she could gather it all in one avid gesture. She hated the memory of Darke County, the lonely back roads, the empty marshes, and the dark line of the woods. "Oh, Annie, I'm glad you came. Everything is different here."

Annie asked gently. "Don't you ever get homesick?"

Lyda shook her head. For bare feet and tattered clothing? For digging potatoes and hoeing weeds? No, she never got homesick for that. "And you won't either, Annie. You don't belong there. The way you talk, the way you smile, even the way you walk—you don't belong to the country. I remember even when you were a baby you looked different. And you did things better. Like cutting out paper dolls—you made them with more life and spirit. You know, Annie, I've had feelings about you."

"But Lyda, I can't even read yet. Not even a child's book."

"That's why you're here! You'll learn all kinds of things. You'll be different here."

"I don't think I could ever forget Swamp Creek and the pasture slough."

"Pasture—you've had enough pasture." She pointed again. "See where the river curves away. We almost went to live in that part of the city, in Oakley or Hyde Park."

"Oakley—" Annie said. "That's a nice name."

"See that building, like a castle above the river. It's the Highland House. Joe wants to take you there."

"What for?"

"Music and dancing and the sight of all the boats on the river. And we'll go to the other places, Lookout House and Bellevue." She pointed again. "Right here on the hilltop is Schuetzenbuckel."

Annie looked at the painted balconies and cupola towers. "What did you call it?"

"Schuetzenbuckel. It's a German name for a shooting club."

Schuetzenbuckel, Annie repeated to herself as they went home to Grand Street. *Schuetzenbuckel.*

Joe Stein wanted to show the city's night life to his wide-eyed sister-in-law. "Vine Street," he said, as they stepped off the horsecar. "There's no gayer street in America."

He was a tall man with a naturally ruddy face that even the gas-lights could not pale. His long stride kept Annie stepping quickly.

They passed the Burnet House with its lights and music. They watched people streaming into the gleaming lobby of Pike's Opera House. They wandered through the Emery Arcade and came out on the street where wienerwurst men, mustard men, oyster peddlers, hot-corn men were shrilling their whistles and blowing their horns. It was a street of wonders—the Atlantic Gardens, the Pacific Gardens, the London Concert Hall, the Melodeon, Kissel's Concert Hall, Wiswell's Art Gallery. They saw the horrors in a waxworks museum, a huge panorama of the Battle of Sedan, the wild animals in the basement of Robinson's Opera House.

Across the canal they were never out of sound of music. Schickling's, Schuler's, Wielert's, the Coliseum—they were all places of sawdust floors, singing waiters, bands playing German waltzes. When they were on the street again Annie heard the sharp sound of rifle fire.

"Where's the shooting?"

He pointed to a row of lighted windows over a beer garden. "It's the Germania Schuetzen Association. They're crazy about target shooting."

"Could we go there?"

"No, but we can go to Charlie Stuttelberg's. Come on."

The shooting gallery was idle, with guns on the counter and Stuttelberg sitting under a gas flare reading the *Cincinnati Abend Post.* At the end of the range gas jets fluttered over a row of metal ducks, another row of big-eared rabbits, and a bull's eye of concentric rings.

Joe picked up a rifle. "I used to be a good shot." He banged away six times, and two ducks fell over in the middle of the line. He handed a gun to Annie. "Try it."

She weighed the gun in her hands and glanced along the barrel. "Do they give prizes?"

Charlie Stuttelberg didn't look up from his paper. "No charge if you ring the bell five times."

"What bell?"

"In the bull's-eye," Joe said.

She swung the gun to her shoulder. The first shot drew a *bong!* from the bull's-eye. Charlie looked up from his paper. She pumped a new shell in. Then she fired fast. The target sounded like an alarm gong, and when she put the gun down the metal still rang with vibration.

Joe stared down at her, and Charlie Stuttelberg jumped up from his chair.

"Lyda told me you hunted quail in the country," Joe said.

She nodded. "Quail are harder to hit than a tin target."

Charlie Stuttelberg picked up another gun. "Try it again. No charge."

She swung the gun up and fired. The bell was silent, but six ducks fell over like a row of dominoes on the metal track.

Charlie Stuttelberg looked at the girl with two braids of hair down her shoulders and her feet tapping the rhythm of the German band across the street. "You don't look like a marksman, but I'll bet you can outshoot Frank Butler."

"Who's he?"

"He's the shooting star at the Coliseum. You been on the stage, Miss?"

"Oh, no."

"Where did you do your shooting?"

"At home, in the country. I shot birds for Mr. Frost's hotel."

"Jack Frost—at the Bevis House. That's where Frank Butler's stopping." When he took off his hat his head shone in the gaslight. He was a small man with a large and drooping mustache. He picked up another gun. "Try one more."

She brought the sights together on the bull's eye—*bong, bong, bong*—and swung down to the row of rabbits. The two end ones fell over, and the last shot dropped the rabbit in the middle.

Charlie Stuttelberg clapped the derby on his bald head. "Come on over to the Bevis House."

"What for?"

"Tell Jack Frost his quail hunter is in town."

On the southwest corner of Court and Walnut, a short block from the canal, stood the four-story Bevis House with the office of the Bevis Coach Line in its cluttered and friendly lobby. Thirty years before it had been a busy packing plant; in its deep storerooms Cincinnati hams and sides of bacon were chilled with ice brought down from Lake Erie. When the packing firms moved to Mill Creek valley the solid building became a hotel, operated by Martin Bevis and W. H. Ridenour. In 1865 young Thomas Alva Edison lived there while working as an operator in the new Cincinnati telegraph exchange. In the middle seventies it came under the management of John B. Frost, who later changed its name to the Globe Hotel.

Jack Frost was an Englishman from the lake country of Cumberland. When he tired of his small farm near the foot of Skiddaw Mountain, he brought his family to America. They tried homesteading in Kansas, but because the lonely life there gave him a hunger for cities and people he came to Cincinnati and the Bevis House. His casual English manner attracted theatrical people, and soon his hotel was a meeting place of singers, actors, musicians, entertainers.

One of the Frost children was a slender dark-haired girl who went to school in Cincinnati as Sarah Frances Frost. She had a natural voice and a natural bearing. At twelve she sang with a juvenile opera company in *H.M.S. Pinafore* and *The Chimes of Normandy;* then she joined Miss Josephine Riley's traveling company, taking her mother's name, Fannie Brough. In 1887, while "Annie Oakley" was being cheered by thousands in Madison Square Garden, she appeared on the New York stage as "Julia Marlowe."

When Charlie Stuttelberg had identified Annie Moses, tall John Frost leaned across the desk. "So you're the hunter from Darke County. You're not as big as my girl Sarah, and she's gone to bed already." He turned to Stuttelberg. "You wouldn't believe it, Charlie —those birds are all shot through the head. We never have our guests spitting out bird shot. You wouldn't think—"

Charlie nodded vigorously. "I believe it. I believe she can outshoot Frank Butler."

Frost's eyes began to twinkle. "Frank thinks well of himself. You know, he shoots the center spot out of a five of spades. He shoots the flame off a candle."

"I've seen him shoot. I'll match this girl."

The hotel man tapped his fingers on the desk. "He's Irish, you know. Jaunty Irish. It might be interesting. You sure she'd have a chance?"

"I'll put fifty dollars on her."

"We might arrange a match at one of the clubs—the Cincinnati Schuetzen Vercin or the Germania Schuetzen Association."

Joe Stein said: "Or at Fairmount. That's where we live."

Frost nodded. "Shooter's Hill."

"Schuetzenbuckel," Annie said. It was her first speech.

Jack Frost slapped the counter. "All right, Fairmount. We'll match this little girl against Frank Butler."

On the wooded St. Clair Heights above the Mill Creek valley the Cincinnati Baptists had built a seminary, but it never attracted more than a handful of students. After the Civil War the rambling frame building was decked with porches and flower-lined balconies and a flagpole was raised above the cupola tower. Rich German food was served in the big dining room, beer was brought to the outdoor tables, and from a balcony a band played between rounds of the *schuetzenfest*. Eventually the building burned, but flags were whipping in the November air when little Annie Moses arrived for a shooting match with the professional Frank Butler.

It was all strange and exciting to a girl from Darke County—the big lounge with antlers over the fireplace, the long dining room looking over the city, the view of a profile Sphinx on the edge of Pancake Hill. Before she had stopped wondering she was led to the target range. There stood a ruddy man, big, blue-eyed, smiling, with a shotgun cradled in his arm. He wore a belted shooting coat and a soft green hat with a jutting feather.

"Mr. Frank Butler—your challenger, Miss Annie Moses."

The marksman stared at her. "This girl—I thought you said—"

"I said there was a crack shot from upcountry. Here she is."

This time his smile was for her, a smile of interest and surprise, of warm and friendly pleasure. She had never seen a man so handsome. He lifted his feathered hat. "It's a pleasure, Miss Moses."

Annie bobbed her head. "Same here," she managed.

Together they went to the shooting station, and Annie was offered her choice of guns from a rack. She lifted a polished gun, balanced it, glanced along the barrel. "All right," she said.

Frank Butler won the toss and took his position.

"Pull!" he called.

The bird sailed out and the gun swung to his shoulder.

"Dead!" cried the referee.

As Annie took her station, she felt lost. A strange place, a strange crowd, a strange gun, a strange man smiling at her. She had never shot clay targets from a mechanical trap; she had never seen a shooting range like this. The gun began shaking in her hands. She brought it to her shoulder, then she lowered it to her waist, and still her hands trembled.

The gallery was dead silent as she waited. She tried to think of the target, but her mind was full of the silent men behind her and the money that hung on her shooting. She wanted to put the gun down, to go home to Darke County. If she were in the woods, watching a covey of quail burst up—then she remembered how they flew. She had told herself many times, and now she told herself again: *You don't sight them. You just swing with them, and when it feels right, pull.* Quail were swifter than clay targets. *When it feels right—*

She forgot all but the gun in her hands and the trap where the clay bird would rise. The wind whipped her skirt and tugged at the ribbon on her hair. She stood lightly balanced, her eyes waiting.

"Pull!"

When the bird arced up the gun rose with a single motion to her shoulder. Her cheek pressed the gunstock, her eyes caught the sailing target. Her finger pressed.

"Dead!" cried the referee.

They were two experts, the big smiling man and the grave small girl, both shooting with instinctive skill. *Pull . . . Dead, Pull . . . Dead, Pull . . . Dead,* the call went on unchanging, until the last shot of the twenty-five.

"Pull!" called Frank Butler. The target came up steeply and quartering to the right. It was an instant longer before the gun sounded. The target sailed on in the sunlight.

"Miss!" the referee cried.

Annie balanced herself, ready to swing from the waist, holding the gun lightly.

"Pull!"

Up came the barrel, her cheek snuggled to the wood. In an instant she corrected for the target's flight. While the gun was swinging her finger pressed.

All her life she remembered the view from Shooter's Hill, widespreading and distant, full of light and color, with the far hills hazy in the sun; and all her life she remembered the referee's high-pitched cry. A year later she was Frank Butler's wife. Two years later she was his partner on the stage. Six years later she was a shooting star and Frank Butler was her manager. Eleven years later she was followed by crowds through the streets of London. She never stopped wondering that it all began with the cry of *Dead!* and the smell of gun smoke on the autumn wind.

The Disappointed Tenderfoot

He reached the West in a palace car where the writers tell us the
    cowboys are,
With the redskin bold and the centipede and the rattlesnake and
    the loco weed.
He looked around for the Buckskin Joes and the things he'd seen
    in the Wild West shows—
The cowgirls gay and the bronchos wild and the painted face of
    the Injun child.
He listened close for the fierce war-whoop, and his pent-up spirits
    began to droop,
And he wondered then if the hills and nooks held none of the
    sights of the story books.

He'd hoped he would see the marshal pot some bold bad man
    with a pistol shot,
And entered a low saloon by chance, where the tenderfoot is
    supposed to dance
While the cowboy shoots at his bootheels there and the smoke of
    powder begrimes the air,
But all was quiet as if he'd strayed to that silent spot where the
    dead are laid.
Not even a faro game was seen, and none flaunted the long, long
    green.
'Twas a blow for him who had come in quest of a touch of the
    real wild woolly West.

He vainly sought for a bad cayuse and the swirl and swish of the
    flying noose,
And the cowboy's yell as he roped a steer, but nothing of this fell
    on his ear.
Not even a wide-brimmed hat he spied, but derbies flourished on
    every side,
And the spurs and the "chaps" and the flannel shirts, the high-
    heeled boots and the guns and the quirts,
The cowboy saddles and silver bits and fancy bridles and swell
    outfits

He'd read about in the novels grim, were not on hand for the likes
    of him.

He peered about for a stagecoach old, and a miner-man with a bag
    of gold,
And a burro train with its pack-loads which he'd read they tie
    with the diamond hitch.
The rattler's whir and the coyote's wail ne'er sounded out as he
    hit the trail;
And no one knew of a branding bee or a steer roundup that he
    longed to see.
But the oldest settler named Six-Gun Sim rolled a cigarette and
    remarked to him:
"The West hez gone to the East, my son, and it's only in tents
    sich things is done."

E. A. Brinninstool

The Wild, Wild West Show

On opening night nine thousand spectators streamed into the Garden, crowding the huge galleries to the roof. In the boxes sat Henry Ward Beecher, General William Tecumseh Sherman, Erastus Wiman, Pierre Lorillard, August Belmont, General Philip H. Sheridan, and the widow of General Custer. The overhead beams were draped with flags and bunting, the arena floor was covered with fresh tanbark. From a side stage the cowboy band, in big hats, chaps, and spurs, played a medley of popular tunes. The music faded, the lights went dim. A ghostly clatter of hoofs filled the vast hall and from the looming mountains came the rich voice of Buffalo Bill: LADIES AND GENTLEMEN: THE WILD WEST PRESENTS THE UNIQUE AND UNPARALLELED SPECTACLE OF WESTERN LIFE AND HISTORY—THE DRAMA OF CIVILIZATION!

    Swinging spotlights, dramatic as a prairie sunset, picked out a group of riders in the scenic entrance. They loped across the plain and pulled up under a purple butte. One spotlight held them there while another swung back to a file of cowboys on half-wild mustangs, then to a band of Mexican vaqueros, and at last to a party of painted Sioux on shaggy ponies. Each raced around the arena and pulled up at the far end. LADIES AND GENTLEMEN: THE WILD WEST PRESENTS THE LOVELY LASS OF THE WESTERN PLAINS, LITTLE SURESHOT, THE ONE AND ONLY ANNIE OAKLEY. The spotlight found her, tiny, graceful, alive, eye-catching and breath-catching on a calico pony under the colored mountains; it raced with her across the tanbark plain. Now came the voice of Frank Richmond, master of ceremonies—LADIES AND GENTLEMEN: THE WILD WEST PRESENTS THE GREAT PLAINSMAN, THE GREAT HUNTER, THE GREAT INDIAN FIGHTER, THE GREATEST SCOUT OF THE OLD WEST —BUFFALO BILL! Amid fanfare the majestic plainsman galloped across the arena and halted his white horse on hind legs, forefeet in the air. The spotlight glittered on silver bridle, spurs, and silver-mounted saddle. The horse, famed Charlie of the buffalo chase, bowed on one knee while Cody swept his Stetson from his flowing hair.

Now the MacKaye "scenario" began. Silence and shadow held the empty plain; then the lights came up like sunrise, showing a "Primeval Forest" with bear, antelope, and elk grazing at its edge. Into the scene trotted two bands of Indians. They joined in a friendly dance, which ended abruptly with the attack of a hostile tribe. In silence the savages fought with bows and arrows, stone hatchets and stone-tipped spears. The lights dimmed on a battleground strewn with dead and dying redmen.

Then came the first interlude, and the first gunfire. Around the ring on an Indian pony raced Annie Oakley, in her fringed skirt and flowered deerskin jacket, shattering targets thrown in the air by a companion rider. She leapt to the ground, seized a rifle from her gun stand, and broke five glass balls thrown simultaneously into the air. She vaulted over the stand, swung a new gun to her shoulder, and shot the flames off a revolving wheel of candles. She was all swiftness, grace, and magic, on horseback and afoot. When she made her quick little curtsy and ran from the ring on twinkling feet, the roof shook with applause. And the Wild West's first indoor audience had been reassuringly introduced to the sound of firearms. The rest of the Show would blaze and crackle.

Scene two opened with the coming of settlers—an emigrant train plodding across the prairie, the wagons pulling into a circle for the night camp. It was a peaceful scene till the Indians came whooping. The whirr of arrows was answered by the rattle of rifles. The Indians fell back, but another peril followed. As sunset faded over the plain a lurid light began. The wagonmaster cried the alarm—*Prairie fire!* Up in MacKaye's light towers the crews worked swiftly, and on the mimic plain the fire came racing. Frantically the teams were caught, the camp dismantled. The prairie schooners rocked away, followed by antelope, elk, and buffalo. The whole prairie was on fire behind them.

After an interlude—cowboys and cowgirls in a Virginia reel on horseback—the floodlights showed a cattle ranch with cowboys roping, riding, skylarking around the dusty corral. Into that careless scene crept the painted Indians. The attack was stealthy; they caught the cowboys off guard and helpless. But while they bound their captives their victorious war whoops drowned a drumming of hoofbeats. With a blaze of gunfire Buffalo Bill and his scouts raced in. A dozen savages lay sprawled in the dust and the rest ran back to the Badlands.

In the next interlude young Johnnie Baker, in an oversized cowboy hat, did some acrobatic shooting, and a Mexican worked magic with a lariat. Then the band swung into *Garry Owen,* the marching song of the Seventh Cavalry—Custer's regiment. A screen of light showed the rolling grasslands of the Little Big Horn, with Custer's men fighting off a ring of howling Sioux. They tightened their circle and the Sioux crept closer. Firing from behind dead horses, rushing in with drawn blades when their guns were empty, the Indians cut down the doomed regiment. At the end one man was left standing, George Armstrong Custer, played by the long-haired King of the Cowboys, Buck Taylor. He fell under a rain of bullets and the furious battleground was still. The Indians moved from one grotesque form to another, taking their last grim trophies. When they were gone the strewn field was as silent as in all the aeons of the geologic past. But a muffled hoofbeat sounded and a lone rider halted a foam-flecked horse. The spotlight held him on the littered field while on the backdrop mountains a light screen spelled the words TOO LATE.

The greatest scout of the Old West bared his head among the fallen, and the scene went dark. Custer had made his last stand.

After a group of Indians had performed the grass dance, the rain dance, the antelope dance, the scenario's final scene showed a mining camp in the Rocky Mountains. To the relay station raced the Pony Express, a dusty rider on a frothing horse. The mailbags were slung onto a new mount; with a staccato of hoofs the rider raced away, toward St. Joe or Sacramento. Then a teamster's voice rang out and wagon wheels sounded; up the rocky road rumbled the storied old Deadwood stage. Bandits lay in ambush. With a volley of pistol fire they halted the six-mule team and cut them loose from the traces. They shot the passengers and carried off the treasure. But at that moment the sky darkened. A howling wind began and a frantic voice cried "Cyclone!" Tumbleweed fled by and a storm of leaves and brush swept the arena. Tents tore loose from their guy ropes and fluttered in the air. As the wind moved on to the painted hills a desolate night fell over the lifeless plain.

When, according to MacKaye's light cue, the lights came up again, the whole Wild West company, soldiers and cowboys, Indians and Mexicans, were assembled, with tiny Annie Oakley smiling beside long-haired Buffalo Bill. An ovation shook the rafters where the light crew mopped their streaming faces. The winter season had begun with triumph.

Annie Oakley's Twilight

For seven years after the World's Fair she continued to travel with the Buffalo Bill show, watching, incidentally, the processes which gradually led to its disintegration. There was, of course, the ending of the partnership between Nate Salsbury and Buffalo Bill and the beginning of a new one with James A. Bailey. The extravagant spending practised by the Colonel, the renting of entire floors of hotels, of the expenditure of money which he believed in his gullible way would continue to flow to him forever. And while he grew poorer, Annie Oakley and her husband, saving always, working in summer with the Wild West and in the winter at trap shooting events where inevitably they obtained not only a chance at the purses, but a share of the gate receipts as well, prepared for the day when they would need travel no more, and when there would be wealth sufficient to keep them always. At last they considered that this time had arrived, and consequently they made known their intention to end their days as an attraction with the Wild West show with the finish of the season of 1901.

The last performance was held. The band played its usual farewell music, "Auld Lang Syne." The show train was loaded and started upon its last journey of the season. Onward, onward through North Carolina it went, headed for the winter quarters—

A crash in the night. The screams of injured, the milling of animals, the rending of steel and wood, the hiss of escaping steam. The show train had met head-on with another, several persons had been killed and more than a hundred injured. Among them was Annie Oakley, pulled unconscious from the wreckage by her husband, and now, in the hospital, unconscious and wavering between life and death. All that night the balance was in doubt, while a watchful husband, stepping at intervals to the bedside of his unconscious wife, watched a strange transformation. The heavy chestnut hair was slowly changing. The next day, the doctors gave the verdict that Annie Oakley would live, but that she might never be able to move or shoot again. The Little Missy which the show world had known was gone. In her place was a mangled, elderly woman with white hair—hair which had been beautiful chestnut only seventeen hours before.

Five operations followed that accident, and years of agony. But the courage of Annie Oakley predominated always. Two years later, a woman walked uncertainly to the traps of a gun club near Nutley, N.J. She fondled a shotgun, lifting it and lowering it, then gazing quizzically along its barrel.

"Pull!" she called, and a target flew forth. There was a lightning movement as a gun went to a feminine shoulder, a crackle of yellow blaze, and in the distance a splintered target. The white haired woman turned and smiled.

"Just as good as ever!" she remarked.

Annie Oakley had "come back."

CHAPTER 11

The Cowboy:
Funny, Tough,
and Lonesome

"What the Cowpoke Saw"

My home is my saddle,
My roof is the sky;
The prairies I'll ride
Till the day that I die.
   —saddle song

THE AMERICAN COWBOY is the last, and in many ways the greatest, of the West's romantic characters. He outlived the explorers and the Indians, the buffalo and the outlaws, the shootouts and the saloon fights, and after him came the dreary monotony of Main Street.

There is no doubt that for us the cowboy's fame owes a powerful debt to the modern mythmakers of film and television. In countless scenes on the movie or TV screen, the cowboy moves in that familiar amble; one moment he leans against the bar with his steady eye on the poker game or the powdered lady in red, or he squats before the fire with a tin plate and a lazy smile; another moment he's riding along the edge of a cattle herd on his way up the Chisholm Trail. Yet for all his notoriety and for all his endurance as a popular American symbol, the cowboy may be more misunderstood than any character before or since.

Certainly he was tough and independent. Madison Avenue knew what it was doing when they invented the Marlboro Man and splashed his lean, leathery look across America's magazines and highway billboards. Less celebrated, though, was the boring routine of the cowboy's life: from sunup to sundown the endless grind of punching cattle, day after day, month after month. We also know of the cowboy's easygoing nature, his wry view of the world (immortalized by Will Rogers), but the image was deceptive. The cowboy's life was a solitary one. He was, in his way, an outcast. His contacts extended mainly to other cowboys, and he found safety and solace in their company. If and when he went to town, it was an escape. So many cowboy tales are about those month-end trips when a night of too much drink and mayhem left him bewildered and broke at sunrise. Then it was back to the ranch again, armed with a new batch of adventures to while away the hours.

Yet, out of the tedium and solitude came the two greatest aspects of the cowpoke's character: his humor and his music. The songs he sang, simple and soulful melodies, caught the essence of the lonely life. Certainly there are many funny, ebullient songs, but the best ones have a lingering melancholy beneath them, a hunger not of the kind banished by bacon and beans, but the sort that cries out for some sense of belonging. "The Kansas Line" and "The Cowboy's Lament" are two of the more popular examples of a body of music that, despite its sentimentalism, moves us in sympathy for those riders of the range.

The cowboy's humor, on the other hand, has no sentiment; it is dry and unerringly sardonic. The cowboy laughs chiefly at himself, at his own choice to live a womanless and foolhardy life. His self-mockery is a credit to his self-knowledge. Many of the following stories in this section were told by cowboys about cowboys, and while there is little brag in them and no grand scenes, there is a sure sense of pride. It is a clean, clear humor that makes the cowboy's wit, like his music, still relevant long after he and many of his kind have passed away. The songs and the stories capture a measure of pain and wisdom without much fuss and make us think that perhaps we could all learn a thing or two from the veterans of the cattle trails.

Home on the Range

Oh, give me a home where the buffalo roam,
Where the deer and the antelope play;
Where seldom is heard a discouraging word,
And the skies are not cloudy all day.

Chorus:

Home, home on the range;
Where the deer and the antelope play;
Where seldom is heard a discouraging word,
And the skies are not cloudy all day.

Where the air is so pure, the zephyrs so free,
The breezes so balmy and light,
That I would not exchange my home on the range
For all the cities so bright.

The red man was pressed from this part of the West,
He's likely no more to return
To the banks of the Red River where seldom if ever
Their flickering campfires burn.

How often at night when the heavens are bright
With the light of the glittering stars,
Have I stood here amazed and asked as I gazed
If their glory exceeds that of ours.

Oh, I love these wild flowers in this dear land of ours;
The curlew I love to hear scream;
And I love the white rocks and the antelope flocks
That graze on the mountain-tops green.

Oh, give me a land where the bright diamond sand
Flows leisurely down the stream;
Where the graceful white swan goes gliding along
Like a maid in a heavenly dream.

Then I would not exchange my home on the range,
Where the deer and the antelope play;
Where seldom is heard a discouraging word,
And the skies are not cloudy all day.

Too Much Talk

Two cowpokes had punched cattle together for years, and one time they were out on a long haul. Each day, the two men would get up, ride off in different directions to corral the herd, and at the end of the day's trek they'd cook dinner and go to sleep. Day after day this continued. One night as they were about to fall off to sleep they heard a bellowing noise coming from the cattle.

"Bull," said the first one.

"Sounds like a steer to me," said the other.

The next day, the two men delivered the cattle to their destination and the first cowboy saddled up his horse to depart.

"Leaving?" asked the other cowboy.

"Yep. Too much damned argument," came the reply.

A Cowboy's Comforts

A cowboy's life was rugged, and out on the range he had few pleasures. There was once this man from back East who thought he would fancy the life of a cowpoke, so he joined up for a cattle drive. The first night, as the men were bedding down, someone tossed the man a piece of wood. "Here, enjoy this," he said. "Tomorrow we're hittin' the plains an' you cain't git no kind of pillow out there." They say the fellow gave up and went home the next day.

No Complaints

You know the rules in a cow camp when they have no regular cook. When anybody complains about the chuck, they have to do the cooking. One cowboy broke a biscuit open and he says, "They are burnt on the bottom and top and raw in the middle and salty as hell, but shore fine, just the way I like 'em."

A Rare Steak

One of our cowboys went to a restaurant in Magdalena one day and ordered a steak. When he cut into it, the blood ran out on his plate, so he called to the waitress. He says, "Take this beef back and have it cooked." She saw he was about half drunk, and she didn't want to bother with him, so she says, "That's done." "Done, hell, I have seen lots of 'em get well that was hurt worse than that."

Advice to a Cowboy

Get up in the morning when you are first called, or you will be apt to rise rapidly on the toe of the foreman's boot. Roll up your bed snug, tie it up tight and firm and lay it near the wagon convenient for loading. Take a good wash. It is most refreshing and prevents sore eyes and other things. If there is no pool or stream of water don't use up all the water in the water butt; remember good drinking water can't be found everywhere, and it is considerable trouble for the cook to fill that butt. Don't open your eyes under water. If it is very dry and dusty and in alkali country don't wash your face at all. It is the experience of those dusty sons of Adam, the bullwackers, that washing the eyeballs in cold water gives you cold in the eyes, makes the lids rough and harsh, induces granulated eyelids, and causes very sore eyes. If you have drawn water from the water barrel just leave the faucet open and the water dropping out and wasting, if you want to get a blessing from the cook. Leave dirty water in the wash pan if you want your brother cowpuncher to love you.

. . . Make yourself spry and useful. Such things are generally relegated to the patient, despised tenderfoot, but you'll lose nothing by such little extra attentions to the cook. Sometimes when you ride into camp hungry, tired, wet, cold and indifferent whether you are alive or dead, you'll be apt to find kept warm for your Royal Bengal Bigness some nice strong coffee and may be a little side dish like brains, or sweetbreads, kidneys, heart, liver or the luscious luxury marrow-gut. They are not regular grub, because they won't go all around, but they are cook's perquisities, and he can give them to whom he likes . . .

Never rush for grub till you have made things up in shape. If the horses are up before breakfast, saddle up, etc. Yes, and don't throw away more than you eat. It would bust any boy in camp if he had to pay the grub bills for the roundup outfit for one season. Don't make a habit of telling vulgar yarns at grub time. Very probably everybody will laugh at the time, but when they get off to themselves and begin to think things over they are sure to sorter lose their good opinion of a chap who seasons his grub with dirty talk. When you are done running your hash mill put your knife, fork and other grub tools on your plate and set them up on the cupboard lid, handy for the cook. If you have time help the cook wash and wipe up the dishes and kettles, and help him to load the mess wagon.

In the evening catch up your quietest, most reliable pony for a night horse. Stake him out to good grass within easy reach . . .

Find out what relief you are to go on, who to call and where they will sleep, so you won't be waking up everybody in camp to find the right man. It makes a cowpuncher fighting mad to wake him up from his needed sleep when not wanted. Double with some boy on the same relief as yourself and make down your boar's nest so as not to take up all the room in the tent. If there is no tent pick out a high, level spot of ground so that you will sleep dry if it rains. A tarpaulin of one solid thick piece of canvass 8 × 16 or 9 × 18 feet is indispensable. Sleep with pants on and stuffed in your socks. Never take the spurs off your boots. Put your boots down first, your chaps on top of them and your jacket over all for a pillow. It's nice to leave your boots outside in the weather and find when you try to pull them on in a hurry that they are either froze stiff as dry rawhide or full of rainwater. Put your hat on top of your blankets under the tarpaulin to keep it from blowing away. A handkerchief tied around your head is not very healthy either when the thermometer is away below zero, or away up hugging 120 close . . .

Have everything ready to rise up, fling on, and skin out like a flash of lightning if there is a stampede, or to get out on time when you are called to go on guard. Remember that the safety of the herd depends on good ponies and good men ready to roll the instant they are needed. If the cattle are restless and there is liability of a stampede, you'd better go to bed just as you are—hat, jacket, pants, boots, spurs, chaps; and if snowing, or raining, your slicker, too—all on. A cowpuncher can sleep anyhow . . .

All in a Day's Work

"One of the slickest things I ever saw in my life," said a veteran army officer, "was a cowboy stopping a cattle stampede. A herd of about 600 or 800 head got frightened at something and broke away pell-mell with their tails in the air and the bulls at the head of the procession. But Mr. Cowboy didn't get excited at all when he saw the herd was going straight for a high bluff, where they would certainly tumble down into the cañon and be killed. You know that when a herd like that gets to going it can't stop, no matter whether the cattle rush to death or not. Those in the rear crowd those ahead, and away they go. I wouldn't have given a dollar a head for the herd, but the cowboy spurred up his mustang, made a little detour, came in right in front of the herd, cut across their path at a right angle, and then galloped leisurely on the edge of the bluff, halted, and looked around at that wild mass of beef coming right toward him. He was as cool as a cucumber, though I expected to see him killed, and was so excited I could not speak.

"Well, sir, when the leaders had got within about a quarter of a mile of him I saw them try to slack up, though they could not do it very quickly. But the whole herd wanted to stop, and when the cows and steers in the rear got about where the cowboy had cut across their path I was surprised to see them stop and commence to nibble at the grass. Then the whole herd stopped, wheeled, straggled back and went to fighting for a chance to eat where the rear guard was.

"You see, that cowboy had opened a big bag of salt he had brought out from the ranch to give the cattle, galloped across the herd's course, and emptied the bag. Every critter sniffed that line of salt, and, of course, that broke up the stampede. But I tell you it was a queer sight to see that man out there on the edge of the bluff quietly rolling a cigarette when it seemed as if he'd be lying under 200 tons of beef in about a minute and a half."

Longrope's Last Guard

"Whoever told you that cattle stampede without cause was talkin' like a shorthorn," says Rawhide Rawlins. "You can bet all you got that whenever cattle run, there's a reason for it. A whole lot of times cattle run, an' nobody knows why but the cows an' they won't tell.

"There's plenty of humans call it instinct when an animal does something they don't savvy. I don't know what it is myself, but I've seen the time when I'd like to a-had some. I've knowed of hosses bein' trailed a thousand miles an' turned loose, that pulled back for their home range, not goin' the trail they come, but takin' cut-offs across mountain ranges that would puzzle a bighorn. An' if you'd ask one of these wise boys how they done it, he'd back out of it easy

by sayin' it's instinct. You'll find cow ponies that knows more about the business than the men that rides 'em.

"There's plenty of causes for a stampede; sometimes it's a green hand or a careless cowpuncher scratchin' a match to light a cigarette. Maybe it's something on the wind, or a tired nighthoss spraddles and shakes himself, an' the poppin' of the saddle leather causes them to jump the bed-ground. Scare a herd on the start, and you're liable to have hell with them all the way. I've seen bunches well trail-broke that you couldn't fog off the bed-ground with a slicker an' six-shooter; others, again, that had had a scare, you'd have to ride a hundred yards away from to spit. Some men's too careful with their herd an' go tiptoein' around like a mother with a sick kid. I've had some experience, an' claim this won't do. Break 'em so they'll stand noise; get 'em used to seein' a man afoot, an' you'll have less trouble.

"There's some herds that you dassen't quit your hoss short of five hundred yards of. Of course it's natural enough for cow-brutes that never see hoss an' man apart to scare some when they see 'em separate. They think the top of this animal's busted off, an' when they see the piece go movin' around they're plenty surprised; but as I said before, there's many reasons for stampedes unknown to man. I've seen herds start in broad daylight with no cause that anybody knows of. The smell of blood will start 'em goin'; this generally comes off in the mornin' when they're quittin' the bed-ground. Now, in every herd you'll find steers that's regular old rounders. They won't go to bed like decent folks, but put in the night perusin' around, disturbin' the peace. If there's any bulls in the bunch, there's liable to be fightin'. I've often watched an old bull walkin' around through the herd an' talkin' fight, hangin' up his bluff, with a bunch of these rounders at his heels. They're sure backin' him up—boostin' an' ribbin' up trouble, an' if there's a fight pulled off you should hear these trouble-builders takin' sides; every one of 'em with his tongue out an' his tail kinked, buckin' an' bellerin, like his money's all up. These night ramblers that won't go to bed at decent hours, after raisin' hell all night, are ready to bed down an' are sleepin like drunks when decent cattle are walkin' off the bed-ground.

"Now, you know, when a cow-brute quits his bed he bows his neck, gaps an' stretches all the same as a human after a night's rest.

Maybe he accidentally tromps on one of these rounders' tails that's layin' along the ground. This hurts plenty, and Mr. Night Rambler ain't slow about wakin' up; he raises like he's overslept an' is afeared he'll miss the coach, leavin' the tossel of his tail under the other fellow's hoof. He goes off wringin' his stub an' scatterin' blood on his rump an' quarters. Now the minute them other cattle winds the blood, the ball opens. Every hoof's at his heels barkin' and bellerin'. Them that's close enough are hornin' him in the flank like they'd stuck to finish him off. They're all plumb hog-wild, an' if you want any beef left in your herd you'd better cut out the one that's causin' the excitement, 'cause an hour of this will take off more taller than they'll put on in a month.

"Cattle like open country to sleep in. I sure hate to hold a herd near any brakes or deep 'royos, 'cause no matter how gentle a herd is, let a coyote or any other animal loom up of a sudden close to 'em an' they don't stop to take a second look, but are gone like a flash in the pan. Old bulls comin' up without talkin' sometimes jump a herd this way, an' it pays a cowpuncher to sing when he's comin' up out of a 'royo close to the bed-ground.

"Some folks'll tell you that cowboys sing their cows to sleep, but that's a mistake, judgin' from my experience, an' I've had some. The songs an' voices I've heard around cattle ain't soothin'. A cowpuncher sings to keep himself company; it ain't that he's got any motherly love for these longhorns he's put to bed an' is ridin' herd on; he's amusin' himself an' nobody else. These ditties are generally shy on melody an' strong on noise. Put a man alone in the dark, an' if his conscious is clear an' he ain't hidin' he'll sing an' don't need to be a born vocalist. Of course singin's a good thing around a herd, an' all punchers know it. In the darkness it lets the cows know where you're at. If you ever woke up in the darkness an' found somebody— you didn't know who or what—loomin' up over you, it would startle you, but if this somebody is singin' or whistlin', it wouldn't scare you none. It's the same with Mr. Steer; that snaky, noiseless glidin' up on him's what scares the animal.

"All herds has some of these lonesomes that won't lie down with the other cattle, but beds down alone maybe twenty-five to thirty yards from the edge of the herd. He's got his own reason for this;

might be he's short an eye. This bein' the case you can lay all you got he's layin' with the good blinker next to the herd. He don't figure on lettin' none of his playful brothers beef his ribs from a sneak. One-eyed hoss is the same. Day or night you'll find him on the outside with his good eye watchin' the bunch. Like Mister Steer, the confidence he's got in his brother's mighty frail.

"But these lonesome cattle I started to tell you about, is the ones that a puncher's most liable to run onto in the dark, layin' out that way from the herd. If you ride onto him singin', it don't startle Mr. Steer; he raises easy, holdin' his ground till you pass; then he lays down in the same place. He's got the ground warm an' hates to quit her. Cows, the same as humans, like warm beds. Many's the time in cool weather I've seen some evil-minded, low-down steer stand around like he ain't goin' to bed, but all the time he's got his eye on some poor, undersized brother layin' near by, all innocent. As soon as he thinks the ground's warm he walks over, horns him out an' jumps his claim. This low-down trick is sometimes practiced by punchers when they got a gentle herd. It don't hurt a cowpuncher's conscience none to sleep in a bed he stole from a steer.

"If you ride sneakin' an' noiseless onto one of these lonesome fellers, he gets right to his feet with dew-claws an' hoofs rattlin', an' is runnin' before he's half up, hittin' the herd like a canned dog, an' quicker than you can bat an eye the whole herd's gone. Cows are slow animals, but scare 'em an' they're fast enough; a thousand will get to their feet as quick as one. It's sure a puzzler to cowmen to know how a herd will all scare at once, an' every animal will get on his feet at the same time. I've seen herds do what a cowpuncher would call 'jump'—that is, to raise an' not run. I've been lookin' across a herd in bright moonlight—a thousand head or more, all down; with no known cause there's a short, quick rumble, an' every hoof's standin'.

"I've read of stampedes that were sure dangerous an' scary, where a herd would run through a camp, upsettin' wagons an' trompin' sleepin' cowpunchers to death. When day broke they'd be fifty or a hundred miles from where they started, leavin' a trail strewn with blood, dead cowpunchers, an' hosses, that looked like the work of a Kansas cyclone. This is all right in books, but the feller that writes 'em is romancin' an' don't savvy the cow. Most stampedes is noisy, but harmless to anybody but the cattle. A herd in a bad storm might drift thirty miles in a night, but the worst run I ever see, we ain't four miles from the bed-ground when the day broke.

"This was down in Kansas; we're trailin' beef an' have got about seventeen hundred head. Barrin' a few dry ones the herd's straight steers, mostly Spanish longhorns from down on the Cimarron. We're about fifty miles south of Dodge. Our herd's well broke an' lookin' fine, an' the cowpunchers all good-natured, thinkin' of the good time comin' in Dodge.

"That evenin' when we're ropin' our hosses for night guard, the trail boss, 'Old Spanish' we call him—he ain't no real Spaniard, but he's rode some in Old Mexico an' can talk some Spanish—says to me: 'Them cattle ought to hold well; they ain't been off water four hours, an' we grazed 'em plumb onto the bed-ground. Every hoof of 'em's got a paunch full of grass an' water, an' that's what makes cattle lay good.'

"Me an' a feller called Longrope's on first guard. He's a center-fire or single-cinch man from California; packs a sixty-foot rawhide riata, an' when he takes her down an' runs about half of her into a loop she looks big, but when it reaches the animal, comes pretty near fittin' hoof or horn. I never went much on these long-rope boys, but this man comes as near puttin' his loop where he wants as any I ever see. You know Texas men ain't got much love for a single rig, an' many's the argument me an' Longrope has on this subject. He claims a center-fire is the only saddle, but I 'low that they'll do all right on a shad-bellied western hoss, but for Spanish pot-gutted ponies they're no good. You're ridin' up on his withers all the time.

"When we reach the bed-ground most of the cattle's already down, lookin' comfortable. They're bedded in open country, an' things look good for an easy night. It's been mighty hot all day, but there's a little breeze now makin' it right pleasant; but down the west I notice some nasty-lookin' clouds hangin' 'round the new moon that's got one horn hooked over the skyline. The storm's so far off that you can just hear her rumble, but she's walkin' up on us slow, an' I'm hopin' she'll go 'round. The cattle's all layin' quiet an' nice, so me an' Longrope stop to talk awhile.

" 'They're layin' quiet,' says I.

" 'Too damn quiet,' says he. 'I like cows to lay still all right, but I want some of the natural noises that goes with a herd this size. I want to hear 'em blowin' off, an' the creakin' of their joints, showin' they're easin' themselves in their beds. Listen, an' if you hear anything I'll eat that rimfire saddle of yours—grass rope an' all.'

"I didn't notice till then, but when I straighten my ears it's quiet as a grave. An' if it ain't for the lightnin' showin' the herd once in a while, I couldn't a-believed that seventeen hundred head of longhorns lay within forty feet of where I'm sittin' on my hoss. It's gettin' darker every minute, an' if it wasn't for Longrope's slicker I couldn't a-made him out, though he's so close I could have touched him with my hand. Finally it darkens up so I can't see him at all. It's black as a nigger's pocket; you couldn't find your nose with both hands.

"I remember askin' Longrope the time.

" 'I guess I'll have to get help to find the timepiece,' says he, but gets her after feelin' over himself, an' holdin' her under his cigarette takes a long draw, lightin' up her face.

" 'Half-past nine,' says he.

" 'Half an hour more,' I says. 'Are you goin' to wake up the next guard, or did you leave it to the hoss-wrangler?'

" 'There won't be but one guard to-night,' he answers, 'an' we'll ride it. You might as well hunt for a hoss thief in heaven as look for that camp. Well, I guess I'll mosey 'round.' An' with that he quits me.

"The lightnin's playin' every little while. It ain't making much noise, but lights up enough to show where you're at. There ain't no use ridin'; by the flashes I can see that every head's down. For a second it'll be like broad day, then darker than the dungeons of hell, an' I notice the little fire-balls on my hoss's ears; when I spit there's a streak in the air like strikin' a wet match. These little fire-balls is all I can see of my hoss, an' they tell me he's listenin' all ways; his ears are never still.

"I tell you, there's something mighty ghostly about sittin' up on a hoss you can't see, with them two little blue sparks out in front of you wigglin' an' movin' like a pair of spook eyes, an' it shows me the old night hoss is usin' his listeners pretty plenty. I got my ears cocked, too, hearing nothin' but Longrope's singin'; he's easy three hundred yards across the herd from me, but I can hear every word:

> *"Sam Bass was born in Injiana,*
> *It was his native home,*
> *'Twas at the age of seventeen*
> *Young Sam began to roam.*
> *He first went out to Texas,*
> *A cowboy for to be;*
> *A better hearted feller*
> *You'd seldom ever see.*

"It's so plain it sounds like he's singin' in my ear; I can even hear the click-clack of his spur chains against his stirrups when he moves 'round. An' the cricket in his bit—he's usin' one of them hollow conchoed half-breeds—she comes plain to me in the stillness. Once there's a steer layin' on the edge of the herd starts sniffin'. He's takin' long draws of the air, he's nosin' for something. I don't like this, it's a bad sign; it shows he's layin' for trouble, an' all he needs is some little excuse.

"Now every steer, when he beds down, holds his breath for a few seconds, then blows off; that noise is all right an' shows he's settlin' himself for comfort. But when he curls his nose an' makes them long draws it's a sign he's sniffin' for something, an' if anything crosses his wind that he don't like there's liable to be trouble. I've seen dry trail herds mighty thirsty, layin' good till a breeze springs off the water, maybe ten miles away; they start sniffin', an' the minute they get the wind you could comb Texas an' wouldn't have enough punchers to turn 'em till they wet their feet an' fill their paunches.

"I get tired sittin' there starin' at nothin', so start ridin' 'round. Now it's sure dark when animals can't see, but I tell you by the way my hoss moves he's feelin' his way. I don't blame him none; it's like lookin' in a black pot. Sky an' ground all the same, an' I ain't gone twenty-five yards till I hear cattle gettin' up around me; I'm in the herd an' it's luck I'm singing an' they don't get scared. Pullin' to the left I work cautious an' easy till I'm clear of the bunch. Ridin's useless, so I flop my weight over on one stirrup an' go on singin'.

"The lightnin' 's quit now, an' she's darker than ever; the breeze has died down an' it's hotter than the hubs of hell. Above my voice I can hear Longrope. He's singin' the 'Texas Ranger' now; the Ranger's a long song an' there's few punchers that knows it all, but Longrope's sprung a lot of new verses on me an' I'm interested. Seems like he's on about the twenty-fifth verse, an' there's danger of his chokin' down, when there's a whisperin' in the grass behind me; it's a breeze sneakin' up. It flaps the tail of my slicker an' goes by; in another second she hits the herd. The ground shakes, an' they're all runnin'. My hoss takes the scare with 'em an' is bustin' a hole in the darkness when he throws both front feet in a badger hole, goin' to his knees an' plowin' his nose in the dirt. But he's a good night hoss an' is hard to keep down. The minute he gets his feet under him he raises, runnin' like a scared wolf. Hearin' the roar behind him he don't care to mix with them locoed longhorns. I got my head turned over my shoulder listenin', tryin' to make out which way they're goin', when there's a flash of lightnin' busts a hole in the sky—it's one of these kind that puts the fear of God in a man, thunder an' all together. My hoss whirls an' stops in his tracks, spraddlin' out an' squattin' like he's hit, an' I can feel his heart beatin' agin my leg, while mine's poundin' my ribs like it'll bust through. We're both plenty scared.

"This flash lights up the whole country, givin' me a glimpse of the herd runnin' a little to my left. Big drops of rain are pounding on my hat. The storm has broke now for sure, with the lightnin' bombardin' us at every jump. Once a flash shows me Longrope, ghostly in his wet slicker. He's so close to me that I could hit him with my quirt an' I hollers to him, 'This is hell.'

" 'Yes,' he yells back above the roar; 'I wonder what damned fool kicked the lid off.'

"I can tell by the noise that they're runnin' straight; there ain't no clickin' of horns. It's a kind of hummin' noise like a buzz-saw, only a thousand times louder. There's no use in tryin' to turn 'em in this darkness, so I'm ridin' wide—just herdin' by ear an' follerin' the noise. Pretty soon my ears tell me they're crowdin' an' comin' together; the next flash shows 'em all millin', with heads jammed together an' horns locked; some's rared up ridin' others, an' these is squirmin' like bristled snakes. In the same light I see Longrope, an' from the blink I get of him he's among 'em or too close for safety, an' in the dark I thought I saw a gun flash three times with no report.

But with the noise these longhorns are makin' now, I doubt if I could a-heard a six-gun bark if I pulled the trigger myself, an' the next thing I know me an' my hoss goes over a bank, lightin' safe. I guess it ain't over four feet, but it seems like fifty in the darkness, an' if it hadn't been for my chin-string I'd a-went from under my hat. Again the light shows me we're in a 'royo with the cattle comin' over the edge, wigglin' an' squirmin' like army worms.

"It's a case of all night riding. Sometimes they'll mill an' quiet down, then start trottin' an' break into a run. Not till daybreak do they stop, an' maybe you think old day ain't welcome. My hoss is sure leg-weary, an' I ain't so rollicky myself. When she gets light enough I begin lookin' for Longrope, with nary a sign of him; an' the herd, you wouldn't know they were the same cattle—smeared with mud an' ga'nt as greyhounds; some of 'em with their tongues still lollin' out from their night's run. But sizin' up the bunch, I guess I got 'em all. I'm kind of worried about Longrope. It's a cinch that wherever he is he's afoot, an' chances is he's layin' on the prairie with a broken leg.

"The cattle's spread out, an' they begin feedin'. There ain't much chance of losin' 'em, now it's broad daylight, so I ride up on a raise to take a look at the back trail. While I'm up there viewin' the country, my eyes run onto somethin' a mile back in a draw. I can't make it out, but get curious, so spurrin' my tired hoss into a lope I take the back trail. 'Tain't no trouble to foller in the mud; it's plain as plowed ground. I ain't rode three hundred yard till the country raises a little an' shows me this thing's a hoss, an' by the white streak on his flank I heap savvy it's Peon—that's the hoss Longrope's ridin'. When I get close he whinners pitiful like; he's lookin' for sympathy, an' I notice, when he turns to face me, his right foreleg's broke. He's sure a sorry sight with that fancy, full-stamped center-fire saddle hangin' under his belly in the mud. While I'm lookin' him over, my hoss cocks his ears to the right, snortin' low. This scares me —I'm afeared to look. Somethin' tells me I won't see Longrope, only part of him—that part that stays here on earth when the man's gone. Bracin' up, I foller my hoss's ears, an' there in the holler of the 'royo is a patch of yeller; it's part of a slicker. I spur up to get a better look over the bank, an' there tromped in the mud is all there is left of

Longrope. Pullin' my gun I empty her in the air. This brings the boys that are follerin' on the trail from the bed-ground. Nobody'd had to tell 'em we'd had hell, so they come in full force, every man but the cook an' hoss-wrangler.

"Nobody feels like talkin'. It don't matter how rough men are—I've known 'em that never spoke without cussin', that claimed to fear neither God, man, nor devil—but let death visit camp an' it puts 'em thinkin'. They generally take their hats off to this old boy that comes everywhere an' any time. He's always ready to pilot you—willin' or not—over the long dark trail that folks don't care to travel. He's never welcome, but you've got to respect him.

" 'It's tough—damned tough,' says Spanish, raisin' poor Long-rope's head an' wipin the mud from his face with his neck-handker-chief, tender, like he's feared he'll hurt him. We find his hat tromped in the mud not far from where he's layin'. His scabbard's empty, an' we never do locate his gun.

"That afternoon when we're countin' out the herd to see if we're short any, we find a steer with a broken shoulder an' another with a hole plumb through his nose. Both these is gun wounds; this ac-counts for them flashes I see in the night. It looks like, when Long-rope gets mixed in the mill, he tries to gun his way out, but the cattle crowd him to the bank an' he goes over. The chances are he was dragged from his hoss in a tangle of horns.

"Some's for takin' him to Dodge an' gettin' a box made for him, but Old Spanish says: 'Boys, Longrope is a prairie man, an' if she was a little rough at times, she's been a good foster mother. She cared for him while he's awake, let her nurse him in his sleep.' So we wrapped him in his blankets, an' put him to bed.

"It's been twenty years or more since we tucked him in with the end-gate of the bed-wagon for a headstone, which the cattle have long since rubbed down, leavin' the spot unmarked. It sounds lone-some, but he ain't alone, 'cause these old prairies has cradled many of his kind in their long sleep."

The Kansas Line

Come all you jolly cowmen, don't you want to go
Way up the Kansas line?
Where you whoop up the cattle from morning till night
All out in the midnight rain?
    The cowboy's life is a dreadful life.
    He's driven through heat and cold;
    I'm almost froze with the water on my clothes,
    A-ridin' through heat and cold.

I've been where the lightning, the lightning,
Tangled in my eyes;
The cattle I could scarcely hold;
I think I heard my boss man say,
"I want all brave-hearted men,
Who ain't afraid to die,
To whoop the cattle from morning till night,
Way up the Kansas line."

Speaking of your farms and your shanty charms,
Speaking of your silver and gold—
Take a cowman's advice, go and marry you a true and lovely
    little wife,
Never to roam, always stay at home;
That's a cowman's, a cowman's advice,
Way up on the Kansas line.

Think I heard the noisy cook say,
"Wake up, boys, it's near the break of day,"
Way up on the Kansas line,
And slowly we will rise with the sleepy-feeling eyes,
Way up on the Kansas line.
    The cowboy's life is a dreary, dreary life
    All out in the midnight rain;
    I'm almost froze with the water in my clothes
    Way up on the Kansas line.

What the Cowpoke Saw

See, I was ridin' along the Blackfoot Ridge on a roundup of some strays and I looked down and saw comin', hellbent, from the south a train doin' sixty miles an hour, sure. Then I looked to the north and there was another train goin' even faster on the same track headin' straight fer the other one. It looked like they were goin' to meet right at the curve of the track.

"What did you do?" asked another cowhand.

"Nothin'."

"You mean, you didn't try to stop them or signal them some way?" asked another man.

"Nope. Didn't think of that."

"Well, what in God's name were you thinkin' about?" cried still another.

"Well, not much, I guess. But I was thinkin' it was sure one hell of a way to run a railroad."

Good-Hearted Cowboys

One hot day in July, 1860, a herdsman was moving his cattle to a new ranch further north, near Helena, Texas, and passing down the banks of a stream, his herd became mixed with other cattle that were grazing in the valley, and some of them failed to be separated. The next day about noon a band of a dozen mounted Texan rangers overtook the herdsman and demanded their cattle, which they said were stolen.

It was before the days of law and courthouses in Texas, and one had better kill five men than to steal a mule worth five dollars, and the herdsman knew it. He tried to explain, but they told him to cut it short. He offered to turn over all the cattle not his own, but they laughed at his proposition, and hinted that they usually confiscated the whole herd, and left the thief hanging on a tree as a warning to others in like cases.

The poor fellow was completely overcome. They consulted apart a few moments and then told him if he had any explanation to make or business to do they would allow him ten minutes to do so, and defend himself.

He turned to the rough faces and commenced: "How many of you have wives?" Two or three nodded. "How many of you have children?" They nodded again.

"Then I know who I am talking to and you'll hear me," and he continued:

"I never stole any cattle; I have lived in these parts over three years. I came from New Hampshire; I failed there in the fall of '57 during the panic; I have been saving; lived on hard fare; I have slept out on the ground; I have no home here; my family remain east; I go from place to place; these clothes I wear are rough and I am a hard-looking customer; but this is a hard country; days seem like months to me, and months like years; married men, you know that but for the letters from home—(Here he pulled out a handful of well-worn envelopes and letters from his wife)—I should get discouraged. I have paid part of my debts. Here are the receipts," and he unfolded the letters of acknowledgement. "I expected to sell out and go home in November. Here is the testament my good old mother gave me; here is my little girl's picture," and he kissed it tenderly and continued: "Now, men, if you have decided to kill me for what I am innocent of, send these home, and as much as you can from these cattle when I'm dead. Can't you send half the value? My family will need it."

"Hold on, now, stop right thar!" said a rough ranger. "Now, I say, boys," he continued, "I say, let him go. Give us your hand, old boy; that picture and them letters did the business. You can go free; but you're lucky, mind ye."

"We'll do more than that," said a man with a big heart, in Texan garb, and carrying the customary brace of pistols in his belt. "Let's buy his cattle here and let him go."

An hour later, he left on horseback for the nearest stage-route, money in his pocket, and as they shook hands and bade him good-by, those cowboys looked the happiest band of men I ever saw.

Tact

There was a fellow out hunting one day when a band of angry cowboys caught up with him, accused him of horse-stealing, and hung him from a nearby tree. Later that day they came across the real thief and realized they'd hung the wrong man. Duty-bound to own up to the mistake, they decided to return the body to the man's wife, and they elected the most well-spoken man in their group to do the talking for the rest of them. The fellow arrived at the home of the dead man, knocked on the door, and presently a lovely woman appeared.

"Ma'am, I b'lieve you're Hank Peter's widder?"

"No, I'm not. I'm his wife."

"Ma'am, I b'lieve you're his widder."

"Listen, young man, I don't know who you are but you have no business annoying me. I'm Hank Peter's wife and you're wasting my time."

The cowboy's face flushed and he fairly shouted, "Ma'am, you ain't his wife, you're his widder an' I've got Hank's dead body back with the boys to prove it!"

Bone Mizell Buries a Buddy

Everybody was there, squatting around the fire: Three Fingers, Axel Jack, the Short Man, Bone Mizell, and me. Axel Jack was telling Bone stories and Bone just smiled and poked at the fire as the bottle was passed around. We all knew if Axel kept it up that Bone, the greatest Florida cowboy that ever lived, the king of the swamp country, would have to say somethin', 'cause Axel Jack can do 'most anything 'cept tell a story.

Axel told us about the time Bone shipped a pal's body back to his rich Yankee folks years after the fella died. "Yessir," said Axel, "Bone went out and dug up his old friend and saw to it that he got buried proper under big marble angels and green grass."

"It's true, ain't it, Bone?" asked Axel, looking at him across the campfire.

When Bone poked the fire one last time and called for the bottle, we knew he was gonna start talkin'.

"Boys," said Bone, "it ain't like Axel says. It ain't like that at all. Nobody knows the real story of Jimmy Maxwell's grave but me an' Joe Dougherty." He thought for a moment, then said, "Maybe tonight's the right time to tell ya'all the straight truth of the matter."

The rest of us got good and settled around the campfire, and Morgan Bonaparte Mizell commenced to talkin'.

"When I first met Jimmy Maxwell, I was workin' cattle near Okeechobee an' he come onto Eli Morgan's place lookin' for work. Well, I knew right off that this boy wasn't no cowpuncher an' didn't know which end of a cow was which, but he had a sly look about him an' was willin'. His fingers were long and smooth and he had a soft laugh like a man that's used to talkin' the ladies down the stream. He had tasted the fine things in life an' he told stories about places I still ain't heard of—an' this was twenty years back or more! Yessir, it must have been a hell of a life that broke ol' Jimmy, 'cause when he got to Okeechobee he had a look about him that said his days were done. He had a terrible cough, an' though he worked like a mule, he never complained 'bout nothin'.

"Joe Dougherty and I kinda looked after Jimmy, an' one day we were sittin' under a tree takin' a break when Jimmy said, grinning, 'Bone, I've been 'round this whole world too many times and I'm tired. I'm going to cash in soon and I want you to do me a favor. Bury me in a nice quiet place like this and leave me alone.'

"I laughed him off, but he made me swear, an' I did. Not long after, Jimmy died—just lay on his back with a smoke in his mouth an' died. He hung 'em up so quiet that we didn't know nothin' till

Joe called to Jimmy and he didn't answer. Well, Joe and I buried Jimmy right there just like we promised, under the moon and stars. No marker, nothin', just like he wanted.

"Some years went by an' Jimmy's folks, rich like I figgered, got wind of his last stand and let it be known that they wanted Jimmy's body buried back North. I only heard 'cause Joe's wife worked in the county clerk's office, where Jimmy's folks had wired money along with a train ticket for the body. So Joe and I got on a wagon an' headed out to the place where Jimmy was buried.

"On the way, I got to thinkin'. Jimmy was tired of the world an' its ways. He said to me that if he ever saw a train or a boat agin, he'd bust out cryin' like a baby. He wanted to put down fer good. Now, anybody here heard of Bob Catlin? He was an old man who had lived on a dirt patch across the river and was so poor that when he died he was buried in an old feed sack. I know that ol' Bob always wanted to have gone somewheres nice in the worst way but could never afford it. I got to thinkin'. Here was one fella wantin' to be left in peace an' the other fella never gettin' the peace he wanted.

"So after Joe an' I had a few more drinks jes' to make the diggin' easier, we did the sensible thing. Boys, it was all my fault an' I talked Joe into it, so if you got a mind to be blamin' somebody, leave him be. But I tell you this—damned if Bob Catlin got his first train ride an' the best, fanciest buryin' a Florida cracker's bones ever did get!"

The Saga of Pecos Bill

Pecos Bill is not a new-comer in the Southwest. His mighty deeds have been sung for generations by the men of the range. In my boyhood days in West Texas I first heard of Bill, and in later years I have often listened to chapters of his history told around the chuck-wagon by gravely mendacious cow-boys.

The stranger in cattle-land usually hears of Bill if he shows an incautious curiosity about the cow business. Some old-timer is sure to remark mournfully:

"Ranchin' ain't what it was in the days Bill staked out New Mexico."

If the visitor walks into the trap and inquires further about Bill, he is sure to receive an assortment of misinformation that every cowhand delights in unloading on the unwary.

Although Bill has been quoted in a number of Western stories, the real history of his wondrous deeds has never been printed. I have here collected a few of the tales about him which will doubtless be familiar to cow-men, but deserve to be passed on to a larger audience.

Bill invented most of the things connected with the cow business. He was a mighty man of valor, the king killer of the bad men, and it was Bill who taught the broncho how to buck. It is a matter of record that he dug the Rio Grande one dry year when he grew tired of packin' water from the Gulf of Mexico.

According to the most veracious historians, Bill was born about the time Sam Houston discovered Texas. His mother was a sturdy pioneer woman who once killed forty-five Indians with a broomhandle, and weaned him on moonshine liquor when he was three days old. He cut his teeth on a bowie-knife, and his earliest playfellows were the bears and catamounts of east Texas.

When Bill was about a year old, another family moved into the country, and located about fifty miles down the river. His father decided the place was gettin' too crowded, and packed his family in a wagon and headed west.

One day after they crossed the Pecos River, Bill fell out of the wagon. As there were sixteen or seventeen other children in the family, his parents didn't miss him for four or five weeks, and then it was too late to try to find him.

That's how Bill came to grow up with the coyotes along the Pecos. He soon learned the coyote language, and used to hunt with them and sit on the hills and howl at night. Being so young when he got lost, he always thought he was a coyote. That's where he learned to kill deer by runnin' them to death.

One day when he was about ten years old a cow-boy came along just when Bill had matched a fight with two grizzly bears. Bill hugged the bears to death, tore off a hind leg, and was just settin' down to breakfast when this cow-boy loped up and asked him what he meant by runnin' around naked that way among the varmints.

"Why, because I am a varmint," Bill told him. "I'm a coyote."

The cow-boy argued with him that he was a human, but Bill wouldn't believe him.

"Ain't I got fleas?" he insisted. "And don't I howl around all night, like a respectable coyote should do?"

"That don't prove nothin'," the cow-boy answered. "All Texans have fleas, and most of them howl. Did you ever see a coyote that didn't have a tail? Well, you ain't got no tail; so that proves you ain't a varmint."

Bill looked, and, sure enough, he didn't have a tail.

"You sure got me out on a limb," says Bill. "I never noticed that before. It shows what higher education will do for a man. I believe you're right. Lead me to them humans, and I'll throw in with them."

Bill went to town with this cow-hand, and in due time he got to enjoyin' all the pleasant vices of mankind, and decided that he certainly was a human. He got to runnin' with the wild bunch, and sunk lower and lower, until finally he became a cow-boy.

It wasn't long until he was famous as a bad man. He invented the six-shooter and train-robbin' and most of the crimes popular in the old days of the West. He didn't invent cow-stealin'. That was discovered by King David in the Bible, but Bill improved on it.

There is no way of tellin' just how many men Bill did kill. Deep down he had a tender heart, however, and never killed women or children, or tourists out of season. He never scalped his victims; he was too civilized for that. He used to skin them gently and tan their hides.

It wasn't long before Bill had killed all the bad men in west Texas, massacred all the Indians, and eaten all the buffalo. So he decided to migrate to a new country where hard men still thrived and a man could pass the time away.

He saddled up his horse and hit for the West. One day he met an old trapper and told him what he was lookin' for.

"I want the hardest cow outfit in the world," he says. "Not one of these ordinary cow-stealin', Mexican-shootin' bunches of amateurs, but a real hard herd of hand-picked hellions that make murder a fine art and take some proper pride in their slaughter."

"Stranger, you're headed in the right direction," answers the trapper. "Keep right on down this draw for a couple of hundred miles, and you'll find that very outfit. They're so hard they can kick fire out of a flint rock with their bare toes."

Bill single-footed down that draw for about a hundred miles that afternoon; then he met with an accident. His horse stubbed his toe on a mountain and broke his leg, leavin' Bill afoot.

He slung his saddle over his shoulder and set off hikin' down that draw, cussin' and a-swearin'. Profanity was a gift with Bill.

All at once a big ten-foot rattlesnake quiled up in his path, set his tail to singin', and allowed he'd like to match a fight. Bill laid down his saddle, and just to be fair about it, he gave the snake the first three bites. Then he waded into that reptile and everlastingly frailed the pizen out of him.

By and by that old rattler yelled for mercy, and admitted that when it came to fightin', Bill started where he left off. So Bill picked up his saddle and started on, carryin' the snake in his hand and spinnin' it in short loops at the Gila monsters.

About fifty miles further on, a big old mountain-lion jumped off a cliff and lit all spraddled out on Bill's neck. This was no ordinary lion. It weighed more than three steers and a yearlin', and was the very same lion the State of Nuevo León was named after down in old Mexico.

Kind of chucklin' to himself, Bill laid down his saddle and his snake and went into action. In a minute the fur was flyin' down the cañon until it darkened the sun. The way Bill knocked the animosity out of that lion was a shame. In about three minutes that lion hollered:

"I'll give up, Bill. Can't you take a joke?"

Bill let him up, and then he cinched the saddle on him and went down that cañon whoopin' and yellin', ridin' that lion a hundred feet at a jump, and quirtin' him down the flank with the rattlesnake.

It wasn't long before he saw a chuck-wagon, with a bunch of cowboys squattin' around it. He rode up to that wagon, splittin' the air with his war-whoops, with that old lion a screechin', and that snake singin' his rattles.

When he came to the fire he grabbed the old cougar by the ear, jerked him back on his haunches, stepped off him, hung his snake around his neck, and looked the outfit over. Them cow-boys sat there sayin' less than nothin'.

Bill was hungry, and seein' a boilerful of beans cookin' on the fire, he scooped up a few handfuls and swallowed them, washin' them down with a few gallons of boilin' coffee out of the pot. Wipin' his mouth on a handful of prickly-pear cactus, Bill turned to the cow-boys and asked:

"Who the hell is boss around here?"

A big fellow about eight feet tall, with seven pistols and nine bowie-knives in his belt, rose up and, takin' off his hat, said:

"Stranger, I was; but you be."

Bill had many adventures with this outfit. It was about this time he staked out New Mexico, and used Arizona for a calf-pasture. It was here that he found his noted horse Widow-Maker. He raised him from a colt on nitroglycerin and dynamite, and Bill was the only man that could throw a leg over him.

There wasn't anythin' that Bill couldn't ride, although I have heard of one occasion when he was thrown. He made a bet that he could ride an Oklahoma cyclone slick-heeled, without a saddle.

He met the cyclone, the worst that was ever known, up on the Kansas line. Bill eared that tornado down and climbed on its back. That cyclone did some pitchin' that is unbelievable, if it were not vouched for by many reliable witnesses.

Down across Texas it went sunfishin', back-flippin', side-windin', knockin' down mountains, blowin' the holes out of the ground, and tyin' rivers into knots. The Staked Plains used to be heavily timbered until that big wind swiped the trees off and left it a bare prairie.

Bill just sat up there, thumbin' that cyclone in the withers, floppin' it across the ears with his hat, and rollin' a cigarette with one hand. He rode it through three States, but over in Arizona it got him.

When it saw it couldn't throw him, it rained out from under him. This is proved by the fact that it washed out the Grand Cañon. Bill came down over in California. The spot where he lit is now known as

Death Valley, a hole in the ground more than one hundred feet below sea-level, and the print of his hip-pockets can still be seen in the granite.

I have heard this story disputed in some of its details. Some historians claim that Bill wasn't thrown; that he slid down on a streak of lightnin' without knockin' the ashes off his cigarette. It is also claimed that the Grand Cañon was dug by Bill one week when he went prospectin'; but the best authorities insist on the first version. They argue that that streak of lightnin' story comes from the habit he always had of usin' one to light his cigarette.

Bill was a great roper. In fact, he invented ropin'. Old-timers who admit they knew him say that his rope was as long as the equator, although the more conservative say that it was at least two feet shorter on one end. He used to rope a herd of cattle at one throw.

This skill once saved the life of a friend. The friend had tried to ride Widow-Maker one day, and was thrown so high he came down on top of Pike's Peak. He was in the middle of a bad fix, because he couldn't get down, and seemed doomed to a lingerin' death on high.

Bill came to the rescue, and usin' only a short calf-loop, he roped his friend around the neck and jerked him down to safety in the valley, twenty thousand feet below. This man was always grateful, and became Bill's horse-wrangler at the time he staked out New Mexico.

In his idle moments in New Mexico Bill amused himself puttin' thorns on the trees and horns on the toads. It was on this ranch he dug the Rio Grande and invented the centipede and the tarantula as a joke on his friends.

When the cow business was dull, Pecos Bill occasionally embarked on other ventures; for instance, at one time he took a contract to supply the S. P. Railroad with wood. He hired a few hundred Mexicans to chop and haul the wood to the railroad line. As pay for the job, Bill gave each Mexican one fourth of the wood he hauled.

These Mexicans are funny people. After they received their share of the wood they didn't know what to do with it; so Bill took it off their hands and never charged them a cent.

On another occasion Bill took the job of buildin' the line fence that forms the boundary from El Paso across to the Pacific. He rounded up a herd of prairie-dogs and set them to dig holes, which by nature a prairie-dog likes to do.

Whenever one of them finished a nice hole and settled down to live in it, Bill evicted him and stuck a fence-post in the hole. Everybody admired his foresight except the prairie-dogs, and who cares what a prairie-dog thinks?

Old Bill was always a very truthful man. To prove this, the cow-boys repeat one of his stories, which Bill claimed happened to him. Nobody ever disputed him; that is, no one who is alive now.

He threw in with a bunch of Kiowa Indians one time on a little huntin'-trip. It was about the time the buffalo were getting scarce, and Bill was huntin' with his famous squatter-hound named Norther.

Norther would run down a buffalo and hold him by the ear until Bill came up and skinned him alive. Then he would turn it loose to grow a new hide. The scheme worked all right in the summer, but in the winter most of them caught colds and died.

The stories of Bill's love-affairs are especially numerous. One of them may be told. It is the sad tale of the fate of his bride, a winsome little maiden called Slue-Foot Sue. She was a famous rider herself, and Bill lost his heart when he saw her riding a catfish down the Rio Grande with only a surcingle. You must remember that the catfish in the Rio Grande are bigger than whales and twice as active.

Sue made a sad mistake, however, when she insisted on ridin' Widow-Maker on her weddin'-day. The old horse threw her so high she had to duck her head to let the moon go by. Unfortunately, she was wearin' her weddin'-gown, and in those days the women wore those big steel-spring bustles.

Well, when Sue lit, she naturally bounced, and every time she came down she bounced again. It was an awful' sad sight to see Bill implorin' her to quit her bouncin' and not be so nervous; but Sue kept right on, up and down, weepin', and throwin' kisses to her distracted lover, and carryin' on as a bride naturally would do under those circumstances.

She bounced for three days and four nights, and Bill finally had to shoot her to keep her from starvin' to death. It was mighty tragic. Bill never got over it. Of course he married lots of women after that.

In fact, it was one of his weaknesses; but none of them filled the place in his heart once held by Slue-Foot Sue, his bouncin' bride.

There is a great difference of opinion as to the manner of Bill's demise. Many claim that it was his drinkin' habits that killed him. You see, Bill got so that liquor didn't have any kick for him, and he fell into the habit of drinkin' strychnine and other forms of wolf pizen.

Even the wolf bait lost its effect, and he got to puttin' fish-hooks and barbed wire in his toddy. It was the barbed wire that finally killed him. It rusted his interior and gave him indigestion. He wasted away to a mere skeleton, weighin' not more than two tons; then up and died, and went to his infernal reward.

Many of the border bards who knew Pecos Bill at his best have a different account of his death.

They say that he met a man from Boston one day, wearing a mail-order cow-boy outfit, and askin' fool questions about the West; and poor old Bill laid down and laughed himself to death.

Edward O'Reilly

Jim

An old nester that had a few cattle and a homestead, better known among the cattlemen as a starve-out, always made it a point to show up at our chuck wagon when we began branding calves. This was a good chance for him to fill up; he was never known to do any work and was more in the way than he was a help. It soon became a by-word when the cowboys saw him ride up to say, "Yonder comes old Jim; when he comes to the outfit it's just like two good men leaving."

An Honorable Genealogy

An Englishman visiting the American West was out in Dodge City and went into a saloon. He called a cowpoke over to the bar and offered to buy him a drink. The cowman agreed. When it came time to pay, the English gentleman realized he had some English currency in his pocket. Holding out a coin to the cowboy, he said, "You see this likeness?"

"Yup," answered the cowboy.

"That, my good man, is His Majesty, the King. He made my grandfather a lord."

The cowboy looked at the coin solemnly, and then he took out a coin of his own. "You see this likeness?" he said, pointing to the Indian profile on the coin.

"I do indeed, sir."

"That, pardner, is a red injun and he made my grandpappy an angel."

Lost in Heaven

. . . I'm jest about as lonesome with this bunch [of newcomers] as old Slabs Tyson said the cowpuncher was who died an' went to heaven. When he got there, all the men folks had dress suits on, their vests cut 'way down to their waistband, an' tails on their coats 'most to their heels. All the women had on lace clothes, an' not much o' them.

Well, the old puncher was jest rigged out regular, and these high-toned folks turned their noses up at him an' wouldn't speak. This went on for some time, till at last one day he saw St. Peter and asked as a special favor if he couldn't get a pass to go down to hell for a few days and see some of the boys, as there wasn't anybody where he was that he was acquainted with. As he'd behaved pretty well, St. Peter gave him a round-trip ticket good for a week, and off he goes.

Well, the very first person he met after he arrived was an old puncher from his home town, who takes an' leads him aroun' an' shows him the sights. Presently they come to an old barn, an' goin' in there, they sees about a thousand people all settin' 'round. They had candles stuck in old bottles and all of 'em was a-playin' poker; some of 'em the puncher did know and some he didn't.

Pretty soon the old feelin' come over him, an' he jest got to itchin' to horn in, especially when he seen what a little some of 'em did know about the national game. As he didn't have any money, and all the boys he knew seemed 'bout broke, he was in a terrible fix. But at last, after gunnin' 'round among the different players, he noticed a feller that was dressed up fit to kill, and seemed kind of out o' place in that bunch, though he sure had a swell stack o' chips in front of him. The puncher got to talkin' to the dude, an' told about gettin' a ticket from St. Peter, good fer a week, an' after then he'd have to return to heaven. One word brought on another, till at last he swapped his return ticket to heaven for the dude's pile o' chips, sayin' he'd rather live in hell with a bunch o' punchers than in heaven with them damn high-toned dudes.

A Cowboy Finds a Friend

I'm talkin' about old times, when cowmen were in their glory. They lived different, talked different, an' had different ways. No matter where you met him, or how he's rigged, if you'd watch him close he'd do something that would tip his hand. I had a little experience back in '83 that'll show what I'm gettin' at.

I was winterin' in Cheyenne. One night a stranger stakes me to buck the bank. I got off lucky an' cash in fifteen hundred dollars. Of course I cut the money in two with my friend, but it leaves me with the biggest roll I ever packed. All this wealth makes Cheyenne look small, an' I begin longin' for bigger camps, so I drift for Chicago. The minute I hit the burg, I shed my cow garments an' get into white man's harness. A hard hat, boiled shirt, laced shoes—all the gearin' known to civilized man. When I put on all this rig, I sure look human; that is, I think so. But them shorthorns know me, an' by the way they trim that roll, it looks like somebody's pinned a card on my back with the word "EASY" in big letters. I ain't been there a week till my roll don't need no string around it, an' I start thinkin' about home.

One evenin', I throw in with the friendliest feller I ever met. It was at the bar of the hotel where I'm camped. I don't just remember how we got acquainted, but after about fifteen drinks we start holdin' hands an' seein' who could buy the most and fastest. I remember him tellin' the barslave not to take my money, 'cause I'm his friend. Afterwards, I find out the reason for this goodheartedness; he wants it all an' hates to see me waste it. Finally, he starts to show me the town an' says it won't cost me a cent. Maybe he did, but I was unconscious, an' wasn't in shape to remember. Next day, when I come to, my hair's sore an' I didn't know the days of the week, month, or what year it was.

The first thing I do when I open my eyes is to look at the winders. There's no bars on 'em, an' I feel easier. I'm in a small room with two bunks. The one opposite me holds a feller that's smokin' a cigarette an' sizin' me up between whiffs while I'm dressin'. I go through myself but I'm too late. Somebody beat me to it. I'm lacin' my shoes an' thinkin' hard, when the stranger speaks:

"Neighbor, you're a long way from your range."

"You call the turn," says I, "but how did you read my iron?"

"I didn't see a burn on you," says he, "an' from looks, you'll go as a slick-ear. It's your ways, while I'm layin' here, watchin' you get into your garments. Now, humans dress up an' punchers dress down. When you raised, the first thing you put on is your hat. Another thing that shows you up is you don't shed your shirt when you bed down. So next comes your vest an' coat, keepin' your hindquarters covered till you slide into your pants, an' now you're lacin' your shoes. I notice you done all of it without quittin' the blankets, like the ground's cold. I don't know what state or territory you hail from, but you've smelt sagebrush an' drank alkali. I heap savvy you. You've slept a whole lot with nothin' but sky over your head, an' there's times when that old roof leaks, but judgin' from appearances, you wouldn't mind a little open air right now."

This feller's my kind, an' he stakes me with enough to get back to the cow country.

A Poor Bet

After being on the ranch for several months working hard with not a day off or a vacation of any kind, the boss told these two cowboys they might go into town and bring back a load of chuck. As soon as they arrived in the city, they went to the hotel, registered, got 'em a room and went up to it. They were hot and dry and immediately ordered something to quench their thirst and cool them off. They were on the third floor in a big room that would accommodate all their friends. They didn't close the door opening out into the hall and welcomed everybody that came by. Finally, a drummer came along, and he joined them. They ordered more drinks and did really put on a party 'til after midnight. Next morning when they woke up, one of them had a leg broke, one arm in a sling, his head bandaged and one eyed blacked. He said to his partner, "What in the world happened last night?" His partner told him, "You bet that drummer you could jump out of that window and fly plumb around this hotel and come back in at the same window." The crippled man said, "You didn't let me, did you?" "Let you hell, I lost ten dollars on you myself."

The Cowboy's Lament

As I walked out in the streets of Laredo,
As I walked out in Laredo one day,
I spied a poor cowboy wrapped up in white linen,
Wrapped up in white linen as cold as the clay.

"Oh, beat the drum slowly and play the fife lowly,
Play the dead march as you carry me along;
Take me to the green valley, there lay the sod o'er me,
For I'm a young cowboy and I know I've done wrong.

"I see by your outfit that you are a cowboy"—
These words he did say as I boldly stepped by.
"Come sit down beside me and hear my sad story;
I am shot in the breast and I know I must die.

"Let sixteen gamblers come handle my coffin,
Let sixteen cowboys come sing me a song.
Take me to the graveyard and lay the sod o'er me,
For I'm a poor cowboy and I know I've done wrong.

"My friends and relations they live in the Nation,
They know not where their boy has gone.
He first came to Texas and hired to a ranchman,
Oh, I'm a young cowboy and I know I've done wrong.

"It was once in the saddle I used to go dashing;
It was once in the saddle I used to go gay;
First to the dram-house and then to the card-house;
Got shot in the breast and I am dying today.

"Get six jolly cowboys to carry my coffin;
Get six pretty maidens to bear up my pall.
Put bunches of roses all over my coffin,
Put roses to deaden the sods as they fall.

"Then swing your rope slowly and rattle your spurs lowly,
And give a wild whoop as you carry me along;
And in the grave throw me and roll the sod o'er me
For I'm a young cowboy and I know I've done wrong.

"Oh, bury beside me my knife and six-shooter,
My spurs on my heel, my rifle by my side,

And over my coffin put a bottle of brandy
That the cowboys may drink as they carry me along.

"Go bring me a cup, a cup of cold water,
To cool my parched lips," the cowboy then said;
Before I returned his soul had departed,
And gone to the round-up—the cowboy was dead.

We beat the drum slowly and played the fife lowly,
And bitterly wept as we bore him along;
For we all loved our comrade, so brave, young, and handsome,
We all loved our comrade although he'd done wrong.

> *Where men lived raw, in the desert's maw,*
> *And hell was nothing to shun;*
> *Where they buried 'em neat, without preacher or sheet,*
> *And writ on their foreheads, crude but sweet,*
> *"This Jasper was slow with a gun."*

The Speckled Yearlin'

April and May rains, followed by good growing weather, had made everything beautiful in the SMS pastures. The turf of curly mesquite grass was like a beautiful rug, painted here and there with wild verbena, star daisies, white and yellow primroses, and the myriad coloring of West Texas flora. Branding time was on, and the SMS Flat Top Mountain outfit had gone into camp at Coon Creek Tank, to begin work the next day.

"Scandalous John," the foreman and wagon boss, had been through the aggravating experience of getting an outfit together. It had been no trouble to find riders—cowboys who knew the game from start to finish—but to secure a cook, a "hoss wrangler" and a hoodlum wagon driver was a problem. No one wants to drive the hoodlum wagon, with the duties of supplying wood and water for camp and branding, helping the cook with his dishes or other odd jobs, unprofessional, from a cowboy standpoint, except so far as they lead to a "riding job," meaning regular cowboy work. The "hoss wrangler" was not hard to find, but whoever takes the job aches all the time to be promoted to a riding job, and is therefore dissatisfied. The hoodlum driver had worked one day, and quit. Scandalous was racking his brain to know where to look for another, and was saddling his horse to hunt for one when Four-Six, one of the cowboys, exclaimed, "Look what's comin'!"

Along the dim pasture road, miles from any dwelling, a figure on foot was approaching—a sight which always attracts attention in the big pasture country, since it is associated in the public mind with suspicion, if the footman is unknown. It often occurs that some one's horse will get away or give out. The rider then makes for the nearest cow camp to borrow a horse; but a man walking needs some explanation, although he is always fed without question. The boys were all quiet and indifferent, as they commonly are in a cow camp when a stranger approaches.

A lad of sixteen, rather the worse for wear, clad in a shirt and ducking trousers, badly frayed, a soft felt hat, full of holes, shoes badly run-down at the heels, and bare toes showing through the uppers, stopped within ten feet of the wagon. Scandalous paused in his saddling to say, "Well, son, in trouble?"

The lad's face, lit up by a broad grin, made an appeal to the whole outfit, and all were attention for his answer. "No, I'm looking for the SMS boss. They told me at the ranch house that he was here, and I'm looking for a job."

"You look hungry, son; come eat, an' then tell us all about it," said Scandalous.

As the lad ate, and refilled his plate and cup, the cook ventured, "Son, you're plumb welcome, but when did you eat last?"

"Night before last," the boy replied. "The brakies give me some bread and meat, but I sure was gittin' ready to eat when I smelt your grub cooking down the road."

"Where be you from, son?"

"I'm from Virginia," came the reply, "and I'm sure glad to get here, and get a job."

"Virginia! A job?" exclaimed Scandalous. "How did you get here, an' how do you know you kin get a job?"

Again that good-natured grin appeared as the lad told his story.

"I walked some, and rode with the brakies some; they was mighty good to me, and give me a card to other brakies; sometimes they'd give me food they cooked in the caboose, and sometimes they took me home. I told them I was coming to the big SMS Ranch to work. I worked on farms some, but hurried as much as I could, to be here branding time. Am I in time?"

The quiet assurance of the boy staggered Scandalous, but he recovered to ask, "How did you know about the SMS Ranch? What made you think you could git a job? Ever done any cow work?"

The lad's grin broadened as he answered: "Well, a feller I worked for down in Virginia had one of them picture books about the SMS Ranch, and I read where it said, 'No use to write for a job,' so I just cum. I kin do anything I start out to do; I wanted to work on a ranch ever since I was a little feller; I can learn to do anything you want done, and I sure am going to work for you."

Scandalous blinked again, and said, "Why, son, we would hev' to hev' permission from your pa and ma, even if we had a job, 'cause you might git hurt."

A shade of sadness swept for a moment over the young face; then it shone again with a new light of conviction.

"I ain't got no pa and ma, I been in the orphan asylum until two years ago, when a fine man, the one with the book, took me on his farm to do chores. I didn't run away from him, neither; he said I was so crazy about comin' I'd better start. I been on the road so long the things he give me wore out. I guess I walked about a month. They told me in town to go to the office, but I was afraid they'd turn me down, so I cum to camp, and I'm a-going to stay and work for nothing."

There is a straight path to the hearts of cowboys, if one knows the way, and Scandalous was glad to hear the chorus from the whole outfit, "Let him stay, Scandalous. We'll help him. Give the little boy a job."

"Reckon you kin drive the hoodlum wagon, 'Little Boy,'" said John, and, like a flash, came this response: "I don't know what a hoodlum wagon is, but I kin drive it."

It was settled. "Little Boy" was hired, and "made good." Every moment that he could get from his work found him in the branding pen, and, as is the custom with cowboys in their work, he often rode big calves. The boys, watching his skill, would get him to pull off "stunts" for visiting cowmen, until it began to be noised about that "Little Boy" in the SMS outfit "was sum calf-rider." Then came the proud day of his life, when an older man was found for the hoodlum wagon. The horse wrangler was promoted to a riding job, and "Little Boy" to horse wrangler.

The boys had from the outset contributed shirts and socks; ducking trousers had been cut off for a makeshift. The first month's wages had provided a fair outfit, including the much-coveted white shirts that cowboys love to have in their "war bags" for special occasions. Succeeding months brought saddle, bridle, spurs, horse blanket and a "hot roll." "Little Boy" was coming on, but had to content himself with shoes until he had all the major necessities, and could acquire the two great luxuries: a $15 John B. hat and $35 handmade stitched top boots.

All through the summer "Little Boy" progressed, first from calves to yearlings in his play time, and then to outlaw broncs, until the boys of the outfit would say, "Thet kid sure kin ride; I'll bet he gets inside the money this fall at the Stamford rodeo."

Anything pertaining to an outlaw horse or steer becomes current gossip in the big pasture country, where horses and cattle form the basis of conversation about the wagon after working hours. Strange stories drifted in about a certain outlaw speckled yearling on the Lazy 7 Ranch—he had thrown every boy with rodeo aspirations who had tried to ride him, and seemed to be getting better all the time. The "Speckled Yearling" was tall, gaunt and quick as a cat. He had a mixed jump and weave that got his men about the third jump, but the boys on the Lazy 7 were keeping him to themselves, with a view of pulling off a prize "stunt" at the Stamford rodeo in September. All the little country towns held rodeos during the summer, with calf and goat roping, bronc busting and steer riding, but the big event was to come, and the boys were ready for it. "Little Boy" had a heart-to-heart talk with his boss, and received permission to ride steers, and tackle the "Speckled Yearlin'," if opportunity permitted.

At last the time for the great event came. Cowboys from 100 miles around were on hand. Professionals were barred. It was to be an event for boys who were in actual service on ranches. The SMS headquarters office was thrown open for all, and the Stamford Inn pulled off an old-time cowboy dance, with old-fashioned "squares" called by old-time punchers, with old-time fiddlers doing the music. The weatherman had done his best; some 2,000 people filled the grandstand, cheering the events of the first day, with now and then a call for the "Speckled Yearlin'," which was not mentioned in the programme.

Any one who had not seen an unprofessional rodeo knows little of real cowboy sport, since it differs in its wild abandon, grace and skill from staged events. As each favored son came on for his "stunt," he was cheered to the echo, and usually he pulled some original antic which sent the crowd wild.

The announcer, riding before the grandstand, waved for silence. "Listen, people: I want you to hear this; it's a surprise, and the big event. No one has ever been able to stay ten jumps on the 'Speckled Yearlin',' from the Lazy 7 Ranch. Nig Clary will now 'ride at' the 'Speckled Yearlin' ' on his own risk; a $50 prize if he stays on; a $25 forfeit if he gets throwed. If he rides him down, a hat collection will be took. If Nig can't ride him some other feller gets a chance tomorrow."

"If Nig can't nobody kin," shouted the grandstand. "Turn him a-loose." A wave from the judges' hands, and, like the cutting off of an electric current, all was still and tense. Then from the mounting chute shot the "Speckled Yearlin'," with Nig Clary up, clinging by two hand-holds to a surcingle and riding bare-back. The yearling was dead-red, with distinct white speckles about the size of one's thumb distributed well over his body. He carried long, sharp horns; his back was on the order of an Arkansas razorback hog. When it came to jumping and weaving his body at the same time, the "Speckled Yearlin' " was the limit.

Nig sat straight for three jumps, began to wobble in the fourth, and was on the ground at the fifth. Still jumping, the yearling turned and made for him, giving Nig only time by a scratch to climb up behind one of the judges.

The second day found "Little Boy" and Scandalous with their heads together. "I know I kin ride him, John, an' I sure want that prize money for my boots an' my John B. They's all I'm needin' to be a real cowboy."

"Yes, I know," said John, "but we're needin' live cowboys, an' I ain't feelin' right 'bout your tryin' thet yearlin'. I'll hev to ask you to waive all blame fer the company, an' if you do git hurt they'll be blamin' me; but if you be bound to ride, us boys will pay the forfeit, if you get throwed."

Again on the second day the announcer waved his hand for silence. "Folks, yesterday the best rider and cowpuncher in Texas rode at the Speckled Yearlin'. Today 'Little Boy' from Flat Top Mountain Ranch says he's goin' to ride him. We hates to let a little orphan boy go agin this here steer, but he sez he ain't a-goin' to git hurt, an' if he does there ain't anybody but him. The management hopes he wins. If he does, git your change ready for a hat prize, an' I'm a-goin' to start it with a five."

As boy and steer came out of the chute, the stillness fairly hurt. Every heart in that great crowd seemed to stop for the first three jumps, but "Little Boy" was sitting tight. From the crowd there came a mighty roar; "Stay with him, 'Little Boy'! He's got a booger on him. Ride him, 'Little Boy'!"

At the tenth jump "Little Boy" was still up, his grin growing broader and his seat getting steadier, while the yearling, maddened by his clinging burden, pitched and weaved, but, like Sinbad's "Old Man of the Sea," "Little Boy" kept "a-ridin'."

The crowd went daft. Every one was standing and shouting. The noise seemed to infuriate the yearling, and, turning from the end of the enclosure, he made straight for the grandstand, struck his head against the protecting wire, stood stock still, and glared, while "Little Boy" sat and grinned. Some one cried "Speech!" and, as stillness came, "Little Boy," still sitting on the dazed steer, broadened his grin and said, "I jest had to ride him. I needed them boots and thet John B. so's I could be a real cowboy, an' this yere Speckled Yearlin's done done it."

Frank J. Hastings

Cowboy's Last Request

Twas good to live when all the range
   Without no fence or fuss,
Belonged in partnership with God,
   The government and us.

With skyline bounds from east to west,
   With room to go and come,
I liked my fellow man the best,
   When he was scattered some.

When my old soul hunts range and rest,
   Beyond the last divide,
Just plant me on some strip of West,
   That's sunny, lone and wide.

Let cattle rub my headstone round,
   And coyotes wail their kin,
Let hosses come and paw the mound,
   But don't you fence me in.

                 Badger Clark, Jr.

CHAPTER 12

The Tall Tales of Swappers, Liars, and Boasters

"The Boy and the Turkeys"

The Tall Tales of Swappers, Liars, and Boasters

"The boy and the turkey"

*"Out there, every prairie-dog hole is a gold mine,
every hill a mountain, every creek a river,
and everybody you meet is a liar."*
—an Easterner's description of the
West in a Montana guidebook

AMERICANS LIKE TO THINK they invented the tall tale or the grand lie. According to folks around American country stoves, nobody can "spin a windy" or "saw off a whopper" like we can in the good old U.S.A. Yet, long before America's love affair with exaggeration began, there were many instances of cultures that enjoyed stretching the truth into the fabulous. Out of eighteenth-century Europe, for example, came one of the most famous liars, Baron Munchausen, a German adventurer who wrote a slim volume of unforgettable whoppers supposedly based on his own wild travels. So distinctive and amusing were these farfetched yarns that even today folklorists refer to tales of improbability as "Munchausens." Readers familiar with Munchausen's book will recognize stories like "The Deep Snow," though I'm sure if you told the poor fellow who tied his horse to the church steeple that the same thing had happened to the Baron, he'd surely get indignant and say that it couldn't possibly snow that much anywhere else.

It's a national characteristic for Americans to exaggerate. Their country is, by all measures, itself an exaggeration. The small, elegant proportions of Europe, for instance, are exploded into the spectacle of the American West. The pastoral meanderings of the Thames are dwarfed by the unceasing flood of the Mississippi, and one could fit the whole of France into the belly of Texas and still leave room for the Alps. Death Valley or the Grand Canyon, the Badlands of Dakota and the plains of Kansas, all had a strong effect on the collective imagination of the people who settled America. When Christopher Columbus reached what is now Haiti, his astonishment at the beauty of the place inspired the first mild exaggeration of the New World. The trees, he said, "are of a thousand kinds and tall, and they seem to touch the sky." As more people came to America, they developed exaggeration into an art form. Those trees to a Carolina farmer might be "so tall it takes two men and a boy to look to the top of them, 'cause one has to start lookin' where the other leaves off."

It is important to remember that simple exaggeration isn't enough to make a good tale tall, or a lie memorable. The art demands wit and a real knowledge of what one is lying about. Some farmers in New England will tell you that the ground is full of rocks, but the artful ones will say their land is so rocky that come springtime they have to shoot their seeds in the cracks with a shotgun. Or perhaps you have heard that folks love to dance in the Appalachians? Well, listen to a local lady's way of telling you: "We love jig dancin' so much 'round here they got to get someone to come the mornin' after and rake the ground of toenails." It is easy enough to fall flat as a windy spinner; the worst complaint against you might be the one made by a fellow who had returned from a visit to a neighboring state: "Hell," he said to his friends, "half the lies those folks tell over there ain't true!"

Bear in mind that another root of the tall tale is simply pride of place, the "spread-eagle oratory," as some call it. Americans, if they aren't bragging about America, are enthusiastic regionalists. The colorful brag or the tale that features some aspect of the local character is another way of celebrating one's own home ground. If you live in a part of the country that is cold or dry or hot, it is a matter of honor that you be sure that your home is the coldest, driest or hottest place of all.

The better your ability to "saw off a whopper," the quicker your capacity to boast with style or lie with wit, the more folks are bound to let you talk. As a card player, a horse trader, a dog swapper, a traveling salesman, even a politician, the ability to make the tale just barely stoop under the truth is a great asset. You might get rebuffed or tossed out on your ear, but folks would remember you for a long time after. The tall tale is, after all, an assertion of pride in our own ability to rewrite the world around us.

A Stubborn Critter

There was this Yankee farmer and he advertised a horse for sale. Well, the people in the immediate vicinity, they knew all about the horse and they didn't want anything to do with it. So this stranger came by and was interested in him and he told the Yankee, "That's a beautiful horse, what do you want for him?"

He said, "$150."

"Well, what's wrong with him?"

"Oh, there's nothing wrong with him."

"Look," said the stranger, "you wouldn't ask less than $350 unless there was something wrong with this horse."

The Yankee said, "No, I've just got no use for him and I want to get rid of him, and I'm willing to sacrifice him."

So the stranger felt his legs and he looked at his hooves and he thumped his belly, and looked at his teeth. Finally he said, "Come on now, what's wrong with this horse?" Then he went over and looked the horse in the eye. "My God," he said, "I believe he's blind."

"No," said the Yankee, "he's not blind."

"Well, open the gate," said the stranger. So the farmer opened the gate and that horse ran out and he ran down and ran right into a tree. The stranger said, "That's what I thought, he's blind."

"No, dammit, he's not blind."

"Well, what made him run into that tree?"

"Oh," said the Yankee, "he just don't give a damn."

The Mare with the False Tail

One time, there was a fellow up in Missouri owned a big, fine-looking saddle mare, except she didn't have no tail, as it had got cut off some way. But there was a wigmaker in Kansas City that fixed a false tail so good you couldn't tell the difference, and it was fastened onto the stub with eelskin and rubber.

The trader that owned the mare got a fine saddle and bridle with silver on it, and he rode around to all the fairs. He would sell the mare for a good price, but he never sold the saddle and bridle. Soon as he got the money in his pocket, he always took off the saddle and bridle, and then he would pull the mare's tail off. She just had a little stub about six inches long, and it was shaved smooth and dyed yellow. It sure did look funny, so all the people would laugh, and the fellow that bought the mare begun to holler for his money back. But the horse trader says the tail does not belong to the mare, because it come off another animal. He says he bought the tail separate in Kansas City, and he has got a bill of sale to prove it. False tails is just like a woman's bustle, and if any gentleman wants a artificial tail, they can go to Kansas City and see the wigmaker, says he.

So then he would go set in the livery stable, and pretty soon the fellow that bought the mare would come around talking turkey. Then the horse trader would say, "I always try to do the right thing, and not work no hardship on the customers. So I will take the mare back, if you will give me twenty dollars for my trouble." That's the way it went all over the country, and sometimes he would sell the mare three or four times in one day. The horse trader was a-living the life of Riley, and putting money in the bank besides.

One day, he rode into a little town in Arkansas, and right away an old man bought the mare for two hundred dollars. When the horse trader pulled the mare's tail off, the old man didn't bat an eye, and he just laughed like the rest of the boys. The horse trader hung around the livery stable all day, but the old man never showed up. The horse trader stayed at the hotel that night, and the next day he borrowed a pony and rode out to the old man's place. He says he don't feel right about the sale, so he will take the mare and give the old man his money back, and no hard feelings.

The old man just laughed, and says he hasn't got no complaint, as a bargain is a bargain. He says he likes the mare fine, and he is going to braid a new tail out of corn shucks, and paint it blue to match his wife's eyes. The horse trader figured the old man must be out of his head. But he had to get the snide mare back somehow, so he offered to pay the two hundred dollars and give the old man ten dollars besides. The old man just laughed louder than ever, and he says the

mare is worth four hundred dollars easy, and she ain't for sale anyhow. So the horse trader come back to town. He set around the hotel
mighty glum, and all the home boys was laughing about it.

Next morning, he went out to see the old man again, and says he
will give two hundred and twenty-five dollars for the snide mare. The
old man says, "Don't talk foolish, because me and my wife has got
attached to the mare now, and she is just like one of the family."
And then he says he knowed that tail was a fake all the time, because
he used to swap horses with the Indians when he was a young fellow.

The horse trader thought about it awhile, and then he says, "Listen, that snide's all I got to live on, and feed a big family. Do you
want to take the bread out of my little children's mouth?" The old
man he says, "No, I wouldn't do nothing like that. Give me three
hundred dollars, and you can have your mare back." The horse
trader started to write a check, but the old man wouldn't take no
check, so they went to the bank, and the horse trader give him three
hundred dollars in cash. All the loafers was a-laughing about it, and
the banker laughed louder than anybody. So then the horse trader
put the mare's tail where it belonged, and he rode out of that town.
He never did come back, neither.

Lots of people up North think the folks that live down in Arkansas are all damn fools. But it ain't so, particular when it comes to
swapping horses and things like that.

How a Dog Made Pete Andrews Rich

I mind them old days right well. Them old boys used to be some
punkins at swappin'. There was Lige Pelton, the snake man. Lige
was a great swapper. Why, he'd ruther swap than eat, an' sometimes
he just had to swap to eat. Lige was no great shakes at workin'. I
mind, one time, Lige started out to cut some ties over on the turn-
pike. Along the road, he met one of the Greening boys. The Green-
ings was great swappers too, an' Lige swapped his ax for a hound

pup. The Greening boys had lots of pups, but they needed an ax. So they swapped.

Lige must have been a little put out by the swap after he done it, because he still needed to git some ties if he was goin' to eat that week. So he went on down the road to Bill McCarty's place, where he met John Hoffman. Now, John Hoffman was a great dog man. He'd buy a good dog any time. Lige showed him the pup. It was a nice pup. The Greening boys had good dogs. Hoffman wanted to buy the pup, but Lige wouldn't sell. "Seems as though it's not fair to the pup to sell him like he was a slave or somethin'," said Lige. "Now, if ye was to say swap I'd take ye on."

"Tell ye what I'll do, Lige," said Hoffman. "I got a lot of ties down to my place that I'm countin' to take down to Shohola. I'll swap ye a small jag of ties for the pup." "Done," said Lige. So they swapped. Lige took the ties to Shohola, bought a new ax, and had a load of groceries, an' that was that.

They was a lot of good swappers down our way when I was a boy. I mind one feller, name of Pete Andrews. This feller was so good that when he died, a few years back, they had to hold an auction to git rid of all the stuff. He had swapped all his life an' he started with only a yaller hound-dog fer capital. This feller started swappin' in his diaper days. They tell of Pete swappin' all the rest of the kids out of their Christmas presents, an' his pappy havin' to buy them all back from Pete. It never did no good, though, because Pete had them all back in a few days.

When Pete was goin' to the Notch school, he had a pocketknife with a handle all pretty colored glass. The kids got all het up over that knife. A lot of them talked swap with Pete, so he swapped the knife to one of the Haas boys for a pair of skates. Pete made the Haas boy believe that he could use the knife the whole year 'round and the skates was good only now an' then when the Shohola Creek was froze over. It was a good swap.

On the way home, Pete swapped the skates to one of the Shields boys for a calf. When he got home with the calf, his pappy swapped him a brood sow for the calf. Come spring, the brood sow had thirteen little ones an' Pete was set up in business.

Pete grew up and got married. He never needed no money. He had a lot of good stock then and a nice piece of land, all got by swappin'. He built a log house an' barn just by swappin'. Course, the neighbors helped with the house an' barn at a raisin'. Pete swapped for a team of mules an' some farm tools, an' give some of his stock in the swap.

But the best of all the yarns about Pete swappin' I shoulda told before, for, after all, this is what set Pete up.

When Pete was about sixteen, his pappy brought home a yaller hound pup an' give it to Pete. The yaller pup grew up to be a big dog an' was just about the beatenest hound-dog in the whole of Pike County. He was about the smartest dog I ever seen, an' Pete claimed that Old Sam, as he called him, could really talk, if ye could understand dog talk, an' Pete allowed he did. Anyway, this yaller hound-dog was Pete's capital. After he got past sixteen, he was on his own an' he traveled around a lot with the yaller dog, an' just swapped. But the big thing was the way Pete trained Old Sam.

In those days, people put a sight of store by a good hound-dog. Pete's yaller hound was a good one an' the whole county was always tryin' to swap Pete out of him, an' this give Pete his big idea.

So one day Pete got ready to go on a swappin' trip. After he started, he fed Old Sam a lot of mush an' other fixin's that dogs like. When Old Sam had swallered it all up, Pete fixed another lot but he did not let Sam eat it. He just let him see it and smell it, then he pulled him away and dragged him off by the chain. On the way down the road, Old Sam kept pullin' back, wantin' to git back to his dish, but Pete dragged him along until he came to Joe Samson's place, a couple miles down the road.

Joe was one of the fellers who was always tryin' to git Old Sam. Him an' Pete talked a while, about swappin' as usual. Pete allowed he was not interested. "Got nothin' to swap just now," said Pete. "What about Old Sam?" said Joe. "Kind o' like to have Old Sam. Give ye the little red heifer for Sam," said Joe. "Nope," said Pete. "Wouldn't swap Old Sam for any heifer ye got; 'sides, Old Sam wouldn't stay with ye. Run home the first time he got loose."

They talked a long time about swappin', an' finally Pete swapped Old Sam for the heifer, two shoats, an' a big goose. But Pete kept tellin' Joe that Sam wouldn't stay with him.

So, the next day, Joe brought the stock over an' took Old Sam home. Well, it turned out just as Pete told him. Old Sam come home the first time he got out an' made for his dish, which Pete kept filled up, waitin' for Sam to come home. Old Sam licked up the food an' Pete kept fillin' the dish up an' Old Sam ate til he was fit to bust.

That afternoon, Joe come over to git Sam, all het up because the dog had run away. Pete took it calm-like. "Told ye Old Sam wouldn't stay with ye," he said. "Wouldn't stay anywhere but to home. Tell ye what I'll do, Joe. I'll give ye back the heifer. Ought to have somethin' for my trouble." Joe allowed that was fair, so he took the heifer an' went home, glad to git somethin' back.

After that, every time Pete went swappin', he filled Sam's dish an' dragged him away when he had half ate. This made Sam long to git back to finish the good fixin's. Pete swapped Old Sam to a lot of fellers in Pike County afore the trick got found out. Then he worked the same trick over in Monroe County, an' along the Wayne County side of the Paupack, an', every time, Old Sam came back. Pete got right smart rich with Old Sam before a rattlesnake bit the hound-dog an' he died.

Crazy for Whiskey

"Some injuns are crazy fer whiskey," said Jack, the brawny cowboy, at the stable. "Last week, I got stopped by this big injun on a fine-lookin' bay. He saw my quart bottle in my saddle bag and started lickin' his lips like his mouth was dry. He didn't speak no English an' I don't speak injun, so he started pointin' at his horse and at my bottle. I swear to ya, he was offerin' his horse fer my whiskey—an' he was throwin' in his saddle as well! Can ya b'lieve it? I swear that he wanted to gimme the finest horse I near 'bout ever saw in my life an' a saddle I coulda sold by itself fer more'n a hunnert dollars, an' all that fer a bottle of hooch that didn't cost me a cent more'n six bucks! Craziest damn trade I ever heard an' I ain't likely ta run by one like it agin."

"Then, where's the hoss, Jack?" asked Pete.

"I didn't make the trade," Jack snarled.

"Why not?"

"Hell, Pete, it was the only whiskey I had on me."

The Fireproof Pitch

Well, I decided to go into the money-safe business. I went out to sell fireproof money safes. I run into a pardner and he said, "What are you selling, Bud?"

I said, "Fireproof money safes."

He said, "Well, that's exactly my business. I sell fireproof money safes."

I said, "Well, I've got a little talk I use in my business, selling safes." I said, "Do you have a talk?"

He said, "Yes, sir."

I said, "Go ahead."

He got up and he said, "Ladies and gentlemen, I'm selling a fireproof money safe. The fireproof safe I'm selling has been tested and tried." He said, "This safe has been put in a ten-room building and fire was set to the building. The building burnt six hours, and after the safe got cool so we could handle it we unlocked it and the money was as bright as ever."

Well, it was my time, you see. I raised up and said, "Well, ladies and gentlemen, I'm selling a money safe, and I want to tell you what we have experienced with this money safe. We put this safe in a ten-story building. We put a rooster instead of money in this safe and locked him up. We set this building afire and it burnt twelve hours. The safe got red hot. After the building burnt down, the safe cooled off, we opened the door of the money safe, and what do you think happened? There stood that rooster with icicles to his tail feathers and he was froze to death."

The Fish-Boning Machine

See here, mister, don't you want somethin' in my line today? I've got a new machine for pickin' bones out of fishes. Now, I tell you it's the darnedest thing you ever did see. Science, you know, is great, and the world is great, and the Atlantic Ocean is great, and the whale is great, but science is greater than all of them; it's bigger than a meetin' house; it takes in all things; it explains parables that will tell you where to find the gizzard in a codfish; it makes out wonderful discoveries; Columbus made out to discover "Cape Cod," and by the aid of his second cousin "Epluribus Unum" made out to discover "America." Well now, the people all thought that was wonderful, but I tell you, this here machine for picking bones out of fishes beats anythin' there is a goin'. All you have to do is to set it on the table and turn a crank, and the fish flies down your throat, and the bones right t'other way. Well, there was a country "green horn" got hold on it t'other day, and he got to turnin' the crank the wrong way, and I tell you the way the bones flew down that feller's throat couldn't be beat. Why, it stuck the feller so full of bones that he couldn't get his shirt off for a whole week.

The Truth About Liars

Of course, there is a great difference in lies, and there are all sorts of liars. There is the fellow who lies for gain, and will swear to you that black is pale blue in order to carry his point. Then there is the flattering liar, the fellow that takes you off to one side and tells you that you can be elected to any office. But the most interesting liar is the fellow who loves to lie so well that he will call you out to your front gate at midnight to tell you one.

Bill Greenfield, a Great Liar

Everything that Bill experienced was remarkable, especially the weather. One time when he was hunting, it got so cold that every morning he had to pound up the air so he could breathe it. Outside the camp he had a saw with twenty-one teeth to the inch—and that should have been fine enough to escape destruction—but the wintry wind blew all the teeth out of the saw. One day Bill froze his feet and hastened to plunge them into a bucket of water to thaw them out. This should have been effective, but he hadn't realized how far the frost had gone. "Well, sir," said Bill, "my feet was so cold, a inch of ice come on top of that water quicker'n you could count two." But Bill recovered in time to go hunting soon after with Abner, his father. They didn't want any more frozen feet; so they set a stump afire to warm themselves, but the cold was still so intense that the blaze, forty feet high, froze in a column. Abner went into a cave to get warm. He tried to talk, but no words came; so, after a pull at a bottle, he and Bill went home. On the next Fourth of July, Bill happened to go into that same cave again, when he was startled to hear Abner's words, just thawing out of the air, saying, "Here, Bill, have a drink."

There were big rains in those days too. Mrs. Wheeler once saw Bill driving past in a downpour, taking a pig home. Later he reported to her that he had driven so fast that he hadn't got a mite wet, but it was a close call, for the pig in the back of the wagon had got drowned. At another time it rained so hard that it took seven men each with a ten-quart pail, working one entire week, to dip up the water that came into camp through a six-inch stove-pipe. The *worst* rain that he reported occurred one day when he took a trip to Saratoga. Standing in a doorway, he observed in front of the store a porkbarrel with both ends knocked out. It rained so hard that the water went into the bunghole faster than it could run out at both ends.

Some of his friends used to say that Bill beat the devil; one day, he told them how true that remark was. He was walking in a field of his father's when he suddenly met that Enemy of Mankind whom Bill's Scottish ancestors named respectfully the Earl of Hell.

"Bill," said the devil, "I need a liar of your talents; you must come with me."

Bill sat down on a stone and began to cry—probably for the first time in his life. Somewhat softened by the spectacle of so great a genius at a loss, Auld Clootie made a concession.

"Bill," he said, "you may ask me to do three things; if you find just one that I cannot manage, you may stay on earth and entertain the County of Saratoga."

At these words Bill grew thoughtful. Pulling up a small sapling he said, "Let me see you pull up that large elm over there."

The devil did it easily.

Picking up a small pebble, Bill turned it around in his hands several times. "Now," he said, "you take that ten-ton boulder over there and do with it just as I've done with this pebble."

"That is easy too," said the devil, performing the feat with nonchalance. "Now, Bill, you have just one more chance."

"I know it," replied Bill, "but I wasn't brought up in the woods to be scared by owls. Those first two jobs would have been easy for me; now here is a hard one for anybody: you go find a bigger liar than Bill Greenfield."

The devil sat down and cried. Then he arose, shook his head, and said, "Bill, you can go."

A Cold Day

One January morning, it was so cold that the forest trees were stiff and they couldn't shake, and the very daybreak froze fast as it was trying to dawn. The tinder box in my cabin would no more ketch fire than a sunk raft at the bottom of the sea. Well, seein' daylight war so far behind time, I thought creation war in a fair way for freezen fast: so, thinks I, I must strike a little fire from my fingers, light my pipe, an' travel out a few leagues, and see about it. Then I brought my knuckles together like two thunderclouds, but the sparks froze up afore I could begin to collect 'em, so out I walked, whistlin' "Fire in the Mountains!" as I went along in three-double-quick time. Well, after I had walked about twenty miles up the Peak O'Day and Daybreak Hill I soon discovered what war the matter. The airth had actually friz fast on her axis, and couldn't turn round; the sun had got jammed between two cakes o' ice under the wheels, an' thar he had been shinin' an' workin' to get loose till he friz fast in his cold sweat. C-r-e-a-t-i-o-n! thought I, this is the toughest sort of suspension, an' it mustn't be endured. Somethin' must be done, or human creation is done for. It was then so anteluvian an' premature cold that my upper and lower teeth an' tongue was all collapsed together as tight as a friz oyster; but I took a fresh twenty-pound bear off my back that I'd picked up on my road, and beat the animal agin the ice till the hot oil began to walk out on him at all sides. I then took an' held him over the airth's axis an' squeezed him till I'd thawed 'em loose, poured about a ton on't over the sun's face, give the airth's cog-wheel one kick backward till I got the sun loose—whistled "Push along, keep movin'!" an' in about fifteen seconds the airth gave a grunt, an' began movin'. The sun walked up beautiful, salutin' me with such a wind o' gratitude that it made me sneeze. I lit my pipe by the blaze o' his top-knot, shouldered my bear, an' walked home, introducin' people to the fresh daylight with a piece of sunrise in my pocket.

A Good Imitation

A Kentuckian imitates the crowing of a rooster so remarkably well that the sun, upon several occasions, has risen two hours earlier by mistake.

John Darling, an Even Bigger Liar

"Some of the most re-markable things," said John Darling, "have happened to me right here to home. I'll never forget that foggy day in early fall when I was shingling the barn. I ain't one to let the weather stop me; so I started good and early and worked hard till noon, encouraging myself with my clarion lung. I knocked off at noon, and when I came back from dinner I had one of the surprises of my life. While I was eating, the sun had come out. Imagine my surprise when I discovered that I had laid the shingles onto the fog forty foot above the roof!

"The most unexpected and beautiful things have happened to me right here on Sand Pond. In summertime, I'm a great hand to go swimming, and, one day, I was feeling specially strong; so I thought I'd see whether I could dive right down to the floor of the Pond out in the middle. Well, by Jeepers, I dove like a fish and landed at the bottom right in an Indian graveyard. I stayed down an hour, walking up and down, reading the names and inscriptions on all them stones. It was one of the prettiest sights I ever saw, and I hated like sin to come up and go back to work.

"You know, boys," John would say, "you know I never shave nor have my hair cut oftener than once a year. Yessir, every May I figure on going down to the barber in Roscoe and getting my whiskers cut off. 'Taint worth while to go oftener than that. Well, last spring I went down, and when the barber cut off my beard, I decided to take it home. Seemed as if there was quite a bit of weight to it; so I took it along, and my old woman poured a little water on it and put it on the stove; and darned if she didn't get seven gallons of maple syrup out of them whiskers! You see, boys, we'd had an extra lot of pancakes that winter.

"I remember a colder winter, though. One day, it was so cold that the fire in my chimley wouldn't draw, and the smoke kept coming into the room. Well, I couldn't stand that; so finally I figured a way to get the smoke up. I whittled a paddle out of a piece of wood, and I fastened it onto the end of a bit of rope. I hung the rope over a nail, and then I stuck the paddle into the fireplace under the smoke. I sat down by the fire and began to pull the rope, like ringing a bell. The paddle kept jerking up and down every time I pulled the rope, and pushed the smoke up the chimley. Well, I sat there a spell, working the paddle and singing songs. (You know, boys, I was born with a clarion lung.) Pretty soon I noticed that the paddle wasn't working so good. It was getting awful heavy and hard to lift, and the smoke seemed harder to push up. Finally I went outside and looked at the chimley. The weather was so cold that the smoke I had paddled had frozen as it came out, and had made a solid column ninety-six feet high in the air. Yessir—that was a real pretty sight all the rest of the winter; and in the spring, when the smoke began to melt, coming out of the air I heard the songs I had sung while I was paddling.

"I remember another day when it was pretty cold. That was when I had that old tomcat that I was so fond of. Well, my old woman, she used to set the jug of pancake-batter behind the stove so it would get light. One day, the cat got into the pancakes, and the old woman took a notion that they was spoilt. She seemed to be pretty mad, and she grabbed a dipperful of boiling water off the stove and went after the cat. I didn't want to see him hurt just for liking pancakes; so I opened the door, and he run for it. Just as he flopped through the door, the old woman let loose with her boiling water. Well, sir, it was so cold that day that the water froze the minute it left the dipper, and when it hit the cat on the head, it was such a heavy chunk of ice that it killed him.

"Speaking of pancakes and syrup—I worked out in California for a man who had some of them tremendous big sugar-bushes. They boiled down so much sap, that the man had to have big pans that weighed one ton each. About that time, mosquitoes out in California used to be pretty brisk, and they was big, too. My boss told me that if I ever heard a sort of thundering sound coming from the sky, I'd better hide quick, because it wouldn't do no good to run.

"Well, I was out in the woods working one day when I heard a sort of *roar, roar, roar* up in the sky that made me look for a place to hide. There wasn't any place except under the big sap-pan, laying bottom-side up on the ground; so I picked up one corner of it and jumped under. Less than a minute later, there was a *crash;* a swarm of mosquitoes had hit that pan so hard that they drove their bills into it. There was some big stones on the ground under the pan where I was; so I picked up a stone and went around clinching all the bills of those mosquitoes onto the inside of the pan. The next thing I knew, they begun to clap their wings and make a sound like as if a big storm was coming. Then the sap-pan begun to lift up slow. It riz up graceful from the ground and over the tree-tops, and the last thing I saw of that sap-pan, it looked no bigger'n a baseball, on the way to China.

"Did I ever have any pets after the old Tom was killed? Well, I got kind of attached to an old sow once . . ."

Big Mosquitoes

A group of men were talking in a Shoshone pool hall about mosquitoes. A little runt of a cowpuncher listened for an hour before he said, "You guys, you ain't seen nothin'. Why, down around Rupert there's real mosquiters. Once, when I was a-wranglin' the critters, I pitched my buffalo robe and staked my hoss; when along comes two mosquiters as big as caribou. They looks me over and one says, 'I don't think he'd make us a meal. He might do for dessert but not for the full helpin's. Let's taste his hoss.' And afore I knowed it, they had that hoss et up clear down to his galluses. Then they looks at me again. 'I tell you,' says one, 'we'll yank the shoes off the hoss and pitch hoss-shoes to see who gits him. They ain't enough in him for dessert for two.' And so they begun pitchin' hoss-shoes and me a-settin' there and shakin' all over. Well, I'd a gone right down a mosquiter's gullet if it hadn't a been they was such ornery cusses. One accused the other of cheatin' and while they was down at the stake a-figgerin' out which shoe was closest, I skinned out like hell and high lightning. For ten miles I could hear them mosquiters after me. They sounded like two airplanes."

Big Wind at Hurley

One time, there was a bad cyclone come through Hurley, up on Spring Creek. Hurley was quite a settlement in them days, with a big gristmill, and more than two hundred people was a-living there. When the storm struck, it tore down a lot of houses, and scared the hell out of everybody in town. That was the time Jack Short got hit on the head with a stick of wood and it pretty near killed him.

A fellow named Alec Hood was coming across his pasture when things begun to turn black. He seen the cloud, and started to run for the creek bank, but he never made it. The wind lifted him clear up over the treetops. Joey Jones run out of the grocery to see what was going on, and quick as a wink he was sucked up in the air too. There was horses, and woodsheds, and turkeys, and even haystacks a-flying along beside him. Them two fellows was whirled round and round, and once they passed so close that they shook hands. "Good-bye, brother," says Alec, and Joey just nodded because he was plumb breathless. It looked like they was both gone goslings for sure.

Everything turned out all right, though. The wind kind of slowed up after while, and finally they come down in a field about three miles from home. Neither one of 'em was hurt a bit. The folks sure was surprised to see them boys, when they come a-walking into town.

There ain't no doubt about them being blowed up in the air, just like they said. There was plenty of folks that seen 'em a-flying over the trees. But maybe the part about shaking hands and saying, "Goodbye, brother!" was made up. The neighbors never did hear nothing about it till several years after the cyclone. It was Alec that told the tale, down at the crossroads store. Joey Jones just grinned, and wagged his head. He never did deny it, though. And everybody knows that funny things do happen sometimes, when one of them big winds hits a settlement like Hurley.

Sandstorm Yarns

As Bill and I were working one hot afternoon, we saw a bank forming in the northwest. We could see a rolling cloud of dust below it, and we knew we were in for another "Panhandle rain." The wind caught us as we ran down the turn-row. Before the sun was shut out, we saw the birds were flying backwards to keep the sand out of their eyes. We also noticed a little flurry in the dirt, and there was a prairie dog, digging straight up, trying to get a breath of air.

We got to the house just before the storm settled down to real business. We ran in at the nearest door and managed to slam it shut, but the sand began to pour through the key hole like shelled corn out of a feed bin. Bill's wife brought her pots, and in the blast got them clean for the first time since they were new. The sand came in faster than we could shovel it out; and on the second day when the sand gave out and the wind started whipping gravel too big for the hole, we just barely had room to stand in the back door and swing our scoops.

We rested until middle afternoon, when the wind died down just before the gravel ran short and the rocks started flying. We went out to stretch our legs a bit and found the old rain barrel chuck full of sand. The barrel had been empty so long that both ends and the bung had fallen out, but the wind had blown dirt in at the bung hole faster than it could run out both ends. The sand blast had worn it down to the size of a pickle keg.

A neighbor came by on a dead run with his combine. I asked him where he was going so fast. He said he'd planted wheat and he was going to harvest it if he had to chase it to the Gulf. We had planted our north section in oats, but we found it covered with barley. During the week, we located our oats five miles to the south, but we never did find out who the owner of the barley was.

Ira and Tom Build Fences

One night in camp, two boys, Ira and Tom, got in rather late. Some of the boys already in camp after having retired to the bunkhouse asked the late comers what they had been doing that day.

Tom sez: "You tell 'em, Iry, 'cause I'm too tired."

Iry sez: "Well, it ain't much to tell, ceptin' that we saved the boss lots of time and money today. He set us out to fence in a section pasture. When we got over there, there wasn't enough fence posts, and in going up a draw I smelt a terrible smell and asked Tom what it might be. He said he didn't think, he knowed already what it was. It was a snake den, and the snakes were crawlin' out to get the sunshine. I sez to him, 'There ain't much sunshine, for it's cold today.'

" 'Well,' sez he, 'mebbe they come out yesterday to warm themselves when it was good and warm and stayed out too late last night and got froze to death.'

"Shore enough, when we got up to this snake den there was somewhere between five and ten thousand rattlesnakes all the way from six to fourteen feet long, lying stretched out and froze stiff. I sez to Tom, 'Right here's where we get our fence posts,' so we jest throwed a rope around a bundle of them and drag 'em to where we was goin' to fence the 'trap' and I'd hold the pointed end of the snake with the rattles on it into the ground, and while Tom'd sit on his horse he'd hammer on the blunt end, that is the end his head's on, with a six pound sledge hammer, and drove him in the ground. We got through by about eleven o'clock, and thinkin' we was through so quick that the boss wouldn't care if we laid down and took a nap. Which we did, an' in the meantime the sun come shinin' out and the boss thought he'd ride over to see how we was gettin' along and caught us sleepin'. I told him he needn't to git mad because we had saved him a lot of time and money, but I wouldn't tell him just how we done it. I told him to come and go with me and I would show him. Well, sir,

I'll be dadgoned if he din't show his appreciation by tellin' me an' Tom to come on down to the bunkhouse and go to sleep, bein' as how we was in such need of sleep and come to the office in the morning and get our money."

One of the boys sez: "Why, Iry, why did he want to fire you, you savin' him all that money expense of cutting fence posts like you did?"

Weather Lore

When smoke drops in a chimney, rain is coming.

When an old tree's limbs start falling, or when you see snakes dropping out of the trees, a mighty storm is coming.

Red sky in the morning, sailor take warning; Red sky at night, sailor's delight.

The first twelve days of January play out the weather for the whole year. Day 1 is January's weather, day 2 is February's, etc.

If the rooster crows before ten in the morning, it's sure to rain.

A circle around the moon means there's bad weather coming.

Lightning is drawn to the eyes of a mule or a horse. Don't work next to either animal during a storm.

Lots of spiders in the fall means a long, tough winter.

Never let a wet dog in your house, or lightning will strike your home.

Cows always come home before a storm.

When a cat begins to wash its face, bad weather is coming soon.

If geese fly high on their way South, there'll be a severe winter.

The brighter the stars, the better the weather.

"Some folks say dat de only way ta stop de rain be de killin' of frogs or mice or sich as dat. Dat ain't right. De onliest cure for big rains is de family singin' all togetha. Yessir, singin'll stop de rain."

The Deep Snow

Schiederhannas saddled his horse one day to take a ride to the court-house. After riding in a heavy snowstorm all day he found the court-house closed. And being weary and tired he stopped, got off his horse, and tied his horse to what he thought was a hitching post. Then he took his blanket from his horse and spread it upon the snow and lay down on it and went to sleep. Awakening the next morning, he looked about for his horse, and to his amazement he saw that the snow was melted, and there was his horse tied to the cross of the church steeple. So he took out his pistol and shot off the strap with which his horse was tied. Down came the horse and Schiederhannas rode away.

The Boy and the Turkeys

One time, there was a boy hid in a corncrib, and he was laying for some wild turkeys that come there to eat the corn. When the turkeys showed up, the boy give a jump right into the middle of the flock and grabbed two of them big gobblers. But the gobblers was stronger than he figured, and they flew off with him hanging onto their legs. The next thing that boy knowed, he was way up in the air, looking down at the treetops.

The boy sure was in a bad fix, but pretty soon he figured out what was the best thing to do. He turned one of them turkeys loose and held onto the other one. The old gobbler flopped his wings like a windmill, but he couldn't quite make it. So down they come, slow and easy. Soon as his feet touched the ground the boy wrung the turkey's neck and started for home.

It was way after dark when he got to the house, because them turkeys had carried him fourteen miles while he was figuring out what to do. The folks didn't believe the story at first, and they was going to give him a licking for lying. But when he showed 'em the big old gobbler, they just didn't know what to think.

Finally the old man says maybe that fool boy is telling the truth, because nobody in this family has got sense enough to make up such a lie out of his own head. And besides, how could he ketch a big wild turkey like that, without a mark on it, only its neck broke?

The folks didn't say much about the turkey story for a week or two, but after a while they got so they would tell it for the gospel truth. And finally the old man told a preacher that he looked out the window just as the two turkeys was carryin' the boy over the tree-tops. "I never would have believed such a tale," says he, "if I hadn't seen it with my own eyes!"

Well-Dressed Turkeys

My great-grandmother, who was a tiny little woman with the soul of a lion, managed to save a few turkeys from the invading Yankees by hiding them upstairs. In time, and by most careful nursing, the flock increased to twenty-six. One day shortly after the close of the war, when things were at the lowest ebb, company came to Winston Place. There was not much to offer them, but great-grandmother did have a huge jar of brandied cherries from an old tree in the orchard. These were served and eaten rather bountifully, the stones being subsequently thrown out into the yard.

After several hours the cook rushed in wringing her hands, "Ole Miss, every single one of them thar turkeys is laying out there in the yard cold stone daid." Grandmother, being a frugal soul, decided she could not let them be a total loss so she had the cook pick all the soft feathers off to save for bed ticks and pillows, leaving only the big wing and tail feathers. The corpses were then thrown in a pile near the back gate.

In a couple of hours the cook came rushing back all agog with excitement, "Ole Miss, for the Lord's sake come see; them thar turkeys is all alive again and strutting around wid dey wings all stretched out and dey tails spread and dey haids to one side looking at each other and saying, 'Ppfft-ppfft,' at each other." Sure enough the birds had gotten dead drunk on the brandied cherry stones and had merely passed out. But, alas, they now faced the rigors of winter in a state of almost complete nudity, and since turkeys are very delicate, they would never survive. So great-grandmother and the cook cut up an old blanket and sewed little woolen jackets on all twenty-six alcoholic turkeys and, incidentally, saved the whole flock.

Some Liars of the Old West

Speakin' of liars, the Old West could put in its claim for more of 'em than any other land under the sun. The mountains and plains seemed to stimulate man's imagination. A man in the States might have been a liar in a small way, but when he comes West he soon takes lessons from the prairies, where ranges a hundred miles away seem within touchin' distance, streams run uphill, and Nature appears to lie some herself.

These men weren't vicious liars. It is love of romance, lack of reading matter, and the wish to be entertainin' that makes 'em stretch facts and invent yarns. Jack McGowan, a well-known old-timer now livin' in Great Falls, tells of a man known as Lyin' Jack, who was famous from Mexico to the Arctic.

McGowan says one of Jack's favorite tales is of an elk he once killed that measured 15-feet spread between the antlers. He used to tell that he kept these horns in the loft of his cabin.

"One time I hadn't seen Jack for years," said McGowan, "when he shows up in Benton. The crowd's all glad to see Jack, an' after a round or two of drinks, asks him to tell them a yarn.

" 'No, boys,' says Jack, 'I'm through. For years I've been tellin' these lies—told 'em so often I got to believin' 'em myself. That story of mine about the elk with the 15-foot horns is what cured me. I told about that elk so often that I knowed the place I killed it. One night I lit a candle and crawled up in the loft to view the horns—an' I'm damned if they was there.' "

Once, up in Yogo, Bill Cameron pointed out Old Man Babcock an' another old-timer, Patrick, sayin', "There's three of the biggest liars in the world."

"Who's the third?" inquired a bystander.

"Patrick's one, an' old Bab's the other two," says Cameron.

This Babcock one night is telling about getting jumped by 50 hostile Sioux, a war party, that's giving him a close run. The bullets an' arrows are tearin' the dirt all around, when he hits the mouth of a deep canyon. He thinks he's safe, but after ridin' up it a way, discovers it's a box gulch, with walls straight up from 600 to 1,000 feet. His only get-away's where he come in, an' the Indians are already whippin' their ponies into it.

Right here old Bab rares back in his chair, closes his eyes, an' starts fondlin' his whiskers. This seems to be the end of the story, when one of the listeners asks:

"What happened then?"

Old Bab, with his eyes still closed, takin' a fresh chew, whispered: "They killed me, b' God!"

The upper Missouri River steamboats, they used to say, would run on a light dew, an' certainly they used to get by where there was mighty little water. X. Beidler an' his friend, Major Reed, are traveling by boat to Fort Benton. One night they drink more than they should. X. is awakened in the morning by the cries of Reed. On entering his stateroom, X. finds Reed begging for water, as he's dying of thirst.

X. steps to the bedside, and takin' his friend's hand, says: "I'm sorry, Major, I can't do anything for you. That damned pilot got drunk too, last night, and we're eight miles up a dry coulee!"

"Cap" Nelse, a well-known old-timer around Benton in the early days, tells of coming south from Edmonton with a string of half-breed carts. They were traveling through big herds of buffalo. It was spring and there were many calves. They had no trouble with the full-grown buffalo, Cap said, but were forced to stop often to take the calves from between the spokes of the cart-wheels!

A traveling man in White Sulphur Springs makes a bet of drinks for the town with Coates, a saloon keeper, that Coates can't find a man that will hold up his hand and take his oath that he has seen 100,000 buffalo at one sight. When the bet's decided, it's agreed to ring the triangle at the hotel, which will call the town to their drinks.

Many old-timers said they had seen that many buffalo, but refused to swear to it, and it looked like Coates would lose his bet until Milt Crowthers showed up. Then a smile of confidence spread over Coates's face as he introduces Crowthers to the drummer.

"Mr. Crowthers," said the traveling man, "how many antelope have you seen at one time?"

Crowthers straightens up and looks wise, like he's turning back over the pages of the past. "Two hundred thousand," says he.

"How many elk?" asks the traveling man.

"Somethin' over a million," replies Crowthers.

"Mr. Crowthers, how many buffalo will you hold up your hand and swear you have seen at one sight?"

Crowthers holds up his hand. "As near as I can figure," says he, "about three million billion."

This is where Coates starts for the triangle, but the traveling man halts him, saying, "Where were you when you saw these buffalo, Mr. Crowthers?"

"I was a boy travelin' with a wagon train," replies Crowthers. "We was south of the Platte when we was forced to corral our wagons to keep our stock from bein' stampeded by buffalo. For five days an' nights 50 men kep' their guns hot killin' buffalo to keep 'em off the wagons. The sixth day the herd spread, givin' us time to yoke up an' cross the Platte, an' it's a damn good thing we did."

"Why?" asks the traveling man.

"Well," says Crowthers, "we no more than hit the high country north of the Platte than, lookin' back, here comes the main herd!"

The Hickory Toothpick

One winter, we sure had a big snow. I was livin' up a ways on Pine Mountain, south side, there where the Poor Fork of The Cumberland runs between The Pine and The Black. And one morning, I tried to open the door, and I couldn't. I'd noticed the snow banked up on the windows, but when I tried the door it looked like the snow had piled up plumb over the house.

I kept my stove goin'. Had me a fairly good pile of wood in the house—and enough rations for a day or two. But after about four days my wood was gone, and the meat, too. I tore out some shelves and kept my fire up. The snow didn't seem to thaw much, and after I'd burned up all my shelves and a couple of chairs I knew I had to get out of there and hunt me some firewood.

So I took the stovepipe down: knocked a few planks loose from around the flue, got my ax and crawled out. Well, the snow went up like a funnel, twenty or thirty feet, where my fire had kept it melted. So I hacked me some toeholds with the ax and finally made it out on top of all that snow. And like I said, it was a big snowfall: plumb over the tops of the tallest trees.

But 'way up on one cliff of Pine Mountain there was one tree—a hickory—the snow hadn't drifted over and buried. So I headed for it. The crust was hard enough to hold me and up I went. I could see directly where other folks' houses were snowed under. Putney, the settlement down at the foot of the mountain, looked like a little patch of doodlebug holes.

Got to that hickory tree finally—and it was full of coons. They'd gone from tree to tree, I reckon, and that hickory was ripe with 'em: frozen fast asleep. So I says, "Well, here's firewood, and meat, too, to do me till a thaw sets in." I shook the coons out. A few rolled down the slope, but I picked up about a dozen: wythed a thin strip of bark off that hickory and tied 'em together by their tails.

Then I cut that tree. Went to trimmin' it. Piled up the limbs right careful, so's I'd have plenty of kindlin'. Oh, I saved every twig! But—don't you know!—when I hacked off that last limb, the log jumped and slid top foremost down the south side of the mountain. There went my stovewood!

I watched it slitherin' down, faster and faster. It was goin' so fast it shot across the bottom and up Black Mountain it flew. I thought it would go right up in the air and over yon' side of The Black. But it slowed down just at the top of the ridge: stopped with its top teeterin' —and here it came back. Scooted across where the river was and headed up The Pine again. I cut me a few heel-holds, stepped down and thought I'd catch it with the ax when it got to me. But when I tried to nail it, it was about four inches too short. Stopped right at me, and down again. Hit through the bottom goin' so fast it was smokin'. Up Black Mountain, clean to the top, and back down this way again. Well I watched it see-sawin' a few times, and finally gathered up my coons and that pile of bresh and made it back to the house. Put the flue and stovepipe back and started my fire.

Well, I lived off coon-meat for about a week. Had to burn up all my chairs, and the table, to keep from freezin'. And I'd started burnin' the bedstead and was fryin' the last of my meat when I heard, drip! drip! drip! And there was a little daylight showin' at the top of the windows. So I shoved on the door, mashed the snow back, and got out. Snow was still about eight foot deep. Got my ax and headed for the nearest tree. Got me a good pile of wood in and fixed the fire till my little stove was red-hot.

Had to go fetch some meal and other rations. I was gettin' a little hungry. So I took off for the store at Putney.

I looked over the country and noticed a sort of trough there between the two mountains where that log had been slidin'. I went right down there. Couldn't see that hickory at all. But when I got to the bottom of that trough I looked, and there—still slidin' back and forth just a few inches—was my log. And—don't you know!—with all that see-sawin' that log had worn down to the size of a toothpick. I leaned over and picked it up. Stuck it in my pocket.

You may not believe me, but—I've kept it to this day.—There. Look at it yourself.

Best toothpick I ever had.

Climbing the Ladder

A man was saying in company that he had seen a juggler place a ladder in the open ground upon one end and mount it by passing through the rounds and stand upon the top erect. Another who was present said he had no doubt of it, as he had seen a man who had done the same thing, but with this addition: that when he arrived at the top, he pulled the ladder up after him.

A Long Name

A man who lived close to Whitakers, North Carolina, had such an outlandish name that it took a Frenchman, a German, and two big Indians to pronounce it. It has never been spelled out, but I hear that there is a Yankee who is going to import a machine from Holland just for that purpose.

A Long High Jump

An old-timer in Lewiston was the first Idahoan to go up in a balloon. According to him, the sponsors of the flight could find nobody who would tackle the bag; and after looking it over, the old-timer said he'd go. "All the folks was lily-livered, but I says if a man could ride herd on some of the toughest broncs in Idaho, he hadn't orter be afraid of a contraption like that. So I says, 'I'll go up in the durned thing,' and I did. They had it tied down, but it warn't long before it give a fair to middlun buck and broke the hobble. And there I was, sailun round and round in the sky all by myself. 'Twarn't so bad at first, but after it got dark and I was still a-sailun I got kinda mad. By gum, I had enough and overboard I jumped. The worst thing is that I sunk clean to my knees in the pavement of Portland."

A Bear for Work

Paul Peavy was in town from his logging camp buying supplies when Ted Chelde asked: "What in darnation you feedun so much honey to lumberjacks for? Ain't that pretty fancy feed for them?"

"This honey ain't for them. It's an investment."

"How come?" propounded Ted.

"Well, I make lumberjacks leave their coats in camp and in freezun weather I get more out of them. But it ain't enough. So I got the idea to make my silvertip cub work too. He's crazy about honey and will climb a rainbow to get it. So I strap a pair of broadaxes on his feet, and give him a sniff at a can and then shin up a tree with it. Up comes Annabel, the axes scoring the tree on two sides. Then I lower the can and down he goes, and raise it and up he shins, just hewing the tree as smooth as a whistle. Then to make railroad ties all I gotta do is chop it over and whack it up into lengths."

A Scared Crow

Shotgun Charlie believes in the worth of scarecrows. He told me that for some years he had one that terrified crows throughout Nash County. In fact, it worked so well that one crow brought back the corn it had stolen three days before.

Hoop Snakes

"When I wus a kid of a boy," said Hite, "hoop snakes wus right smart common in these parts. Why, in th' hot months of summer, 'specially in dog-days, a feller would sometimes see two or three of 'em rollin' 'round in that thar holler. See that ol' snag t' th' right o' that pin oak? A feller named Pod Warner wus a-diggin' sprouts thar on th' side of th' hill one day when a hoop snake took its tail in its mouth an' started rollin' toward him. Pod saw it comin' an' jist had time t' jump out'n th' way. It wus comin' hell-bent-fer-'lection, Pod said, an' he had t' jump quick as a ghost when a rooster crows. I guess th' snake had its eyes on Pod, fer when it missed him, it hit slabdab into that thar tree. It rammed its pizen stinger into it, fer th' leaves begin t' fall off an' in two-three months th' tree wus dead.

"At another time," continued Hite, "Aunt Steller Bonham wus pickin' blackberries on a bluff above Clabber Crick. She heerd a noise in th' bresh above her, an' lookin' up saw a hoop snake rollin' straight fer her. Snakes alive, she wus scairt! It wus as big 'round as yer arm an' made a loop th' size of a bar'l hoop. She didn't have time t' git out'n th' way, but throwed up th' bucket she had blackberries in t' keep th' thing frum hittin' her square in th' face. When she swung th' bucket, th' snake dodged an' jist ripped her dress with th' p'int of its tail. Th' ol' woman warshed her dress th' next day an' th' pizen in it turned three tubs o' warsh water plumb green. Hoop snakes is powerful pizen."

The Swollen Hoe Handle

One time, I's choppin' out corn in a new ground, bad weed patch, you know. Man, that bad weeds is hard work, too. So they's a big rattlesnake come wigglin' down through the weed patch and bit my hoe handle and that hoe handle begin swellin' up, you know, and got so big finally, I couldn't carry it. I had to lay it down. And finally it got so I couldn't drag it, and so I rolled it off to the bottom, off of the mountain—we had a cornfield way back in the mountain, a big new ground. And so I took it in. It kept swellin'. I took it to a sawmill and sawed lumber and built me a hog pen, helt twelve hogs. And when I got my hogs all in there and the swellin' begin to go out of the wood—that timber—and there it was. I had bad luck. It squez up and choked all my hogs to death.

The Soft-Soaped Mule

About seventy-five years ago, the Collingswood Lumber Company began to cut timber in the Paupack River Valley marking the boundary between Pike and Wayne counties. Timber was cut in winter and floated downstream at flood stage in spring and summer.

When the first heavy cut of timber was made, the rivermen charged with floating the logs found that the main stream was lost when the river rose to a stage of six or more feet. Instead of floating toward the big sawmill at Wilsonville, Wayne County, the logs drifted all over the forest wherever vagrant streams carried them. Even when rafts were spiked together the stream could not be followed when the oxbow country was reached. Thus too many logs were lost.

Finally, the company rigged up a flat-bottomed boat with a paddle wheel at the the stern propelled by a horse walking a treadmill. The boat made its way upstream and came back towing rafts of logs. The towboat worked all right at flood stage; but when the water receded and the river returned to its natural course, too much time was lost going around the oxbow loops through which the river wound its way down the valley. The worst place on the river was in front of the Schuman farm, where the loops were so close they resembled a bunch of shoestrings folded together.

So a canal was dug across the loops to force the river to flow on a straight course. Then it was found that a horse could not take the hard work on the treadmill. Mules were substituted, but they, too, failed to bear the strain. At length, it was suggested that only a canal mule, inured to long-sustained strains, could fill the bill. After a long search, one was located on a farm near the notch.

It was a big black mule answering to the name of "Old Satan." Old Satan had seen service with Sherman in the Civil War and had put in many years on the Delaware & Hudson Canal. The farmer had obtained it in a trade for a hog one dark night. Probably both traders had been stuck; the hog was one of those famous Pike County razorbacks and the mule lived up to its name. The farmer found Old Satan the blackest, ugliest, most ornery, and least desirable mule in Pike County. Old Satan fought off work and when put into the barn kicked everything to pieces. He would chase the dogs and scare the women and children.

The farmer in desperation was about to shoot Old Satan when one day a remarkable thing happened. The mule was in the yard kicking things around as usual when suddenly he discovered a half barrel of soft soap that the women had made and hidden under a few boards near the kitchen. Old Satan knocked the boards off and drank the soft soap to the last drop.

The soft soap worked a miracle in Old Satan. He now became mild, good-natured, gentle, and quite agreeable to work. He played with the children. The farmer rode him to town, and the women hooked him to the buckboard and drove to church on Sundays. Old Satan was soft-soaped for life.

The tough old mule became a great boon in a country where soap was scarce. One Sunday morning one of the hired hands could not shave because he lacked soap. Then he remembered that after each rain Old Satan broke out in a thick lather. The mule lathered so easily that the boys used to say, "The soft soap is coming out of him." So this hired hand took a cup of warm water, poured it over Satan, worked up a thick lather, and shaved . . .

Can Rats Read?

One time, there was an old man come through the settlement afoot. His clothes was kind of ragged, with a funny-looking hat on his head. So when he went past the old Ragsdale place, that big boy with the buck teeth throwed some wet corncobs at him. The old man seen who was a-throwing them cobs, but he just kept on walking down the road.

When the old man come to Bud Henderson's house, he stopped to get a drink of water. Him and Bud got to talking, and pretty soon Sally Henderson cooked up a good supper, with hot cornbread and fried meat. It was the first victuals the old man had eat that day, and he drunk three cups of coffee. While they was eating, a big rat run across the floor, and Sally says, "The rats is the worst I ever seen." After supper they set out on the porch awhile, and then Bud says there is an extra bed and the old man better stay with them all night. And so he done it.

Next morning, Sally give the old man a fine breakfast, and he says, "You folks sure have treated me right, so I am going to get rid of them rats for you. All you got to do is give me a pencil and a piece of paper." And also, he says, "What is the name of them people down the road where they got a big boy with buck teeth?" Sally says their name is Ragsdale, but they are a kind of mean family, so her and Bud don't have no truck with them. The old man set down and wrote a letter like this:

DEAR MISTER RAT you have been here a long time and wore out your welcome, these folks are fixing to concrete the cellar and build a new corncrib very tight, so you will not get much to eat from now on, and they are going to put out poison besides. You better take all your kinfolks and move over to Ragsdale's place with a red roof only a quarter mile down the road. Because there is lots of corn and a smokehouse full of meat and a big cellar with all kind of vegetables laying around. You will be happy there, and you can live right under the kitchen, as the Ragsdales haven't got no cats, and there is only one dog very old and pretty near blind. This is the truth as you can ask the rats in town because they all know me, and I would not fool you. A FRIEND TO RATS.

He wrapped the letter around a raw potato and stuck it down a hole in the floor. Then he wrote another letter and wrapped it around an ear of corn and throwed it under the barn. And then he wrote another letter and wrapped it around a slice of bacon and put it under the smokehouse. "Well, in three days the rats will all be gone, and they will be better off at Ragsdale's anyhow," he says. "And that big boy with the buck teeth better think twice before he throws some more wet cobs at people." And with that the old man picked up his little satchel and walked on down the road.

Bud and Sally didn't say nothing till the old man was out of sight, and then they had to laugh. Sally says, "Well, I have heard about conjuring rats, but I never seen it done before." And Bud says, "It is all foolishness, because everybody knows rats can't read writing, and them old-timers sure have got some funny notions," he says. Sally just laughed, and she says, "Well, he is a nice old man anyhow, and I'm glad we give him some hot victuals and a bed to sleep in for a change." Bud says he is glad too, and then they never thought no more about it.

It was about a week after that when Sally says, "Bud, have you seen any rats lately?" Bud looked kind of funny, and finally he says, "No, I ain't." So then both of them watched careful, but they never seen no signs of a rat. And then they heard folks talking how the Ragsdales was just eat out of house and home with rats, and they was even jumping on the beds and biting the children of a night. The Ragsdale people tried cats and traps and poison, but it didn't seem to do no good.

Bud and Sally never did talk much about the rat conjure, and Bud still says he don't believe no rat could read them letters. But there ain't no rats at Henderson's to this day, and the Ragsdale place is just a-swarming with 'em. Maybe it is because Bud and Sally always treat everybody right, instead of throwing cobs at old men that come down the road.

The Cat with the Wooden Paw

Jack Storme was the local cooper and blacksmith of Thebes, Illinois. He had a cat that stayed around his shop. The cat was the best mouser in the whole country, Jack said. He kept the shop free of rats and mice. But, one day, the cat got a forepaw cut off. After that, he began to grow poor and thin and didn't take any interest in anything, because he wasn't getting enough to eat.

So, one day, Jack decided to fix him up a wooden paw. He whittled one out with his knife and strapped it on the maimed leg. After that, the cat began to grow sleek and fat again. Jack decided to stay at the shop one night to see how the cat managed it with his wooden paw.

After dark, the cat got down in front of a mouse-hole and waited. Pretty soon a mouse peered out cautiously. Quick as a flash the cat seized it with his good paw and knocked it on the head with his wooden one. In no time, that cat had eighteen mice piled up before the hole.

The Boomer's Hound

THIS TALE IS a favorite railroad yarn. Dogs are particularly loved by the men of the rails, and railroad lore is filled with stories about the courage and loyalty of the canine. A boomer is a drifter, a worker who goes from job to job and knows his way among the engines and the switches. The term dates back to the pioneer days of "boom towns," when workers flooded in from all over to take advantage of the brief and spectacular lives of such places.

A boomer fireman is never long for any one road. Last year, he may have worked for the Frisco, and this year he's heaving black diamonds for the Katy or the Wabash. He travels light and travels far and doesn't let any grass grow under his feet when they get to itching for the greener pastures on the next road of the next division or maybe to hell and gone on the other side of the mountains. He doesn't need furniture and he doesn't need many clothes, and God knows he doesn't need a family or a dog.

When the Boomer pulled into the roadmaster's office looking for a job, there was that sooner hound of his loping after him. That hound would sooner run than eat and he'd sooner eat than fight or do something useful like catching a rabbit. Not that a rabbit would have any more chance than a snowball in hell if the sooner really wanted to nail him, but that crazy hound dog didn't like to do anything but run and he was the fastest thing on four legs.

"I might use you," said the roadmaster. "Can you get a boarding place for the dog?"

"Oh, he goes along with me," said the Boomer. "I raised him from a pup just like a mother or father and he ain't never spent a night or a day or even an hour far away from me. He'd cry like his poor heart would break and raise such a ruckus nobody couldn't sleep, eat or hear themselves think for miles about."

"Well, I don't see how that would work out," said the roadmaster. "It's against the rules of the road to allow a passenger in the cab, man or beast, or in the caboose, and I aim to put you on a freight run, so you can't ship him by express. Besides, he'd get the idea you wasn't nowhere about and pester folks out of their wits with his yipping and yowling. You look like a man that could keep a boiler popping off on an uphill grade, but I just don't see how we could work it if the hound won't listen to reason while you're on your runs."

"Why, he ain't no trouble," said the Boomer. "He just runs alongside, and when I'm on a freight run he chases around a little in the fields to pass the time away."

"That may be so, I do not know;
It sounds so awful queer.
I don't dispute your word at all,
But don't spread that bull in here,"

sang the roadmaster.

"He'll do it without half trying," said the Boomer. "It's a little bit tiresome on him having to travel at such a slow gait, but that sooner would do anything to stay close by me, he loves me that much."

"So spread that on the grass to make it green," said the roadmaster.

"I'll lay my first paycheck against a fin* that he'll be fresh as a daisy and his tongue behind his teeth when we pull into the junction. He'll run around the station a hundred times or so to limber up."

"It's a bet," said the roadmaster.

On the first run, the sooner moved in what was a slow walk for him. He kept looking up into the cab where Boomer was shoveling in the coal.

"He looks worried," said the Boomer. "He thinks the hog law† is going to catch us, we're making such bad time."

The roadmaster was so sore at losing the bet that he transferred the Boomer to a local passenger run and doubled the stakes. The sooner speeded up to a slow trot, but he had to kill a lot of time, at that, not to get too far ahead of the engine.

Then the roadmaster got mad enough to bite off a drawbar. People got to watching the sooner trotting alongside the train and began thinking it must be a mighty slow road. Passengers might just as well walk; they'd get there just as fast. And if you shipped a yearling calf to market, it'd be a bologna bull before it reached the stockyards. Of course, the trains were keeping up their schedules the same as usual, but that's the way it looked to people who saw a no-good, mangy sooner hound beating all the trains without his tongue hanging out an inch or letting out the least little pant.

It was giving the road a black eye, all right. The roadmaster would have fired the Boomer and told him to hit the grit with his sooner

* Five dollar bill
† Rule forbidding excessive overtime

and never come back again, but he was stubborn from the word go and hated worse than anything to own up he was licked.

"I'll fix that sooner," said the roadmaster. "I'll slap the Boomer into the cab of the Cannon Ball, and if anything on four legs can keep up with the fastest thing on wheels I'd admire to see it. That sooner'll be left so far behind it'll take nine dollars to send him a post card."

The word got around that the sooner was going to try to keep up with the Cannon Ball. Farmers left off plowing, hitched up, and drove to the right-of-way to see the sight. It was like a circus day or the county fair. The schools all dismissed the pupils, and not a factory could keep enough men to make a wheel turn.

The roadmaster got right in the cab so that the Boomer couldn't soldier on the job to let the sooner keep up. A clear track for a hundred miles was ordered for the Cannon Ball, and all the switches were spiked down till after that streak of lightning had passed. It took three men to see the Cannon Ball on that run: one to say "There she comes," one to say "There she is," and another to say, "There she goes." You couldn't see a thing for steam, cinders, and smoke, and the rails sang like a violin for a half hour after she'd passed into the next county.

Every valve was popping off and the wheels three feet in the air above the roadbed. The Boomer was so sure the sooner would keep up that he didn't stint the elbow grease; he wore the hinges off the fire door and fifteen pounds of him melted and ran right down into his shoes. He had his shovel whetted to a nub.

The roadmaster stuck his head out of the cab window, and—whoosh!—off went his hat and almost his head. The suction like to have jerked his arms from their sockets as he nailed a-hold of the window seat.

It was all he could do to see, and gravel pinged against his goggles like hailstones, but he let out a whoop of joy.

"THE SOONER! THE SOONER!" he yelled. "He's gone! He's gone for true! Ain't *nowhere* in sight!"

"I can't understand that," hollered the Boomer. "He ain't *never* laid down on me yet. It just ain't like him to lay down on me. Leave me take a peek."

He dropped his shovel and poked out his head. Then he whooped even louder than the roadmaster had.

"He's true blue as they come!" the Boomer yelled. "Got the interests of the company at heart too. He's still with us."

"Where do you get that stuff?" asked the roadmaster. "I don't see him nowhere. I can't see hide nor hair of him."

"We're going so fast half the journal boxes are on fire and melting the axles like hot butter," said the Boomer. "The sooner's running up and down the train hoisting a leg above the boxes. He's doing his level best to put out some of the fires. That dog is true blue as they come and he's the fastest thing on four legs, but he's only using three of them now."

Sam Patch, the Jumping Man

To the Ladies and Gentlemen of
Western New-York and of Upper Canada

All I have to say is, that I arrived at the Falls too late, to give you a specimen of my Jumping Qualities, on the 6th inst.; but on Wednesday, I thought I would venture a small Leap, which I accordingly made, of Eighty Feet, merely to convince those that remained to see me, with what safety and ease I could descend, and that I was the TRUE SAM PATCH, and to show that Some Things could be Done as well as Others; which was denied before I made the Jump.

Having been thus disappointed, the owners of Goat Island have generously granted me the use of it for nothing; so that I may have a chance, from an equally generous public, to obtain some remuneration for my long journey hither, as well as affording me an opportunity of supporting the reputation I have gained, by Aero-Nautical Feats, never before attempted, either in the Old or New World.

I shall, Ladies and Gentlemen, on Saturday next, Oct.

17th, precisely at 3 o'clock, P.M. LEAP at the FALLS OF
NIAGARA, from a height of 120 to 130 feet (being 40 to 50
feet higher than I leapt before), into the eddy below. On my
way down from Buffalo, on the morning of that day, in the
Steam-Boat Niagara, I shall, for the amusement of the Ladies, doff my coat and Spring from the Mast head into the
Niagara River.

SAM PATCH

Buffalo, Oct. 12, 1829.   *Of Passaic Falls, New Jersey.*

The biographical data about Samuel Patch prior to his first public
jumping exploit in 1827 are extremely slight. He spent his early years
in Pawtucket, Rhode Island, where he worked in Samuel Slater's
cotton mill and made running jumps into the Pawtucket River from
nearby roofs, thus earning the plaudits of his townsmen. Moving to
Paterson, New Jersey, still a cotton spinner, Sam eluded the consta-
bles and jumped seventy feet from the highest cliff overlooking the
scenic Passaic Falls to steal the show from Timothy Crane, who was
then pulling the first bridge across the chasm. Exhilarated by the
notoriety he received, Patch took to electrifying crowds in New
Jersey and New York with descents from bridges, until Niagara Falls
provided his crowning conquest.

Apparently plans to blast off a portion of Table Rock, treacher-
ously overhanging the chasm from the Canadian bank, suggested to
Buffalo citizens the idea of securing an additional attraction. They
invited the Jersey jumper to perform, and also decided to send the
shallow-draught schooner *Superior* careening over the falls. (Two
years earlier the unseaworthy brig *Michigan* had floated down the
rapids with an animal crew of bears, foxes, geese, and a buffalo, plus
an effigy of Andrew Jackson, before fascinated thousands.) Patch
accepted, but as the handbill quoted above indicates, he missed the
festival day, and the throngs saw a ship fall and smash, rather than a
man leap and live. On the next day Sam did demonstrate his powers
to a limited audience with a preliminary plunge of some seventy feet
from the lower end of Goat Island. Robbed of his rightful turnout,
however, Patch publicized a second and greater leap for the follow-

ing week. For these exhibitions, the wooded islet splitting the cataract in an uneven half between the American and the Horseshoe Falls provided a logical springboard. Observers congregated on the island and lined the American and Canadian shores. For this second leap the platform on Goat Island stood about two-thirds the elevation of the 160-foot-high neighboring banks, a fearful height when scanned from the depths below.

On a rainy Saturday, Sam boldly climbed the perpendicular ladder to the scaffold, ignoring tearful farewells and protestations from persons at the foot. Before ascending, he shed his shoes and coat and tied a handkerchief about his neck. Atop the ladder, which had been built from four trees spliced together and fastened by ropes running back upon Goat Island, he mounted the narrow, reeling platform. It was barely large enough for a man to sit upon, and for ten minutes he displayed his poise and tested the stand, while the spectators repeatedly cheered. At length he rose upright, took the handkerchief from his neck, tied it about his waist, waved his hand, kissed the American flag which flew over his head, and stepped off steadfastly in the swirling flood. A general cry of "He's dead, he's lost!" swept through the crowd, according to one account; a second reports a benumbed silence, broken only by joyous congratulations when Sam's head burst out of the waters. While handkerchiefs waved and huzzas roared, the Jumping Hero swam briskly to the shore, to inform his first onrushing admirer, "There's no mistake in Sam Patch!" Unanimously the surrounding group exclaimed, "This is the real Sam Patch!" The *Buffalo Republican* commented: "The jump of Patch is the greatest feat of the kind ever effected by man. He may now challenge the universe for a competitor."

Flushed with the publicity of press notices and the public excitement, Sam turned to Rochester and the Genesee Falls for a new conquest. By now the newspapers of the nation were playing up Sam enthusiastically, and his sponsors determined to provide a still greater, climactic feat, by erecting a twenty-five-foot scaffold on the rock's brow to extend the jump to a distance of 125 feet. In the posters Sam announced, with unwitting irony: "HIGHER YET! SAM'S LAST JUMP. SOME THINGS CAN BE DONE AS WELL AS OTHERS. THERE IS NO MISTAKE IN SAM PATCH." Monroe and Ontario counties poured out for the November 13 leap; schooners and coaches ran excursions; betting ran high in the local bars as to the outcome; nearby roofs and windows and both banks swarmed with the curious. But when Sam walked out on the grassy, tree-covered rock that divided the greater and lesser branches of the cataract, at two P.M. (his pet bear was to jump at three), and climbed up to the platform, some spectators thought he staggered and lacked his usual aplomb. Some assert that the jumper was reeling drunk; others stoutly deny that he took more than a glass of brandy to counteract the chilly day. Sam made a brief speech: Napoleon was a great man and conquered nations, Wellington was a greater and conquered Napoleon, but neither could jump the Genesee Falls—that was left for him to do. Then he jumped. But this time the descent lacked its usual arrowy precision. One third of the way down his body began to droop, his arms parted from his sides, he lost command of his body and struck the water obliquely with arms and legs extended. He did not reappear before the horror-stricken assemblage. Dragging for the body proved unsuccessful, perhaps because of pinioning branches on the river bed. Nor was it found until the following March 17, when a farmer broke the ice to water his horses at the mouth of the Genesee near Lake Ontario. The black kerchief was still tied about the waist. An autopsy revealed a ruptured blood vessel and dislocation of both shoulders. The body was buried in a nameless grave and lay long forgotten in the Charlotte cemetery, until it was finally identified by a board head-marker reading, "Here lies Sam Patch; such is Fame." Since the removal of the marker, controversy has arisen as to Sam's real whereabouts.

The High Divers

You ask me why I'm all bunged up this way, going on crutches, both arms busted, and what may still be a fractured skull. The doctor ain't sure about that yet. I'll live, I guess, but I don't know what for.

I can't never be a high diver any more. I'll go to selling razor blades, like as not, and there's plenty doing that already.

Eddie La Breen is to blame for it all. High diving was an easy and high-paying profession before he tried to root me and every other performer out of it. I would go traveling in the summer with a carnival company, and my high dive would be a free feature attraction. The local merchants would kick in for signs to put on my ladder and advertise their goods. Sometimes I'd make a little spiel from the top of the ladder just before I dived off into the tank.

Eddie La Breen called himself "The Human Seal." He bragged that he could dive higher into shallower water than any man alive. I was pretty good myself, being billed as Billie the Dolphin, spectacular and death-defying high diver extraordinary.

I'm doing all right with Miller's Great Exposition Shows, using a 25-foot ladder and diving into a ten-foot tank. Big crowds of people would come from miles around to see me, and not a soul ever seemed dissatisfied until we happen to be playing Omaha on a lot not over ten blocks away from where Eddie La Breen is playing with Barker's World's Fair Shows.

Just when I come up out of the tank and start to take a bow one night, I hear somebody say: "That ain't *nothing*. You ought to see Eddie La Breen over on Farnum Street diving twice as high into water half as deep."

I found out it's so. Eddie has been diving into five feet of water from a fifty-foot ladder, and Mr. Miller threatens to let me go if I can't do as well.

It sure looked high when I got up there and I could feel my nose scraping on the bottom of the tank just as I made the upturn. But I'm no slouch at the high dive myself, and Eddie La Breen ain't going to outdo me if I can help it.

I added the fire act to my dive too, and most of the time I could hardly see where to dive. For the fire act you have a little bit of gasoline pouring into the tank. It stays right on top of the water, and when you fire it, it makes a fearful sight, splashing fire in every direction when you hit the water.

Eddie sends me word that I might as well give up. "I'm going to dive next from a thousand feet into a tank of solid concrete," he says, "and I'll do it while playing the ukulele, eating raw liver, and keeping perfect time. Why, when I was a kid of ten or so I could dive off a silo onto the dew in the grass, bellybuster, and never even grunt when I lit."

He didn't do quite that, but he did enough. He raised his ladder to a hundred feet, and kept only two and a half feet of water in the tank.

I practiced and practiced and got a few bruises, but I cut that depth to two feet and I raised my ladder to a hundred and fifty feet.

By this time, Eddie sent word he was good and mad, and he's going to call himself the Minnow. "You know how a minnow just skitters along on top of a pond," he says. "Well, that's the way I'll light on that tank. From two hundred feet I'll dive into six inches of water and just skim off without hardly making a bubble."

If ever a man practiced hard to make a shallow dive, that was me. I did that minnow dive in four inches of water from a height of 250 feet, lit right on my feet after barely touching the water, and didn't even muss my hair.

When Eddie makes it from 300 feet into three inches, I'm a little put out, but I don't give up. I tell Miller to get me a good heavy bath mat and soak it good all day. First time I hit that bath mat it sort of knocked me dizzy. You know how it is when you have the breath knocked out of you and all you can do is croak like a frog. But I got better and better at it until I hardly puffed at all.

I beat Eddie La Breen fair and square, but he wasn't man enough to admit it or to take it like a man. He showed that he was rotten to the core and treacherous from the word go.

We were playing Sheboygan, Wisconsin, and I had no idea that Eddie was anywhere within miles. I had heard that Barker had told him to pack his keister and get out when I bested him.

When I hit that bath mat that night I thought my time had come. That was six months ago, and look at me now. Still on crutches, and lucky if I ever get off of them.

What happened? Well, sir, I don't know anybody but Eddie who wanted to have done me that dirt. They had soaked my heavy bath mat in water, all day, the same as usual, but they must have let it get out of their sight some time or other, because some one had wrung it out practically dry. That's the way I had it done to me. I heard somebody say later that a man answering to the description of Eddie La Breen had been seen lurking around the show grounds that evening.

And if he didn't do it, who did?

Jack Conroy

Casey at the Bat

It looked extremely rocky for the Mudville nine that day;
The score stood two to four, with but one inning left to play.
So, when Cooney died at second, and Burrows did the same,
A pallor wreathed the features of the patrons of the game.

A straggling few got up to go, leaving there the rest,
With that hope which springs eternal within the human breast.
For they thought: "If only Casey could get a whack at that,"
They'd put even money now, with Casey at the bat.

But Flynn preceded Casey, and likewise so did Blake,
And the former was a pudd'n, and the latter was a fake.
So on that stricken multitude a deathlike silence sat;
For there seemed but little chance of Casey's getting to the bat.

But Flynn let drive a "single," to the wonderment of all.
And the much-despisèd Blakey "tore the cover off the ball."
And when the dust had lifted, and they saw what had occurred,
There was Blakey safe at second, and Flynn a-huggin' third.

Then from the gladdened multitude went up a joyous yell—
It rumbled in the mountaintops, it rattled in the dell;
It struck upon the hillside and rebounded on the flat;
For Casey, mighty Casey, was advancing to the bat.

There was ease in Casey's manner as he stepped into his place,
There was pride in Casey's bearing and a smile on Casey's face;
And when responding to the cheers he lightly doffed his hat,
No stranger in the crowd could doubt 'twas Casey at the bat.

Ten thousand eyes were on him as he rubbed his hands with dirt,
Five thousand tongues applauded when he wiped them on his
    shirt;
Then when the writhing pitcher ground the ball into his hip,
Defiance glanced in Casey's eye, a sneer curled Casey's lip.

And now the leather-covered sphere came hurtling through the
    air,
And Casey stood a-watching it in haughty grandeur there.
Close by the sturdy batsman the ball unheeded sped;
"That ain't my style," said Casey. "Strike one," the umpire said.

From the benches, black with people, there went up a muffled
    roar,
Like the beating of the storm waves on the stern and distant
    shore.
"Kill him! kill the umpire!" shouted someone on the stand;
And it's likely they'd have killed him had not Casey raised his
    hand.

With a smile of Christian charity great Casey's visage shone;
He stilled the rising tumult, he made the game go on;
He signaled to the pitcher, and once more the spheroid flew;
But Casey still ignored it, and the umpire said, "Strike two."

"Fraud!" cried the maddened thousands, and the echo answered
    "Fraud!"
But one scornful look from Casey and the audience was awed;
They saw his face grow stern and cold, they saw his muscles
    strain,
And they knew that Casey wouldn't let the ball go by again.

The sneer is gone from Casey's lips, his teeth are clenched in hate,
He pounds with cruel vengeance his bat upon the plate;
And now the pitcher holds the ball, and now he lets it go,
And now the air is shattered by the force of Casey's blow.

Oh, somewhere in this favored land the sun is shining bright,
The band is playing somewhere, and somewhere hearts are light;
And somewhere men are laughing, and somewhere children shout,
But there is no joy in Mudville—Mighty Casey has struck out.

                                        Ernest Lawrence Thayer

Febold Feboldson,
the Most Inventingest Man

Although the history books have never given him credit, the inventingest man to hit this country was Febold Feboldson. According to Bergstrom Stromberg, his famous great-uncle taught Eli Whitney, Robert Fulton, Alexander Graham Bell, Luther Burbank and Thomas Edison all they knew about inventing—and still had thousands of ideas left over.

Why, Febold could even invent animals. In the Year of the Many Rains, for instance, the weather was so wet that all the chickens in the country were dying of starvation. Their feet just sank into the mud and they mired down, unable to get out and forage eats.

The situation was, to say the least, becoming desperate, but as usual, Febold came to the rescue. He put webbed feet on the chickens, then flattened their bills so that they would be better adapted to probe water or mud while looking for grub. Unthinkingly, the great Swede had invented a new species of fowl. They took to the water and were so satisfied with their new equipment that they would not allow it to be taken off. They even tried to swim and the Indians, amused at the way the fowl kept tipping and going under the water, called them ducks.

Febold was a great person to fret over lost energy. He even worried about his dogs and the energy they wasted by turning around three times before lying down. Little things like that kept him thinking. Febold realized, of course, that this was a hangover from the days when dogs were wild and ranged in country covered with tall grass; the untamed canines had to turn around several times to flatten the grass before they could lie down.

The Swede devised a scheme to utilize this wasted energy. He made soft beds for the dogs on circular treadmills, then told the dogs

long-winded stories of his experiences. Although they were accustomed to leading a dog's life, the animals found that Febold's highly
colored accounts, entertaining at first, soon became repetitious re-
hashes of tales told over and over again. This made the dogs sleepy—
which was just what Febold expected. When they started to lie down,
they turned around several times; this started the treadmill which, in
turn, started the windmill which pumped water for Febold's stock.

Just as the dogs were ready to lie down, the Swede would shout
"Sic 'em!" The dogs woke up immediately and Febold continued his
story. The procedure proved satisfactory for a while and provided
plenty of water in the tanks during the dry weather.

One night, however, Febold started for bed. He was quite sleepy
but on his way upstairs he got to thinking. After three hours, he
suddenly discovered that he was not on the stairs at all but had
inadvertently stepped onto one of the treadmills. He rushed to the
tank to see what had become of all the water he had pumped. To his
dismay, he discovered that the water had run into a small hole in the
ground, then back into the well. The same water had been used over
and over again.

Appalled at this atrocious waste of energy Febold pulled up the
well and threw it away—leaving the water standing there.

Once while passing through a swamp along the south side of the
Dismal River, Febold attempted to light his pipe and caused a terrific
explosion. After much investigation, the Swede determined the
cause: a kind of marsh gas, escaping upward from the swamp, was
highly inflammable.

"Why not utilize the gas for heating purposes?" queried Febold.

He hurried home, gathered up all the buffalo robes he could find,
sewed them together and made a huge cover for the swamp. With the
help of his pet gopher, Lizzie, he dug tiny tunnels from the swamp to
the various tepees in the Dirtyleg Indian village. The gas was then
piped from the marsh to the redskins' wigwams. A little gas was lost
by outside competition when curious moles tried to hook on to the
gas line, but the loss was slight.

Febold even went so far as to freeze a number of gopher holes
during one winter, then dug them up and laid them across the ice on

the Dismal River to supply a suburb of the Dirtyleg village on the north bank. With the first thaw, however, the pipe melted and the Swede decided that the iced gopher holes were not at all practical.

Whenever corn-shucking time rolls around, Bergstrom Stromberg recalls the contest between his great-uncle and Swan Swanson, an obscure ancestor of Stromberg himself on his mother's side.

A shot was fired to start the contest. Febold was driving a pair of Jack Rabbit mules (in those days jack rabbits grew to be nearly as large as mules do nowadays) and was soon in the lead, with Swanson close behind. Febold husked faster and faster, one ear after another flying against the bang-board and into the wagon box. The box began to get warm—and warmer—until the corn began to pop. The popped corn soon filled the wagon and ran out onto the ground. Febold's mules saw the popcorn and, thinking it was snow, began to shiver and shake like a tent-show dancer at the county fair. Soon they were so cold they froze to death! Swanson's team, close behind, also saw the popcorn snow, and dropped dead in their tracks. Febold was adjudged the winner, since he had been in the lead.

Poor Febold! He now had no money, no team, no work! He went home, heartsick. Next morning when he went out where his mules lay dead, the ground was covered with animals—wolves, foxes, bears and skunks. They had been attracted by the dead mules and, coming up close, had seen the drifts of popcorn. They, too, had froze to death.

Well, to make a long story short, Febold got out his hunting knife and began to skin those animals. He was busy until late spring and made more money on the sale of the furs than he would have made farming in five years.

In the meantime, gold had been discovered in California, and many wagon trains headed west were caught in the deep snows that covered Nebraska. Instead of thawing with the coming of spring, the snows remained throughout the summer until the next winter when more snow fell; the phenomenon was called the Year of the Petrified Snow. As a result of Nebraska's inhospitable weather, the '48ers were held up in their gold rush and became '49ers.

At that time Febold was operating an ox train between San Francisco and Kansas City because the snow prevented him from doing anything else. Since he was the only plainsman able to withstand the winter weather that year, the '48ers appealed to him for help. His secret was to load his wagon with sand from Death Valley, California; neither he nor his oxen grew cold because the sands of the desert never lost their heat. He sold this sand to the gold rushers at fifty dollars a bushel. It was really a preposterous price but the frozen prospectors were glad to pay it.

In January, 1849, the prospectors began their westward trek over the snow-covered plains in their prairie schooners. Before they reached the Rockies, however, the jolting of the wagons had scattered the sand and covered every bit of the Petrified Snow. That's the reason, according to Bergstrom Stromberg, who handed down this tale of the fabulous Febold, that the prairies are so all-fired hot in the summertime.

Febold cursed himself twenty times a day for the next twenty years for selling the '48ers that torrid sand. He spent the next twenty years attempting various schemes to moderate the climate. Deciding nothing could be done about Nebraska weather, the Swede went to California. But that's another story.

Gib Morgan and the Whickles

Wherever oilmen gather, whether in an exclusive club or in an engine house in eastern Texas, the chances are that the talk will eventually swing to Gib Morgan and his stories. Oilmen tell me that they have heard the stories in the steamy jungles of India, deep in the Malay country, in the arctic cold of Siberia—wherever oil is found. To the younger generation of oilmen, Morgan is a legend. He has been dead many years, but his amazing tales live and grow and appear to have an astonishing vitality and durability. To us of the older generation, the man was very real. As a youngster I saw and heard him, and believed too many of his salty and fantastic tales.

Gib Morgan was the minstrel of the oil fields. If he had a home, he spent most of his time away from it. He was a fiercely proud old vagabond, a tall, angular individual with buttermilk-blue eyes, a sweeping, grizzled mustache, and a mellow, persuasive voice that helped to give a semblance of verity to the stories he told so vividly. There was something distinctive about him, although he dressed as did most oilmen of the day. Perched jauntily on the side of his head was the inevitable, sand-pumping-splashed, black derby hat. He usually wore a blue flannel shirt, open at the throat. His pants were the jeans worn by all oilmen, and he wore high, laced boots of good leather. Possibly his individuality came from the way he walked and the way he would flip a casual and friendly hand in greeting to a drilling crew as he passed.

We never knew when he was going to visit our little town of Pleasantville in Venango County. Often, of a late afternoon, he would be seen plodding up a dusty road, swinging his arms, chewing intently on a gigantic wad of Spearhead eatin' tobacco, and looking straight ahead. His coming was news. Oil-field workers suddenly found that it was necessary for them to go to town that night. In the bar of the Eagle House there would be a private session limited to about two dozen oilmen. To be invited to be present was the equivalent of a royal command. After Gib had been primed with rye, the session would be ready to start, and the door of the long, narrow barroom would be locked. No one could enter or leave until the session was ended, the last story told, and the final drink downed.

Morgan usually stood at the end of the bar, with a tall water glass of whisky at his elbow. Every time he took a swallow, which was often, the bartender would instantly refill the glass, whereupon Gib would gaze at him reproachfully. Until he had absorbed what he considered the requisite volume of alcohol, he would remain somewhat aloof. A good showman, Morgan knew the value of suspense and used it to advantage. Eventually he'd start talking. Maybe someone would be complaining that the production of a certain well was declining sharply. Gib would look at the man, and a toothy smile would momentarily flash behind the heavy mustache.

"Whickles!" he would say, with a slight cough. That was the kick-off, the traditional signal for someone to ask a leading question designed to launch a story from Morgan.

"What in the world are whickles, Gib?" Sam Wilson or some other oil producer would ask.

Morgan would sneer thinly, gloomily note that his glass had been refilled, and drink most of it. His pale eyes would light up, and his deep, resonant voice could be easily heard.

"Whickles!" he would snort. "Mean to tell you ain't heard about whickles? What manner of oilmen are you? Them whickles is what causes your oil production to go down, gents!"

And then would come the story. Morgan told it slowly, persuasively, with dramatic pauses. When he was spinning his tale, it would be as quiet in the bar as a funeral home.

Before the time of any man present, Gib would begin, bachelor Mont Morrison lived in a little shack at Skunk Hollow. Morrison, a pumper, owned two canaries by which he set great store. The male bird, according to Morgan, was a rather delicate creature named Oscar. The bird had a great fondness for dried-apple pie, a weakness shared by his owner.

One day Morrison, partially overtaken with drink, made a dried-apple pie, but neglected to let the apples first stand in water and expand. He gave Oscar a liberal piece that the bird hungrily gobbled. "Gentlemen, that there bird swole up as big as a eagle and exploded forthwith," Gib Morgan related solemnly. Morrison, fortunately, had not tasted the pie, which was rapidly swelling. He did, however, witness what had happened to Oscar and forthwith decided never to drink again.

The unhappy accident left the other canary, a flighty female named Minnie, in a lonely world that she did not relish. Removed from the solace of drink, Morrison had plenty of time on his hands and vainly tried to console Minnie. She became peckish about her food, sang gloomy songs, and generally brooded. One bright spring day Morrison noted that Minnie seemed to have perked up a bit. She took a bath and preened her feathers. She warbled a few gay bars of music and sat perched with her head on one side, her eyes bright with expectancy. The cage had been hung out in the morning sun; pretty soon Morrison noticed a gigantic bumblebee buzzing around the cage in a most amorous manner. The bee was literally strutting in the air, diving, twisting, floating to a dead stop, and fluttering his wings daintily. To such antics Minnie gave feminine encouragement, singing gay trifles of jigs and reels, dancing up and down on the perch, and even uttering silly sounds of endearment.

It burst upon Morrison that he was witnessing a love affair. It was something that touched his heart, and he decided to further the cause by opening the door of Minnie's cage. She stepped out daintily and tried to fly. Years of confinement severely handicapped her, and the first time she tried to do a power dive, she lost control and struck the ground smartly on her stomach. The big bee alighted and solicitously examined the inert canary; she recovered almost immediately. Presently, the two of them flew away, the bumblebee circling the slow-winged Minnie and still stunting.

"It was a right pretty sight," Morgan related. Every morning the two of them would come back for food. Then, after an absence, they returned one morning with a brood of children.

"Them offspring was whickles, a cross between a canary and a bumblebee, embracin' the worst qualities of both parents. They growed fast, intermarried, had terrific appetites. And tempers! One day Mont brushed one of the youngsters outa his hair a little rough-like. The whickle uttered a sort of a banshee war cry, and ten of his brothers and sisters made for poor Morrison and stang him fore and aft. He swore some stingers were over an inch long. Just before he passed out he hollered for mercy to the parents. He swore that Minnie and her husband was sittin' on the kitchen table, titterin' and eggin' the kids on and takin' great joy in his misery."

Morgan would pause, wipe the long mustache with a graceful gesture, and stare unseeingly across the smoky room. Then his eyes would turn solemnly toward the bar and the filled glass of rye. He would start just a little and look very sad. "Me, I'm a temperate man," he would interpolate. "But when I tell this story, it grieves me and a little rye helps.

"Well, gents, Morrison was badly swole when he woke. He hurt considerable. He felt that the only thing that would cure him was plenty of swigs of likker. He went over to Cash-Up and after he had managed to swaller a quart or so, he started to feel better. He tried to tell the bartender about the whickles and got throwed out for his pains. Hurt his feelin's.

"The whickles and the parents never returned to Morrison's shack. But one day Mont was comin' back from Shamburg with a gallon of applejack. He had partook pretty liberal and after he had sung some duets with himself, he laid down to take himself a little nap. He forgot to put the cork back in the jug, which was a bad mistake. He woke up to the sound of a terrible buzzin', and a sound of singin'. He lay there, quiet as a mouse. He told me that he was afraid to move. The whickles, almost a thousand of them by this time, was engaged in drinkin' up that applejack. They enjoyed it, too. They was even good-natured. They had formed a sort of a singin' society and sung songs, very rowdy ones, too, in a sort of a cross between a canary's voice and the buzzin' of a bumblebee. Off-key, the singin' was very loud and kinda wicked.

"Eventually, they flew off without disturbin' Morrison. It was about this time that wells around Skunk Hollow started to dry up. Producers claimed it was due to a lot of things, but Morrison knew better. He discovered that the whickles had acquired a taste for crude oil. They was a new breed of critters, so it was reasonable that they should find food the easiest way. They was millions of them by this time. One day Morrison saw the whole string of them divin' out of the sky into the lead line of one of the best wells on the Benedict farm. Within a week, that well's production fell off terrible. Morrison, being a sensible feller, jacked up his courage with a little redeye and went off to see old man Benedict. He told him about the whickles and outlined a scheme for capturing them. He suggested that Benedict place a dozen jugs of whisky on the ground around the well. Eventually, the whickles would come out and drink the likker and fall down dead drunk. They could then be captured and destroyed. Did old man Benedict foller his advice? He did not! Instead, he heaved a sucker-rod wrench at poor old Mont and danged near hit him.

"Mont died of a broken heart. I was the only other man he took into his confidence. Me, I'm open-minded. Your oil wells are producin' less and less oil, and you don't do nothin' about it. Whickles is robbin' you blind. If you was smart, you'd put whisky—

rye whisky—in jugs around your ailin' wells. You could go out in the mornin' and find the ground covered with drunken whickles. Yessir!"

No one dared to laugh aloud, but the crowd would smother its laughter in quiet chuckles. One oil producer, we had heard, had taken Morgan's advice and placed three jugs of whisky around a well. When he returned in the morning, all he found was an empty jug and Gib Morgan sound asleep on the ground. Morgan simply stated that he had come out to watch the experiment and had carelessly fallen asleep. He did not, however, explain why the empty jug was cradled in his arms.

Gib's Biggest Rig

Another time he was in Texas he had better luck. It was fitting, Gib thought, though only a coincidence, that the biggest oil rig ever built should be built in the biggest state in the union. It all came about like this.

There was a certain region down in Texas where the Standard rockhounds figured that there was oil under the ground, but they hadn't been able to get to it. They had sent their crack drilling crews and production men down, but the formation above the oil sand was so cavy that they hadn't been able to make a hole. They would start with a twenty-four-inch bit and case with a twenty-two-inch casing. Then they would make a few more feet of hole and would have to set a twenty-inch casing. They would cut a little more ditch and then they would have to case again. And it would go on like that until the casing became too small for the tools to go through, and after all that expense they would have to abandon the hole.

Finally John D. himself called Gib in and showed him the logs of all the wells they had tried to make, and said, "Gib, do you think you can make me a hole down to the oil sand?"

Gib looked at the logs a while and then he said, "John D., if you'll put up the money, I'll put down the hole."

"It's a deal," said John D., and they shook hands on it, but they didn't drink, both being temperance men.

First Gib went over to Pittsburgh to see the Oil Well Supply Company and told them how to make the special tools he wanted, some big tools and some little tools. Then he went to Texas and started putting up the rig.

The derrick covered an acre of ground, and since Gib expected to be there for some time he fixed it up nice. He weatherboarded it on the outside and plastered it on the inside. It was so high that he had it hinged in two places so that he could fold it back to let the moon get by. It took a tool dresser fourteen days to climb to the top to grease the crown pulleys. That is the reason Gib had to hire thirty tool dressers. At any time there would be fourteen going up, fourteen coming down, one on the top and one on the ground. A day's climbing apart he built bunk houses for the men to sleep in. These bunk houses had hot and cold showers and all the modern conveniences.

By the time the derrick was up, the tools began to arrive from Pittsburgh. The biggest string of tools reached to within ten feet of the crown block. The drill stem was twelve feet in diameter. At the first indication of caving, Gib cased the well with thousand-barrel oil tanks riveted together. This reduced the hole to twenty feet. He put on an eighteen-foot bit and made about fifty feet of hole before he had to case again. Down about five hundred feet he had to go to a smaller bit, one about six feet in diameter. At a thousand feet he was using standard tools. At two thousand feet he was using his specially made small tools and casing with one-inch tubing. But he hadn't figured it quite fine enough, for he hadn't got the oil sand when the smallest drill he had wouldn't go through the tubing. But that didn't stump Gib. He brought in the well with a needle and thread.

How Gib Invented Rubber Boots

This was not Gib's first experience with rubber. Fact is that it was Gib that invented rubber boots, which in some respects was a mighty fine thing. But if he could have foreseen all the consequences of his invention, he never would have made it.

It all happened some twenty odd years ago when he was in East India putting down a bunch of wells for the Burmah Oil Company Limited.

When Gib went to the Fiji Islands he knew enough about the country to take along three or four extra pairs of boots for himself and each member of the crew. But it didn't occur to him to do this when he went to India. He had always heard that India was the seat of an ancient and mature civilization, and he naturally assumed that in a civilized country one would be able to buy shoes wherever he went. When he got there, however, he noticed that all the natives who didn't wear sandals were barefooted; and when his boots began to wear out, he started looking for a new pair. He went to every store for a hundred miles around, but not one pair of boots or shoes of any kind could he find for sale. He and his men patched up their boots the best they could. They cut off pieces of belting for soles, but the uppers were getting more and more ragged and they saw that it wouldn't be long until they would be barefooted like the natives. The men were getting madder and madder and were threatening to quit and go back to God's country where a man could buy a pair of Wisconsin boots if he had the money.

Gib saw that something had to be done if the work was to go on, so he studied and studied and after a while he hit upon a solution so simple that he wondered why he had not thought of it before—especially since he was right in the middle of the rubber country where the natives were bringing in gum from the forests every day.

First he got some pure para gum. Then he took off his boots, that is as much of his boots as was left, which was just barely enough to hang to his feet, and covered his socks with a layer of rubber, making the soles especially thick. When he got them done he had the other men take off their boots, that is what was left of them, and he covered their socks in the same way.

In some ways the new boots were better than leather, especially when the rainy season came. The men were pleased and went about their work with a new will and cut more ditch per day than they had ever done before.

Then just as everybody was feeling happy a most unfortunate accident occurred. One day Gib's tool dresser climbed the derrick to grease the crown pulleys. Gib never did know how it came about, for he was a good workman and had never done anything like that before, but for some reason he fell off. He hit the ground rubber boots first and bounced up twice as high as the derrick. When he hit the ground the second time, he bounced out of sight and didn't come down for two hours. When he went up the third time, he didn't come down for two days. Gib got to figuring, and he figured it out that if he went up again, he wouldn't come down in less than twenty-four days, and Gib knew that no man could live for twenty-four days without food or drink. So as much as he hated to do it, Gib had to shoot him to keep him from starving to death.

How Gib Saved His Tool Dresser

If, however, Gib had then known some of the things he later learned when he was drilling in the big pasture country of West Texas he could have saved the poor toolie's life and himself all the regret he felt every time he got to thinking about having invented rubber boots.

Fact is he was so cut up about the tool dresser that when he got back to the United States, he didn't feel like taking out a patent on his invention. If he had he would have been a rich man, for it wasn't long before rubber boots began to appear in all the oil fields of the United States. Gib remembered the first pair ever seen in the Bradford area. He was drilling there at the time, and one midnight his tool dresser came on tour with a pair on. It was raining and the ground was muddy all around the rig. About two o'clock in the morning it began to freeze, and by daylight the derrick was a cone of ice and the ground was as hard as pavement. The crown pulley got to squeaking and the toolie said he would go up and grease it. Gib told him to be careful and he said he would. He greased the pulley all right but on his way down he slipped and fell. He began bouncing just as the toolie in India had done and was soon out of sight.

Gib cut the bailer loose, tied a hondo in the sand line, and made a loop just as he had seen the cowboys do in Texas. When the tool dresser came down and started up again, Gib lassoed him around the neck, threw in the clutch and reeled him in. The man was forever grateful to him for saving him from a horrible death.

CHAPTER 13

Paul Bunyan
and
His World

"Why the Great Lakes Have No Whales"

*"He was the king pin of 'em all,
the greatest logger in the land."*
—The American Lumberman

IMAGINE SOMEONE BIGGER than Pecos Bill with his boots on, smarter than Febold Feboldson, tougher than Mike Fink, funnier than Gib Morgan—he is Paul Bunyan, king of the lumberjacks. He cleared a continent from Maine to the Pacific, and wherever you hear the sound of a saw or a deep voice calling, "Timber!" you might find Paul nearby. At least that is what they say.

Bunyan may have been born of the legends that came out of the timber drives in French Canada or Michigan, but there is no real evidence of it. His real birthplace appears to be the creative mind of a young advertising writer for the Red River Lumber Company in Minnesota named W. B. Laughead. Out of an assortment of logging lore and tales with which he was familiar, Laughead fashioned the first mighty muscles of Paul and his friends in a little booklet given to customers. No one remembers if Paul helped the sales (the original intention, of course) but he grew, quick as a twig-snap, into an American legend. He suited a country that put a premium on size, humor, strength, and zest, and American ingenuity wasted little time expanding his world. What a contrast Paul Bunyan is to the mythical giants of other places. Would Hercules or Thor make us laugh so?

Look at some of his friends: Babe, his blue ox, who was so strong she could be hitched to forty miles of winding road and pull it straight and true; Johnny Inkslinger, Paul's tireless accountant, who went through nine barrels of ink a day keeping the logging records in order. There was Ole, the blacksmith, who had a special iron mine on Lake Superior and kept it going twenty-four hours a day just to keep Babe shod. The camp cook, Slim, made flapjacks for the crew's breakfast on a grill so big it had to be kept greased by seven boys skating over it with hams strapped to their feet. His dining room had tables so long that waiters sent down to the other end often never came back, though their grandchildren sometimes did.

Paul's loggers like to tell of the time Ole and Slim both arrived in camp for the first time. Paul was in a hurry, and without even looking up from his desk (this was before Johnny Inkslinger and Paul were having a terrible time with figuring out his payroll), he ordered Ole the blacksmith to the kitchen and Slim the cook to the forge. Neither man wanted to argue with their new boss, so they each went where they were told. Poor Paul didn't know of his mistake until Ole's biscuits arrived at the table so hard that the loggers cracked their teeth. As for Ole, he was soaking Babe's sore hoof in a tub of oatmeal that smelled so good the whole camp was hungry. Paul realized his mistake and, to everyone's relief, swapped them into their proper jobs.

The old-time logger is gone now, the logging camps are vine-wild and empty. No one knows for certain what happened to Paul Bunyan. They say that Babe died from eating too many flapjacks on a hot summer day, and some claim they heard Paul was in Alaska. You can bet that he has gone to a place where the forests are thick and the axes sharp. It really doesn't matter where he is, because, as you will see in the following pages, he has left enough of himself behind to keep us laughing.

America has an exuberant folklore, a tradition of wit that possesses the rare capacity to reinvent itself over and over. Bunyan's world came from the same imagination that spawned the cowboy humor, the lies of Jim Bridger, and the countless whoppers and tall tales that have filled this book. Old Paul is a suitable finale to the collection. He is an American creation, blood and bone made from a marvelous spirit that shall endure forever and ever.

Paul Bunyan's Birth

If what they say is true, Paul Bunyan was born down in Maine. And he must have been a pretty husky baby, too, just like you'd expect him to be, from knowin' him afterwards.

When he was only three weeks old he rolled around so much in his sleep that he knocked down four square miles of standin' timber and the government got after his folks and told 'em they'd have to move him away.

So then they got some timbers together and made a floatin' cradle for Paul and anchored it off Eastport. But every time Paul rocked in his cradle, if he rocked shoreward, it made such a swell it came near drownin' out all the villages on the coast of Maine. The waves was so high Nova Scotia came pretty near becomin' an island instead of a peninsula.

That wouldn't do, of course, and the government got after 'em again and told 'em they'd have to do somethin' about it. They'd have to move him out of there and put him somewheres else, they was told. So they figured they'd better take him home again and keep him in the house for a spell.

But it happened Paul was asleep in his cradle when they went to get him. They had to send for the British Navy, and it took seven hours of bombardin' to wake him up. Then, when Paul stepped out of his cradle, it made such a swell it caused a seventy-five foot tide in the Bay of Fundy. Several villages were swept away, and seven of the invincible English warships were sunk to the bottom of the sea.

Well, Paul got out of his cradle then, and that saved Nova Scotia from becomin' an island, but the tides in the Bay of Fundy are just as high as they ever were.

So I guess the old folks must have had their hands full with him, all right. And I ought to say, the King of England sent over and confiscated the timbers in Paul's cradle and built seven new warships to take the place of the ones he'd lost.

When Paul was only seven months old, he sawed off the legs from under his dad's bed one night. The old man noticed when he woke up in the mornin' that his bed seemed considerable lower than it used to be, so he got up and investigated. Sure enough, there were the legs all sawed off from under it and the pieces layin' out on the floor.

Then he remembered he'd felt somethin' the night before, but he'd thought he must be dreamin'—the way you dream that you're fallin' down sometimes when you first go off to sleep. He looked around to see who could have done it and there was Paul layin' there sound asleep with his dad's cross-cut saw still held tight in his fist and smilin' in his sleep as pretty as anythin'.

He called his wife, and when she came in he said to her, "Did you feel anythin' in the night?"

"No," she said. "Is anythin' wrong?"

"Well, just look here," he said. And he showed her the four-by-eights layin' there on the floor and the saw in their kid's hand.

"I didn't light the lamp when I went to get up this mornin'," she said, "and I guess I didn't notice it."

"Well, he's done it, anyway," said the old man. "I'll bet that boy of ours is goin' to be a great logger someday. If he lives to grow up, he's goin' to do some great loggin' by and by, you just see—a whole lot bigger than any of the men around here have ever done."

And they was right, all right. There ain't never been loggin' before nor since like Paul Bunyan done.

Babe, Paul Bunyan's Blue Ox

Paul Bunyan couldn't of done all the great loggin' he did if it hadn't been for Babe the Blue Ox. I believe I mentioned helpin' to take care of him for a couple of months when I first come to camp, and then I helped measure him once afterwards for a new yoke Ole had to make for him. He'd broke the one he had when Paul was doin' an extra quick job haulin' lumber for some millmen down in Muskegon one summer, and Ole had to make him a new one right away and so we had to take Babe's measurements.

I've forgot most of the other figgurs, but I remember he measured forty-two axhandles between the eyes—and a tobacco box—you could easy fit in a Star tobacco box after the last axhandle. That tobacco box was lost and we couldn't never take the measurements again, but I remember that's what it was. And he weighed accordin'. Though he never was weighed that I know of, for there never was any scales made that would of been big enough.

Paul told Ole he might as well make him a new log chain too while he was at it—they generally never lasted no more'n about two months anyway, the way Babe pulled on 'em—and so we measured him up for the chain too. It generally took about four carloads of iron every time he had to have a new one.

Babe was so long in the body, Paul used to have to carry a pair of field-glasses around with him so as he could see what he was doin' with his hind feet.

One time Babe kicked one of the straw bosses in the head, so his brains all run out, but the cook happened to be handy and he filled the hole up with hotcake batter and plastered it together again and he was just as good as ever. And right now, if I'm not mistaken, that boss is runnin' camp for the Bigham Loggin' Company of Virginia, Minnesota.

Babe was so big that every time they shod him they had to open up a new iron mine on Lake Superior, and one time when Ole the Blacksmith carried one of his shoes a mile and a half he sunk a foot and half in solid rock at every step.

His color was blue—a fine, pretty, deep blue—and that's why he was called the Blue Ox—when you looked up at him the air even looked blue all around him. His nose was pretty near all black, but red on the inside, of course, and he had big white horns, curly on the upper section—about the upper third—and kind of darkish brown at the tip, and then the rest of him was all that same deep blue.

He didn't use to be always that blue color though. He was white when he was a calf. But he turned blue standin' out in the field for six days the first winter of the Blue Snow, and he never got white again. Winter and summer he was always the same, except probly in July— somewheres about the Fourth—he might maybe've been a shade lighter then.

I've heard some of the old loggers say that Paul brought him from

Canada when he was a little calf a few days old—carried him across Lake Champlain in a sack so he wouldn't have to pay duty on him. But I'm thinkin' he must of been a mighty few days old at the time or Paul couldn't of done it, for he must of grown pretty fast when he got started, to grow to the size he did. And then besides there's them that says Paul never had him at all when he was a little fellow like that, but that he was a pretty fair sized calf when Paul got him. A fellow by the name of O'Regan down near Detroit is supposed to of had him first. O'Regan didn't have no more'n about forty acres or so under cultivation cleared on his farm and naturally that wasn't near enough to raise feed for Babe, and so he's supposed to of sold him the year of the Short Oats to Paul Bunyan. I don't know exactly. It's all before my time. When I went to work for Paul, and all the time I knowed him, the Ox was full grown.

Babe was as strong as the breath of a tote-teamster, Paul always said, and he could haul a whole section of timber with him at a time —Babe'd walk right off with it—the entire six hundred forty acres at one drag, and haul it down to the landin' and dump it in. That's why there ain't no section thirty-seven no more. Six trips a day six days a week just cleaned up a township, and the last load they never bothered to haul back Saturday night, but left it lay on the landin' to float away in the spring, and that's why there quit bein' section 37's, and you never see 'em on the maps no more.

The only time I ever saw Babe on a job that seemed to nearly stump him—but that sure did look like it was goin' to for awhile, though—durin' all the time I was with Paul was one time in Wisconsin, down on the St. Croix. And that was when he used him to pull the crooks out of eighteen miles of loggin' road; that come pretty near bein' more'n the Ox could handle. For generally anything that had two ends to it Babe could walk off with like nothin'.

But that road of all the crooked roads I ever see—and I've seen a good many in my day—was of all of 'em the crookedest, and it's no wonder it was pretty near too much for Babe. You won't believe me when I tell you, but it's the truth, that in that stretch of eighteen miles that road doubled back on itself no less than sixteen times, and made four figure 8's, nine 3's, and four S's, yes, and one each of pretty near every other letter in the alphabet.

Of course the trouble with that road was, there was too much of it, and it didn't know what to do with itself, and so it's no wonder it got into mischief.

You'd be walkin' along it, all unsuspectin', and here of a sudden you'd see a coil of it layin' behind a tree, that you never knowed was there, and layin' there lookin' like it was ready to spring at you. The teamsters met themselves comin' back so many times while drivin' over it, that it begun to get on their nerves and we come near havin' a crazy-house in camp there. And so Paul made up his mind that that there road was goin' to be straightened out right then and there, and he went after it accordin'.

What he done was, he went out and told Bill to bring up the Blue Ox right away, and hitch him to the near end of the road.

Then he went up and spoke somethin' kind of low to Babe, and then afterwards he went out kind of to one side himself, and Babe laid hold, and then is the time it come pretty near breakin' the Ox in two, like I said.

"Come on, Babe! Co-ome on, Ba-abe!" says Paul, and the Ox lays hold and pulls to the last ounce of him. If I live to be a hundred years old I never hope to see an ox pull like that again. His hind legs laid straight out behind him nearly, and his belly was almost down touchin' the ground.

It was one beeg job, as the Frenchmen would of said. And when the crooks finally was all out of that there piece of road, there was enough of it to lay around a round lake we skidded logs into that winter, and then there was enough left in the place where it'd been at first to reach from one end to the other.

I've always been glad I saw Babe on that pull, for it's the greatest thing I ever saw him do—in its way, anyway.

Bill, that took care of the Blue Ox, generally went by the name of Brimstone Bill at camp and the reason was because he got to be so awfully red-hot tempered. But I never blamed him, though. Havin' that Ox to take care of was enough to make a sinner out of the best fellow that ever lived. Of all the scrapin' and haulin' you'd have to do to keep him lookin' anywheres near respectable even, no one would ever think.

And the way he ate—it took two men just to pick the balin' wire out of his teeth at mealtimes. Four ton of grain wasn't nothin' for Babe to get away with at a single meal, and for the hay—I can't mention quantities, but I know they said at first, before he got Windy Knight onto cuttin' it up for nails to use in puttin' on the cook-house roof, Paul used to have to move the camp every two weeks to get away from the mess of haywire that got collected where Babe ate his dinner. And as for cleanin' the barn and haulin' the manure away—

I remember one night in our bunkhouse as plain as if it'd been yesterday. I can see it all again just like it was then. That was one time afterwards, when we was loggin' down in Wisconsin.

There was a new fellow just come to camp that day, a kind of college fellow that'd come to the woods for his health, and we was all sittin' around the stove that night spinnin' yarns like we almost always done of an evenin' while our socks was dryin'. I was over on one end, and to each side of me was Joe Stiles, and Pat O'Henry—it's funny how I remember it all—and a fellow by the name of Horn, and Big Gus, and a number of others that I don't recollect now, and over on the other end opposite me was Brimstone Bill, and up by me was this new fellow, but kind of a little to the side.

Well, quite a number of stories had been told, and some of 'em had been about the Blue Ox and different experiences men'd had with him different times and how the manure used to pile up, and pretty soon that there college chap begun to tell a story he said it reminded him of—one of them there old ancient Greek stories, he said it was, about Herukles cleanin' the Augaen stables, that was one of twelve other hard jobs he'd been set to do by the king he was workin' for at the time, to get his daughter or somethin' like that. He was goin' at it kind of fancy, describin' how the stables hadn't been cleaned for some time, and what a condition they was in as a consequence, and what a strong man Herukles was, and how he adopted the plan of turnin' the river right through the stables and so washin' the manure away that way, and goin' on describin' how it was all done. And how the water come through and floated the manure all up on top of the river, and how there was enough of it to spread over a whole valley, and then how the manure rolled up in waves again in the river when it got to where it was swifter—and it was a pretty good story and he was quite a talker too, that young fellow was, and he had all the men listenin' to him.

Well, all the time old Brimstone Bill he sat there takin' it all in, and I could see by the way his jaw was workin' on his tobacco that he was gettin' pretty riled. Everythin' had been quiet while the young fellow was tellin' the story, and some of us was smokin', some of us enjoyin' a little fresh Star or Peerless maybe and spittin' in the sandbox occasionally which was gettin' pretty wet by this time, and there wasn't no sound at all except the occasional sizzle when somebody hit the stove, or the movin' of a bench when somebody's foot or sock would get too near the fire, and the man's voice goin' along describin' about this Herukles and how great he was and how fine the stables looked when he got through with 'em, when all at once Brimstone Bill he busted right into him:

"You shut your blamed mouth about that Herik Lees of yourn," he says. "I guess if your Herik Lees had had the job I've got for a few days, he wouldn't of done it so easy or talked so smart, you young Smart Alec, you—" and then a long string of 'em the way Bill could roll 'em off when he got mad—I never heard any much better'n him —they said he could keep goin' for a good half hour and never repeat the same word twict—but I wouldn't give much for a lumberjack who couldn't roll off a few dozen straight—specially if he's worked with cattle—and all the time he was gettin' madder'n madder till he was fairly sizzlin' he was so mad. "I guess if that Mr. Lees had had Babe to take care of he wouldn't of done it so easy. Tell him he can trade jobs with me for a spell if he wants to, and see how he likes it. I guess if he'd of had to use his back on them one hundred and fifty jacks to jack up the barn the way I got to do he wouldn't of had enough strength left in him to brag so much about it. I just got through raisin' it another sixty foot this afternoon. When this job started we was workin' on the level, and now already Babe's barn is up sixteen hundred foot. I'd like to see the river that could wash that pile of manure away, and you can just tell that Herik Lees to come on and try it if he wants to. And if he can't, why then you can just shut up about it. I've walked the old Ox and cleaned 'im and doctored 'im and rubbed 'im ever since he was first invented, and I know what it is, and I ain't goin' to sit here and let you tell me about any Mr. Lees or any other blankety blank liar that don't know what he's talkin' about tellin' about cleanin' barns—not if I know it." And at it he goes again blankety blank blank all the way out through the door, and slams it behind him so the whole bunkhouse shook, and the stranger he sits there and don't know hardly what to make of it. Till I kind of explained to him afterwards before we turned in, and we all, the rest of 'em too, told him not to mind about Bill, for he couldn't hardly help it. After he'd been in camp a few days he'd know. You couldn't hardly blame Bill for bein' aggravated—used to be a real good-natured man, and he wasn't so bad even that time I was helpin' him, but the Ox was too much for any man, no matter who.

Heavy-Timbered Land

"Is the land well timbered?" inquired a person of a Wolverine who was offering a tract of land for sale. "It is a most almighty piece of land, and so heavy timbered that a hummingbird could not fly through it," replied the vender. "As I was passing upon the road alongside of it the other evening, I heard a loud cracking and crashing in the trees, so I looked to see what it was, and I'm darned if it were not the moon trying to get through the branches, but 'twas so tarnation thick she couldn't do it, so down she went, and I had to go home in the dark."

Why the Great Lakes Have No Whales

The weather was charging in a column of clouds. This was evident to the boss logger as he approached Saginaw Bay. Here the clouds thinned toward the eastern horizon. More light filtered through, and the raindrops ran. The waters of the bay itself were unthickened. Yet enough mud had poured in from the big river to prove that it was not a disagreeable element for whales. The whole host of bucks disported frolicsomely as Babe the Blue Ox played pitch and fetch with them, showing that the mud rain had not dampened their spirits in the least.

"I knowed it," said Paul triumphantly to himself. "The deep-water kin of carps, that's what whales are. And they'll tame to the halter just as easy as carps do, that's what I'll bet, by the old hospitality of the great fish of Jonah!"

Hope surged on in the boss logger's heart as he watched Babe swing a pine tree in his jaws and pitch it far over the bay. The buck whales spouted and leaped under the arc of the flying pine, butting each other with thunderous thuds, their eyes shining with eagerness and excitement. None of the other whales displayed resentment or envy when the victor in the race fetched the tree back to Babe to pitch again.

"Just as kind and friendly as they were in Jonah's time, whales are," Paul Bunyan thought on, his sublime idea striking deeper than ever in his mind. "Let me handle 'em right, and they'll take to log driving like they were born to it."

It was not yet the time for whale-taming, however. This first day had to be devoted to preparations. Skirting the shore until the bank of Round River was reached, Paul then unshouldered the great net and stretched it across the mouth of the bay. Now he had a stout whale-pen, from which there could be no escape. The inspired boss logger then spent the rest of the day working the leather from the stores into enormous bridles and saddle girths, and in hewing pines into the form of pack-saddle crosstrees. At nightfall he counted his sets and then took a census of the bucks in his impromptu whale-pen.

"One outfit apiece, and fifty-nine left over for extras," concluded the boss logger, with a sigh of satisfaction. "Tomorrow I start to tame 'em down and break 'em in."

He called Babe, who was yet unwearied from the long day of pitching pines a mile. The buck whales now noticed the logger. They observed him with suspicion and backed timidly from the shore. But Paul Bunyan was sure that he could lull all their doubts. Even now the whales saw that their playmate trusted him implicitly. This was already a strong point in his favor. In the camp stores was stuff which should entirely win their trust. Paul thanked his lucky stars for Snoose Mountain. It was his sagacious surmise that the magic ore would be a treat for whales.

"The Big Swede," reasoned Paul, "is a fish-eater and a snoose-lover. Whales also eat fish. Ergo, whales should also love snoose. The Blue Ox, on the other hand, is herbivorous, and snoose is not native to his nature. Yet he enjoys playing with whales even as he does with Hels. All in all, I vow that these whales here are more like a Swede than an ox. They'll be eating out of my hand tomorrow."

With that botanical boast, Paul Bunyan clucked at Babe. Hero and ox vanished in the deep shadows of the thick clouds up river. The buck whales wallowed and drowsed, waiting for the murky morning to bring their playfellow again.

Again the sun had risen unseen. Paul Bunyan labored to break whales to the bridle and pack-saddle. His method had been thought out shrewdly during the night. In the taming he must soften firmness with kindness, and in the breaking he must toughen kindness with firmness again. Softly, shrewdly, firmly, kindly, toughly, he proceeded from buck to buck, day after day, ignoring the downpour from the apparently limitless reserves of mud clouds, tempering each of the friendly-spirited mammals to his purpose.

For kindness Paul would woo one of the shy and suspicious creatures with a hogshead of snoose, holding it out betwixt a thumb and forefinger, and coaxing in a fine tone.

"Come on, buck. Come, boy, now," Paul would wheedle, his voice murmuring as gently through his beard as a spring breeze through green grass. "Come, boy. Co'! Co'! Hopsy daisy! There's the whale. Co', lad. Come, boy. Wrap your lips around this snoose here. There's a dozy lad! That's being a whale, buck!"

Slowly and gingerly the shy young buck whale would swim toward the ingratiating logger; halting now and again, wriggling his flukes, hoisting his snout above the water and cocking one questioning eye at Paul Bunyan; then the whale would get one salty and peppery sniff of the powerful panacea; and his tongue would loll out, fairly streaming with his hunger for the barreled hundredweight of the rarest delicacy known to whales and Swedes. His mouth watering more and more, the buck whale would edge closer, on and on, and finally he would cast off all restraint and boldly leap to grab the dainty with one snap of his jaws.

As the whale snapped, a bridle would be slipped like lightning over his head, and a pine-tree bit would be thrust between his snapping jaws. But now this mattered nothing to the buck. For an hour he would be quivering only from the ravishing emotions that coursed from the hundred pounds of snoose wadded in his cheek. Paul Bunyan's sagacity had reasoned aright. The whales and the Big Swede were brothers under their hides.

At last all the buck whales were wooed and won by the kindness of Paul Bunyan. Now he needed to call firmness into play. Time pressed. Day followed day as bee follows bee in hiving-time. Steadily the black battalions of the weather rolled on. And just as steadily the Big Muddy thickened. Back in camp the shanty boys were once more reverting to a state of human nature. If the weather won, they might never be fit for logging again. So Paul Bunyan hastened.

In his haste he was sometimes harsh with the whales. More than one felt the lash of the whale whip when he reared rebelliously under the trees of the pack-saddle or balked against the pull of the bridle reins, his eyes glittering stubbornly from the shadows of the blinders. Then the lash would fall, and the whale would be forced into sullen submission. Most of the punished bucks could be mollified with snoose. Only a few were natural outlaws and trouble-makers, remaining sullen and stubborn to the end.

Eventually every whale was at least outwardly tractable. Paul Bunyan, with a sigh of weariness and relief, tied his new work-whales together and started up river for the rollways.

The boss logger tramped the river trail, a rope woven and spliced from young pine trees swinging from his hands. At the other end of the rope the most snoose-loving and kind-tempered bucks led the herd. They swam with laborious energy against the current of mud, the less tractable bucks following in fair order. The outlaws were kept in line by Babe, who would dash into the river and snap at the flukes of any buck who tried to start a stampede. The Blue Ox was the playfellow of whales no longer. He was all business when it came to getting out the logs. So discipline was maintained. By nightfall the whales were all tethered up river from the rollways.

Babe remained on watch. Paul Bunyan retired for a bit of rest in his private hill. The drive should start at dawn.

An hour before the time for dawnbreak the shanty boys heard the Big Feller's voice rolling through the shadows.

"Roll out or roll up! It's down the river, men!"

Every jack grumbled from his blankets as he heard the old driving call. In each shanty the embers on the open camboose fireplace glowed a deep red. Not a ray from the sky touched the square smoke-hole in the roof. The drops of mud rain spattered down, hissing on the embers as they baked dry.

"The Big Feller's waited too long," the jacks complained. "It'll simply be bog and sink with the logs now. This here's one spring he won't make a drive. Ol' Paul seems to be losin' his holt."

Paul Bunyan smiled grimly through his beard as he heard the growling and grumbling from the shanties. He was entirely tolerant of it all. It had been a miserable wait. The weather had to bear all the blame. The men would be his bully jacks again as soon as they learned what a famous drive was in store. Just as soon as they saw that they were to ride and drive whales this morning, the men would realize that everything had indeed come out in the wash.

Paul Bunyan let the news wait. The jacks were still growling and grumbling as they started for the rollways in the dim light of dawn.

This was the sorriest-looking gang of woodsmen that ever marched a river trail. Every jack was mud-caked, from the tassel of his cap to the spikes of his boots. Mackinaws were stiff and drab. All beards were stiff and black. The men moved in a shambling march, now and again breaking into a goosestep to shake the mud from their boots. They dragged their peaveys, their shoulders slumped, their eyes fixed in dull, dismal stares at the muddy trail.

Paul Bunyan marched in the lead. His head was up, his cap seeming to touch the lowering clouds. Beside him labored Johnny Inkslinger, the logarithms which he used in scaling logs shielded by a vast umbrella attached to his figuring pencil. Hels Helson tramped blindly, entirely occupied with the gluey ball of snoose and mud that yet persisted in clinging to one or the other of his hands. From up the river sounded an eager moo of welcome.

To the right of the trail the pines wearily dripped and plopped from the mud rain pouring ever and anon from the sky. Their black boughs sagged, too burdened to stir in the hardest wind. Mud puddles spotted the forest floor. The creeks gurgled with thick, heaving floods. The Big Muddy oozed on in a sluggish current, its body soggy and dark. The clouds rolled dolorously.

Paul Bunyan led the march past the rollways. When he called a halt, his men were still slumped and staring dismally at the trail. They looked up sullenly as the boss logger roared:

"Seventeen peavey men to each rollway there! All others take to the whales! One jack to a buck! Mount whales, men! For the first time in history we're driving logs down a mud river! For the first time in botany we're driving logs with whales! Boots and saddles and charge, by the four hossback riders of the old Apocalipsy!"

For the second time this morning the boss logger of the North Woods smiled through his beard at his shanty boys. This time it was not a grim smile, but proud and fond. Here in the grand old Saginaw timber country the men had grown to be true jacks at heart. They were showing it now. Give them something they could get a grip on, and all would keep the faith.

Certainly there was nothing bigger for the jacks to get a grip on than whales. And how they were taking hold! At first they were smitten blank with amazement at seeing a huge herd of whales tethered along the river bank, each one humped under a pack-saddle, champing a bit, and staring out from bridle blinders. But all the jacks quickly recovered. Their hearts thumped and the hair on their chests stiffened valiantly as the Big Feller roared them on:

"Mount whales, men! Ride 'em handsome and high!"

Forgetting fears and doubts and all other particles of human nature, the jacks swarmed down the river banks, picked mounts, and swung boldly up. Some trouble ensued. Here an outlaw took the bit in his teeth and charged off in a runaway down river, his rider vainly tugging at the reins, until Babe floundered out, his jaws snapping as he herded the outlaw back into line. There another outlaw lunged, bucking blindly up river, heaving his rider in convulsive jumps, until the lash of Paul Bunyan's whale whip quoiled him down. Several such scenes were enacted in the river of mud.

But at last the columns were formed in good order. Hogsheads of snoose were passed round. The whales settled down. Even the outlaws munched in apparent resignation. Atop his mount every proud jack stared at his neighbor with shining eyes. And now this yell rolled along the river:

"You can't stop the Big Feller from pulling off a spring drive! Not even a mud rain can beat him, you betcher!"

The worst was indeed over. The only other threat of trouble was from a troop of calves which had followed the herd up from the whale-pen. The calves found the Big Swede standing knee-deep in the stream, still addled over his snoose and mud ball. The calves decided to play leapfrog with Hels, so they charged his legs and knocked him down. Then they discovered that by butting him in the ribs they could tickle him into convulsions. Hels rolled and laughed helplessly, downing barrels of mud every time he opened his cavernous mouth, until Paul tossed some snoose downstream. The calves rushed away to chase snoose, and Hels was saved. In the turmoil he had wiped the perplexing sticky ball on his shirt, so now he was free of it and ready to break out the rollways.

Hels Helson stood at ready where the mud river surged along the rollways. Johnny Inkslinger opened his logarithms, his umbrella pencil shedding the drops of mud rain. The peavey men poised their tools. The first whale, a huge, docile buck, was halted in place for loading.

"Timber!" roared Paul Bunyan. "Let 'er roll!"

The river roared back at him as the log banks broke. The peavey men swarmed the heaving slopes of tumbling logs like grasshoppers. Down at the bottom the Big Swede scooped the timbers in his cleaned paws and stacked them high in the pack-saddle trees, binding the tiers. Above the back of each whale towered a pyramid of logs. On the top log, the binder, crouched the jack in charge; his arms stiff, his hands steady as he gripped the reins slanting down to the bit in the jaws of his whale mount. So the first column of whales moved ponderously on in the mud river.

In an hour a squadron was lined up in ranks, four abreast. The whales rested at ease, heaving in the sluggish swells of the stream. Paul Bunyan kept his whale whip uncoiled, but he was to swing its lash no more. Even the outlaws held an unbroken formation, as squadron after squadron fell into line. At last the boss logger stared at emptied rollways.

"Down the river!" commanded Paul Bunyan.

The river thundered and boiled from threshing flukes.

"Yay, whales!" bawled the jacks.

The drive was on.

On in a huge sweep swam the buck whales, bearing the logs irresistibly down the muddy tide and round the first big bend. A cheer burst from the deeps of Paul Bunyan's heart for the magnificent sight. His pride in his shanty boys knew no bounds now. The purpose and the plan had been his, but the fulfillment was theirs. For once his distrust of the human nature inherent in all men was smothered.

There they stood, genuine timber savages, true bullies of the woods! Down the river and round the bend the jacks drove the logs on the backs of whales! Every jack kept his calks set solidly in the top log of his pyramid, sprung his knees, hunched shoulders, clenched his fists, and solidly held a tight rein. The snouts of the whales were

618   PAUL BUNYAN AND HIS WORLD

up, their jaws gaped as they fought the bit; and as they lunged through the sucking and dragging mud at blinding speeds, their drivers bravely yelled:

"Yay, whales! Show 'em all the colors of your flukes there!"

So the drive rounded the big bend. Paul Bunyan cut through the timber to beat the drive to the river's mouth. The rest was easy, the battle was won. In the bay he would unload the logs, boom them, and then set the whales free. The great logger was content. In this first encounter he had licked the weather even as he had beaten the wild young rivers. This day Paul Bunyan had made history, and botany as well.

But one eventuality marred Paul Bunyan's triumph. In never another spring did the whale herds swim up from deep salt water and jump Niagara to use Round River as a calving- and nursing-ground. The bridle, the bit, the blinders, the pack-saddle, and the whale whip were bitter memories to all the bucks. Even the ones who were urged to return by fond recollections of snoose and of playing pitch and fetch with Babe considered that Paul Bunyan had taken advantage of the hospitable and friendly nature of whales, so famous since Jonah's time. The outlaws were utterly intolerant. They refused to believe that Paul Bunyan might receive them differently in fine weather.

Thus the Great Lakes, the mighty sons of Round River, Father of Waters, remain barren of whales to this day.

For the lamentable lack Paul Bunyan may be blamed. But who can find the heart to blame him? He had to whip the weather. He had to get out the logs.

The Lumberman's Song

Come all you sons of freedom
    That run the Saginaw stream,
Come all you roving lumber boys,
    And listen to my theme.
We'll cross the Tittabawassee,
    Where the mighty waters flow,
And we'll range the wildwoods over
    And once more a-lumbering go.

Chorus:
    And once more a-lumbering go.
    And we'll range the wildwoods over
    And once more a-lumbering go.

When the white frost takes the valley,
    And the snow conceals the woods,
Each farmer has enough to do
    To earn the family food.
With the week no better pastime
    Than to hunt the buck and doe,
And we'll range the wildwoods over
    And once more a-lumbering go.

You may talk about your farms,
    Your houses and fine ways,
And pity us poor shanty boys
    While dashing in our sleighs;
While round a good campfire at night
    We'll sing while the wild winds blow,
And we'll range the wildwoods over
    And once more a-lumbering go.

With our axes on our shoulders
    We'll make the woods resound,
And many a tall and stately tree
    Will come tumbling to the ground.
With our axes on our shoulders,
    To our boot tops deep in snow,
And we'll range the wildwoods over
    And once more a-lumbering go.

When navigation opens,
    And the waters run so free,

We'll drive our logs to Saginaw,
Then haste our girls to see.
They will welcome our return,
And we'll in raptures flow;
And we'll stay with them through summer
And once more a-lumbering go.

When our youthful days are ended,
And our jokes are getting long,
We'll take us each a little wife
And settle on a farm.
We'll have enough to eat and drink,
Contented we will go;
And we'll tell our wives of our hard times
And no more a-lumbering go.

Chorus:
And no more a-lumbering go.
We'll tell our wives of our hard times
And no more a-lumbering go.

The Round Drive

Paul logged in Michigan for about five years after that, and then we went up into Wisconsin, to a new part where we hadn't never been before. One year, I know, up there, we was loggin' on a river that we didn't even know the name of till we happened to find out the next spring when we was pretty near ready to leave anyway.

That spring Shot Gunderson, Joe Murphy, Pete Hackett, and myself was goin' to take the drive down for Paul; and then we had a number of others along too—they was most of 'em pretty good rivermen—and then for good luck we had Pete Legoux along. I'll have to stop and tell about Pete some time, for he sure was about as fool a Frenchman as you ever want to see. One time I remember he made Paul pretty good and mad at him.

Paul had a raft of logs in the river that he was goin' to take down to the mill afterwards but that he wanted to tie up for the time bein' till he could get another lot out first. Well, the way it was, Paul himself was out on the boom fastenin' up the boom chains, and the river was roarin' along pretty fast right there, and he'd left Pete up at the other end by the windlass with the anchor, and when he got the boom in just the right location to suit him, he yells to Pete, "Drop the anchor, Pete!"

And Pete he looks down at the anchor and he sees there ain't no rope on it, and he yells back to Paul:

"Hey, Paul, no string on hank'."

But course with the roar of the river and all the noise it made, Paul didn't hear, and he yells again, "Drop the anchor, Pete. What's the matter with you? Drop the anchor, I said."

And then Pete he drops the anchor. "What Paul say, she go," he says to himself. "Paul, he ees ze boss and he make all ze monee from log. When he say, 'Drop ze hank',' I drop ze hank'. By Gar! Eef Paul say drop ze horse, I drop ze horse."

And so the minute Paul let go, the boom went spinnin' down the rapids, naturally, and the anchor was safe in the mud at the bottom of the river, and Paul would of liked to've fell in and got drowned if he hadn't of turned the log he was on around and made it float up river so's he could get to land. And he sure was mad at Pete that time.

But here now I've been tellin' all about Pete, when I was goin' to tell about the Round Drive. And for that matter that ain't all about Pete Legoux neither—I'll have to tell the rest some other time, I guess.

Well, there was Shot Gunderson and Joe Murphy, and Pete Hackett and myself and a number of others and we was goin' to take the drive down that spring. There'd been this river close to where we was loggin' and we'd been puttin' all the logs we got out that winter into this river we was on—about twenty-six million feet I reckon these must of been in all—and Paul told us to take 'em down to a mill somewheres and sell 'em.

Well, we didn't know where we was exactly, but we figgured if we followed the "usual plan and drove the way the river ran," like they say in the poetry, we'd come out somewheres, and so we started out.

Hackett was cookin' for the gang and Joe and me and Shot was takin' turns actin' as river-boss, and we was movin' along havin' a gay time, laughin' and talkin' and singin', and that's the way we went on down the river for about two weeks or three pretty near, and nothin' happened all that time, and then what did we do one day but run by a camp that looked pretty near as big as ours, and we wondered who it was that was loggin' there, naturally.

But of course we didn't stop to investigate, because we didn't think so very much about it then, but kept right on goin'.

And then pretty soon, after about another two or three weeks or so, we passed another camp that looked even bigger than the first one had done. There was the same cook-house pretty near like in our own camp, with the stove-pipe and the smoke comin' out of it, and there was the barns for the cattle and the manure piles and everythin', and the stacks of wood that the bull-cooks had got in, behind the cook-shanty, and the blacksmith-shop and all, and all just exactly like we had in our camp—only not quite so big, of course, but pretty near—and we wondered who it was that was loggin' on anythin' like that scale, almost like Paul, and was apin' his methods like that, and we talked about it almost every day after that for the next couple of weeks. And then I'll be jiggered if we didn't run into another camp again, just the same as the other two that we'd passed before.

So that time we thought we'd stop and investigate, and we did.

"I'm goin' to go ashore," I says. "I don't care what the rest of you is goin' to do."

And Shot Gunderson, he says, "I'm with you, Angus. Just wait a minute. I'll go up with you."

And the two of us went up towards the camp.

"If we find out who the fellow is, runnin' this outfit," says Shot, "we'll just tell him Paul's got all the land in this part of the state preempted, and he'd better be thinkin' about movin' out if he knows what's good for him.

"And Paul's got a patent on them there kind of skid sleds," he says, "and this feller'd better not be usin' 'em, or he'll find out."

"Looks like he's got a blue ox to log with too," I says. "Look at that barn up there." For there was a big barn just like Babe's up on the hill.

"Paul will sure be mad when he finds out about this," Shot says.

And by that time we was pretty near up to the commissary, and we was all ready with what we was goin' to say to that boss when we found him, and here if we didn't run right plank, slam into Paul himself as big as you please, sittin' on the commissary steps in the sunshine whittlin' on a jackpine. By George, we was some surprised.

You see the way that was, the river we'd been on was round and hadn't no outlet, and we'd been goin' round and round the same way all them eight weeks we'd been out, and them three camps we'd passed had been nothin' but our own camp all the time.

"Ef we go roun' an' roun' some more, las' we go to hal," says Pete Legoux. And I guess that time Pete would of been about right.

And so that was the end of the Round Drive. Well, that is, of course, we had to get the logs out, but Paul fixed that up all right. What he done was, he just called Sourdough Sam, the cook.

"Sam," he says, "make up a good stiff batch of sourdough biscuit dough, and when I get ready, you put it in where I tell you to."

And then he goes out right away and spades out a channel through a ridge that's between the river and a lake over on the other side, that's got an outlet. And next mornin' Sam dumps his sourdough in the big tank and hitches Babe to it and hauls it out and dumps it in the river, and it riz right up and filled the channel and floated the logs right out into the lake, and so then Shot and I and Joe and the rest of 'em started out again, gay as ever. And then we knowed it was the Round River we'd been loggin' on that winter.

How Paul Bunyan Cleared
North Dakota
(Originally titled "The Kingdom of North Dakota")

Soon after Paul had finished digging the St. Lawrence River he received a letter from the King of Sweden. It seems that the King had heard of Paul Bunyan through Ole the Big Swede. He wanted Paul to cut down all the trees in North Dakota so the Swedes could settle there and farm the land. The King wrote that he wanted this job done in one month so the farmers could plant their grain at once. All the trees were to be cut up and made into toothpicks for the Swedish army.

When this huge job was finished, all the Swedes in North America were to settle in the New Kingdom of North Dakota and farm the land. This was about the largest job that Paul ever attempted. He soon gathered his men together and started moving his camp to North Dakota. When they all arrived, he built the largest camp the world had ever seen.

The bunks in the new sleeping quarters were eighteen decks high and the men in the top bunks had to get up an hour earlier in the morning in order to get down to breakfast on time. The dining room was longer than ever, and the boy that drove the salt and pepper wagon around the tables would only be halfway around by nightfall. He would stay overnight at the other end and drive back the next day.

Paul had to finish the job in one month, so he hired the Seven Axemen. They were famous woodsmen and could cut down trees faster than anyone except Paul himself. They were all cousins, and each was named Frank. It was very confusing, because every time Paul shouted "Frank!" all the Seven Axemen would drop their work and run over to see what he wanted.

The Seven Axemen used great double-bitted axes that an ordinary man could not lift. When the axes became dull they would start a round, flat rock rolling down the hillside and run beside it holding the blades of their axes against the rock until they were sharp again.

No matter how fast they worked, the huge job was always being delayed. Paul began to have bad luck. First, Babe the Blue Ox lost his heavy iron shoes in a swamp, and a new mine had to be opened to get enough iron to make him a new set.

Next came the great fog that covered the earth like a blanket. It was so thick that the fish in the river couldn't tell where the water left off and the fog began. They swam around in the fog and got lost among the trees in the forest. When the fog disappeared, thousands of small fish were left in the woods many miles from the nearest stream.

The Seven Axemen had to chop a tunnel in the fog from the

kitchen to the dining room so the cooks could serve food. The fog even got into the coffee and made it so weak the men wouldn't drink it. At night the men had to sleep with mosquito netting over their heads to keep the tadpoles from getting in their ears.

Finally the fog went away, but all the blankets and shirts were so wet it took fourteen days to dry them out.

At last all the trees were cut down and split into toothpicks, but still the King of Sweden wasn't satisfied. He wrote Paul another letter which said, "My farmers will not be able to till the soil with all the stumps," and the farmers refused to settle in the new Kingdom of North Dakota.

Paul called Johnnie Inkslinger into the office and said, "You are good at solving problems. What are we going to do about the stumps?" Johnnie Inkslinger thought and thought for seven days and nights.

"We will send for several large fire hoses and flood the ground with water," said Johnnie Inkslinger finally. "Babe the Blue Ox, as you all know, doesn't like to get his feet wet, for that gives him a cold in the head.

"With water all over the ground, he will walk on the stumps. He is so heavy his huge hoofs will drive the stumps into the ground."

The men did as Johnnie said. They covered the whole country with water. Babe roamed all over North Dakota, stepping very carefully from stump to stump to avoid getting his feet wet. His heavy weight drove the stumps six feet under ground.

The King of Sweden was finally satisfied, and to this day there isn't a single tree or stump in the whole state of North Dakota.

Tony Beaver Meets Paul Bunyan

TONY BEAVER WAS Pennsylvania's greatest lumberjack. He was a mighty hero to lumbermen in neighboring states as well. Some of his feats were as great as Paul Bunyan's, and if you asked a logger in Pennsylvania who the greatest of the lumber kings was, he'd shout, "Tony Beaver," and dare you to disagree. Bunyan's and Beaver's legends got so big that they had to meet. Here is the memorable tale of their showdown.

Did any of you folks what's reading this book ever hear tell of that great lumberjack, Paul Bunyan, what lives up North somewheres? They say that feller kin burl a log so fast he'll skin it clean outer its bark, and then run to shore on the bubbles; and in his camp they uses a holler tree for a dinner horn—he sure must be a regular two-fisted Jim-bruiser of a feller, and I'm aiming now to tell you-all about the time him and Tony Beaver met up right face to face. That sure was somepen to see, and I'm mighty glad I was there to see it. Out of it too come the biggest kinder eye-opener for Tony and Paul both.

The first news us fellers in Tony Beaver's crew had of Paul Bunyan was one time when a strange logger come by the Eel River camp singing a little song—

> "Paul Bunyan growed a mighty tree,
> Its branches scratched the sky;
> And when he felled the doggoned thing
> It ripped a hole on high."

"Hey, stranger!" Big Henry yells at him. "That song's all right, but you got the names twisted. It wasn't no Paul Somebody growed that tree; it was Tony Beaver hisself, and well I recollect the time."

"I never heard tell of no Tony Beaver," says the stranger, "but Paul Bunyan I know well, being one of his hands in the Big Onion Camp. In Paul's camp now," he says, setting down on a stump and biting him off a big chaw of terbacker (you-all mind what I tole you right at the beginning, the bigger the chaw, the bigger the lie?), "they got a griddle for frying the batter cakes the fellers eats so big that the onliest way they kin grease the thing is to have six men skate over it with a slab of fat meat on each foot."

"Welcome to Eel River!" says Big Henry. "It's right here in Tony Beaver's camp you belong—only first you got to git them names straight."

"I hate to git things wrong," says the stranger, looking like he was doing his best to hit the truth; "and it's a fact I made a slip when I said Paul Bunyan needs six men to grease that there griddle. It's really eight he uses, and in a pinch I've seen as many as ten or twenty hands skating over it, with them slabs of bacon on they feets. It sure is hot work for the fellers! Every slide they make they leave a trail of smoke behind 'em, and they have to keep stomping they feet *all* the time to stomp the flames out."

"Look ahere, stranger, didn't you hear me say that was Tony Beaver you was talking erbout?" says Big Henry, gitting mighty restless.

"Paul Bunyan is the man I'm speaking of," says the t'other, buttoning up his mouth in a right stubborn way.

"That's a—" says Big Henry, and sidesteps. "That's a—" he says ergin, riding right up to the word and jumping off jest in time.

"If the word yer aiming at is 'lie,' hit it!" says the stranger, standing up kinder dangerous.

"Well," says Big Henry, knowing he has to be polite to company, "we don't have to *say* nothing erbout lies in this camp, for Tony Beaver's got a trick for ketching 'em. He's invented him some sticky lie-paper that ketches lies as fast as fly-paper ketches flies. Hey! Truth-Teller! Fetch out yer lie-paper!" he hollers at me.

I come a-running with the thing, and Big Henry and me swishes it all erbout in the air where the stranger'd been talking.

"Here, now, we'll jest see what's what!" says Big Henry. But no, sir! We didn't ketch nary ernother lie.

"Hey! Looks like I've been telling the truth all erlong!" says the strange hand, kinder tickled, and some s'prised too. "Or else somepen's the matter with the paper—mebbe you fellers in this camp has sorter overworked it."

"Somepen's wrong, sure," says Big Henry, mightily outdone. "There, now!" he says, looking down the trail. "Here comes ole Preacher Mutters! He's got all kinds er book sense if he ain't got no other kind. Mebbe he kin straighten things out. Hey, Brother Mutters!" he bawls. "Did you ever hear tell of a feller by the name of Paul Bunyan?"

The ole preacher claws his fingers through his beard for a spell, looking as earnest as a billy goat. "It's *John Bunyan* you mean—him as writ that holy book, *The Pilgrim's Progress,*" he says, rolling back his eyes, and tipping up his chin to let them pious words trickle down his throat, like a ole hen drinking.

"That's news to me," says the stranger. "Paul mought of had a brother by the name of John, but I never heared tell of him. The Bunyan I'm speaking of," he says, gitting into his stride ergin, "has the biggest bees a feller ever did see. Each one of 'em's big as a full-grown ox, and Paul crossed 'em a while back with a gang of moskeeters, and the offsprings of that wedding is the awfulest critters a person ever did see, for they has stings both before and behind."

"That sure don't sound like nothing I ever heared tell of *John* Bunyan," says the preacher, shaking his head mightily mystified.

"Looks like the bunion's on the t'other foot, then," says the stranger, acting smart.

"It ain't no Paul Bunyan, ner no John neither—it's Tony Beaver! And I'm here to tell the world so!" says Big Henry, jumping up.

But it was the stranger got in the furst lick. *"Paul Bunyan!"* he says, putting his fist in the word, and landing it on Big Henry's jaw.

"Tony Beaver!" Big Henry bellers back, placing his name on the t'other's nose.

"Hol' on, brothers! Hol' on!" the preacher bellers, reaching out and trying to peacify the two. But pore ole feller! *Bang!* he got a *Paul* on the side of his head, and *Biff!* a *Tony* tuck him in the chist, bowling him over flat on the ground with the wind knocked outer him.

He lay there for quite a spell gaping up at the sky. "No," he says at last, kinder talking to hisself. "No, that Paul Bunyan surely ain't no kin at all to John."

But jest erbout then Tony Beaver hisself happens up on the scene, toting that little boy on his shoulder what's sech a great buddy of hisn.

The little feller kin walk all right now since that time his crippled foot got suppled up dancing to the big music, but all the same he ain't going to give up his seat on Tony's shoulder to nobody.

"Here, now! Here! What's all this erbout?" Tony hollers. With that he scoops ole Brother Mutters up offn the ground, steps right in betwixt the two fighting fellers, and had everything ca'med down jest in no time.

"But look ahere, Tony," says Big Henry, still all worried up. "Here's a strange hand telling some of your doings, and tacking 'em all on to a logger by the name of Paul Bunyan—or mebbe his furst name's John."

"No, *sir!* It ain't John Bunyan!" says Brother Mutters, feeling hisself all over to see was he fatally busted.

"I wished you-all could see that blue ox, Babe, of Paul's," says the strange hand, going right erlong like nothing hadn't happened. "He measures all of forty-two axe handles and a plug of terbacker acrost his forehead—forty-two, that is, of Paul's axe handles; that 'ud be erlong erbout one hundred and seventy-five of any common hand's. An' his nose is so fer away from his years he can't hear hisself snort."

"Well, *that* ain't nothing," chips in the young-un setting up on Tony Beaver's shoulder mighty proud, for he jest thinks Tony Beaver makes the world go round, and measuring it all off wide with both arms. "Tony, he's got him a yoke er steers so big it takes a crow a week to fly betwixt the horns of one of 'em."

"Shake, young feller," says the stranger. "If yer needing a job, I'd be glad to take you up to Paul; he's looking for stout hands like you right this minute."

"I thank you," says the little feller, all swelled up, "but I got jest erbout all I kin han'le right here he'ping Tony out."

"I've heared tell of that Paul Bunyan afore now," says Tony, scratching his year more like he was some kinder varmint than a human. "If he's the great logger you say he is, tell him to come on up Eel River, and him and me'll have a contest and find out which is the best feller."

"That's the *very* trick!" Big Henry hollers out.

"All right, I'll take your word to Paul—*he'll* show you-all somepen," says the stranger, laying back his years, and making ready to shoot for his own shanty.

"Tony Beaver'll show *him* somepen!" the little feller hollers after him, cocking up his head, flapping his arms and crowing out "Err—erk—Err—erk—Err—*Roooo!*" like that joky feller in camp has learned him to.

Well, it wa'n't hardly no time after that 'fore Paul Bunyan come up Eel River with a whole parcel of hands from his camp. There was

Charlie the Swede, Big Ole, and a whole heap more, besides Johnny
Inkslinger, Paul's timekeeper, with his fountain pen as big as a saw-
log—no, I dunno's it's quite *that* big—I got to recollect I'm the
Truth-Teller.

Well, sirs! When they met, Tony and Paul sure did set a swift pace
in manners!

"Welcome to Eel River, Mr. Bunyan," says Tony.

"Pleased to meet you, Mr. Beaver," says Paul. "Me and my crew
put out from the Big Onion camp the minute I got your word, but
mebbe I'm a bit late gitting here. What's the time?"

"It's any time you say, Mr. Bunyan," says Tony.

"How's that, Mr. Beaver?" says Paul.

"Jest like I say—name the time you want, and it's yourn."

"Well, I *was* aiming to hit your camp at sunup, but now looks like
it's nigh midday," says Paul.

"Sunup she shall be!" says Tony. With that he reaches in his
pocket and hauls out a handful of time, and *swish!* thar she was right
back at sunup ergin, with the dew fresh on the grass, and all the little
birds chirping up to sing.

"That's a mighty handy trick," says Paul. "Inkslinger, make a
note of that."

The timekeeper laid aholt of his pen, and the scratch-scratching of
it was like a million katydids ripsawing on they hind legs in fall
weather.

"We had bad luck with the time in our camp the winter of the blue
snow," says Paul. "There was mighty little forage that year, and
Babe, that ox of mine, busted into the granary where the time was
kep' and chawed it all up 'fore we could make him quit—all, that is,
'cept the leap years. Even Babe couldn't stomick *them.*"

"My time is yours, Mr. Bunyan. Jest help yerself; take right smart,
take darned nigh all," says Tony, showing his manners.

"I thank you," says Paul. "I fetched you a present of a couple of
my bees. The pair of 'em'll make you along about twenty tons er
honey a month. Here, Ole! Fetch up them bees!" he hollers out.

Big Ole brung the bees up, and I wished you could er seen 'em!
Each one of 'em was as big as a ox, and they was loaded down with
log chains to keep 'em from flying erway.

"We had 'em check they stings with the timekeeper while we was traveling," says Paul. "But Johnny Inkslinger's got 'em all labeled which ones goes behind and which before, and kin slip 'em right into place whenever you say."

Tony casts his eye over 'em, and they sure did give him back a mighty mean look, with both of 'em buzzing like a sawmill cutting through white oak.

"Well," he says, "let's git better acquainted afore we give 'em back they weepons."

After that the stunts betwixt Paul Bunyan and Tony Beaver commenced. But pshaw! It looked like there wasn't a pin to choose betwixt the two of 'em. If Tony Beaver tore a white oak up by the roots and pitched it acrost Eel River, Paul Bunyan'd pull up a red oak and toss it over the ridge. And if Paul set the calks of his boots nigh fifty feet up in the face of a cliff, Tony'd jump across Eel River and back ergin and never tech ground on the t'other side. So there they was—pull Dick, pull Tom—wasting a lot er sweat and nothing gitting settled. But d'reckly all hands got to noticing that that little boy belonging to Tony's camp kep' a-hollering all the time for Tony no matter which feller done the trick. "Aw, look at Tony Beaver jumping acrost Eel River! Aw, look at Tony stomping his boots up yander on the rocks!" he'd holler.

That made Paul's hands kinder mad. "Look ahere, young feller, your man ain't doing it all! That was Mr. Bunyan what set his calks in the face of the cliff," Big Ole tells him.

The little feller looks at him kinder big-eyed and s'prised, and then he says, "Aw, you fool me!" an' kep' right erlong hollering "Looky! Look at Tony!" for everything that happened.

But Paul hisself didn't git mad. He looks at the little feller for a spell, and then he throws back his head and busts out with a great big round "Haw, haw, haw!"

"What's hitting your funny bone, brother?" Tony asks him, for by now the two of 'em was gitting mighty thick.

"There's a big laf coming from somewhere's," says Paul, kinder sniffing up the air like he was a hound dawg. "I can't tell where it's heading from, but when she busts she sure will be a big one. I'm funny that way," he says; "I kin sense a joke and commence to laf when it's still all of ten miles off—be damned if I can't! *Aw—oh!"* he says, clapping his hand to his mouth, "I didn't go to let that word fly out before the little feller!"

"Take it back then, brother!" says Tony.

"How kin I? I spit that word out so hard it's nigh half a mile down the skidways of the past by now."

"I kin git it back for you!" says Tony, bawling to his hands to fetch him around his riding horse.

Now that nag of Tony's sure is swift, but it ain't so much its swiftness that's peculiar as it's the way they got him saddled. Tony had a chore boy in his camp a while back what appeared to be jest a fool for want er sense, and one time the feller fetched the horse round with the saddle facing the tail. "I saddled him thataway so's you kin ride both going and coming," he says, his mouth gaping open at his own smartness.

"Well, there ain't one grain er sense to that," says Tony, "and jest for that very reason I b'lieve it's true." With that he jumps on the beast, and dogged if he couldn't do jest like the fool said, ride both going and coming. It sure is a swift way er traveling, and the onliest way I know of that a person kin be in two places at onced.

Well, Tony jumps on his beast now, and takes out *pluckety-pluck* after that cuss word Paul had let fly. Riding thataway, it wa'n't hardly no time 'fore he come up with it. But course I don't have to tell none er you-all that if there's one thing a cuss word hates worse'n another it is to be taken back once it's loose. So, with Tony right atop of it, that word turned a kind of a somersault, and tuck back up the road ergin, its years laid, flat, jest scooting for—Well, to name the place that "damn" was heading for I'd have to let out another cuss word, which I ain't aiming to do; so I'll jest say it was making for home, and let it go at that.

"There she goes! Head her off! *Head her!"* Tony bawls, checking up his beast, and turning erbout with the gravel flying off into the bresh, and the trail smoking behind him.

All hands from both camps spread out acrost the road whooping and hollering for all they was wurth. But, with them hollering in front, and Tony whooping up behind, that "damn" word commenced to squawk and to fly like a skeered guinea hen. All us hands

made a jump for it, but it sailed right over the heads of every one
'cept Paul. He give sech a master leap that it landed him atop of a
white oak tree, and from there he bounded over on to a low-hanging
cloud, ketching that cuss word on the way.

"Aw, *looky!* Look at Tony up in the clouds!" the little feller
screeches out, dancing eround and all carried erway.

"That ain't Mr. Beaver up yander; it's Mr. Bunyan," Paul's hands
hollers back at him, clean outdone.

Well, sirs! Things sure commenced to look bad for Paul. That
cloud had been jest drifting erlong, hanging low in a kind of a doze,
but when Paul landed down on its back, all so sudden, it give a great
bound, and headed for the sky like a skeered racer, with Paul hung
up on it, and no way er reaching ground ergin. More'n that, the
cloud was right thin, and it looked like, heavy as Paul is, he mought
fall spang through it any minute. Every step he tuck he went down
waist-deep in the thing; and it's the truth, time and ergin the fellers
seen his boots come dangling through the bottom side of the cloud
with nothing but air betwixt them and destruction. All of Paul's
hands sets up a turrible yammering, hollering up at him to "take
keer" and "mind out" and "don't fall," and all like that, like the
feller would fall if he could he'p hisself. Tony's hands, wanting to
show they manners, they hollered too. Johnny Inkslinger, what's the
greatest cal'ulator the world has ever knowed, unlimbered his fountain pen and commenced to figger out the distance from the ground,
Paul's weight, and all like that, so's they'd know how bad he'd be
busted when he drapped.

"Git ready for the wurst, boys, for he'll be nothing but fractions
when he hits," he says, figgering and sniffling, with the ink and tears
all spluttering out together.

But erbout then Big Ole lets out a great yell. "It's all right! Ole
Paul's all right! He's kicking him up a thunderstorm!" he hollers.

Sure 'nough, when we-all looked we seen that Paul was milling
'round in the cloud, trompling on it and teasing it, making the thing
so mad that it was gitting blacker and blacker every minute, till
d'reckly it all fires up and busts out in er turrible storm, swearing
and spitting out thunder and lightning at him. Paul waits jest long
enough to pick him a good streak of lightning, and then he slides to

the ground on it all safe and sound, 'cept his pants was some scorched, and a person could smell singed whiskers. But the cuss word, it was burnt to a crisp.

"I have to thank ole Pecos Bill for that trick," says Paul, breshing hisself off. "Bill, he's that great cattle man they got down in Texas. He kin take a cyclone by the year, ride it acrost three states, and slide to ground on the lightning whenever he gits ready."

"I knowed you was all right, Tony. I knowed you'd slide down on the lightning streak," says the little feller.

"Now look a-here, buddy, you got to git things straight," says Tony, kinder worried. *"That's* Mister Bunyan," he says, pointing at Paul, "and *this* here is me. It was him, not me, slided down on the lightning streak."

The little feller looks at him mighty big-eyed and earnest, doing his best to onderstand, but in the end he says, jest like he had afore, "Aw, you fool me!"

At that Paul Bunyan lets out ernother great crackling laf, shrugging up his shoulders, and rubbing his elbows erginst his ribs. "That big laf's gitting closer, I kin feel it tickling my funny bones," he says.

Tony Beaver looks and looks at the little feller in a kind of a daze.

"Well, I will be dogged!" he says, like big news had struck him.

"Haw, haw, haw! Do you reckon it kin be true, brother?" says Paul.

"Well, there's one way to find out. Come on, let's take it!" says Tony. With that he takes the little boy up on his shoulder, and, not saying nothing to none of us, him and Paul went off into the bresh together.

Tony, he led along through the woods till they come to a little clear spring running out from under the roots of a witch-hazel bush. "Now then, buddy, you work us a charm," he says to the little feller. With that he breaks off a switch from the witch-hazel like what you've seen a water doctor use, and gives it to the young-un to whip through the spring for a spell. Then he says to Paul, "Look, brother, and tell me what you kin see." And standing right side by side they both of 'em looked down into the water.

"I see myself and nobody else," says Paul. "What do you see, brother?"

"I see myself and nobody else," says Tony.

So there you see how it was: after the little feller had charmed the water it showed 'em the truth—what the young-un had sensed all erlong—that Tony and Paul was one and the same feller, only dressed up in different skin and bones, and going under the name er Paul Bunyan in one part er the world and Tony Beaver in ernother. Did any of you folks ever meet yer very own self right face to face? Well, I ain't neither, and I know mighty well I ain't craving to. No, sir! If there's another me—Jerry Dan Doolittle—roaming around the world dressed up in another body, I'll jest thank him to keep erway from me for according to my figgering *one* of us is a-plenty. You'd think it would be a powerful awesome sight to meet up with yerself, but dogged if it tuck them two fellers thataway.

"So you're me an' I'm you!" says Tony with a great "Haw, haw!"

"I'm you an' you're me, and I wouldn't be s'prised if ole Pecos Bill from down yander in Texas wasn't mixed up with us, too," says Paul. "And what did I tell you erbout a big laf coming?"

With that the two of 'em jest laid back, whooping and hollering and laffing fit to bust the sky wide open.

FURTHER READING

IN THE SEARCH for good folklore one is often best served by starting close to home. There is always interesting material in the memories of one's family elders or the recollections of a neighbor. For those with a greater appetite, however, I offer a brief reading list of sources in addition to the ones credited earlier in my acknowledgments. Many of them are out of print and others are hard to find, but each is worth the time required to track it down. In addition, numerous folklore journals and folk archives are available across the country. Some of the earliest and most enduring folklore can be found in the newspapers and almanacs of the nineteenth century, the best of which is William T. Porter's *Spirit of the Times*. And, finally, the folklore collected under the guidance of the Federal Writers' Project of the WPA is an embarrassment of riches.

Abrahams, Roger D. *Deep Down in the Jungle*. Folklore Associates, Hatboro, PA, 1964.

Allsopp, Frederick W. *Folklore of Romantic Arkansas*. Grolier Society, New York, 1931.

Alvord, Thomas G. *Paul Bunyan and Resinous Rhymes of the North Woods*. Derrydale Press, New York, 1934.

Aswell, James (ed). *God Bless the Devil!* Harper & Bros., New York, 1947.

Baldwin, James Glover. *The Flush Times of Alabama and Mississippi*. Americus, GA, 1853.

Bell, Horace. *Reminiscences of a Ranger*. Los Angeles, 1881.

Botkin, Benjamin A. *A Treasury of American Folklore*. Crown Publishers, New York, 1944. (See also his many other regional folklore treasuries.)

Bradford, Roark. *John Henry*. Harper & Bros., New York, 1931.

Brewer, John M. *American Negro Folklore*. Quadrangle/New York Times Book Company, New York, 1968.

Brown, Frank C. *Collection of North Carolina Folklore*. Duke University Press, Durham, NC, 1954–61.

Buel, J. W. *The Border Outlaws*. St. Louis, 1881.

Buffum, George T. *Smith of Bear City and Other Frontier Sketches.* Grafton Press, New York, 1906.

Burke, T. A. *Polly Peablossom's Wedding and Other Tales.* Philadelphia, 1869.

Callison, John. *Bill Jones of Paradise Valley, Oklahoma.* M. A. Donohue, Kingfisher, OK, 1941.

Chittick, V.L.O. *Ring-Tailed Roarers.* Caxton Printers, Caldwell, ID, 1941.

Clemens, Samuel L. (Mark Twain). *The Adventures of Huckleberry Finn.* 1884.

Clough, Benjamin C. *The American Imagination at Work.* Alfred A. Knopf, New York, 1947.

Collins, Earl. *Folk Tales of Missouri.* Christopher Publishing House, Boston, 1935.

Crockett, Col. David. *Exploits and Adventures in Texas.* London, 1837. (See also the endlessly rich versions of the Crockett Almanacs.)

Evans, Joe M. *A Corral Full of Stories.* McMath Company, El Paso, TX, 1939.

Field, Joseph. *The Drama in Pokerville.* Philadelphia, 1847.

———. *Three Years in Texas. Magazine of History,* Boston, 1836. Paperback: William Abbatt, Tarrytown, NY, 1925.

Gerrard, Lewis. *Wah-To-Yah and the Taos Trail.* Philadelphia, 1850.

Grinnell, George Bird. *Pawnee Hero Stories and Folk Tales.* New York, Charles Scribner's Sons, 1899.

Haliburton, Thomas C. *The Americans at Home.* Hurst & Blackett, London, 1854.

Hall, James. *Tales of the Border.* Philadelphia, 1836.

———. *Legends of the West.* Philadelphia, 1836.

Harris, Joel Chandler. *Nights with Uncle Remus.* Houghton Mifflin, Boston, 1883.

Haywood, Charles. *A Bibliography of North American Folklore and Folksong.* Dover Publications, New York, 1961.

Hoig, Stan. *The Humor of the American Cowboy.* Caxton Printers Ltd., Caldwell, ID, 1958.

Hough, Emerson. *The Story of the Outlaw.* A. L. Burt Company, New York, 1907.

————. *The Story of the Cowboy*. Hodder & Stoughton, London, 1927.

House, Boyce. *Tall Talk from Texas*. The Naylor Company, San Antonio, TX, 1944.

Inman, Col. Henry. *Buffalo Jones: Forty Years of Adventure*. Kansas City, 1899.

Jackson, Thomas. *On a Slow Train Through Arkansaw*. T. W. Jackson Publishing Co., Chicago, 1903.

Jones, C. C. *Negro Myths from the Georgia Coast*. State Co., Columbia, SC, 1888.

Kittredge, George Lyman. *The Old Farmer and His Almanack*. William Ware & Co., Boston, 1904.

————. *Witchcraft in Old and New England*. Harvard University Press, Cambridge, MA, 1929.

Levinge, Sir Richard Augustus. *Echoes from the Backwoods*. London, 1858.

Longstreet, A. B. *Georgia Scenes, Characters, Incidents etc.* 1855.

MacKaye, Percy. *Weathergoose—woo!* Longmans, Green & Co., New York, 1929.

————. *Tall Tales of the Kentucky Mountains*. George H. Doran Co., New York, 1926.

McKnight, Charles. *Our Western Border*. J. C. McCurdy & Co., Philadelphia, 1876.

Masterton, James R. *Tall Tales of Arkansas*. Houghton Mifflin, Boston, 1943.

Mather, Cotton. *Magnalia Christi Americana: Or, The Ecclesiastical History of New England*. (2 vols.) Russell & Russell, New York, 1967.

Meine, Franklin J. (ed). *The Crockett Almanacs*. Caxton Club, Chicago, 1955.

Montague, Margaret. *Up Eel River*. Macmillan, New York, 1927.

Porter, William T. (ed). *Big Bear of Arkansas and Other Sketches*. Philadelphia, 1845.

————. *A Quarter Race in Kentucky*. Philadelphia, 1847.

Reynard, Elizabeth. *The Narrow Land*. Houghton Mifflin, Boston, 1934.

Ruxton, Frederick. *Life in the Far West*. London, 1849.

Sandburg, Carl. *The People, Yes.* Harcourt, Brace & Co., New York, 1936.

Thomas, Robert. *The Farmer's Almanac.* Boston, 1795.

Thorp, N. Howard. *Pardner of the Wind.* Caxton Printers, Caldwell, ID, 1945.

Watterson, Henry. *Oddities in Southern Life and Character.* Houghton Mifflin, Boston, 1882.

INDEX OF TALL TALES AND LEGENDS

INDEX OF BALLADS AND VERSE

INDEX OF SUPERSTITIONS AND MISCELLANEOUS LORE

18741